Lecture Notes in Computer Science　　10996

Commenced Publication in 1973
Founding and Former Series Editors:
Gerhard Goos, Juris Hartmanis, and Jan van Leeuwen

Editorial Board

More information about this series at http://www.springer.com/series/7412

Jie Zhou · Yunhong Wang
Zhenan Sun · Zhenhong Jia
Jianjiang Feng · Shiguang Shan
Kurban Ubul · Zhenhua Guo (Eds.)

Biometric Recognition

13th Chinese Conference, CCBR 2018
Urumqi, China, August 11–12, 2018
Proceedings

 Springer

Editors
Jie Zhou
Tsinghua University
Beijing
China

Jianjiang Feng
Tsinghua University
Beijing
China

Yunhong Wang
Beihang University
Beijing
China

Shiguang Shan
Chinese Academy of Sciences
Beijing
China

Zhenan Sun
Chinese Academy of Sciences
Beijing
China

Kurban Ubul
Xinjiang University
Urumqi
China

Zhenhong Jia
Xinjiang University
Urumqi
China

Zhenhua Guo
Tsinghua University
Shenzhen
China

ISSN 0302-9743   ISSN 1611-3349   (electronic)
Lecture Notes in Computer Science
ISBN 978-3-319-97908-3   ISBN 978-3-319-97909-0   (eBook)
https://doi.org/10.1007/978-3-319-97909-0

Library of Congress Control Number: 2018950102

LNCS Sublibrary: SL6 – Image Processing, Computer Vision, Pattern Recognition, and Graphics

This Springer imprint is published by the registered company Springer Nature Switzerland AG
The registered company address is: Gewerbestrasse 11, 6330 Cham, Switzerland

Preface

Security and privacy issues are topics of growing concern in the Internet era and as a result of the growing demand for anti-terrorism activity. This has raised great interest in biometric technology, which provides substantial advantages over traditional password-or token-based solutions. Biometric recognition systems have been extensively deployed worldwide in law enforcement, government, and consumer applications. In China, thanks to the huge population using the Internet and smart phones as well as to the great investment of the government in security and privacy protection, the biometric market is rapidly growing and biometric research keeps attracting the attention of numerous scholars and practitioners. These researchers have been addressing various biometric problems, promoting diverse biometric techniques, and making significant contributions to the biometrics field. The Chinese Conference on Biometric Recognition (CCBR), an annual conference held in China, provides an excellent platform for biometric researchers to share their progress and advances in the development and applications of biometric theory, technology, and systems.

CCBR 2018 was held in Urumqi during August 11–12, 2018, and was the 13rd in the series, which has been successfully held in Beijing, Hangzhou, Xi'an, Guangzhou, Jinan, Shenyang, Tianjin, Chengdu, and Shenzhen since 2000. CCBR 2018 received 112 submissions, each of which was reviewed by at least three experts from the Program Committee. Based on the rigorous review comments, 78 papers were selected for presentation. These papers comprise this volume of the CCBR 2018 conference proceedings covering a wide range of topics: face recognition and analysis; hand-based biometrics; eye-based biometrics; gesture, gait, and action; emerging biometrics; feature extraction and classification theory; and behavioral biometrics.

We would like to thank all the authors, reviewers, invited speakers, volunteers, and Organizing Committee members, without whom CCBR 2018 would not have been successful. We also wish to acknowledge the support of the Chinese Association for Artificial Intelligence, Institute of Automation of Chinese Academy of Sciences, Springer, and Xinjiang University for sponsoring this conference. Special thanks are due to Prof. Kurban Ubul and Mr. Hao Gui for his hard work in organizing the conference.

August 2018

Jie Zhou
Yunhong Wang
Zhenan Sun
Zhenhong Jia
Jianjiang Feng
Shiguang Shan
Kurban Ubul
Zhenhua Guo

Organization

Advisors

Anil K. Jain	Michigan State University, USA
Tieniu Tan	Institute of Automation, Chinese Academy of Sciences, China
David Zhang	The Hong Kong Polytechnic University, Hong Kong, SAR China
Jingyu Yang	Nanjing University of Science and Technology, China
Xilin Chen	Institute of Computing Technology, Chinese Academy of Sciences, China
Jianhuang Lai	Sun Yat-sen University, China

Honorary Chair

Wushouer Silamu	Xinjiang University, China

General Chairs

Jie Zhou	Tsinghua University, China
Yunhong Wang	Beihang University, China
Zhenan Sun	Institute of Automation, Chinese Academy of Sciences, China
Zhenhong Jia	Xinjiang University, China

Program Chairs

Jianjiang Feng	Tsinghua University, China
Shiguang Shan	Institute of Computing Technology, Chinese Academy of Sciences, China
Zhenhua Guo	Graduate School at Shenzhen, Tsinghua University, China
Kurban Ubul	Xinjiang University, China

Program Committee

Caikou Chen	Yangzhou University, China
Cunjian Chen	Canon Information Technology (Beijing), China
Fanglin Chen	National University of Defense Technology, China
Weihong Deng	Beijing University of Posts and Telecommunications, China
Yuchun Fang	Shanghai University, China
Lunke Fei	Guangdong University of Technology, China
Keren Fu	Shanghai Jiao Tong University, China
Quanxue Gao	Xidian University, China
Shenghua Gao	ShanghaiTech University, China

Yongxin Ge	Chongqing University, China
Xun Gong	Southwest Jiaotong University, China
Zhe Guo	Northwestern Polytechnical University, China
Hu Han	Institute of Computing Technology, Chinese Academy of Sciences, China
Zhenyu He	Harbin Institute of Technology Shenzhen Graduate School, China
Ran He	Institute of Automation, Chinese Academy of Sciences, China
Qingyang Hong	Xiamen University, China
Dewen Hu	National University of Defense Technology, China
Di Huang	Beihang University, China
Wei Jia	Hefei University of Technology, China
Xiaoyuan Jing	Wuhan University, China
Wenxiong Kang	South China University of Technology, China
Zhihui Lai	Shenzhen University, China
Huibin Li	Xian Jiaotong University, China
Weijun Li	Institute of Semiconductors, Chinese Academy of Sciences, China
Wenxin Li	Peking University, China
Zhifeng Li	Shenzhen Institutes of Advanced Technology, Chinese Academy of Sciences, China
Dong Liang	Nanjing University of Aeronautics and Astronautics, China
Shengcai Liao	Institute of Automation, Chinese Academy of Sciences, China
Eryun Liu	Zhejiang University, China
Feng Liu	Shenzhen University, China
Heng Liu	Anhui University of Technology, China
Manhua Liu	Shanghai Jiao Tong University, China
Yiguang Liu	Sichuan University, China
Zhi Liu	Shandong University, China
Guangming Lu	Harbin Institute of Technology Shenzhen Graduate School, China
Jiwen Lu	Tsinghua University, China
Xiao Luan	Chongqing University of Posts and Telecommunications, China
Haifeng Sang	Shenyang University of Technology, China
Chao Shen	Xi'an Jiaotong University, China
Fumin Shen	University of Electronic Science and Technology of China, China
Linlin Shen	Shenzhen University, China
Kejun Wang	Harbin Engineering University, China
Yiding Wang	North China University of Technology, China
Yi Wang	Hong Kong Baptist University, Hong Kong, SAR China
Xiangqian Wu	Harbin Institute of Technology, China
Lifang Wu	Beijing University of Technology, China
Xiaohua Xie	Sun Yat-sen University, China

Yuli Xue	Beihang University, China
Haibin Yan	Beijing University of Posts and Telecommunications, China
Gongping Yang	Shandong University, China
Jinfeng Yang	Civil Aviation University of China, China
Jucheng Yang	Tianjin University of Science and Technology, China
Wankou Yang	Southeast University, China
Yingchun Yang	Zhejiang University, China
Shiqi Yu	Shenzhen University, China
Weiqi Yuan	Shenyang University of Technology, China
Baochang Zhang	Beihang University, China
Lei Zhang	The Hong Kong Polytechnic University, Hong Kong, SAR China
Lin Zhang	Tongji University, China
Man Zhang	Institute of Automation, Chinese Academy of Sciences, China
Yongliang Zhang	Zhejiang University of Technology, China
Zhaoxiang Zhang	Institute of Automation, Chinese Academy of Sciences, China
Cairong Zhao	Tongji University, China
Qijun Zhao	Sichuan University, China
Weishi Zheng	Sun Yat-sen University, China
Xiuzhuang Zhou	Capital Normal University, China
En Zhu	National University of Defense Technology, China
Wangmeng Zuo	Harbin Institute of Technology, China

Publicity Chairs

| Wei Jia | HeFei University of Technology, China |
| Askar Hamdulla | Xinjiang University, China |

Doctoral Consortium Chairs

Zhaoxiang Zhang	Institute of Automation, Chinese Academy of Sciences, China
Shiqi Yu	Shenzhen University, China
Tuergen Yibulayin	Xinjiang University, China

Publication Chairs

Angelo Marcelli	University of Salerno, Italy
Jinfeng Yang	Shenzhen University, China
Liejun Wang	Xinjiang University, China

Organizing Committee Chair

| Huicheng Lai | Xinjiang University, China |

Organizing Committee

Halimulati Maimaiti	Xinjiang University, China
Alimjan Aysa	Xinjiang University, China
Wenzhong Yang	Xinjiang University, China

Contents

Hand-Based Biometrics

Dorsal Hand Vein Recognition Method Based on Multi-bit
Planes Optimization.   3
   Haoxuan Li, Yiding Wang, and Xiaochen Jiang

A Novel Finger-Knuckle-Print Recognition Based
on Batch-Normalized CNN 11
   Yikui Zhai, He Cao, Lu Cao, Hui Ma, Junyin Gan, Junying Zeng,
   Vincenzo Piuri, Fabio Scotti, Wenbo Deng, Yihang Zhi, and Jinxin Wang

A New Hand Shape Recognition Algorithm Based
on Delaunay Triangulation 22
   Fu Liu, Shoukun Jiang, Bing Kang, and Tao Hou

Finger Vein Recognition Based on Weighted Graph Structural
Feature Encoding 29
   Shuyi Li, Haigang Zhang, Guimin Jia, and Jinfeng Yang

Fingerprint Pore Extraction Using Convolutional Neural Networks
and Logical Operation 38
   Yuanhao Zhao, Feng Liu, and Linlin Shen

Palmprint Recognition Using Siamese Network. 48
   Dexing Zhong, Yuan Yang, and Xuefeng Du

A Cylinder Code-Based Partial Fingerprint Matching Algorithm
for Small Fingerprint Scanners 56
   Xiangwen Kong, Yumeng Wang, Rongsheng Wang, Changlong Jin,
   and Hakil Kim

Optimal Parameter Selection for 3D Palmprint Acquisition System 66
   Xu Liang, Gang Wu, Yan He, and Nan Luo

Gesture, Gait and Action

Residual Gating Fusion Network for Human Action Recognition 79
   Junxuan Zhang and Haifeng Hu

Study on Human Body Action Recognition 87
   Dong Yin, Yu-Qing Miao, Kang Qiu, and An Wang

Multi-view Gait Recognition Method Based on RBF Network   96
  Yaru Qiu and Yonghong Song

Video Emotion Recognition Using Local Enhanced Motion History
Image and CNN-RNN Networks.   109
  Haowen Wang, Guoxiang Zhou, Min Hu, and Xiaohua Wang

A Video Surveillance System Based on Gait Recognition   120
  Dexin Zhang and Haoxiang Zhang

Plantar Pressure Data Based Gait Recognition by Using Long
Short-Term Memory Network.   128
  Xiaopeng Li, Yuqing He, Xiaodian Zhang, and Qian Zhao

Improving Gait Recognition with 3D Pose Estimation   137
  Weizhi An, Rijun Liao, Shiqi Yu, Yongzhen Huang, and Pong C. Yuen

Cross-Cascading Regression for Simultaneous Head Pose Estimation
and Facial Landmark Detection.   148
  *Wei Zhang, Hongwen Zhang, Qi Li, Fei Liu, Zhenan Sun, Xin Li,
  and Xinxin Wan*

Real Time Violence Detection Based on Deep Spatio-Temporal Features   157
  Qing Xia, Ping Zhang, JingJing Wang, Ming Tian, and Chun Fei

Selecting the Effective Regions for Gait Recognition
by Sparse Representation   166
  Jiaqi Tan, Jiawei Wang, and Shiqi Yu

A Method of Personnel Location Based on Monocular Camera
in Complex Terrain   175
  Yanqiong Liu, Gang Shi, Qing Cui, Yuhong Sheng, and Guoqun Liu

Feature Extraction and Classification Theory

LPPNet: A Learning Network for Image Feature Extraction
and Classification   189
  Guodong Li, Haishun Du, Meihong Xiao, and Sheng Wang

Design of Multimodal Biometric Information Management System
Based on Commercial Systems   198
  Wei-Jian Zhu, Chuan-Zhi Zhuang, Jing-Wei Liu, and Ming Huang

Supervised Group Sparse Representation via Intra-class
Low-Rank Constraint.   206
  *Peipei Kang, Xiaozhao Fang, Wei Zhang, Shaohua Teng, Lunke Fei,
  Yong Xu, and Yubao Zheng*

Partial Multi-view Clustering via Auto-Weighting Similarity Completion   214
Chen Min, Miaomiao Cheng, Jian Yu, and Liping Jing

Phase Retrieval by the Inverse Power Method   223
Qi Luo, Hongxia Wang, and Jianyun Chen

Robust Discriminative Principal Component Analysis   231
Xiangxi Xu, Zhihui Lai, Yudong Chen, and Heng Kong

Guided Learning: A New Paradigm for Multi-task Classification.   239
Jingru Fu, Lei Zhang, Bob Zhang, and Wei Jia

An Image Fusion Algorithm Based on Modified Regional Consistency
and Similarity Weighting   247
Tingting Yang and Peiyu Fang

Face

Discriminative Weighted Low-Rank Collaborative Representation
Classifier for Robust Face Recognition   257
Xielian Hou, Caikou Chen, Shengwei Zhou, and Jingshan Li

Face Expression Recognition Using Gabor Features and a Novel Weber
Local Descriptor   265
*Jucheng Yang, Meng Li, Lingchao Zhang, Shujie Han, Xiaojing Wang,
and Jie Wang*

Face Synthesis for Eyeglass-Robust Face Recognition   275
Jianzhu Guo, Xiangyu Zhu, Zhen Lei, and Stan Z. Li

Single Shot Attention-Based Face Detector.   285
Chubin Zhuang, Shifeng Zhang, Xiangyu Zhu, Zhen Lei, and Stan Z. Li

Local Directional Amplitude Feature for Illumination Normalization
with Application to Face Recognition   294
Chitung Yip, Haifeng Hu, and Zhihong Chen

Facial Expression Bilinear Encoding Model   302
Haifeng Zhang, Wen Su, and Zengfu Wang

Face Clustering Utilizing Scalable Sparse Subspace Clustering
and the Image Gradient Feature Descriptor.   311
Mingkang Liu, Qi Li, Zhenan Sun, and Qiyao Deng

Fusing Multiple Deep Features for Face Anti-spoofing.   321
Yan Tang, Xing Wang, Xi Jia, and Linlin Shen

Sensitive Information of Deep Learning Based Face
Anti-spoofing Algorithms.   331
  Yukun Ma, Lifang Wu, and Meng Jian

Weighted Softmax Loss for Face Recognition via Cosine Distance   340
  Hu Zhang, Xianliang Wang, and Zhixiang He

Improving Large Pose Face Alignment by Regressing 2D and 3D
Landmarks Simultaneously and Visibility Refinement   349
  Xu Luo, Pengfei Li, Fuxuan Chen, and Qijun Zhao

RGB-D Face Recognition: A Comparative Study of Representative
Fusion Schemes   358
  Jiyun Cui, Hu Han, Shiguang Shan, and Xilin Chen

An ICA-Based Other-Race Effect Elimination for Facial
Expression Recognition   367
  Mingliang Xue, Xiaodong Duan, Wanquan Liu, and Yuehai Wang

ClusterFace: Clustering-Driven Deep Face Recognition   377
  Lingjiang Xie, Cuican Yu, Huibin Li, and Jihua Zhu

Sketch Synthesized Face Recognition with Deep Learning Models   387
  Wei Shao, Zhicheng Chen, Guangben Lu, Xiaokang Tu,
  and Yuchun Fang

Face Anti-spoofing to 3D Masks by Combining Texture
and Geometry Features   399
  Yan Wang, Song Chen, Weixin Li, Di Huang, and Yuhong Wang

An Illumination Augmentation Approach for Robust Face Recognition   409
  Zhanxiang Feng, Xiaohua Xie, Jianhuang Lai, and Rui Huang

Robust Face Recognition with Deeply Normalized Depth Images   418
  Ziqing Feng and Qijun Zhao

MobileFaceNets: Efficient CNNs for Accurate Real-Time Face
Verification on Mobile Devices.   428
  Sheng Chen, Yang Liu, Xiang Gao, and Zhen Han

Eye-Based Biometrics

Gabor Filtering and Adaptive Optimization Neural Network for Iris
Double Recognition.   441
  Shuai Liu, Yuanning Liu, Xiaodong Zhu, Zhen Liu, Guang Huo,
  Tong Ding, and Kuo Zhang

Efficient Method for Locating Optic Disc in Diabetic Retinopathy Images . . .   450
  Aili Han, Anran Yang, and Feilin Han

Research on Security of Public Security Iris Application   459
  Li Li, Shengguang Li, Shiwei Zhao, and Lin Tan

Hybrid Fusion Framework for Iris Recognition Systems.   468
  *He Zhang, Jing Liu, Zhiguo Zeng, Qianli Zhou, Shengguang Li,
  Xingguang Li, and Hui Zhang*

Design of a Long Distance Zoom Lens for Iris Recognition   476
  Xiaoyu Lv, Wenzhe Liao, Kaijun Yi, and Junxiong Gao

Efficient Near-Infrared Eye Detection Utilizing Appearance Features   486
  Qi Wang, Ying Lian, Ting Sun, Yuna Chu, and Xiangde Zhang

Attention Detection by Learning Hierarchy Feature Fusion
on Eye Movement.   497
  *Bing Liu, Peilin Jiang, Fei Wang, Xuetao Zhang, Haifan Hao,
  and Shanglin Bai*

Emerging Biometrics

An Efficient 3D Ear Recognition System Based on Indexing   507
  Qinping Zhu and Zhichun Mu

Actual Radiation Patterns-Oriented Non-deterministic Optical Wireless
Channel Characterization   517
  Jupeng Ding, Chih-Lin I, Ruiyue Xie, Huicheng Lai, and Chi Zhang

Detection of the Toe-off Feature of Planar Shoeprint Based on CNN.   528
  Xiangyu Meng, Yunqi Tang, and Wei Guo

Identification of the Normal/Abnormal Heart Sounds Based
on Energy Features and Xgboost.   536
  Ting Li, Xing-rong Chen, Hong Tang, and Xiao-ke Xu

Muscle Synergy Analysis for Stand-Squat and Squat-Stand Tasks
with sEMG Signals   545
  Chao Chen, Farong Gao, Chunling Sun, and Qiuxuan Wu

ECG Based Biometric by Superposition Matrix in Unrestricted Status   553
  Gang Zheng, Xiaoxia Sun, Shengzhen Ji, Min Dai, and Ying Sun

Ear Alignment Based on Convolutional Neural Network   562
  Li Yuan, Haonan Zhao, Yi Zhang, and Zeyu Wu

Evaluation of Outdoor Visible Light Communications Links Using Actual
LED Street Luminaries 572
   Jupeng Ding, Chih-Lin I, Chi Zhang, Baoshan Yu, and Huicheng Lai

Readback Error Classification of Radiotelephony Communication Based
on Convolutional Neural Network 580
   Fangyuan Cheng, Guimin Jia, Jinfeng Yang, and Dan Li

Determination of Sex Discriminant Function Analysis in Chinese
Human Skulls 589
   Wen Yang, Xiaoning Liu, Fei Zhu, Guohua Geng, and Kang Li

Fast and Robust Detection of Anatomical Landmarks Using Cascaded
3D Convolutional Networks Guided by Linear Square Regression 599
   *Zi-Rui Wang, Bao-Cai Yin, Jun Du, Cong Liu, Xiaodong Tao,
   and Guoping Hu*

An Automated Brain Tumor Segmentation Framework
Using Multimodal MRI 609
   Haifeng Zhao, Shuhai Chen, Shaojie Zhang, and Siqi Wang

Video-Based Pig Recognition with Feature-Integrated Transfer Learning 620
   Jianzong Wang, Aozhi Liu, and Jing Xiao

Integrating Multi-scale Gene Features for Cancer Diagnosis 632
   *Peng Hang, Mengjun Shi, Quan Long, Hui Li, Haifeng Zhao,
   and Meng Ma*

Behavioral Biometrics

A Novel Multiple Distances Based Dynamic Time Warping Method
for Online Signature Verification 645
   Xinyi Lu, Yuxun Fang, Qiuxia Wu, Junhong Zhao, and Wenxiong Kang

The Detection of Beard Behavior of Taxi Drivers Based
on Traffic Surveillance Video 653
   *Zuyun Wang, Xunping Huang, Kebin Jia, Pengyu Liu,
   and Zhonghua Sun*

Robust Recognition Algorithm for Fall Down Behavior 662
   Wei Yan, Jianbin Xie, Peiqin Li, and Tong Liu

Multi-source Interactive Behavior Analysis for Continuous
User Authentication on Smartphones 669
   Xiaozi Liu, Chao Shen, and Yufei Chen

Character-Based N-gram Model for Uyghur Text Retrieval.   678
Turdi Tohti, Lirui Xu, Jimmy Huang, Winira Musajan,
and Askar Hamdulla

Multi-task Network Learning Representation Features of Attributes
and Identity for Person Re-identification   689
Junqian Wang and Mengsi Lyu

BoVW Based Feature Selection for Uyghur Offline Signature Verification. . .   700
Shu-Jing Zhang, Mahpirat, Yunus Aysa, and Kurban Ubul

Research on the Methods for Extracting the Sensitive Uyghur
Text-Images for Digital Forensics   709
Yasen Aizezi, Anniwaer Jiamali, Ruxianguli Abdurixiti,
and Kurban Ubul

A Study on the Printed Uyghur Script Recognition Technique
Using Word Visual Features.   719
Halimulati Meimaiti

Multilingual Offline Handwritten Signature Recognition Based
on Statistical Features   727
Kurban Ubul, Xiao-li Wang, Ahat Yimin, Shu-jing Zhang,
and Tuergen Yibulayin

HMM-Based Off-Line Uyghur Signature Recognition   736
Long-Fei Mo, Hornisa Mamat, Mutallip Mamut, Alimjan Aysa,
and Kurban Ubul

Author Index   745

Hand-Based Biometrics

Dorsal Hand Vein Recognition Method Based on Multi-bit Planes Optimization

Haoxuan Li[(✉)], Yiding Wang, and Xiaochen Jiang

North China University of Technology, Beijing, China
lhxlihaoxuan@sina.com

Abstract. With the development of technology, how to improve the accuracy of dorsal hand vein recognition has become the focus of current research. In order to solve this problem, this paper proposes a dorsal hand vein image recognition method which is based on multi-bit planes and Deep Learning network. The multi-bit planes can not only fully use the gray information of the images but also their intrinsic relationship between the bit planes of the images. In addition, the bit plane with less information is removed according to the Euclidean distance, and a new bit planes sequence is formed, and the accuracy of the recognition of the dorsal hand vein is improved. The algorithm is tested on the real dorsal hand vein database, and the recognition accuracy is more than 99%, which proves the effectiveness of the algorithm.

Keywords: Dorsal hand vein recognition · Multi-bit planes
SqueezeNet network · Euclidean distance

1 Introduction

In the current society, with the continuous development of technology, especially the innovation of information technology, traditional authentication measures, such as passwords, cards, and keys, can no longer satisfy people's security requirements [1]. Due to its uniqueness and long-term stability, the dorsal hand vein is widely used in many fields, such as companies, factories, airports, schools, and so on.

At present, the traditional dorsal hand vein recognition algorithm is still limited to the classic algorithms to extract feature points from the original image, such as SIFT, LBP, PCA and so on [2, 3], and then use the classifier to identify. It cannot fully use the image's gray information and there are factors such as rotation, light and so on [4].

In recent years, convolutional neural network (CNN) have become the focus of research in the field of biometrics [5]. Deep learning is based on the automatic extraction of feature information of large data through the network and the use of iterative training to generate classifiers. The effectiveness of classification and recognition is significantly improved. The sequence of bit planes is obtained from grayscale information that preserves the grayscale profile of the hand veins. It can completely represent all the image information, and the internal relationship between each bit plane is unique. However, not every bit plane can effectively represent the information of image, that is to say such bit plane is of high interference. The bit plane with less information is removed according to the Euclidean distance [6], and a new suitable bit

J. Zhou et al. (Eds.): CCBR 2018, LNCS 10996, pp. 3–10, 2018.
https://doi.org/10.1007/978-3-319-97909-0_1

planes sequence is formed. The gray information of images is fully utilized. The SqueezeNet network [7] is adaptable to application of multiple fields. Therefore, the combine of the suitable multi-bit planes and the SqueezeNet network is the main point of this paper.

2   The Generation of Multi-bit Planes

2.1   Collection of Images

This paper uses a reflective infrared light source and an infrared light wave of a wavelength of 850 nm to collect the dorsal hand vein images from a CCD camera with an infrared filter. The device is shown in Fig. 1. The appearance of the device is shown in Fig. 1(a) and the internal structure of the device is shown in Fig. 1(b).

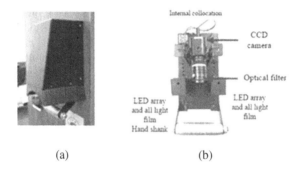

(a)   (b)

Fig. 1. Image collection equipment

The original images are shown in Fig. 2(a), (b), and (c) are three people's dorsal hand vein images.

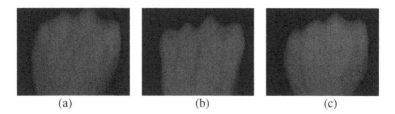

(a)   (b)   (c)

Fig. 2. Original dorsal hand vein images

2.2   Preprocessing of Image

Since the Otsu threshold segmentation method (OTSU) [8] has a good segmentation effect on the target background, and the great difference of gray scale between the dorsal hand vein and the background, this paper uses the OTSU to segment the vein images. The segmented image is shown in Fig. 3.

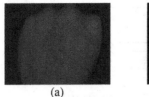 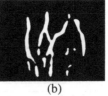

(a)   (b)

Fig. 3. Segmentation of Image

In order to obtain bit planes sequence, it is necessary to obtain a grayscale image which only retains original grayscale vein. The binary image Fig. 3(b) is multiplied with the original image Fig. 3(a) to obtain a grayscale dorsal hand vein image by:

$$G(x, y) = T(x, y) \times M(x, y) \tag{1}$$

Where $M(x, y)$ denotes original image, $T(x, y)$ denotes binary image, and $G(x, y)$ denotes grayscale image. The grayscale image is shown in Fig. 4.

Fig. 4. Grayscale Image

In order to obtain more image information, the multi-bit planes are to be researched. The concept of the bit plane is illustrated by a 256-level grayscale image. If each pixel of the image is from 0 to 255, each pixel value can be represented by an eight-bit binary number, such as $b_7, b_6, b_5, b_4, b_3, b_2, b_1, b_0$. Each bit has a value of 0 or 1, and each pixel can be divided into eight bits by:

$$I = b_7 \times 2^7 + b_6 \times 2^6 + b_5 \times 2^5 + b_4 \times 2^4 + b_3 \times 2^3 + b_2 \times 2^2 + b_1 \times 2^1 + b_0 \times 2^0 \tag{2}$$

Each item in formula (2) represents a plane of pixels. The bit plane is shown in Fig. 5.

The eight bits planes are shown in Fig. 6(b) to (i).

As shown in the below images in Fig. 6, the 2nd (c), 5th(f), 6th(g), 7th(h), and 8th(i) bit planes can completely represent the informative image, but the 1st(b), 3rd(d), and 4th (e) bit planes contain little image information and may interfere with the recognition result. Therefore, it is necessary to optimize the bit planes sequence.

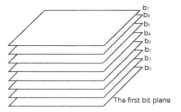

Fig. 5. Bit plane diagram

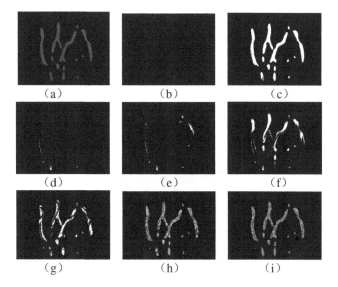

Fig. 6. Bit plane sequence

3 Optimization of Multi-bit Planes

In the abovementioned multi-bit planes, the first, third, and fourth planes contain little image information and may affect the overall recognition result. Eight groups of single-bit plane are tested Through SqueezeNet network training. The recognition rates of the first, third, and fourth bit planes are very low, all less than 0.8. The experimental results are shown in Table 1.

This paper uses the Euclidean distance to exclude situations where different people are highly correlated in same bit planes. The Euclidean distance is the actual distance between two points in two-dimensional space by:

$$dis(X; Y) = \sum_{x \in X} \sum_{y \in Y} \sqrt{(x_i - x)^2 + (y_i - y)^2} \tag{3}$$

Table 1. Single bit plane training and test results

Bit-plane	1st	2nd	3rd	4th	5th	6th	7th	8th
Recognition rate	0.02	0.98	0.70	0.60	0.86	0.92	0.96	0.98

The Euclidean distance between the same bit planes of every two different samples are calculated, and the numbers of a bit plane's Euclidean distance of 100 samples will come to be 4950. The average Euclidean distance of a bit plane are shown in Table 2.

Table 2. The average Euclidean distance of each bit plane

Bit-plane	1st	2nd	3rd	4th	5th	6th	7th	8th
Euclidean Distance	0	0.903	0.109	0.278	0.714	0.602	0.541	0.480

According to Table 2, the mean values of Euclidean distance of the 1st 3rd and 4th bit plane are obviously low and does not exceed 0.3. It is proved that there is little difference between the 1st, 3rd, and 4th planes of every two samples, when such bit planes are tested, the testing results may be wrong. In short, this paper will form a new bit planes sequence according to the abovementioned experiment, the new experimental sequence includes the 2nd, 5th, 6th, 7th, and 8th bit planes.

4 Classification Experiment Based on SqueezeNet Network

With the development of technology, CNN have been widely used in the field of computer vision. Compared with traditional pattern recognition methods, CNN have the advantages of self-adaptive and automatic feature extraction. After a large amount of data training and iteration, CNN achieves the best results. This paper selects the SqueezeNet network for training and testing. Compared with the traditional CNN, it has the advantage of ensuring a high performance with less parameters, and the model is more concise. SqueezeNet's performance advantages rely mainly on the Fire Module structure. The SqueezeNet network model is small and belongs to the light network. Therefore, in practical applications, micro-processors can be used for calculations to facilitate subsequent development. Because of the small sample, the deep network cannot play an advantage, and may even cause the phenomenon of overfitting. Therefore, the SqueezeNet network is suitable for this work as a shallow network. The Fire Module structure consists of two sub-layers, the squeeze layer and the expand layer, which are connected by an activation function. SqueezeNet network structure shown in Fig. 7.

There are 100 samples (100 people), each person is collected 20 dorsal vein images (one hand), among them 18 images as the training set and the 2 images as the testing set. The TensorFlow framework is applied to The SqueezeNet network, the hardware configuration includes the Intel core i5 7500 CPU, and the GTX1080Ti GPU. Comparing two optimizers, Root Mean Square Propagation (RMSProp) and Adaptive

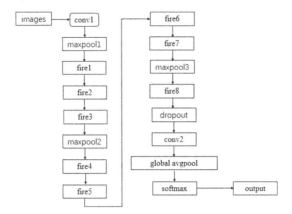

Fig. 7. SqueezeNet network structure

Table 3. Training results under different optimizers and elimination rates

Optimizer	Dropout ratio	Loss
RMSProp	0.4	0.05485
	0.5	0.00157
	0.6	0.01321
Adam	0.4	0.00637
	0.5	0.00065
	0.6	0.00109

moment estimation (Adam) [9], parameters are optimized through setting the elimination rate in the dropout layer. The experimental results are shown in Table 3.

As shown in Table 3, loss function value of the Adam optimizer is lower than RMSProp, and the loss function value is the lowest when the elimination rate is 0.5. Therefore, the best elimination rate is 0.5, and the Adam is as optimizer chooses for training. What's more, this paper chooses cross-entropy algorithm [10] as loss value.

This paper uses two kinds of schemes to verify the Experimental result. The first scheme uses a multi-bit planes image to train the data set. Five bits planes images include 10000 samples, among them 9000 images are used as a training set and 1000 pictures as a testing set. The input of network is a sequence of images including the 2nd, 5th, 6th, 7th, and 8th bit planes per person. The testing set is also a sequence of images for five bits planes of each person of. The flow chart of the algorithm is shown in Fig. 8.

The second scheme is to merge the training models of the 2nd, 5th, 6th, 7th, and 8th bit planes to get the final recognition result. The weights of the single-bit plane training model fusion are a = b = c = d = e = 0.2. The flow chart of the algorithm is shown in Fig. 9.

Recognition rates of the two schemes are shown in Table 4.

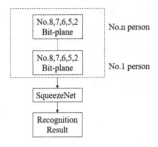

Fig. 8. Flow chart of the Multi-bit plane image network model

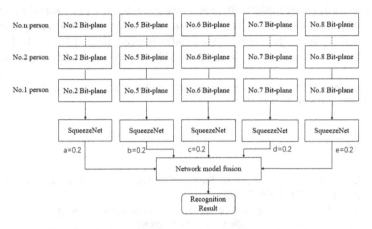

Fig. 9. Single bit plane network model fusion flow chart

Table 4. Comparison of experimental schemes

Experimental schemes	Recognition rate
Single bit-plane model fusion	0.98
Multi-bit planes sequence	1.00

Comparing two recognition rates in Table 4, we can know that at the aspect of classification recognition rate of the multi-bit planes model is superior than the single-bit plane fusion model. In addition, comparing with the traditional algorithms, such as PCA and LBP, recognition rates of dorsal hand vein is greatly improved through our algorithm. The several Recognition rates are shown in Table 5.

Table 5. The recognition rate of different algorithms

Name	Recognition rate
LBP	0.94
PCA	0.90
Ours	1.00

5 Conclusion

According to the problem of recognition rate of dorsal hand vein is not very ideal, this paper proposes a method which is based on multi-bit planes and SqueezeNet network.

This paper selects the suitable bit planes sequence through Euclidean distance. The intrinsic connection between the bit planes is used to achieve the best recognition rate. The dorsal hand vein images are processed and optimized through our method, then be trained and tested through CNN, which proves the superiority of this algorithm.

Acknowledgment. This work was supported by the National Natural Science Fund Committee of China (NSFC no. 61673021).

References

1. Jian, L.I., Sheng, C.X., Han, Z., et al.: Survey of research on identity management. Comput. Eng. Des. **30**(6), 1364–1365 (2009)
2. Wang, Y.X., Liu, T.G., Jiang, J.F., et al.: Hand vein recognition using local SIFT feature analysis. J. Optoelectron. Laser **20**(5), 681–684 (2009)
3. Luo, Y.T., Zhao, L.Y., Zhang, B., et al.: Local line directional pattern for palmprint recognition. Pattern Recognit. **50**(1), 26–44 (2016)
4. Jia, W., Hu, R.X., Lei, Y.K., et al.: Histogram of oriented lines for palmprint recognition. IEEE Trans. Syst. Man Cybern. Syst. **44**(3), 385–395 (2014)
5. Syafeeza, A.R.: Convolutional neural networks for face recognition and finger-vein biometric identification (2014)
6. Wang, L., Zhang, Y., Feng, J.: On the Euclidean distance of images. IEEE Trans. Pattern Anal. Mach. Intell. **27**(8), 1334–1339 (2005)
7. Iandola, F.N., Han, S., Moskewicz, M.W., et al.: SqueezeNet: AlexNet-level accuracy with 50x fewer parameters and <0.5 MB model size (2016)
8. Otsu, N.: A threshold selection method from gray-level histograms. IEEE Trans. Syst. Man Cybernet. **9**(1), 62–66 (2007)
9. Wilson, A.C., Roelofs, R., Stern, M., et al.: The marginal value of adaptive gradient methods in machine learning (2017)
10. Farahnak-Ghazani, F., Baghshah, M.S.: Multi-label classification with feature-aware implicit encoding and generalized cross-entropy loss. In: Electrical Engineering, pp. 1574–1579. IEEE (2016)

A Novel Finger-Knuckle-Print Recognition Based on Batch-Normalized CNN

Yikui Zhai[1], He Cao[1], Lu Cao[1(✉)], Hui Ma[1], Junyin Gan[1],
Junying Zeng[1], Vincenzo Piuri[3], Fabio Scotti[3], Wenbo Deng[1],
Yihang Zhi[2], and Jinxin Wang[1]

[1] School of Information Engineering, Wuyi University,
Dongchengstr. 22, Jiangmen 529020, China
yikuizhai@163.com, caohe115@163.com,
caolu20001742@163.com, mahuiwuyi@163.com,
junyinggan@163.com, zengjunying@163.com,
wenbodeng92@163.com, 18326410857@163.com
[2] School of Computer, Wuyi University,
Dongchengstr. 22, Jiangmen 529020, China
yihangzhi0@163.com
[3] Dipartimento Di Informatica, Universita' degli Studi di Milano,
Milan 26013, CR, Italy
{vincenzo.piuri,fabio.scotti}@unimi.it

Abstract. Traditional feature extraction methods, such as Gabor filter and competitive coding, have been widely used in finger-knuckle-print (FKP) recognition. However, these methods focus on manually designed features which may not achieve satisfying results on FKP images. In order to solve this problem, a novel batch-normalized Convolutional Neural Network (CNN) architecture with data augmentation for FKP recognition is proposed. Firstly, a novel batch-normalized CNN is designed specifically for FKP recognition. Then, random histogram equalization is adopted as data augmentation here for training the CNN in FKP recognition. Meanwhile, batch-normalization is adopted to avoid overfitting during network training. Extensive experiments performed on the PolyU FKP database show that compared with traditional feature extraction method, the proposed method can not only extract more discriminative features, but also improve the accuracy of FKP recognition.

Keywords: Finger-knuckle-print · Batch-normalized · Data augmentation

1 Introduction

Due to the huge market demand of personal authentication, it has attracted much attention in the academic and industry fields. Biometric authentication [1–4] can provide higher security than normal computer passwords which are utilize in applications such as: bank security, computer security system and national ID card etc. Over the past few decades, researchers have focused on the use of biometric traits, like face, fingerprint, iris, palmprint, hand vein, voice, gait etc. In recent years, hand-based biometrics have attracted more attention compared to other biometrics identifiers.

© Springer Nature Switzerland AG 2018
J. Zhou et al. (Eds.): CCBR 2018, LNCS 10996, pp. 11–21, 2018.
https://doi.org/10.1007/978-3-319-97909-0_2

Biometrics, such as palmprint [1], hand geometry [2], fingerprint [3] and hand vein [4], have been fully researched.

Owing to the uniqueness of FKP, FKP can be considered as a distinctive biometric identifier technique [5, 6]. The unique advantages of the FKP, compared with other biometrics are as follows: the surface of FKP is not easy to be abraded because people usually hold things with the inner side of their hands. Because of non-contact characteristic the collection of the FKP, the users usually have higher acceptance [7]. As such, FKP is considered one of the most promising personal identification technologies of the future.

However, to the best of our knowledge, these are no investigations about the application of convolution neural network for FKP recognition. Hence, we designed a novel batch-normalized CNN with deep learning method for FKP recognition to improve recognition accuracy. Compared with traditional methods, the proposed CNN could extract more distinctive features and achieve satisfying recognition performance. The main contributions of this paper are as follows: (i) A novel CNN architecture specialty for FKP recognition is designed. (ii) Histogram equalization method as a data augmentation method is adopted to get more training data for FKP recognition. (iii) Batch-normalization is utilized to prevent overfitting in CNN, respectively.

The rest of this paper is structured as follows: Sect. 2 introduces the existing FKP recognition methods. Section 3 presents the proposed batch-normalized CNN architecture. Section 4 describes the recognition process of FKP images. Section 5 shows and analyses the experimental results. Finally, Sect. 6 presents the conclusions.

2 Related Work

Many recent studies on FKP recognition attempt to generate distinctive and robust feature representation for FKP images. Woodard et al. [8, 9] built a 3D hand database and extract 3-D features from finger surface for authentication. Due to the high cost and time consuming of 3D acquisition equipment, the real-time performance of the bio-metrics system is affected. And there is no effective system for the extraction of the characteristics of the outer surface of the finger. Kumar et al. [10, 11] extracted finger-back surface image features to personal authentication by subspace analysis methods. Subspace analysis is widely used in face recognition task because it has the characteristics of strong distinctive, low computational cost, it is easy to realize and good separability; however, it cannot effectively extract the line features, such as FKP images. Zhang et al. [12] used Gabor filters to extract the feature and use the competitive coding (CompCode) to encode it, as the final feature representation for FKP images. Later, Zhang et al. [5] used Gabor filter to extract the orientation information and magnitude information of FKP images. In [13], the coefficient of the Fourier transform of the FKP images as features, and the similarity of the images is calculated by band-limited phase-only correlation technique. To obtain more FKP images, Morales et al. [14] used Gabor filter to enhance the FKP lines, then adopted Scale Invariant Feature Transform (SIFT) to extract features. Le et al. [15] proposed a robust feature presentation and matching method based on Speeded-Up Robust Features (SURF). This method is robust, which is invariant to the change of rotation, scale and viewpoint. Barinath et al. [16] used a combination of SIFT and SURF to enhance the texture of FKP images. Owing to the complementarity of the two described approaches, the FKP recognition method made great progress. Li et al. [17] used a high-order steerable filter to extract continuous orientation feature maps, an Adaptive Steerable Orientation Coding Scheme (ASOC) is proposed. Yang et al. [18] proposed a Fisher discriminant analysis framework for FKP recognition. Zhang et al. [19] used RCode1 and RCode2 to code feature, improving the FKP recognition rate; however, these methods could not achieve desirable FKP recognition results.

3 Batch-Normalized CNN

A novel CNN architecture specifically for FKP recognition has been designed. The batch-normalized CNN architecture is shown in Fig. 1, which includes 4 convolution layers and 3 fully connected layers. 'C' denotes the convolution layer, the maxpooling layer and the full connection layer are represented by 'MP' and 'FC', respectively. During the training stage, the input of the CNN is a 220 × 110 grayscale image; all the images are cropped into 110 × 110 randomly as the input of the entire network. The parameters of each layer are optimized based on multiple experimental verification. Owing to the small FKP database, the solution to avoid overfitting is crucial. Hence, to prevent the training overfitting, a dropout layer is adopted in the proposed CNN and a batch of normalized layer is added after each convolution layer. Details of the network structure and parameters of batch-normalized CNN are shown in Table 1.

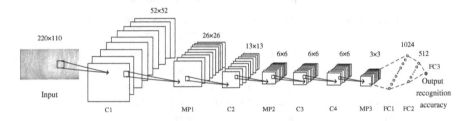

Fig. 1. The batch-normalized CNN architecture.

3.1 Batch-Normalized Convolutional Neural Networks

Due to the change of parameters of the previous network layers during the training process, the input of other layers will be affected. This leads to a large amount of computation from deep neural networks. This may reduce the speed of training, requiring lower learning rates and a careful parameter initialization. This makes training models notoriously difficult to saturating nonlinearities [21].

Batch normalization can be used for activation sets in a network. Here, we consider a affine transform followed by an element nonlinearity:

$$z = g(Wu + b) \tag{1}$$

where W and b represent the parameters that the model needs to optimize. Function $g(\cdot)$ represents a non-linearity function such as ReLU. Batch normalization is applied to the all convolutional layers and the full connected layers. And BN transform is added by normalizing $x = Wu + b$ before non-linearity. The input layer u should be normalized, because u is the output of another non-linear layer whose distribution may change during the training process. This also limits the first and second phases of the input layer and mitigating the covariance shift. On the contrary, since $Wu + b$ has symmetry and a non-sparse distribution, normalizing is more likely to produce a stable distribution of the excitation function.

Note that the subsequent mean subtraction can cancel the effects of bias b, so bias b can be ignored, as a result, $z = g(Wu + b)$ can be replaced with:

$$z = g(BN(Wu)) \tag{2}$$

A pair of parameters $\gamma(k)$ and $\beta(k)$ are optimized at each layer, where BN transform is utilized.

For convolutional layers, we also require that the normalization should obey the convolutional property, so that the same feature maps at different locations using different elements are normalized in the same way. In order to achieve this, all the activations at all locations are normalized in a mini-batch. Given a feature map, all the activation of a given feature map adopts the same linear transformation.

Table 1. Comparison of network model architecture.

Layer name	Alexnet [20]	Batch-normalized CNN
Input	224	220×110
Conv1	96,11 $\times$ 11 kernels	96,7 $\times$ 7 kernels
Conv2	256,5 $\times$ 5 kernels	128,5 $\times$ 5 kernels
Conv3	384,3 $\times$ 3 kernels	128,3 $\times$ 3 kernels
Conv4	384,3 $\times$ 3 kernels	128,3 $\times$ 3 kernels
IP1	4096	1024
IP2	4096	512
IP3	1000	165
Loss	Softmax	Softmax
Convolution kernels	1376	480

3.2   ReLU Activation Function

Compared with traditional saturated nonlinear activation functions, such as tanh and sigmoid, etc. ReLU (Rectified Linear Units), as non-saturated nonlinear activation function, has a faster network convergence speed. During forward propagation sigmoid and tanh function requires exponential calculation, while ReLU only needs to set a threshold value. In this paper, we utilized ReLU as the activation function of the CNN architecture, which mimics the characteristics of a unilateral and a sparse activation of biological neurons. ReLU activation function can be expressed as:

$$f(x) = \max(0, x) \tag{3}$$

When the input is less than or equal to 0, the response is 0, otherwise the response directly equals its own value. Due to the characteristics of the ReLU function, the output has some sparsity, which can speed up the network convergence and make the CNN have a stronger classification ability.

$$f'(x) \begin{cases} 0, & x \leq 0 \\ 1, & x > 0 \end{cases} \tag{4}$$

By Eq. (4), the gradient is not saturated, only when $x > 0$, $f'(x) = 1$; therefore, in the process of backward propagation, the problem of gradient dispersion can be alleviated and the parameters of CNN can be updated quickly.

4   FKP Recognition Process

The recognition process of FKP images is divided into two stages: training and testing. Training stage includes three parts: ROI extraction, data augmentation and batch-normalized CNN training. The quality of the training data is critical to the training of the network, so it is necessary to ensure that the adopted database is effective. Firstly, we adopted a two-stage center point detection [22] to improve the positioning accuracy in skewed conditions. Secondly, histogram equalization method is utilized to obtain more data for the FKP recognition. Finally, the preprocessed training data is used as an input to train the proposed CNN model. The testing stage includes two parts: data preprocessing (ROI extraction) and identifying results. First, preprocessing testing data, and then the trained model is adopted to recognize FKP images.

4.1   ROI Extraction

The FKP images have a lot of background noise, which will do harm to the recognition rate. [23, 24] shows that the recognition performance of FKP image recognition highly depends on the accuracy of ROI extraction. This paper used a more effective two-stage center point detection method [22] to extract ROI of FKP images. The method has two stages: center point preliminary detection and center point secondary precise positioning. For more details, please refer to [22]. In Fig. 2, the first row are the original FKP images of four people in the PolyU FKP database [25] and images in the second row are the ROI images, respectively.

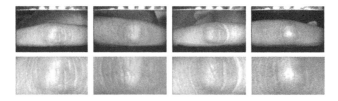

Fig. 2. Original FKP images and ROI images.

(a)   (b)

Fig. 3. (a) FKP ROI image, (b) FKP ROI image with histogram equalization.

4.2 Data Augmentation via Random Histogram Equalization

As shown in Fig. 3(a), the FKP ROI image has been curved with an nonuniform reflections, resulting in a low contrast; hence, we augmented the FKP ROI images by histogram equalization method to a better texture image distribution. Additionaly, PolyU database is small, which will bring limitations to the algorithm, making it appear overfitted in the learning process. Inspired by [26], histogram equalization was used with different levels to augment the FKP data, which significantly improve the classification results. In general, the FKP database after histogram equalization will satisfy the requirement of the data quantity and avoids the overfitting phenomenon.

Given an image, the gray level is distributed $0 \leq r \leq 1$ after normalization. For any r within [0,1] interval, it can be transformed as:

$$s = T(r) \tag{5}$$

The transformation function $T(r)$ should satisfy two conditions: firstly, it increases monotonously in [0,1] interval to ensure the grayscale of the image changes from white to black orderly. Secondly, after the mapping transformation, the value of s must be guaranteed within the [0,1] interval. The discrete form of r's probability density function is as follows:

$$P_r(r_k) = \frac{n_k}{n} \tag{6}$$

Among them, $P_r(r_k)$ represents the distribution of image gray level, r_k represents the discrete gray level, where $0 \leq r_k \leq 1$, $k = 0,1,2..., n\text{-}1$. n denotes the total number of pixels, and n_k denote the number of r_k appearing in the image, respectively. Image histogram equalization can be expressed as:

$$S_r = T(r_i) = \sum_{i-0}^{k} \frac{n_i}{n} \tag{7}$$

where k is the gray level, $0 \le r_k \le 1$, $k = 0,1,2..., n-1$. The original FKP image and FKP image after histogram equalization is shown in Fig. 3(a) and (b).

By setting different thresholds (low-in, high-in, low-out and high-out) and using the transformation function ($T(r)$), the amount of the training images will be 360 times more than the original database. The values that are smaller than the low-in values will be mapped to low-out, while the values that bigger than high-in values will be mapped to high-out, and the values between low-in and high-in will be transformed into [low-out, high-out] by $T(r)$.

5 Experimental Results

The experiment was configured with on a desktop computer with Intel Xeon E5-2620v2, 2.1 GHz CPUs, 80 GB RAM, a single NVIDIA Tesla K20c, on Windows 10 operation system. The training and testing of the proposed CNN model are based on the publicly available Caffe Library [29].

5.1 PolyU Database

Extensive experiment is performed on PolyU FKP database, which shows the performance of the proposed CNN architecture. The database's images were obtained by collecting finger images from 165 volunteers, with a ratio of nearly 3:1 for male and female. Among them, the proportion of people aged 20–30 and 30–50 years is close to 7:1. All images are collected in two sessions. In each session, the volunteer's left index, left middle, right index and right middle images were collected, each using 6 images, respectively. Overall, the database contained 7920 images of 660 different fingers from 165 volunteers. The average finger image collection time interval from the first to the second session was 25 days. Among them, the maximum and minimum collected time intervals between two sessions were 196 days and 14 days, respectively. After ROI extraction and data augmentation, the final image size was 220 × 110. Here, we use the histogram equalization mentioned in Sect. 4.2 to augment the data.

5.2 Configuration of Training Parameters

Training parameters are set as follows:

(1) prepare data sets, and divide the PolyU database into 6:1:5 as training, validation, and test data sets, respectively. More specifically, the training set randomly selected 6 images from each subject. The same method is used to complete the preparation of the validation sets and test sets.

(2) we set the momentum to 0.9, the weight decay of all the convolution layers and the first fully connected layer is 5e−4, and the fixed learning rate is 0.001. Randomly initialized the tunable network parameters and started the training of the network.

(3) during the training process, when the verification accuracy is no longer trending upwards, then reducing the learning rate to continue training until the verification accuracy is no longer increasing.

(4) the test results were obtained by selecting the model with the highest verification accuracy and the least loss.

(5) we set the dropout rate to 0.5, which gets the best performance.

5.3   FKP Experimental Results

The recognition results are shown in Table 2, where LI denotes left index finger, LM denotes left middle finger, RI denotes right index finger and RM denotes right middle finger.

Table 2. Comparison results of proposed FKP recognition algorithms and other algorithms.

Recognition method	Finger			
	LI	LM	RI	RM
	TTR(%)	TTR(%)	TTR(%)	TTR(%)
BP [30]	92.6	92.5	93.2	93.0
Ordinal Code [31]	97.3	95.9	96.3	95.9
BOCV [32]	97.6	97.6	97.6	97.7
RLOC [33]	97.8	97.7	97.9	97.7
SRC [34]	98.7	98.7	98.4	98.0
Comp Code [35]	98.0	98.0	98.2	98.1
AlexNet	85.6	86.5	85.2	85.2
AlexNet with AD	88.3	90.2	86.8	89.9
Batch-normalized CNN	89.7	92.1	87.1	91.3
Batch-normalized CNN with AD	99.1	98.9	99.4	98.3

To verify the effect of the augmented data on the proposed CNN architecture, the contrast experiment was added. Experimental results show the effectiveness of the proposed CNN on augmentation data used in this paper. The training of network model is relying on the scale of training data; hence, increasing the training sample can improve network testing performance.

From the experimental results, we know that Comp Code accuracy is 98.0%, 98.0%, 98.2% and 98.1%, respectively. The proposed CNN on the proposed augmented data can obtain the state-of-the-art recognition accuracy of 99.1%, 98.9%, 99.4% and 98.3%, correspondingly. Compared with the state-of-the-art methods, such as AlexNet, BP [30], Ordinal Code [31], BOCV [32], RLOC [33], SRC [34] and Comp Code [35], the structure proposed in this paper has achieved the best results.

6   Conclusion

In this paper, we proposed a novel batch-normalized CNN for FKP recognition. A data augmentation method of random histogram equalization and a dropout layer were adopted to prevent overfitting during training in the proposed neural network architecture. Experimental results on finger-knuckle-print database established by the PolyU show that the batch-normalized CNN could achieved satisfying results in recognizing finger-knuckle-print.

Acknowledgments. This work is supported by National of Nature Science Foundation Grant (No. 61372193, No. 61771347), Guangdong Higher Education Outstanding Young Teachers Training Program Grant (No. SYQ2014001), Characteristic Innovation Project of Guangdong Province (No. 2015KTSCX 143, 2015KTSCX145, 2015KTSCX148), Youth Innovation Talent Project of Guangdong Province (No. 2015KQNCX172, No. 2016KQNCX171), Science and Technology Project of Jiangmen City (No. 201501003001556, No. 201601003002191), and China National Oversea Study Scholarship Fund.

References

1. Fei, L., Wen, J., Zhang, Z., et al.: Local multiple directional pattern of palmprint image, 3013–3018. In: The 23rd International Conference on Pattern Recognition (ICPR) (2016)
2. Bapat, A., Kanhangad, V.: Segmentation of hand from cluttered backgrounds for hand geometry biometrics. In: IEEE Region 10 Symposium (TENSYMP), pp. 1–4 (2017)
3. Chatterjee, A., Bhatia, V., Prakash, S.: Anti-spoof touchless 3D fingerprint recognition system using single shot fringe projection and biospeckle analysis. Opt. Lasers Eng. **95**, 1–7 (2017)
4. Huang, D., Zhang, R., Yin, Y., et al.: Local feature approach to dorsal hand vein recognition by centroid-based circular key-point grid and fine-grained matching. Image Vis. Comput. **58**, 266–277 (2017)
5. Zhang, L., Zhang, L., Zhang, D., et al.: Online finger-knuckle-print verification for personal authentication. Pattern Recogn. **43**(7), 2560–2571 (2010)
6. Zhang, L., Zhang, L., Zhang, D., et al.: Ensemble of local and global information for finger-knuckle-print recognition. Pattern Recogn. **44**(9), 1990–1998 (2011)
7. Kumar, A., Ravikanth, C.: Personal authentication using finger knuckle surface. IEEE Trans. Inf. Forensics Secur. **4**(1), 98–110 (2009)
8. Woodard, D.L, Flynn, P.J.: Personal identification utilizing finger surface features. In: IEEE Conference on Computer Vision and Pattern Recognition (CVPR), vol. 2, pp. 1030–1036 (2005)
9. Woodard, D.L., Flynn, P.J.: Finger surface as a biometric identifier. Comput. Vis. Image Underst. **100**(3), 357–384 (2005)
10. Ravikanth, C., Kumar, A.: Biometric authentication using finger-back surface. In: IEEE Conference on Computer Vision and Pattern Recognition, pp. 1–6 (2007)
11. Kumar, A., Ravikanth, C.: Personal authentication using finger knuckle surface. IEEE Trans. Inf. Forensics Secur. **4**(1), 98–110 (2009)
12. Zhang, L., Zhang, L., Zhang, D.: Finger-knuckle-print: a new biometric identifier. In: IEEE International Conference on Image Processing (ICIP), pp. 1981–1984 (2009)

13. Zhang, L., Zhang, L., Zhang, D.: Finger-knuckle-print verification based on band-limited phase-only correlation. In: Jiang, X., Petkov, N. (eds.) CAIP 2009. LNCS, vol. 5702, pp. 141–148. Springer, Heidelberg (2009). https://doi.org/10.1007/978-3-642-03767-2_17

14. Morales, A., Travieso, C.M., Ferrer, M.A., et al.: Improved finger-knuckle-print authentication based on orientation enhancement. Electron. Lett. **47**(6), 380–381 (2011)

15. Le, Z.: Finger knuckle print recognition based on surf algorithm. In: The Eighth International Conference on Fuzzy Systems and Knowledge Discovery (FSKD), vol. 3, pp. 1879–1883 (2011)

16. Badrinath, G.S., Nigam, A., Gupta, P.: An efficient finger-knuckle-print based recognition system fusing SIFT and SURF matching scores. In: Qing, S., Susilo, W., Wang, G., Liu, D. (eds.) ICICS 2011. LNCS, vol. 7043, pp. 374–387. Springer, Heidelberg (2011). https://doi.org/10.1007/978-3-642-25243-3_30

17. Li, Z., Wang, K., Zuo, W.: Finger-knuckle-print recognition using local orientation feature based on steerable filter. In: Huang, D.-S., Gupta, P., Zhang, X., Premaratne, P. (eds.) ICIC 2012. CCIS, vol. 304, pp. 224–230. Springer, Heidelberg (2012). https://doi.org/10.1007/978-3-642-31837-5_33

18. Yang, W., Sun, C., Zhang, L.: A multi-manifold discriminant analysis method for image feature extraction. Pattern Recogn. **44**(8), 1649–1657 (2011)

19. Zhang, L., Li, H.: Encoding local image patterns using riesz transforms: with applications to palmprint and finger-knuckle-print recognition. Image Vis. Comput. **30**(12), 1043–1051 (2012)

20. Krizhevsky, A., Sutskever, I., Hinton, G.E.: Imagenet classification with deep convolutional neural networks. In: Advances in Neural Information Processing Systems, pp. 1097–1105 (2012)

21. Ioffe, S., Szegedy, C.: Batch normalization: accelerating deep network training by reducing internal covariate shift. In: International Conference on Machine Learning (ICML), pp. 448–456 (2015)

22. Yu, H., Yang, G., Wang, Z., et al.: A new finger-knuckle-print ROI extraction method based on two-stage center point detection. Int. J. Sig. Process. Image Proc. Pattern Recogn. **8**(2), 185–200 (2015)

23. Meraoumia, A., Chitroub, S., Bouridane, A.: Palmprint and finger-knuckle-print for efficient person recognition based on log-gabor filter response. Analog Integr. Circ. Sig. Process **69**(1), 17–27 (2011)

24. Xiong, M., Yang, W., Sun, C.: Finger-knuckle-print recognition using LGBP. In: Liu, D., Zhang, H., Polycarpou, M., Alippi, C., He, H. (eds.) ISNN 2011. LNCS, vol. 6676, pp. 270–277. Springer, Heidelberg (2011). https://doi.org/10.1007/978-3-642-21090-7_32

25. PolyU Finger-Knuckle-Print Database: http://www.comp.polyu.edu.hk/~biometrics (2010)

26. Kirthiga, R., Ramesh, G.: Efficient FKP based recognition system using k-mean clustering for security system. SSRG Int. J. Electron. Commun. Eng. 1–7 (2016)

27. Konda, K., Bouthillier, X., Memisevic, R., et al.: Dropout as data augmentation. Computer. Science **1050**, 29 (2015)

28. Srivastava, N., Hinton, G., Krizhevsky, A., et al.: Dropout: a simple way to prevent neural networks from overfitting. J. Mach. Learn. Res. **15**(1), 1929–1958 (2014)

29. Jia, Y., Shelhamer, E., Donahue, J., et al.: Caffe: convolutional architecture for fast feature embedding. In: Proceedings of the 22nd ACM International Conference on Multimedia, pp. 675–678 (2014)

30. Leung, H., Haykin, S.: The complex backpropagation algorithm. IEEE Trans. Signal Process. **39**(9), 2101–2104 (1991)

31. Sun, Z., Tan, T., Wang, Y., et al. Ordinal palmprint representation for personal identification. In: IEEE Conference on Computer Vision and Pattern Recognition (CVPR), vol. 1, pp. 279–284 (2005)
32. Guo, Z., Zhang, D., Zhang, L., et al.: Palmprint verification using binary orientation co-occurrence vector. Pattern Recogn. Lett. **30**(13), 1219–1227 (2009)
33. Jia, W., Huang, D.S., Zhang, D.: Palmprint verification based on robust line orientation code. Pattern Recogn. **41**(5), 1504–1513 (2008)
34. Wright, J., Yang, A.Y., Ganesh, A., et al.: Robust face recognition via sparse representation. IEEE Trans. Pattern Anal. Mach. Intell. **31**(2), 210–227 (2009)
35. Kong, A.W.K., Zhang, D.: Competitive coding scheme for palmprint verification. In: The 17th International Conference on Pattern Recognition (ICIR), vol. 1, pp. 520–523 (2004)

A New Hand Shape Recognition Algorithm Based on Delaunay Triangulation

Fu Liu[(⊠)], Shoukun Jiang, Bing Kang, and Tao Hou

College of Communication Engineering,
Jilin University, Changchun 130022, China
liufu@jlu.edu.cn

Abstract. In this paper, we present a new hand shape recognition algorithm based on Delaunay triangulation. When collecting hand shape images by a non-contact acquisition equipment, the degree of stretching of fingers may cause finger root contour deformation, which leads to unstable central axis and width features. Thus, we propose to form a more robust and non-parametric finger central axis extraction algorithm, by using a Delaunay triangulation algorithm. We show that our robust algorithm achieves the recognition rate of 99.89% on our database, while the mean time of feature extraction is 0.09 s.

Keywords: Hand shape recognition · Delaunay triangulation
Finger central axis

1 Introduction

Hand shape recognition plays an important role in biometric, because of its convenience, stability, security and uniqueness. The feature extraction of hand shape recognition mainly includes two parts: finger geometry [1–4] and finger contour [5, 6].

One of the main problems in hand recognition is that the root contour deformation caused by the degree of stretching of fingers increases the difficulty of recognition algorithms [7]. To solve this problem, Liu presents a hand shape recognition algorithm unrelated to finger root contour [8, 9], which improves the central axis location algorithm. Li also proposes an algorithm based on finger skeleton [10]. Wang uses Voronoi diagram to extract a more robust finger central axis [11].

However, they are, to some extent, effective, and the processes are time consuming. The Voronoi diagram algorithm needs to be delineated the area of finger central axis in advance, this may cause that there are some noise points in the area, which will lead an adverse impact on the central axis extraction. Therefore, we propose a hand shape recognition based on Delaunay triangulation [12]. First, we adopt a new way to get the circumcenters of the contour; second, we design an algorithm to find the circumcenters which use to fit the finger central axis; then we extract the width features and applies them to recognition. The experimental result show that the proposed algorithm achieves the recognition rate of 99.89% on our database, while the mean time of feature extraction is 0.09 s.

© Springer Nature Switzerland AG 2018
J. Zhou et al. (Eds.): CCBR 2018, LNCS 10996, pp. 22–28, 2018.
https://doi.org/10.1007/978-3-319-97909-0_3

2   Finger Contour Extraction

The original hand image and hand shape contour are shown in Fig. 1. In Fig. 1(b), the asterisks and circles are finger root points, the stars are the fingertips. The formula (1–2) are used to find the fingertips and finger root points.

$$dis(i) = \|(x_i - x_0, y_i - y_0)\|_2, i = 1, 2, \ldots, n \tag{1}$$

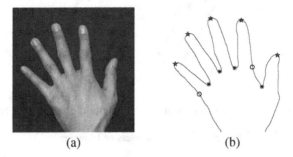

(a)   (b)

Fig. 1. Original image and contour

Where (x_0, y_0) is the center point of wrist, (x_i, y_i) is the coordinates of the ith contour point. n is the number of contour points.

$$\begin{cases} \text{fingertip} & \text{if } \frac{d(dis(i))}{d(i)} = 0 \&\& \frac{d^2(dis(i))}{d(i^2)} < 0 \\ \text{finger root} & \text{if } \frac{d(dis(i))}{d(i)} = 0 \&\& \frac{d^2(dis(i))}{d(i^2)} > 0 \end{cases} \tag{2}$$

With the fingertips and finger root points, we extract the finger contours (Fig. 2) without thumb because of its great freedom. From (a)–(d), the contours are little finger, ring finger, middle finger and index finger. The root contours are distorted, which can influence feature extraction and recognition.

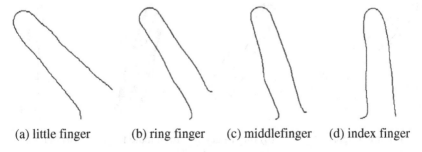

(a) little finger   (b) ring finger   (c) middlefinger   (d) index finger

Fig. 2. Four finger contours

3   Finger Central Axis and Features Extraction

Calculate the Delaunay triangulation of the finger contours, we can obtain the circumcenters of the triangles in all Delaunay triangulation and corresponding sets of vertexes. The points in Fig. 3(a–d) are the circumcenters of triangles.

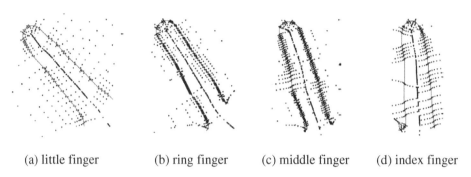

(a) little finger   (b) ring finger   (c) middle finger   (d) index finger

Fig. 3. The circumcenters of triangles

From Fig. 3, there are sets of circumcenters in symmetric axis of each finger contour, we will find those circumcenters and fit the central axis. The finger central axis meets the following conditions:

(a) The central axis must be in the contour area (closed area formed by connecting contour endpoints);
(b) The central axis must be in the middle of the finger contour.

Corresponding to the above conditions, the circumcenters which are used to fit the central axis must meet the following conditions:

(a) The circumcenters must be in the contour area (Fig. 4);
(b) The corresponding vertexes of each circumcenter must be distributed on both sides of the contour.

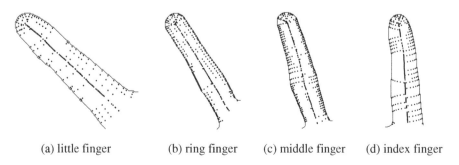

(a) little finger   (b) ring finger   (c) middle finger   (d) index finger

Fig. 4. The circumcenters in contour area

The formula (3) is used to calculate the angle of circumcenter to any two corresponding vertexes, θ is the angle, $(x_i, y_i), i = 1, 2, \cdots, n$ is the circumcenter, (x_{l1}, y_{l1}) and (x_{l2}, y_{l2}) are any two corresponding vertexes.

$$\theta(l) = \arccos\left(\frac{(x_{l1} - x_i)(x_{l2} - x_i) + (y_{l1} - y_i)(y_{l2} - y_i)}{\|(x_{l1} - x_i, y_{l1} - y_i)\|_2 \|(x_{l2} - x_i, y_{l2} - y_i)\|_2}\right) \tag{3}$$

For each circumcenter, if $\exists l, \theta(l) > 90$, no operation; else delete this circumcenter. To reduce the amount of calculation, we use formula (4) instead of formula (3), because if $\theta(l) \in [0, 180°]$, the necessary and sufficient condition that $\theta(l) > 90°$ is $\lambda(l) < 0$. So, we only need to calculate $\lambda(l)$ instead of $\theta(l)$, which can reduce some calculation. For each circumcenter, if $\exists l, \lambda(l) < 0$, no operation; else delete this circumcenter.

$$\lambda(l) = (x_{l1} - x_i)(x_{l2} - x_i) + (y_{l1} - y_i)(y_{l2} - y_i) \tag{4}$$

All the circumcenters that conform to the above conditions are shown in Fig. 5(a–d). The circumcenters near fingertips are filtered out. We use the least squares algorithm to fit the finger central axis, which can reduce the impact of outliers. In formula (5–6), $\bar{x}$ is the mean value of the abscissa of all circumcenters, k and b are the slope and intercept. The fitted straight lines are the central axis of fingers. The straight lines in Fig. 4(e–h) are the proposed central axis.

$$k = \frac{\overline{xy} - \bar{x}\bar{y}}{\overline{x^2} - \bar{x}^2} \tag{5}$$

$$b = \bar{y} - k\bar{x} \tag{6}$$

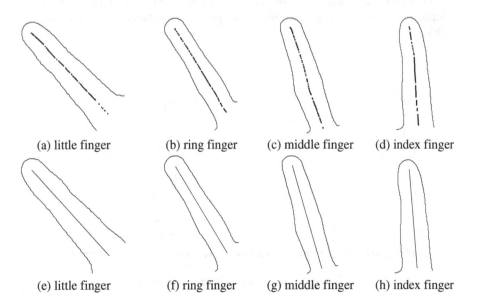

(a) little finger   (b) ring finger   (c) middle finger   (d) index finger

(e) little finger   (f) ring finger   (g) middle finger   (h) index finger

Fig. 5. Circumcenters and central axis of four fingers

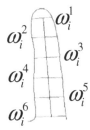

Fig. 6. Feature extraction diagram

We use the same feature extraction method as [7], Fig. 6 is feature extraction diagram. $F_i = \left[N_i, \omega_i^1, \omega_i^2, \cdots, \omega_i^n\right], i = 1, 2, 3, 4$ is the feature vector, N_i is the number of features, The width of the horizontal lines are $\omega_i^1, \omega_i^2, \cdots, \omega_i^n$, which are the width features. The distance between adjacent horizontal lines is 10 pixels.

4   Results and Analysis

The central axis extraction results with different algorithms are shown as Fig. 6. Figure 7 illustrates that the root contour deformation influences the result of central axis of (a) and (b), this is because the central axis in (a) and (b) depend on the fingertips and the root to some extent. From (c) and (d), the fingertips points hardly affect the central axis due to the use of statistics around fingertips. However, the central axis is short than others because of the thinning algorithm (block in (c)), this reduces the number of width features which leads to a lower recognition rate. The proposed method weakens the influence of the fingertips and finger root points and retains as many features as possible.

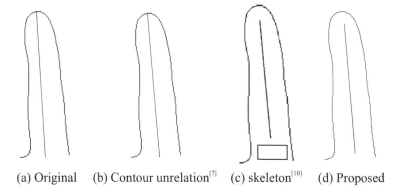

(a) Original   (b) Contour unrelation[7]   (c) skeleton[10]   (d) Proposed

Fig. 7. The results with different algorithms

We use the same recognition algorithm as [7]. The recognition results with different central axis extraction algorithms are shown in Table 1. By comparison with other algorithms, we only use 0.09 s to extract features and the recognition rate reaches 99.89%. The feature extraction time of [9] is less than the proposed algorithm, but they take lots of time at the training stage and the recognition rate is less than the proposed algorithm.

Table 1. The recognition rate and feature extraction time with different central axis extraction algorithms

Algorithm	Recognition rate (%)	Feature extraction time (s)
Fusion feature + PSO [9]	98.61	0.05
Voronoi diagram [11]	98.952	2.5
Root contour unrelation [7]	99.51	0.08
Finger skeleton [10]	99.62	0.2
Proposed	**99.89**	**0.09**

5   Conclusion

In this paper, we propose a hand shape recognition algorithm, in which central axis is extracted by Delaunay triangulation, making it insensitive to the degree of stretching of fingers. The main characteristics of this work are as follows:

(1) we adopt a new way to get the circumcenters of the contour;
(2) we design an algorithm to find the circumcenters which use to fit the finger central axis.

The experimental results show that the proposed algorithm is insensitive to the degree of stretching of fingers, the recognition rate is 99.89% and feature extraction time is 0.09 s.

Acknowledgments. This study is supported by National Natural Science Foundation of China (NO. 61503151), Natural Science Foundation of Jilin Province (NO. 20160520100JH), Industrial Innovation Special Fund Project of Jilin Province (NO. 2017C032-4, NO. 2017C045-4).

References

1. Guo, J.M., Hsia, C.H., Liu, Y.F., et al.: Contact-free hand geometry-based identification system. Expert Syst. Appl. **39**(14), 11728–11736 (2012)
2. Yuan, W., et al.: Hand shape identification method based on finger relative length. J. Optoelectron. Laser **5**(20), 685–689 (2009)
3. Yuan, W., et al.: Analysis of relationship between finger width and recognition rate. Opt. Precis. Eng. **7**(17), 1730–1736 (2009)
4. Kang, W., Wu, Q.: Pose-invariant hand shape recognition based on finger geometry. IEEE Trans. Syst. Man Cybern. Syst. **44**(11), 1510–1521 (2017)

5. Bakina, I., Mestetskiy, L.: Hand shape recognition from natural hand position. In: 2011 International Conference on Hand-Based Biometrics (ICHB), vol. 1, no. 6, pp. 17–18 (2011)

6. Duta, N.: A survey of biometric technology based on hand shape. Pattern Recogn. **43**(11), 2797–2806 (2009)

7. Liu, F., Gao, L., LI, W., Liu, H.: A new hand shape recognition algorithm unrelated to the finger root contour. In: Sun, Z., Shan, S., Sang, H., Zhou, J., Wang, Y., Yuan, W. (eds.) CCBR 2014. LNCS, vol. 8833, pp. 522–529. Springer, Cham (2014). https://doi.org/10.1007/978-3-319-12484-1_60

8. Liu, F., et al.: Hand shape recognition based on fusion features of fingers and particle swarm optimization. Opt. Precis. Eng. **6**(23), 1774–1782 (2015)

9. Liu, F., et al.: Hand recognition based on finger-contour and PSO. In: International Conference on Intelligent Computing and Internet of Things, pp. 35–39. IEEE (2015)

10. Wenwen, L., et al.: A method of hand-shape recognition based on extraction of finger skeleton. J. Cent. South Univ. (Sci. Technol.) **47**(3), 777–783 (2017)

11. Wang, S., et al.: A new hand shape positioning algorithm based on Voronoi diagram. In: Chinese Control Conference, pp. 4117–4121 (2016)

12. Biniaz, A., Dastghaibyfard, G.: A faster circle-sweep Delaunay triangulation algorithm. Adv. Eng. Softw. **43**(1), 1–13 (2012)

Finger Vein Recognition Based on Weighted Graph Structural Feature Encoding

Shuyi Li, Haigang Zhang, Guimin Jia, and Jinfeng Yang[(⊠)]

Tianjin Key Lab for Advanced Signal Processing,
Civil Aviation University of China, Tianjin, China
jfyang@cauc.edu.cn

Abstract. The finger-vein recognition performance is usually sensitive to illumination and pose variation. Exploring suitable feature representation method is therefore significant for finger-vein recognition improvement. In this paper, we propose a novel feature encoding method based on local graph structure (LGS), which behaves better in improving the matching accuracy of features. In terms of the variations of veins in running direction, oriented Gabor filters are firstly used for venous region enhancement. Then, a symmetric cross-weighted local graph structure (SCW-LGS) is proposed to locally represent the gradient relationships among the pixels in a neighborhood of the Gabor enhanced images. Based on SCW-LGS, a multi-orientation feature encoding method is developed for vein network feature representation. Experimental results show that the proposed approach achieves better performance than the state-of-the-art approaches on finger-vein recognition.

Keywords: Feature encoding · Finger-vein recognition · Local graph structure
Gabor filter

1 Introduction

As a new approach of personal identification, finger-vein recognition has attracted much attention due to its natural living anti-counterfeit [1, 2]. Compared with traditional biometric patterns (e.g. fingerprint, face, iris and palm print), finger-vein pattern has some advantages in uniqueness, universality, permanence and security [2–4]. Hence, the finger-vein recognition technology has been widely used in various fields, such as computer login, security inspection, ATM certification, etc.

The quality of finger-vein images is often degraded seriously due to light scattering in the biological tissues [5, 6], which is unfavorable for reliable feature representation. So the scattering removal task is usually implemented for finger-vein image quality improvement. Noteworthily, from another viewpoint, the vein network itself has inherently scattering characteristics due to biological variations of finger tissues. Therefore, to some extent, the imaging properties of human fingers in NIR light are beneficial for expressing the discriminability of finger veins. In this respect, the encoding-based methods are usually considered to be effective in representing this kind of characteristics related with image properties [7].

© Springer Nature Switzerland AG 2018
J. Zhou et al. (Eds.): CCBR 2018, LNCS 10996, pp. 29–37, 2018.
https://doi.org/10.1007/978-3-319-97909-0_4

In recent years, many feature encoding algorithms related to graph structure have been proposed [8–10]. In 2011, Abusham et al. first proposed a Local Graph Structure (LGS) algorithm used for face recognition [8]. The proposed LGS was non-symmetric and represented more left-handed neighbor pixels than the right-handed ones. To make encoded features symmetric, Mohd et al. proposed a symmetrical LGS (SLGS) algorithm [9], which utilized the spatially symmetrical information around the target pixel. Based on SLGS, Dong et al. put forward a Multi-Orientation Weighted SLGS (MOW-SLGS) algorithm for finger-vein recognition [10]. Unfortunately, the LGS-based algorithms do not still consider the full relationships between the target pixel and its surrounding ones. Moreover, in MOW-SLGS algorithm, the scheme of assigning different weights for symmetric pixels often leads to imbalance of feature representation.

To overcome the limitations of the above algorithms, we propose a new symmetrical cross-weighted local graph structure (SCW-LGS). The SCW-LGS can fully exploit position and gradient information among the surrounding pixels. Experimental results show that the proposed method improves the robustness of finger-vein features in expression.

2   Feature Encoding Algorithm

The proposed procedure of finger-vein feature encoding algorithm is shown in Fig. 1. Firstly, the texture of finger-vein ROI images is enhanced by using a bank of Gabor filters. Second, the SCW-LGS operator is proposed to encode the finger-vein images. Finally, the encoded images are uniformly divided into non-overlapping blocks, and the histograms of all blocks are concatenated into a vector for feature representation.

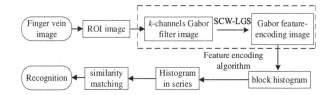

Fig. 1. Finger-vein recognition process based on Gabor-SCW-LGS

2.1   Finger-Vein Enhancement

The even-symmetric Gabor filter can extract the flexible texture information of finger-vein effectively, which is defined as [11, 12]

$$G(x, y, \theta_k, f_k) = \frac{1}{2\pi\sigma^2} \exp\left\{ -\frac{1}{2} \left(\frac{x_{\theta_k}^2}{\sigma_x^2} + \frac{y_{\theta_k}^2}{\sigma_y^2} \right) \right\} \cos(2\pi f_k x_{\theta_k}), \tag{1}$$

Where

$$\begin{bmatrix} x_{\theta_k} \\ y_{\theta_k} \end{bmatrix} = \begin{bmatrix} \cos\theta & \sin\theta \\ -\sin\theta & \cos\theta \end{bmatrix} \begin{bmatrix} x \\ y \end{bmatrix},$$

σ is the scale of the Gabor filter, k ($= 1, 2,..., K$) is the channel number, θ_k and f_k respectively denote the orientation and the central frequency of the kth filter. Let $I(x, y)$ be an original finger-vein image and $I_k(x, y)$ be the kth Gabor filtered image, then

$$I_k(x,y) = I(x,y) \otimes G(x,y,\theta_k,f_k), \tag{2}$$

where the symbol "$\otimes$" denotes two-dimensional convolution. Some Gabor filtered images are shown in Fig. 2. Some details about the used Gabor operation can found in [13].

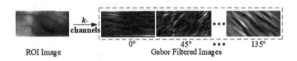

Fig. 2. The finger-vein enhanced image

2.2 SCW-LGS

In order to make full use of gradient and orientation information among surrounding pixels in the enhanced image, a novel feature encoding method based on local graph structure is proposed. For a center pixel, we respectively select three pixels in the left and the right of $n \times n$ neighborhoods, as shown in Fig. 3. These pixels are used to constitute a graph structure of SCW-LGS.

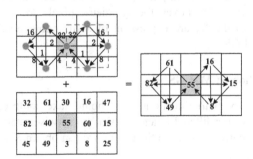

Fig. 3. The structure of SCW-LGS ($n = 3$, 0° orientation)

Fig. 4. The encoding process in SCW-LGS

The SCW-LGS operation is shown in Fig. 4. Starting from a center pixel, on the right square neighborhood, the gray values of four pixels are compared one by one along the direction of the graph. If the gray value becomes larger, the edge between the two adjacent pixels is encoded to 1, otherwise, it is 0. Similarly, the same encoding process is done on the left side. Thus, a new value is generated for each pixel according to Eqs. (3) and (4).

$$F_{\theta_k} = \sum_{i=1}^{6} p(g_i - f_i)2^{6-i} + \sum_{j=1}^{6} q(g_j - f_j)2^{6-j}, \quad (k = 1, 2, \cdots, K), \qquad (3)$$

$$p(x), q(x) = \begin{cases} 1, x \geq 0 \\ 0, x < 0 \end{cases}, \qquad (4)$$

where g_i and f_i (g_j and f_j) represent two pixel values to be compared on the right (left) sides, F_{θ_k} represents the encoded value of the target pixel in θ_k direction. For instance, $k = 1$, as shown in Fig. 4,

$F_{\theta_1} = (000100)_2 + (110110)_2$
$\quad = (0 \times 32 + 0 \times 16 + 0 \times 8 + 1 \times 4 + 0 \times 2 + 0 \times 1)$
$\quad + (1 \times 32 + 1 \times 16 + 0 \times 8 + 1 \times 4 + 1 \times 2 + 0 \times 1) = 58.$

Thus, this proposed algorithm is able to not only express the relationships between the target pixel and the surrounding pixels, but also consider the hidden relationships among surrounding pixels. Moreover, the symmetric pixels are weighted equally on right and left sides, so the feature expression of surrounding pixels becomes more equilibrium in SCW-LGS.

2.3   Multi-orientation SCW-LGS

As Gabor features vary with directions, we should take multi-orientation feature encoding method for Gabor filtered images. Counterclockwise rotating the SCW-LGS from 0° to θ_k ($K = 4$, corresponding to Sect. 2.1), we can obtain K structures of SCW-LGS, as shown in Fig. 5.

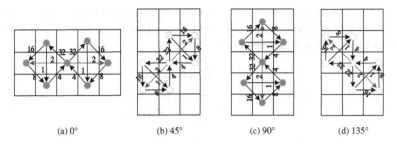

(a) 0°   (b) 45°   (c) 90°   (d) 135°

Fig. 5. Multi-orientation SCW-LGS operators ($K = 4$)

Using Eqs. (3) and (4), the K encoded values of the target pixel can be obtained. Considering the optimal response of the Gabor filters in K orientations, the final encoded value can be computed by

$$F(x, y) = \arg \max_{\theta_k \in (0°, 180°)} (F_{\theta_k}).$$ (5)

After the above steps, we can obtain the final feature coded image, as show in Fig. 6. Inspired by the good power of Gabor filter in capturing specific texture feature from any orientation of an image, the multi-orientation SCW-LGS extends SCW-LGS into arbitrary orientation. Hence, this proposed method has superior orientation selectivity and is able to more effectively describe the position information and gradient information in the neighborhood.

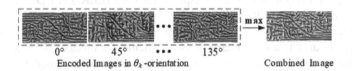

0°   45°   •••   135°   Combined Image
Encoded Images in θ_k-orientation

Fig. 6. The feature encoded image by multi-orientation SCW-LGS

3 Feature Matching

In this section, for convenience, a histogram-based method is used for finger-vein feature representation. Referring to [14], an encoded finger-vein image is first divided equally into M non-overlapping blocks. Then, the local gray histograms corresponding to these M blocks are built accordingly. Assuming that $H^i (i = 1, 2,..., M)$ denotes the histogram of the ith block, the global histogram H of an encoded finger-vein image is defined as

$$H = (H^1, H^2, \cdots, H^M).$$ (6)

Here, the intersection coefficient between two histograms is used for measuring the similarity of two finger-vein images [15, 16]. Given two histograms, $H_1(i)$ and $H_2(i)$, the intersection coefficient can be computed by

$$S(H_1(i), H_2(i)) = \frac{\sum\limits_{i=1}^{L} \min[H_1(i), H_2(i)]}{\sum\limits_{i=1}^{L} H_1(i)}, \tag{7}$$

where L is the dimension of a histogram. Thus, two finger-vein images will tend to be more similar as the value of $S(\cdot)$ increasing.

4 Experiments and Analysis

The finger-vein images used in our experiments are all from a homemade finger-vein image acquisition system. The database contain 500 individuals and each individual contains 10 finger-vein images. In this paper, we randomly select 600 images of 100 individuals (6 images of each individual) as experimental database. Considering recognition efficiency and matching accuracy, we perform the experiment with $K = 4$.

4.1 Parameter Selection

Noticeably, the size of the neighborhood n constituting the SCW-LGS and the number of image division blocks M are two important parameters that can make a big influence on the performance of the proposed method in finger-vein recognition. In order to find the suitable parameters n and M, some equal error rates (EERs) in ROCs are listed in Table 1 by changing the values of n and M.

From Figs. 7(a), (b) and (c), we can see that ROCs vary with n. By observing these ROCs corresponding to a same image division scheme, for instance, $M = 6$, 7 or 8, we find that the recognition performance is optimal when neighborhood size is 5×5 ($n = 5$). Hence, a 5×5 neighborhood is better in expressing the local relationships around the central pixel as well as insensitivity to noise.

From Fig. 7(d), it can be noted that the proposed method can also perform best when the size of a block is 7×7 ($M = 7$), using SCW-LGS with 5×5 neighborhood. This shows that a suitable image division scheme, for instance, $M = 7$, is desirable for recognition performance improvement. Hence, $n = 5$ and $M = 7$ are two optimal parameters for the proposed SCW-LGS based method in finger-vein recognition.

4.2 Comparisons

In order to evaluate the performance of the proposed method, some common feature encoding methods (LLBP [17], SLGS [9] MOW-SLGS [10]) and the state-of-the-art deep learning method [18] are used for comparisons here. As shown in Fig. 8 and Table 2, the EER of the proposed method is reduced to 0.15%, which is the lowest among the five method. This shows that the proposed Gabor-SCW-LGS method is powerful in improving matching accuracy rate of finger-vein recognition.

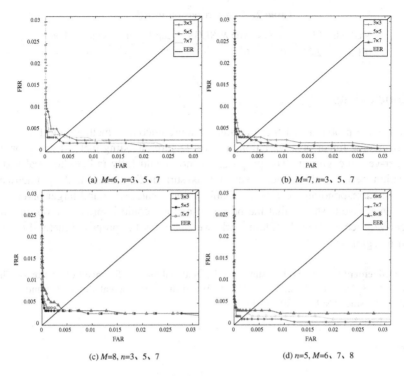

(a) $M=6$, $n=3$、5、7

(b) $M=7$, $n=3$、5、7

(c) $M=8$, $n=3$、5、7

(d) $n=5$, $M=6$、7、8

Fig. 7. ROCs of different parameters n and M

Table 1. Comparisons on EER(%)

Neighborhood	Blocks		
	6×6	7×7	8×8
3×3	0.39	0.33	0.38
5×5	0.27	0.15	0.33
7×7	0.36	0.30	0.34

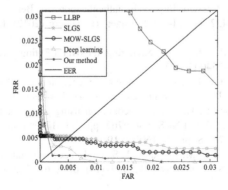

Fig. 8. ROCs of different methods

Table 2. Comparisons on EER(%)

Methods	LLBP	SLGS	MOW-SLGS	Deep learning	Our method
(EER/%)	2.22	0.53	0.47	0.33	0.15

5 Conclusions

To address the problem that the traditional feature encoding method could not effectively overcome finger pose variation, a novel feature encoding method was proposed for finger-vein recognition. The proposed method could fully utilize the local texture information between the target pixel and its surrounding ones, and symmetrically assign the corresponding weights to reliably extract features around target pixels. The experimental results shown that the proposed method could improve the performance of finger-vein recognition. In future work, we can apply the proposed method to other pattern recognition.

Acknowledgements. This work is supported by National Natural Science Foundation of China (No. 61502498, No. 61379102, NO. U1433120) and the Fundamental Research Funds for the Central Universities (NO. 3122017001).

References

1. Miura, N., Nagasaka, A., Miyatake, T.: Feature Extraction of finger-vein patterns based on repeated line tracking and its application to personal identification. Mach. Vis. Appl. **15**, 194–203 (2004)
2. Yang, J.F., Shi, Y.H.: Finger-vein ROI localization and vein ridge enhancement. PRL **33** (12), 1569–1579 (2012)
3. Yang, J.F., Shi, Y.H., Jia, G.M.: Finger-vein image matching based on adaptive curve transformation. PR **66**, 34–43 (2017)
4. Yang, W., Hu, J., Wang, S.: A finger-vein based cancellable bio-cryptosystem. In: Lopez, J., Huang, X., Sandhu, R. (eds.) NSS 2013. LNCS, vol. 7873, pp. 784–790. Springer, Heidelberg (2013). https://doi.org/10.1007/978-3-642-38631-2_71
5. Kim, H.-G., Lee, E.J., Yoon, G.-J., Yang, S.-D., Lee, E.C., Yoon, S.M.: Illumination normalization for SIFT based finger vein authentication. In: Bebis, G., et al. (eds.) ISVC 2012. LNCS, vol. 7432, pp. 21–30. Springer, Heidelberg (2012). https://doi.org/10.1007/978-3-642-33191-6_3
6. Yang, J.F., Zhang, B., Shi, Y.H.: Scattering removal for finger-vein image restoration. Sensors **12**(3), 3627–3640 (2012)
7. Jia, W., Zhang, B., Lu, J.T., et al.: Palmprint recognition based on complete direction representation. IEEE Trans. Image Process. **26**(9), 4483–4498 (2017)
8. Abusham, E.E.A., Bashir, H.K.: Face recognition using local graph structure (LGS). In: Jacko, J.A. (ed.) HCI 2011. LNCS, vol. 6762, pp. 169–175. Springer, Heidelberg (2011). https://doi.org/10.1007/978-3-642-21605-3_19
9. Abdullah, M.F.A., Sayeed, M.S., Muthu, K.S., et al.: Face recognition with symmetric local graph structure (SLGS). Expert Syst. Appl. **41**(14), 6131–6137 (2014)

10. Dong, S., Yang, J.C., Chen, Y., et al.: Finger vein recognition based on multi-orientation weighted symmetric local graph structure. KSII Trans. Internet Inf. Syst. **9**(10), 4126–4142 (2015)
11. Yang, J.F., Yang, J.: Multi-channel gabor filter design for finger-vein image enhancement. In: Fifth ICIG. IEEE Computer Society, pp. 87–91 (2009)
12. Yang, J., Shi, Y., Yang, J.: Finger-vein recognition based on a bank of gabor filters. In: Zha, H., Taniguchi, R.-I., Maybank, S. (eds.) ACCV 2009. LNCS, vol. 5994, pp. 374–383. Springer, Heidelberg (2010). https://doi.org/10.1007/978-3-642-12307-8_35
13. Yang, J.F., Shi, Y.H.: Finger-vein network enhancement and segmentation. PAA **17**(4), 783–797 (2014)
14. Jia, W., Hu, R.X., Lei, Y.K., et al.: Histogram of oriented lines for palmprint recognition. IEEE Trans. Syst. Man Cybern. **44**(3), 385–395 (2014)
15. Luo, Y.T., Zhao, L.Y., Zhang, B., et al.: Local line directional pattern for palmprint recognition. PR **50**(C), 26–44 (2014)
16. Swain, M.J., Ballard, D.H.: Color indexing. IJCV **7**(1), 11–32 (1991)
17. Lu, Y., Yoon, S., Xie, S.J., et al.: Finger vein recognition using generalized local line binary pattern. KSII Trans. Internet Inf. Syst. **8**(5), 1766–1784 (2014)
18. Qin, H., EI-Yacoubi, M.A.: Deep representation-based feature extraction and recovering for finger-vein verification. IEEE Trans. Inf. Forensics Secur. **12**(8), 1816–1829 (2017)

Fingerprint Pore Extraction Using Convolutional Neural Networks and Logical Operation

Yuanhao Zhao[1], Feng Liu[1,2(✉)], and Linlin Shen[1]

[1] College of Computer Science and Software Engineering,
Shenzhen University, Shenzhen, Guangdong, China
feng.liu@szu.edu.cn
[2] School of Computer Science and Software Engineering,
Shenzhen University, Shenzhen, Guangdong, China

Abstract. Sweat pores have been proved to be discriminative and successfully used for automatic fingerprint recognition. It is crucial to extract pores precisely to achieve high recognition accuracy. To extract pores accurately and robustly, we propose a novel coarse-to-fine detection method based on convolutional neural networks (CNN) and logical operation. More specifically, pore candidates are coarsely estimated using logical operation at first; then, coarse pore candidates are further judged through well-trained CNN models; precise pore locations are finally refined by logical and morphological operation. The experimental results evaluated on the public dataset show that the proposed method outperforms other state-of-the-art methods in comparison.

Keywords: Pore extraction · Convolutional neural network · Logical operation

1 Introduction

Since Galton quantified the uniqueness of fingerprints in 1872, fingerprints have been widely used for human identification [1–3]. Fingerprints are identified by their features. Level 1 features are the overall global ridge flow patterns, including singular points, deltas and cores. Level 2 features refer to ridge ending and ridge bifurcation, namely minutiae points and level 3 features are defined as the dimensional attributes of the ridges, such as sweat pores, ridge contour, and ridge edge features. Similar to Level 1 and Level 2 features, Level 3 features are also permanent, immutable and unique [4]. Past research studies of fingerprint identification based on Level 3 features are mainly focused on sweat pores. This feature is used for more accurate fingerprint matching because of its large amount and better performance compared to other features [5, 6]. Recent studies prove that pores can greatly increase the accuracy of fingerprint recognition [7–13]. Therefore, a precise pore extraction and locating influence the pore matching directly. The accuracy of pore extraction from fingerprints is an important step in whole fingerprint recognition.

In the literature, there are several studies on the extraction of pore features from fingerprint samples, in particular, of the coordinates of pores. The existing pore

© Springer Nature Switzerland AG 2018
J. Zhou et al. (Eds.): CCBR 2018, LNCS 10996, pp. 38–47, 2018.
https://doi.org/10.1007/978-3-319-97909-0_5

extraction methods are generally divided into two categories. One is the model-based method which uses different techniques to estimate the shape of pores from the samples, such as: Gabor filters [6], DAPM filters [13], wavelet transforms [14], watershed segmentation [15], or morphological operators [16, 17]. The other is the learning-based method that mainly uses convolutional neural networks (CNN) to estimate the location of pores from the samples, such as: Labati's model [18], Wang's U-Net model [19] and DeepPore model [20].

Adaptive pore extraction is a very difficult problem because there exist so many kinds of pore shape. The shape of pores from different person might be quite different. Sometimes, the shape of the pores in the fingerprints from the same person can also be different. Convolutional neural networks (CNN) seem to be a good solution for pore extraction because of its large learning capacity. Convolutional neural networks' capacity can be controlled by varying their depth and breadth. They also make strong and mostly correct assumptions about the nature of images [21]. The CNN can use several filters to extract the most distinctive features from images. Furthermore, CNN don't need any prior knowledge because the weights of filters can be learned automatically from training data images during training. With a large quantity of training data, CNN can extract discriminative features and achieve high accuracy in classification tasks. For these reasons, CNN is widely used to extract features in biometrics.

Due to the large learning capacity of CNN, learning-based methods outperform model-based methods in accuracy. However, the existing learning-based methods are still not good enough. Because of the various kinds of pore shape and limited by training type of samples, CNN is not sensitive enough to distinguish false types from true types. To solve this problem, we propose a novel method to extract the pores from fingerprint images using CNN and logical operation. The method includes three parts: *(i)* coarse estimation of pore candidates using logical operation; *(ii)* further judgement of pore candidates through well-trained CNN models; *(iii)* pore location refinement by logical and morphological operation. The effectiveness of the proposed method was proved by our experimental results.

The rest of this paper is organized as follows. Section 2 introduces our proposed method step by step. Section 3 reports and analyzes the evaluation results. Section 4 finally concludes the paper.

2   Methodology Statement

The flowchart of the proposed method is shown in Fig. 1. The method can be roughly divided into three steps: *(i)* coarse detection of pore candidates using logical operation; *(ii)* CNN judgement of pore candidates; *(iii)* refinement by logical and morphological operation after judgement. These steps will be introduced detailedly in the following subsections.

2.1   Coarse Detection of Pore Candidates

The CNN can be used for sweat pore extraction after training. Considered that CNN test on each pixels will produce big calculation quantities, it is reliable to propose a coarse detection to test images in order to select candidate position of the pore first. Coarse detection of pore candidates consists of a series of logical operations.

As shown in Fig. 2, it is required to get binary and ridge images of test fingerprint images. First, using Bernsen's binary method [25] to get binary images, which is based on partial adaptive thresholds. Adaptive thresholds achieve better performance than global threshold in fingerprint image binaryzation [26]. Then using Lin's enhance method [27] to get ridge images and get the candidate position of test image by implementing XOR operating on ridge images and binary images pixel by pixel. In test step, testing with CNN only operates in these candidate pixels. This detecting step will reduce the calculation quantity, also help to improve recognition accuracy because it greatly removes the impossible position of the pore.

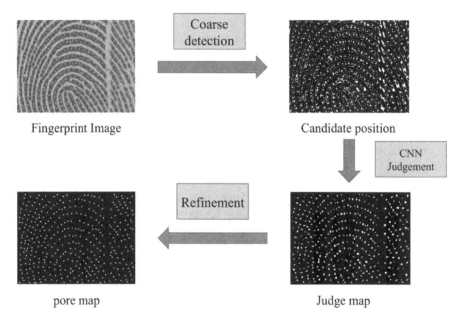

Fig. 1. The flowchart of the proposed method.

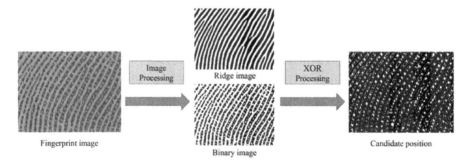

Fig. 2. The flow chart of detecting pore candidates.

2.2 CNN Architecture and Implement Details

Inspired by VGGNet [22], this paper proposed "Judge-CNN" architecture. The purpose of this network is to judge if there is a pore in the center area of the input image or not. Therefore, the CNN is used to solve binary classification problems in this study. That is, when labeling the training data, if there is a pore's centroid located in the center of the input patch, they are labeled as positive samples. Otherwise, the patch is labeled as negative samples.

The architecture of judge-net is illustrated in Fig. 3. The network is composed of 5 convolution layers and 2 fully-connected layers, and finally a softmax output layer. All layers apart from the output layer followed by a rectified linear unit (ReLU) [21] and all of them share a standard set of hyper-parameters. The input image is set to 11×11. The same to VGGNet [22], the convolutional filter size is set to 3×3 with a stride of 1. The number of filters in the convolutional layers is set to $2^{\lceil l/2 \rceil + 4}$, where l is the layer number. The two fully-connected layers consist of 128, 32 nodes, respectively. In order to prevent overfitting, both of them use dropout [23] with a ratio of 0.5. One drawback of our architecture can be inferred is that because of the input image size limit, the pores which located in each boundary side of the image perhaps cannot be detected very well.

In order to make the CNN network achieve better capacity of judgement. It is necessary to select the training data strictly. The training data selection area is produced as Fig. 4. When we get a fingerprint image which pores' centroid were labeled with ground truth, we assume a threshold d to calculate if each pixel is sufficiently near to a pore. Using Euclidean distance to calculate the distance between each pixel to its nearest pore centroid. Defining d_p and d_n to denotes positive distance and negative distance, respectively. As shown in Fig. 4, the areas which all the pixels' distance is higher than d_n, we label it the negative area. On the other hand, the areas which all the pixels' distance is lower than d_p, we label it the positive area. The d_p and d_n are empirically set to 3 and 5, respectively. As for the other area besides the positive and negative area, it can be labeled the ignored area.

Then we select a location (pixel) in the fingerprint image for training data randomly to get enough positive and negative samples from corresponding area. Each training data is a patch of size 11×11 cropped from the fingerprint image whose center is a selected pixel. In order to prevent ambiguous training data labels, it is important not to pick a patch whose center is located in the ignored area.

In order to improve the robustness of the model trained, we use data augmentation. A random selection of grayscale transformation, contrast variation and noise degradation were applied to every patche once it was picked up from the fingerprint image. The parameters for this augmentation were also randomly selected within limits. Furthermore, a random rotation and picture flipping were applied to patches. Millions of training samples were picked up by this means.

The training implementation details are stated as follows. Initializing the weights in each layer from a zero-mean Gaussian distribution with standard deviation 0.01. Training adopted stochastic gradient descent as optimization method with 0.9 momentum. Mini-batch is set to 256, base learning-rate is set to 0.005 and reduced every 10,000 iteration and max-iteration is set to 50,000. When the loss is converged

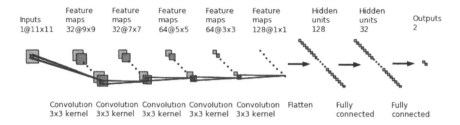

Fig. 3. "Judge-CNN" architecture for candidate pore judgement.

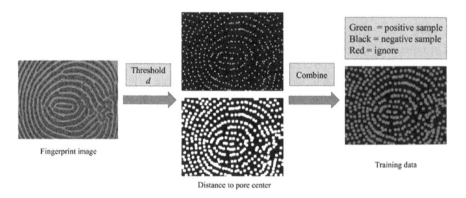

Fig. 4. Training data selection in an automatic way.

for a sufficient period, training can be stopped manually. Caffe [24] framework was used to implement the network training and testing. Workstation's CPU is 2.8 GHz RAM 32 GB and GPU is NVIDIA Quadro M5000 M 8 GB. All methods were implemented using MATLAB.

2.3 Refinement

After getting judged map through CNN judge on candidate pore map, it is necessary for us to propose a refinement step to make the test result better. As shown in Fig. 5, the refinement step includes two substeps, the elimination step and locating step. The same to the coarse detection step, the refinement step implements through logical transformation operation.

The elimination step aims mainly to eliminate false detected results. There are many false detected pores in the judge map. Many of them are located in the valley area in original test input fingerprint images, because the ridge image has wider ridge than the binary image and the CNN judge net cannot remove them completely. So we implement morphology erosion processing to get thinner ridge image from ridge image. The thinner ridge image has smaller ridge width than the original ridge image. Then, we get eliminated judge map from by implementing XOR operating on judge map and thinner ridge map pixel by pixel. By this way, a lot of false detected pores can

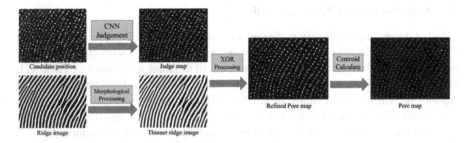

Fig. 5. The flow chart of refinement step.

be removed. But in the same time, this operation will remove also some true detected pores whose center is located far from ridge skeleton (most of them are open pores with small size).

The Last step is to get pore map by calculating all the connected components' centroid from the eliminated judge map. The coordinates of each pixel which is centroid in the eliminated judge map stands for the location of each detected pore. We discard the white regions with area equal or less than an empirical threshold before calculating the centroids.

3 Experimental Results and Analysis

3.1 Databases and Protocols

In the experiment, High-Resolution-Fingerprint (HRF) database [7] from PolyU were used to evaluate the performance of pore extraction. The HRF database contains 30 fingerprint images with ground truth of pores labeled manually. Each image has a spatial size of 320 pixels by 240 pixels and a resolution of 1200dpi. The labels denote that there are 12,767 pores in the database totally.

In this paper, k-fold cross validation strategy [9] is used for evaluating the performance. We choose k = 5 in experiment, 3 folds of them for training, 1 fold for validation and 1 fold for testing. Each fold is composed of 6 different images and were mutual exclusion with other folds. The performance of the method is calculated by averaging the accuracy of five testing folds.

Two figures of merit are used for evaluating the performance: the true detection rate (R_T) and the false detection rate (R_F) [10]. R_T represents the ratio of the number of detected real pores to the number of all true pores present in the image, where R_F indicates the ratio of the number of falsely detected pores to the total number of detected pores. If the Euclidean distance between the coordinate of the detected pore and ground truth label is less than d pixels, it is considered that the pore is detected correctly. Setting $d = rw/2$, where rw is the average ridge width in the image. Obviously, the algorithm performs the best while R_T and R_F are one and zero, respectively, which indicates all pores were detected correctly.

3.2 Validation of the Proposed Method

A skill of decreasing test position of pore is introduced in Sect. 2.1. The compress rate of the method is decided by the size of window during binary processing. Where w denotes the size of window ($2 \times w+1$), the result of different w is shown in Table 1. It is obvious that with the growth of window size, the compress rate becomes higher. That indicates the calculation quantity of CNN is reduced greatly. Compared with w = 0 (test on all 230 by 310 pixels) and w = 1, the result shows that testing only on candidate position can reduce the calculations and make better performance. Considering that R_F is reduced obviously because many invalid regions were removed when choosing candidate position, R_T is improved slightly, maybe because many regions of two or more pores have connected when all positions are tested. That will lead mistakes when picking up the centroid of candidate region and cause lower R_T. But with the growth of w, more candidate positions are removed, so the R_T decreases. Reducing the candidate region will also cause higher R_F because the detected pores decreased.

Table 1. Average performance metrics in percentage and standard deviation (in parenthesis)

w	0	1	2	3	4
R_T	93.92(1.09)	94.27(0.72)	93.70(0.85)	92.75(0.98)	91.61(1.12)
R_F	14.52(3.51)	8.62(0.83)	10.45(1.37)	10.54(1.48)	10.28(1.48)
Compress	0%	74.47%	80.69%	82.82%	83.53%

Before computing the centroid of each white region, a refinement step is introduced in Sect. 2.3. Because of the performance, we choose the accuracy w = 1 as our best result for the following experiment. The result after refinement is shown in Table 2. As inferred before, the refinement step removes all the candidate pixels far away from ridge. It can prevent candidate pore appearing in the impossible position well but remove genuine pore which is located far from ridge skeleton at the same time. It is obvious that after refinement, R_F is reduced to be half nearly after refinement. Meanwhile, the R_T is slightly decreased but kept at the same level as a non-refined result.

Table 2. Average performance metrics contrast while the parameter w = 1

Refinement	Non refine	After refine
R_T	94.27(0.72)	93.14(1.43)
R_F	8.62(0.83)	4.39(1.44)

3.3 Comparison with the-State-of-the-Art Methods

Comparing the result of the proposed method with other existing method according to the R_T and R_F. The existing method including model-based method such us Jain's model [6], Adapt. DoG and DAPM [13], morphology-based method such us Xu's method [17], CNN-based methods such us Labati's model [18] and DeepPore [20]. The comparison results are shown in Table 3. It can be seen that the proposed method achieves lower R_F and more standard deviation than other methods. As for R_T, the proposed method achieves similar results as DeepPore method and better results than other methods. Some extraction results are shown in Fig. 6, which demonstrates the effectiveness of the proposed method. Most of pores were detected correctly. As illustrated in Sect. 2.2, due to the limit of input image, most of the pores which located in each boundary side of the image are lost.

Table 3. Average performance metrics in percentage and standard deviation (in parenthesis) of six different state-of-the-art method

	Gabor Filter [6]	Adapt. Dog [13]	DAPM [13]	Xu et al. [17]	Labati et al. [18]	DeepPore [20]	Proposed Method
R_T	75.90(7.5)	80.80(6.5)	84.80(4.5)	85.70	84.69(7.81)	93.09(4.63)	93.14(1.43)
R_F	23.00(8.2)	22.20(9.0)	17.60(6.3)	11.90	15.31(6.2)	8.64(4.15)	4.39(1.44)

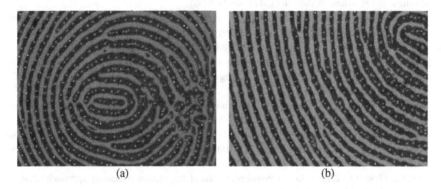

(a) (b)

Fig. 6. Examples of the pores detected by the proposed method. The true predictions are denoted by green dots, where the miss pores and false predictions are yellow and red, respectively. (Color figure online)

4 Conclusion

This paper proposed a new pore extraction method based on deep learning. Combined with logical operation, the CNN model achieves better results than the state-of-the-art methods on the benchmark database. The experimental results showed that both of R_T and R_F are improved. Furthermore, the standard deviation is reduced to one third when it is compared with DeepPore method. Meanwhile, the proposed method is demonstrated to be robust to gray and contrast variation of fingerprint images.

References

1. Yoon, S., Jain, A.K.: Longitudinal study of fingerprint recognition. In: Proceedings of the National Academy of Sciences of the United States of America, vol. 112, no. 28, p. 8555 (2015)
2. Peishan, X., Yuzhen, Y.: HPTLC fingerprint identification of commercial ginseng drugs - reinvestigation of HPTLC of ginsenosides. J. High Resolut. Chromatogr. **10**(11), 607–613 (2015)
3. Liu, F., Zhang, D., Shen, L.: Study on novel curvature features for 3D fingerprint recognition. Neurocomputing. **168**(C), 599–608 (2015)
4. Thornton, J.: Setting standards in the comparison and identification. In: Proceedings of 84th Annual Training Conference of the Cali- fornia State Division of IAI. Laughlin, Nevada (2000)
5. Kryszczuk, K., Drygajlo, A., Morier, P.: Extraction of level 2 and level 3 features for fragmentary fingerprints. In: Proceedings of the 2nd COST275 Workshop, vol. 27, no. 2, pp. 290–304 (2004)
6. Jain, A.K., Chen, Y., Demirkus, M.: Pores and ridges: fingerprint matching using level 3 features. IEEE Trans. PAMI. **4**(1), 477–480 (2006)
7. Zhao, Q., Zhang, L., Zhang, D., Luo, N.: Direct pore matching for fingerprint recognition. Adv. Biometrics ICB. **5558**, 597–606 (2009)
8. Kryszczuk, K., Morier, P., Drygajlo, A.: Study of the distinctiveness of level 2 and level 3 features in fragmentary fingerprint comparison. In: Maltoni, D., Jain, Anil K. (eds.) BioAW 2004. LNCS, vol. 3087, pp. 124–133. Springer, Heidelberg (2004). https://doi.org/10.1007/978-3-540-25976-3_12
9. Jain, A.K., Chen, Y., Demirkus, M.: Pores and ridges: high-resolution fingerprint matching using level 3 features. IEEE Trans. Pattern Anal. Mach. Intell. **29**(1), 15–27 (2007)
10. Liu, F., Zhao, Q., Zhang, L., Zhang, D.: Fingerprint pore matching based on sparse representation. In: Proceedings of the 20th International Conference on Pattern Recognition (2010)
11. Liu, F., Zhao, Q., Zhang, D.: A novel hierarchical fingerprint matching approach. Pattern Recogn. **44**(8), 1604–1613 (2011)
12. Liu, F., Zhao, Y., Shen, L.: Feature guided fingerprint pore matching. In: Zhou, J., et al. (eds.) CCBR 2017. LNCS, vol. 10568, pp. 334–343. Springer, Cham (2017). https://doi.org/10.1007/978-3-319-69923-3_36
13. Zhao, Q., Zhang, D., Zhang, L., Luo, N.: Adaptive fingerprint pore modeling and extraction. Pattern Recognit. **43**(8), 2833–2844 (2010)
14. Abhyankar, A., Schuckers, S.: Towards integrating level-3 Features with perspiration pattern for robust fingerprint recognition. In: IEEE International Conference on Image Processing, vol. 59, no. 1, pp. 3085–3088. IEEE (2010)
15. Malathi, S., Maheswari, S., Meena, C.: Fingerprint pore extraction based on marker controlled watershed segmentation. In: The International Conference on Computer and Automation Engineering, vol. 3, pp. 337–340. IEEE (2010)
16. da Silva Teixeira, R.F., Leite, N.J.: On adaptive fingerprint pore extraction. In: Kamel, M., Campilho, A. (eds.) ICIAR 2013. LNCS, vol. 7950, pp. 72–79. Springer, Heidelberg (2013). https://doi.org/10.1007/978-3-642-39094-4_9
17. Xu, Y., Lu, G., Liu, F., Li, Y.: Fingerprint pore extraction based on multi-scale morphology. In: Zhou, J., et al. (eds.) CCBR 2017. LNCS, vol. 10568, pp. 288–295. Springer, Cham (2017). https://doi.org/10.1007/978-3-319-69923-3_31

18. Labati, R., Genovese, A., Muñoz, E., Piuri, V., Scotti, F.: A novel pore extraction method for heterogeneous fingerprint images using convolutional neural networks. Pattern Recognit. Lett. (2017)
19. Wang, H., Yang, X., Ma, L., Liang, R.: fingerprint pore extraction using U-Net based fully convolutional network. In: Zhou, J., et al. (eds.) CCBR 2017. LNCS, vol. 10568, pp. 279–287. Springer, Cham (2017). https://doi.org/10.1007/978-3-319-69923-3_30
20. Jang, H., Kim, D., Mun, S., Choi, S., Lee, H.: Deeppore: fingerprint pore extraction using deep convolutional neural networks. IEEE Signal Process. Lett. 24(12), 1808–1812 (2017)
21. Krizhevsky, A., Sutskever, I., Hinton, I.G.: ImageNet classification with deep convolutional neural networks. In: International Conference on Neural Information Processing Systems, vol. 60, no. 2, pp. 1097–1105 (2012)
22. Simonyan, K., Zisserman, A.: Very deep convolutional networks for large-scale image recognition. Comput. Sci. (2014)
23. Hinton, G., Srivastava, N., Krizhevsky, A., Sutskever, I., Salakhutdinov, R.: Improving neural networks by preventing co-adaptation of feature detectors. Comput. Sci. 3(4), 212–223 (2012)
24. Jia, Y., Shelhamer, E., Donahue, J., Karayev, S., Long, J.: Caffe: convolutional architecture for fast feature embedding, pp. 675–678 (2014)
25. Bernsen, J.: Dynamic thresholding of grey-level images. In: International Conference on Pattern Recognition (1986)
26. Maltoni, D., Maio, D., Jain, A.K., Prabhakar, S.: Handbook of Fingerprint Recognition. Springer, London (2009). https://doi.org/10.1007/978-1-84882-254-2
27. Lin, H., Wan, Y., Jain, A.K.: Fingerprint image enhancement: algorithm and performance evaluation. IEEE Trans. Pattern Anal. Mach. Intell. 20(8), 777–789 (1998)

Palmprint Recognition Using Siamese Network

Dexing Zhong$^{(\boxtimes)}$, Yuan Yang, and Xuefeng Du

Xi'an Jiaotong University, Xi'an 710049, Shaanxi, People's Republic of China
`bell@xjtu.edu.cn`

Abstract. Recently, palmprint representation using different descriptors under the incorporation of deep neural networks, always achieves significant recognition performance. In this paper, we proposed a novel method to achieve end-to-end palmprint recognition by using Siamese network. In our network, two parameter-sharing VGG-16 networks were employed to extract two input palmprint images' convolutional features, and the top network directly obtained the similarity of two input palmprints according to their convolutional features. This method had a good performance on PolyU dataset and achieved a high recognition outcome with an Equal Error Rate (EER) of 0.2819%. To test the robustness of the proposed algorithm, we collected a palmprint dataset called XJTU from the practical daily environment. On XJTU, the EER of our method is 4.559%, which highlighted a promising potential of the usage of palmprint in personal identification system.

Keywords: Palmprint recognition · Siamese network
Convolutional Neural Networks · Feature extraction

1 Introduction

Previously, people tended to use password and ID cards for personal identification, yet they are easily stolen or forgotten. With the rapid development of information technology, biometric authentication receives increasingly more attention because of its convenience, safety and uniqueness [1]. A person's biological characteristics can be used in identification including fingerprint [2], face [3], vein figuration [4], iris [5], palmprint [6], skin texture [7], *etc.* While a single biological feature, such as human face and fingerprint recognition technologies, has been widely researched today, the development direction of biometric authentication technology is to employ multi-biological feature fusion instead of focusing on the single-mode features. Palmprint has singular points, minutiae points, principal lines, texture, wrinkles, and ridges, which can provide plenty of details and features for recognition [8, 9]. Moreover, Palmprint image is easy to collect and is ideal for identity authentication, so it has become a promising field in practical application. Therefore, there is a great research value in algorithms on palmprint-based authentication.

In this paper, we presented a system that can directly generate the similarity of two input palmprint images. It is very suitable for verification (Is this the same person), recognition (Who is this person) and clustering (Finding those images belonging to the same sampler among various palmprints) [10]. The system was trained on a small

J. Zhou et al. (Eds.): CCBR 2018, LNCS 10996, pp. 48–55, 2018.
https://doi.org/10.1007/978-3-319-97909-0_6

dataset of palmprint images. Transfer learning is used to optimize the performance of this system under the condition that the dataset is not very large. In addition, it has been tested on our own dataset collected in a practical environment and our proposed method is proven to have a good performance as well.

In summary, we made the following contributions: (1) As far as we are concerned, this paper makes the first attempt to directly obtain an index representing the similarity of two palmprints through the learnable method. (2) We flexibly used transfer learning to increase the accuracy and robustness of the experimental result in order to overcome the constraint that the dataset for training is not very large. (3) The proposed method not only performed well on the public palmprint database PolyU, but also showed an obvious advantage on our realistic dataset XJTU.

The rest of this paper is organized as follows: in Sect. 2, we review the literature in this area; Sect. 3 describes our whole network architecture and training procedure; in Sect. 4, we present some quantitative results of our method. Section 5 is the conclusion of this paper and we raise the potential outlook for future work.

2   Related Work

Until now, a number of researches concerning palmprint recognition have been conducted and many valuable viewpoints to enhance its performance have also been proposed. Fourier response and Gabor amplitude based quality estimation method [11], Adaboost algorithm [12], and learning for high resolution palmprint minutiae based quality estimation method [13], *etc.* were applied to evaluate the quality of certain minutiae. Early works, such as [14, 15] focused on classical and uncomplicated methods to classify and match the palmprint images.

In recent years, researchers have a strong interest in deep neural networks (DNN) [16]. Owing to the fact that deep neural networks have better scaling properties compared to other machine learning methods such as Support Vector Machines (SVM), Principal Component Analysis (PCA) and Linear Discriminant Analysis (LDA) [17]. It is widely used especially in multimedia and vision applications [18]. Hence, researchers began to utilize DNN to solve palmprint recognition problems. Zhao *et al.* [19] proposed an overview of deep learning in palmprint recognition. Liu *et al.* [1] used Convolutional Neural Networks (CNN) to carry out contactless recognition. And a novel extracting measure based on CNN for region of interest (ROI) of palmprint is presented in [20].

As what has been already mentioned, we solved palmprint recognition by comparing the similarity of two palmprint images. The traditional approaches to compare palmprints consist of two key components: a feature descriptor and a squared Euclidean distance. Most feature descriptors used hand-crafted feature as DAISY [21] or SIFT [22]. Previously, Cheng *et al.* [18] proposed a method called deep convolutional features based supervised hashing (DCFSH), which implemented learnable palmprint coding representation by integrating CNN and supervised Hashing, but it is not an end-to-end method for palm recognition. Our approach considered CNN as a feature descriptor and directly outputted an index to demonstrate the similarity of two input palmprints by a fully connected neural network.

3   Method

We proposed the method by referring to the structure of Siamese network [23]. It is made up of two key components as Fig. 1 shown. The first component is a feature descriptor. Moreover, it is comprised of two CNN structures that still consists of a series of convolutional, ReLU and max-pooling layers. The two CNN branches share the same architecture and the same set of weights. The second component is a decision network. It is a fully connected neural network which has two linear fully connected layers, a ReLU activation layer and a Sigmoid activation layer.

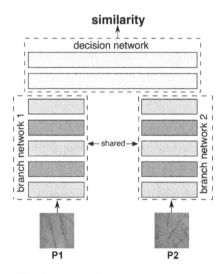

Fig. 1. The architecture of our network.

3.1   Feature Extraction

As what has been discussed above, two parameter-sharing VGG-16 [24] were designed to extract palmprint convolutional features. It differs from the original VGG-16 in the number of 'fc2' and 'fc3' layer outputs because of the change of dataset classes. The architecture of the VGG-16 used in this paper is shown in Table 1.

We trained our VGG-16 as a multi-class palmprint recognition task. Due to the fact that the palmprint dataset we used is too small to meet the training needs of VGG-16, if we still conducted training in small datasets with no modification, it will be extremely time-consuming while the corresponding results will not be satisfactory. Hence, we referred to the VGG-16 learned by a source task (ImageNet) to help learning our task. Then, we retrained the parameters on 'fc2' and 'fc3' layer based on the pre-trained VGG-16 network. The reason why only 'fc2' and 'fc3' were trained will be mentioned in the Sect. 4.2. The goal of training is to maximize the probability of the correct class (palmprint Id). We achieved this by minimizing the cross-entropy loss using stochastic gradient descent (SGD). Finally, we took the output of each palmprint image on 'fc3' layer as its palmprint feature vector (500×1).

Table 1. Architecture of the VGG-16 used in this paper.

Layer	Output	Layer	Output
input	$3 \times 224 \times 224$	conv4	$512 \times 28 \times 28$
conv1	$64 \times 224 \times 224$		$512 \times 28 \times 28$
	$64 \times 224 \times 224$		$512 \times 28 \times 28$
max_pool1	$64 \times 112 \times 112$	max_pool4	$512 \times 14 \times 14$
conv2	$128 \times 112 \times 112$	conv5	$512 \times 28 \times 28$
	$128 \times 112 \times 112$		$512 \times 28 \times 28$
max_pool2	$128 \times 56 \times 56$		$512 \times 28 \times 28$
conv3	$256 \times 56 \times 56$	max_pool5	$512 \times 7 \times 7$
	$256 \times 56 \times 56$	fc1	4096
	$256 \times 56 \times 56$	fc2	1024
max_pool3	$256 \times 28 \times 28$	fc3	500
		softmax	500

3.2   Verification Method

The similarity of two palmprint images was obtained from the decision network by inputting the combination of their features as Fig. 1 shows. The training set of the training decision network is a 1000×1 vector formed by linking the feature vectors of two palmprints (500×1) and a label indicating whether they are from the same person.

Decision network is a fully connected neural network consisting of two linear fully connected layers (1000×100, 100×1) that are separated by a ReLU activation layer. The output layer is activated by a Sigmoid function.

When training the decision network, we took two pictures randomly from the training set as a training sample. If they are from the same person, we assigned the value 1 to the tag, and if not, the tag was assigned the value of 0. The ratio of positive versus negative samples in each batch is 1:2.

4   Experiments

In the system we proposed, we need to train feature extraction network and decision network separately on the palmprint dataset. Two datasets for experimentation will be used. One is the public dataset PolyU, and the other is our own realistic dataset XJTU. The ratio of training sets versus testing sets in all experiments is 1:1.

4.1   Datasets

PolyU from Hong Kong Polytechnic University is an authoritative public palmprint dataset (shown as Fig. 2). It is collected in semi-closed environment with a stable uniform light provided. In contrast, more research value exists in the images of XJTU (shown in Fig. 3) collected from the practical daily environment because it may be relatively closer to the practical application of palmprint recognition. Specific information about these two databases is provided in Table 2.

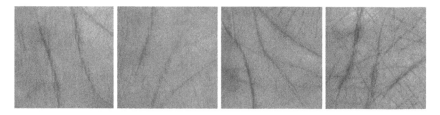

Fig. 2. Palmprint ROI images in PolyU.

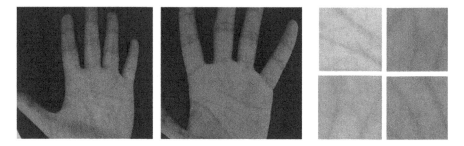

Fig. 3. Palmprint images and ROI images in XJTU.

Table 2. Comparison between PolyU and XJTU.

Item	PolyU	XJTU
Environment	Semi-closed black box	Open source
Light source	Stable uniform source	Natural light
Hand state	Fixed	Freely move
Size (Samples/Subject)	6000/500	2078/114
Resolution	128 × 128	640 × 480

4.2 Training of VGG-16

The number of layers needed to be retrained in transfer learning is determined by the following two factors: (1) the size of target task dataset (2) the similarity between the source and target tasks. These two factors are difficult to quantify. Therefore, we need to carry out a comparative experiment. We retrained some layers in VGG-16 as a multi-class palmprint recognition task for roughly 400 times of iteration over the PolyU dataset. The results are shown in Table 3.

Table 3. Comparison of recognition results in training different layers.

Retrained layer	Accuracy
fc3	98.9%
fc3, fc2	99.6%
fc3, fc2, fc1	96.1%

According to Table 3, the performance of only retrain 'fc3' and 'fc2' layer is better than others. Accordingly, we retrained 'fc3' and 'fc2' layer in VGG-16 and considered the output of 'fc3' as the final palmprint feature.

4.3   Results on PolyU Dataset

As mentioned in Sect. 4.2. We first retrained 'fc3' and 'fc2' layers in VGG-16 as a multi-class palmprint recognition task on training set of PolyU. Then, we trained the decision network through the image pairs from PolyU training set.

Finally, The EER on PolyU test set is 0.2819%. And the ROC curve is shown in Fig. 4.

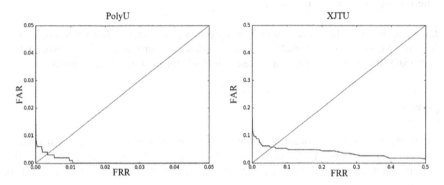

Fig. 4.   The ROC curve on PolyU and XJTU.

4.4   Results on XJTU Dataset

To test the robustness of the algorithm, we also tested on XJTU dataset. We first retrained 'fc3' and 'fc2' layers in VGG-16 as a multi-class palmprint recognition task on XJTU. Then, the decision network was trained through the image pairs from XJTU training set.

Finally, The EER on XJTU test set is 4.559%. And the ROC curve is shown in Fig. 4.

4.5   Experimental Setting and Time Complexity

A quad-core Intel CPU i7-7700 and a NVIDIA GPU GTX1060 with 6G memory power was used in this article. The training section took a total of 12 h. It takes about 0.012 s to calculate the similarity of a pair of input palmprint images.

5 Conclusion

In this paper, we proposed a palmprint recognition method using Siamese network, which can directly derive the similarity index of two input palmprints. Besides, our method also implemented end-to-end recognition. Two parameter-sharing VGG-16 networks were employed to extract two input palmprints' convolutional features, and the top network obtained the similarity of two input palmprints according to their convolutional features. The EER of this method on PolyU test set was 0.2819%. Moreover, on our realistic dataset XJTU, the EER was 4.559%.

In the future work, we will further improve the overall network structure to reduce the EER especially on the XJTU dataset. In order to optimize the end-to-end training, we will carry out more research by integrating the decision network and the two CNNs as one training session in the future.

Acknowledgements. This work is supported by grants from National Natural Science Foundation of China (No. 61105021), Natural Science Foundation of Shaanxi, China (No. 2015JQ6257) and the Fundamental Research Funds for the Central Universities.

References

1. Liu, D., Sun, D.M.: Contactless palmprint recognition based on convolutional neural network. In: Baozong, Y., Qiuqi, R., Yao, Z., Gaoyun, A.N. (eds.) Proceedings of 2016 IEEE 13th International Conference on Signal Processing, pp. 1363–1367. IEEE, New York (2016)
2. Rivalderia, N., Gutierrez-Redomero, E., Alonso-Rodriguez, C., Dipierri, J.E., Martin, L.M.: Study of fingerprints in Argentina population for application in personal identification. Sci. Justice **57**, 199–208 (2017)
3. Chu, Y.J., Ahmad, T., Bebis, G., Zhao, L.D.: Low-resolution face recognition with single sample per person. Signal Process. **141**, 144–157 (2017)
4. Chen, L.K., Wang, J., Yang, S.Y., He, H.B.: A finger vein image-based personal identification system with self-adaptive illuminance control. IEEE Trans. Instrum. Meas. **66**, 294–304 (2017)
5. Liu, N.F., Liu, J., Sun, Z.N., Tan, T.: A code-level approach to heterogeneous iris recognition. IEEE Trans. Inf. Forensic Secur. **12**, 2373–2386 (2017)
6. Jia, W., et al.: Palmprint recognition based on complete direction representation. IEEE Trans. Image Process. **26**, 4483–4498 (2017)
7. Bianconi, F., Chirikhina, E., Smeraldi, F., Bontozoglou, C., Xiao, P.: Personal identification based on skin texture features from the forearm and multi-modal imaging. Skin Res. Technol. **23**, 392–398 (2017)
8. Kong, A., Zhang, D., Kamel, M.: A survey of palmprint recognition. Pattern Recognit. **42**, 1408–1418 (2009)
9. Zhang, L., Li, L.D., Yang, A.Q., Shen, Y., Yang, M.: Towards contactless palmprint recognition: a novel device, a new benchmark, and a collaborative representation based identification approach. Pattern Recognit. **69**, 199–212 (2017)
10. Schroff, F., Kalenichenko, D., Philbin, J.: FaceNet: a unified embedding for face recognition and clustering. In: Proceedings of 2015 IEEE Conference on Computer Vision and Pattern Recognition, pp. 815–823. IEEE, New York (2015)

11. Liu, C., Wang, H., Feng, J.: High-resolution palmprint minutiae extraction based on gabor phase and image quality estimation. Acta Sci. Nat. Univ. Pekin. (China) **51**, 384–390 (2015)
12. Feng, J.F., Liu, C.J., Wang, H., Sun, B.: High-resolution palmprint minutiae extraction based on Gabor feature. Sci. China-Inf. Sci. **57**, 1–15 (2014)
13. Wang, H., Liu, C.-J., Fu, X., Feng, J.-F.: Quality estimation algorithm based on learning for high-resolution palmprint minutiae. J. Softw. (China) **25**, 2180–2186 (2014)
14. Wang, Y.X., Ruan, Q.Q.: Dual-tree complex wavelet transform based local binary pattern weighted histofram method for palmprint recognition. Comput. Inform. **28**, 299–318 (2009)
15. Yang, X., Cheng, K.T.: Local difference binary for ultrafast and distinctive feature description. IEEE Trans. Pattern Anal. Mach. Intell. **36**, 188–194 (2014)
16. Krizhevsky, A., Sutskever, I., Hinton, G.E.: ImageNet classification with deep convolutional neural networks. Commun. ACM (USA) **60**, 84–90 (2017)
17. Taigman, Y., Yang, M., Ranzato, M., Wolf, L.: DeepFace: closing the gap to human-level performance in face verification. In: Proceedings of 2014 IEEE Conference on Computer Vision and Pattern Recognition, pp. 1701–1708. IEEE, New York (2014)
18. Cheng, J., Sun, Q., Zhang, J., Zhang, Q.: Supervised hashing with deep convolutional features for palmprint recognition. In: Zhou, J., et al. (eds.) CCBR 2017. LNCS, vol. 10568, pp. 259–268. Springer, Cham (2017). https://doi.org/10.1007/978-3-319-69923-3_28
19. Zhao Dandan Pan, X., Pan, X., Luo, X., Gao, X.: Palmprint recognition based on deep learning. In: Proceedings of 6th International Conference on Wireless, Mobile and Multi-Media (ICWMMN 2015), pp. 214–216 (2015)
20. Bao, X.J., Guo, Z.H.: Extracting region of interest for palmprint by convolutional neural networks. In: Lopez, M.B., Hadid, A., Pietikainen, M. (eds.) Proceedings of 2016 Sixth International Conference on Image Processing Theory, Tools and Applications, pp. 1–6. IEEE, New York (2016)
21. Tola, E., Lepetit, V., Fua, P.: A fast local descriptor for dense matching. In: Proceedings of 2008 IEEE Conference on Computer Vision and Pattern Recognition (CVPR), pp. 1–8 (2008)
22. Lowe, D.G.: Distinctive image features from scale-invariant keypoints. Int. J. Comput. Vis. **60**, 91–110 (2004)
23. Bromley, J., et al.: Signature verification using a siamese time delay neural network. Int. J. Pattern Recognit. Artif. Intell. **7**, 669–688 (1993)
24. Simonyan, K., Zisserman, A.: Very deep convolutional networks for large-scale image recognition. Comput. Sci. **15**, 1–14 (2014)

A Cylinder Code-Based Partial Fingerprint Matching Algorithm for Small Fingerprint Scanners

Xiangwen Kong[1], Yumeng Wang[1], Rongsheng Wang[1],
Changlong Jin[1(✉)], and Hakil Kim[2]

[1] Department of Computer Science, Shandong University at Weihai,
Weihai, Shandong Province, China
kxwkaoyan@163.com, kt2meng@163.com,
wangrsl412@mails.jlu.edu.cn, cljin@sdu.edu.cn
[2] School of Information and Communication Engineering,
INHA University, Incheon, Korea
hikim@inha.ac.kr

Abstract. To solve the problem of partial fingerprint matching difficulty caused by very small fingerprint sensors on mobile terminals, this paper presents a Cylinder Code-based partial fingerprint matching algorithm. The algorithm is inspired by the Minutia Cylinder Code (MCC) structure, and keeps the original MCC structure characteristics while reducing data redundancy. In addition, ridge points are added in the algorithm, which solve the feature loss caused by the small size of the sensors. The proposed algorithm are tested on the FVC2002 database and compared with four well-known matching algorithms. The results show the proposed method has excellent comprehensive performance and ability to apply to light architecture that other algorithms cannot match.

Keywords: Partial fingerprint · Matching · Minutia cylinder code
Ridge point

1 Introduction

Due to some mobile applications, such as mobile payments, require a more secure and accurate partial fingerprint matching system to protect privacy, partial fingerprint matching algorithms still need to be improved. Researchers often fuse minutiae with non-minutia features, such as level 3 features [1–4], together to increase the reliability of partial fingerprint matching results. Level 3 features are tiny and unstable features on fingerprint, such as incipient ridges, creases, warts scars, pores, ridge concave, ridge convex, and so on. However, it is hard to detect reliable level 3 features by sensors with a resolution below 1000dpi, and high-resolution sensors are not standard for all mobile terminals.

There are also some partial fingerprint matching algorithms based on SIFT [5] or A-KAZE [6] feature. SIFT and A-KAZE feature are commonly used for object recognition and image matching. Their advantage is they can obtain a lot of feature

© Springer Nature Switzerland AG 2018
J. Zhou et al. (Eds.): CCBR 2018, LNCS 10996, pp. 56–65, 2018.
https://doi.org/10.1007/978-3-319-97909-0_7

points even if the area of partial fingerprint images are small. However, the algorithms are susceptible to noise and distortion and have a high computational complexity.

Ridge line is the basis of fingerprint, which is very stable. However, ridge line-based matching algorithm [7] is too time consuming, therefore, Fang et al. [8] used ridge points sampled from ridge line instead of the whole ridge line in matching process, and the results showed a very good matching capabilities while reducing the runtime. Even at low resolutions, reliable ridge points can be obtained, and its computational complexity of matching is not high.

Inspired by the original MCC [9] structure, this paper proposes a novel partial fingerprint matching algorithm based on the Modified Feature Point Cylinder Code (MFPCC) structure. The MFPCC are built for minutiae and ridge points, respectively. In local matching, local similarity is obtained through simple and efficient vector correlation calculation. Global similarity is obtained by iterative relaxation algorithm in global matching. The final matching score is derived by considering the global similarity of minutiae and ridge points.

The rest of this paper is organized as follows, Sect. 2 analyzes MCC[1] and proposes a new matching algorithm, Sect. 3 applies the proposed algorithm over the FVC2002 DB1 and FVC2002 DB3 and discuss the experimental results. The conclusion is reported in Sect. 4.

2   Fingerprint Matching Using Cylinder Code

The proposed algorithm is based on the modified MCC structure. The equations of this paper follow the writing rules in the original MCC. Equations or symbols that are not specifically mentioned have the same meaning as in the original MCC algorithm written by Raffaele et al. [9].

2.1   Analyzation and Modification of MCC Structure

The MCC-based matching algorithm is the state-of-the-art minutiae-based matching algorithms. It has invariant characteristics for translation and rotation, and robustness to distortion and slight spurious feature points. Besides, it is binary coded and low reversible. It is worth mentioning that MCC can be efficiently implemented on light architectures, which ensures that fingerprint identification applications against external attacks.

These advantages are the premise that MCC applies to partial fingerprint matching. But at the same time, MCC has some defects that cannot be ignored. MCC takes a long time to construct and only utilizes minutia features, so it is hard to be applied directly to partial fingerprint matching. Analysis of MCC reveals that there are very large redundancies between the data stored in layers[2]. To deal with these drawbacks, a modified MCC for partial fingerprint matching is proposed in the paper. By changing

---

[1] MCC mentioned in this paper refers to MCC8b.

[2] The cylinder of original MCC structure is divided into six layers in height, and each layer is divided into 8×8 cells.

the calculation method of contribution for each cell, the modified structure halves the layers number of the original MCC and greatly reduces the construction time of MCC.

The modified structure is as follows. The local structure associated to a given $center = (x_{center}, y_{center}, \theta_{center})$ (minutia or fingerprint ridge point) is represented by a cylinder with radius R and height $\left[-\frac{\pi}{2}, \frac{\pi}{2}\right]$ whose base is centered on the *center* location, see Fig. 1.

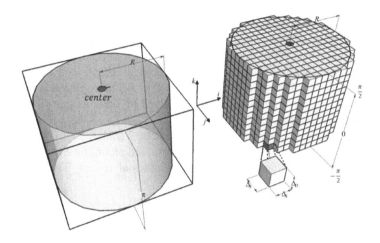

Fig. 1. The picture is quoted from the literature [9].

The cylinder is enclosed inside a cuboid whose base is aligned according to the *center* direction θ_{center}; the cuboid is discretized into $N_S \times N_S \times (N_D/2)$ cells ($N_S = 8$, $N_D = 6$). Each cell can be uniquely identified by three indices (i, j, k). For each cell (i, j, k), a numerical value $C_{SCC}(i, j, k)$ is calculated by accumulating contributions from each *point$_t$* belonging to the neighborhood $N_{p_{i,j}}$ of $p_{i,j}$:

$$C_{SCC}(i,j,k) = \begin{cases} \Psi\left(C^D_{SCC}(p_{i,j}, d_{\varphi_k}) \sum_{point_t \in N_{p_{i,j}}} \left(C^S_{SCC}(point_t, p_{i,j})\right)\right) \\ \qquad\qquad if\, \xi_m(p_{i,j}) = valid \\ \qquad invalid \qquad otherwise \end{cases} \tag{1}$$

Where, *point* can be minutia or relevant ridge point; $p_{i,j}$ is the two-dimensional point corresponding to the center of the cells with indices i, j.

$$N_{p_{i,j}} = \{point_t \in point; d_S(point_t, p_{i,j}) \leq 3\sigma_S\}. \tag{2}$$

$C^S_{SCC}(point_t, p_{i,j})$ is the spatial contribution that *point$_t$* gives to cell (i, j, k); it is defined as a function of the Euclidean distance between *point$_t$* and $p_{i,j}$:

$$C^S_{SCC}(point_t, p_{i,j}) = G_S(d_S(point_t, p_{i,j})). \tag{3}$$

$C_{SCC}^D(p_{i,j}, d_{\varphi_k})$ is the directional contribution of $point_t$; it is defined as a function of:
(1) d_{φ_k}, and (2) the different angles between θ_{center} and the orientation angles of $p_{i,j}$.
Intuitively, the contribution is high when (1) and (2) are close to each other:

$$C_{SCC}^D(p_{i,j}, d_{\varphi_k}) = G_D(d_\phi(d_{\varphi_k}, d_o(center, ori_{p_{i,j}}))). \tag{4}$$

Where, d_o calculates the angle between *center* and orientation angles, and the result range is $\left[-\frac{\pi}{2}, \frac{\pi}{2}\right]$.

The modified MCC proposed in this paper changes calculation method of directional contributions of the cell in the original MCC. It changes calculation method from accumulating directional contribution from all minutiae belonging to the neighborhood of the cell to only calculating directional contributions from orientation angle of the cell center position $p_{i,j}$.

New directional contributions calculation method is independent of the feature points in the neighborhood of cell, so it is no longer necessary to cyclically accumulate directional contributions of each feature point in the neighborhood like the original MCC. And orientation angles don't have direction, so the height of cylinder changes from $[-\pi, \pi]$ to $\left[-\frac{\pi}{2}, \frac{\pi}{2}\right]$ and the number of layers changes from N_D to $N_D/2$.

The modified structure greatly reduces the runtime in calculating the contribution of each cell and halves the total number of calculations for the contribution of cells. The speed of structure construction is greatly increased. In Sect. 3, the matching performance of MCC and MFPCC is evaluated. The result proves that MFPCC effectively improves the construction speed of MCC while retaining the matching performance. Equation (1) shows that MFPCC has a flexible parameter selection mode. The different selection of *center* (center point) and *point* (neighborhood point) forms different structures. Partial fingerprint matching algorithm proposed in this section is based on the Modified Feature Point Cylinder Code-Minutia (MFPCC-M) structure and Modified Feature Point Cylinder Code-Ridge Point (MFPCC-RP) structure, which are extended from the MFPCC structure.

2.2   Extraction of Ridge Point

The sampling method of ridge is as follows:

Find the connection ridges for each minutia, ending point has a connection ridge and bifurcation point has three connection ridges.

(1) Trace from the minutia, equidistant sampling on connecting ridges (45 pixels).
(2) Starting from neighboring ridge points, equidistant sampling on both sides of ridges, see Fig. 2.
(3) In the paper, the sampling points from related ridges are called relevant ridge points; all relevant ridge points are called fingerprint ridge points.

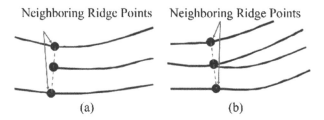

Fig. 2. (a) 3 related ridges and 1 connection ridge for ending point. (b) 5 related ridges and 3 connection ridge for bifurcation point.

2.3   Build Modified Feature Point Cylinder Code-Minutia Structure

In order to increase the uniqueness of minutiae, the proposed method builds MFPCC structure for each minutia, known as MFPCC-M structure, which can store the distribution of other minutiae and relevant ridge points in its neighborhood.

For each cell in MFPCC-M, two numerical value $C_m^m(i,j,k)$ and $C_m^{rp}(i,j,k)$ are calculated by Eq. (1), which respectively represent the contribution of minutiae belonging to the cell neighborhood and the contribution of relevant ridge points belonging to the cell neighborhood.

The calculation of $C_m^m(i,j,k)$ is the same as $C_{SCC}(i,j,k)$, but variables *center* in Eq. (4) and *point* in Eq. (1) represents minutia. Each minutia will get a corresponding $N_S \times N_S \times (N_D/2)$ size data structure C_m^m.

The calculation of $C_m^{rp}(i,j,k)$ is the same as $C_{SCC}(i,j,k)$, but variables *center* in Eq. (4) represents minutia and *point* in Eq. (1) represents relevant ridge point. Each minutia will get a corresponding $N_S \times N_S \times (N_D/2)$ size data structure C_m^{rp}. The two data structures are transformed into a vector c_m of $N_S \times N_S \times N_D$ dimensions through a linear function and the corresponding cell validity is stored in the vector $\hat{c}_m$. Figure 3(a), (b) and (d) show a MFPCC-M structure.

2.4   Build Modified Feature Point Cylinder Code-Ridge Point Structure

In order to increase the matching features, proposed method builds MFPCC structure for each fingerprint ridge point, known as MFPCC-RP structure, which can store the distribution of other minutiae in its neighborhood.

For each cell in MFPCC-RP, a numerical value $C_{rp}^m(i,j,k)$ is calculated by Eq. (1), which represent the contribution of minutiae belonging to the cell neighborhood.

When calculating $C_{rp}^m(i,j,k) = C_{SCC}(i,j,k)$, *center* in Eq. (4) represents fingerprint ridge point and *point* in Eq. (1) represents minutia. Each fingerprint ridge point will get a corresponding $N_S \times N_S \times (N_D/2)$ size data structure C_{rp}^m. The data structure is transformed into a vector c_{rp} of $N_S \times N_S \times (N_D/2)$ dimensions through a linear function and the corresponding cell validity is stored in the vector $\hat{c}_{rp}$. Figure 3(c) and (e) show a MFPCC-RP structure.

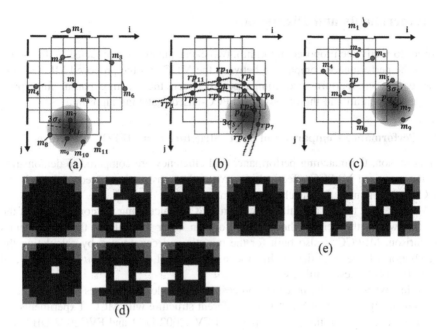

Fig. 3. (a) Distribution of adjacent minutiae in MFPCC-M associated to minutia m. (b) Distribution of relevant ridge points in MFPCC-M associated to minutia m. (c) Distribution of adjacent minutiae in MFPCC-RP associated to ridge point rp. (d) The cell values of MFPCC-M associated to minutia m. Figures 1, 2 and 3 show the contribution of minutiae belonging to the cell neighborhood, and Figs. 4, and 6 show the contribution of ridge points belonging to the cell neighborhood. (e) The cell values of the MFPCC-RP associated to ridge point rp. Black denotes 0, white denotes 1, and grey denotes invalid area.

2.5   Matching Strategy

Since the feature structure has been transformed into a fixed-length feature vector, the structure similarity can be obtained by simple and fast binary vector correlation calculation. In the calculation, the matching between minutiae points and the matching between ridge points are followed. The minutia pairs and ridge point pairs with higher similarity are taken as candidate feature point pairs for global matching.

We use the Local Similarity Sort with Releasing (LSS-R) algorithm proposed in [5] to obtain the global score. The basic idea is to iteratively modify the local similarities based on the compatibility among feature points (in the candidate feature point pairs) relationships. After iteration, the efficiency of genuine matching will be high and the efficiency of impostor matching will be low. The final score is obtained by averaging the updated local similarity of feature point pairs with higher efficiency.

3 Experiments and Discussions

In order to verify the proposed algorithm, two experiments are conducted in this work. One is the performance comparison between the MCC and the proposed MFPCC, the other one is the performance comparison between the existing partial fingerprint matching algorithm and the proposed MFPCC-based matching algorithm.

3.1 Performance Comparison of MCC Structure and MFPCC Structure

In this section, the matching performance and efficiency are compared to demonstrate that the proposed MFPCC effectively improves the construction speed of the original MCC while retaining the matching performance.

MCC is built for the minutia and constructed by calculating the contribution of the minutiae within the neighborhood. Therefore, in order to facilitate the experimental comparison, MFPCC is also built for the minutia and constructed by calculating the contribution of the minutiae within the neighborhood, where *point* in Eq. (1) and *center* Eq. (4) represent minutia.

In this experiment, the matching process and the adopted features are the same as the original [9] except that MFPCC has different structure with MCC. Experiments are conducted over the full fingerprint images of FVC2002 DB1 and FVC2002 DB2, and there are 2800 genuine matching and 4950 impostor matching for each dataset.

As shown in Table 1, the Equal Error Rates (EER) of MFPCC and MCC are basically the same, but MFPCC is about 5 times faster than MCC in the stage of structure establishment. The runtime difference indicates that the drawbacks of MCC construction speed are eliminated, and scope of application of the structure has also been extended. It is possible to apply the structure to partial fingerprint matching. MFPCC is basis of the algorithm proposed in this paper.

Table 1. Performance of fingerprint matching on DB1 and DB2 of FVC2002.

EER	DB1a	DB2a	T_{cs}^a	T_m^b
MCC	1.25%	0.96%	5.4 ms	6.1 ms
MFPCC	1.25%	0.96%	1.1 ms	3.6 ms

[a]Average runtime to create the local structure.
[b]Average runtime to match.

3.2 Performance Evaluation of the Proposed Algorithm

In order to obtain a complete fingerprint template by mosaicking, commercial fingerprint-authentication systems in mobile terminals require users to input multiple impressions in the enrollment process. In the verification process, partial fingerprint images are inputted by the small fingerprint scanning and matched with the complete fingerprint template stored.

To simulate the real situation, the images in the FVC 2002 DB1 and FVC 2002DB3 datasets are cropped to partial fingerprint patches. Among the eight impressions for each finger, the last four impressions are used to generate partial fingerprint patches and the first four impressions are used as the complete fingerprint template (the highest score of the first four in matching is final matching score). A total of 20 (=5 × 4 fingers) query partial fingerprint patches were randomly generated from the foreground regions of the last four impressions, and the screening condition is the generated partial fingerprint patches should contain 90% foreground region.

Three different sizes of patches are considered, and a total of 2000 (=20 × 100 fingers) patches and 100 templates are generated for each pre-defined size. Each dataset will perform 2000 (=100 fingers × 20 patches) genuine matching and 9900 (the first patch of 100 fingers × 99 templates) imposter matching. Tables 2 present the results (EERs) of the proposed algorithm, and Fig. 4 shows the ROC curves of the proposed algorithm.

Table 2. Performance of proposed algorithm on the partial fingerprint datasets simulated on DB1 and DB3 of FVC2002.

2002 (pixel^2)	192 × 184	160 × 152	136 × 128
DB1	0.42%	0.52%	1.11%
2002 (pixel^2)	184 × 184	152 × 152	136 × 136
DB3	1.83%	2.51%	3.93%

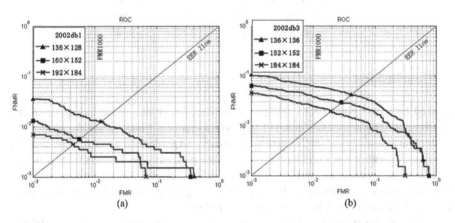

Fig. 4. ROC curves of partial fingerprint matching on FVC2002: (1) DB1, (2) DB3.

The matching performance of the proposed algorithm are also compared with four well-known matching algorithms. Due to the time, this paper does not implement the four algorithms, and the experimental results of the four well-known matching algorithms come from the literature [10].

As shown in Tables 3 and 4, the proposed algorithm has better EER than the matching method except RSF matcher. However, the proposed algorithm has more advantages than RSF matcher in time complexity and security. In summary, the proposed algorithm have good comprehensive performance in accuracy, security, speed, and light architecture, and have unique advantages compared with other matching algorithms.

Table 3. EER of five algorithms in DB1 of FVC2002.

Image size (pixel^2)		192×184	160×152	136×128
Sensing area (mm^2)		9.8×9.3	8.1×7.7	6.9×6.5
EER(%)	MCC [9]	0.40	6.69	25.26
	RRP [8]	0.55	2.94	6.65
	A-KAZE [6]	1.15	2.35	4.95
	RSF [10]	**0.25**	0.54	1.20
	Proposed	0.42	**0.53**	**1.12**

Table 4. EER of five algorithms in DB3 of FVC2002.

Image size (pixel^2)		184×184	152×152	136×136
Sensing area (mm^2)		9.3×9.3	7.7×7.7	6.9×6.9
EER(%)	MCC [9]	2.80	9.78	22.61
	RRP [8]	2.50	4.86	7.58
	A-KAZE [6]	10.35	13.72	16.00
	RSF [10]	**1.50**	**2.50**	**3.90**
	Proposed	1.83	2.52	3.94

4 Conclusions

Inspired by the original MCC, this paper presents a Cylinder Code-based partial fingerprint matching algorithm for small fingerprint scanners which solves the problem of insufficient minutiae and MCC data redundancy. Experimental results show that the proposed algorithm has excellent comprehensive performance. In particular, it is portable to light architecture and can provide perfect security for fingerprint matching systems on mobile terminals. With the increasing emphasis on fingerprint privacy security, this feature will have an important influence.

However, the proposed algorithm cannot be properly performed if a partial fingerprint image does not contain any minutia points due to its low quality or its small size. Accordingly, in future we plan to further improve MFPCC structure and try to solve this problem.

Acknowledgments. This work is supported by the Natural Science Foundation of Shandong Province, China (No. ZR2014FM004).

References

1. Chen, Y., Jain, A.: Dots and incipients: extended features for partial fingerprint matching. In: Proceedings of the 2nd Biometrics Symposium, pp. 1–6 (2007)
2. Jain, A.K., Chen, Y., Demirkus, M.: Pores and ridges high-resolution fingerprint matching using level 3 features. IEEE Comput. Soc. **29**, 15–27 (2007)
3. Kryszczuk, K.M., Drygajlo, A., Morier, P.: Extraction of level 2 and level 3 features for fragmentary fingerprints. In: Proceedings of the Second Cost Action Workshop, vol. 27, pp. 290–304 (2004)
4. Zhao, Q., Zhang, D., Zhang, L., Luo, N.: High resolution partial fingerprint alignment using pore-valley descriptors. Patt. Recogn. **43**, 1050–1061 (2010)
5. Yamazaki, M., Li, D., Isshiki, T., Kunieda, H.: Sift-based algorithm for fingerprint authentication on smartphone. In: Proceedings of the 6th International Conference of Information and Communication Technology for Embedded Systems, pp. 1–5 (2015)
6. Mathur, S., Vijay, A., Shah, J., Das, S., Malla, A.: Methodology for partial fingerprint enrollment and authentication on mobile devices. In: Proceedings of the 9th International Conference on Biometrics, pp. 1–8 (2016)
7. Feng, J., Ouyang, Z., Cai, A.: Fingerprint matching using ridges. Patt. Recogn. **39**, 2131–2140 (2006)
8. Fang, G., Srihari, S.N., Srinivasan, H.: Use of ridge points in partial fingerprint matching. In: Biometric Technology for Human Identification IV, pp. 4–35 (2007)
9. Cappelli, R., Ferrara, M., Maltoni, D.: Minutia cylinder-code: a new representation and matching technique for fingerprint recognition. IEEE Trans. Patt. Anal. Mach. Intell. **32**, 2128–2141 (2010)
10. Lee, W., Cho, S., Choi, H., Kim, J.: Partial fingerprint matching using minutiae and ridge shape features for small fingerprint scanners. Expert Syst. Appl. **87**, 183–198 (2017)

Optimal Parameter Selection for 3D Palmprint Acquisition System

Xu Liang[1], Gang Wu[2], Yan He[2], and Nan Luo[2,3(✉)]

[1] Harbin Institute of Technology (Shenzhen), Shenzhen, China
1042110615@qq.com
[2] The Institute of Automation,
Heilongjiang Academy of Sciences, Harbin, China
wugang@haai.com.cn, 820494227@qq.com,
nanluo1980@163.com
[3] Shenzhen Institue of the Hong Kong Polytechnic University, Shenzhen, China

Abstract. 3D palmprint recognition system have been widely studied in recent years. More and more 3D palmprint feature extraction and matching methods are proposed. However, most of the existing image acquisition systems are based on commercial equipment which has high cost, big equipment volume, over-high precision and long 3D data generation time. What's more, those systems are not designed specialized for palmprint. Most of their parameters are not suitable for 3D palmprint acquisition. Those shortcomings have seriously hindered the applications of 3D palmprint identification. In this paper, we developed a new scheme to tune the initial system parameters to balance the tradeoff of device cost, volume, and data generation time. The samples collected by our proposed device have proved its effectiveness and advantages. The system is easy to implement and will promote the application of 3D palmprint.

Keywords: 3D palmprint measurement · Phase-shifting error
Structured-light imaging

1 Introduction

Nowadays, a lot of biometrics applications are based on 3D information. Such like face ID in iPhone and gesture recognition in Kinect. 3D information has its natural advantages in background subtraction, posture estimation and accuracy improvement. Compared with 2D palmprint recognition, 3D palmprint image can provide depth information of the principle, wrinkle and ridge lines. Hence, these years more and more researches are focused on 3D palmprint recognition. Kanhangda *et al.* [1, 2] utilizes the commercial laser scanning measurement device to capture 3D palms under different postures. Then he designed several methods to estimate and correct the hand postures. Zhang *et al.* [5] achieved high speed 3D palmprint identification using collaborative representation. Li *et al.* [6] further decreased the final EER (Equal Error Rate) by refining the 2D palmprint image based on the global information obtained from the 3D palm surface.

© Springer Nature Switzerland AG 2018
J. Zhou et al. (Eds.): CCBR 2018, LNCS 10996, pp. 66–76, 2018.
https://doi.org/10.1007/978-3-319-97909-0_8

There are four kinds of methods to capture 3D palmprint:

(1) Laser scanning based triangulation measurement [1];
(2) Depth sensor based 3D measurement;
(3) Stereo vision based 3D measurement [9];
(4) Structured-Light based high precision 3D measurement [4].

Most laser scanning equipment, such like VIVID 910, is designed for general 3D reconstruction. The long measurement time (0.5 ~ 2.5 s) and long working distance (0.6 ~ 1.2 m) is not suitable for palmprint recognition. Depth sensor can provide real-time 3D frame, but the data contains much noise. Low SNR (signal to noise ratio) and low resolution are their problems. Stereo camera based system [9, 10] can only provide 3D information of the matched points between the current image pairs. Hence its resolution and precision are not sufficient for palmprint recognition. Compared with them, structured-light imaging method performs better. It could obtain high precision and it is easy to implement. Based on structured-light technique, Zhang *et al.* [3] designed the first 3D palmprint acquisition device. As shown in Fig. 1, the device contains a plate for putting palm, several pegs to limit the palm position and a top cover to ensure the internal lighting conditions. The current largest 3D palmprint public benchmark is also collected by this device. Many 3D palmprint recognition methods [4, 5, 7, 8] have been proposed based on this device. But they haven't did research on the system design and parameter optimization. The big volume of the final device has seriously affected its application ranges.

  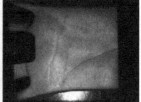

Fig. 1. The existing 3D palmprint measurement systems.

The main shortcomings of the existing 3D palmprint measurement system are as following:

(1) Expensive;
(2) Big volume;
(3) Long generation time.

Current studies have developed many feature extraction and matching methods to improve the accuracy of 3D palmprint recognition. But, no more high-precision 3D palmprint measurement devices are proposed. The existing problems have become the key factors that limited the development of 3D palmprint recognition. For this reason, we consider doing some work to balance the tradeoff of device cost, volume, and data generation time, trying to further reduce the device volume and decrease the equipment cost. Only in this way, can 3D palmprint recognition be widely used in practice.

In the rest of the paper, Sect. 2 describes different models of the structured-light measurement. Based on the cross light model, Sect. 3 proposed our scheme to optimize the initial structure parameters. Section 4 shows the experimental results, Sect. 5 draws the conclusions.

2   Brief Introduction of Structured Light Based Reconstruction

The principle of structured-light measurement is projecting a set of predesigned grating patterns to the measured object and using a camera to capture the distorted grating patterns which is modulated by the object height. Generally, those systems are consisted of a CCD camera, a projector and an enclosure.

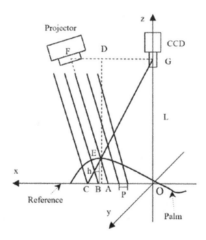

Fig. 2. Illustration of the parallel light model.

2.1   Parallel Light Model

As shown in Fig. 2, the user's palm is put on the reference plane whose height is set to be zero. L is the vertical distance from the camera lens to the supporting plane. P is the wavelength of the grating patterns on the plane. D is the horizontal distance between the camera and the projector. Since $\triangle AEC \sim \triangle FEG$, we have:

$$\frac{L-h}{h} = \frac{D}{\overrightarrow{CA}} \tag{1}$$

$$\overrightarrow{CA} = \frac{\phi_{CA}}{2\pi} \times P \tag{2}$$

Suppose (x, y) is one point of the captured 2D image, then according to (1) and (2), the corresponding height of this point in 3D space is:

$$h(x,y) = \frac{-L\phi_{CA}}{\phi_{CA} + \frac{2\pi D}{P}} \tag{3}$$

ϕ_{CA} can be obtained by (4). It is the phase difference between point C and point A.

$$\phi_{CA} = \phi_{OC} - \phi_{OA} \tag{4}$$

$\phi(x, y)$ is calculated using phase shifting algorithm [11, 12, 13]. However, parallel light model requires the values of P are fixed and equal on the reference plane. But, in practice, this is difficult to realize. Besides, the over-complex hardware will greatly increase the cost and volume of the device.

2.2   Cross Light Model

Compared with parallel light model, cross light model is closer to the actual situation. But once the projector's optical axis is not prependicular to the reference plane, the projected wavelength of the grating pattern is not fixed (as shown in Fig. 3). Complex algorithms are needed to rectify the distorted wavelength. For palmprint recognition, if we set P to be the average wavlength $\overline{P}$, the final measurement error can be decreased to an interval which is acceptable after tunning the structure parameters. In practice, this requirement is easier to meet. This model could facilitate the system calibration process. Since the primary task of this paper is making a study on initial parameters selection, the calibration procedure is not described here.

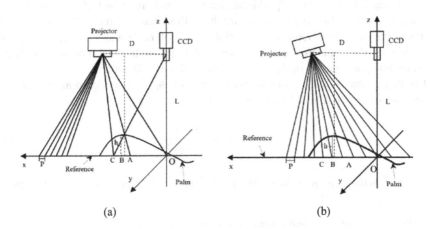

(a)   (b)

Fig. 3. Illustration of cross light model.

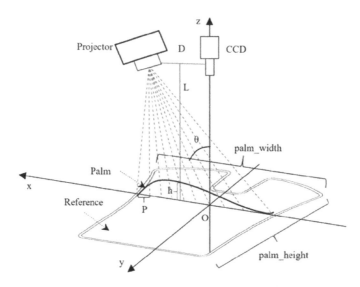

Fig. 4. Illustration of the system structure.

3   Optimal Parameters Selection

3.1   Measurement Error Analysis

The performance of cross light model not only depends on structure parameters of L, D and P, but also the size and scale of the measured object. The goal of this work is to design a 3D palmprint acquisition device, whose precision can meet the requirements of the existing 3D recognition algorithms. Since the final precision is determined by the structure parameters. In order to make sure the built system could achieve the required precision, we need to determine the initial values of L, D and P according to the constraints of the measured palm, before traditional system calibration procedure. Based on this purpose, we designed a system model as following:

Let $\Delta\phi_{CA}$ stands for the measurement error of ϕ_{CA}, then according to (3), the measurement error of h could be assembled by:

$$\Delta h(x, y) = \frac{-L\Delta\phi}{\Delta\phi + \frac{2\pi D}{\overline{P}}} \tag{5}$$

Where $\overline{P}$ is the average wavelength of the current grating pattern. From (5) we have the following regularities:

(1) Smaller $\Delta\phi$ could obtain higher precision;
(2) Smaller L can achieve higher precision;
(3) Bigger D can obtain higher system precision;
(4) Smaller $\overline{P}$ can obtain higher system precision.

Hence, the system precision is high related with the parameters of L, D, P and phase error $\Delta\phi$. Generally, phase error $\Delta\phi$ is caused by random noise, such like the electronic noise from the projector and CCD sensor. For a given system, it is limited into an interval, its range can be assembled by experiments. The captured modulated pattern image is as following:

$$I(x,y) = I'(x,y) + I''(x,y)\cos(\phi(x,y) + \delta) \qquad (6)$$

Where $I'(x,y)$ stands for the image captured without grating projecting, $I''(x,y)$ stands for the modulus of the grating pattern, and δ is the initial phase. The sequential grating images are designed based on different δ. After establishing equations, $\phi(x,y)$ can be obtained using Eq. (7). $I_1 \sim I_4$ are images captured under different multiples of δ.

$$\phi(x,y) = \tan^{-1}\left(\frac{I_4 - I_2}{I_1 - I_3}\right) \qquad (7)$$

We use the implemented device to measure the reference plane whose height should be zero theoretically. Figure 5(a) shows the obtained phase distribution of the reference plane Fig. 5(b) shows the 3D information of the selected point on the corresponding line of the reference plane. The SNR of the selected camera is 59db. According to the experimental results, $\Delta\phi$ is smaller than 0.1.

(a)   (b)

Fig. 5. The measurement data of the reference plane. (a) The phase distribution. (b) 3D information of the selected points.

3.2   Parameters Optimization and Selection

The device is designed specialized for palmprint acquisition, the projecting area should be bigger than the size of the palm. In Fig. 4, *palm_height* and *palm_width* are the height and width of the measured palm. Since there exist constrains in this structure. We should optimize system parameters under the constraints of the target. The prototype of the proposed system is shown in Fig. 6.

Fig. 6. The prototype of the proposed system.

In summary, the goal of our work is:

$$\underset{L,D,P}{\arg\min}\{\Delta h(x,y) = \frac{-L\Delta\phi_{CA}}{\Delta\phi_{CA} + \frac{2\pi D}{\overline{P}}}\}$$

$$s.t. \begin{cases} \dfrac{1}{u} + \dfrac{1}{v} = \dfrac{1}{f} \\[2mm] \dfrac{u}{v} = \dfrac{W_{palm}}{W_{CCDsensor}} \\[2mm] L \approx u \\[2mm] \theta_{min} \leq \theta = \arctan(D/L) \leq \theta_{max} \\[2mm] D_{min} \leq D \leq D_{max} \\[2mm] \overline{P} = \dfrac{W_{palm}}{C_{grating}} = \dfrac{W_{palm}}{W_{img}/P_{img}} \geq P_{min} \end{cases} \tag{8}$$

Where u, v, f are object distance, image distance and focus-length. In order to decrease the lens distortion and reduce the system cost, 12 mm focus length is an optimal choice for the camera lens. W_{palm} is the width of the palm, we set it as 90 mm according to the statistical information of the size of human palm. $W_{CCDsensor}$ is the width of the CCD sensing area, which can be found in the specifications of the camera's datasheet. Then L is approximate equal to u. θ is the inclination angle between projector's optical axis and vertical direction (as shown in Fig. 4). If θ is too big, some part of the palm will be out of the camera's DOF (depth-of-field). Since grating patterns are easily affected by the out of focus blur, θ should be smaller than 30 degrees. According to (5), smaller D will decrease the measurement accuracy. On the contrary, if D is too big, it will increase the volume of the device and the captured image also will suffer from bigger distortions of inclination. $\overline{P}$ is the grating wavelength length in millimeter, $C_{grating}$ is the count of the grating period on the plane. W_{img} is image with of the projector, P_{img} is grating wavelength in pixel. Smaller grating period could generate high measurement accuracy, but subjecting to the restrictions of the projector quality, camera SNR and palm surface reflective characteristics, the grating's period couldn't be too small. Hence, we set P_{img} to be 16 pixels for general projectors.

4 Experimental Results and Analysis

We implement the system by a low cost projector. Figure 7 shows the structure of the final system.

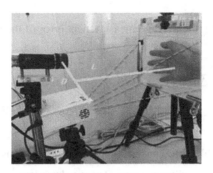

Fig. 7. The acquisition system and structure parameters

According to the specific requirements of 3D palmprint recognition, the hardware parameters of the projector, CCD camera and camera lens are selected as following:

Table 1. Parameters of the hardware module

Items	Optimal selected hardware parameters
Filed of view	115 mm × 90 mm
Depth of filed	25 mm
Camera pixel	737 × 575
Object distance	240 mm
Focus	12 mm
Projector frequency	60 Hz
Projector resolution	1024 × 768
Filed of view	120 mm × 90 mm

Based on the hardware framework, using the strategy proposed in Sect. 3.2, the final optimized parameters are listed in Table 2. The final captured data are shown in Fig. 8. Table 3 compares the proposed and the existing 3D palmprint acquisition systems.

Table 2. Technical parameters of the proposed system.

Items	Parameters
θ	27.5°
$C_{grating}$	48
L	240 mm
D	125 mm
P	1.875 mm
$\Delta\phi$	<0.1

Then according to (5), the average measurement error of the reference plane can be assembled as:

$$\overline{\Delta h}(x,y) \leq \frac{240 \times 0.1}{0.1 + \frac{2\pi \times 125}{1.875}} \approx 0.057 \text{ mm}$$

Table 3. Comparisons of the existing systems.

Reference	Projector	System price	Device volume (mm^3)	Measurement error
[4]	Customized	>9000.0 $	275 × 255 × 325	0.05 mm–0.1 mm
Our system	COOLUX A3	<800.0 $	160 × 140 × 180	≤ 0.057 mm

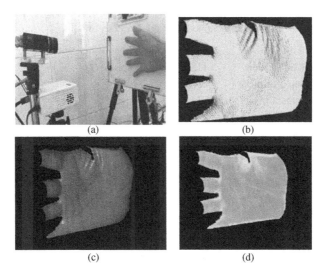

(a) (b) (c) (d)

Fig. 8. The generated 3D palm images. (a) The 3D palmprint acquisition system. (b) Points cloud of the captured 3D palmprint. (c) Triangulated 3D palmprint. (d) Curvature map of the 3D palmprint.

5 Conclusion

The goal of this paper is to find out a scheme to determine the initial structure parameters before system calibration. Parameters of L, D and P are selected according to the information of the measured palm and the precision requirements of the existing 3D palmprint recognition algorithms. Without losing measurement precision, this scheme can decrease the time cost of system design and testing. Based on the designed initialization parameter, the system can achieve higher precision after further calibration. For summary, the core of our strategy is starting with a simplified model and calculating the set of initial parameters. Then, refine the parameters based on the previous result to achieve higher precision. Compared with the previous system, the new system implemented by initialized parameters has advantages of low cost and smaller volume. Based on this, it can further promote the development and application of 3D palmprint recognition.

References

1. Kanhangad, V., Kumar, A., Zhang, D.: Contactless and pose invariant biometric identification using hand surface. IEEE Trans. Image Process. **20**(5), 1415–1424 (2011)
2. Kanhangad, V., Kumar, A., Zhang, D.: A unified framework for contactless hand verification. IEEE Trans. Inf. Forensics Secur. **6**(3), 1014–1027 (2011)
3. Li, W., Zhang, D., Lu, G., Luo, N.: A novel 3-D palmprint acquisition system. IEEE Trans. Syst. Man Cybern. Part A Syst. Hum. **42**(2), 443–452 (2012)
4. Zhang, D., Lu, G., Li, W., Zhang, L., Luo, N.: Palmprint recognition using 3-D information. IEEE Trans. Syst. Man Cybern. Part C Appl. Rev. **39**(5), 505–519 (2009)
5. Zhang, L., Shen, Y., Li, H., Lu, J.: 3D palmprint identification using block-wise features and collaborative representation. IEEE Trans. Pattern Anal. Mach. Intell. **37**(8), 1730–1736 (2015)
6. Li, W., Zhang, L., Zhang, D., Lu, G., Yan, J.: Efficient joint 2D and 3D palmprint matching with alignment refinement. In: 2010 IEEE Computer Society Conference on Computer Vision and Pattern Recognition. Presented at the 2010 IEEE Computer Society Conference on Computer Vision and Pattern Recognition, pp. 795–801 (2010)
7. Aggithaya, V.K., Zhang, D., Luo, N.: A multimodal biometric authentication system based on 2D and 3D palmprint features. In: Proceedings of the SPIE 6944, Biometric Technology for Human Identification V. Presented at the Biometric Technology for Human Identification V, International Society for Optics and Photonics, p. 69440C (2008)
8. Zhang, D., Lu, G.: 3D Palmprint classification by global features. In: 3D Biometrics, pp. 135–152. Springer, New York (2013). https://doi.org/10.1007/978-1-4614-7400-5_8
9. Bingöl, Ö., Ekinci, M.: Stereo-based palmprint recognition in various 3D postures. Expert Syst. Appl. **78**(15), 74–88 (2017)
10. Bingöl, Ö., Ekinci, M.: 3D palmprint pose estimation using stereo camera. In: 2013 21st Signal Processing and Communications Applications Conference (SIU). Presented at the 2013 21st Signal Processing and Communications Applications Conference (SIU), pp. 1–4 (2013)

11. Srinivasan, V., Liu, H.C., Halioua, M.: Automated phase-measuring profilometry of 3-D diffuse objects. Appl. Opt. **23**(18), 3105 (1984)
12. Berryman, F., Pynsent, P., Cubillo, J.: A theoretical comparison of three fringe analysis methods for determining the three-dimensional shape of an object in the presence of noise. Opt. Lasers Eng. **39**(1), 35–50 (2003)
13. Tribolet, J.: A new phase unwrapping algorithm. IEEE Trans. Acoust. Speech Sig. Process. **25**(2), 170–177 (1997)

Gesture, Gait and Action

Residual Gating Fusion Network for Human Action Recognition

Junxuan Zhang and Haifeng Hu[✉]

School of Electronic and Information Engineering, Sun Yat-sen University,
Guangzhou, China
huhaif@mail.sysu.edu.cn

Abstract. Most of the recent works leverage Two-Stream framework to model the spatiotemporal information for video action recognition and achieve remarkable performance. In this paper, we propose a novel convolution architecture, called *Residual Gating Fusion Network* (RGFN), to improve their performance by fully exploring spatiotemporal information in residual signals. In order to further exploit the local details of low-level layers, we introduce *Multi-Scale Convolution Fusion* (MSCF) to implement spatiotemporal fusion at multiple levels. Since RGFN is an end-to-end network, it can be trained on various kinds of video datasets and applicative to other video analysis tasks. We evaluate our RGFN on two standard benchmarks, i.e., UCF101 and HMDB51, and analyze the designs of convolution network. Experiments results demonstrate the advantages of RGFN, achieving the state-of-the-art performance.

Keywords: Human action recognition · Video analysis
Spatiotemporal fusion · Convolutional neural network

1 Introduction

Learning discriminative video representation is a key task in the field of video action recognition. Previous works mainly utilize the hand-craft local features such as Space Time Interest Points [1] and trajectory-based methods [2] to describe the visual information and motion pattern of video. However, one limitation is that they lack the ability to model global semantic representation. Recently, human action recognition has gain significant improvement by applying deep convolutional neural network (CNN). Among the methods based on CNN, Two-Stream network [3] shows its power to video recognition and provide great inspirations for follow-up works. By leveraging Two-Stream framework, many researchers try to obtain discriminative video representation by jointly modelling the appearance and motion cues and combining them together. For instance, Feichtenhofer et al. [4] fuse the spatial stream and temporal stream through convolution fusion such that channels that have correlations are put in correspondence. Wang et al. [5] model long-term temporal structure by fusing the Two-Stream features extracted from several video segments. Diba et al. [14]

© Springer Nature Switzerland AG 2018
J. Zhou et al. (Eds.): CCBR 2018, LNCS 10996, pp. 79–86, 2018.
https://doi.org/10.1007/978-3-319-97909-0_9

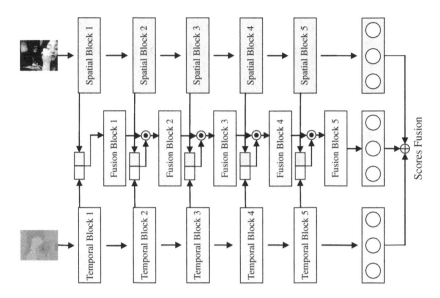

Fig. 1. Illustration of our Spatiotemporal Residual Gating Network architecture.

modify the Two-Stream framework by adopting bilinear fusion for long term information encoding. While these works achieve remarkable performance, most of them apply late fusion (LF) for spatial and temporal features at the last pooling layer or fully-connected layer. However, these approaches only model the high-level global spatiotemporal information while leaving the low-level local details (e.g., corners or edges at the shallow layers) in frames not fully fused, which is far from enough for action recognition. Therefore, we consider the combination of low-level features and deep-level features and provide systematic justification for the design of spatiotemporal fusion.

Based on the above analysis, this paper proposes a *Residual Gating Fusion Network* (RGFN) for action recognition. More specifically, three contributions are made in our work. Firstly, RGFN is an end-to-end convolution network which can be applicative to various kinds of video analysis tasks. Secondly, we propose *Multi-Scale Convolution Fusion* (MSCF) to explore spatiotemporal correlation at multiple levels and incorporate them into a complete model. Thirdly, we experimentally evaluate several fusion strategies and discuss how to effectively fuse the features for improvement.

2   Residual Gating Fusion Network

To fully utilize multiple levels of spatiotemporal information, we propose an end-to-end training architecture, called RGFN. In the following, we will present the detail of RGFN.

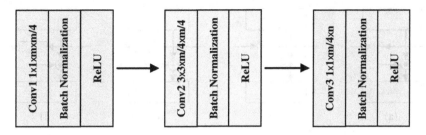

Fig. 2. The structure of the fusion block in our RGFN. It stacks the convolution layers, BN layers and ReLU layers to construct a bottleneck structure. "m" and "n" denote the number of input and output channels.

2.1 Network Architecture

Before introducing RGFN, we first revisit the base architecture ResNets [6]. ResNets contain five convolutional blocks and one prediction layer. Similar to other CNNs, ResNets apply 3×3 filters for feature extraction and a bank of 1×1 filters for dimensionality expansion and reduction. ResNets operate on the images with size 224×224 and will be pooled five times by stride two. Followed by a global average pooling, the obtain $1 \times 1 \times 2048$ feature maps are fed into the fully connected layer for classification. The residual connection can be expressed as,

$$x^{l+1} = \xi(x^l + \Psi(x^l, \{W\})) \tag{1}$$

where x^l is the input of lth layer, Ψ is the combination of a set of layer including convolution layer, batch normalization layer and ReLU, W is the weights of convolution layer and ξ denotes the ReLU.

Based on ResNets, this paper proposes a novel architecture called RGFN for action recognition. As shown in Fig. 1, Two-Stream framework is leveraged to construct RGFN. In our work, spatial and temporal residual features extracted from each convolution block are concatenated as spatiotemporal features. In this way, the useful information in two types of residual signals can be fully retained. Since the spatiotemporal features from different convolution blocks have different spatial scales, we fed them into a fusion block for scale transformation and knowledge exploration. In our work, the fusion signals obtained from fusion block are treated as gating signals to modulate the spatiotemporal features. Formally, the fusion process can be expressed as

$$x_f^{l+1} = \Phi^{l+1}([x_s^{l+1}, x_t^{l+1}] \odot \xi(x_f^l), \{W_f^{l+1}\}) \tag{2}$$

where x_f^l, x_s^l and x_t^l denote the output of lth fusion block, l^{th} spatial convolution block and l^{th} temporal convolution block respectively, Φ denotes the operation in fusion block, $\xi \equiv ReLU$, W_f^{l+1} are the parameters of Φ^{l+1} and $\odot$ denotes the element-wise product operation.

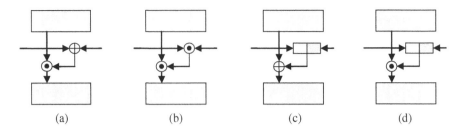

Fig. 3. Different types of feature interactions for three stream features.

A significant advantage of this arrangement is that the higher level features can be modulated by the fusion signals obtained from lower level layers. Thus, it allows the low-level features to be directly connected to the high-level features, which enables gradients to be propagated directly from the deeper layers to shallower layers without the concern of gradient vanishing. In addition, some literatures show that direct injection of new features will change the learned structure of the network during training due to great change of propagated gradients. In some cases, such changes will lead to inferior performance. Hence, to avoid the destruction of the learned structure, spatial and temporal features are put together into an independent stream instead of direct injection to the original two streams.

2.2   Multi-scale Convolution Fusion

Many previous works only allow spatial features and temporal features to interact via LF with simple element-wise addition or element-wise product operations. Such designs do not support fully exploiting spatiotemporal cues in two streams features. Instead, we introduce MSCF for spatiotemporal fusion, which hierarchically fuses spatial and temporal features through five convolution fusion blocks. The structure of fusion block is shown in Fig. 2. Considering the computation efficiency, we adopt the bottleneck design for the fusion block to reduce the parameters. For each fusion block, we use a stack of three convolution layers with 1×1, 3×3 and 1×1 convolution kernels respectively. Each convolution layer is followed by a batch normalization layer and a ReLU layer. Theoretically, our MSCF has similar performance to LF if we cut the connection of the low-level fusion features. Assuming that the low-level features contains the discrimination of actions, our MSCF can achieve the performance no less than LF by accumulating the multiple levels of features. Since there are numerous ways for interaction among three types of features, i.e., spatial features, temporal features and fusion features, we propose four types of interactions (Fig. 3) for three streams features. In the experiments, we will conduct ablation studies to evaluate their performances and analyze the designs of different interactions.

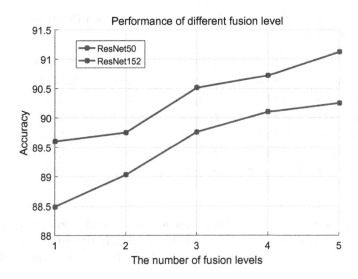

Fig. 4. Performance of different fusion levels (%) on the first split of UCF101.

3   Experiments

3.1   Datasets

We conduct experiments on two popular datasets, i.e., UCF101 [7] and HMDB51 [8]. The HMDB51 dataset contains 51 action categories with 6,766 video clips. The UCF101 dataset contains 101 action classes with 13,320 video clips. Both of them have more than 100 video clips for each action category. Following the standard evaluation scheme, we report the average accuracy over three splits on both UCF101 and HMDB51.

3.2   Implementation Details

Spatial stream and temporal stream are first separately trained on UCF101. Then we following the two-step procedure for learning our RGFN. Firstly, to avoid the domination of trained spatial stream and temporal stream, we learn fusion stream and explore spatiotemporal information by fixing the parameters of spatial stream and temporal stream. In this step, we start with a learning rate of 10^{-2} and lower it twice by a factor of 10 after every 1500 iterations. We use a batch size of 32 for ResNet50 and 16 for ResNet152. In the second step, we train RGFN using the following objective function,

$$Loss = CE(S_s) + CE(S_t) + CE(S_f) + CE(S_s + S_t + S_f) \qquad (3)$$

where S_s, S_t and S_f denotes the spatial, temporal and fusion score vectors respectively, CE denotes the cross entropy loss. Since the final decision is based on the average score of three streams, the forth term in loss function can further

Table 1. Classification accuracy (%) on the first splits of UCF101 under different feature interaction methods.

	ResNet50	#Parameters	ResNet152	#Parameters
spatial	81.50	95.1 M	81.86	234.1 M
temporal	84.51	95.3 M	84.01	234.4 M
interaction (a)	89.08	214.8 M	89.52	492.8 M
interaction (b)	89.12	214.8 M	89.98	492.8 M
interaction (c)	89.87	281.8 M	90.33	559.8 M
interaction (d)	**90.25**	281.8 M	**91.12**	559.8 M

improve accuracy. It is worth noting that we use a small learning rate of 10^{-4} with only 500 iterations for the second step to sightly fine-tune our RGFN in order to preserve the learned structure of spatial stream and temporal stream.

3.3   Analysis on Different Fusion Levels

To understand the influence of low-level features, we evaluate our RGFN with different fusion levels on first split of UCF101. Fusion level m denotes that there are last m fusion blocks are retained in our RGFN. For example, fusion level 2 denotes that the fusion block 5 and 4 are retained and the other fusion blocks are removed, so that only last two levels of features are incorporated into the fusion stream. In the experiments, we validate 5 fusion levels with two CNNs, namely ResNet50 and ResNet152. The results are shown in Fig. 4. Note that the results are only obtained by the fusion stream. From Fig. 4, we observe that the performance improves as the fusion levels increases, which implies that low-level features contain useful information as deep-level features do and we can enhance the discriminative power of features by accumulating multiple levels of features. Besides, from the comparison between ResNet50 and ResNet152, we also find that deeper model has greater power for representation and improve the performance.

3.4   Analysis on Feature Interaction and Fusion

In Sect. 2.2 we introduce four types of feature interactions. In this section, we provide experiments for different types of feature interactions. The proposed four types of interactions are shown in Fig. 3 and Table 1 reports the their accuracies on the first split of UCF101. From the table we can see that all interactions have clear improvement compared to the original spatial stream and temporal stream, which proves all interactions can effectively implement spatiotemporal fusion. Next, we first focus on interaction (a) and (b). From the table we know that (b) sightly performs better than (a), which implies that multiplicative gating interaction provides stronger signal correlation for spatiotemporal fusion. Similar phenomenon can be seen in the comparison of (c) and (d). We also observe that (c) and (d)

Table 2. Performance comparisons (%) with the state-of-the-art methods on UCF101 and HMDB51 (3 splits).

	UCF101	HMDB51
C3D (3 nets+linear SVM) [11]	85.20	-
Long-term ConvNets [12]	91.70	64.80
Long-term ConvNets+iDT [12]	92.70	67.20
Two-Stream ConvNet [3]	88.00	59.40
Multiple Dynamic Images [9]	89.10	65.20
TDD+iDT [10]	91.50	65.90
Two-Streams Fusion [4]	92.50	65.40
Key Volume Mining [13]	93.10	63.30
Two-Stream (ResNet50) [6]	90.03	62.81
RGFN-ResNet50 (3 streams)	92.11	63.93
RGFN-ResNet50 (3 streams+iDT)	93.31	67.02
Two-Stream (ResNet152) [6]	89.14	62.35
RGFN-ResNet152 (3 streams)	92.57	64.36
RGFN-ResNet152 (3 streams+iDT)	**93.64**	**67.78**

performs better than (a) and (b). We conjecture that concatenation of spatial and temporal features can preserve more information, thus improving performance. As a price, interactions (c) and (d) need more parameters than (a) and (b).

3.5   Comparison with State-of-the-art

We conclude the experimental results of current state-of-the-art and compare our RGFN with them on three splits of UCF101 and HMDB51. As a final results, we adopt score fusion to three streams to gain improvement. We apply $L2-normalization$ to all three scores and average them to obtain the prediction output. As seen in Table 2, we achieve 92.11%/63.93% with ResNet50 and 92.57%/64.36% with ResNet152 on UCF101/HMDB51. RGFN combining 3 streams make improvement over the Two-Stream (ResNet50/ResNet152) by 2.08% and 3.43% on UCF101 and 1.12% and 2.01% on HMDB51, which indicates that incorporating multiple levels of features is an effective way to increase the discriminative power for deep learning. Since many recent works show that combining with hand-craft features can further improve the performance due to their complementation, we apply $L2-normalization$ to the SVM scores of Fisher Vector encoded iDT features and combine them with the overall scores of 3 streams to obtain the final decisions. Then we obtain 93.31%/67.02% with ResNet50 and 93.64%/67.78% with ResNet152 on UCF101/HMDB51, which performs the best among the state-of-the-art models. This proves that deep learned features and hand-craft features are complementary and can facilitate each other to improve performance.

4   Conclusion

In this paper, we propose a novel end-to-end convolution architecture, called RGFN for video action recognition, aiming to combine multiple levels of features into the network to improve recognition performance. We validate RGFN on two popular datasets, namely UCF101 and HMDB51. The improvements shown in experimental results strongly proves the effectiveness of the proposed RGFN.

Acknowledgement. This work was supported in part by the National Natural Science Foundation of China under Grant 61673402, Grant 61273270, and Grant 60802069, in part by the Natural Science Foundation of Guangdong under Grant 2017A030311029, Grant 2016B010109002, Grant 2015B090912001, Grant 2016B010123005, and Grant 2017B090909005, in part by the Science and Technology Program of Guangzhou under Grant 201704020180 and Grant 201604020024, and in part by the Fundamental Research Funds for the Central Universities of China.

References

1. Laptev, I.: On space-time interest points. In: ICCV, vol. 1, pp. 432–439 (2003)
2. Wang, H.: Action recognition with improved trajectories. In: ICCV, pp. 3551–3558 (2014)
3. Simonyan, K., Zisserman, A.: Two-stream convolutional networks for action recognition in videos. In: NIPS, pp. 568–576 (2014)
4. Feichtenhofer, C.: Convolutional two-stream network fusion for video action recognition. In: CVPR, pp. 1933–1941 (2016)
5. Wang, L.: Temporal segment networks: towards good practices for deep action recognition. ACM Trans. Inf. Syst. **22**(1), 20–36 (2016)
6. He, K.: Deep residual learning for image recognition. In: CVPR, pp. 770–778 (2016)
7. Soomro, K.: UCF101: a dataset of 101 human actions classes from videos in the wild, CRCV-TR-12-01 (2012)
8. Kuehne, H.: HMDB: a large video database for human motion recognition. In: ICCV (2011)
9. Bilen, H.: Dynamic image networks for action recognition. In: CVPR, pp. 3034–3042 (2016)
10. Wang, L.: Action recognition with trajectory-pooled deep-convolutional descriptors. In: CVPR, pp. 4305–4314 (2015)
11. Du, T.: Learning spatiotemporal features with 3D convolutional networks. In: ICCV, pp. 4489–4497 (2016)
12. Varol, G.: Long-term temporal convolutions for action recognition. TPAMI, **PP**(99), 1 (2016)
13. Zhu, W.: A key volume mining deep framework for action recognition. In: CVPR, pp. 1991–1999 (2016)
14. Diba, A.: Deep temporal linear encoding networks. In: CVPR (2017)

Study on Human Body Action Recognition

Dong Yin[1,2(✉)], Yu-Qing Miao[3,4(✉)], Kang Qiu[1,2], and An Wang[1]

[1] School of Information Science and Technology,
USTC, Hefei 230027, Anhui, China
{yindong, anwang}@ustc.edu.cn, qk0208@mail.ustc.edu.cn
[2] Key Laboratory of Electromagnetic Space Information
of CAS, Hefei 230027, Anhui, China
[3] School of Computer Science and Information Security,
GUET, Guilin 541004, Guangxi, China
miaoyuqing@guet.edu.cn
[4] Key Laboratory of Intelligent Processing of Image and Graphics,
GUET, Guilin 541004, Guangxi, China

Abstract. A novel human body action recognition method based on Kinect is proposed. Firstly, the key frame of the original data is extracted by using the key frame extraction technology based on quaternion. Secondly, the moving pose feature based on the motion information of each joint point is constituted for the skeleton information of each key frame. And, combined with key frame, online continuous action segmentation is implemented by using boundary detection method. Finally, the feature is encoded by Fisher vector and input to the linear SVM classifier to complete the action recognition. In the public dataset MSR Action3D and the dataset collected in this paper, the experiments show that the proposed method achieves a good recognition effect.

Keywords: Action recognition · Kinect · Support vector machine
Fisher vector

1 Introduction

In recent years, home service robots have developed rapidly. The human motion detection and recognition has become an important research topic in the field of robot application. Due to the expensive and complex design of robot equipment, it is a very successful way to study human action recognition by using cheap and good Kinect.

In action recognition technology, scholars have been studied a lot. Wang [1] proposed a combination representation called global Gist feature and local patch coding to identify actions reliably. Kwak [2] proposed an algorithm which could be efficiently applied to a real-time intelligent surveillance system. Vinagre [3] presented a geometric correspondence between joints called Trisarea feature. It was defined as the area of the triangle formed by three joints. He [4] proposed self-taught learning features and unsupervised learning pre-processing. Das Dawn [5] presented a comprehensive review on STIP-based methods. These methods had achieved good results in human motion recognition.

© Springer Nature Switzerland AG 2018
J. Zhou et al. (Eds.): CCBR 2018, LNCS 10996, pp. 87–95, 2018.
https://doi.org/10.1007/978-3-319-97909-0_10

In recent years, neural networks have been developed rapidly and applied widely in video image processing. Ijjina [6] proposed an approach using genetic algorithms (GA) and deep convolutional neural networks (CNN). Wu [7] gave a review of various state-of-the-art deep learning-based techniques. Sargano [8] presented a method based on a pre-trained deep CNN model for feature extraction & representation followed by a hybrid Support Vector Machine (SVM) and K-Nearest Neighbor (KNN) classifier for action recognition. Ma [9] addressed the problems of both general and also fine-grained action recognition in video sequences. Their work sought to improve fine-grained action discrimination, while also retaining the ability to perform general recognition.

To sum up, scholars have done a lot of work on human action recognition, and have achieved fruitful results. However, due to factors such as background, illumination and occlusion, recognition based on color video is still difficult to achieve satisfactory results. As the function of Kinect is enhanced and the price is low, people have developed and studied on its platform. It is gradually applied to robot, medical treatment, education and so on. Therefore, based on Kinect V2, we carried out the action recognition method of depth information and skeleton information. And we finally transplant the method to the robot.

2 Relevant Theoretical Basis

With the rise of artificial intelligence, the traditional human-computer interaction mode has been unable to meet the demands of people. The way to transfer information through action becomes a more friendly and natural choice. Human action recognition is a comprehensive subject, which involves many fields.

2.1 Device of Kinect

Kinect, which was launched in September 2010 by Microsoft, is a peripheral applied to the XBOX360 host. Its sensor contains a depth sensor, a color camera and a microphone array. Kinect uses optical coding to get deep data and provides information about body skeleton and joints. Each joint is represented by a three-dimensional coordinate. Figure 1 shows the sketch map of extraction skeleton.

(a)   (b)   (c)   (d)   (e)

Fig. 1. Sketch map of Kinect extraction skeleton information. (a) Kinect device (b) Input depth map (c) Distribution of body parts (d) 3D joint point (e) Output 3D skeleton

2.2 Action Features Extraction

Feature extraction is divided into feature-joint, feature-joint selection and dynamic features. The feature-joint point is the feature extracted from the skeleton information, which can represent the relationship between the joint points of the human body, and can be divided into three subcategories: spatial, geometric and key attitude features. The feature-joint selection refers to extract the most influential parts of the body from all joints. Ofli [10] put forward a feature representation method called "maximum information" joint sequence to describe human action. The dynamic feature refers to the characteristics of skeleton sequence as a 3D trajectory and modeling the dynamics of time series.

2.3   Action Classification Recognition

Action classification algorithm can be divided into dynamic time warping algorithm, generative model and discriminant model. The warping algorithm is a dynamic programming based nonlinear regularization, which has been widely used in speech recognition early. The generative model, which is the dynamic classifier, is usually modeled on the joint probability distribution $P(x, y)$, and the $P(y_i|x)$ is obtained by the Bayes formula, and the largest y_i of $P(y_i|x)$ is selected as the recognition result. The discriminant model named static classifier models directly the probability $P(y|x)$.

3   Our Method

Based on Kinect and robot oriented applications, a human action recognition system framework is presented in this paper, as shown in Fig. 2. It includes three major modules: Data Acquisition, Continuous Action Segmentation and Action Recognition.

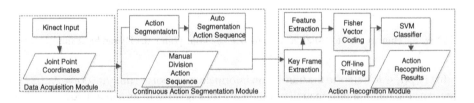

Fig. 2. Proposed system framework of human body action recognition.

Data Acquisition gets joint point coordinators from Kinect. Continuous Action Segmentation divides the start and end frames of the action. One is calibrated manually by user, another is auto. In Action Recognition, the current frame has been judged which belongs to the action. The extracted action will be encoded. The Fisher vector is input into the pre-trained model, and the recognition results are obtained.

3.1   Key Frame Processing

Key frames refer to the important frames that can be extracted from them and represent the motion characteristics. In this paper, we use a simple and efficient approximate algorithm. Firstly, use quaternion to describe the action information of the human body, and based on it, define the distance between frames and frames. Secondly, decide the key frames whose distance is larger than a threshold.

As the original data obtained by Kinect is 3D coordinate sequence of each joint point, the Kinect V2 obtains 25 joint points per frame. We use 21 points shown as Fig. 3(a). In order to make full use of this chain structure, a tree model is used to represent the human body structure shown as Fig. 3(b). No.1 point is selected as the root node and the other 20 joints are used as children nodes. The distance between each node and root is a fixed value. While the distance between elbow and shoulder point is the length of arm, the space position of elbow is determined only by the rotation information of elbow relative to shoulder. So we can use a discrete time vector function to represent motion information at t time.

$$m(t) = [p(t), \ q_2(t), \ q_3(t), \ \ldots, \ q_{21}(t)]. \tag{1}$$

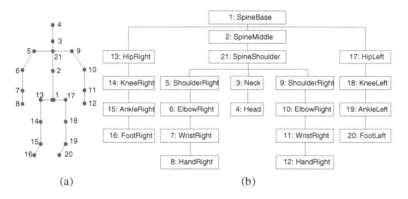

(a)   (b)

Fig. 3. Human skeleton stratification model. (a) Joint points (b) Hierarchical model

In (1), $p(t) \in R^3$ refers to the translation information of root at t time. $q_i(t)(i = 2,...,21)$ represents the rotation information of i joint at t time relative to its parent node.

It is simple and fast to express the rotation information with the quaternion method. Given $s = w \in R$ and $V = (x, y, z) \in R^3$, quaternion $q \in S^4$ is defined as:

$$q = [s, -V] = [w, \ x, \ y, \ z]. \tag{2}$$

In (2), s represents the scalar part of quaternion q, V represents 3D vector part. The root node translation information is $p(t) = (x_t, y_t, z_t)$. We need to find out the rotation axis and angle. Sign $P_p(t)$ to the coordinate of parent node and $P_c(t)$ to the coordinate of child node at t time. Rotation axis u and angle θ are defined as:

$$u = P_p(t) \times P_c(t), \theta = \arccos\left(\left(P_p(t) \bullet \cdot P_c(t)\right)/\left(\left|P_p(t)\right| \bullet \cdot|P_c(t)|\right)\right). \tag{3}$$

Using u and θ, we can get the rotational and action information in the form of quaternion. Then, we use moving pose (MP) which proposed by Zanfir [11] to extract the feature of joint points. The MP feature is Taylor form in (4), δP is the first-order differential, and $\delta^2 P$ is the second-order.

$$X_t = \left[P_t, \delta P_t, \delta^2 P_t\right]. \tag{4}$$

Each node extracts 3D P_t, δP_t and $\delta^2 P_t$, which constitute 6D dynamic characteristics. So the feature of each joint is a 9D vector, and each frame can extract a feature of 21×9.

3.2 Feature Coding

The Fisher vector combines the advantages of generative and discriminant model. The first- and second- order statistical features are included in addition to the zero-order.

The feature is represented as $X = \{x_t, \ t = 1,2,...,T\}$. We will get the Fisher core based on gradient function shown as formula (5).

$$K(X, Y) = G_\lambda^{X\prime} F_\lambda^{-1} G_\lambda^Y. \tag{5}$$

In (5), G is the Fisher vector, F is information matrix. Since the final Fisher vector does not contain the time sequence information of the action, that is to say, any Fisher vector is the same, and more specifically, the two opposite actions, such as "stand up" and "sit down", have the same Fisher vector when the time sequence information is not considered. To distinguish these movements, we need to carry out a sequence like Pyramid. The N layer is divided into n non-overlapping sub-sequence. This paper uses 3 layers, and the final encoding is composed of the Fisher vectors of the $(1 + 2 + 3)$ sub-sequence, that is, the eigenvectors of the 6 segments of the action sequence are calculated respectively. Finally, the corresponding Fisher vector is stitched together.

3.3 Action Classification

Support vector machine (SVM) is a classifier for solving two classification problems. It cannot be used to solve the multiple classification problem directly. In order to apply it to the multiple classification problem of action recognition, it needs to be popularized. This paper uses "one to one" strategy.

The "one to one" strategy refers to the assumption that the training samples have N categories. From which, two classes are taken as positive and negative samples of the two classification SVM, then a total of $N (N - 1)/2$ two classification problems can be formed, and each of them is trained to get the SVM classifier. When testing, the test samples are entered into the classifiers to vote on the classification results. The category of the largest number of votes is the result of the identification.

4 Experiments and Analysis

The platform used in the paper is CPU/Intel i7-4790, Memory/8 GB, Kinect v2, Windows 8.1, Microsoft VS 2013, Windows SDK 2.0, LibSVM 3.22, OpenCV 2.4.10.

4.1   Public Dataset – MSR Action3D

The MSR Action3D data set is collected by a static generation of Kinect sensors at the Microsoft Institute, including twenty movements, such as hand waving, drawing, clapping and bending. The data set was performed by 10 experimenters. Each action was performed 2 ~ 3 times, and finally there were 544 sets of experimental data.

The 20 actions are divided into three subsets. Each subset is composed of 8 actions, as shown in Table 1. AS1 and AS2 collect some similar actions, while AS3 sets some complex actions. In experiment, when calculating Fisher vector, the number K of Gauss elements in GMM is set to 128, and the normalized parameter of energy normalization $\alpha = 0.3$. The comparison of recognition rate in Tables 2 and 3 show that our method has a certain improving extent, which proves the effectiveness.

Table 1.   Three subsets of MSR Actions3D.

Action Set 1 (AS1)	Action Set 2 (AS2)	Action Set 3 (AS3)
Horizontal arm wave	High arm wave	High throw
Hammer	Hand catch	Forward kick
Forward punch	Draw ×	Side kick
High throw	Draw √	Jogging
Hand clap	Draw O	Tennis swing
Bend	Two hand wave	Tennis serve
Tennis serve	Forward kick	Golf swing
Pickup & Throw	Side boxing	Pickup & Throw

Table 2.   The comparison of recognition rate in MSR Actions3D with three subsets.

Method	AS1	AS2	AS3	Average
Histogram of 3D Joints [12]	87.98	85.48	63.46	78.97
EigenJoints [13]	74.50	76.10	96.40	82.33
Skeletal Quad [14]	88.39	86.61	94.59	89.86
Lie Group SE(3) [15]	95.29	83.87	98.22	92.46
Our method	93.81	90.09	96.30	**93.40**

Table 3.   The comparison of recognition rate in MSR Actions3D with whole dataset.

Method	Recognition rate
Actionlet Ensemble [16]	88.20
Histogram of Norms in 4D [17]	88.89
Lie Group SE(3) [15]	89.48
The moving pose [11]	91.70
Our method	**92.08**

4.2 Own Dataset – PAR718

Based on the application scene of the home service robot, we build a data set called PAR718 in this paper. It collects 10 common movements in living rooms, including sitting, drinking water, staying, calling, which are performed by 14 experimenters (9 women and 5 men). Each performing is done two times for per movement, so the dataset has 280 action sequences in total. The length of the action is from 47 frames to 220 frames, with a total of 26633 frames.

Figure 4 is the depth map sequence of the key frame extracted from the "drink water" movement. The original sequence has 101 frames and 30 key frames are extracted.

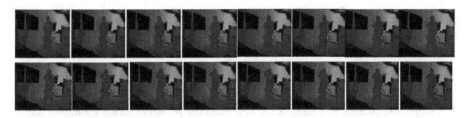

Fig. 4. The key frame sequences extracted from "drink water". From left to right, up to down, the numbers are 1st, 4th, 8th, 12th, 17th, 20th, 22th, 24th, 29th, 31th, 37th, 44th, 66th, 72th, 75th, 77th.

Figure 5 is the obfuscation matrix. In this experiment of feature extraction and action recognition classification, the K is 128 and $\alpha = 0.3$ when the energy is normalized. 280 action sequences are divided into training set and testing set. The accuracy is 98.57% (138/140). From Fig. 5, most of the actions are correctly identified, except for reading and writing, because they are too similar.

	Sitting	Standing Up	Drinking	Calling	Stretching	Walking	Squating	Reading	Applauding	Strowing
Sitting	1.00	0.00	0.00	0.00	0.00	0.00	0.00	0.00	0.00	0.00
Standing Up	0.00	1.00	0.00	0.00	0.00	0.00	0.00	0.00	0.00	0.00
Drinking	0.00	0.00	1.00	0.00	0.00	0.00	0.00	0.00	0.00	0.00
Calling	0.00	0.00	0.00	1.00	0.00	0.00	0.00	0.00	0.00	0.00
Stretching	0.00	0.00	0.00	0.00	1.00	0.00	0.00	0.00	0.00	0.00
Walking	0.00	0.00	0.00	0.00	0.00	1.00	0.00	0.00	0.00	0.00
Squating	0.00	0.00	0.00	0.00	0.00	0.00	1.00	0.00	0.00	0.00
Reading	0.00	0.00	0.00	0.00	0.00	0.00	0.00	0.95	0.00	0.00
Applauding	0.00	0.00	0.00	0.00	0.00	0.00	0.00	0.00	1.00	0.00
Strowing	0.00	0.00	0.00	0.00	0.00	0.00	0.00	0.00	0.00	0.93

Fig. 5. The obfuscation matrix of own dataset.

5 Conclusion

Human action recognition based on vision has become a research hotspot nowadays. The difficulty of human action recognition based on deep data and human skeleton information is greatly reduced in target segmentation, and the accuracy is greatly improved. This paper mainly studies the human action recognition method based on the 3D skeleton sequence obtained by Kinect, and puts forward a new framework of human body action recognition, which has achieved good recognition effect on the common dataset MSR Action3D and own dataset PAR718. Further effective identification of high similarity actions is the next step in this paper.

Acknowledgments. This paper is supported by the Guangxi Natural Science Foundation Project (2014GXNSFAA118395), the research project of Guangxi Colleges & Universities Key Laboratory of Intelligent Processing of Image and Graphics (GIIP201706), the National Natural Science Foundation Project (61763007), the key project of the Guangxi Natural Science Foundation (2017GXNSFDA198028).

References

1. Wang, Y., Li, Y., Ji, X.: Human action recognition based on global gist feature and local patch coding. Int. J. Signal Process. Image Process. Pattern Recognit. **8**(2), 235–246 (2015)
2. Kwak, N., Song, T.: Human action recognition using accumulated moving information. Int. J. Multimed. Ubiquitous Eng. **10**(10), 211–222 (2015)
3. Vinagre, M., Aranda, J., Casals, A.: A new relational geometric feature for human action recognition. In: Ferrier, J.-L., Gusikhin, O., Madani, K., Sasiadek, J. (eds.) Informatics in Control, Automation and Robotics. LNEE, vol. 325, pp. 263–278. Springer, Cham (2015). https://doi.org/10.1007/978-3-319-10891-9_15
4. He, J.: Self-taught learning features for human action recognition. In: Proceedings of 2016 3rd International Conference on Information Science and Control Engineering, ICISCE 2016, pp. 611–615, 31 October (2016)
5. Dos Dawn, D., Shaikh, S.: A comprehensive survey of human action recognition with spatio-temporal interest point (STIP) detector. Visual Comput. **32**(3), 289–306 (2016)
6. Ijjina, E., Chalavadi, K.: Human action recognition using genetic algorithms and convolutional neural networks. Pattern Recognit. **59**, 199–212 (2016)
7. Wu, D., Sharma, N., Blumenstein, M.: Recent advances in video-based human action recognition using deep learning: a review. In: 2017 International Joint Conference on Neural Networks, IJCNN 2017–Proceedings, vol. 2017-May, pp. 2865–2872, 30 June (2017)
8. Sargano, A., Wang, X., Angelov, P., Habib, Z.: Human action recognition using transfer learning with deep representations. In: Proceedings of the International Joint Conference on Neural Networks, vol. 2017-May, pp. 463–469, 30 June (2017)
9. Ma, M., Marturi, N., Li, Y., Leonardis, A., Stolkin, R.: Region-sequence based six-stream CNN features for general and fine-grained human action recognition in videos. Pattern Recognit. **76**, 506–521 (2018)
10. Ofli, F., Chaudhry, R., Kurillo, G.: Sequence of the most informative joints (SMIJ): a new representation for human skeletal action recognition. J. Vis. Commun. Image Represent. **25**(1), 24–38 (2014)
11. Zanfir, M., Leordeanu, M., Sminchisescu, C.: The moving pose: an efficient 3D kinematics descriptor for low-latency action recognition and detection. In: Proceedings of the IEEE International Conference on Computer Vision, pp. 2752–2759 (2014)
12. Xia, L., Chen, C., Aggarwal, J.: View invariant human action recognition using histograms of 3D joints. In: 2012 IEEE Computer Society Conference on Computer Vision and Pattern Recognition Workshops (CVPRW), pp. 20–27 (2012)

13. Yang, X., Tian, Y.: Effective 3D action recognition using eigenjoints. J. Vis. Commun. Image Represent. **25**(1), 2–11 (2014)
14. Evangelidis, G., Singh, G., Horaud, R.: Skeletal quads: human action recognition using joint quadruples. In: 2014 22nd International Conference on Pattern Recognition (ICPR), pp. 4513–4518 (2014)
15. Vemulapalli, R., Arrate, F., Chellappa, R.: Human action recognition by representing 3D skeletons as points in a lie group. In: Proceedings of the IEEE Conference on Computer Vision and Pattern Recognition, pp. 588–595 (2014)
16. Wang, J., Liu, Z., Wu, Y.: Mining actionlet ensemble for action recognition with depth cameras. 2012 IEEE Conference on Computer Vision and Pattern Recognition (CVPR), pp. 1290–1297 (2014)
17. Tang, S., et al.: Histogram of oriented normal vectors for object recognition with a depth sensor. In: Lee, K.M., Matsushita, Y., Rehg, James M., Hu, Z. (eds.) ACCV 2012. LNCS, vol. 7725, pp. 525–538. Springer, Heidelberg (2013). https://doi.org/10.1007/978-3-642-37444-9_41

Multi-view Gait Recognition Method Based on RBF Network

Yaru Qiu[1] and Yonghong Song[2(✉)]

[1] School of Software Engineering, Xi'an Jiaotong University,
Xi'an 710049, Shaanxi, China
`mihuqiu@126.com`
[2] School of Electronic and Information Engineering, Xi'an Jiaotong University,
Xi'an 710049, Shaanxi, China
`songyh@mail.xjtu.edu.cn`

Abstract. Gait is an important biometrics in human identification, but the view variation problem seriously affects the accuracy of gait recognition. Existing methods for multi-view gait-based identification mainly focus on transforming the features of one view to another view, which might be unsuitable for the real applications. In this paper, we propose a multi-view gait recognition method based on RBF network that employs a unique view-invariant model. First, extracts the gait features by calculating the gait individual image (GII), which could better capture the discriminative information for cross view gait recognition. Then, constructs a joint model, use the DLDA algorithm to project the model and get a projection matrix. Finally, the projected eigenvectors are classified by RBF network. Experiments have been conducted in the CASIA-B database to prove the validity of the proposed method. Experiment results shows that our method performs better than the state-of-the-art multi-view methods.

Keywords: Gait recognition · RBF network · Invariant feature

1 Introduction

Gait recognition, as an emerging biometric identification technology, can be recognized at long distance or low resolution, and it is difficult to hide and conceal. Gait recognition has a wide application and development prospect in the field of biometric identification and video monitoring based on the above advantages. Gait recognition methods are divided into model-based method [1, 2] and model-free method [3–5] according to the difference of feature representation. These works show that the gait recognition is feasible in human identification at a distance. However, the recognition accuracy is easily influenced by factors such as the change of view angles [6]. Therefore, it is of great theoretical and practical significance to study gait recognition method to improve gait recognition rate and solve the view variation problem.

Most existing gait recognition methods heavily depend on the accuracy of view angle estimation, which need to create an independent model for each gallery and probe angle pair. Bodor *et al.* [7] applied image-based rendering on a 3-D model to automatically reconstruct gait features. Zhang *et al.* [8] proposed a view-independent gait

© Springer Nature Switzerland AG 2018
J. Zhou et al. (Eds.): CCBR 2018, LNCS 10996, pp. 96–108, 2018.
https://doi.org/10.1007/978-3-319-97909-0_11

recognition algorithm using Bayesian rules and a 3-D linear model. Zhao *et al.* [9] proposed an array of multiple cameras to capture a set of video sequences. Markihara *et al.* [10] designed a view transformation model (VTM) in the frequency-domain features nor the spatial domain, while the method RSVD-VTM proposed in [11] is in the spatial domain. Kusakunniran *et al.* [12] took the view transformation as a regression problem. These methods can cope with view variations and achieve good results. However, the transformation process may fail to work because either complete gait feature mapping or single-pixel mapping is sensitive to self-occlusion. And some researchers paid close to transform features from two views into a common discriminative subspace. Bashi *et al.* [13] used canonical correlation analysis (CCA) to model the correlation of gait sequences from different views. But CCA is an unsupervised dimensionality reduction method without exploiting the label information. Zhang *et al.* [14] proposed a discriminative projection with list-wise constraint (DPLC) to deal with view variance. Portillo *et al.* [15] employed a unique view invariant model. These two method that proposed in recent years achieved better performance. However, the recognition rate will decrease obviously in the condition of larger view variants.

In this paper, we use the gait individual image to extract the view-invariant feature. We create a joint projection model that don't need to create independent models for classification at different view angles. This is particularly useful in practical situations where the probe data be acquired at a view angle that does not exist in the gallery data. Moreover our proposed RBF network for classification can significantly improve the recognition rate.

The remainder of this paper is organized as follows. Section 2 briefly reviews the existing work for multi-view gait recognition. Section 3 describes the proposed method in detail. Experiments and analysis are presented in Sect. 4. Section 5 gives the conclusion.

2   Related Work

Gait recognition methods aimed at solving problems related to varying view angles can be classified as: 3D reconstruction method, view transformation-based method and view invariant method.

The 3D reconstruction methods [7–9] are used to reconstruct the 3D model from the 2D images, and then project the model to a target view for recognition. These methods perform well for fully controlled and cooperative multi-camera environments. However, their computational cost is usually high and not suitable for the reality.

The view transformation-based methods [10–12] are to transform the feature vectors from one domain to another by estimating the relationship between two domains, which mostly employ singular value decomposition (SVD). These methods has achieved good results, however, these methods need to establish a separate transformation model for each pair of views and recognition accuracy degrades when the target view and the views used for training are significantly different. Moreover, they usually suffer under-sampling problem [16].

The view invariant methods [13–15] transform samples of different views into a common space, through two invariant features for gait recognition. The view-invariant feature can be independent from the view, and it can be also be applied in the case of fewer gait sequences. Subspace learning-based method is one of the commonly used method, which project features into a subspace that is learned from training data and then estimate a set of view-invariant features.

The JDLDA method proposed by Jose Portillo [15] is a new subspace learning-based method, which employs gait energy images (GEIs) as the feature and uses direct linear discriminant analysis (DLDA) to create a single projection model, finally use KNN for classification. The advantage of JDLDA method is not required to create independent projection models and it can handle high-dimensional feature problem. However, the recognition rate will decrease obviously in the condition of larger view variants. This is because when the view variants is relatively large, the gait energy image (GEI) suffers large difference, which can cause interference to the recognition result. In addition, using KNN as the classifier, although it is easy to realize, but the recognition rate is low when the gallery view is different from the probe view. Thus, we employ gait individual image (GII) to extract more discriminative view-invariant feature and propose to use RBF network for classification. Experimental results on the CASIA-B database [6], which is one of the most widely used multi-view gait database, demonstrate the effectiveness of the proposed method.

3   Proposed Method

Our proposed framework is illustrated in Fig. 1. The dataset is first split into test and training classes. The training classes are used to create a single joint model for all view angles available for training by using DLDA. The result of this is a transformation matrix W. The test classes are further split into gallery and probe subsets; the former is used to train the RBF network, while the latter is used to test the result. It consists of three main stages: extract gait features, subspace learning using DLDA, and RBF classification. We describe in detail three stages next.

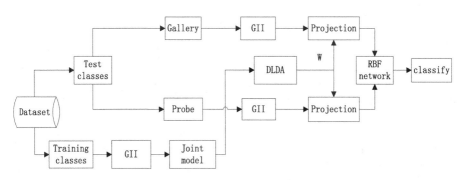

Fig. 1. Proposed framework

3.1 Extract Gait Features

To solve the first problem, we use gait individual image (GII) in the following to extract view-invariant gait features.

Assuming that silhouettes have been extracted from original human walking. First we compute gait energy image as follows:

$$G(x,y) = \frac{1}{N}\sum_{t=1}^{N} F_t(x,y) \tag{1}$$

where N is the number of available frames in a gait sequence, $F_t(x,y)$ is the t th frame, x and y are 2-D image coordinates.

GEI has better recognition capability at the same view, but when the view changes, the recognition rate will decrease. So we use a novel representation named gait individual image (GII) to bridge the gap between different views. GII for person in view is defined as the follows:

$$I_P^v(x,y) = G_P^v(x,y) - \frac{1}{M}\sum_{m=1}^{M} G_m^v(x,y) \tag{2}$$

where M is the total number of GEIs in training data from the gallery or probe view, $G_m^v(x,y)$ is the m th GEI in view v.

Figure 2 shows the comparison of GEI and GII under different views. In detail, body part in legs, arms and head, and contour of the trunk in GII are important parts which contain rich information for cross-view gait recognition. It can be observed from Fig. 2 that GEI suffers deformation as the view varies, but GII just change a little as the view ranges from 18° to 144° except 0° or 180°. Therefore, GII is more robust than GEI when the view changes, it can be used to represent the gait features of multi-view.

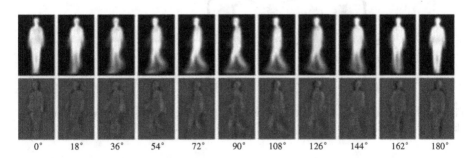

Fig. 2. Comparison of GEI and GII under 11 different views. All the image belongs to the same person. The images in first raw correspond to GEI, and the second correspond to GII.

3.2   Subspace Learning Using DLDA

The proposed method estimates a joint projection model which avoids creating a model independently for each view angle.

Once GIIs of all sequences with different view angles for each person k are obtained by Eq. 2, these GIIs are concatenated to generate the k-class input matrix:

$$X_k(d, m_k) = I_{j,k,v}(x, y) \tag{3}$$

which has a size of $d \times m_k$ where d is the total number of pixels in each GII. We normalized GII to 240*240, thus $d = 240 \times 240 = 57600$; and the size of $m_k = J \times V$, where J is the number of sequences per class and V is number of angles per class. Then, the training set X is generated by concatenating all input:

$$X = [X_1|X_2|...X_K] \tag{4}$$

The size of the training set X is therefore $d \times M$, where $M = \sum_{k=1}^{K} m_k$ denotes the total number of GIIs of all classes. Figure 3 shows the generation of training set X.

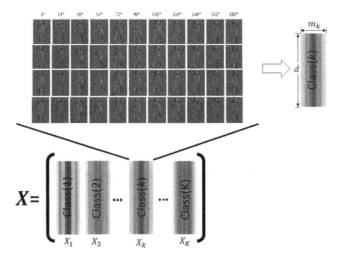

Fig. 3. Illustration of the joint model constructed by using the training data corresponding to K-classes using gait individual images of the CASIA-B database [6].

Since the size of X is too large, a dimensionality reduction method must be used. By using DLDA, we obtain a transformation matrix **W** that projects the data into a low dimensional subspace with an appropriate class separability. More details about DLDA refer to [15].

3.3   RBF Classification

Radial basis function (RBF) networks [17] belong to one of major neural networks, and draw many researchers' attention because of good performance in many application fields. The proposed method use RBF network for classification. Figure 4 shows the typical RBF structure. It consists of three layers: input layer, hidden and output layer.

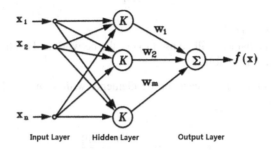

Fig. 4. RBF Structure.

A standard choice of basis function is the Gaussian:

$$\Phi(x) = \exp(-\frac{||x - \mu||^2}{2\sigma^2}) \tag{5}$$

Radial basis function makes an approximation based training data, and Gaussian function is used mostly as the radial basis function. In order to train RBF networks first we use unsupervised learning method k-means to find the centers of the hidden nodes. Given input matrix $X = [X_1, X_2, \ldots, X_n]$, thus get the hidden nodes' central matrix $C = [C_1, C_2, \ldots, C_n]$, and then calculate the variance of the hidden nodes according to distance among each data centers using the following:

$$\sigma_j = \min||c_j - c_i|| \tag{6}$$

We consider the centers as perception and input the gallery dataset again decide the weights w of the output nodes by pseudo-inverse. The training algorithm is as follow:

1. Calculate the outputs from each gallery elements with Gaussian basis function at each j th center:

$$\phi_{ij}(x) = \exp(-\frac{||x_i - c_j||^2}{2\sigma_j^2}) \tag{7}$$

where $i = 1, 2, \ldots n; j = 1, 2, \ldots N$ and x_i is the vector of gallery dataset.

2. Compute the correlation matrix and estimate the weight:

$$y_i = f(X_i)W = (w_1, w_2, \ldots, w_n)^T \tag{8}$$

$$y = t^T = (y_1, y_2, \ldots, y_N)^T \tag{9}$$

$$y = HW \tag{10}$$

Thus, weight $W = H^{-1}y$.

Finally, the probe dataset will be used to test the network and evaluate the accuracy. The algorithm of test is as follow:

1. Calculate the outputs from each probe elements with Gaussian basis function at each j th center:

$$\phi_{tj}(x) = \exp(-\frac{||x_t - c_j||^2}{2\sigma_j^2}) \tag{11}$$

where $t = 1, 2, \ldots n$; $j = 1, 2, \ldots N$ and x_t is the vector of probe dataset.

2. Get the corresponding target vector of probe elements:

$$T \arg et = \phi_{tj}W \tag{12}$$

3. Compare with probe dataset to get the number of the items NC. Evaluation function would be used to get the accuracy of this network:

$$Accuracy = \frac{NC}{N_{probe}}\% \tag{13}$$

Repeat above steps for several times and record the average results.

4   Experiments and Analysis

In this section, we will introduce our experiment setting, evaluate the performance of our method by comparing with other state-of-the-art algorithm.

4.1   Experiment Settings

We performed experiments on the CASIA B to verify the validity of our method. CASIA B gait dataset [6] is one of the largest public multi-view gait datasets, which consists of 124 subjects captured from 11 views. The view range is from 0 to 180° with 18° interval between two nearest views. For each individual, six gait sequences were captures under normal conditions, two sequences were captures when the people walking with a bag, and the other two sequences were captured when the people wearing a coat. In our experiment, we only use the data captured under normal conditions.

To compare the effectiveness of our method compare against JDLDA method. We set the same experiment settings as [15]. The dataset is divided in two classes: the training classes, which consists of 24 subjects and the test classes, which has the remaining 100 subjects. In the test classes, the first 4 normal walking sequences of each subjects are put into the gallery set and the others into the probe set.

4.2   The Effectiveness of GII Feature

The first experiment is to evaluate the effectiveness of GII compare against GEI. GEI and GII were used as the gait features, and KNN was used for classification. Figure 5 shows the comparison of recognition GII and GEI as the gait feature at different probe views.

As illustrated in Fig. 5, the proposed method outperforms the original method almost at all probe angle and gallery angle pairs. And the recognition rates of some angles increased by about 10%. It can be explained that the proposed method can extract better gait feature which can be robust to view variations.

4.3   The Effectiveness of RBF Classification

The second experiment is to evaluate the effectiveness of RBF compare against KNN. Using the same gait features, the RBF network and KNN classifier were used for classification. Figure 6 shows the comparison of RBF and KNN as the classifier at different probe views.

As illustrated in Fig. 6, the recognition rate of proposed method is obviously better than the original method at all view. The original method suffers decrease when the angle between the gallery and the probe is large, especially as the probe angle is $0°$ and $180°$, and the proposed method significantly improves the recognition rates of these two angles. It proves that the proposed method can handle large view variation well. In addition, the recognition rate of proposed method is above 50% in the angle of $54°$, $72°$, $90°$, $108°$, $126°$. In particular, the result is close to 100% when the gallery angle and probe angle are same. Therefore, it can be explained that RBF network can significantly enhance the recognition results, and prove that the proposed method is feasible.

4.4   Comparison with the State-of –the-Art

In order to better illustrate the performance of the proposed method, we also compare the proposed method with some state-of-the-art methods. We compared the recognitions with some view transformation-based methods and view invariant methods. They are GEI+PCA [6], GEI+SVD [10], GEI+SVR [11], GEI+CCA [13], GEI+DPLCR [14] and GEI+SPAE [18].

In this experiment, we follow the similar experiment setting as [18], and choose $54°$, $90°$ and $126°$ as probe views. We select one view angle as probe view, and the rest

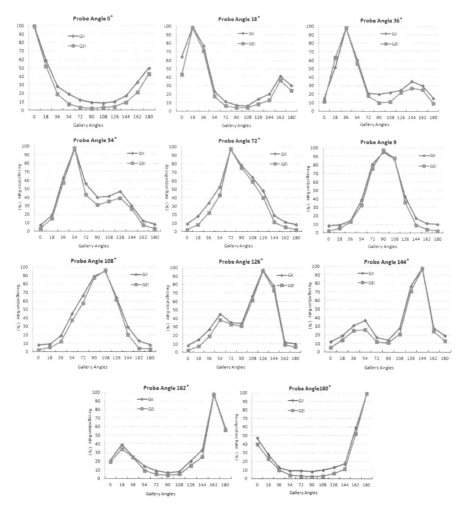

Fig. 5. Comparison of GEI and GII under 11 different views. The blue lines are achieved by the proposed method.

10 view angles as gallery views. Thus, there are totally 3 × 10 combinations of the probe view and gallery view. Tables 1, 2 and 3 shows the recognition rates of different methods for probe view 54°, 90° and 126°, respectively. And we also compare the average recognition rates of each probe angle. From the results we can find that the proposed method provides very competitive recognition rates comparison with others, except the gallery view is 0° and 180°. The reason for the poor recognition at these two angles is mainly because GII at these two angles is quite different from other angles, this causing interference to the recognition results. And the average recognition rates for each probe angle are much higher than others. The results show that the proposed method can achieve state-of-the-art performance.

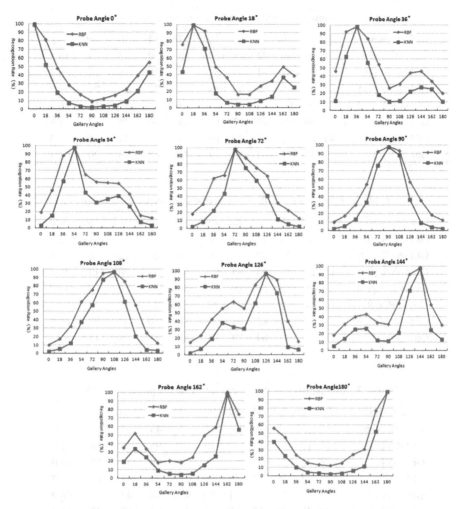

Fig. 6. Comparison of KNN and RBF under 11 different views. The blue lines are achieved by the proposed method.

Here we want to emphasis that the proposed method contains only one model for any view as [18], which don't need to create independent models at different view angles and estimate the view angle. It is feasible in practical application. Moreover, Most of the results are superior to GEI+SPAE and our proposed method has only three network layers, which is much less than GEI+SPAE.

At the probe view 54°, the recognition rate of our method in the angle of 36°, 108°, 126°, 144°, 162° is the highest, in the angle of 0°, 18°, 72°, 90° is the second highest. Moreover, the average accuracy of our method is 64.3%. It is 1% higher than the second highest rate 63.3% by GEI+SPAE, and much higher than others. In particular, in the angle of 36° and 72°, the recognition rate can reach above 90%.

Table 1. Comparisons with the state-of-the-art at probe view 54°.

Gallery view	0°	18°	36°	72°	90°	108°	126°	144°	162°	180°	Avg.
GEI+PCA [6]	4	9	30	22	18	17	38	19	2	3	16.2
GEI+SVD [10]	13	46	87	81	49	31	27	19	18	16	38.7
GEI+SVR [11]	22	64	95	93	59	51	42	27	20	21	49.4
GEI+CCA [13]	22	56	94	88	51	47	43	27	17	15	46.0
GEI+DPLCR [14]	23	64	95	**95**	**77**	69	61	50	25	17	57.6
GEI+SPAE [18]	**40**	**75**	91	83	70	65	73	67	44	**25**	63.3
Our method	29	73	**95**	93	73	**71**	**75**	**68**	**46**	20	**64.3**

Table 2. Comparisons with the state-of-the-art at probe view 90°.

Gallery view	0°	18°	36°	54°	72°	108°	126°	144°	162°	180°	Avg.
GEI+PCA [6]	3	4	7	17	82	88	22	2	1	1	22.7
GEI+SVD [10]	7	11	22	52	75	79	45	26	12	6	33.5
GEI+SVR [11]	16	22	36	63	95	95	65	38	20	13	46.3
GEI+CCA [13]	12	18	30	55	89	91	51	32	16	8	40.2
GEI+DPLCR [14]	16	24	44	74	96	97	71	43	**55**	14	53.4
GEI+SPAE [18]	**34**	**47**	54	82	94	96	86	**60**	39	**27**	**61.9**
Our method	18	27	**60**	**84**	**99**	**98**	**88**	58	24	15	57.1

Table 3. Comparisons with the state-of-the-art at probe view 126°.

Gallery view	0°	18°	36°	54°	72°	90°	108°	144°	162°	180°	Avg.
GEI+PCA [6]	2	5	13	29	21	15	37	43	2	4	17.1
GEI+SVD [10]	16	17	21	31	42	53	80	95	49	14	41.8
GEI+SVR [11]	22	26	26	42	57	78	98	98	74	19	54.0
GEI+CCA [13]	21	18	26	34	54	75	91	97	63	18	49.7
GEI+DPLCR [14]	17	30	52	62	71	80	96	94	44	23	56.9
GEI+SPAE [18]	**38**	48	55	65	80	81	90	97	**72**	**38**	**66.4**
Our method	25	**51**	**63**	**67**	**88**	**81**	**98**	**99**	65	18	65.5

At the probe view 90°, the recognition rate of our method in the angle of 36°, 54°, 72°, 108°, 126° is the highest, in the angle of 0°, 18°, 144° is the second highest. In particular, in the angle of 72° and 108°, the recognition rate is close to 100%.

At the probe view 126°, the recognition rate of our method in the angle of 18°, 36°, 54°, 72°, 90°, 108°, 144° is the highest, in the angle of 0° is the second highest. In particular, in the angle of 108° and 144°, the recognition rate is close to 100%.

5 Conclusion

In this paper, we proposed a view-invariant gait recognition method based on RBF network. The proposed method use GII to extract invariant gait feature and construct a single joint model. To further improve the performance, RBF network is presented to classify. Experiment results on CASIA-B demonstrate the superiority of the proposed method compared with the state-of-the-arts. It is very suitable for practical applications in surveillance. In feature, we will study how to improve the performance for large view variants (e.g., view 0° and view 180°).

References

1. Tafazzoli, F., Safabakhsh, R.: Model-based human gait recognition using leg and arm movements. Eng. Appl. AI **23**(8), 1237–1246 (2010)
2. Yam, C.Y., Nixon, M.S., Carter, J.N.: Automated person recognition by walking and running via model-based approaches. Pattern Recogn. **37**(5), 1057–1072 (2004)
3. Han, J., Bhanu, B.: Individual recognition using gait energy image. IEEE Trans. Pattern Anal. Mach. Intell. **28**(2), 316–322 (2006)
4. Zhang, E., Zhao, Y., Xiong, W.: Active energy image plus 2DLPP for gait recognition. Signal Process. **90**(7), 2295–2302 (2010)
5. Wang, C., Zhang, J., Wang, L.: Human identification using temporal information preserving gait template. IEEE Trans. Pattern Anal. Mach. Intell. **34**(11), 2164–2176 (2012)
6. Yu, S., Tan, D., Tan, T.: A framework for evaluating the effect of view angle, clothing and carrying condition on gait recognition. In: ICPR, vol. 4, pp. 441–444 (2006)
7. Bodor, R., Drenner, A., Fehr, D.: View-independent human motion classification using image-based reconstruction. Image Vis. Comput. **27**(8), 1194–1206 (2009)
8. Zhang, Z., Troje, N.F.: View-independent person identification from human gait. Neurocomputing **69**(1–3), 250–256 (2005)
9. Zhao, G., Liu, G., Li, H.: 3D gait recognition using multiple cameras. In: FG, pp. 529–534 (2006)
10. Makihara, Y., Sagawa, R., Mukaigawa, Y., Echigo, T., Yagi, Y.: Gait recognition using a view transformation model in the frequency domain. In: Leonardis, A., Bischof, H., Pinz, A. (eds.) ECCV 2006. LNCS, vol. 3953, pp. 151–163. Springer, Heidelberg (2006). https://doi.org/10.1007/11744078_12
11. Kusakunniran, W., Wu, Q., Li, H.: Support vector regression for multi-view gait recognition based on local motion feature selection. In: CVPR, pp. 974–981 (2010)
12. Kusakunniran, W., Wu, Q., Zhang, J.: Gait recognition under various viewing angles based on correlated motion regression. IEEE Trans. Circ. Syst. Video Technol. **22**(6), 966–980 (2012)
13. Bashir, K., Xiang, T., Gong, S.: Cross view gait recognition using correlation strength. In: BMVC, pp. 1–11 (2010)
14. Zhang, Z., Chen, J., Wu, Q.: GII representation-based cross-view gait recognition by discriminative projection with list-wise constraints. IEEE Trans. Cybern. **88**(99), 1–13 (2017)
15. Portillo-Portillo, J., Leyva, R., Sanchez, V.: Cross view gait recognition using joint-direct linear discriminant analysis. Sensors **17**(1), 6 (2017)

16. Tao, D., Li, X., Wu, X.: General tensor discriminant analysis and gabor features for gait recognition. IEEE Trans. Pattern Anal. Mach. Intell. **29**(10), 1700–1715 (2007)
17. Alldrin, N., Smith, A., Turnbull, D.: Classifying facial expression with radial basis function networks, using gradient descent and K-means (2003)
18. Yu, S., Wang, Q., Shen, L.: View invariant gait recognition using only one uniform model. In: ICPR, pp. 889–894 (2016)

Video Emotion Recognition
Using Local Enhanced Motion History Image
and CNN-RNN Networks

Haowen Wang[1,2(✉)], Guoxiang Zhou[1], Min Hu[1,2(✉)],
and Xiaohua Wang[1,2]

[1] School of Computer and Information,
Hefei University of Technology, Hefei, China
2016170718@mail.hfut.edu.cn, zgxhfut@163.com,
{jsjxhumin,xh_wang}@hfut.edu.cn
[2] Anhui Province Key Laboratory of Affective Computing and Advanced
Intelligent Machine, Hefei 230009, China

Abstract. This paper focus on the issue of recognition of facial expressions in video sequences and propose a local-with-global method, which is based on local enhanced motion history image and CNN-RNN networks. On the one hand, traditional motion history image method is improved by using detected human facial landmarks as attention areas to boost local value in difference image calculation, so that the action of crucial facial unit can be captured effectively, then the generated LEMHI is fed into a CNN network for categorization. On the other hand, a CNN-LSTM model is used as an global feature extractor and classifier for video emotion recognition. Finally, a random search weighted summation strategy is selected as our late-fusion fashion to final predication. Experiments on AFEW, CK+ and MMI datasets using subject-independent validation scheme demonstrate that the integrated framework achieves a better performance than state-of-arts methods.

Keywords: Video emotion recognition · Motion history image
LSTM · Facial landmarks

1 Introduction

Convolutional Neural Networks [1] were developed to ease the process of feature selection and give better results than already existing machine learning methods. Many researchers have developed similar methods [2] based on CNN for human expression recognition. However, Hosseini et al. [3] show that finding an appropriate feature for the given problem may be still important since they can enhance the performance of CNN-based algorithms. Encouraged by this conclusion, we aim to find a hand-craft feature to improve the performance of CNN.

Compared to single-image recognition, the temporal correlations between image frames of a video provide additional motion information for video recognition. Therefore it is important to extract dynamic texture for facial expression recognition. MHI [4] has been proved to effectively extract dynamic texture to address the problem of facial

© Springer Nature Switzerland AG 2018
J. Zhou et al. (Eds.): CCBR 2018, LNCS 10996, pp. 109–119, 2018.
https://doi.org/10.1007/978-3-319-97909-0_12

expression recognition. MHI is firstly proposed to detect human movement and one of its advantages is that a range of times may be encoded in a single frame. Traditional MHI pay attention to all of movements occurred in while ignoring the subtle movements. However, subtle movements can be used to distinguish the movements of crucial components of face (e.g., opening of mouth and raising of eyebrows).

Facial landmarks are naturally locator of facial components, Hasani et al. [5] replace the shortcut in residual unit of their 3D CNN with element-wise multiplication of facial landmarks and the input tensor of the residual unit, finally achieve a desirable performance for video facial expression recognition, but this method is computationally expensive due to its complex network structure and numerous parameters. We address the limitations of MHI and Enhanced 3D CNN by element-wise multiplication of facial landmarks and difference image that update MHI template, which generate attention-aware dynamic features that enable more distinct representations of subtle movement of different facial parts.

In this paper, we proposed a novel method named LEMHI, which extracts temporal relations of consecutive frames in a video sequence using MHI, with facial landmarks used to emphasize on more expressive facial components. Furthermore, we follow the intuition of temporal segment LSTM by Ma et al. [6] and utilize VGG networks and temporal segment LSTM to classify video human expression. Then a random search weighted summation strategy is selected as our late-fusion fashion to combine each predication scores of two models into the final score.

2 Related Work

2.1 Motion History Image

The motion history image (MHI) approach is a view-based temporal template method which is simple but robust in representing movements. MHI H(x, y, t) can be computed from an update function $\Psi(x, y, t)$:

$$H(x,y,t) = \begin{cases} \tau & if \quad \psi(x,y,t) = 1 \\ \max(0, H_\tau(x,y,t-1) - \delta) & otherwise \end{cases} \quad (1)$$

Here, (x, y) and t show the position and time, (x, y, t) signals object's presence (or motion) in the current video image, the duration τ decides the temporal extent of the movement, and σ is the decay parameter. This update function is called for every new video frame analyzed in the sequence. Usually, the MHI is generated from a binarized image, obtained from frame subtraction, using a threshold ξ:

$$\psi(x,y,t) = \begin{cases} 1 & if \ D(x,y,t) \geq \xi \\ 0 & otherwise \end{cases} \quad (2)$$

where $D(x, y, t)$ is defined with difference distance Δ as:

$$D(x,y,t) = |B(x,y,t) - B(x,y,t \pm \Delta)| \tag{3}$$

Here, $B(x, y, t)$ is the intensity value of pixel location with coordinate (x, y) at the t frame of the image sequence.

2.2 Long Short Term Memory Network

An LSTM network (Fig. 1) computes a mapping from an input sequence $x = (x_1, \ldots, x_t)$ to an output sequence $y = (y_1, \ldots, y_t)$ by calculating the network unit activations using the following equations iteratively from $t = 1$ to t:

$$i_t = \sigma(W_{ix}x_t + W_{im}m_{t-1} + W_{ic}c_{t-1} + b_i) \tag{4}$$

$$f_t = \sigma(W_{fx}x_t + W_{fm}m_{t-1} + W_{fc}c_{t-1} + b_f) \tag{5}$$

$$c_t = f_t \odot c_{t-1} + i_t \odot g(W_{cx}x_t + W_{cm}m_{t-1} + b_c) \tag{6}$$

$$o_t = \sigma(W_{ox}x_t + W_{om}m_{t-1} + W_{oc}c_t + b_o) \tag{7}$$

$$m_t = o_t \odot h(c_t) \tag{8}$$

$$y_t = W_{ym}m_t + b_y \tag{9}$$

where the W terms denote weight matrices, the b terms denote bias vectors, σ is the logistic sigmoid function, i and f, o and c are respectively the input gate, forget gate, output gate and cell activation vectors, all of which are the same size as the cell output activation vector m, $\odot$ is the element-wise product of the vectors, g and h are the cell input and cell output activation functions, generally tanh.

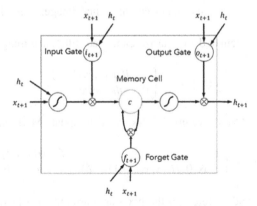

Fig. 1. A simple LSTM block with input, output, forget gates and memory cell.

3   Proposed Method

3.1   Local Enhanced Motion History Image

Although MHI is widely employed by various research groups for action recognition, it is still difficult to capture these subtle motions of facial component, meanwhile, there is usually background noise when MHI is generated.

Fortunately, we have the advantage of extracting facial landmarks and using this information to improve the recognition rate. Naturally we apply facial landmarks to traditional MHI to differentiate between the importance of main facial components (such as eyebrows, lip corners) and other parts of the face which are less expressive of facial expressions as well as control the background noise. The concrete practice is as follows:

Firstly the difference image D(x, y, t) obtained from frame subtraction, then attention-aware mask of facial landmarks M(x, y, t) is generated by detected facial landmarks. M(x, y, t) is defined as follows:

$$M(x, y, t) = \begin{cases} \alpha & (x, y) \in L \\ \alpha - 0.1\alpha d_{M(L,P)} & (x, y) \in W \\ 1 & otherwise \end{cases} \tag{10}$$

Here L is a set of landmarks coordinates while W represents set of coordinates of pixels that surround landmarks, weight α can be seen as a weight assigned to every pixels of mask, it is obvious that landmarks have the highest weights α while their surrounding pixels have lower weights proportional to their distance from the corresponding facial landmark. We choose Manhattan distance $d_{M(L, P)}$ as mentioned distance with a linear weight function. An element-wise multiplication of the mask M(x, y, t) and difference image D(x, y, t) is defined as follows:

$$E(x, y, t) = M(\text{x,y,t}) \circ D(x, y, t) \tag{11}$$

Where E(x, y, t) represents enhanced difference image, $\circ$ is Hadamard product symbol.

A threshold ξ is calculated to binarize enhanced difference image:

$$\psi(x, y, t) = \begin{cases} 1 & if\ E(x, y, t) \geq \xi \\ 0 & otherwise \end{cases} \tag{12}$$

Like the traditional MHI, we utilize Ψ(x, y, t) to update MHI template as follows:

$$H(x, y, t) = \begin{cases} \tau & if\quad \psi(x, y, t) = 1 \\ \max(0, H_\tau(x, y, t - 1) - \delta) & otherwise \end{cases} \tag{13}$$

The landmarks window refers to the pixel area around each landmark, the size of window will affect the capturing of facial movement. As shown in Fig. 3, a small window find it is hard to completely cover the areas of main facial component.

Larger windows mean that there may be overlaps between different windows. Furthermore, flexible enhancement weight α can also lead to diverse recognition rate. The influence of enhancement weight and landmarks window on recognition rate will be investigated in the following experimental part (Fig. 2).

Fig. 2. Contrast of MHI template and LEMHI template. It shows that local enhanced MHI with facial landmarks facilitate capturing subtle motions of crucial face component and the background noises are restrained effectively.

8x8   20x20   30x30

Fig. 3. Masks with diverse landmark windows

3.2 Cross Temporal Segment LSTM

LEMHI pay more attention to important facial components while ignoring motions of inferior part of face such as cheeks, which results in inadequate features exploiting. To address this problem, we train a Cross Temporal Segment LSTM with CNN features exploited from every fames. Here CNN plays a role in spatial features exploiting with Temporal Segment LSTM take up extracting temporal features. The structure of our Cross Temporal Segment LSTM is shown in Fig. 4.

Formally, given a video V with t frames $\{f_1, f_2, f_3, \ldots f_t\}$, we divide $\{f_1, f_2, f_3, \ldots f_t\}$ into K segments $\{T_1, T_2, T_3, \ldots T_4\}$ of equal durations. Then the spatial-temporal network models can be represented as follows:

$$N(f_1, f_2, \cdots f_t) = F_{softmax}(F_{fc}(h_k)) \tag{14}$$

$$h_k = R(h_{k-1}, p_k; w_r) \tag{15}$$

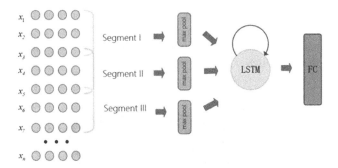

Fig. 4. Cross temporal segment LSTM architecture.

$$p_k = p(F_{cov}(f_i; w_c), \cdots F_{cov}(f_j; w_c)) \quad f_i, \cdots f_j \in T_k \tag{16}$$

F_{cov} is the function representing a Convolution operation with parameters w_c which operates on every frame in snippet T_k and return CNN features, P is a pool operation. R is update function in LSTM, P_k is input of this function while h_{k-1} is hidden state of LSTM, the outputs h_k connected with an fully connection layer and softmax function for predicts the probability of each expression class for the whole video. Meanwhile, we choose the widely used standard categorical cross-entropy loss as final loss and stochastic gradient descent (SGD) to learn the model parameters.

3.3   Integrated Framework of LEMHI-CNN and CNN-RNN

In many classification tasks, the fusion of different predication results can effectively improve the accuracy of individual prediction results [2]. Considering the complementarity between LEMHI-CNN model and the CNN-RNN model, a late fusion fashion is implemented to this two models. The overview of the integrated framework is shown in Fig. 5. This system can be divided into two parts. In the first model, video RGB image sequence is used as the input, and the VGG16 model after the FER2013 pre-training is selected as the spatial feature extractor for its best emotion fine-tuning

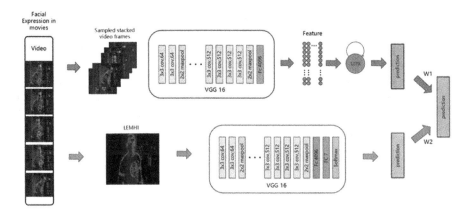

Fig. 5. The overview of the integrated framework

performances [2], followed by our CTSLSTM network which play a role in exploiting temporal features.

Especially, different layer of VGG network have different capacity to encode features. We empirically evaluated several layers of VGG network for feature exploiting, among all of these layers, FC-6 layer is used to report our final recognition accuracies for its excellent ability in encoding features [7].

The second model takes the LEMHI feature of video frame sequence as input, using conventional VGG16 as feature classifier to get predication results.

For the results obtained from these two parts, we adopt the weighted fusion method. Assume that prediction vector obtained from CNN-RNN is P while prediction vector get from LEMHI-CNN is Q, then the final prediction can be defined as follows:

$$R = \lambda P + (1-\lambda) Q, \quad 0 \leq \lambda \leq 1 \tag{17}$$

R represents final prediction result, here weight λ is determined by random search method. Weights λ are sampled uniformly from [0.0, 1.0] followed by per class rescaling, so that they sum up to 1. Then the best sampled weights are chosen based on the validation performance. After an initial random search with 100,000 iterations, we perform a local random search around the best set of weights found so far. This local random search consists of sampling weights from a Gaussian with mean set to the current best set of weights and standard deviation σ of 0.5. The current best λ is updated as soon as a new best is found. After every 100,000 iterations, the σ is decreased by a factor of 0.9 and the local search is stopped when σ is smaller than 0.0001.

4   Experiment and Result

In this section, we briefly review the databases we used for evaluating our method. We then report the results of our experiments using these databases and compare the results with the state of the arts.

4.1   Face Expression Databases

Since our method is designed for video emotion recognition, databases that contain only independent unrelated still images of facial expressions such as SFEW, FER2013 cannot be training or testing data for our method. We evaluate our proposed method on MMI, extended CK+, AFEW which contain videos of annotated facial expressions. Video sequences in MMI and CK+ database are collected in a strict controlled setting with near frontal poses, consistent illumination and posed expressions while AFEW is a dynamic temporal facial expressions data corpus extracted from movies with realistic real world environment. The extended Cohn-Kanade database (CK+) contains 593 videos from 123 subjects and there are 773 movie segments for training and 383 movie segments for validation in AFEW. However, the test set of AFEW is not considered as our training data or test data for the reason that it is not labeled.

All of sequences from CK+, MMI and AFEW are normalized uniformly by three steps: (1) face detect. (2) face align. (3) input normalization. After pre-processing we get sequences of 224×224 size face image as our input tensor, while each sequence has 16 frames.

4.2   Experimental Results

We use subject-independent scheme to evaluate the performance of the proposed framework with each database is split into training and validation sets in a strict subject independent manner. In all the experiment we report the results using 5-fold cross-validation technique and then averaging the recognition rates over five folds.

According to AFEW database, there are several sequences failed to be located facial landmarks due to facial occlusion and large angle of head rotation, all of these sequences are not considered as our training or test data for LEMHI-CNN models.

The first experiment aims to investigate the effectiveness of the LEMHI features, and is conducted on the CK+ dataset. As the performance of LEMHI might rely on the size of landmarks window and the value of enhancement weight α, we conducted our experiment using different sizes and α. Table 1 shows that better performances are achieved using 2 than using the larger or smaller weight. Also, using windows with size 20×20 gives the best performances.

The second experiment compares the performance difference between the MHI and LEMHI features. The recognition rates in using MHI and LEMHI which employs facial landmarks are summarized in Fig. 6. As is shown, no matter MMI or CK+, the performance of LEMHI-VGG model in each database obviously better than MHI-VGG model.

The third experiment investigates the effectiveness of our CNN-RNN model on three different databases, Fig. 7 shows the resulting confusion matrices of our model on these databases. Additionally, an experiment is carried out to explore the relationships between number of segments and accuracy. As is shown in Table 2. It is obvious that less segments with more frames in one segments result in higher accuracy probably because it preserves more spatial features.

In last experiment we test our integrated framework on three datasets. Table 3 shows the results using two individual model separately, and the final accuracy achieved by integrated framework. Comparing to other state-of-the art works, our framework outperforms others in CK+ databases while achieves comparable results in AFEW and MMI. It should be mentioned that some methods achieve high accuracy in AFEW since it incorporates extra audio information. Thus, we can also conclude that the combination of two models improves the recognition rate.

Table 1. Accuracy of LEMHI using several combinations of different landmark window and α on classification of seven facial expressions on CK+ dataset with subject-independent validation.

	30×30	20×20	10×10	5×5
$\alpha = 1.5$	80.84	79.36	77.32	71.84
$\alpha = 2.0$	81.21	**83.22**	78.39	71.31
$\alpha = 2.5$	79.49	81.30	77.94	69.64
$\alpha = 3.0$	72.63	77.34	70.26	67.32

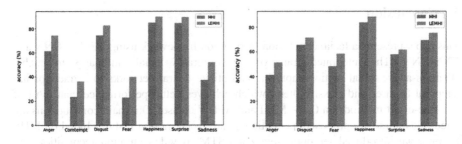

Fig. 6. Recognition rates of all expressions using MHI and LEMHI on CK+ and MMI datasets.

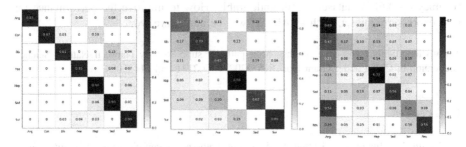

Fig. 7. Recognition rates of VGG-CTSLSTM on CK+, MMI and AFEW (from left to right).

Table 2. The relationship between number of segments and accuracy. Frames represent the number of frame in one segments, for example, when there are 5 frames in each segment, all 16 frames can be divided into 4 segments due to one frame overlapping.

Segments	Frames	Accuracy (MMI, CK+)
4	5	62.4, 81.3
5	4	66.5, 86.4
7	3	**68.8, 87.6**

Table 3. Accuracy of LEMHI-VGG, VGG-CTSLSTM and Integrated framework respectively evaluated on CK+, MMI and MMI.

Datasets	State of art method	VGG-CTSLSTM	LEMHI-VGG	Fusion
CK+	84.1[20], 84.4[21], 88.5[22], 92.4 [23], 93.2[9]	87.6	83.2	**93.9**
MMI	63.4[23], 75.12[24], 86.7[25], 78.51 [26], 77.5[9]	68.8	66.5	78.4
AFEW	37.6[27], 53.8[27], 59.02[3]	45.6	43.7	**51.2**

5   Conclusion

This paper presents a facial expression recognition framework using LEMHI-CNN and CNN-RNN. The integrated framework incorporates facial landmarks to enable attention-aware facial motion capturing and utilize neural networks to extract spatial-temporal features and classify them, which achieves better performance than most of the state-of-art methods on CK+, MMI and AFEW dataset. Our main contributions are three folds. First, we proposed a attention-aware facial motion features based on MHI. Second, we introduced temporal segment LSTM to video emotion recognition and improve it. Third, we integrate two models with late fusion based on random weight search.

Although we achieve a comparable accuracy on CK+ and MMI dataset, the accuracy on AFEW dataset is still undesirable. How to improve the performance on wild expression dataset, such as AFEW, will be our future work.

Acknowledgments. This research has been partially supported by National Natural Science Foundation of China under Grant Nos. 61672202, 61502141 and 61432004.

References

1. Lecun, Y., Huang, F.J., Bottou, L.: Learning methods for generic object recognition with invariance to pose and lighting. In: Computer Vision and Pattern Recognition, CVPR 2004 (2004)
2. Fan, Y., Lu, X., Li, D., Liu, Y.: Video-based emotion recognition using CNN-RNN and C3D hybrid networks. In: ACM International Conference on Multimodal Interaction, pp. 445–450. ACM (2016)
3. Hosseini, S., Lee, S.H., Cho, N.I.: Feeding hand-crafted features for enhancing the performance of convolutional neural networks (2018)
4. Koelstra, S., Pantic, M., Patras, I.: A dynamic texture-based approach to recognition of facial actions and their temporal models. IEEE Trans. Pattern Anal. Mach. Intell. **32**(11), 1940–1954 (2010)
5. Hasani, B., Mahoor, M.H.: Facial expression recognition using enhanced deep 3D convolutional neural networks (2017)
6. Ma, C.Y., Chen, M.H., Kira, Z., et al.: TS-LSTM and temporal-inception: exploiting spatiotemporal dynamics for activity recognition (2017)
7. Razavian, A.S., Azizpour, H., Sullivan, J., et al.: CNN features off-the-shelf: an astounding baseline for recognition. In: IEEE Conference on Computer Vision and Pattern Recognition Workshops, pp. 512–519. IEEE Computer Society (2014)
8. Mayer, C., Eggers, M., Radig, B.: Cross-database evaluation for facial expression recognition. Pattern Recogn. Image Anal. **24**(1), 124–132 (2014)
9. Lee, S.H., Yong, M.R.: Intra-class variation reduction using training expression images for sparse representation based facial expression recognition. IEEE Trans. Affect. Comput. **5**(3), 340–351 (2017)
10. Taheri, S., Qiu, Q., Chellappa, R.: Structure-preserving sparse decomposition for facial expression analysis. IEEE Trans. Image Process. **23**(8), 3590–3603 (2014)

11. Liu, M., Li, S., Shan, S., Wang, R., Chen, X.: Deeply learning deformable facial action parts model for dynamic expression analysis. In: Cremers, D., Reid, I., Saito, H., Yang, M.-H. (eds.) ACCV 2014. LNCS, vol. 9006, pp. 143–157. Springer, Cham (2015). https://doi.org/10.1007/978-3-319-16817-3_10
12. Liu, M., Shan, S., Wang, R., et al.: Learning expressionlets on spatio-temporal manifold for dynamic facial expression recognition. In: IEEE Conference on Computer Vision and Pattern Recognition, pp. 1749–1756. IEEE Computer Society (2014)
13. Shan, C., Gong, S., Mcowan, P.W.: Facial expression recognition based on Local Binary Patterns: a comprehensive study. Image Vis. Comput. **27**(6), 803–816 (2009)
14. Fan, X., Tjahjadi, T.: A dynamic framework based on local Zernike moment and motion history image for facial expression recognition. Pattern Recogn. **64**, 399–406 (2017)
15. Yao, A., Shao, J., Ma, N., et al.: Capturing AU-aware facial features and their latent relations for emotion recognition in the wild. In: ACM on International Conference on Multimodal Interaction, pp. 451–458. ACM (2015)

A Video Surveillance System
Based on Gait Recognition

Dexin Zhang[1] and Haoxiang Zhang[2(✉)]

[1] Tianjin Academy for Intelligent Recognition Technologies,
TEDA MSD-G1 10F, TEDA Tianjin Economic-Technological
Development Area, Tianjin, China
[2] School of Electronic and Information Engineering,
Ningbo University of Technology,
201 Fenghua Road, Ningbo 315211, Zhejiang, China
sean_public@qq.com

Abstract. Gait recognition is a biometric technology with unique advantages over other conventional ones, and its wide applications are yet to come. The proposed system applies gait recognition over existing video camera networks, converting them into powerful surveillance systems. It provides an efficient way of searching through the accumulated videos, saving human reviewers from tedious and inefficient work. The system also enables various scenarios from different cameras to be processed in parallel so different equipment at different locations can be coordinated to work together thus greatly improve the efficiency for searching and tracing subject persons. The system is adopted by policing department and has showed outstanding robustness and effectiveness.

Keywords: Biometrics · Gait recognition · Video cameras · CCTV

1 Introduction

Theory advances and technical progress has been seen in biometrics in recent years [1–4], which helped to boost the interest for their wide range of potential applications. Biometric technologies exploit the biological characters of humans, such as face, fingerprint, iris, vein, and gait etc. to recognize or verify the identity of individuals. Among them, gait recognition is also a powerful technique [5–8], which has yet to receive enough attention. Comparing to other popular biometric techniques, such as fingerprint, face, iris, and so on, gait is a bit far from the human's physical body, that is, it does not record any character embedded in a body, but instead, a whole set of motion patterns when walking, which allows some unique advantages over other biometric technologies.

In this paper, we propose a system that exploits gait recognition technique to process gigantic amount of video files to search for target persons. This offers an excellent solution for policing and public security purposes. The proposed system could automatically carry on the whole process without the need of human reviewers to watch every video clip. It not only liberates the viewers from the screen, but also delivers very high efficiency and accuracy. The system has been adopted in practice, and already showed its power by solving real life investigation and searching cases.

© Springer Nature Switzerland AG 2018
J. Zhou et al. (Eds.): CCBR 2018, LNCS 10996, pp. 120–127, 2018.
https://doi.org/10.1007/978-3-319-97909-0_13

The rest of the paper is organized as following, Sect. 2 introduces the background of gait recognition technique; Sect. 3 introduces the gait techniques used in the system; Sect. 4 presents the structure and design of the system; Sect. 5 concludes the paper.

2 Background

Gait refers to the way a person walks, rather than anything directly embedded in the body [1, 5]. In contrast to some other biometric features, there are some obvious advantages for using gait instead, its acquisition is easy and convenient, requiring no more than a brief video clip of a walking pedestrian. This means no specific devices are needed for acquisition. Hence it is also much easier to be introduced to real world applications, that is, the existing Close circuit TV (CCTV) systems could be upgraded to intelligent system with almost no more on site installation or hardware modifications.

Gait information can be obtained from a long distance away from the object people. As the the application and installation of CCTV systems become more and more pervasive, it is much easier to obtain the gait information and find an objective person. It is very difficult for any individuals to hide the way and style of walking before all video cameras [9, 10], therefore, with the help of gait recognition technologies, it would be virtually impossible for anyone to hide from such a massive grid of monitoring eyes. On one hand, large network of cameras provides a very wide range of coverage, an almost seamless record of pedestrians. So, in case of any event or crime investigations, enough data can be checked through. On the other hand, though, a complete coverage results in a huge amount of videos. To search for a specific individual is like finding a needle in haystack.

Gait recognition technology works as a perfect fit in such a scenario. CCTV systems have shown their fastest growth in the past few decades. All kinds of video cameras have been installed, almost everywhere, and the number is still growing exponentially. However such growth was achieved while little was considered about how to search through the data. Gait recognition can be applied to systems of various cameras installed over the years. This way, the system efficiency is boosted to a much higher level.

3 Gait-Based Video Monitoring System

This section details the technologies and structure of the systems. The system is installed in the back end of the monitoring system to search through the recorded videos. Considering the actual camera performance and practical conditions, we choose gait as the biometric characters to use in this system.

In the proposed system, gait recognition is exploited to deal with some difficult investigation cases in which cameras are too far away from the subject to record clear face image. Meanwhile, the system is robust to some distortions. It is able to detect the target individual even if the subject wears different clothes, or deliberately carry some cover, such as an umbrella. Multiple cameras can also be coordinated to set up strict surveillance over specific suspect or target people, dynamic gait comparison point, and cross-scenario gait tracking. Other functions include.

3.1   Gait Recognition Procedure

A video based gait recognition system consists four functioning modules, Video Capture, Motion Detection, Feature Extraction, and Classification. Motion detection involves background modelling, Foregrounds detection, and binary segmentation, as shown in Fig. 1.

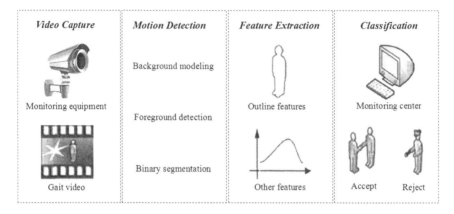

Fig. 1. The framework of gait recognition System

Gait recognition is very convenient to be applied to the videos straightaway, and it could tolerate fairly poor quality of video signals, thus applicable to most available real-world CCTV systems.

3.2   The Information Acquisition for Gait Recognition

Unlike face recognition or other typical biometric technologies, gait recognition does not rely on image details to work [11, 12]. Gait recognition is a long-distance, non-intrusive process and does not require cooperation of the subject person, which means it is very easy to obtain relevant information. The cycle of walking could be roughly divided into supporting phase, swinging phase, and the acquired information should include multiple complete copies of such cycle. And cautions should be taken to include various outlook style, angles, and background scenarios. Figure 2 below shows a typical gait acquisition procedure.

Fig. 2. The gait information acquisition

3.3   The Process of Gait Recognition

Gait recognition mainly consists 3 major steps, human shape detection, human segmentation, and gait recognition. First, motion detection and segmentation is applied to outlined human figures, and distinguish the real human subjects. Then, the resultant shapes of segmentation undergoes some pre-processing, and then the key features are extracted. The exact chosen features could be different according to the actual conditions. In the end, the extracted features are classified, and then compared against the collected database for identity recognition or verification. Alarms would be raised if a target is found. Figure 3 presents this process.

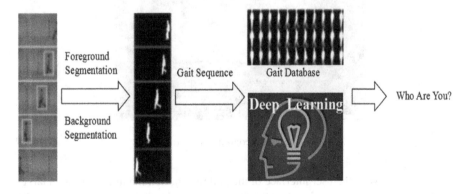

Fig. 3. The process of gait recognition.

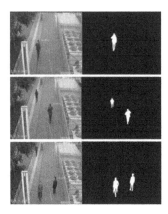

Fig. 4. Subject outline shape extraction

Figure 4 presents a real example of such process. The input to gait recognition system is a piece of video series, presented in the left column. The system then takes the video and perform background modeling, motion detection, and then extract the outline shape of the subject, shown in the right column.

At this stage, the subjects are clearly extracted from a complicated scenario, and their walking styles are clearly revealed. The system then needs to extract the the key features, and compare with the database for recognition judgment.

Fig. 5. The gait recognition user interface

Figure 5 above is the user interface of the gait recognition module. It shows a target subject is recognized to an colored rectangle block is used to indicate the position in the image.

3.4   Cross-Scenario Gait Recognition and Tracing

The proposed system has been adopted by the policing department, where the system is used to extract the each joint's movements, recognize the gait features of suspects. In order to improve the efficiency and robustness, especially to overcome the suspects' deliberate cover-up, some new functions are introduced into the system.

Fig. 6. Registration of the subject's gait information

The first one is to coordinate all the relevant cameras according to the available time, location and target person's information. The tracing can be performed over multiple cameras. With the help of the map, the route of the subject's movement is clearly showed. And the user can easily choose to view any cameras along the route. This function enables various parties to share information, and the commanders to coordinate resources, which greatly improves the efficiency. The software provides a convenient interface for it. Once the target person is confirmed in one scenario, his/her gait features could be registered, and the subject will be marked once it appear in other scenarios. Figures 5 and 6 show an example of this procedure (Fig. 7).

Fig. 7. Track the target and trigger the alarm for cross-scenes

3.5 Gait Recognition with Cover Ups

The usage of CCTV cameras are widely known, so it is not surprising that some experienced criminals would try to hide their identities before cameras, such as changing clothes, wearing masks, or even use umbrella to cover themselves up. Such difficulties are taken into consideration when designing the systems. Since gait recognition focuses on the movement of joints, it is naturally more resilient to such cover up. Figures 8 and 9 show an example that different clothing can not hide the subject's identity.

Fig. 8. Registration of the subject's gait information (subject wears trousers)

Fig. 9. Result of the subject's gait recognition (subject wears shorts)

4 Practical Performance of the System

The proposed system is adopted by many public security departments for improving their video monitoring systems, and showed outstanding performances and greatly increased the efficiency of their daily management and coordinating work.

According to many on-site experiments, the system could achieve an impressive performance, as shown in Table 1 below.

Table 1. Processing performance of the proposed system

Detection range	≥ 30 m daytime ≥ 20 m nighttime
Maximum concurrent subjects	≤ 10
Recognition accuracy	$\geq 85\%$
Processing time	≤ 190 ms

5 Conclusion

Biometrics technologies, especially gait recognition, are very suitable for helping to make the normal CCTV monitoring system intelligent, so that the management and searching of the recorded videos could be performed by machines, thus greatly improving efficiency and accuracy. We propose a system that takes these advantages of gait technologies and provides a fast, efficient, and accurate system. It has been installed and used in public security departments of various places. Practice shows that the system has an outstanding performance, and helped to solve many real cases.

References

1. Zhao, W., et al.: Face recognition: a literature survey. ACM Comput. Surv. **35**(4), 399–458 (2003)
2. Ahonen, T., Hadid, A., Pietikinen, M.: Face description with local binary patterns: application to face recognition. IEEE Trans. Pattern Anal. Mach. Intell. **28**(12), 2037 (2006)
3. Zhang, H.: A multi-model biometric image acquisition system. Biometric Recognition. LNCS, vol. 9428, pp. 516–525. Springer, Cham (2015). https://doi.org/10.1007/978-3-319-25417-3_61
4. Ding, C., Tao, D.: Trunk-branch ensemble convolutional neural networks for video-based face recognition. IEEE Trans. Pattern Anal. Mach. Intell. **40**(4), 1 (2017). PP. 99
5. Collins, R.T., Gross, R., Shi, J.: Silhouette-based human identification from body shape and gait. In: IEEE International Conference on Automatic Face and Gesture Recognition, Proceedings, pp. 366–371. IEEE (2002)
6. Ngo, T.T., Makihara, Y., et al.: Similar gait action recognition using an inertial sensor. Pattern Recogn. **48**(4), 1289–1301 (2015)
7. Marín-Jiménez, M.J., Castro, F.M., et al.: On how to improve tracklet-based gait recognition systems. Pattern Recogn. Lett. **68**, 103–110 (2015)
8. Kastaniotis, D., Theodorakopoulos, I., et al.: A framework for gait-based recognition using Kinect. Pattern Recogn. Lett. **68**, 327–335 (2015)
9. Gribbin, T.C., Slater, L.V., et al.: Differences in hip–knee joint coupling during gait after anterior cruciate ligament reconstruction. Clin. Biomech. **32**, 64–71 (2016)
10. Zhang, T., Venture, G.: Individual recognition from gait using feature value method. Cybern. Inf. Technol. **12**(3), 86–95 (2012)
11. Liu, Z., Sarkar, S.: Improved gait recognition by gait dynamics normalization. IEEE Trans. Pattern Anal. Mach. Intell. **28**(6), 863–876 (2006)
12. Wang, L., Ning, H., Tan, T., Hu, W.: Fusion of static and dynamic body biometrics for gait recognition. IEEE Trans. Circ. Syst. Video Technol. **14**(2), 149–158 (2004)

Plantar Pressure Data Based Gait Recognition by Using Long Short-Term Memory Network

Xiaopeng Li, Yuqing He$^{(\boxtimes)}$, Xiaodian Zhang, and Qian Zhao

Key Laboratory of Photoelectronic Imaging Technology and System,
Ministry of Education of China, School of Optoelectronics,
Beijing Institute of Technology, Beijing 10081, China
yuqinghe@bit.edu.cn

Abstract. As a kind of continuous time series, plantar pressure data contains rich contact of time information which has not been fully utilized in existing gait recognition methods. In this paper, we proposed a new gait recognition method based on plantar pressure data with a Long Short-Term Memory (LSTM) network. By normalization and dimensionality reduction, the raw pressure data was converted to feature tensor. Then we feed the LSTM network with the feature tensors and implement classification recognition. We collected data from 93 subjects of different age groups, and each subjects was collected 10 sets of pressure data. The experiment results turn out that our LSTM network can get high classification accuracy and performs better than CNN model and many traditional methods.

Keywords: Gait recognition · LSTM · Plantar pressure data

1 Introduction

Gait is a biological behavior that can be perceived at a long distance. Gait recognition has attracted increasing attention in the field of biometrics in recent years. Compared with other biometric identification technology, gait recognition has the advantages of non-contact, difficult to disguise and easy to collect. Currently, gait recognition is mainly divided into two categories based on the way of obtaining information. One is to extract the visual features of the human gait from video information [1, 2], and the other is based on force sensing system by extracting gait kinetic information [3]. The recognition of gait features in video information has yielded a lot of results such as Gait Energy Image (GEI). However, the quality of the video, climate disturbances, and clothing occlusion will have a significant effect on the recognition effect. The cost of training and testing data acquisition is very high. Comparatively speaking, the collection of plantar pressure has various advantages such as long-effecting distance and no privacy-intrusion problem.

There has been much research on biometric recognition by using plantar pressure data. Feng et al. [4] explored a static plantar pressure gait clustering algorithm which used the non-negative matrix factorization and a fuzzy C-means algorithm to cluster the sample objects after dimension reduction. Xia et al. [5] proposed a gait recognition algorithm based on spatio-temporal histogram of oriented gradient of plantar pressure

© Springer Nature Switzerland AG 2018
J. Zhou et al. (Eds.): CCBR 2018, LNCS 10996, pp. 128–136, 2018.
https://doi.org/10.1007/978-3-319-97909-0_14

distribution. Pataky et al. [6] used plantar pressure image dimensionality reduction processing and feature extraction to generate the peak pressure image (PPI), and the nearest neighbor algorithm was used to identify the subjects. Li et al. [7] used PPI as the input to feed a convolutional neural network (CNN) to realize the recognition.

As a kind of recursive neural network, Long Short-Term Memory is suitable for processing data related to time series [8] and there has been much progress in video information gait recognition. Liao et al. [9] proposed a pose-based temporal-spatial network to extract the temporal-spatial features and achieves good performance in both carrying and clothing conditions. Xie et al. [10] proposed a temporal-then-spatial recalibration scheme to alleviate complex variations and the scheme significantly boost the performance of skeleton-based action recognition. However, there is not much research on gait recognition using time series plantar pressure data by LSTM.

In this paper, we proposed a dynamic foot pressure identification algorithm based on LSTM network. The identification is completed by building a multi-layer LSTM network and using pre-conditioned plantar pressure dynamic sequence. Some parameters of LSTM networks are optimized in order to get the better classification results. We trained and tested the network in a plantar pressure dataset which built by ourselves and compared with other algorithms.

The rest of paper is organized as follows. In Sect. 2, the algorithm framework, data preprocessing and the LSTM model is introduced. In Sect. 3, the experimental results are shown and compared with other methods. Section 4 gives the conclusions.

2   Methods

The implementation of the algorithm is divided into three procedures. First, preprocess the time series pressure data to obtain a normalized two-dimensional vector. Second, build the LSTM network model and feed the pre-processed data with label into the network. Finally, we used the trained model for identification. The flowchart of the proposed algorithm is shown in Fig. 1.

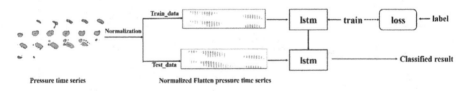

Fig. 1. The flowchart of the proposed algorithm

2.1   Data Preprocessing

Each person's foot pressure data is a continuous time series, which contains rich information. However, the original data cannot be used directly as the input of LSTM. We performed a two-part preprocessing operation on the raw data.

Normalize the Plantar Data. As we all know, the data as input of a neural network must be uniform in size. However, the size of each person's feet and the walking speed are not the same. So the normalization is necessary. The specific operation is as follows:

- Find the maximum size of all stress matrices (a_max, b_max) and place each person's stress matrix (a, b) in the upper left part of a empty matrix of size (a_max, b_max) to ensure each person's pressure matrix has the same size. The reason why we do this operator instead of directly resize the feet with a same size is that each person's foot size information is also an important classification feature.
- Find the largest frame number of all pressure time series (frame_max), and add some blank normalization matrices to ensure each person has the same number of pressure metrics in time series. The process is shown in Fig. 2.

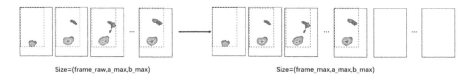

Size=(frame_raw,a_max,b_max)   Size=(frame_max,a_max,b_max)

Fig. 2. The normalization of pressure time series

Dimensionality Reduction of Plantar Data. The input required by LSTM is a two-dimensional tensor data as is shown in Fig. 3. Therefore, the plantar data of each frame needs dimension reduction to obtain a one-dimensional vector, and then the multi-frame data is arranged in two dimensions to the required two-dimensional feature tensor.

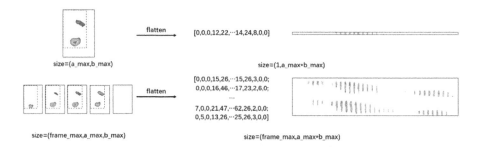

size=(a_max,b_max)   flatten   [0,0,0,12,22,···14,24,8,0,0]   size=(1,a_max*b_max)

[0,0,0,15,26,···15,26,3,0,0;
0,0,0,16,46,···17,23,2,6,0;
···
7,0,0,21,47,···62,26,2,0,0;
0,5,0,13,26,···25,26,3,0,0]

size=(frame_max,a_max,b_max)   size=(frame_max,a_max*b_max)

Fig. 3. The dimensionality reduction of plantar data

2.2   LSTM Networks for Recognition

LSTM is a time-recursive neural network [11] that is suitable for processing and predicting important events with relatively long time intervals and time series delays. It consists of an input layer, hidden layers and an output layer.

The input to the LSTM neural network is a normalized reduced-dimensional pressure time series X. The expression of X is as followed:

$$X = (X_1; X_2; \ldots, X_t, \ldots, X_{last}) \tag{1}$$

The row vector X_t of the normalized reduced-dimensional pressure time series is the input of the LSTM hidden layer at time t. The expression of X_t is as followed, x_n is the pressure value of a pixel on the detector at time t and $x_{a\_max \times b\_max}$ is the last pressure value.

$$X_t = (x_1, x_2, \ldots, x_n, \ldots x_{a\_max \times b\_max}) \tag{2}$$

Each row vector produces a hidden layer output through a multi-layered unidirectionally propagating LSTM hidden layer. The output of all the row vectors constitutes a time series $\mathbf{h}$. The expression of $\mathbf{h}$ is as followed:

$$\mathbf{h} = (h_1, h_2, \ldots, h_t, \ldots, h_{last}) \tag{3}$$

The output of the LSTM hidden layer is a time series. Liu [14] averaged the output time series of LSTM hidden layer. The classification accuracy was about 3% higher than that of using the last hidden layer output. We used both h_{mean} in Eq. 4 and h_{last} as the output of the hidden layer to figure out which method is more effective. $last$ represents the number of vectors in Eq. 3's $\mathbf{h}$.

$$h_{mean} = \frac{\sum_{t=1}^{last} h_t}{last} \tag{4}$$

h_{mean} and h_{last} will be processed by full connected layer and softmax layer. The results y_{mean} in Eq. 5 and y_{last} in Eq. 6 are the predicted classification result which reflected the probability of belonging to each class. Using the prediction results to train the model [13], we apply the cross-entropy loss function (CELoss) in Eq. 7. CELoss is used to measure the difference between the predicted probability distribution y_i and the standard probability distribution p_i.

$$y_{mean} = softmax(h_{mean}) \tag{5}$$

$$y_{last} = softmax(h_{last}) \tag{6}$$

$$CELoss = -\sum_i y_i \log p_i \tag{7}$$

The algorithm structure diagram is shown in Fig. 4.

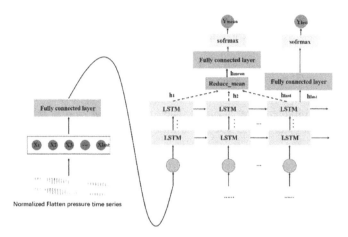

Fig. 4. Our LSTM structure diagram

3 Experimental Results

3.1 Dataset

The data in this study is collected by 93 people including 62 males and 31 females in different age groups. Each person is collected 10 sets of plantar pressure time series. Each set of data consists of a series of 160–200 frames plantar pressure matrices and the maximum pressure matrix is 39×26. The plantar pressure data used in this study is obtained by the Footscan® system from a research institute [16]. This system can be used for barefoot or wearing shoes walking, running and other different static or dynamic foot plantar pressure measurement. The total measuring plate is 200×40 cm, contains a total of 16384 pressure sensors.

To ensure the validity of the measurement data, each testee needs warm-up and be familiar with the basic test process. During the test, the testees walk according to their own walking habits and speed. The sampling frequency of the system is set to 126 Hz. The procedure of data acquisition is shown in Fig. 5.

Fig. 5. The procedure of data acquisition

3.2 Optimization of Network Parameters

We use the TensorFlow framework to train and test the model of the plantar pressure identification algorithm. TensorFlow is the second generation of artificial intelligence learning system developed by Google based on DistBelief. It is a system that transmits complex data structures to the artificial intelligence neural network for analysis and processing. The experimental hardware configuration is 2.5 GHz CPU, 8G memory, NVIDIA GeForce GTX1050ti, 4G GDDR5.

We trained our algorithmic model with the normalized plantar pressure series. In order to optimize LSTM network parameters, we experimented with multiple sets of parameters for training, we changed the number of hidden layers, the number of hidden layer neurons, the processing method of the hidden layer output, and the batch size. The comparison results are shown in Fig. 6.

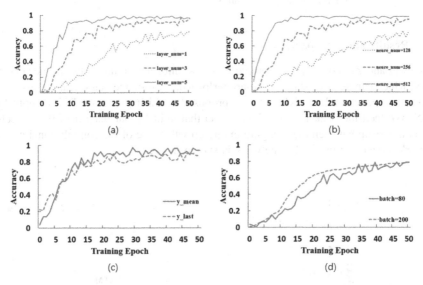

Fig. 6. The comparison results of changing different parameters. Where the figure a, b, c and d respectively change number of hidden layers, the number of hidden layer neurons, the processing method of the hidden layer output and the batch size.

It can be seen that it's better to select multiple layers of hidden layers. The number of neurons in the hidden layer cannot be too small, otherwise the recognition rate is low. By comparison, it is found that the accuracy of using h_{mean} is higher than that of using h_{last} as the output. Obviously, h_{mean} contains more spatial and temporal information. The experimental results show that the lager the batch is, the faster the recognition rate increases. But batch size cannot be too large, or it will consume too much memory space.

Dropout processing was performed on the hidden layer of Multi-RNN-Cell to prevent over-fitting. The training rate will attenuate during the training. It was reduced by 0.2 times for every 8 train epochs. Batch processing was operated on the training data to increase efficiency. The optimal parameters of the network are listed in Table 1.

Table 1. The parameters of the proposed LSTM network

Parameter	Parameter value
Classification classes	93
Number of hidden layers	3
Number of hidden layer neurons	500
Learning rate	0.0001
Batch size	80
Dropout_keep_probability	0.5

3.3   Results and Comparison

Simonyan and Zisserman [12] captured temporal information under the framework of CNN, which can achieve state-of-the-art performance on image classification tasks. As a comparison, we built a CNN network proposed by Li [6] who use PPI as input for CNN. We feed the peak pressure image data that built by our dataset of 93 subjects. The comparison between the recognition rate growth curve of the convolutional neural network model and the LSTM network is shown in Fig. 7.

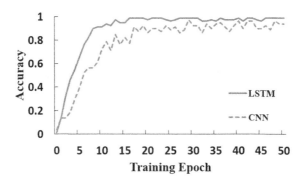

Fig. 7. The comparison of recognition rate between CNN and LSTM

To compare the proposed method with traditional gait recognition methods, we have implemented two other algorithms [15] which also use plantar pressure data. The input features of the two traditional algorithm include PPI and Spatio-Temporal Histogram of Oriented Gradients (STHOG). The comparative results evaluated by a s-fold cross-validation are shown in Table 2.

Table 2. The comparison of different methods

Method	The input	Accuracy (%)	Execution time (s)
SVM	PPI	82.79	0.035
SVM	STHOG	86.53	0.021
CNN of Li's [7]	PPI	94.51	0.015
LSTM proposed	Feature vector	98.75	0.31

The results in Table 2 shows that the methods based on neural network performed better results compared with traditional methods. The LSTM method proposed has a higher accuracy than the method based on CNN. We think this is because LSTM can make full use of the link of plantar pressure data in terms of time, and CNN can not catch such a link. As for the execution time, the method based on CNN performs best and the LSTM-based method has a bit longer execution time. This result is not strange since the two-dimensional tensor as the input of LSTM is much larger than the PPI in size.

4   Conclusion

In this paper, we proposed a new LSTM-based method for gait recognition by using plantar pressure data. The LSTM can realize the feature extraction and classification automatically. Unlike many traditional and CNN methods, LSTM network can fully utilize the connection at each frame of plantar pressure data. Experimental results show that the proposed method can obtain a high recognition accuracy and achieve better performs than CNN network and other traditional methods.

References

1. Ben, X., Meng, W., Yan, R., Wang, K.: An improved biometrics technique based on metric learning approach. Neurocomputing **97**, 44–51 (2012)
2. Ben, X., Zhang, P., Meng, W., Yan, R., Yang, M., Liu, W., Zhang, H.: On the distance metric learning between cross-domain gaits. Neurocomputing **208**, 153–164 (2016)
3. Pujol, E., Müller, B., Coll, R., et al.: Gait pattern recognition by foot pressure measurement in patients with intra-articular calcaneus fractures. In: World Congress of the International Society of Physical and Rehabilitation Medicine (2009)
4. Feng, Y., Li, Y., Luo, J.: Learning effective gait features using LSTM. In: 23rd International Conference on Pattern Recognition, ICPR 2016, Cancún, Mexico, 4–8 December 2016, pp. 325–330 (2016)
5. Xia, R., Ma, Z., Yao, Z., Sun, Y.: Gait recognition based on spatio-temporal HOG feature of plantar pressure distribution. J.PR & AI. **26**(6), 529–536 (2013)
6. Pataky, T.C., Mu, T., Bosch, K., Rosenbaum, D., Goulermas, J.Y.: Gait recognition: highly unique dynamic plantar pressure patterns among 104 individuals. J. R. Soc. Interface **9**, 790–800 (2012)

7. Li, Y., et al.: A convolutional neural network for gait recognition based on plantar pressure images. In: Zhou, J., et al. (eds.) CCBR 2017. LNCS, vol. 10568, pp. 466–473. Springer, Cham (2017). https://doi.org/10.1007/978-3-319-69923-3_50

8. Greff, K., Srivastava, R., Koutník, J., et al.: LSTM: a search space odyssey. IEEE Trans. Neural Netw. Learn. Syst. **28**(10), 2222–2232 (2016)

9. Liao, R., Cao, C., Garcia, E.B., Yu, S., Huang, Y.: Pose-based temporal-spatial network (PTSN) for gait recognition with carrying and clothing variations. In: Zhou, J., et al. (eds.) CCBR 2017. LNCS, vol. 10568, pp. 474–483. Springer, Cham (2017). https://doi.org/10.1007/978-3-319-69923-3_51

10. Xie, C., Li, C., Zhang, B., Chen, C.: Memory attention networks for skeleton-based action recognition. IJCAI (2018). arXiv: 1804.08254

11. Hochreiter, S., Schmidhuber, J.: Long short-term memory. Neural Comput. **9**(8), 1735–1780 (1997)

12. Simonyan, K., Zisserman, A.: Two-stream convolutional networks for action recognition in videos. In: Advances in Neural Information Processing Systems, pp. 568–576 (2014)

13. Zhang, K., Huang, Y., Du, Y., et al.: Facial expression recognition based on deep evolutional spatial-temporal networks. IEEE Trans. Image Process. **26**, 4193–4203 (2017)

14. Liu, Y.-H., Liu, X., Fan, W., Zhong, B., Du, J.-X.: Efficient audio-visual speaker recognition via deep heterogeneous feature fusion. In: Zhou, J., et al. (eds.) CCBR 2017. LNCS, vol. 10568, pp. 575–583. Springer, Cham (2017). https://doi.org/10.1007/978-3-319-69923-3_62

15. Xia, Y., Ma, Z., Yao, Z., Sun, Y.: Gait recognition based on spatio-temporal HOG of plantar pressure distribution. Pattern Recognit. Artif. Intell. **26**, 529–536 (2013)

16. Huang, H., Qiu, J., Liu, T., et al.: Similarity of center of pressure progression during walking and jogging of anterior cruciate ligament deficient patients. Plos One **12**(1) (2017)

Improving Gait Recognition with 3D Pose Estimation

Weizhi An[1], Rijun Liao[1], Shiqi Yu[1(✉)], Yongzhen Huang[2], and Pong C. Yuen[3]

[1] College of Computer Science and Software Engineering, Shenzhen University,
Shenzhen 518060, China
{anweizhi2016,2150230306}@email.szu.edu.cn, shiqi.yu@szu.edu.cn
[2] National Laboratory of Pattern Recognition, Institute of Automation,
Chinese Academy of Sciences, Beijing 100190, China
yongzhen.huang@nlpr.ia.ac.cn
[3] Department of Computer Science, Hong Kong Baptist University,
Hong Kong SAR, China
pcyuen@comp.hkbu.edu.hk

Abstract. Gait is a kind of attractive biometric feature for human identification in recent decades. The view, clothing, carrying and other variations are always the challenges for gait recognition. One of the possible
solutions is the model based methods. In this paper, 3D pose is estimated
from 2D images are used as the feature for gait recognition. So gait can
be described by the motion of human body joints. Besides, the 3D pose
has better capacity for view variation than the 2D pose. Experimental
results also prove that in the paper. To improve the recognition rates,
LSTM and CNNs are employed to extract temporal and spatial features. Compared with other model-based methods, the proposed one has
achieved much better performance and is comparable with appearance-
based ones. The experimental results show the proposed 3D pose based
method has unique advantages in large view variation. It will have great
potential with the development of pose estimation in future.

Keywords: Gait recognition · 3D pose · LSTM · CNNs

1 Introduction

Gait as a kind of biometric feature has a great potential for human identification
at a distance. Compared with other kinds of biometric features such as fingerprint, iris, palmprint and face, gait has unique advantages like non-contact, hard
to fake. Therefore, gait recognition has attracted more and more attention in the
computer vision field. Although many creative works have been proposed on gait
recognition, it is still a challenge task due to view variation, clothing occlusion,
carrying bags which could reduce the recognition rate drastically.

There are mainly two kinds of methods for gait recognition: the appearance-
based methods and the model-based ones. The appearance based methods [16,19,

© Springer Nature Switzerland AG 2018
J. Zhou et al. (Eds.): CCBR 2018, LNCS 10996, pp. 137–147, 2018.
https://doi.org/10.1007/978-3-319-97909-0_15

20,23] usually extract appearance features from human silhouettes. The appearance based methods were popular in the pass decades for the efficiency of feature extraction. However, this kind of methods are easily affected by shape changes like clothing and carrying bags. The recognition accuracy could also drop rapidly when evaluated under clothing, carrying conditions. Another category of methods is based on human models which employ modelling human body and local movement patterns of different body parts. Many model-based methods [11,13,14,22] employ static structures of body and motion. It is evident that the model-based methods can be insensitive to occlusions, clothing changing and some other variations. But it was challenging to build an accurate human model in the past. It mainly relies on markers attached on human bodies or using special sensors to track body joints.

With the development of the pose estimation which can directly extract human pose from images, gait recognition also benefited from that. There are some pose-based gait recognition methods in the literature [3,8,9]. It can be easily understood that human joints are insensitive under the carrying bags and clothing conditions if the joints can be estimated accurately. Some pioneer researchers have worked on gait recognition based one human pose. Liang et al. [8] use skeleton data acquired from the Kinect sensors. Feng et al. [3] use the human body joint heatmap as the feature for gait recognition. They feed the joint heatmap of consecutive frames to Long Short Term Memory (LSTM) to extract the gait features. Our prior work [9] proposed a 2D pose-based gait recognition method and used the temporal-spatial network (PTSN) to extract the gait feature. Different from the method in [9], 3D pose feature is used in the proposed method. Experimental results also show that the 3D pose feature is superior to 2D feature.

Our contributions in this paper are: (1) The 3D pose is estimated directly from 2D images from one camera only, and camera calibration and special senors and markers are not needed. (2) LSTM and CNNs are combined to capture both temporal and spatial information from consecutive 3D pose. (3) Only one uniform 3D pose model is needed which can handle view, carrying and clothing variations.

The rest of the paper is organized as follows. Section 2 describes the proposed 3D pose model. Experiments and evaluation are presented in Sect. 3. The Sect. 4 conclude the conclusions.

2   3D Pose Feature Extraction

3D human pose contains more information than 2D [9]. Compared with 2D pose [9], the pose information of our proposed method is in the three dimension, which is definitely beneficial to dealing with view problem. In addition, we use the center loss rather than contrastive loss to constrain the gait feature, which can reduce the complexity in the training process and improve the performance of gait recognition. It is inherently view invariant because it is in a 3D space. Given the 3D human model, the feature at any view can be synthesized

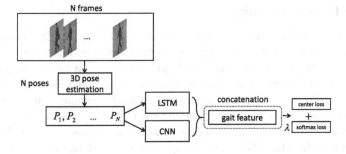

Fig. 1. The framework of the proposed method.

from the 3D model. The proposed method employs the 3D pose information estimated from 2D images by CNN. It is inspired by the facial expression recognition method in [21]. We extract temporal features based on 3D pose from consecutive frames by LSTM, and spatial features by CNN. A multiple loss strategy is employed to enhance the gait feature extraction and improve recognition rates. The framework of the proposed method is shown in Fig. 1.

2.1   3D Pose Estimation

Estimating a high accuracy 3D pose is a challenge because it can be cast as a nonlinear optimization problem [7]. Recently, Chen *et al.* [2] explore 3D human pose estimation from single RGB image and it is straightforward to implement with off-the-shelf 2D pose estimation systems and 3D mocap libraries. It outperforms almost all state-of-the-art 3D pose estimation system, so we use it to obtain the gait pose which contains 14 joints. The 14 joints are Nose, Neck, Right Shoulder, Right Elbow, Right Wrist, Left Shoulder, Left Elbow, Left Wrist, Right Hip, Right Knee, Right Ankle, Left Hip, Left Knee, Left Ankle, Right Eye, Left Eye, Right Ear and Left Ear. Some gait RGB images and the correspondent 3D pose are show in Fig. 2.

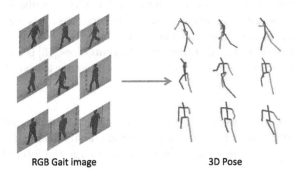

RGB Gait image   3D Pose

Fig. 2. Some gait RGB images and the correspondent 3D pose estimated from the RGB images.

2.2   The Feature Learning

In the proposed architecture there are two networks. They are LSTM and CNNs respectively. The size of the input data is $N \times 42$ where N stands for N consecutive frames selected from a video and 17 body joints (each joint has its position with (x, y, z). The consecutive poses can be considered as dynamic variation so we implement LSTM as a temporal network to extract dynamic features from the consecutive poses. Another network based on CNNs is constructed to extract features from still poses. The dynamic features extracted by LSTM and the spatial features by the CNNs are finally concatenated as our gait feature to improve the recognition.

LSTM for Temporal Feature: Since that gait is the walking style and different person has different gait. Gait can also be regarded as the dynamic motion of different body joints in the temporal space. LSTM is a network which is good at extracting features in the temporal domain. It contains self-connected memory units. It can improve long range contextual information of in the temporal domain. So it is effective in capturing dynamic information. We put the joint positions into a LSTM network to extract the temporal feature.

CNNs for Spatial Feature: A CNNs model is also designed in the proposed method to extract the spatial information. We want to emphasis here that the input of CNNs is the pose data which is the same with the one to LSTM. For most CNNs based gait recognition methods, the input is 2D images which is the appearance data. The input is a global representation of a gait sequence. As illustrated in Table 2, we implemented ResNet [4] which add shortcut and can help to extract deep global information. Then, the LSTM and CNNs are fused to extract temporal and spatial gait features in a gait sequence. At last, the temporal gait feature and the spatial one are concatenated as the feature.

2.3   Loss Functions

After the gait feature extraction by LSTM and CNNs, a multi-loss strategy is involved to improve the recognition rate. For gait features, it is a great challenge that intra-class is larger than inter-class sometimes. The softmax loss [12] can help to enlarge the inter-class distance, and the center loss [15] is good at reducing the intra-class distance. So the softmax loss and the center loss are fused to boost our network.

Softmax Loss. Our networks can learn discriminant features under the supervision of the gait labels. The softmax loss could classify each gait pose into the correspondent subject, and it also effectively to enlarge the inter-class distance. It is defined as:

$$L_S = -\sum_{i=1}^{m} \log \frac{e^{W_{y_i}^T x_i + b_{y_i}}}{\sum_{j=1}^{n} e^{W_j^T x_i + b_j}} \qquad (1)$$

where $x_i \in \mathbb{R}^d$ is the ith feature that belongs to the y_ith class. d, $W \in \mathbb{R}^{d \times n}$ and $b \in \mathbb{R}^d$ denote the feature dimension, last connected layer and bias term, respectively.

Center Loss. In gait recognition many challenges such as the view variation can cause the recognition rate to drop drastically because the intra-class distance is mostly greater than the inter one. The center loss is effective to reduce the intra-class distance. It is defined as:

$$L_C = \frac{1}{2} \sum_{i=1}^{m} ||x_i - c_{y_i}||_2^2 \tag{2}$$

where $c_{y_i} \in \mathbb{R}^d$ is the y_ith class center of pose features. When the distance between the pose and its correspondent center is large, it adds penalty so that the intra-class can be reduced.

Fusion of Loss Functions. To enlarge the inter-class distance and reduce the intra-class one, the softmax lass and the center loss are fused. They are fused as follows.

$$L = L_S + \gamma L_c \tag{3}$$

where γ is to balance the weight of two loss functions, and in our experiment the γ is set to value 0.005.

3   Experimental Results and Analysis

3.1   Dataset

CASIA-B gait dataset [18] is one of the largest public gait databases in this world, and it contains 124 subjects captured from 11 views with the view range from $0°$ to $180°$ with $18°$ interval between two nearest views. The set of view angles are $\{0°, 18°, \cdots, 180°\}$. There are 10 sequences for each subject, 6 sequences of normal walking (NM), 2 sequences of walking with bag (BG) and 2 sequences of walking with coat (CL). The CASIA-B dataset consists 13640 video sequences and with 2 or 3 gait cycles in each sequence.

3.2   Implementation Details

The experimental setting of the proposed method is the same with those in [9]. All the gait data including "nm", "bg" and "cl" are all involved. The first 62 subjects are put into the training set and the remaining 62 ones into the test set. In the test set, the first 4 normal walking sequences of each subjects are put into the gallery set and the others into the probe set as shown in Table 1.

According to our framework in Fig. 1, the 3D pose is estimated from images using the method in [2]. The 3D pose contains 14 joints. The height of the

Table 1. Experimental setting on CASIA-B dataset.

Training	Test	
	Gallery Set	Probe Set
ID: 001-062	ID: 063-124	ID: 063-124
NM01-NM06	SNM01-NM04	NM05-NM06
BG01-BG02, CL01-CL02		BG01-BG02, CL01-CL02

Table 2. Implementation details of the CNN.

Layers	Number of filters	Filter size	Stride	Activation function
Conv.1	32	3×3	1	P-ReLU
Conv.2	64	3×3	1	P-ReLU
Pooling.1	N	2×2	2	N
Conv.3	64	3×3	1	P-ReLU
Conv.4	64	3×3	1	P-ReLU
Eltwise.1	Sum operation between Pooling.1 and Conv.4			
Conv.5	128	3×3	1	P-ReLU
Pooling.2	N	2×2	2	N
Conv.6	128	3×3	1	P-ReLU
Conv.7	128	3×3	1	P-ReLU
Eltwise.2	Sum operation between Pooling.2 and Conv.7			
Conv.8	128	3×3	1	P-ReLU
Conv.9	128	3×3	1	P-ReLU
Eltwise.3	Sum operation between Eltwise.2 and Conv.9			
Conv.10	128	3×3	1	P-ReLU
FC.1	512	N	N	N

subjects in the images is not fixed because the distance between the subjects and the camera is not fixed. So the human pose is normalized to a fixed size. To be specifically, it is that the distance between the neck and the hip is normalized to a fixed size.

The 3D pose joint data of train set are fed into the networks. The details of our networks involving CNNs and LSTM are shown in Table 2 and Table 3 respectively.

3.3 Impact of Temporal Network

The proposed method combines the LSTM and CNNs to extract temporal and spatial features respectively. To evaluate the efficiency of the LSTM, experiments are carried out with only CNNs with exactly the same train and set settings. We compute the average recognition rates under the view variation, carrying and

Table 3. Implementation details of LSTM

Layers	Activation function
FC	ReLU
FC	ReLU
FC	ReLU
FC	ReLU
LSTM	N

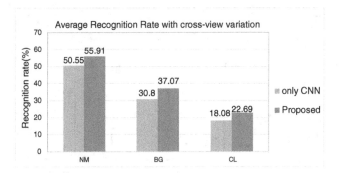

Fig. 3. The cross-view average recognition comparison between proposed and only using CNNs model on CASIA-B dataset.

clothing conditions. From the results shown in Fig. 3, we can find that the proposed method outperforms the method with CNNs only. It shows the efficiency of the temporal information by LSTM.

3.4 Comparisons with 2D Pose

Our prior work in [9], named as PTSN, is a 2D pose based gait recognition method. Different from the 3D joint positions extracted from images, it is only the 2D positions used in [9]. The proposed method is compared with PTSN under the cross-view variations to evaluate that the 3D pose is more robust to view variation. The experimental design of the proposed method is the same with that of PTSN as shown in Table 1. Figure 4 shows the recognition rates of PTSN and the proposed method at each probe angle. It is clearly shown that the proposed can achieve much better results especially when there is a larger view variation. That means the proposed method is more robust to view variation.

3.5 Comparison with Other Cross-View Methods

We compared the proposed method with some other sate-of-the-art works. They are FD-VTM [10], RSVD-VTM [5], RPCA-VTM [23], R-VTM [6], GP+CCA [1], C3A [17] and PTSN [9]. For the limitation of space, we only selected the results

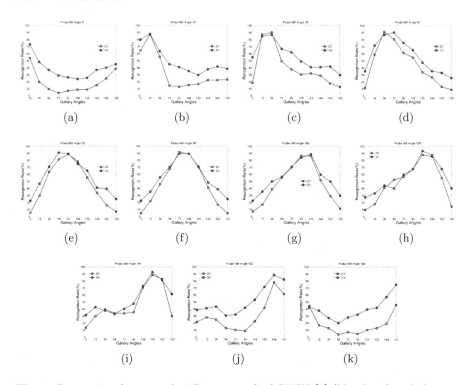

Fig. 4. Comparison between the 2D pose method PTSN [9] (blue lines) and the proposed method (red lines). (Color figure online)

of 54°, 90°, 126° probe angles. It is the same setting with that in [9]. The experimental results are shown in Fig. 5.

We want to emphasize here that only the positions of 14 joint are taken as the input. No other kinds of appearance based features are sent into the networks. From the results, we can find that the proposed method performs well in large view variation especially. The results also show that the proposed 3D model owns advantages in handling cross-view condition.

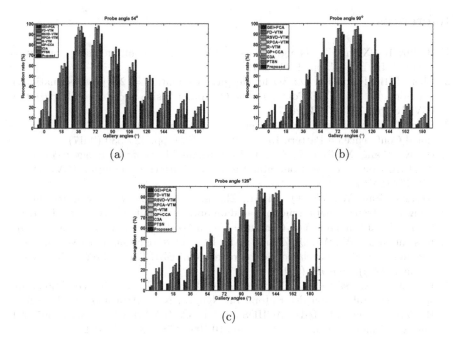

Fig. 5. Comparing with existing methods at probe angles (a) 54°, (b) 90° and (c) 126° on CASIA-B dataset. The gallery angles are the rest 10 angles except the corresponding probe angle.

4   Conclusions and Future Work

In this paper, we proposed a gait recognition method based on 3D body pose to handle the cross-view variations. A 3D pose estimation method based on CNN is used to estimate the position of human body joints. Then the positions in a sequence can be sent to neural networks to train the networks. Since 3D pose is used in the proposed method, the proposed method is more robust to view variation and others. Experimental results also prove that. Even only the joint positions are used for recognition, state-of-the-art recognition rates are achieved.

Human pose estimation is just improved greatly in these several years with the progress of deep learning. We surely believe that the pose estimation will achieve better performance in future. The work in the paper shows that 3D pose can benefit gait recognition a lot. Gait recognition will be continually benefited by the development of human pose estimation, human body modeling and related topics.

Acknowledgment. The work is supported by the strategic new and future industrial development fund of Shenzhen (Grant No. 20170504160426188).

References

1. Bashir, K., Xiang, T., Gong, S.: Cross view gait recognition using correlation strength. In: BMVC, pp. 1–11 (2010)
2. Chen, C.H., Ramanan, D.: 3D human pose estimation = 2D pose estimation + matching. In: The IEEE Conference on Computer Vision and Pattern Recognition (CVPR), pp. 7035–7043 (2017)
3. Feng, Y., Li, Y., Luo, J.: Learning effective gait features using LSTM. In: International Conference on Pattern Recognition (ICPR), pp. 325–330 (2017)
4. He, K., Zhang, X., Ren, S., Sun, J.: Deep residual learning for image recognition. In: IEEE Conference on Computer Vision and Pattern Recognition (CVPR), pp. 770–778 (2016)
5. Kusakunniran, W., Wu, Q., Li, H., Zhang, J.: Multiple views gait recognition using view transformation model based on optimized gait energy image. In: IEEE International Conference on Computer Vision Workshops, pp. 1058–1064 (2010)
6. Kusakunniran, W., Wu, Q., Zhang, J., Li, H.: Gait recognition under various viewing angles based on correlated motion regression. IEEE Trans. Circuits Syst. Video Technol. **22**(6), 966–980 (2012)
7. Kwolek, B., Krzeszowski, T., Michalczuk, A., Josinski, H.: 3D gait recognition using spatio-temporal motion descriptors. In: Nguyen, N.T., Attachoo, B., Trawiński, B., Somboonviwat, K. (eds.) ACIIDS 2014. LNCS (LNAI), vol. 8398, pp. 595–604. Springer, Cham (2014). https://doi.org/10.1007/978-3-319-05458-2_61
8. Liang, Y., Li, C.T., Guan, Y., Hu, Y.: Gait recognition based on the golden ratio. Eurasip J. Image Video Process. **2016**(1), 22 (2016)
9. Liao, R., Cao, C., Garcia, E.B., Yu, S., Huang, Y.: Pose-based temporal-spatial network (PTSN) for gait recognition with carrying and clothing variations. In: Zhou, J., et al. (eds.) CCBR 2017. LNCS, vol. 10568, pp. 474–483. Springer, Cham (2017). https://doi.org/10.1007/978-3-319-69923-3_51
10. Makihara, Y., Sagawa, R., Mukaigawa, Y., Echigo, T., Yagi, Y.: Gait recognition using a view transformation model in the frequency domain. In: Leonardis, A., Bischof, H., Pinz, A. (eds.) ECCV 2006. LNCS, vol. 3953, pp. 151–163. Springer, Heidelberg (2006). https://doi.org/10.1007/11744078_12
11. Nash, J.M., Carter, J.N., Nixon, M.S.: Dynamic feature extraction via the velocity hough transform. Pattern Recogn. Lett. **18**(10), 1035–1047 (1997)
12. Sun, Y., Wang, X., Tang, X.: Deep learning face representation from predicting 10,000 classes. In: IEEE Conference on Computer Vision and Pattern Recognition (CVPR), pp. 1891–1898 (2014)
13. Tanawongsuwan, R., Bobick, A.: Gait recognition from time-normalized joint-angle trajectories in the walking plane. In: IEEE Conference on Computer Vision and Pattern Recognition, p. 726 (2001)
14. Wang, L., Tan, T., Hu, W., Ning, H.: Automatic gait recognition based on statistical shape analysis. IEEE Trans. Image Process. **12**(9), 1120–1131 (2003)
15. Wen, Y., Zhang, K., Li, Z., Qiao, Y.: A discriminative feature learning approach for deep face recognition. In: Leibe, B., Matas, J., Sebe, N., Welling, M. (eds.) ECCV 2016. LNCS, vol. 9911, pp. 499–515. Springer, Cham (2016). https://doi.org/10.1007/978-3-319-46478-7_31
16. Wu, Z., Huang, Y., Wang, L., Wang, X., Tan, T.: A comprehensive study on cross-view gait based human identification with deep CNNs. IEEE Trans. Pattern Anal. Mach. Intell. **39**(2), 209–226 (2016)

17. Xing, X., Wang, K., Yan, T., Lv, Z.: Complete canonical correlation analysis with application to multi-view gait recognition. Pattern Recogn. **50**(C), 107–117 (2016)
18. Yu, S., Tan, D., Tan, T.: A framework for evaluating the effect of view angle, clothing and carrying condition on gait recognition. In: International Conference on Pattern Recognition (ICPR), pp. 441–444 (2006)
19. Yu, S., Wang, L., Hu, W., Tan, T.: Gait analysis for human identification in frequency domain. In: International Conference on Image and Graphics, pp. 282–285 (2004)
20. Yu, S., Wang, Q., Shen, L., Huang, Y.: View invariant gait recognition using only one uniform model. In: 23rd International Conference on Pattern Recognition (ICPR 2016), pp. 889–894 (2016)
21. Zhang, K., Huang, Y., Du, Y., et al.: Facial expression recognition based on deep evolutional spatial-temporal networks. IEEE Trans. Image Process. **26**(9), 4193–4203 (2017)
22. Zhao, G., Liu, G., Li, H., Pietikainen, M.: 3D gait recognition using multiple cameras. In: International Conference on Automatic Face and Gesture Recognition, pp. 529–534 (2006)
23. Zheng, S., Zhang, J., Huang, K., He, R., Tan, T.: Robust view transformation model for gait recognition. In: 2011 18th IEEE International Conference on Image Processing (ICIP), pp. 2073–2076. IEEE (2011)

Cross-Cascading Regression for Simultaneous Head Pose Estimation and Facial Landmark Detection

Wei Zhang[1,2,3], Hongwen Zhang[1,2], Qi Li[1], Fei Liu[1], Zhenan Sun[1,2], Xin Li[4], and Xinxin Wan[4(✉)]

[1] Center for Research on Intelligent Perception and Computing, National Laboratory of Pattern Recognition, Institute of Automation, Chinese Academy of Sciences, Beijing, China
{wei.zhang,hongwen.zhang}@cripac.ia.ac.cn,
{qli,fei.liu,znsun}@nlpr.ia.ac.cn
[2] University of Chinese Academy of Sciences, Beijing, China
[3] School of Information Science and Technology, Southwest Jiaotong University, Chengdu, China
[4] The National Computer Network Emergency Response Technical Team/Coordination Center of China, Beijing, China
{lixin,wanxx}@cert.org.cn

Abstract. Head pose estimation and facial landmark localization are crucial problems which have a large amount of applications. We propose a cross-cascading regression network which simultaneously perform head pose estimation and facial landmark detection by integrating information embedded in both head poses and facial landmarks. The network consists of two sub-models, one responsible for head pose estimation and the other for facial landmark localization, and a convolutional layer (channel unification layer) which enables the communication of feature maps generated by both sub-models. To be specific, we adopt integral operation for both pose and landmark coordinate regression, and exploit expectation instead of maximum value to estimate head pose and locate facial landmarks. Results of extensive experiments demonstrate that our approach achieves state-of-the-art performance on the challenging AFLW dataset.

Keywords: Facial landmark detection · Head pose estimation
Cross-cascading regression · Integral regression
Deep convolutional network

1 Introduction

Head pose estimation and facial landmark localization have drawn much attention from computer vision community as they are of great significance and broad applications in problems such as face verification, face animation, and emotion recognition.

© Springer Nature Switzerland AG 2018
J. Zhou et al. (Eds.): CCBR 2018, LNCS 10996, pp. 148–156, 2018.
https://doi.org/10.1007/978-3-319-97909-0_16

Traditionally, head pose estimation and facial landmark localization are treated as independent problems and seldomly be studied jointly.

Thanks to the development of Deep Convolutional Neural Networks (DCNN), there has been significant progress on both head pose estimation and facial landmark localization [1–3] and recent methods generally adopt DCNN as their main building blocks. One of the major advantages of DCNN is its capability of performing end-to-end optimization, especially for multitask problems [4] where related tasks can benefit from each other. Facial landmark detection algorithms could be roughly classified into two categories, detection based methods and regression based methods. At present, most best performing methods are detection based, in which heatmaps indicating the probability of the precense of the facial landmarks are generated and the exact locations of landmarks are determined according to maximum likelihood. However, since the operation of taking maximum value is not differentiable, it breaks the back propagation chain required for end-to-end learning. Intuitively, head pose estimation and facial landmark detection are not isolated problems and low-level facial representations could be shared by the two objectives, thus they attract the attention of many researchers [5,6].

The motivation of this work is to integrate information from head pose and facial landmarks for improving the performance of both facial landmark detection and head pose estimation on arbitrary faces, taking advantages of DCNN. In this work, we propose a novel network architecture named Cross-Cascading Regression network which integrates information from both pose and landmarks, and simultaneously perform head pose estimation and facial landmark detection. Since our network structure is topological symmetric, we expand a single network module by consecutively appending multiple modules together at the end which achieves finer prediction.

To overcome the obstacle of non-differentiable operations, we adopt integral regression [7], and use expectation instead of maximum value to locate landmarks. The loss of the network consists of two components: classification and regression.

The proposed method achieves comparable or better results in comparison with state-of-the-art algorithms on the challenging dataset AFLW [8] for both head pose estimation and facial landmark detection. With more blocks stacked, the performance improves significantly.

2   Related Works

In this section, we introduce some related works in facial landmark localization and head pose estimation. Traditionally, these two problems are addressed as independent problems.

Facial Landmark Localization. There are two distinct families of methods for facial landmark localization: detection based and regression based methods. Detection based methods handle facial landmark detection as a heat map prediction problem, and many explorations have been made such as stacked architectures, residual connections, and multiscale processing. Newell et al. [9] proposed the Stacked Hourglass Network, which incorporates multi-resolution features and improves scores on 2D pose estimation challenges significantly. On the other hand, facial landmark detection is essentially a regression problem. Typically, regression based methods use cascaded regressors to predict land-marks' coordinates directly from intensities of input images. Cao et al. [10] used a vectorial regression function to infer the whole facial shape from the input. Xiong et al. [11] proposed a Supervised Descent Method (SDM) for minimiz-ing a Non-linear Least Squares (NLS) function to optimize the performance of facial feature detection. Although regression based methods have been widely used, the performance is still not satisfactory. The idea that using information from different tasks to constrain the solution space is also a optional approach to achieve better results. Zhang et al. [5] trained a multi-task network which optimizes facial landmark detection together with correlated tasks such as head pose estimation and facial attribute inference. Huang et al. [6] proposed a unified FCN framework named DenseBox to accomplish landmark localization and face detection simultaneously. Wu et al. [12] propose an iterative cascade method for simultaneous facial landmark detection, head pose estimation, and facial defor-mation analysis.

Head Pose Estimation. Head pose estimation usually serves as a by-product of facial landmark detection, which means the precision of head pose estimation is closely related to the accuracy of landmark detection. However, extremely relevant information can disturb prediction precision. It also fails to make the utmost of facial information. The research of independent head pose estimation is rare. Nataniel et al. [3] trained a multi-loss convolutional neural network on 300W-LP to estimate pose directly from input image through joint binned pose classification and regression.

3   Approach

In this section, we present the technical details of Cross-cascading Regression Network. The proposed model consists of two sub-networks, which performs head pose estimation and facial landmark localization simultaneously with intermedi-ate facial feature sharing. Specifically, the network takes a face image as input, and outputs heatmaps where each per-pixel indicates the likelihood for loca-tions of key points. Meanwhile, it outputs three float numbers which indicate the degrees of yaw, pitch and roll, and a combination of information maps for further processing.

3.1   Head Pose Estimation

The pose estimation sub-network aims at getting appraisals of three Euler angles Y, P and R (Y denotes yaw, P denotes pitch and R denotes roll). Since the range of head poses is divided into N classes, we adopt a N-way softmax layer at

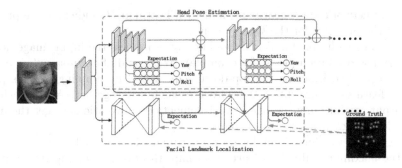

Fig. 1. Our cross-cascading regression network consists of head pose estimation sub-network and facial landmark localization sub-network

the top of the sub-network, generating the probability distribution of the head pose in the input image over N classes.

Instead of inferring head pose from the estimated landmarks, we directly predicted intrinsic Y, P, R from image intensities through joint binned pose classification and regression [3], which avoids irrelevant information damaging the prediction accuracy so that the module has greater robustness.

For network training, an cross-entropy loss is employed:

$$\mathcal{L}_{pc} = -\sum_p y_p \log \hat{y}_p \tag{1}$$

where y_p is the target probability distribution of head pose, and $\hat{y}_p$ is the predicted head pose probability distribution.

Inspired by [3], we also add a regression loss to improve the performance of head pose prediction, which is the Mean Square Error between the predicted pose and ground truth. The total loss of pose estimation sub-network is:

$$\mathcal{L}oss_p = \mathcal{L}_{pe} + \alpha_1 \mathcal{L}_{pc} = \sum_{k=1}^{3} \left\| Q_k - \hat{Q}_k \right\|_2 + \alpha_1 \mathcal{L}_{pc} \tag{2}$$

where α_1 is the balance factor, k indicates the k_{th} pose, Q_k and $\hat{Q}_k$ refers to the predicated and ground truth pose, respectively.

The pose estimation sub-network is built upon ResNet50 [13], with three fully-connected layers appended at the end to predict each angle independently. Pervious convolutional layers of the backbone network are shared by all of these fully-connected layers. By enabling back-propagation of the regression results of head pose angles, network learns to obtain fine-grained pose predictions.

3.2 Facial Landmark Localization

The design of the facial landmark localization sub-network is based on the Hourglass Networks [9] which has shown outstanding results on human pose estimation. We adapted the idea to the case of facial landmark localization. The output of the sub-network are k heatmaps, and each heatmap H_k indicates the probability of the presence for the k_{th} key point.

Several convolutional and max pooling layers process the input image down to a very low resolution (4×4, for example). At the end of down-sampling operations, the network begins the top-down sequence of upsampling. In this procedure, features across different scales are combined together. After reaching the output resolution, we applied two 1-demention convolutions to get the final prediction, which is a set of heat maps.

In general, the final joint location coordinate is obtained as the location with the maximum value in a learnt heatmap. However, obtaining the location possessing the maximum value is non-differentiable, which breaks down the end-to-end training framework. On the other hand, since the size of heatmap is usually smaller than inputs, it also produces quantization error. We modifies the max operation to operation of taking expectation, formulated as

$$J_k = \sum_{p_y=1}^{H} \sum_{p_x=1}^{W} p \cdot \hat{H}_k(p) \tag{3}$$

where H and W are the height and width of predicted heatmap $\hat{H}_k$.

In addition, we adopt the Mean Square Error as a loss function $\mathcal{L}_{lc}$ to calculate the loss between predicted heat maps and ground truth, formulated as follows:

$$\mathcal{L}_{lc} = \sum_{k=1}^{M} \left\| H_k - \hat{H}_k \right\|_2 \tag{4}$$

where M indicates the number of landmarks, $\hat{H}_k$ is the predicted heatmap for the k_{th} landmark.

In a similar way, we added a regression loss to improve the performance of facial landmark estimation, which is the Mean Square Error of predicted landmarks and ground truth. The total loss of landmark sub-network is:

$$\mathcal{L}oss_l = \mathcal{L}_{le} + \alpha_2 \mathcal{L}_{lc} = \sum_{k=1}^{M} \left\| J_k - \hat{J}_k \right\|_2 + \alpha_2 \mathcal{L}_{lc} \tag{5}$$

where α_2 is the balance factor, M indicates the number of landmarks, J_k and $\hat{J}_k$ are the predicated and ground truth landmark coordinates, respectively.

3.3   Cross Cascading Regression

Inspired by [14], in order to make full use of the information of head pose and facial landmarks, we design Cross-cascading Regression Network which connects facial landmark localization and head pose estimation together.

Through several convolutional and max pooling layers, the input image is processed down to a lower resolution, which is applicable for facial landmark localization sub-network and head pose estimation sub-network to take as input.

At the same time, after obtaining the predicted head pose, two deconvolutional layers are added to compute the upsampling features. To match the number of channels of the facial landmark localization's output features and the upsampling features, we set a convolutional layer serves as channel unification layer. With the convolutional layer for channel unification, these feature maps are associated together, which enables the communication between head pose and facial landmark information. The output of head pose estimation sub-network is the summation of facial landmark heatmaps, the upsampling features and intermediate features of head pose estimation sub-network.

We adopt the coarse-to-fine strategy and extend network further by stacking a block at the end, feeding the combination of information maps achieved by former block as input into the following. Moreover, to facilitate the efficiency of information communication, we insert the pose information map into the intermediate structure of hourglass network in the next block. The structure of our network is shown in Fig. 1.

Since Cross-cascading Regression Network consists of two sub-networks completing the head pose estimation and facial landmark localization simultaneously, the loss function must give consideration to the information of both head pose and facial key points, which is formulated as follows:

$$\mathcal{Loss} = \mathcal{Loss}_p + \lambda \cdot \mathcal{Loss}_l \qquad (6)$$

where λ indicates the relative importance of the two terms.

4   Experiment

4.1   Dataset

We train our network on AFLW datasets. AFLW is a challenging dataset which consists of 24386 images of human faces in the wild, with head pose ranging from $0°$ to $120°$ for yaw and up to $90°$ for pitch and roll. It also provides at most 21 key points for each face. In our experiments, we train on a subset of the dataset, which contains nearly 20000 images, and keep the rest for evaluation. For each sample image, the facial area is cropped out and then resized into 256×256 for normalization.

4.2   Implementation Details

The network is implemented using Pytorch framework. The variance σ of the 2D Guassians in heatmap is set to 1. For invisible landmarks, the ideal estimations are defined as 0. During training, the learning rate is fixed to $2.5e-4$. Instead of taking the max activated location as the final prediction, we use the expectations of the output heatmaps to predict landmarks, and the predicted pose is the expectation of each output angle computed based on the output classification features.

4.3   Evalution Metric

To evaluate a facial landmark localization algorithm, we adopt the widely used Normalized Mean Error (NME) as the evaluation metric, which can be formulated as follows:

$$NME = \frac{1}{n} \sum_{i=1}^{n} \frac{\|x_i - x_i^*\|_2}{l} \tag{7}$$

where l denotes the normalized distance and n is the number of facial landmarks involved in the evaluation. In our experiment, l is the width (or height) of the face bounding box which is square for test samples in AFLW, and n indicates the number of visible landmarks.

4.4   Comparison with State of the Arts

We compare our Cross-cascading Regression network (CCR) with state-of-the-art head pose estimation and facial landmark detection approaches, results are shown in Tables 1 and 2. The result shows that our Cross-cascading regression Network achieves better or comparable performance when compared with state-of-the-art methods, which justifies the effectiveness of combining pose and landmark information explicitly.

Table 1. Mean Average Error (MAE) of Euler angles across different methods on AFLW.

Methods	Yaw	Pitch	Roll	MAE
Multi-loss ResNet50 [3] (α=1)	6.26	5.89	3.82	5.324
Multi-loss AlexNet [3] (α=1)	7.79	7.41	6.05	7.084
KEPLER [1]	6.45	**5.85**	8.75	7.017
Patacchiola, Cangelosi [15]	11.04	7.15	4.40	7.530
CCR (two blocks stacked)	**5.22**	**5.85**	**2.51**	**4.527**

Fig. 2. Results of landmark detection and pose estimation generated from Cross-cascading Regression network. The red axis points towards the front of the face, green pointing downward and blue pointing to the side. (Color figure online)

Table 2. Normalized Mean Error (NME) of facial landmark detection across different methods on AFLW.

Methods	NME
CDM [16]	12.44
RCPR [17]	7.85
ESR [10]	8.24
Hyperface [18]	4.26
FRTFA [19]	4.23
PIFA [20]	6.80
CCL [21]	5.85
CCR (two blocks stacked)	5.72

5   Conclusion

In this work, we propose a novel network architecture named Cross-cascading Regression Network which consists of two sub-networks. The proposed model performs head pose estimation and facial landmark localization simultaneously with compact information communication. We extend our network architecture by stacking multiple blocks end-to-end, feeding the combination of information maps achieved by former block as input into the next, which achieves a coarse-to-fine prediction scheme. Our loss function consists of regression loss and classification loss, and the prediction of pose and landmarks are calculated by binned results. The proposed method achieves superior, or at least comparable performance in comparison with state-of-the-art methods on challenging datasets AFLW, which demonstrates the effectiveness of combining information from differenct tasks and the significance of cascading.

Acknowledgments. This work is supported by the National Natural Science Foundation of China (Grant No. 61427811, 61273272, 61573360).

References

1. Kumar, A., Alavi, A., Chellappa, R.: KEPLER: keypoint and pose estimation of unconstrained faces by learning efficient H-CNN regressors. In: IEEE International Conference on Automatic Face and Gesture Recognition (FG) (2017)
2. Amador, E., Valle, R., Buenaposada, J.M., Baumela, L.: Benchmarking head pose estimation in-the-wild. In: Mendoza, M., Velastín, S. (eds.) Progress in Pattern Recognition, Image Analysis, Computer Vision, and Applications (2018)
3. Ruiz, N., Chong, E., Rehg, J.M.: Fine-grained head pose estimation without keypoints. In: IEEE Conference on Computer Vision and Pattern Recognition (CVPR Workshops) (2018)
4. Kokkinos, I.: UberNet: training a 'universal' convolutional neural network for low-, mid-, and high-level vision using diverse datasets and limited memory. In: IEEE Conference on Computer Vision and Pattern Recognition (CVPR) (2017)

5. Zhang, Z., Luo, P., Loy, C.C., Tang, X.: Facial landmark detection by deep multi-task learning. In: European Conference on Computer Vision (ECCV) (2014)
6. Huang, L., Yang, Y., Deng, Y., Yu, Y.: DenseBox: unifying landmark localization with end to end object detection, vol. abs/1509.04874 (2015)
7. Sun, X., Xiao, B., Liang, S., Wei, Y.: Integral human pose regression, volume arXiv:abs/1711.08229 (2017)
8. Köstinger, M., Wohlhart, P., Roth, P.M., Bischof, H.: Annotated facial landmarks in the wild: a large-scale, real-world database for facial landmark localization. In: IEEE International Conference on Computer Vision Workshops (ICCV Workshops) (2011)
9. Newell, A., Yang, K., Deng, J.: Stacked hourglass networks for human pose estimation. In: European Conference on Computer Vision (ECCV) (2016)
10. Cao, X., Wei, Y., Wen, F., Sun, J.: Face alignment by explicit shape regression. In: IEEE Conference on Computer Vision and Pattern Recognition (CVPR) (2012)
11. Xiong, X., De la Torre, F.: Supervised descent method and its applications to face alignment. In: IEEE Conference on Computer Vision and Pattern Recognition (CVPR) (2013)
12. Wu, Y., Gou, C., Ji, Q.: Simultaneous facial landmark detection, pose and deformation estimation under facial occlusion. In: IEEE Conference on Computer Vision and Pattern Recognition, (CVPR) (2017)
13. He, K., Zhang, X., Ren, S., Sun, J.: Deep residual learning for image recognition. In: IEEE Conference on Computer Vision and Pattern Recognition (CVPR) (2016)
14. Güler, R.A., Neverova, N., Kokkinos, I.: DensePose: dense human pose estimation in the wild. In: IEEE Conference on Computer Vision and Pattern Recognition (CVPR) (2018)
15. Head pose estimation in the wild using convolutional neural networks and adaptive gradient methods. In: Pattern Recognition (2017)
16. Yu, X., Huang, J., Zhang, S., Yan, W., Metaxas, D.N.: Pose-free facial landmark fitting via optimized part mixtures and cascaded deformable shape model. In: IEEE International Conference on Computer Vision (ICCV) (2013)
17. Burgos-Artizzu, X.P., Perona, P., Dollár, P.: Robust face landmark estimation under occlusion. In: IEEE International Conference on Computer Vision (ICCV) (2013)
18. Ranjan, R., Patel, V.M., Chellappa, R.: Hyperface: a deep multi-task learning framework for face detection, landmark localization, pose estimation, and gender recognition. In: IEEE Transactions on Pattern Analysis and Machine Intelligence (TPAMI) (2017)
19. Bhagavatula, C., Zhu, C., Luu, K., Savvides, M.: Faster than real-time facial alignment: a 3d spatial transformer network approach in unconstrained poses. In: International Conference on Computer Vision (ICCV) (2017)
20. Jourabloo, A., Liu, X.: Pose-invariant 3d face alignment. In: IEEE International Conference on Computer Vision (ICCV) (2016)
21. Zhu, S., Li, C., Loy, C.C., Tang, X.: Unconstrained face alignment via cascaded compositional learning. In: IEEE Conference on Computer Vision and Pattern Recognition (CVPR) (2016)

Real Time Violence Detection
Based on Deep Spatio-Temporal Features

Qing Xia$^{(\boxtimes)}$, Ping Zhang$^{(\boxtimes)}$, JingJing Wang, Ming Tian, and Chun Fei

School of Optoelectronic Science and Engineering of UESTC,
University of Electronic Science and Technology of China, Chengdu, China
qingxiacool@gmail.com, pingzh@uestc.edu.cn

Abstract. Typical manually-selected features are insufficient to reliably detect violence actions. In this paper, we present a violence detection model that is based on a bi-channels convolutional neural network (CNN) and the support vector machine (SVM). The major contributions are twofolds: (1) we fork the original frames and the differential images into the proposed bi-channels CNN to obtain the appearance features and the motion features respectively. (2) The linear SVMs are adopted to classify the features and a label fusion approach is proposed to improve detection performance by integrating the appearance and motion information. We compared the proposed model with several state-of-the-art methods on two datasets. The results are promising and the proposed method can achieve real-time performance of 30 fps.

Keywords: Violence detection
Bi-channels convolution neural network
Deep spatio-temporal features · Label fusion

1 Introduction

Public security affairs have been drawing more and more attention to communities. Violence detection in videos is of great importance to make people alert in scenes such as streets, schools, and prisons. Due to negative factors, such as the low resolution of surveillance video, the varing illumination, occlusion and complex backgrounds, it is difficult to detect violence actions. Although great progress has been made in this domain in the latest decade, there are still a long way to go to solve this problem.

Currently, there are two feature description methods for video violent detection, based on the global features and the local features respectively. Local feature description methods are most based on how to detect the Spatio-Temporal Interest Points (STIP) [1], the Histogram of Oriented Gradient (HOG) [2] or Histograms of Oriented Optical Flow (HOF) [3] descriptors. De Souza et al. [4] found that spatio-temporal features outperform pure spatial features through comparing the STIP and the scale invariant feature transform (SIFT) [5]. However, Hassner et al. [6] found that such feature descriptors cannot work well on

© Springer Nature Switzerland AG 2018
J. Zhou et al. (Eds.): CCBR 2018, LNCS 10996, pp. 157–165, 2018.
https://doi.org/10.1007/978-3-319-97909-0_17

crowded scenes like the Crowd Violence dataset they presented. Nievas et al. [7] that Motion SIFT [8] outperforms the STIP. Xu et al. [9] further improved these works by substituting the bag-of-words step with a sparse coding scheme to encode MoSIFT features for violent detection.

Although the local features methods demonstrate good performance on providing accurate representation of the motion, they may not accurate enough when the scene is crowded. Therefore, global feature based methods have been proposed. Wang et al. [10] used histograms based on optical flow for abnormal behavior recognition. Cong et al. [11] proposed a new feature descriptor: Multiscale Histogram of Optical Flow (MHOF). To detect abnormal behaviors in crowed scene, Gnanavel et al. [12] combined MHOF with Edge Oriented Histogram (EOH) to obtain the motion context. Other methods that are based on Histogram of Optical Flow Orientation (HOFO) descriptor were also proposed to detect abnormal behavior in crowded scenes.

The existing local and global features methods work fine on some scenes, but they are designed subjectively for specific tasks, which are limited in other applications. In recent years, the deep convolution neural networks methods have been developed to deal with the violence detection. Simonyan et al. [13] proposed a two-steam convolution neural network (CNN) for action recognition. Ding et al [14] proposed a 3D ConvNet method to detect violence action. Dong et al. [15] proposed a method for the violence detection by using the information of acceleration. Meng et al. [16] integrated the trajectory information into the CNN to improve the performance of violence detection.

In this paper, we present a method that is based on the bi-channels CNN with SVM. The contributions in this paper can be summarized as follows:

- A violence detection model based on a bi-channels convolutional neural network (CNN) and SVM is proposed. Features from different layers of the two channel network are accordingly compared to choose the best ones.
- A new label fusion is first proposed, which effectively combines the appearance and motion information to improve the accuracy of the detection.
- Real-time performance is achieved and the accuracy is superior to the most of the state-of-the- art methods.

The remainder is organized as follows: the proposed framework is introduced in Sect. 2, then experiments are presented in Sect. 3. The conclusion is drawn in Sect. 4.

2   Our Approach

Figure 1 shows that a bi-channels network framework for violence detetion is proposed, which consists of three parts: feature extraction, SVM training and label fusion. Firstly, two features are extracted based on the structure of the bi-channels CNN. The original video frame is used as one channel input to extract the appearance features and the difference of adjacent frames is used as another input to extract the motion feature. Then, two linear SVMs are adopted as the appearance and motion classifier respectively. Finally, the violence detection result is obtained by using a label fusion method which combines the appearance information with the motion information. Detailed description of each part is presented in the following subsections.

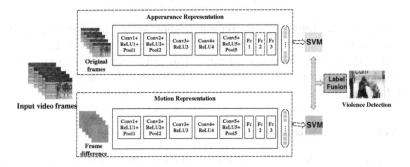

Fig. 1. An overview of the proposed bi-channels network framework.

2.1   Feature Extraction

Still frames in videos always carry a lot of information about scenes and objects in videos. Some violence always occurs in specific scenes. For instance, supposing someone holding a big stick or a gun is fighting with someone else, this violence is close to the scene with the big stick or the gun. The deep CNN which operates on the still frames has effectively performed in many visual tasks such as image classification [17]. In this paper, we use the pre-trained VGG-f model on ImageNet dataset to obtain appearance on still frames. The so-called appearance feature, as shown in Fig. 2a, is obtained by directly using the original images as the input of the first channel. The feature extracted in this way is called the appearance feature.

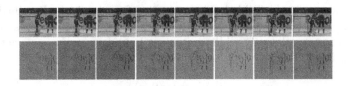

Fig. 2. Schematic of appearance and motion images. (a) First row: appearance images. (b) Second row: motion images.

Since violence is always described with motion information like the kick or hit on purpose. The second channel of the framework aims to learn the effective motion features which have got excellent performance in action classification. Christoph et al. proposed two-steam network to realize action recognize and they used optical flow map as one input of one steam network in [18], but its disadvantage is that the computation is complex and difficult to achieve real-time performance. In order to improve efficiency, we use the difference of adjacent frames instead of optical flow map to describe the motion information as another input:

$$F_{input} = F_t - F_{t-1}, \tag{1}$$

where F_{input} is the difference of adjacent frames as another channel input, F_t is the current frame and F_{t-1} is the previous frame. As shown in Fig. 2(b), the image after the frame difference contains the difference between the original adjacent images. The extracted feature from the frame difference is so-called motion feature.

2.2   Network Architecture

In this paper, we use the public pre-trained VGG-f [19] network model to extract appearance features and motion features.

Table 1. The architecture of VGG-f

Arch.	Conv1	Conv2	Conv3	Conv4	Conv5	Full6	Full7	Full8
CNN	$64 \times 11 \times 11$	$256 \times 5 \times 5$	$256 \times 3 \times 3$	$256 \times 3 \times 3$	$256 \times 3 \times 3$	4096	4096	1000
-	st.4, pad 0	st.1, pad 2	st.1, pad 1	st.1, pad 1	st.1, pad 1	Drop-	Drop-	soft-
F	LRN, ×2pool	LRN, ×3	-	-	×2 pool	out	out	max

As shown in Table 1, the architecture contains 5 convolution layers (Conv 1–5) and 3 fully-connected layers (Full 1–3). The details of each of the convolutional layers are given in three sub-rows: the first specifies the number of convolution filters and their receptive field size as *"num × size × size"*; the second indicates the convolution stride ("st.") and spatial padding ("pad"); the third row indicates if Local Response Normalisation (LRN) [17] is applied, and the max-pooling downsampling factor. The dimension of each fully-connected layer is also shown in the Table 1. The activation function is the Rectified Linear Uints (ReLU) function because the ReLU function has the advantages of unilateral suppression, a relatively wide excitement boundary, and sparse activation, as shown in Eq. (2).

$$f(x) = max(0, x) \tag{2}$$

As shown in Fig. 2, the original video frames and its adjacent frames differences are respectively used as the inputs of the bi-channels neural network to obtain appearance and motion feature vectors.

2.3   Classifier

For violence detection in videos, it is a binary classification problem. To reduce the influence of non-linearity, we choose the linear SVM as classifier. As shown in Fig. 1, we use two SVM classifiers to train and test separately, thus two labels are obtained by different classifiers: $label_a$ represents the classification result of appearance feature while $label_m$ represents the classification result of motion feature.

2.4   Label Fusion

A new measure of label fusion is proposed to combine the appearance information with the motion information as shown in Eq. (3).

$$Label_F = threshold_\delta(\beta * label_a + (1 - \beta) * label_m) \tag{3}$$

$$threshold_t(f) = \begin{cases} 1 & if\,(f \geq t) \\ 0 & if\,(f < t) \end{cases}, \tag{4}$$

where $label_a$ and $label_m$ respectively represent the labels of appearance feature and motion feature, δ represents the threshold value for label fusion, and $Label_F$ represents the label after fusion. β represents the weighting coefficient, and the larger its value, the greater the influence of the apparent feature on the violence detection. Equation (4) is a simple threshold function, if the value f is bigger than the threshold t, then the result would be 1.

$$Label = threshold_\tau(\sum_T Label_F) \tag{5}$$

In our model, the violence is continuous in time domain, which means for the $Label_F$, the label of violent behavior can not exist in isolation. Therefore, a threshold τ is taken on the time axis to eliminate these isolated points. If the detected violence is less than the threshold τ within the length of time T, then the detection result is considered an wrongly predicted point as shown in Eq. (5). In general, the larger the value of T, the longer the prediction of the algorithm will be delayed.

3   Experiment and Result

3.1   Data Sets

We conducted our experiments on two datasets: Hockey Fight [7] and Violent Crowd [6] dataset respectively. Figure 3 shows some sample frames from these datasets.

The Hockey Fights dataset contains 1,000 short videos about the National Hockey League (NHL), each video consists of 50 frames with a resolution of

Fig. 3. Sample frames of violent scenes from two data sets. (a) First row: Hockey Fight. (b) Second row: Crowd Violence.

360×288 pixels. This dataset has several challenges: blurring caused by differences in perspective, camera movement, and other people appearing in the video, especially fast-moving arms and legs, also presents a challenge to frame-based motion extraction.

Crowd violence is a dataset released by Hassner et al., which consists of 246 video sequences collected from YouTube which have been captured in a variety of arenas (as opposed to the Hockey Fight). These videos have a resolution of 320×240 and video lengths range from 50 to 150 frames. The challenge with this dataset is the image quality which is affected by compression artifacts, motion blur, text overlay, flash lights, and varying temporal resolutions.

3.2   Implement Details

The VGG-f model used in this paper is pre-trained on ImageNet dataset. As shown in Table 1, the VGG-f model contains three fully-connected layers and the output of each fully-connected layer can be the extracted features. In order to select the most suitable feature as output, we have compared the classification accuracy of each fully-connected layer as a feature.

When verifying the performance of different layer features, 10-fold cross-validation method is used. The classification results of 10 times are shown in Fig. 4, and the average comparison of 10-fold cross-validation is shown in Fig. 4. It can be seen that the classification accuracy of the first fully-connected layer as a feature is higher than that of the other layers. Thus, the output of the first fully-connected layer of VGG-f is selected.

In order to verity the feasibility of the fusion framework, the appearance feature and the motion feature are separately tested as separate features. As shown in Table 2, the detection accuracy of the fusion method is superior to that of the one feature method. This indicates that the label fusion method in this paper is significantly effective.

The fusion coefficient β used in this paper is tested on two different data sets respectively, the result shows that when the value of the fusion coefficient β is 0.5, the accuracy rate will be the highest. The threshold δ is given an empirical value of 0.4. As to the isolated points, the length of time T selected in this paper is 20 frames and the threshold τ is 8 frames, which means the delay time of this method is about one second.

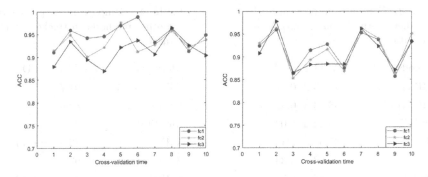

Fig. 4. Classification results from different fully-connected layers on two datasets.

Table 2. Performance comparison of using different features on two datasets.

ACC ± SD(%)	Hockey fight	Violent crowd
Appearance accuracy	94.72 ± 3.6	91.46 ± 2.69
Motion accuracy	84.56 ± 4.85	75.87 ± 4.07
Fusion accuracy	**95.90 ± 3.53**	**93.25 ± 2.34**

3.3 Experimental Results

In this section, we compare the proposed method with the state-of-the-art methods on the Hockey Fights and Crowd Violence dataset. Not only the traditional spatio-temporal features based method such as HOG [2], HOF [2], MoSIFT [8], ViF [6] and LaSIFT [20], but also Two-streams [13] and two-steam+IDT [16] these CNN-based approach are compared.

The Crowd Violence dataset is especially designed to evaluate violence in crowded scene. Table 3 shows the comparison results on this dataset between the proposed and other methods. Our proposed method outperforms the others, especially for those spatiotemporal features (HOF, HOG, MoSIFT). Spatio-temporal descriptors perform bad mainly since crowded scenes seriously affect their needed scene and motion information. The proposed bi-channels network performs much better than HOF and HOG features, which proves that deep-learned features learn more discriminative information than hand-crafted features and more robust even in crowded scenes. We also compare our method with methods based on CNN. As the results shown, the proposed method in this paper also outperforms these methods on this crowded dataset.

The Hockey Fight dataset is especially used to evaluate violence detection systems in uncrowded scenes. Table 4 shows the comparison results of the proposed method and other methods on the Hockey Fight dataset. It can be seen that the performance of the proposed method is significantly higher than that based on the traditional hand-crafted features. Compared with the CNN-based methods, the proposed method performs better than [13] because the proposed

Table 3. Comparison of proposed and other methods on Crowd Violence dataset.

Methods	ACC ± SD(%)
STIP (HoG)	57.43 ± 0.37
STIP (HoF)	58.53 ± 0.32
MoSIFT	83.42 ± 8.03
ViF	81.3 ± 0.21
Two-streams	91.83 ± 3.34
LaSIFT	93.12 ± 8.77
Two-stream+IDT	92.5
Proposed	**93.25 ± 2.34**

Table 4. Comparison of proposed and other methods on Hockey Fight dataset.

Methods	ACC ± SD(%)
STIP (HoG)	91.7
STIP (HoF)	88.6
MoSIFT	90.9
ViF	82.90 ± 0.14
Two-streams	93
LaSIFT	94.42 ± 2.82
Two-stream+IDT	**98**
Proposed	95.90 ± 3.53

label fusion method effectively combines the appearance and motion feature. However, the performance of the proposed method is not good enough compared with the method of [16]. That is because this dataset contains people violence behaviors at a comparatively short distance. The method of [16] performs better since the trajectory information is utilized, which takes advantage of the method of improved trajectory to capture long-term action information.

This proposed method is tested on platform i5 6300HQ and can reach a real time performance about 30 fps.

4   Conclusion

In this paper, a method based on bi-channels CNN is proposed for violence detection. Original frames and differential images are used as inputs of bi-channels neural network to obtain appearance features and motion features respectively, which effectively utilizes the spatio-temporal features in the videos. Additionally, two linear SVMs are adopted to classify the features and a label fusion approach is proposed to improve the accuracy of violence detection in videos. The experimental results on different databases verify that the proposed method outperforms the state-of-the-art methods in various realistic scenes. It is noted that the proposed method can achieve real-time performance. In the future we will consider more efficient ways to extract spatio-temporal features and more reliable fusion approaches.

References

1. Laptev, I., Lindeberg, T.: On space-time interest points. Int. J. Comput. Vision **64**(2–3), 107–123 (2005)
2. Dalal, N., Triggs, B.: Histograms of oriented gradients for human detection. IEEE Computer Society Conference on Computer Vision and Pattern Recognition. In: CVPR 2005, pp. 886–893 (2005)

3. Dalal, N., Triggs, B., Schmid, C.: Human detection using oriented histograms of flow and appearance. In: Leonardis, A., Bischof, H., Pinz, A. (eds.) ECCV 2006. LNCS, vol. 3952, pp. 428–441. Springer, Heidelberg (2006). https://doi.org/10. 1007/11744047_33

4. De Souza, F.D.M., Chvez, G.C., Do Valle Jr., E.A., Arajo, A.D.A.: Violence detection in video using spatio-temporal features. In: Graphics, Patterns and Images, pp. 224–230 (2011)

5. Lowe, D.G.: Distinctive image features from scale-invariant keypoints. Int. J. Comput. Vision **60**(2), 91–110 (2004)

6. Hassner, T., Itcher, Y., Kliper-Gross, O.: Violent flows: real-time detection of violent crowd behavior. In: Computer Vision and Pattern Recognition Workshops, pp. 1–6 (2012)

7. Bermejo Nievas, E., Deniz Suarez, O., Bueno García, G., Sukthankar, R.: Violence detection in video using computer vision techniques. In: Real, P., Diaz-Pernil, D., Molina-Abril, H., Berciano, A., Kropatsch, W. (eds.) CAIP 2011. LNCS, vol. 6855, pp. 332–339. Springer, Heidelberg (2011). https://doi.org/10.1007/978-3-642-23678-5_39

8. Chen, M.Y., Hauptmann, A.: Mosift: recognizing human actions in surveillance videos. Ann. Pharmacother. **39**(1), 150–152 (2009)

9. Xu, L., Gong, C., Yang, J., Wu, Q., Yao, L.: Violent video detection based on mosift feature and sparse coding, pp. 3538–3542 (2014)

10. Wang, T., Snoussi, H.: Detection of abnormal visual events via global optical flow orientation histogram. IEEE Trans. Inf. Forensics Secur. **9**(6), 988–998 (2014)

11. Cong, Y., Yuan, J., Liu, J.: Abnormal event detection in crowded scenes using sparse representation. Pattern Recogn. **46**(7), 1851–1864 (2013)

12. Gnanavel, V.K., Srinivasan, A.: Abnormal event detection in crowded video scenes. In: Satapathy, S.C., Biswal, B.N., Udgata, S.K., Mandal, J.K. (eds.) Proceedings of the 3rd International Conference on Frontiers of Intelligent Computing: Theory and Applications (FICTA) 2014. AISC, vol. 328, pp. 441–448. Springer, Cham (2015). https://doi.org/10.1007/978-3-319-12012-6_48

13. Simonyan, K., Zisserman, A.: Two-stream convolutional networks for action recognition in videos, vol. 1, pp. 568–576 (2014)

14. Tran, D., Bourdev, L., Fergus, R., Torresani, L., Paluri, M.: Learning spatiotemporal features with 3D convolutional networks. iN: International Conference on Computer Vision, ICCV 2015, pp. 4489–4497 (2015)

15. Dong, Z., Qin, J., Wang, Y.: Multi-stream deep networks for person to person violence detection in videos, vol. 662, pp. 517–531 (2016)

16. Meng, Z., Yuan, J., Li, Z.: Trajectory-pooled deep convolutional networks for violence detection in videos. In: Liu, M., Chen, H., Vincze, M. (eds.) ICVS 2017. LNCS, vol. 10528, pp. 437–447. Springer, Cham (2017). https://doi.org/10.1007/ 978-3-319-68345-4_39

17. Krizhevsky, A., Sutskever, I., Hinton, G.E.: Imagenet classification with deep convolutional neural networks. Commun. ACM **60**(6), 84–90 (2017)

18. Feichtenhofer, C., Pinz, A., Zisserman, A.: Convolutional two-stream network fusion for video action recognition, pp. 1933–1941, January 2016

19. Chatfield, K., Simonyan, K., Vedaldi, A., Zisserman, A.: Return of the devil in the details: delving deep into convolutional nets (2014)

20. Senst, T., Eiselein, V., Kuhn, A., Sikora, T.: Crowd violence detection using global motion-compensated lagrangian features and scale-sensitive video-level representation. IEEE Trans. Inf. Forensics Secur. **12**(12), 2945–2956 (2017)

Selecting the Effective Regions for Gait Recognition by Sparse Representation

Jiaqi Tan[1], Jiawei Wang[2], and Shiqi Yu[1(✉)]

[1] College of Computer Science and Software Engineering, Shenzhen University,
Shenzhen 518060, China
chriatinatan0704@gmail.com, shiqi.yu@szu.edu.cn
[2] College of Physics and Energy, Shenzhen University, Shenzhen 518060, China
2014180065@email.szu.edu.cn

Abstract. In gait recognition the variations of clothing and carrying conditions can change the human body shape greatly. So the gait feature extracted from human body images will be greatly affected and the performance will decrease drastically. Thus in this paper, we proposed one gait recognition method to improve the robustness towards these variations. The main idea is to select effective regions by sparse representation. If the region can be represented by features from gait data without variations, that means the region is not occluded by some objects. Experimental results on a large gait dataset show that the proposed method can achieve high recognition rates, and even outperform some deep learning based methods.

Keywords: Gait recognition · Sparse representation · HOG features
Gait energy image

1 Introduction

Gait is a behavioral biometric that can identify different persons. Compared with face, iris and finger print, gait can be acquired at a distance and gait feature can be extracted from low resolution images. Based on these advantages, gait recognition can be applied in various kinds of fields especially in video surveillance. In the past few decades, great strides have been made in gait recognition. Many gait recognition methods have been proposed. Methods to gait recognition mainly fall into two categories, one is model-based methods [10,12,14,23] which built models for human bodies and movements of different body parts. The other one is appearance-based (model-free) approaches [15,20,21,24] which extracts the gait feature directly from images. Appearance-based methods are more popular in the past few years. And the Gait Energy Image(GEI) [5] can be regarded as the most popular gait feature.

Gait recognition is still a challenging problem due to the variations in clothing conditions, carrying conditions, views, etc. In recent years, there are many methods based on deep learning which were proposed to improve the recognition

© Springer Nature Switzerland AG 2018
J. Zhou et al. (Eds.): CCBR 2018, LNCS 10996, pp. 166–174, 2018.
https://doi.org/10.1007/978-3-319-97909-0_18

rate. Yu *et al.* [18] employed one deep model based on auto-encoder to extract invariant gait feature. In the method GaitGAN [17] a GAN model is trained as a regressor to generate invariant gait images that is side view images with normal clothing and without carrying bags. In [15] it also shows that CNNs can achieve encouraging results.

Another category of methods to reduce the variations effect in gait recognition is based on sparse representation. In [4] sparse representation is used to create new distance metric to remove the polluted part of GEI. Xu *et al.* [16] used locality-constrained group sparse representation (LGSR) based on previous sparse methods as a classification method. This method has a good enforcement on both the group sparsity and local smooth sparsity, which leads to a robust performance on low-resolution datasets. In [8], Lai *et al.* focus on the matrix representation-based human gait recognition and propose a sparse bilinear discriminant analysis (SBDA) method based on sparse algorithm in [9]. These methods based on sparse representation have a natural advantage to remove the occlusions of clothings and carried objects. Most previous methods based on sparse representation take the whole human body image as a sample in a high dimensional space to find a sparse linear combination of samples in the gallery set.

In this paper, a gait recognition method based on sparse representation is proposed. The difference between most other related methods and our method is that the samples we used are pixels but not the whole images. We use sparse representation to find the effective regions in images to remove the occlusion regions automatically. The experimental results show that the proposed method is effective to remove variations. Besides, we did not use the original GEI as the features to sparse analysis beacuse we found that HOG [2] owns a better capability for gait recognition.

The rest of the paper is organized as follows. Section 2 describes the proposed sparse representation for variants reduction. Experiments and evaluations are presented in Sect. 3. Section 4 concludes the paper.

2   Proposed Method

The proposed method mainly focuses on the variations of clothing and carrying conditions. The present of different clothing and carrying objects can change the shape of the human bodies. We want to analyze the contribution of different human body parts, and remove the body parts which have less and even negative effect. Our idea is straightforward but how to evaluate and select the parts is challenging.

The framework of the feature extraction is shown in Fig. 1. Firstly we take GEI (gait energy image) [5] as the raw feature for its robustness. Later on we found that HOG (Histogram of oriented gradients) [2] is has greater capability for gait recognition. So we extract HOG from GEI. The most important part of the proposed method is how to evaluate the contribution of different parts. Thus, sparse representation is involved to select effective regions.

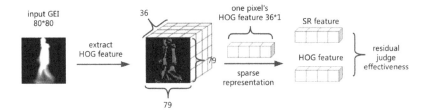

Fig. 1. The procedure of extracting effective regions

2.1 Gait Energy Image

GEI (gait energy image) [5] is the average of silhouettes in a gait video sequences. It has been widely used in many methods in gait recognition for its robustness and capability of distinguish different persons. It is defined in the following equation.

$$G(x,y) = \frac{1}{N} \sum_{t=1}^{N} I(x,y,t) \tag{1}$$

where N determines how many frames are involved in the sequence, I represents an human body silhouette image, t indicates the tth frame of the sequence and x and y are the spacial coordinates.

2.2 HOG Feature

GEI image can be accurately described by the distribution of intensity gradients or edge directions, and HOG [2] can count the occurrences of gradient orientation of an image locally. HOG is successfully used in many fields to describe image regions. Assuming that the size of our input image is $k \times k$ pixel, and we set the cell size of HOG to 1 pixel and use the default block size (2×2 cells per block). The number of directions is set to 9.

The gradient value and direction of pixel at (x, y) are:

$$\begin{cases} \Delta G(x,y) = \sqrt{G_x(x,y)^2 + G_y(x,y)^2} \\ \theta(x,y) = \tan^{-1} \dfrac{G_y(x,y)}{G_x(x,y)} \end{cases} \tag{2}$$

Finally, we cast the gradient direction of pixel at (x, y) into $180°$ and count the occurrences of gradient orientation of each pixel. For an input GEI image whose size is $k \times k$ pixels, the size of its output HOG feature vector should be $(k-1) \times (k-1) \times 36$.

2.3   Orthogonal Matching Pursuit for Sparse Representation

Simply use the HOG feature in gait can not perform well under clothing and carrying conditions because HOG can not remove the occlusion caused by clothing and carried objects. In order to find the effective regions, we introduced Orthogonal Matching Pursuit (OMP) [11] algorithm and composed a best matching projection (BMP) to evaluate the effectiveness of different positions. As mentioned above, for an input GEI the size of its HOG feature would be $(k-1)\times(k-1)\times 36$. Each pixel can be represented by a vector of length 36. In order to analyze the effectiveness of each pixel's HOG we applied OMP algorithm [11] on its HOG feature.

OMP algorithm is a sparse approximation algorithm which can find the BMP (best matching projection) of multidimensional data onto the span of an overcomplete dictionary A. For analyzing the carrying or clothing condition image, if the input pixel can be effectively represented by samples in the dictionary A then we can conclude that there is not occlusion at the position. Otherwise, it can be in the occlusion region by variations of clothing or carrying.

To evaluate the effectiveness of the pixel located at (i,j) from the probe set, all the HOG feature vectors at pixel (i,j) from the gallery set as the dictionary $A = [a_1, a_2, \cdots, a_n]$. If y is the feature vector of one sample at (i,j) from the probe set, if we want to get the BMP of pixel y, we need to solve the following equation:

$$y = Ax \tag{3}$$

where x is the coefficient vector $([x_1, x_2, \cdots, x_n]$, x_i represents the ith coefficient according to sample pixel a_i).

The residual between y's BMP and y is:

$$\|y - Ax\|^2 \tag{4}$$

OMP can find the best x to minimize the residual. It is a greedy algorithm to find a non-zero element for x each time. Considering that our final goal is to evaluate the effectiveness of the pixel, thus we do not need to get the minimal residual by more non-zero elements in x. So we set the number of non-zero elements in x to 10 and get the BMP using the corresponding 10 samples. The implementation of OMP algorithm steps are shown in Algorithm 1.

After 10 loops we can have a residual value of $\|y - Ax\|^2$ for this position. Then we applied the OMP algorithm on each pixel of all the GEI images in the probe set and add up the residual value by each pixel and get a $(k-1) \times (k-1)$ residual sum output. Then we set a threshold for residual sum value as 35 experimentally and select the valid pixel according to residual sum output. Figure 2 shows the valid pixel's template for clothing condition and carrying condition under $90°$.

Finally, we applied the template on all the relevant condition GEI images, set the invalid pixel's data in both probe set and gallery set to zero and put the final data to the classifier. The classifier we used is the nearest neighbor classifier with L1 distance.

Algorithm 1. OMP algorithm

Input: Testing pixel HOG feature: y, dictionary: A

Output: coefficient x for sparse representation, residual value e between y and Ax

1: initial: $e_n = y$ and $n = 1$
2: **repeat**
3:    Find $a_i \in A$ with maximum inner product $| < e_n, a_i > |$
4:    $a_n \leftarrow < e_n, a_{\gamma_n} > /||a_{\gamma_n}||^2$;
5:    $e_{n+1} \leftarrow e_n - a_n a_{\gamma_n}$;
6:    $n \leftarrow n + 1$;
7: **until** $n >$Overlap threshold

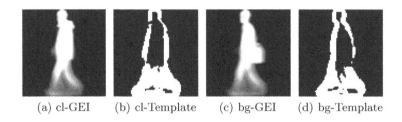

(a) cl-GEI   (b) cl-Template   (c) bg-GEI   (d) bg-Template

Fig. 2. Valid pixel's template for clothing and carrying condition at view 90°

3 Experiments and Analysis

3.1 Dataset

The proposed method was evaluated by the CASIA-B dataset [19]. In CASIA-B dataset there are 124 subjects. For each subject there are 6 sequences of normal walking condition, 2 sequences of walking in a coat and 2 sequences of walking with a bag. It is a suitable dataset to evaluate the robustness to variations of clothing and carrying conditions.

3.2 Experimental Design

At the beginning of the experiment, considering the size of the input image is relatively small so we set the cell size of the HOG as 1 pixel, set the block size as 2 cells and stride as 1 pixel, then we can get a $79 \times 79 \times 36$ HOG feature vector from an input GEI image (the size of the input GEI image is 80×80). When applying Sparse representation algorithm we set the threshold of residual value as 35. We designed three experiments A, B and C to evaluate the proposed method in walking normally (NM), dressed in a coat (CL) and carried a bag (BG) respectively.

Experiment A is to evaluate the recognition accuracy under normal walking condition. The first 4 normal sequences are put into the gallery set, and the remaining 2 are put into the probe. Since we mainly focus on the variations of clothing and carrying objects, the experiments are carried out at 11 views. But there is not view variation. That means the view angles of the probe and the gallery are the same.

Experiment B is similar with Experiment A. The only difference is that the data in the probe set is gait with the variation of clothing. This experiment can be used to evaluate the robustness to the variation of clothing.

Experiment C is designed to evaluate the variation of carrying objects. The 2 sequences of carrying a bag of each subject are put into the probe set.

3.3 Comparisons with the Original HOG

Firstly we want to prove the effectiveness of the sparse presentation in the proposed method. So we carried out the three experiments using the original HOG feature and the nearest neighbor classifier. The experimental results are listed in Table 1. There are 11 experiments for each experimental design. So there are 33 experiments altogether. The average classification rates are also listed in the last column in the table.

Table 1. Correct classification rates (%) of the original HOG.

	0°	18°	36°	54°	72°	90°	108°	126°	144°	162°	180°	Ave.
Exp. A nm-nm	99.19	96.77	93.14	91.93	97.17	95.16	95.16	97.98	97.58	95.96	97.98	96.18
Exp. B nm-cl	49.60	50.81	53.23	53.63	68.95	63.31	58.87	55.65	55.65	55.24	45.97	55.54
Exp. C nm-bg	75.80	76.20	80.24	79.03	83.06	82.66	79.83	76.61	73.38	78.22	73.38	72.80

Table 2. Correct classification rates (%) of the proposed method (HOG+SP) which selects effective regions based on sparse representation.

	0°	18°	36°	54°	72°	90°	108°	126°	144°	162°	180°	Ave.
Exp. A nm-nm	99.19	99.19	97.98	97.58	97.98	97.58	98.38	99.19	98.38	99.19	99.19	98.53
Exp. B nm-cl	75.81	76.21	80.24	79.03	83.06	82.66	79.84	76.61	73.39	78.23	73.39	78.04
Exp. C nm-bg	88.70	85.88	84.67	84.67	89.51	84.67	83.87	89.51	89.51	86.69	91.93	87.24

The correct classification rates of the proposed method are listed in Table 2. The experimental designs are exactly the same with those in Table 1. From the results in the two tables, we can find that selecting effective regions based on sparse representation can improve the correct classification rates greatly. Especially there is variation of clothing, the CCR improved to 78.04% from 55.54%. Even for experiment A there is not variation. The CCR is also improved.

3.4 Comparisons with the State-of-the-Art

Before the comparisons, we want to emphasis that the proposed method is not a deep learning based one. Currently the deep learning based gait recognition has made a great progress and can achieve very high recognition rates. From the results in Table 3 we can find that the proposed method achieves comparable performance compared with the state-of-the-art, and even outperforms some deep learning based methods. The results show that the effective region selection based on sparse representation is successful in improving the robustness of occlusions.

Table 3. Comparisons with the state-of-the-art

Gallery-Probe	Exp. A nm-nm	Exp. B nm-cl	Exp. C nm-bg
GEI [19]	97.7	28.9	67.8
GPPE [6]	93.36	22.44	56.12
GEnl [1]	98.3	33.5	86.3
GaitGAN [17]	**98.75**	41.50	72.72
GEI+2DLPP [22]	95.2	44.35	55.65
SPAE [18]	97.58	45.45	72.14
WDMD [13]	96.77	50.40	71.37
STIPs [7]	95.4	52.0	60.9
PTSN [10]	96.92	68.11	85.78
Masked GEI+CDA [3]	98.57	77.78	86.46
Distance matric [4]	97.6	**79.0**	87.1
Proposed method	98.53	78.04	**87.24**

4   Conclusions

In the proposed method, we use the sparse representation to select the effective regions in images for gait recognition. Experimental results show that the proposed method is robust to variations of clothing and carrying conditions. The proposed method is successful in removing the occlusion regions and achieves very good results.

Acknowledgment. The work is supported by the strategic new and future industrial development fund of Shenzhen (Grant No. 20170504160426188).

References

1. Bashir, K., Xiang, T., Gong, S.: Gait recognition using gait entropy image. In: 3rd International Conference on Crime Detection and Prevention (ICDP 2009), pp. 1–6, January 2009
2. Dalal, N., Triggs, B.: Histograms of oriented gradients for human detection. In: IEEE Conference on Computer Vision and Pattern Recognition (CVPR 2005), vol. 1, pp. 886–893, June 2005
3. Dupuis, Y., Savatier, X., Vasseur, P.: Feature subset selection applied to model-free gait recognition. Image Vis. Comput. **31**(8), 580–591 (2013)
4. Gong, M., Xu, Y., Yang, X., Zhang, W.: Gait identification by sparse representation. In: 2011 Eighth International Conference on Fuzzy Systems and Knowledge Discovery (FSKD), vol. 3, pp. 1719–1723, July 2011
5. Han, J., Bhanu, B.: Individual recognition using gait energy image. IEEE Trans. Pattern Anal. Mach. Intell. **28**(2), 316–322 (2006)
6. Jeevan, M., Jain, N., Hanmandlu, M., Chetty, G.: Gait recognition based on gait pal and pal entropy image. In: 2013 IEEE International Conference on Image Processing, pp. 4195–4199, September 2013
7. Kusakunniran, W.: Recognizing gaits on spatio-temporal feature domain. IEEE Trans. Inf. Forensics Secur. **9**(9), 1416–1423 (2014)
8. Lai, Z., Xu, Y., Jin, Z., Zhang, D.: Human gait recognition via sparse discriminant projection learning. IEEE Trans. Circ. Syst. Video Technol. **24**(10), 1651–1662 (2014)
9. Lai, Z., Xu, Y., Yang, J., Tang, J., Zhang, D.: Sparse tensor discriminant analysis. IEEE Trans. Image Process. **22**(10), 3904–3915 (2013)
10. Liao, R., Cao, C., Garcia, E.B., Yu, S., Huang, Y.: Pose-based temporal-spatial network (PTSN) for gait recognition with carrying and clothing variations. In: Zhou, J., et al. (eds.) CCBR 2017. LNCS, vol. 10568, pp. 474–483. Springer, Cham (2017). https://doi.org/10.1007/978-3-319-69923-3_51
11. Pati, Y.C., Rezaiifar, R., Krishnaprasad, P.S.: Orthogonal matching pursuit: recursive function approximation with applications to wavelet decomposition. In: Proceedings of 27th Asilomar Conference on Signals, Systems and Computers, vol. 1, pp. 40–44, November 1993
12. Tanawongsuwan, R., Bobick, A.: Gait recognition from time-normalized joint-angle trajectories in the walking plane. In: IEEE Conference on Computer Vision and Pattern Recognition, p. 726 (2001)
13. Wang, J., Garcia, E.B., Yu, S., Zhang, D.: Windowed DMD for gait recognition under clothing and carrying condition variations. In: Zhou, J. (ed.) CCBR 2017. LNCS, vol. 10568, pp. 484–492. Springer, Cham (2017). https://doi.org/10.1007/978-3-319-69923-3_52
14. Wang, L., Tan, T., Hu, W., Ning, H.: Automatic gait recognition based on statistical shape analysis. IEEE Trans. Image Process. **12**(9), 1120–1131 (2003)
15. Wu, Z., Huang, Y., Wang, L., Wang, X., Tan, T.: A comprehensive study on cross-view gait based human identification with deep CNNS. IEEE Trans. Pattern Anal. Mach. Intell. **39**(2), 209–226 (2016)
16. Xu, D., Huang, Y., Zeng, Z., Xu, X.: Human gait recognition using patch distribution feature and locality-constrained group sparse representation. IEEE Trans. Image Process. **21**(1), 316–326 (2012)
17. Yu, S., Chen, H., Reyes, E.B.G., Poh, N.: Gaitgan: invariant gait feature extraction using generative adversarial networks. In: 2017 IEEE Conference on Computer Vision and Pattern Recognition Workshops (CVPRW), pp. 532–539. IEEE (2017)

18. Yu, S., Chen, H., Wang, Q., Shen, L., Huang, Y.: Invariant feature extraction for gait recognition using only one uniform model. Neurocomputing 239, 81–93 (2017)
19. Yu, S., Tan, D., Tan, T.: A framework for evaluating the effect of view angle, clothing and carrying condition on gait recognition. In: 18th International Conference on Pattern Recognition (ICPR 2006), vol. 4, pp. 441–444 (2006)
20. Yu, S., Wang, L., Hu, W., Tan, T.: Gait analysis for human identification in frequency domain. In: International Conference on Image and Graphics, pp. 282–285 (2004)
21. Yu, S., Wang, Q., Shen, L., Huang, Y.: View invariant gait recognition using only one uniform model. In: 23rd International Conference on Pattern Recognition (ICPR 2016), pp. 889–894 (2016)
22. Zhang, E., Zhao, Y., Xiong, W.: Active energy image plus 2DLPP for gait recognition. Signal Process. **90**(7), 2295–2302 (2010)
23. Zhao, G., Liu, G., Li, H., Pietikainen, M.: 3D gait recognition using multiple cameras. In: International Conference on Automatic Face and Gesture Recognition, pp. 529–534 (2006)
24. Zheng, S., Zhang, J., Huang, K., He, R., Tan, T.: Robust view transformation model for gait recognition. In: 18th IEEE International Conference on Image Processing (ICIP), pp. 2073–2076. IEEE (2011)

A Method of Personnel Location Based on Monocular Camera in Complex Terrain

Yanqiong Liu[1], Gang Shi[1,2(✉)], Qing Cui[1], Yuhong Sheng[1], and Guoqun Liu[3]

[1] Xinjiang University, Urumqi 830046, Xinjiang, China
shigang@xju.edu.cn
[2] Tsinghua University, Beijing 100084, China
[3] Shandong University, Qingdao, Shandong, China

Abstract. This article proposed a method based on monocular camera for locating people in complex terrain. The coordinates of the person in the 3D space are derived from the image coordinates of the person's and the feature points in the model of the complex terrain. First, using the monocular camera, camera internal parameters and image coordinate system and combining some reference points in the three-dimensional world coordinate system, the three-dimensional point cloud of complex terrain can be obtained. And the 3D model of a complex terrain can be obtained by triangles generated by the region growing method. Second, the TensorFlow object detection model is used to detect people in the frame image of the video. The lower midpoint of the marked rectangular used to identify the person in image is taken as the person's image coordinate point. The person's 3D coordinates can be obtained from the person's image coordinates combined with the 3D coordinates of the feature points in the already established model. Finally, the positioning of people in a complex terrain based on monocular camera can be done.

Keywords: Personnel position · Monocular camera
Complex terrain · 3D modeling · TensorFlow · Object detection

1 Introduction

The object positioning based on the monocular camera has a high value in practical applications. For example, in the new driver's auxiliary system, the emergency brake of the car and the adaptive cruise control are all dependent on the object detection in the video [5,6]. And the positioning of personnel in the surveillance system can be used for security or analysis human behavior and many other occasions. However, most current surveillance systems use monocular

The authors were supported in part by NSFC (Grant No. 61462086, 61563050, 61262023), National Science and Technology Major Project (Grant No. MJ-2015-D-066).

© Springer Nature Switzerland AG 2018
J. Zhou et al. (Eds.): CCBR 2018, LNCS 10996, pp. 175–185, 2018.
https://doi.org/10.1007/978-3-319-97909-0_19

cameras, and most of terrains under monocular cameras are complex. The object positioning in the two-dimensional image generated by the monocular camera has a large limitations in complex terrains. For example, in map navigation, two-dimensional images do not know the terrain very well. The current detection of moving objects in most surveillance systems is not differentiated between humans and objects. That results a high error rate in practical applications such as security alarms. To sum up, it is of great significance to study the method of locating people in the complex terrain under a monocular camera.

At present, the object positioning technology is mainly divided into two categories: Calibration and No-Calibration object positioning technology. There are calibration positioning technologies: positioning based on the Radio frequency identification (RFID) [15], Wireless location technology based on Zigbee [2,7] and Location Based Service [9]. No-calibration object positioning contains calculate aberration in binocular camera, Frame-Difference method (FD) [3,12] and background subtraction [16] etc.

In this article, we use monocular cameras and laser range finder to obtain the three-dimensional coordinates of the hill feature points on the campus of Xinjiang University. Finally build a 3D model of the hill. The frame image of the video in the terrain is converted into a NumPy object, and the Tensorflow Object Detection model is input to obtain the image coordinates of the character in the frame image. A feature point in the three-dimensional model is taken as a reference point, and the reference point three-dimensional coordinates and the image coordinate of the character are combined. Find the three-dimensional coordinates of the character. Finally, the human body positioning in a complex terrain based on a monocular camera is realized.

When the three-dimensional model is created, triangles with small angles or long side lengths are prone to be generated, which lead to error topology and abnormal borders when the 3D model is created. In this article, 3D Model built via the Delaunay Triangulation [1,13]. The interior of any circumscribed circle of any Delaunay triangle cannot contain any other point. Lawson proposed the principle of maximizing the minimum angle [10]. Every two adjacent triangles form the diagonal of the convex quadrilateral. After exchange, the minimum angles of the six interior angles no longer increase. By the method, the model will be built as expected.

The rest of the paper is organized as follows. In next Section, it will introduce the hardwares and software composition of the system of personnel positioning and tracking in complex scenes and introduce the implementation methods of the system. In Sect. 3, we give the algorithm for building the 3D model, and the steps of creating the 3D model are analyzed. In Sect. 4, We discusses the implement method of personnel positioning and trajectory tracking in 3D models. In Sect. 5, based on the Sects. 3 and 4, we take the hill in the campus of Xinjiang University as example to build 3D model, and draw the trajectory of a person in the model. Section 6 discusses some related work, and finally, the paper is Concluded in Sect. 7.

The contribution of this article includes two parts: (1) In this paper, we can create complex 3D models of complex terrain only by a monocular camera and a laser range-finder. (2) Compared with the traditional two-dimensional positioning, this paper provides a location method in complex 3D scene.

2 System Composition

The system consists of two parts: hardware and software. The hardware equipment includes a monocular camera and a laser range-finder. The focal length of the monocular camera used in this study is 3.81 mm, and the limited-range of the laser range-finder is 800 m. The software uses Pycharm as the development environment. The development language is python language. Human detection realized via the TensorFlow object detecton model. The creation of the model and personnel location tracking utilizes the PIL image processing standard library.

3 Create the 3D Model of Complex Terrain

3.1 Get Three-Dimensional Points

Select the image in the video, and use the frame image as the background model to get the three-dimensional coordinates of the points. Shown in the Fig. 1.

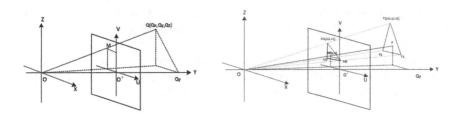

Fig. 1. Get three-dimensional points   **Fig. 2.** Object detection

(1) O is the origin of the world coordinate system, O_1 is the origin of two-dimensional coordinates based on the image center noted as (u_{center}, v_{center}), the length of O and O_1 is written as f_1. M(u, v) is the corresponding point of the point Q to be measured on the image.

(2) L represents the straight line distance from the point Q to the camera.

(3) f is the camera focal length, f_1 is the efficient focal distance of the camera.

$$OM = \sqrt{u^2 + v^2 + f_1^2} \tag{1}$$

$$\frac{Q_y}{f_1} = \frac{L}{OM} \tag{2}$$

$$Q_y = \frac{L}{OM} * f_1 \tag{3}$$

$$\frac{Q_z}{v} = \frac{Q_y}{f_1} \tag{4}$$

$$Q_z = \frac{Q_y}{f_1} * v \tag{5}$$

$$\frac{Q_x}{Q_z} = \frac{u}{v} \tag{6}$$

$$Q_x = \frac{u}{v} * Q_z \tag{7}$$

In formula (1), the length of OM is derived from Pythagorean theorem. Formula (2), (4) and (6) got by the ratio relations based on similar triangles. Formula (3), (5) and (7) are derived from formula (2), (4) and (6), respectively.

Finally, the coordinates of Q point are obtained as (Q_x, Q_y, Q_z), and so on, three-dimensional coordinates of all the key points can be obtained, then the three-dimensional scene coordinates of the monocular camera can be obtained.

3.2   Create a Three-Dimensional Coordinate System

Generate a three-dimensional model of triangular patches by region seeds growing (RSG) [11].

(1) Select the Seed and Build the Initialization Queue. In order to save space, circular linked list will be established as storage structure. List l_1: active edge list, list l_2: triangular list, list l_3: boundary point linked list. And initialize l_1, l_2, l_3 are empty lists.

From the point cloud, the largest point of the h-coordinate and its two neighboring points are selected to construct the seed triangle. The three sides of the seed triangle are used to initialize the active edge list l_1.

(2) Select the Best Match. The selection of the best matching point is a combination of two methods:

(1) the minimum corner product.
(2) the side length limitation principle.

The purpose is to prevent the generation of narrow triangles from generating errors or to prevent the generation of abnormal boundaries.

a. Minimum corner product: When the best matching point is the adjoining boundary point of the current edge: the minimum internal angle of the triangle formed by the candidate point and the two ends of the current edge should be less than a certain threshold. When the candidate points are outliers or other boundary points: The minimum internal angle of the triangle formed by the candidate point and the two ends of the current edge should be less than a certain threshold.

b. Side length limit Principle: In order to save space, circular linked list will be established as storage structure. List l_1: active edge list, list l_2: triangular list, list l_3: boundary point linked list.

When the candidate points are selected, the length of the edge is limited to a certain threshold to prevent the generation of wrong topology and abnormal boundaries.

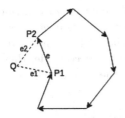

Fig. 3. Best-match point a outside point

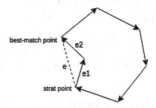

Fig. 4. Best-match point a start point

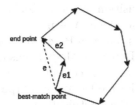

Fig. 5. Best-match point a end point

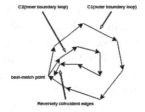

Fig. 6. Point is other point

(3) Update and Mark Boundaries. The boundary update is different because of the selection of the best matching point, including the following cases:

Case 1: The best match point is outside point shown in Fig. 3.

Two new edges e_1, e_2. e_1 are formed by the current edge start point p_1 and the out point Q, denoted by $e_1(p_1, Q)$, and e_2 is composed of the outer point Q and the end point p_2 of the current side, denoted as (Q, p_2).

Case 2: The best match point is the adjacency point of the current edge start point shown in Fig. 4.

Two new inner edges e_1, e_2, a new edge e and a new inner point Q are generated. The new edge e is inserted into the edge queue l_1, the inner edges e_1, e_2 are deleted from the edge queue l_1, and the inner point Q is deleted from the point queue l_3. The resulting new triangle inserts the triangle queue l_2.

Case 3: The best match point is the adjacency point of the current edge end point shown in Fig. 5.

Processing method is the same as case 2.

Case 4: The best matching point is the other boundary point that is not adjacent to the current starting point or end point shown in Fig. 6.

The new edges e_1, e_2. e_1 are the starting points of the current edge and the best matching points. e_2 is composed of the best matching point and the ending point of the current edge. The best boundary ring is divided into two at the best matching point. For ring c_1 and outer boundary ring c_2, in order to ensure that there are only one boundary ring in the process of splitting, check whether the new edges e_1 and e_2 overlap with a boundary edge in boundary rings c1 and c_2. If there is a boundary e and e_1 or e_2 coincide, if the new edge e_1 coincides with the boundary edge e, mark the boundary edge e and the new edge e_1 as a dead edge. The new edge e_2 enters the linked list l_1, and then deletes the current edge e, if both e_1, e_2 are equal to The current side e does not coincide, then e_1, e_2 successively enter the linked list l_1, and then delete the current edge e.

4 Tracking People in a Complex 3D Scene

4.1 Human Recognition in the Frame Image by TensorFlow Object Detection Model

The detection of people in the video and the acquisition of the person's image coordinates mainly include the following steps. First, OpenCV is used to cut the frame of the video, the frame image is converted into a NumPy object and the NumPy object is input into the TensorFlow Object Detection Model. TensorFlow Object Detection provides five models. ssd_mobilenet, ssd_inception, rfcn_resnet, faster_rcnn_resnet, faster_rcnn_inception_resnet. The model finally outputs an object boxes of a dictionary data type that contains the identification rectangles, labels, and degrees of recognition of the identified objects. Select the coordinates of the midpoint of the lower edge of the rectangular box labeled person as the person's image coordinates.

4.2 Draw a Human Trajectory

Identify people in the frame image by TensorFlow Object Detection Model. After many tests, the probability that the object is identified as a person in the video is more than 85% and it can be determined as a person. Take the middle point of the bottom of the marked rectangle as the human position, and mark it as M(u, v) in the image shown in Fig. 2. P is the point of M in the world coordinate system. T1, T2, T3 are the three vertices of the triangular including the point P in the model. The reference point of the coordinates of the point P in this study is the highest point among the three vertices of the triangle in which P is located, all of which are recorded as T1. According to the following 4 steps, we can calculate the P(x, y, z) in three-dimensional coordinates.

Step 1: U-V coordinate projection for three dimensional model.

Step 2: Determining triangle marked as (T_1, T_2, T_3) of point M is on the U-V coordinate system.

Step 3: According to the following formula, we get the actual height of the three-dimensional spatial coordinate point P(x, y, z) corresponding to point M.

$$\frac{z_1}{z} = \frac{v_1}{v} \tag{8}$$

Step 4: Get x, y by formula 5, formula 7 and formula 8.

Through the above steps, the location of a person in three-dimensional space by a frame image can be realized. According to the same method, the video can be processed in this way frame by frame. Finally, the trajectory of a person in the three-dimensional space model can be obtained.

5   Implementation

5.1   Get the Three-Dimensional Coordinates of All Marking Points and Build 3D Model

Based on the above methods, the experiments in this paper are carried out on the hills in the campus of Xinjiang University. The background image and its processing are shown in Figs. 7, 8, 13 and 14. The 3D coordinates of the feature points in the background frame image are shown in Table 1.

Fig. 7. Marked image   **Fig. 8.** Gray image

According to the above method based on the data in Table 1 of the experiment, we can obtained the three-dimensional model of the actual complex terrain under the monocular camera shown in Fig. 15.

Moving objects detection and setting in 3D models are based on deep learning object detection and face recognition methods.

5.2   Human Detection and Trajectories Drawing

Each key frame is converted as a NumPy Object, and input TensorFlow object detection model to detect and identify moving objects and record track coordinates.

It is finally drawn in an image with a three-dimensional model. By processing frames one by one, the trajectory of personnel in three-dimensional space model can be obtained shown in Figs. 9, 10, 11, 12.

Table 1. The three-dimensional coordinates of the actual measurement points.

Point	X	Y	Z	Point	X	Y	Z
Q_1	−12.44042598	17.16697681	2.073554521	Q_{16}	−2.689149452	22.56753174	2.525668119
Q_2	−12.17169807	17.67308294	2.149529301	Q_{17}	−1.223682252	22.63218146	2.506766555
Q_3	−7.047518315	11.92849613	1.433924206	Q_{18}	0.129703096	22.46221796	2.497374154
Q_4	−9.541230267	17.92509236	1.794391136	Q_{19}	1.291866401	24.73372356	2.939482947
Q_5	−6.890008767	14.15907951	1.281378114	Q_{20}	−0.070458402	17.89643403	1.646847709
Q_6	−4.15040249	7.628091408	0.284701994	Q_{21}	−0.332410574	15.63560848	1.332925363
Q_7	−2.787642677	9.432432149	0.611498882	Q_{21}	−1.367231499	7.821549569	0.320252423
Q_8	−7.536392966	17.10164217	1.780186689	Q_{23}	−0.168503705	7.379300184	0.105363236
Q_9	−7.015441982	17.83111004	1.905729136	Q_{24}	0.524083432	12.96596023	1.050889375
Q_{10}	−7.885089951	18.68295567	2.212532703	Q_{25}	2.031785009	12.13338697	1.010797119
Q_{11}	−6.888410826	17.4965635	1.869973926	Q_{26}	2.202059209	17.12213385	1.680755397
Q_{12}	−6.950186673	19.44215215	2.286111328	Q_{27}	3.833658058	13.5242937	1.156486847
Q_{13}	−5.859086938	19.01458367	1.969331947	Q_{28}	3.677358724	11.9443621	0.966834979
Q_{14}	−5.791712517	20.81738178	2.393179323	Q_{29}	2.220195066	6.206121203	0.067762373
Q_{15}	−3.943244106	18.10091571	1.708422386	Q_{30}	5.906003825	10.98724344	0.922813098

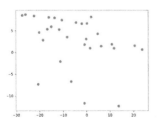

Fig. 9. Object detection

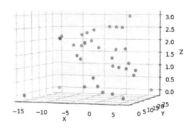

Fig. 10. Object detection

Fig. 11. Object detection

Fig. 12. Object detection

Fig. 13. Points in image

Fig. 14. Three dimensional scatter point

Finally, the trajectories of people or objects under complex terrain are solved. The results of the experiment are shown in Fig. 16.

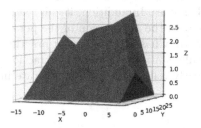

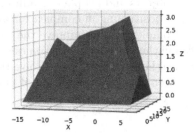

Fig. 15. 3D model of complex terrain   **Fig. 16.** The trajectory of person

6   Related Work

The Background subtract [4] is a method of detecting an object by a difference between the current image and the background image. In the Revolving camera, because the background changes at any time, the efficiency of object detection by the Background subtract will be greatly reduced. $D_i(x, y)$ is the motion area, $I_i(x, y)$ is the i-th frame image, $B_{i-1}(x, y)$ is the background model.

$$D_i(x, y) = I_i(x, y) - B_{i-1}(x, y) \tag{9}$$

The Frame-difference method is a comparison of pixel points on an image of a video adjacent frame. If a pixel point changes, it is a motion area, thereby detecting a moving object in the video. $D_i(x, y)$ is the motion area, $I_i(x, y)$ is the i-th frame image, $B_{i-1}(x, y)$ is the (i−1)-th frame image.

$$D_i(x, y) = I_i(x, y) - I_{i-1}(x, y) \tag{10}$$

The disadvantages of other technologies are high cost, poor signal anti-interference ability and high error in batch object identification. In comparison, using this method to locate more precisely and at lower cost. This article uses deep learning [8,14] based on Tensorflow's object recognition model to identify whether the object in the surveillance system is human and locate the target's foot in the 3D terrain under the monocular camera. Eventually it can obtain the positioning of people in the 3D terrain under the monocular camera.

7   Conclusion

This article uses a monocular camera, camera parameters and image coordinate system, combining a laser range finder to measure the heights of several reference points in a three-dimensional world coordinate system, constructing a three-dimensional digital model of complex terrain. And then use a deep learning object detection method. Finally, draw the trajectory of the person or the measured object under complex terrain. Compared to the recognition and positioning of objects and people in traditional 2D images, this article addresses the problem of positioning in complex terrain 3D scenes. In addition, it can reduce the time complexity and improve the efficiency in the application of the person identified in the video as the person tag. This study has very important practical significance. For example, it can solve the traffic statistics of tourist attractions in smart scenic spots. In addition, it can greatly reduce the false alarm rate in the security system.

References

1. IEEE Conference on Computer Vision and Pattern Recognition Workshops, CVPR Workshops 2004, 27 June–2 July 2004, Washington, DC, USA. IEEE Computer Society (2004)
2. 4th International Symposium on Computational Intelligence and Design, ISCID 2011, 28–30 October 2011, Hangzhou, China, vol. 2. IEEE Computer Society (2011)
3. Bang, J., Kim, D., Eom, H.: Motion object and regional detection method using block-based background difference video frames. In: 2012 IEEE International Conference on Embedded and Real-Time Computing Systems and Applications, RTCSA 2012, 19–22 August 2012, Seoul, Korea (South), pp. 350–357 (2012)
4. Berjón, D., Cuevas, C., Morán, F., García, N.N.: Real-time nonparametric background subtraction with tracking-based foreground update. Pattern Recognit. **74**, 156–170 (2018)
5. García, F., Prioletti, A., Cerri, P., Broggi, A.: PHD filter for vehicle tracking based on a monocular camera. Expert Syst. Appl. **91**, 472–479 (2018)
6. Goro, K., Onoguchi, K.: Road boundary detection using in-vehicle monocular camera. In: Proceedings of the 7th International Conference on Pattern Recognition Applications and Methods, ICPRAM 2018, 16–18 January 2018, Funchal, Madeira - Portugal, pp. 379–387 (2018)
7. Guo, X., Li, Y.: Underground personnel positioning system based on zigbee. In: 4th International Symposium on Computational Intelligence and Design, ISCID 2011, 28–30 October 2011, Hangzhou, China, vol. 2, pp. 298–300 (2011)
8. Gupta, S.: Deep learning in rectified Gaussian nets. Ph.D. thesis, University of California, San Diego, USA (2018)
9. Kiefer, P., Huang, H., Van de Weghe, N., Raubal, M. (eds.): LBS 2018. LNGC. Springer, Cham (2018). https://doi.org/10.1007/978-3-319-71470-7
10. Lawson, C.L.: Transforming triangulations. Discrete Math. **3**(4), 365–372 (1972)
11. Long, C., et al.: A new region growing algorithm for triangular mesh recovery from scattered 3d points. Trans. Edutainment **6**, 237–246 (2011)
12. Ning, C., Fei, D.: Flame object segmentation by an improved frame difference method. In: Third International Conference on Digital Manufacturing & Automation, ICDMA 2012, 31 July–2 August 2012, Guilin, China, pp. 422–425 (2012)
13. Snoeyink, J. (ed.): Proceedings of the Eleventh Annual Symposium on Computational Geometry, 5–12 June 1995, Vancouver, B.C., Canada. ACM (1995)

14. Wongsuphasawat, K., et al.: Visualizing dataflow graphs of deep learning models in tensorflow. IEEE Trans. Vis. Comput. Graph. **24**(1), 1–12 (2018)
15. Xu, H., Ding, Y., Li, P., Wang, R., Li, Y.: An RFID indoor positioning algorithm based on bayesian probability and K-nearest neighbor. Sensors **17**(8), 1806 (2017)
16. Yao, G., Lei, T., Zhong, J., Jiang, P., Jia, W.: Comparative evaluation of background subtraction algorithms in remote scene videos captured by MWIR sensors. Sensors **17**(9), 1945 (2017)

Feature Extraction and Classification Theory

LPPNet: A Learning Network for Image Feature Extraction and Classification

Guodong Li, Haishun Du[(✉)], Meihong Xiao, and Sheng Wang

School of Computer Science and Information Engineering, Henan University,
Kaifeng 475004, China
gdli_henu@qq.com, mhxiao_henu@qq.com, jddhs@vip.henu.edu.cn,
wangsheng1910@163.com

Abstract. PCANet is a very simple learning network for image classification. Inspired by PCANet, we propose a new learning network, referred to as LPPNet, for image feature extraction and classification. Different from PCANet, LPPNet takes the class information and the local geometric structure of data into account simultaneously. In LPPNet, local preserving projections (LPP) is first employed to learn filters, and then binary hashing and block histograms are used for indexing and pooling. Experimental results on several image datasets verify the effectiveness and robustness of LPPNet for image feature extraction and classification.

Keywords: LPPNet · Learning network · Feature extraction
Image classification

1 Introduction

Feature extraction plays an important role in the fields of machine learning and pattern recognition due to its contributions to solving the problem of "the curse of dimensionality" [1] and alleviating the computational burden. Many feature extraction techniques have been proposed in the past several decades. Among them, principal component analysis (PCA) [2] and linear discriminant analysis (LDA) [3] are the two most well-known ones. However, PCA and LDA only focus on the global Euclidean structure of data. This may lead to a consequence that they can not faithfully approximate data distribution in the feature subspace. Inspired by the nonlinear manifold learning techniques [4,5], many linear manifold learning based methods [6–9] have been designed for considering the local geometric structure of data in feature extraction. Recently, with the rapid development of deep learning, Chen et al. [10] proposed a simple learning network, namely PCANet, for image feature extraction and classification. Although PCANet has achieved promising performance, it does not consider the class information and the local geometric structure of data, which are essential to the classification tasks.

To address the disadvantages of PCANet, in this paper, we propose a new learning network, referred to as LPPNet, for image feature extraction and

J. Zhou et al. (Eds.): CCBR 2018, LNCS 10996, pp. 189–197, 2018.
https://doi.org/10.1007/978-3-319-97909-0_20

classification. In LPPNet, local preserving projections (LPP) [6], which takes the class information and the local geometric structure of data into account simultaneously, is first employed to learn the filters, and then binary hashing and block histograms are used for indexing and pooling.

The remainder of this paper is organized as follows. In Sect. 2, The details of the proposed LPPNet are presented. Experimental results on several image datasets are reported in Sect. 3. Finally, Sect. 4 concludes this paper.

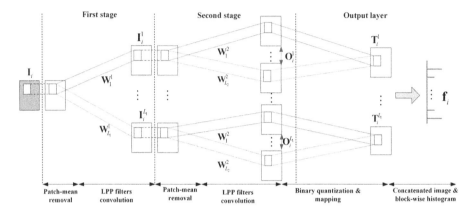

Fig. 1. The block diagram of the proposed LPPNet

2 LPPNet

Given N training samples $\{\mathbf{I}_i\}_{i=1}^N$ of size $m \times n$ belonging to C classes, and assume that the patch size is $k_1 \times k_2$ in all the stages. The proposed LPPNet model is shown in Fig. 1 and only the LPP filters need to be learned from the input images $\{\mathbf{I}_i\}_{i=1}^N$.

2.1 First Stage

Around each pixel, we take a patch of $k_1 \times k_2$ and collect all patches of the i-th image, i.e., $\mathbf{x}_{i,1}, \mathbf{x}_{i,2}, ..., \mathbf{x}_{i,\tilde{m}\tilde{n}} \in \mathbb{R}^{k_1 k_2}$, where $\mathbf{x}_{i,j}$ represents the j-th vectorization patch in $\mathbf{I}_i$, $\tilde{m} = m - \lceil k_1/2 \rceil$, $\tilde{n} = n - \lceil k_2/2 \rceil$, and $\lceil z \rceil$ is the smallest integer greater than or equal to z. Subtracting the patch mean from each patch, we can get $\tilde{\mathbf{X}}_i = [\tilde{\mathbf{x}}_{i,1}, \tilde{\mathbf{x}}_{i,2}, ..., \tilde{\mathbf{x}}_{i,\tilde{m}\tilde{n}}]$, where $\tilde{\mathbf{x}}_{i,j} = \mathbf{x}_{i,j} - \left(\mathbf{1}^{\mathrm{T}}\mathbf{x}_{i,j}/k_1 k_2\right)\mathbf{1}$ is a mean-removed patch, and $\mathbf{1}$ is an all-one vector with proper dimension. Stacking $\tilde{\mathbf{X}}_i$ ($i = 1, 2, ..., N$) into a matrix, we obtain $\tilde{\mathbf{X}} = [\tilde{\mathbf{X}}_1, \tilde{\mathbf{X}}_2, ..., \tilde{\mathbf{X}}_N] \in \mathbb{R}^{k_1 k_2 \times N\tilde{m}\tilde{n}}$.

LPP preserves the local geometric structure of data within a family of filters, i.e.,

$$\frac{1}{2} \min_{\mathbf{W} \in \mathbb{R}^{k_1 k_2 \times L_1}} \sum_{i=1}^N \sum_{j=1}^N \sum_p^{\tilde{m}\tilde{n}} \sum_q^{\tilde{m}\tilde{n}} \left\| \mathbf{W}^{\mathrm{T}} \tilde{\mathbf{x}}_{ip} - \mathbf{W}^{\mathrm{T}} \tilde{\mathbf{x}}_{jq} \right\|_2^2 G_{ip,jq}, \tag{1}$$

where $G_{ip,jq}$ is the similarity between the p-th block of the i-th image and the q-th block of the j-th image. Here, we assume that the similarity between the patch of i-th image and the patch of j-th image that are in same location is equal to the similarity between the i-th image and j-th image, and zero otherwise. This assumption is intuitively reasonable. For example, there are two face images with same size. Obviously, the patches of two face images that are in the same location look similar, and the patches that are in different location have little to do with each other. So, the weight $G_{ip,jq}$ can be defined as follows:

$$G_{ip,jq} = \begin{cases} S_{ij}, & p = q \\ 0, & \text{otherwise} \end{cases}, \qquad (2)$$

where S_{ij} is the similarity between the i-th image and j-th image, and its definition is as follows:

$$S_{ij} = \begin{cases} \exp\left(\| \text{vec}(\mathbf{I}_i) - \text{vec}(\mathbf{I}_j) \|_2^2 / t\right), & \mathbf{I}_j \in N_k(\mathbf{I}_i) \text{ or } \mathbf{I}_i \in N_k(\mathbf{I}_j) \\ 0, & \text{otherwise} \end{cases}, \qquad (3)$$

where $\text{vec}(\mathbf{A})$ is the vectorization operation of a matrix $\mathbf{A}$, $N_k(\mathbf{I}_i)$ indicates the set of the k nearest neighbors of the image $\mathbf{I}_i$ in the same class, and t is a parameter that can be determined empirically. Therefore, the optimization problem of (1) is reduced as follows:

$$\frac{1}{2} \min_{\mathbf{W} \in \mathbb{R}^{k_1 k_2 \times L_1}} \sum_{i=1}^{N} \sum_{j=1}^{N} \sum_{p=1}^{\tilde{m}\tilde{n}} \left\| \mathbf{W}^{\mathrm{T}} \tilde{\mathbf{x}}_{ip} - \mathbf{W}^{\mathrm{T}} \tilde{\mathbf{x}}_{jp} \right\|_2^2 S_{ij}. \qquad (4)$$

Following some simple algebraic steps, we can see that

$$\frac{1}{2} \sum_{i=1}^{N} \sum_{j=1}^{N} \sum_{p=1}^{\tilde{m}\tilde{n}} \left\| \mathbf{W}^{\mathrm{T}} \tilde{\mathbf{x}}_{ip} - \mathbf{W}^{\mathrm{T}} \tilde{\mathbf{x}}_{jp} \right\|_2^2 S_{ij} = \mathrm{Tr}\left[\mathbf{W}^{\mathrm{T}}(\mathbf{F} - \mathbf{E})\mathbf{W}\right], \qquad (5)$$

where $\mathbf{F} = \sum_{i=1}^{N} \tilde{\mathbf{X}}_i D_{ii} \tilde{\mathbf{X}}_i^{\mathrm{T}}$, $\mathbf{E} = \sum_{i=1}^{N} \sum_{j=1}^{N} \tilde{\mathbf{X}}_i S_{ij} \tilde{\mathbf{X}}_j^{\mathrm{T}}$, and $D_{ii} = \sum_j S_{ij}$. Moreover, we impose a constraint on the optimization problem of (4) as follows:

$$\mathbf{W}^{\mathrm{T}} \mathbf{F} \mathbf{W} = \mathbf{I}, \qquad (6)$$

where $\mathbf{I}$ denotes an identity matrix with proper dimension. Thus, the optimization problem of (4) is reformulated as:

$$\min_{\mathbf{W} \in \mathbb{R}^{k_1 k_2 \times L_1}} \mathrm{Tr}\left[\mathbf{W}^{\mathrm{T}}(\mathbf{F} - \mathbf{E})\mathbf{W}\right] \text{ s.t. } \mathbf{W}^{\mathrm{T}} \mathbf{F} \mathbf{W} = \mathbf{I}. \qquad (7)$$

Obviously, $\mathbf{W} = [\mathbf{w}_1, \mathbf{w}_2, ..., \mathbf{w}_{L_1}] \in \mathbb{R}^{k_1 k_2 \times L_1}$ can be obtained by the L_1 Eigenvectors of the corresponding L_1 largest Eigenvalues of the following generalized Eigenvalue problem:

$$\mathbf{E}\mathbf{w} = \lambda \mathbf{F}\mathbf{w}. \qquad (8)$$

Usually, the larger the Eigenvalue is, the more important the corresponding Eigenvector is. Therefore, we define the importance measure of an Eigenvector based on the corresponding Eigenvalue as follows:

$$\varepsilon_l = \lambda_l \bigg/ \sum_{l=1}^{L_1} \lambda_l, \quad l = 1, 2, \cdots, L_1, \tag{9}$$

where λ_l is the l-th Eigenvalue of the L_1 largest Eigenvalues. Based on the important measures, the weighted LPP filters of the first stage can be obtained as follows:

$$\mathbf{W}_l^1 = \mathrm{mat}_{k_1, k_2}(\varepsilon_l \mathbf{w}_l), \quad l = 1, 2...L_1, \tag{10}$$

where $\mathrm{mat}_{k_1, k_2}(\mathbf{v})$ is a function that maps a vector $\mathbf{v} \in \mathbb{R}^{k_1 k_2}$ to a matrix $\mathbf{V} \in \mathbb{R}^{k_1 \times k_2}$.

2.2 Second Stage

Suppose the l-th filter output of the first stage is

$$\mathbf{I}_i^l = \mathbf{I}_i * \mathbf{W}_l^1, \qquad i = 1, 2, ...N, \tag{11}$$

where $*$ represents the 2D convolution, and the boundary of $\mathbf{I}_i$ is zero-padded before the 2D convolution to make $\mathbf{I}_i^l$ have the same size as $\mathbf{I}_i$. As in the first stage, we also collect all patches of $\mathbf{I}_i^l$ and subtract the patch mean from each patch, and then get $\tilde{\mathbf{Y}}_i^l = [\tilde{\mathbf{y}}_{i,l,1}, \tilde{\mathbf{y}}_{i,l,2}, ..., \tilde{\mathbf{y}}_{i,l,\tilde{m}\tilde{n}}] \in \mathbb{R}^{k_1 k_2 \times \tilde{m}\tilde{n}}$, where $\tilde{\mathbf{y}}_{i,l,p}$ is the p-th mean-removed patch in $\mathbf{I}_i^l$. Defining $\tilde{\mathbf{Y}}^l = \left[\tilde{\mathbf{Y}}_1^l, \tilde{\mathbf{Y}}_2^l, ..., \tilde{\mathbf{Y}}_N^l\right] \in \mathbb{R}^{k_1 k_2 \times N\tilde{m}\tilde{n}}$ and stacking $\tilde{\mathbf{Y}}^l$ ($l = 1, 2, \cdots, L_1$) into a matrix, we obtain $\tilde{\mathbf{Y}} = \left[\tilde{\mathbf{Y}}^1, \tilde{\mathbf{Y}}^2, ..., \tilde{\mathbf{Y}}^{L_1}\right] \in \mathbb{R}^{k_1 k_2 \times L_1 N\tilde{m}\tilde{n}}$.

As in the first stage, we give the optimization problem as follows:

$$\frac{1}{2} \min_{\mathbf{W} \in \mathbb{R}^{k_1 k_2 \times L_2}} \sum_{l=1}^{L_1} \sum_{k=1}^{L_1} \sum_{i=1}^{N} \sum_{j=1}^{N} \sum_{p}^{\tilde{m}\tilde{n}} \sum_{q}^{\tilde{m}\tilde{n}} \left\| \mathbf{W}^{\mathrm{T}} \tilde{\mathbf{y}}_{l,i,p} - \mathbf{W}^{\mathrm{T}} \tilde{\mathbf{y}}_{k,j,q} \right\|_2^2 Q_{lip,kjq}, \tag{12}$$

where $Q_{lip,kjq}$ is the similarity between the p-th block of $\mathbf{I}_i^l$ and the q-th block of $\mathbf{I}_j^k$. Similarly, we assume that the similarity between the patch of $\mathbf{I}_i^l$ and the patch of $\mathbf{I}_j^l$ that are in same location is equal to the similarity between $\mathbf{I}_i^l$ and $\mathbf{I}_j^l$, and zero otherwise. That is to say, the similarity $Q_{lip,kjq}$ can be defined as follows:

$$Q_{lip,kjq} = \begin{cases} H_{i,j}^l, & l = k \text{ and } p = q \\ 0, & \text{otherwise} \end{cases}, \tag{13}$$

where $H_{i,j}^l$ is the similarity between the i-th image and j-th image of the l-th filter output, and its definition is as follows:

$$H_{i,j}^l = \begin{cases} \exp\left(\| \mathrm{vec}(\mathbf{I}_i^l) - \mathrm{vec}(\mathbf{I}_j^l) \|_2^2 / t\right), & \mathbf{I}_i^l \in N_k(\mathbf{I}_j^l) \text{ or } \mathbf{I}_j^l \in N_k(\mathbf{I}_i^l) \\ 0, & \text{otherwise} \end{cases}, \tag{14}$$

where vec($\mathbf{A}$) is the vectorization operation of a matrix $\mathbf{A}$, $N_k(\mathbf{I}_i^l)$ indicates the set of the k nearest neighbors of the image $\mathbf{I}_i^l$ in the same class, and t is a parameter that can be determined empirically. So, the optimization problem of (12) can be reduced as follows:

$$\frac{1}{2} \min_{\mathbf{W} \in \mathbb{R}^{k_1 k_2 \times L_2}} \sum_{l=1}^{L_1} \sum_{i=1}^{N} \sum_{j=1}^{N} \sum_{p=1}^{\tilde{m}\tilde{n}} \left\| \mathbf{W}^{\mathrm{T}} \tilde{\mathbf{y}}_{l,i,p} - \mathbf{W}^{\mathrm{T}} \tilde{\mathbf{y}}_{l,j,p} \right\|_2^2 H_{i,j}^l. \tag{15}$$

Following some simple algebraic steps, we can see that

$$\frac{1}{2} \sum_{l=1}^{L_1} \sum_{i=1}^{N} \sum_{j=1}^{N} \sum_{p=1}^{\tilde{m}\tilde{n}} \left\| \mathbf{W}^{\mathrm{T}} \tilde{\mathbf{y}}_{l,i,p} - \mathbf{W}^{\mathrm{T}} \tilde{\mathbf{y}}_{l,j,p} \right\|_2^2 H_{i,j}^l = \mathrm{Tr} \left[\mathbf{W}^{\mathrm{T}} (\mathbf{M} - \mathbf{N}) \mathbf{W} \right], \tag{16}$$

where $\mathbf{M} = \sum_{l=1}^{L_1} \sum_{i=1}^{N} \tilde{\mathbf{Y}}_i^l \tilde{R}_{ii}^l \tilde{\mathbf{Y}}_i^{l\,\mathrm{T}}$, $\mathbf{N} = \sum_{l=1}^{L_1} \sum_{i=1}^{N} \sum_{j=1}^{N} \tilde{\mathbf{Y}}_i^l H_{i,j}^l \tilde{\mathbf{Y}}_j^{l\,\mathrm{T}}$, and $R_{ii}^l = \sum_j H_{i,j}^l$.

As in the first stage, we also impose a constraint on the optimization problem of (15) as follows:

$$\mathbf{W}^{\mathrm{T}} \mathbf{M} \mathbf{W} = \mathbf{I}, \tag{17}$$

where $\mathbf{I}$ denotes an identity matrix with proper dimension. Then, the optimization problem of (15) can be reformulated as follows:

$$\min_{\mathbf{W} \in \mathbb{R}^{k_1 k_2 \times L_2}} \mathrm{Tr} \left[\mathbf{W}^{\mathrm{T}} (\mathbf{M} - \mathbf{N}) \mathbf{W} \right], \quad \text{s.t. } \mathbf{W}^{\mathrm{T}} \mathbf{M} \mathbf{W} = \mathbf{I}. \tag{18}$$

Obviously, $\mathbf{W} = [\mathbf{w}_1, \mathbf{w}_2, ..., \mathbf{w}_{L_2}] \in \mathbb{R}^{k_1 k_2 \times L_2}$ can be obtained by the L_2 Eigenvectors of the corresponding L_2 largest Eigenvalues of the following generalized Eigenvalue problem:

$$\mathbf{N} \mathbf{w} = \beta \mathbf{M} \mathbf{w}. \tag{19}$$

As in the first stage, we also give the importance measures, η_k ($k = 1, 2, ...L_2$), of the Eigenvectors and obtain the L_2 weighted LPP filters of the second stage as follows:

$$\mathbf{W}_k^2 = \mathrm{mat}_{k_1,k_2}(\eta_k \mathbf{w}_k), \quad k = 1, 2, ...L_2. \tag{20}$$

2.3   Output Stage

For each input $\mathbf{I}_i^l$ of the second stage, there are L_2 outputs $\mathcal{O}_i^l = \{\mathbf{I}_i^l * \mathbf{W}_k^2\}_{k=1}^{L_2}$. We binary these outputs to obtain $\{\mathrm{H}(\mathbf{I}_i^l * \mathbf{W}_k^2)\}_{k=1}^{L_2}$, in which $\mathrm{H}(\cdot)$ is a Heaviside function whose values are ones for positive entries and zeros otherwise. On each pixel, we treat the vector of L_2 binary bits as a decimal number and convert the L_2 outputs in $\mathcal{O}_i^l$ into a single integer-value matrix $\mathbf{T}_i^l = \sum_{k=1}^{L_2} 2^{k-1} \mathrm{H}(\mathbf{I}_i^l * \mathbf{W}_k^2)$, whose every entry value is an integer in range $[0, 2^{L_2} - 1]$.

For each of L_1 matrices $\mathbf{T}_i^l$ $(l = 1, 2, ..., L_1)$, we firstly divide it into B blocks and then compute the 2^{L_2} bins' histogram in each block. Furthermore, we concatenate the B histograms into a vector $\mathrm{Bhist}(\mathbf{T}_i^l)$. Finally, Stacking the L_1 vectors $\mathrm{Bhist}(\mathbf{T}_i^l)$ $(l = 1, 2, ..., L_1)$ into a vector, we can obtain the feature vector $\mathbf{f}_i$ of an input image $\mathbf{I}_i$ as follows:

$$\mathbf{f}_i = [\mathrm{Bhist}(\mathbf{T}_i^1), \cdots, \mathrm{Bhist}(\mathbf{T}_i^{L_1})]^{\mathrm{T}} \in \mathbb{R}^{(2^{L_2})L_1 B}. \tag{21}$$

3   Experiments

In this section, we conduct experiments to evaluate the performance of the proposed LPPNet. We compare the proposed LPPNet with PCA [2], LDA [3], LPP [6], PCANet [10], and LDANet [10]. In all experiments, the parameters of LPPNet is set to $L_1 = L_2 = 8$, $k_1 = k_2 = 5$, and $B = 16$. Moreover, the nearest neighbor classifier with Chi-squared distance measure is employed for classification.

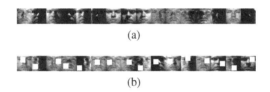

(a)

(b)

Fig. 2. Example images on the Extended Yale B dataset: (a) some example images of one subject; (b) several example images with white block occlusions.

3.1   Experiments on the Extended Yale B Dataset

The Extended Yale B dataset [11] contains 2414 front face images of 38 individuals. Each individual contains about 64 images, taken under various laboratory-controlled lighting conditions. Every image is manually cropped and resized to 32×32 pixels. We design two group experiments on this dataset. In the first group, we randomly select 32 image each individual for training, and the remainder for testing. In the second group, we randomly select 32 images each individual for training, and the rest images, each of which is occluded by randomly located square white block with size of 11×11 pixels, for testing. Figure 2(a) shows some example images of one subject on this dataset, and Fig. 2(b) gives several example images with white block occlusions on this dataset. We independently perform all the methods 5 times, and then report the average classification accuracies. The best classification accuracies and the corresponding standard deviations of all the methods are listed in Table 1. It can be seen that LPPNet outperforms the other methods in each scenario.

3.2   Experiments on the CMU PIE Dataset

The CMU PIE dataset [12] consists of over 40,000 face images of 68 individuals. Images of each individual were acquired across 13 different poses, under 43 different illumination conditions, and with 4 different expressions. Figure 3(a) shows some example images of one subject on this dataset. Here, we use a near frontal pose subset, namely C07, for experiments, which contains 1629 images of 68 individuals. Each individual has about 24 images in C07, and all the images are manually cropped and resized to 32 × 32 pixels. On this dataset, we also do two group experiments. In the first group, 12 images per individual are chosen for training, and the rest for testing. In the second group, 12 images per individual are selected for training, and the rest images, each of which is occluded by randomly located square white block with size of 11 × 11 pixels, for testing. Figure 3(b) shows some example images with white block occlusions on this dataset. All the methods are independently perform 5 times, and then the average classification accuracies are reported. Table 2 gives the best classification accuracies and the corresponding standard deviations of all the methods. Again, LPPNet achieves best performance in each scenario.

Table 1. The best classification accuracies (%) and the corresponding standard deviation (%) of all the methods on the Extended Yale B dataset.

Methods	Un-occluded		Occluded	
	Accuracy	Std	Accuracy	Std
PCA	68.20	0.81	37.05	0.67
LDA	91.09	0.86	47.71	0.47
LPP	92.77	0.47	54.97	0.48
PCANet	92.77	0.37	92.44	0.84
LDANet	93.49	1.04	92.49	1.49
LPPNet	**94.42**	0.52	**94.32**	0.76

(a)   (b)

Fig. 3. Example images on the CMU PIE dataset: (a) some example images of one subject; (b) several example images with white block occlusions.

Table 2. The best classification accuracies (%) and the corresponding standard deviation (%) of all the methods on CMU PIE dataset.

Methods	Un-occluded		Occluded	
	Accuracy	Std	Accuracy	Std
PCA	84.33	1.56	34.15	0.63
LDA	93.09	0.85	37.88	1.66
LPP	95.08	0.84	47.77	0.70
PCANet	94.88	1.27	94.69	1.06
LDANet	95.57	0.91	94.64	0.95
LPPNet	**96.24**	0.83	**95.69**	0.84

4   Conclusions

In this paper, we proposed a new learning network, namely LPPNet, to address the disadvantages of PCANet. By considering both the class information and the local geometric structure of data in filters learning, LPPNet outputs more discriminative features. That is to say, LPPNet is more suitable for image classification tasks. The experimental results on several image datasets verify the effectiveness and robustness of LPPNet for image feature extraction and classification.

Acknowledgments. This work is supported in part by the NSFC-Henan Talent Jointly Training Foundation of China (no. U1504621) and the Key Scientific Research Project of University in Henan Province of China (no. 18A120001).

References

1. Jain, A.K., Duin, R.P.W., Miao, J.: Statistical pattern recognition: a review. IEEE Trans. Pattern Anal. Mach. Intell. **22**(1), 4–37 (2000)
2. Turk, M., Pentland, A.: Eigenfaces for recognition. J. Cogn. Neurosci. **3**(1), 71–86 (1991)
3. Belhumeur, P.N., Hespanha, J.P., Kriegman, D.J.: Eigenfaces vs. fisherfaces: recognition using class specific linear projection. IEEE Trans. Pattern Anal. Mach. Intell. **19**(7), 711–720 (2002)
4. Tenenbaum, J.B., Silva, V.d., Langford, J.C.: A global geometric framework for nonlinear dimensionality reduction. Science **290**(5500), 2319–2323 (2000)
5. Roweis, S.T., Saul, L.K.: Nonlinear dimensionality reduction by locally linear embedding. Science **290**(5500), 2323–2326 (2000)
6. He, X., Yan, S., Hu, Y., Niyogi, P., Zhang, H.: Face recognition using Laplacianfaces. IEEE Trans. Pattern Anal. Mach. Intell. **27**(3), 328–340 (2005)
7. Lai, Z., Xu, Y., Yang, J., Shen, L., Zhang, D.: Rotational invariant dimensionality reduction algorithms. IEEE Trans. Cybern. **47**(11), 3733–3746 (2017)
8. Shi, X., Guo, Z., Lai, Z., Yang, Y., Bao, Z., Zhang, D.: A framework of joint graph embedding and sparse regression for dimensionality reduction. IEEE Trans. Image Process. **24**(4), 1341–1355 (2015)

9. Wang, Q., Gao, Q., Xie, D., Gao, X., Wang, Y.: Robust dlpp with nogreedy ℓ_1 minimization and maximization. IEEE Trans. Neural Netw. Learn. Syst. **29**(3), 738–743 (2018)
10. Chan, T.H., Jia, K., Gao, S., Lu, J., Zeng, Z., Ma, Y.: PCANet: a simple deep learning baseline for image classification? IEEE Trans. Image Process. **24**(12), 5017–5032 (2015)
11. Georghiades, A.S., Belhumeur, P.N., Kriegman, D.J.: From few to many: illumination cone models for face recognition under variable lighting and pose. IEEE Trans. Pattern Anal. Mach. Intell. **23**(6), 643–660 (2001)
12. Sim, T., Baker, S., Bsat, M.: The CMU pose, illumination, and expression database. IEEE Trans. Pattern Anal. Mach. Intell. **25**(12), 1615–1618 (2010)

Design of Multimodal Biometric Information Management System Based on Commercial Systems

Wei-Jian Zhu[1,2(✉)], Chuan-Zhi Zhuang[1], Jing-Wei Liu[1], and Ming Huang[3]

[1] Key Laboratory of Network Data Science and Technology, Institute of Computing Technology, Chinese Academy of Sciences, Beijing 100190, China
{zhuweijian,zhuangchuanzhi,liujingwei}@software.ict.ac.cn
[2] University of Chinese Academy of Sciences, Beijing 100049, China
[3] East China University of Science and Technology, Shanghai 200237, China
huangming@mail.ecust.edu.cn

Abstract. In these years, Biometric technology has passed through its establishment and maintains a good momentum of growth. With the development and reform of social transformation, it seems almost inevitable that the public safety issues have increasingly become a focus. Biometric technology can effectively prevent infringement, obtain the criminal evidence and maintain the public safety. Many standards related to biometric identification in public security area are about to be implemented. Biometric identification will exploit better development opportunities. However, unimodal biometric may not be able to achieve the desired requirement for public security, especially for criminal in the civilian law enforcement environment. It has been found that unimodal biometric shows some inherent drawbacks in universality and accuracy. Hence, this paper proposes the design of multimodal biometric information management system (MBIMS) to create a collaborative platform by acquiring biometric data from multi-commercial systems, defines the data flow API and applies the prototype system successfully in the field of public security.

Keywords: Biometric · Personal identification · System fusion
Public security

1 Introduction

With the development and social transformation in China, the prevention and management of public security is facing with the period of sharp pressure and this has become a major issue of practical significance. How to accurately identify a person's identity is a key issue. The use of biometric to confirm the individual identity is not a new concept. Biometric identification as a reliable and effective method has been applied in high security fields [1]. With the implementation of many China national standards related to biometric identification in this year, the biometric identification industry will usher in another period of rapid growth. How to intelligent, efficient and rapid realization of the collection, capture and processing of related personnel information, this challenge brings strong requirement from biometric technology applications. Some novel multi-biometric acquisition and identification equipment are also deployed in public security

© Springer Nature Switzerland AG 2018
J. Zhou et al. (Eds.): CCBR 2018, LNCS 10996, pp. 198–205, 2018.
https://doi.org/10.1007/978-3-319-97909-0_21

applications. For example, United States security agencies have adopted a hand-held biometric collector (secure electronic enrollment kit) which can collect the iris, face information and fingerprint of the target people. These information can be fed back into a reliable and accurate individual biological database, which can be used to effect evidence collection and people identification. The police departments are also equipped with such gathering devices in China [2]. Some local public security bureaus have already collected millions of biometric samples with those equipments. As the most widely used field, the application of biometric identification technology can effectively prevent and protect in public security. However, most of the existing biometric technology are based on single-mode biometric. It has been found that the single modal biometric shows some inherent drawbacks in accuracy and universality [3].

One of the method on solving these problems is to make use of multimodal biometric technology, but the research and discussion of multi-biometric identification based on data fusion technology is still in its infancy. In addition, there is no strong correlations between different types of biological characteristics. The relevant researches combined the multi-biological characteristics with different fusion strategy, and the applicable scenarios have limitations [4].

On the other hand, some of comprehensive and perfect enterprise have emerged with the biometric recognition industry expands rapidly, they launched a series of commercial products which are powerful and have high promotion rate for single biometric applications. They play an irreplaceable role to public security, criminal investigation and public security management. It would be a great waste if not fully utilized them.

2 Previous Multimodal Biometrics Work

No single biometric is expected to effectively meet all the requirements imposed by public security. Although there is a certain scope of application of the single-mode biometric identification technology, there is not a strong method to solve all problems of recognition in complex situations [5]. Because each method has its owns pros and cons, how to effectively combine multiple method will be a trend of future research [6], how to obtain all kinds of information of maximum and organically combine together, this also is a universal topic. Multimodal biometrics are expected to alleviate some of the limitations of unimodal biometric systems. Thus, a properly designed multimodal biometric system can improve matching accuracy.

More and more attention has been paid to the researchers. Some of the multimodal biometric technology utilized different biometric features to establish application systems [7]. Brunelli et al. [8] combined the face and voice traits of an individual for identification. Oliveira et al. [9] brought a summary about fusion of face and gait for biometric recognition. Gowda et al. [10] investigated in robust about face and fingerprint fusion. Ross and Jain [11] addressed the problem of information fusion in biometric systems by combining information. Sarhan et al. [12] proposed the study for different modalities in biometric fusion. The identification accuracy can be significantly improved by utilizing those traits.

However, the multimodal biometric recognition technology is still in the stage of exploring research. There are still many problems to be solved: the biological characteristics of species selection to fusion, there is rarely related research to confirm the optimal combination. The key points of fusion algorithm design and optimization need to be further studied [13, 14]. The criterion of fusion criterion should be further standardized and unified [1, 15]. Therefore, it is necessary to choose which kinds of biological characteristics as the object of information fusion, and what fusion algorithms to adopt at all levels are subject to further research and experiments [4, 5, 16, 17].

The above various factors have led to much the real application of biometric fusion recognition system to realize the difficulty of how to integrate theory with practice, to make more biometrics for real application is an important research content [18].

3   Proposed Work

The core of biometrics is to acquire biological characteristics and convert them into digital information, using reliable matching algorithms to complete the process of verification and identification for personal identity. With the gradual improvement of technical standards and the popularization of applications in various fields, commercial biometrics industry has been started a number of enterprises with leadership advantages in the market.

In recent years, biometrics recognition technology has made a remarkable progress and obtained certain achievements, especially in the field of face recognition and fingerprint recognition, which have been widely used in the field of public security. Here are some classic representatives of the commercial systems which applied in the public security bureau in a certain city.

3.1   Fingerprint and Palmprint

Fingerprint has been used for personal identification in public security for many decades. The palmprint contains pattern of ridges and valleys very like the fingerprint. Beijing Hisign technology limited company is widely regarded as the most comprehensive and perfect enterprise in Chinese multi-biometrics industry, especially in fingerprint and palmprint technology.

Its market share is higher in the public security. The biometric database of public security size becomes larger and larger. Up to now, the fingerprint data stored in the database is over 8 millions, and rapidly increased with 100 thousands per year in a certain city. The Hisign's fingerprint system has a C/S system framework which more complication and low expansibility.

3.2   Genetic Analysis

Human-specific quantitative PCR has been developed for public security use and is the preferred DNA quantification technique with high accurate [19].

The amount of information that can be gleaned from a single quantification reaction using commercially available quantification kits. Thermo Fisher Scientific Inc. is the world leader in life sciences research. Applied biosystems integrated systems is widely applied in public security for genetic analysis. Applied biosystems integrated systems is for real-time, digital and end point PCR. DNA specialty technology [20] has become a very important routine technical means for public security organs to crack down on criminal crime and maintain social stability. Its database is up to 2 million in a public security bureau of the certain city.

3.3 Face Identification

Facial attributes are probably the most common biometric features used to recognize person. The public security applications of facial recognition range from a static to a dynamic in a cluttered background. Beijing Megvii technology limited company (Face++) has been widely applied in identity authentication in the public security field. The police can timely confirm unknown identity, trace suspects, conduct real-time monitoring. The database size is up to 5 million with high grown rate in a certain city. Using the face recognition system, the police can import it into permanent resident database and criminal database, and used it in the investigation.

3.4 Voiceprint Recognize

As a leading provider of intelligent speech technology, the intelligent speech technology of Iflytek limited company takes the largest market share among all business entities in the security field. The Interveri is a professional voiceprint recognition engine launched by Iflytek to meet the public security demand. The voiceprint database is up to 3 million in a certain city.

3.5 Development of MBIMS

With the widely application of the system described above, the industry leading company has made considerable progress in recent years, especially in face identification, fingerprint identification have good application results and high recognition. How to combining different characteristics and different identification methods to establish an identification fusion system based on current commercial system characteristics.

In this paper, the design of MBIMS is elaborated based on them, try to create a collaborative platform to connect the biological characteristics of the distributed database, such as hardware and software resources, defines the API interface between system and data flow, provides single mode and biometric identification fusion more unified application layer interface functions. The interface embraces specifications and defines an API for executing tasks related to verification and identification. The model block diagram is shown in Fig. 1.

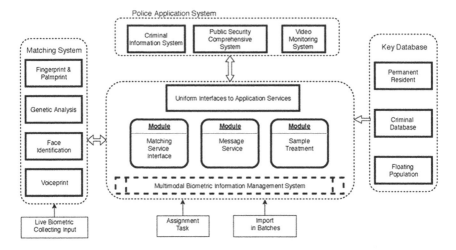

Fig. 1. Multimodal biometric information management system model block diagram.

Implement unified interface to personnel information data (such as ID card information, mobile phone info) distributed to palmprint, face, DNA and other professional comparison system, many biological characteristics for specific information storage and comparative analysis. The upper application interface can also be connected with professional systems such as police summary and criminal investigation, and the sharing application of personnel data can be used to support the export of the standard FPT file of the ministry of public security. Figure 2 demonstrates the working process of biometric task.

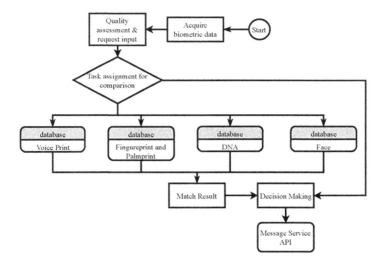

Fig. 2. Biometric comparison task process diagram.

MBIMS uses data access object to encapsulate the access between persistent data, provide a consistent API interface for the business application layer, and flexibly switch the data access policy at runtime. The service-oriented architecture system provides HTTP access with the bioapi as the specification, and JSON format data as the interface and data interface persistence layer integration solution. It gives out a brief example to realize it as shown in Table 1.

Table 1. Simple interface architecture to access system API.

Variable	Type	Remark
dispatch_id	int	task ID
ob_code	string	biometric system unique number
in_ob_code	string	internal ID of commercial system
file	object	information File
source_object	json	original information
result	array/json	return result
similarity	double	comparing bio-sequences similarity
object_info	json	accessorial information
remark	string	probably none

Database structure definition and object store structure definition are realized in the MBIMS. Table 2 shows a simple example about the main structure of the system database.

Table 2. Management system database structure definition.

Field	Type	Remark
TASK_BIOLOGICAL_ID	VARCHAR2(64)	relevancy ID
TASK_ID	VARCHAR2(64)	task ID
OB_ID	VARCHAR2(64)	object ID
UNKNOW_OB_ID	VARCHAR2(64)	unknown object ID
BIOLOGICAL_ID	VARCHAR2(64)	biometrics ID
BIOLOGICAL_TYPE	NUMBER(6)	1:face, 4:voice, 8:finger and palm, 16:DNA
SYSTEM_CODE	VARCHAR2(64)	system unique number
SYSTEM_NAME	VARCHAR2(64)	system
SORT_NUM	VARCHAR2(10)	task sort number
INTERFACE_TYPE	NUMBER(3)	1:XML 2:JSON 3:STRING 4:CUSTOMIZE
SERVICE_IP	VARCHAR2(64)	interface service address
SERVICE_PORT	VARCHAR2(64)	interface ports

The functional design focuses on the main aspects of content: to be able to provide all kinds of single mode state biometric identification module and unified data interface, including user registration, sample storage, identity recognition and other content. To realize the electronic process management of biological characteristics standardized inspection and management, biometric sample collection, transfer, inspection, processing, warehousing, etc. The management of the related identification, inspection and treatment of biological characteristics samples is in accordance with the standard of CNAS-CL08:2013 and ISO/IEC 17025:2005 and the internal management requirements of the end user.

It is necessary to fully utilize commercial systems in biometric analysis. To efficient realizes multibiological feature combination comparison and confidence evaluation by means of the existing system. The key point of combining them together is to realize uniform standard and resource interoperability which is guiding further research in the future.

4 Conclusion

This paper presents the multimodal biometric information management system (MBIMS) which take convenient and reliable features full advantage of the convenience of the commercial systems. It conducts security management provides stronger support for security inspection and criminal investigation in the field of public security.

Acknowledgments. This work was supported in part by Shanghai Public Security Bureau and by Shanghai Municipal People's Government. We also wish to express thanks to Jiangsu Qingtian Information Technology Co., Ltd.

References

1. Arora, P., Bhargava, S., Srivastava, S., Hanmandlu, M.: Multimodal biometric system based on information set theory and refined scores. Soft. Comput. **21**, 5133–5144 (2017)
2. Maity, S., Abdel-Mottaleb, M., Asfour, S.S.: Multimodal biometrics recognition from facial video via deep learning. Sig. Image Process. Int. J. **8**, 1–9 (2017)
3. Raju, A., Udayashankara, V.: Biometric person authentication: a review. In: 2014 International Conference on Contemporary Computing and Informatics (IC3I), pp. 575–580. IEEE (2014)
4. Kadam, A., Ghadi, M., Chavan, A., Jawale, P., Student, B.: Multimodal biometric fusion. Int. J. Eng. Sci. 12554 (2017)
5. Ghayoumi, M.: A review of multimodal biometric systems: fusion methods and their applications. In: 2015 IEEE/ACIS 14th International Conference on Computer and Information Science (ICIS), pp. 131–136. IEEE (2015)
6. Geng, A.-L., Liu, L.: The investigation on multimodal biometric recognition (2015)
7. Jain, A.K., Ross, A., Prabhakar, S.: An introduction to biometric recognition. IEEE Trans. Circ. Syst. Video Technol. **14**, 4–20 (2004)
8. Brunelli, R., Falavigna, D.: Person identification using multiple cues. IEEE Trans. Pattern Anal. Mach. Intell. **17**, 955–966 (1995)

9. Oliveira, E.L., Lima, C.A., Peres, S.M.: Fusion of face and gait for biometric recognition: systematic literature review. In: Proceedings of the XII Brazilian Symposium on Information Systems on Brazilian Symposium on Information Systems: Information Systems in the Cloud Computing Era, vol. 1, p. 15. Brazilian Computer Society (2016)

10. Gowda, H.S., Kumar, G.H., Imran, M.: Robust multimodal biometric verification system based on face and fingerprint. In: 2017 International Conference on Advances in Computing, Communications and Informatics (ICACCI), pp. 243–247. IEEE (2017)

11. Ross, A., Jain, A.: Information fusion in biometrics. Pattern Recogn. Lett. **24**, 2115–2125 (2003)

12. Sarhan, S., Alhassan, S., Elmougy, S.: Multimodal biometric systems: a comparative study. Arab. J. Sci. Eng. **42**, 443–457 (2017)

13. Shobana, D., Logeshwari, A., Maheswari, S.U.: A study on multimodal biometrics system (2017)

14. Barra, S., Casanova, A., Fraschini, M., Nappi, M.: Fusion of physiological measures for multimodal biometric systems. Multimedia Tools Appl. **76**, 4835–4847 (2017)

15. Shanmugasundaram, K., Mohamed, A.S.A., Ruhaiyem, N.I.R.: An overview of hand-based multimodal biometrie system using multi-classifier score fusion with score normalization. In: 2017 International Conference on Signal Processing and Communication (ICSPC), pp. 53–57. IEEE (2017)

16. Kumar, D.: A review in various approaches of feature extraction and feature fusion in multimodal biometric system IEEE Trans. Syst. Man Cybern. Part C (Appl. Rev.) **40**(4), 384–395 (2017)

17. Gupta, K.: Advances in multi modal biometric systems: a brief review. In: 2017 International Conference on Computing, Communication and Automation (ICCCA), pp. 262–267. IEEE (2017)

18. Kumar, K., Farik, M.: A review of multimodal biometric authentication systems. Int. J. Sci. Technol. Res. **5**, 12 (2016)

19. Zupanic Pajnic, I., et al.: Prediction of autosomal STR typing success in ancient and Second World War bone samples. Forensic Sci. Int. Genet. **27**, 17–26 (2017)

20. Beck, M.B., Rouchka, E.C., Yampolskiy, R.V.: Finding data in DNA: computer forensic investigations of living organisms. In: Rogers, M., Seigfried-Spellar, K.C. (eds.) ICDF2C 2012. LNICST, vol. 114, pp. 204–219. Springer, Heidelberg (2013). https://doi.org/10.1007/978-3-642-39891-9_13

Supervised Group Sparse Representation via Intra-class Low-Rank Constraint

Peipei Kang[1], Xiaozhao Fang[1(✉)], Wei Zhang[1], Shaohua Teng[1], Lunke Fei[1],
Yong Xu[2], and Yubao Zheng[3]

[1] School of Computer Science and Technology, Guangdong University of Technology,
Guangzhou 510006, China
ppkanggdut@126.com, xzhfang168@126.com, {weizhang,shteng}@gdut.edu.cn,
flksxm@126.com
[2] Bio-Computing Research Center, Shenzhen Graduate School,
Harbin Institute of Technology, Shenzhen 518055, China
yongxu@ymail.com
[3] Department of Infectious Diseases,
The Third Affiliated Hospital of Sun Yat-Sen University, Guangzhou 510630, China
guangzhouzyb@126.com

Abstract. Group sparse representation (GSR) which uses the group structure of training samples as the prior knowledge has achieved extensive attention. However, GSR represents a new test sample using the original input features for least reconstruction, which may not be able to obtain discriminative reconstruction coefficients since redundant or noisy features may exist in the original input features. To obtain more discriminative data representation, in this paper we propose a novel supervised group sparse representation via intra-class low-rank constraint (GSRILC). Instead of representing the target by the original input features, GSRILC attempts to use the compact projection features in a new subspace for data reconstruction. Concretely, GSRILC projects data sharing the same class to a new subspace, and imposes low-rank constraint on the intra-class projections, which ensures that samples within the same class have a low rank structure. In this way, small intra-class distances and large inter-class distances can be achieved. To illustrate the effectiveness of the proposal, we conduct experiments on the Extended Yale B and CMU PIE databases, and results show the superiority of GSRILC.

Keywords: Group sparse representation · Intra-class low-rank
Discriminative data representation · Subspace learning

1 Introduction

It is well known that data representation plays an important role in the field of computer vision due to its great significance for follow-up analysis [1], and people tend to use regularization norms for obtaining simple but identifiable data

© Springer Nature Switzerland AG 2018
J. Zhou et al. (Eds.): CCBR 2018, LNCS 10996, pp. 206–213, 2018.
https://doi.org/10.1007/978-3-319-97909-0_22

representation. The sparse representation (SR) based and low-rank representation based feature learning methods have raised wide attention since they utilize the l_1 norm or l_2 norm constrained regularization or the low-rank constraint on the reconstruction matrix to make it recognitive, such as the sparse representation based classification (SRC) [2], the collaborative representation based classification (CRC) [3], the structured low-rank representation for classification (SLRRC) [4], and the structure-constrained low-rank representation (SC-LRR) [5]. Different from the SR based methods, group sparse representation (GSR) [6] also obtains satisfied performance and it is turned out to outperform SR based methods [7,8]. For the SR based methods, when samples from two different classes are similar, or the dictionary is not over-complete, the target from one class may be represented by samples from other classes, causing incorrect recognition result. However, samples sharing the same class are likely to be grouped together so that the structure of data is group-sparse. GSR treats this kind of group-sparse structure as prior knowledge, and aims to represent the target data by grouped (same class) samples, therefore the GSR based methods perform better.

However, some issues may exist since the above mentioned methods represent the new sample by original input features, and the original feature based representation may be disturbed by some redundant or noisy features. In recent years, [9,10] have revealed that the combinations of features are more discriminative than individual features. That is to say, features in a new subspace are probably more reliable. But how to achieve better recognition ability when we project data to the new subspace? Low-rank representation considers that data from the same class are close in new feature spaces and lie in the same subspace.

With this in mind, in this paper we propose a new supervised group sparse representation via intra-class low-rank constraint (GSRILC). To obtain more compact and discriminative data representation, we use a projection matrix to project original features to a more compact subspace and constrain intra-class data to be low-rank, which ensures that data is reconstructed by its same class of samples.

The main contributions of this paper are as follows.

(1) Different from GSR that reconstructs data by original features, GSRILC achieves compact data representation in a new subspace, which eliminates the negative effect from redundant or noisy features.
(2) GSRILC enhances the group structure by imposing the intra-class low-rank constraint, which is beneficial for data reconstruction within the same class and improving the discrimination of the new representation.

The reminder of this paper is organized as follows. We introduce the model, optimization and some analyses of the proposal in Sect. 2, and conduct experiments based on two face image data sets in Sect. 3. Finally we conclude this paper in Sect. 4.

2   Supervised Group Sparse Representation via Intra-class Low-Rank Constraint

Before the detail of GSRILC, we introduce the notations of the variables first. We denote matrix by capital letters. Specifically, $X \in R^{d \times n}$ is the training set with n samples, and the sample dimensionality is d. We define $X = [X^{(1)}, X^{(2)}, ..., X^{(c)}]$ from c classes, and $X^{(i)}$ is one of the training set where all the training samples are from i-th class. $Y \in R^{d \times m}$ denotes the test set containing totally m test samples. Besides, for a matrix $Q \in R^{m \times n}$, we have the Frobenius norm of Q as $||Q||_F^2 = \sum_{i=1}^{m} \sum_{j=1}^{n} Q_{ij}^2 = tr[Q^T Q]$. And the $L_{2,1}$ norm of Q is defined as $||Q||_{2,1} = \sum_{i=1}^{m} \sqrt{\sum_{j=1}^{n} Q_{ij}^2} = 2tr[Q^T D Q]$, where D is a diagonal matrix with $D_{ii} = \frac{1}{2||q_i||_2}$. Further more, the nuclear norm of Q is the convex approximation of low-rank constraint on Q, and $||Q||_* = \sum_{i=1}^{r} \delta_i$, where δ_i is one of the r singular values of Q.

2.1   Model of GSRILC

Considering that data representation in GSR may be disturbed by noisy features, we hope to find appropriate representations in a new subspace where the following characteristics need to be met.

(1) Data structure should be consistent with the real structure. That means data from the same class still keep in one group in the subspace and vice versa.

(2) The subspace should be discriminative enough to tell the labels of new samples.

It is natural that we introduce matrix $W \in R^{d \times r}$ to project original d-dimensional samples to a lower dimensionality of r. In order to achieve the first property of preserving data structure, we use the label information of training set, and impose the intra-class low-rank constraint on every group of projections, so the real group structure is preserved. It is formulated as (1).

$$\min \sum_{i=1}^{c} ||W^T X^{(i)}||_* \tag{1}$$

To fulfill the second property, i.e., telling the labels of test samples, we reconstruct every test sample by training samples in subspace, and classify it to the class with least group reconstruction error. In detail, we regard the training set as a dictionary, and represent test samples $Y \in R^{d \times m}$ by the dictionary, which is formulated as (2),

$$\min \frac{1}{2}||W^T Y - W^T X Z||_F^2 \tag{2}$$

where $Z \in R^{n \times m}$ is the reconstruction matrix. To obtain group-sparse representation, we enforce $l_{2,1}$ norm constraint on the reconstruction matrix Z as formula (3), because it is convex and can select class-specific samples across all data points with some sparsity [11].

$$\min ||Z||_{2,1} \tag{3}$$

Integrating the above three objectives into one framework, and imposing orthogonal constraint $W^T W = I$ to make the problem tractable, we obtain the final target (4),

$$\min_{W,Z} \frac{1}{2}||W^T Y - W^T X Z||_F^2 + \frac{\lambda_1}{2}||Z||_{2,1} + \lambda_2 \sum_{i=1}^{c} ||W^T X^{(i)}||_* \quad s.t. \quad W^T W = I \tag{4}$$

where λ_1 and λ_2 are tradeoff parameters.

2.2   Solution to GSRILC

We use the alternating direction method of multipliers (ADMM) [12] to solve problem (4). Define $A = W^T X$ to facilitate the optimization, then the corresponding augmented Lagrangian function is described as (5),

$$J = arg \min_{W,Z,A,P} \quad \frac{1}{2}||W^T Y - W^T X Z||_F^2 + \frac{\lambda_1}{2}||Z||_{2,1} + \lambda_2 \sum_{i=1}^{c} ||A^{(i)}||_*$$
$$+ \frac{\mu}{2}||A - W^T X + \frac{P}{\mu}||_F^2 \quad s.t. \quad W^T W = I \tag{5}$$

where $A^{(i)}$ is the counterpart of $X^{(i)}$ in new subspace, P is the Lagrange multiplier, and μ is the penalty parameter.

We alternatively update each variable of A, Z, W and P with other variables fixed. The iteration will stop when objective value is stable.

Step 1. Update A: Denoting $H = W^T X - \frac{P}{\mu}$, it will be clear to find that the optimization problem related to A can be transformed to the optimization about $A^{(i)}$. We solve each $A^{(i)}$ independently, and then join all $A^{(i)}$ to form A, $A = [A^{(1)}, A^{(2)}, ..., A^{(c)}]$. The way of updating $A^{(i)}$ is as Eq.(6),

$$A^{(i)} = \Theta_{\lambda_2/\mu}(H^{(i)}) \tag{6}$$

where Θ is the singular value thresholding (SVT) shrinkage operation.

Step 2. Update Z: Z can be updated by (7), where $U_{ii} = \frac{1}{2||z_i||_2}$, and z_i is the i-th row of Z. Note that (7) is derived by setting the partial derivative to Z as 0.

$$Z = (X^T W W^T X + \lambda_1 U)^{-1}(X^T W W^T Y) \tag{7}$$

Step 3. Update W: Solve W by (9) with A and Z fixed. The optimization problem about W is not easy to solve directly due to the non-convex constraint. Enlightened by [13] that can get the approximate solution during iterations based on gradient, we suppose $W(t)$ as the result of the t-th iteration of W, then the skew-symmetric matrix $\bigtriangledown = GW(t)^T - W(t)G^T$, where G is the gradient of optimization about W. Denoting $D = A + P/\mu$, we have Eq. (8) for calculating G.

$$G = YY^TW - XZY^TW - YZ^TX^TW$$
$$+ XZZ^TX^TW - \mu XD^T + \mu XX^TW \qquad (8)$$

We update W by the following Eq. (9). It is clear that an initial W is required. For fast convergence, we adopt PCA [14] to initialize W by selecting the eigenvectors corresponding to the smallest r eigenvalues of $[X, Y]^T$.

$$W(t+1) = (I + \frac{\tau}{2}\bigtriangledown)^{-1}(I - \frac{\tau}{2}\bigtriangledown)W(t) \qquad (9)$$

where τ is the iteration step size.

Step 4. Update P, μ: Lagrange multiplier P and penalty parameter μ are updated by Eq. (10),

$$P = P + \mu(A - W^TX)$$
$$\mu = min(\rho\mu, \mu_{max}) \qquad (10)$$

where ρ and μ_{max} are two constants.

2.3   Computational Complexity and Convergence

The main computational consumptions lie in solving A, Z and W. Specifically speaking, the SVT operation for solving A is based on a $r \times n_i$ matrix with computational complexity of $O(n_i^3)$, so the whole computation about updating A in one iteration is $O(\sum_{i=1}^{c} n_i^3)$. For updating Z and W, the inverse operation can be seen on a $n \times n$ matrix and a $d \times d$ matrix with the computational complexity of $O(n^3)$ and $O(d^3)$ respectively. Totally, the whole computational complexity of this algorithm is approximately $O(t(n^3 + d^3 + \sum_{i=1}^{c} n_i^3))$, where t denotes the number of iterations.

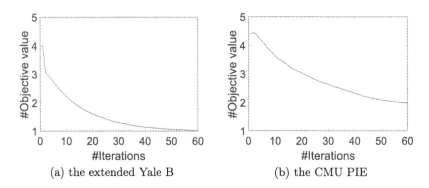

(a) the extended Yale B   (b) the CMU PIE

Fig. 1. The objective value versus iterations on the (a) extended Yale B and (b) PIE databases.

We testify its convergence property through experiments on the Extended Yale B and PIE face databases by showing the objective value with 60 iterations in Fig. 1. It is obvious that the objective value decreases along with the iterations, and finally stays stable, which proves the convergence of the proposal. Note that during this experiment, 10 samples of each class are randomly selected as training set, the remaining as test set.

2.4   Classification Detail

In this section, we introduce the detailed way for the classification of GSRILC. For a test sample y_i that is the i-th column of Y, we use every training set $X^{(j)}$ in X to reconstruct it. Suppose $\delta_{X^{(j)}}$ denotes the column indexes of $X^{(j)}$, then the corresponding reconstruction coefficient of y_i is $Z_i^{(j)}$ which represents the elements of the i-th column and $\delta_{X^{(j)}}$-th rows of Z. After projecting y_i to the new subspace by W, we classify y_i to the class that wins the least reconstruction error, i.e., $y_i \in \min_j ||W^T y_i - W^T X^{(j)} Z_i^{(j)}||_F^2$, $j = 1, 2, ..., c$.

3   Experiment Results

The Extended Yale B collects 2414 images from 38 people, 59–64 images for each one. In this database, there are illumination changes from different directions for every person, and we resize every picture to $32 \times 32 = 1024$ pixels.

The CMU PIE face database is collected by Carnegie Mellon University. This database contains 41368 images from 68 people, with different poses, illuminations and expressions. In this experiment, we only select a subset of five near front poses for training and test. Specifically speaking, we select C05 (look left), C07 (look up), C09 (look down), C27 (look forward) and C29 (look right) under different illuminations and expressions, thus we have totally 11554 pictures and an average of 170 per person. We also cropped every image into 32×32 pixels in advance.

Figure 2 shows the relationship between classification accuracy and dimensionality on the two data sets where 10 samples of each class are randomly selected as training set, the remaining as test set. It can be seen that the classification accuracy increases with the increase of projection dimensionality, but when the dimensionality reaches a certain value, the classification accuracy no longer changes. The reason is that a certain dimensional subspace is able to cover the information of data, but too few features are not enough to embody the difference.

Tables 1 and 2 report the classification accuracies for various methods on the two databases. For all methods, we perform four groups of experiments, where different number of samples (10, 15, 20, 25) per class are selected for training, and the remaining for test. Note that we repeat each group of experiment for 30 times and give the mean results. It can be seen that GSRILC performs best among all the compared methods. The main reason may be that GSRILC obtains a more discriminative data representation by utilizing the group information compared with others.

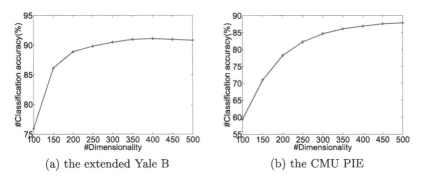

(a) the extended Yale B   (b) the CMU PIE

Fig. 2. The curves of classification accuracy versus the dimensionality on the (a) extended Yale B, (b) CMU PIE,

Table 1. Classification accuracies (%) for various methods on the Extended Yale B face database

Alg.	10	15	20	25
SRC [2]	87.8 ± 0.3	92.6 ± 0.6	94.4 ± 0.6	96.7 ± 0.5
CRC [3]	86.1 ± 0.5	90.7 ± 0.3	93.0 ± 0.2	94.1 ± 0.3
SLRRC [4]	85.5 ± 0.4	91.4 ± 0.6	94.0 ± 0.5	95.6 ± 0.7
SC-LRR [5]	85.6 ± 0.4	88.7 ± 0.8	92.8 ± 0.3	94.5 ± 0.8
ILRDFL [15]	86.8 ± 0.7	91.3 ± 0.6	93.9 ± 0.8	95.5 ± 0.6
GSRILC	$\mathbf{91.3 \pm 0.5}$	$\mathbf{93.9 \pm 0.5}$	$\mathbf{95.5 \pm 0.5}$	$\mathbf{97.1 \pm 0.4}$

Table 2. Classification accuracies (%) for various methods on the CMU PIE face database

Alg.	10	15	20	25
SRC [2]	76.4 ± 0.3	88.1 ± 0.2	90.2 ± 0.5	93.4 ± 0.2
CRC [3]	83.8 ± 0.4	88.3 ± 0.3	91.0 ± 0.6	93.2 ± 0.3
SLRRC [4]	80.8 ± 0.3	86.7 ± 0.1	89.6 ± 0.3	91.8 ± 0.2
SC-LRR [5]	86.9 ± 0.4	90.2 ± 0.6	92.6 ± 0.7	94.0 ± 0.5
ILRDFL [15]	84.7 ± 0.6	90.3 ± 0.5	93.2 ± 0.6	94.1 ± 0.7
GSRILC	$\mathbf{87.2 \pm 0.0}$	$\mathbf{91.2 \pm 0.0}$	$\mathbf{93.2 \pm 0.0}$	$\mathbf{94.2 \pm 0.0}$

4   Conclusion

In this paper, we propose a novel supervised group sparse representation method via intra-class low-rank constraint. By projecting data to a new subspace, we obtain compact data representation and weaken the influence of noisy features. The intra-class low-rank constraint on class-specific data ensures the discrimination of subspaces and enhances the group sparse representation. Experiments on two face image data sets show the superiority of this proposal. We leave the problem of high computational complexity to the future.

Acknowledgments. This work is supported in part by the Natural Science Foundation of China under Grants 61772141, 61702110, 61603100, Guangdong Provincial Natural Science Foundation under Grant 17ZK0422, Guangdong Provincial Science and Technology Project under Grants 2015B090901016, 2016B010108007, and Guangzhou Science and Technology Project under Grants 201804010347.

References

1. Fang, X.Z., et al.: Approximate low-rank projection learning for feature extraction. IEEE Trans. Neural Netw. Learn. Syst. **99**, 1–14 (2018)
2. Wright, J., Yang, A.Y., Ganesh, A., Sastry, S.S., Ma, Y.: Robust face recognition via sparse representation. IEEE Trans. Pattern Anal. Mach. Intell. **31**(2), 210–227 (2009)
3. Zhang, L., Yang, M., Feng, X.C.: Sparse representation or collaborative representation: which helps face recognition? In: 2011 IEEE International Conference on Computer Vision, pp. 471–478. IEEE (2011)
4. Zhang, Y.M.Z., Jiang, Z.L., Davis, L.S.: Learning structured low-rank representations for image classification. In: IEEE Conference on Computer Vision and Pattern Recognition, pp. 676–683. IEEE Computer Society (2013)
5. Tang, K.W., Liu, R.S., Su, Z.X., Zhang, J.: Structure-constrained low-rank representation. IEEE Trans. Neural Netw. Learn. Syst. **25**(12), 2167–2179 (2014)
6. Yuan, M., Lin, Y.: Model selection and estimation in regression with grouped variables. J. Royal Stat. Soc. **68**(1), 49–67 (2006)
7. Majumdar, A., Ward, R.K.: Classification via group sparsity promoting regularization. In: IEEE International Conference on Acoustics, Speech and Signal Processing, pp. 861–864. IEEE (2009)
8. Gao, L.W., Li, Y.Q., Huang, J.Z., Zhou, S.G.: Semi-supervised group sparse representation: model, algorithm and applications. In: European Conference on Artificial Intelligence, pp. 507–514. IOS Press (2016)
9. Li, Z.C., Liu, J., Tang, J.H., Lu, H.Q.: Robust structured subspace learning for data representation. IEEE Trans. Pattern Anal. Mach. Intell. **37**(10), 2085–2098 (2015)
10. Fang, X.Z., Teng, S.H., Lai, Z.H., He, Z.S., Xie, S.L., Wong, W.K.: Robust latent subspace learning for image classification. IEEE Trans. Neural Netw. Learn. Syst. **99**, 1–14 (2017)
11. Ren, C.X., Dai, D.Q., Yan, H.: Robust classification using $l_{2,1}$-norm based regression model. Pattern Recogn. **45**(7), 2708–2718 (2012)
12. Boyd, S., Parikh, N., Chu, E., Peleato, B., Eckstein, J.: Distributed optimization and statistical learning via the alternating direction method of multipliers. Found. Trends Mach. Learn. **3**(1), 1–122 (2010)
13. Wen, Z.W., Yin, W.T.: A feasible method for optimization with orthogonality constraints. Math. Program. **142**(1–2), 397–434 (2013)
14. Turk, M., Pentland, A.: Eigenfaces for recognition. J. Cogn. Neurosci. **3**(1), 71–86 (1991)
15. Zhou, P., Lin, Z.C., Zhang, C.: Integrated low-rank-based discriminative feature learning for recognition. IEEE Trans. Neural Netw. Learn. Syst. **27**(5), 1080–1093 (2016)

Partial Multi-view Clustering via Auto-Weighting Similarity Completion

Chen Min, Miaomiao Cheng, Jian Yu, and Liping Jing[✉]

Beijing Key Lab of Traffic Data Analysis and Mining,
Beijing Jiaotong University, Beijing 100089, China
{minchen,chengmiaomiao,jianyu,lpjing}@bjtu.edu.cn

Abstract. With the development of data collection techniques, multi-view clustering (MVC) becomes an emerging research direction to improve the clustering performance. However, most MVC methods assume that the objects are observed on all the views. As a result, existing MVC methods may not achieve satisfactory performance when some views are incomplete. In this paper, we propose a new MVC method, called as partial multi-view clustering via auto-weighting similarity completion (**PMVC-ASC**). The major contribution lies in jointly learning the consensus similarity matrix, exploring the complementary information among multiple distinct feature sets, quantifying the contribution of each view and splitting the similarity graph into several informative submatrices, each submatrix corresponding to one cluster. The learning process can be modeled via a joint minimization problem, and the corresponding optimization algorithm is given. A series of experiments are conducted on real-world datasets to demonstrate the superiority of **PMVC-ASC** by comparing with the state-of-the-art methods.

Keywords: Multi-view clustering · Partial data
Similarity completion

1 Introduction

With the increasing of advanced information technology, multi-view data are very ubiquitous in many real world applications. Beneath the prosperous studies of the multi-view data, there is a fundamental problem that the data from one view or more than one view are inaccessible. For example, in social platform (such as Facebook and Flickr), more and more digital images are uploaded to the websites, but only partial images are annotated by users. In this case, the data usually contain two kinds of objects, one having full views' information while the other having partial views' information, which are called as partial data [2] and incomplete data [10,14]. Because of partial multi-view data, most existing multi-view learning methods are inevitably degenerate or even fail. In this paper, we consider unsupervised partial multi-view learning, i.e., partial

© Springer Nature Switzerland AG 2018
J. Zhou et al. (Eds.): CCBR 2018, LNCS 10996, pp. 214–222, 2018.
https://doi.org/10.1007/978-3-319-97909-0_23

multi-view clustering (PMVC), which is a challenging task for lacking supervised information to guide the learning process.

PMVC aims to sufficiently divide the objects into different groups and has received considerable attention in the area of artificial intelligence and machine learning. A surge of methods have been proposed, which can be roughly divided into two categories (i) exploring the complementary and consistency among multiple views by identifying the common representation [2,4,7,10,12], and (ii) filling the missing information via kernel completion technique [3,6,8,9,15]. Although the above PMVC methods generally provide promising results, they have two main drawbacks. Firstly, the existing methods usually treat all views equally, ignoring their differences when contributing to the learning process. For instance, the text view plays a more important role than the visual view in image-text processing. Secondly, the existing completion methods are all based on the kernel matrices and can only fit kernel-based multi-view clustering.

In this paper, thus, we propose a novel partial multi-view clustering model (**PMVC-ASC**), which contains three components. The first one is to learn the consensus correlations among objects with complete views. The nearly parameter-free weight of each view is automatically determined and iteratively updated. The second part is to effectively complete the missing correlations among objects with partial views by exploiting the relations between the obtained correlations and the missing correlations. The third component is to constrain the clusters from the correlation graph. We integrate the two pipelined stets (multi-view representation learning and clustering) into one optimization framework. Moreover, to efficiently and effectively seek the solution of the joint optimization problem, an iterative optimization algorithm is designed. Extensive experiments on benchmark datasets are conducted to demonstrate the superiority of **PMVC-ASC** over the state-of-the-art methods.

The rest of this paper is organized as follows. The proposed model and its optimization algorithm are given in Sects. 2 and 3 respectively. In Sect. 4, a series of experiments on real world datasets are conducted to demonstrate the clustering performance. Finally, Sect. 5 draws a brief conclusion.

2   The Proposed Model

Given a multi-view dataset with n data objects, each object in the v-th view is described with d^v features. Our goal is to perform multi-view representation learning and multi-view clustering simultaneously. In order to sufficiently explore the complementary information among multiple views, we propose a novel partial multi-view clustering model (**PMVC-ASC**). It consists of three components: the first one for adaptive local structure learning to obtain the incomplete similarity matrix, the second one for similarity matrix completion, and the last one for constraining the clusters from the completed similarity matrix. These three components are iteratively performed so that they affect each other until the optimal stage is obtained. Moreover, the weight of each view is automatically identified for better clustering performance.

In the whole paper, all the vectors are written as lowercase while the matrices are written as uppercase. For an arbitrary matrix X, x_i denotes the i-th row of X and x_{ij} denotes the j-th elements in x_i. X^T and $tr(X)$ stand for the transpose and trace of X, respectively. $\|X\|_F$ denotes the Frobeneous (F) norm of X. $\|v\|_2$ represents the l_2 norm of vector v. Moreover, $\mathbf{1}$ and I mean all the elements of a column vector are one and the identity matrix, respectively.

2.1   Adaptive Local Structure Learning

For partial multi-view data, the i-th object x_i^v may not have information in the v-th view, i.e., the entries in the v-th data matrix X^v are empty. For simplicity, we assign zeros to these missing entries. Let M^v indicate the index set for the observed objects pairs in data matrix X^v, where $m_{ij}^v = 1$ represents that both i-th and j-th objects exist in the v-th view, otherwise $m_{ij}^v = 0$. Let $q_{ij}^v = m_{ij}^v / \sum_v m_{ij}^v$ and $m_{ij} = m_{ij}^1 \vee \cdots \vee m_{ij}^v$.

To capture the correlations hidden in the observed multi-view objects, we adopt the idea of adaptive local structure learning [11] on the partial multi-view data. The neighbors of x_i are defined by its probabilistic neighbors. For the i-th object, all the data objects can be connected to it as a neighbor with probability s_{ij}. Usually, a smaller distance d_{ij}^v between two objects x_i^v and x_j^v should be assigned with a larger probability s_{ij}. Considering the contribution of each view may be different, a more reasonable manner is to weight these views with suitable strengths. Then, the probabilities $s_{ij}|_{m_{ij}=1}$ can be determined via

$$\min_S \sum_v \omega_v \sum_{\{i,j|m_{ij}^v=1\}} q_{ij}^v d_{ij}^v s_{ij} \quad \text{s.t.} \quad 0 \leqslant s_{ij} \leqslant 1. \tag{1}$$

where ω_v is the weight of the v-th view.

2.2   Similarity Matrix Completion

As multi-view data have different feature sets, the correlations among partial objects (i.e., $m_{ij} = 0$) can not be directly obtained. Here, $m_{ij} = 0$ indicates that all elements of $\{m_{ij}^1, \cdots, m_{ij}^v\}$ are zero. As a result, the similarity matrix is incomplete, which makes the existing multi-view clustering methods inevitably degenerate or even fail. To address it, we apply matrix completion on the incomplete similarity matrix by taking advantage of the obtained correlations among objects. Intuitively, if objects i and k are close to each other, and j and k are close to each other, the distance between i and j is very likely to be small. In this case, we can complete the similarity $s_{ij}|_{m_{ij}=0}$ with $h_{ij} = \sum_{k=1}^K s_{ik} \times s_{kj}$ (K is the number of objects with complete views), which can be formulated as

$$\min_S \sum_{\{i,j|m_{ij}=0\}} (s_{ij} - h_{ij})^2 \quad \text{s.t.} \quad 0 \leqslant s_{ij} \leqslant 1. \tag{2}$$

2.3 Structured Optimal Graph

Inspired by [1] (for single-view data), we integrate the subspace learning and spectral clustering into one framework to deal with multi-view clustering. Our goal is to assign one object into only one cluster, thus, with the aid of similarity matrix, clustering problem can be modeled via

$$\sum_{i,j=1}^{n} \|f_i - f_j\|_2^2 s_{ij} = 2Tr(F^T L_S F) \quad \text{s.t.} \ \ F^T F = I. \tag{3}$$

here $F \in \mathscr{R}^{n \times c}$ is cluster indicator matrix with c clusters. $L_S = D_S - \frac{S^T + S}{2}$ is the Laplacian matrix of S. D_S is a diagonal matrix and its i-th diagonal element is defined as $D_S(i,i) = \sum_j \frac{(s_{ij}+s_{ji})}{2}$.

By combining (1), (2) and (3), we can get the proposed **PMVC-ASC** model

$$\min_S \sum_v \omega_v \sum_{\{i,j|m_{ij}^v=1\}} q_{ij}^v d_{ij}^v s_{ij} + \beta \sum_{\{i,j|m_{ij}=0\}} (s_{ij} - h_{ij})^2 + \alpha \|S\|_F^2 + 2\lambda Tr(F^T L_S F)$$

$$\text{s.t.} \ \ s_i^T 1 = 1, 0 \leqslant s_{ij} \leqslant 1, F^T F = I. \tag{4}$$

where β and λ are trade-off parameters. The third item is added to avoid trivial solution where only the nearest object of x_i is assigned with 100% probability and other objects be 0.

3 The Optimization Algorithm

Obviously, problem (4) is not a joint convex optimization problem. In order to find its optimal solution, we adopt the iterative minimization technique via solving the following subproblems alternatively.

3.1 Update S

S can be updated by fixing ω_v and F, then (4) with S can be partitioned into two parts. In the i-th row, we set $\sum_{j=1}^n (s_{ij}|m_{ij}=1) = l_i$ and $g_i = 1 - l_i$. l_i is set to be 1 in the first iteration and $1 - g_i$ in the following iteration. In each iteration, g_i is changed and the updating of g_i is described at the end of this subsection. $s_{ij}|m_{ij}=1$: Let $d_{ij} = \sum_v q_{ij}^v d_{ij}^v + \lambda \|f_i - f_j\|_2^2$, which represents the weighted distance between objects x_i and x_j. Due to the independence assumption among objects, we can update s_i one by one, then (4) can be rewritten as

$$\min_{s_i} \sum_j (d_{ij} s_{ij} + \alpha s_{ij}^2) \quad \text{s.t.} \ \ s_i^T 1 = l_i, 0 \leqslant s_{ij} \leqslant 1. \tag{5}$$

Let $d_i \in \mathscr{R}^{n \times 1}$ with the j-th elements as d_{ij}, then the above problem (5) becomes

$$\min_{s_i} \|s_i + \frac{1}{2\alpha} d_i\|_2^2 \quad \text{s.t.} \ \ s_i^T 1 = l_i, 0 \leqslant s_{ij} \leqslant 1. \tag{6}$$

To deal with constrained optimization, we introduce its Lagrangian function

$$\mathscr{L}(s_i, \theta, \varphi_i) = \|s_i + \frac{1}{2\alpha_i}d_i\|_2^2 - \theta(s_i^T \mathbf{1} - l_i) - \varphi_i^T s_i \quad (7)$$

here θ and φ_i are Lagrangian multipliers. According to the KKT condition, the optimal solution of s_i containing exact k non-zero elements is

$$s_{ij}|_{m_{ij}=1} = -\frac{d_{ij}}{2\alpha_i} + \frac{l_i}{k} + \frac{1}{2k\alpha_i}\sum_{j=1}^{k}d_{ij} \quad (8)$$

And α is set to be

$$\alpha = \frac{1}{n}\sum_{i=1}^{n}\alpha_i = \frac{1}{n}\sum_{i=1}^{n}(\frac{k}{2l_i}d_{i,k+1} - \frac{1}{2l_i}\sum_{j=1}^{k}d_{ij}) $$

where $d_{i1}, d_{i2}, \ldots, d_{in}$ are sorted in ascending order.
$s_{ij}|_{m_{ij}=0}$: Let $d_{ij}^f = \|f_i - f_j\|_2^2$, the problem (4) about each s_i can be written as

$$\min_{s_i} \sum_{j}(\beta\|s_i - h_i\|_2^2 + \alpha s_i^2 + \lambda d_i^{fT} s_i) \quad \text{s.t.} \ 0 \leqslant s_{ij} \leqslant 1. \quad (9)$$

Its Lagrangian function can be formulated as

$$\mathscr{L}(s_i, \varphi_i) = \beta\|s_i - h_i\|_2^2 + \alpha s_i^2 + \lambda d_i^{fT} s_i - \varphi_i^T s_i \quad (10)$$

here φ_i is Lagrangian multiplier. According to KKT condition, s_i can be updated via

$$s_{ij}|_{m_{ij}=0} = \frac{\beta h_{ij} - \lambda d_{ij}^f}{2\beta + 2\alpha} \quad (11)$$

After obtaining $s_{ij}|_{m_{ij}=0}$, g_i is updated by $g_i = \sum_{j=1}^{n}(s_{ij}|_{m_{ij}=0})$.

3.2 Update ω_v and F

When fixing S, (4) with respect to F becomes

$$\min_{F \in \mathscr{R}^{n \times c}, F^T F = I} Tr(F^T L_S F) \quad (12)$$

Equation (12) is the same as spectral clustering given the similarity S. The optimal solution of F can be obtained by calculating the first c eigenvectors of L_S.

ω_v can be updated with $\omega_v = 0.5/(\sum_{i,j} m_{ij}^v d_{ij}^v s_{ij})^{\frac{1}{2}}$ via the optimization method in [13]. It is clearly shown that once the similarity matrix S is obtained, the weight of each view ω_v is automatically determined. In addition, more compact the data in one view is, more contributions the view makes to the clustering result. This method to set the weight of each view has the advantage of less time to tune the parameter and considering the internal information of the data without noise.

4 Experiment Results and Discussion

In this section, a series of experiments are conducted to validate **PMVC-ASC** by comparing with the state-of-the-art partial multi-view clustering methods.

4.1 Experimental Setting

Datasets. In this paper, we evaluate the proposed method on three widely used multi-view datasets: *COIL*, *UCI-HD*, and *MNIST*. *COIL-20*[1] consists of 1440 images with 20 categories. Three features (1024 Intensity, 3304 LBP, and 6750 Gabor) are extracted as three views. *UCI-HD*[2] contains 0-9 handwritten digits data with 2000 instances from UCI repository. It includes two feature sets, 216 profile correlations (FAC) and 240 pixel averages in 2×3 windows (PIX). *MNIST*[3] is a handwritten digit dataset including 10000 examples (10 categories) with three feature sets.

Methodology. To validate the effectiveness of **PMVC-ASC**, we compare it with five recently published approaches as baselines, including three typical subspace methods: MIC [7], GPMVC [4] and USL [5] and two important kernel completion methods: MKKIK [6] and CKKM [3]. The parameters of all approaches are carefully set for fairness. For MKKIK and CKKM, Gaussian kernels are generated by setting widths as the mean of all pair-wise object distances. Three widely used metrics are adopted to evaluate the clustering performances: accuracy (ACC), normalized mutual information (NMI), and adjusted rand index (ARI). The higher value indicates better clustering quality.

4.2 Results and Discussion

To simulate the partial multi-view setting, we randomly select a small fraction of objects as complete data with all-view information, while the remaining objects as the incomplete data which are randomly described by only one view (this is much harder than that the incomplete data are described by more than one view). Such process is repeated 10 times and the average results are recorded. Partial Example Ratio (PER) records the fraction of incomplete objects.

Effect of Parameters. There are three important parameters (β, λ, k) in the proposed model **PMVC-ASC**. In experiments, trade-off parameters β and λ are tuned from 10^{-2} to 10^3 and 10^{-9} to 10^2, respectively. The number of nearest neighbors k is tuned from 1 to 50 with step 1, as shown in Fig. 1.

It can be seen that the clustering performance becomes better as β increases, which suggested that similarity matrix completion is effective for

---

[1] http://www.cs.columbia.edu/CAVE/software/softlib/.

[2] http://archive.ics.uci.edu/ml/datasets.html.

[3] http://yann.lecun.com/exdb/mnist/.

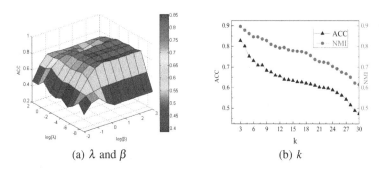

(a) λ and β (b) k

Fig. 1. Effect of parameters (a) β, λ and (b) k on PMVC-ASC for three-view data *COIL*.

clustering result. The results reach the best when $\beta = 100$. We believe this is because larger β can enforce $s_{ij} = h_{ij}$ to preserve the efficacy of similarity completion. Figure 1(b) indicates that **PMVC-ASC** performs best at the middle point $k = 3$. The reason is that small k can not optimally characterize the data structure, while large k may introduce noisy information. Other two datasets have the similar trends and the following experiments are conducted with the optimal settings.

Clustering Performance. The first experiment is conducted on *MNIST* by varying the fraction of partial objects (PER) from 99% to 90% with step of 1%. Note that larger PER makes learning task more difficult. Figure 2(a) shows the clustering results obtained by six methods. Obviously, all methods suffer from large PER. Fortunately, **PMVC-ASC** consistently outperforms baselines and achieves the promising result even with a large fraction of missing data, esp., $PER = 99\%$.

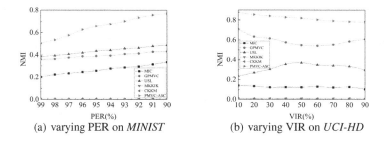

(a) varying PER on *MINIST*   (b) varying VIR on *UCI-HD*

Fig. 2. Comparing clustering performance (NMI) under varying (a) PER on *MNIST* and (b) VIR on *UCI-HD*.

In real application, one view may be much more incomplete than others. We simulate this situation by setting the value of view's imbalance ratio (VIR) on two-view data *UCI-HD*. Let $VIR^v = n^v / \sum_v n^v$, where n^v is the number of partial instances in the v-th view. Figure 2(b) gives the effect of VIR^{FAC}. As expected, **PMVC-ASC** consistently outperforms all baselines with different VIR values.

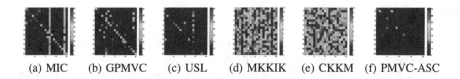

(a) MIC   (b) GPMVC   (c) USL   (d) MKKIK   (e) CKKM   (f) PMVC-ASC

Fig. 3. Confusion matrices (clustering result) of six methods on *COIL*.

To investigate the proposed model **PMVC-ASC**, the confusion matrices obtained by six methods on *COIL* are listed in Fig. 3. It clearly shows that **PMVC-ASC** has ability to separate the partial multi-view objects well, while other methods can not.

Table 1. Comparing PMVC-ASC with five baselines on clustering three partial multi-view datasets in term of ACC, NMI and ARI.

Methods	ACC			NMI			ARI		
	COIL	UCI-HD	MNIST	COIL	UCI-HD	MNIST	COIL	UCI-HD	MNIST
MIC [7]	0.5529	0.1495	0.2705	0.5782	0.1228	0.2008	0.3575	0.0013	0.0903
GPMVC [4]	0.5215	<u>0.4695</u>	0.3085	<u>0.7009</u>	<u>0.5469</u>	0.2572	<u>0.3951</u>	<u>0.3151</u>	0.1231
USL [5]	<u>0.5631</u>	0.3415	<u>0.4075</u>	0.6312	0.3269	<u>0.3870</u>	0.3624	0.1652	<u>0.2634</u>
MKKIK [6]	0.1007	0.1340	0.1152	0.0468	0.0100	0.0022	0.0005	0.0008	0.0002
CKKM [3]	0.1021	0.1325	0.1128	0.0491	0.0121	0.0018	0.0011	0.0015	0.0001
PMVC-ASC	**0.8278**	**0.8250**	**0.4292**	**0.8969**	**0.8193**	**0.5070**	**0.7537**	**0.7592**	**0.3093**

Table 1 lists the comparison results on three datasets, where the best and second best results are marked in bold and underlined respectively. Since the number of instances is small in *COIL* and *UCI-HD*, we test the results with $PER = 90\%$. For *MNIST*, the results are obtained with $PER = 99\%$. As expected, **PMVC-ASC** is superior to all baselines, which confirms that the structured optimal graph constraint, similarity completion, and considering the different contributions of different view are helpful for partial MVC. As compared with the best baseline, **PMVC-ASC** obtained more than 5%, 27% and 50% relative gain (on all metrics) for *MNIST*, *COIL* and *UCI-HD* respectively.

5   Conclusions

In this paper, we propose a novel partial multi-view representation learning model. It can simultaneously represent the partial multi-view data and determine the clusters from the new representation of data. Moreover, the importance of each view can be automatically identified for extracting proper volume of information from each view. The experiments on real-world datasets demonstrate that **PMVC-ASC** consistently and significantly outperforms the popular existing partial multi-view clustering methods.

References

1. Li, C., Vidal, R.: Structured sparse subspace clustering: a unified optimization framework. In: Proceedings of CVPR (2015)
2. Li, S., Jiang, Y., Zhou, Z.: Partial multi-view clustering. In: Proceedings of AAAI (2014)
3. Ye, Y., Liu, X., Liu, Q., Yin, J.: Consensus kernel-means clustering for incomplete multiview data. Comput. Intell. Neurosci. **2017**, 11 (2017)
4. Rai, N., Neigi, S., Chaudhury, S.: Partial multi-view clustering using graph regularized NMF. In: Proceedings of ICPR (2016)
5. Yin, Q., Wu, S., Wang, L.: Unified subspace learning for incomplete and unlabeled multi-view data. Pattern Recognit. **67**, 313–327 (2017)
6. Liu, X., Li, M., Wang, L., Dou, Y., Yin, J., Zhu, E.: Multiple Kernel k-means with incomplete kernels. In: Proceedings of AAAI (2017)
7. Shao, W., He, L., Yu, P.S.: Multiple incomplete views clustering via weighted non-negative matrix factorization with $L_{2,1}$ regularization. In: Appice, A., Rodrigues, P.P., Santos Costa, V., Soares, C., Gama, J., Jorge, A. (eds.) ECML PKDD 2015. LNCS (LNAI), vol. 9284, pp. 318–334. Springer, Cham (2015). https://doi.org/10.1007/978-3-319-23528-8_20
8. Trivedi, A., Rai, P., Daume, H.: Multiview clustering with incomplete views. In: Proceedings of NIPS (2010)
9. Shao, W., Shi, X., Yu, P.: Clustering on multiple incomplete datasets via collective kernel learning. In: Proceedings of ICDM (2013)
10. Zhao, L., Chen, Z., Yang, Y., Wang, Z., Leung, V.: Incomplete multi-view clustering via deep semantic mapping. Neurocomputing **275**, 1053–1062 (2018)
11. Nie, F., Wang, X., Huang, H.: Clustering and projected clustering with adaptive neighbors. In: Proceedings of ACM SIGKDD (2014)
12. Zhao, H., Liu, H., Fu, Y.: Incomplete multi-modal visual data grouping. In: Proceedings of IJCAI (2016)
13. Nie, F., Cai, G., Li, X.: Multi-view clustering and semi-supervised classification with adaptive neighbours. In: Proceedings of AAAI (2017)
14. Xu, C., Tao, D., Xu, C.: Multi-view learning with incomplete views. IEEE Trans. Image Process. **24**(12), 5812–5825 (2015)
15. Bhadra, S., Kaski, S., Rousu, J.: Multi-view kernel completion. Mach. Learn. **106**(5), 713–739 (2017)

Phase Retrieval by the Inverse Power Method

Qi Luo[1,2(⊠)], Hongxia Wang[1,2], and Jianyun Chen[1,2]

[1] College of Science, National University of Defense Technology,
Changsha 410073, Hunan, People's Republic of China
[2] Beijing Institute of Graphics, Beijing 10029, People's Republic of China
luoqi_nudt@outlook.com, whx8292@hotmail.com, cjy2918@163.com
http://www.ccbr2018.xju.edu.cn/

Abstract. Phase retrieval is to recover signals from phaseless linear measurements. The most efficient methods to tackle this problem are nonconvex gradient approaches, which however generally need an elaborate initialized guess to ensure successful reconstruction. The inverse power method is proposed to provide a more accurate initialization. Numerical experiments illustrate the higher accuracy of the proposed method over other initialization methods. And we further demonstrate the iterative use of the initialization method can obtain an even better estimate.

Keywords: Phase retrieval · Spectral method · Inverse power method

1 Introduction

Phase retrieval is to recover the signal $x \in \mathbb{C}^n$ from the phaseless measurement:

$$b_i = |\langle a_i, x \rangle|, \quad 1 \leq i \leq m, \tag{1}$$

where the measuring vectors a_i in $\mathbb{C}^n$. The measuring matrix $A = [a_1, \cdots, a_m]$ is assumed to be full-rank. The applications of phase retrieval exists widely in many fields of sciences and engineering, including X-ray crystallography [1], molecular imaging [2], biological imaging [3] as well as astronomy [4]. To avoid the illness of problem, it is proved that m should be larger than $2n - 1$ in real-valued case or $4n - 4$ in complex-valued case [5,6], which we call the information limit in phase retrieval.

The nonlinear inverse problem in (1) is generally known to be NP-hard [7]. Therefore, without adopting effective heuristic function, it is almost impossible to find the solution in tolerable time when n is relatively large. The efficient and practical approaches to this problem are generally nonconvex and can be roughly categorized into two types: alternating projection algorithms (also referred as fixed point algorithms) [8,9] and gradient-descent methods [10,11].

Work in this paper was supported by NSF grants 61571008.

© Springer Nature Switzerland AG 2018
J. Zhou et al. (Eds.): CCBR 2018, LNCS 10996, pp. 223–230, 2018.
https://doi.org/10.1007/978-3-319-97909-0_24

The crucial step for nonconvex methods is an elaborate initialization. Namely, one usually needs a good estimate of the true solution to ensure the probability of successful reconstruction. In fact, many nonconvex gradient-like method, e.g. the Wirtinger flow method [10] and the Amplitude flow method [12] degenerate to be convex if the initialization lies around the true solution. As more accurate initializer is proposed, the nonconvex method can performs even better when m is below the information limit in phase retrieval [13].

Related work is presented in Sect. 2. In Sect. 3, a more accurate initialization method, called the inverse power method is proposed in this paper. And through numerical experiments, the effectiveness and superior accuracy are illustrated in Sect. 4.

2   Related Work

Current initialization methods include the spectral method [8], the truncated spectral method [14] and the null vector method [15]. For the convenience of the notation, the measuring vectors are normalized to unit vectors before the initialization step, namely $\|a_i\| = 1$.

The spectral method is a linear algebraic initializer by the maximization problem:

$$x_{\text{spec}} = \arg\max\left\{\|\text{diag}(b)A^*x\|^2 : x \in \mathbb{C}^n, \|x\| = \|x_0\|\right\}, \tag{2}$$

where $\text{diag}(b)$ is a function that returns a square diagonal matrix with the elements of vector b on the main diagonal.

The truncated spectral method is a modification of the spectral method. This method first select a part of measuring vectors which have the largest inner product with the true solution x. Then an estimate can be obtained by finding the vector that is most coherent with the selected set of vectors. Specifically, the truncated spectral vector method is to solve the maximization problem:

$$x_{\text{t-spec}} = \arg\max\left\{\|\text{diag}(1_\tau \odot b)A^*x\|^2 : x \in \mathbb{C}^n, \|x\| = \|x_0\|\right\}, \tag{3}$$

where $\odot$ stands for element-wise multiplication, and 1_τ is the characteristic function of the set

$$\{i : b(i) \leq \tau\|x_0\|\} \tag{4}$$

with some preset threshold value $\tau \in (0, 1)$.

The null vector method is proposed from another viewpoint: the orthogonality between vectors. A set of *weak* vectors that are most orthogonal to x are selected from the measuring vectors. And through seeking the vector which is most orthogonal to the *weak* vectors, one can obtain an estimate of the x. Mathematically speaking, the *weak* vector set is denoted as $I \subset \{1, \cdots, m\}$ and its complement I_c are defined such that $b_i \leq b_j$ for all $i \in I$ and $j \in I_c$. Then the null vector method can be formulated as

$$x_{\text{null}} = \arg\min \left\{ \left\| A_I^* x \right\|^2 : x \in \mathbb{C}^n, \|x\| = \|x_0\| \right\}. \tag{5}$$

To make use of the available power method, Chen convert (5) into a maximization problem [15]:

$$x_{\text{null}} = \arg\max \left\{ \left\| A_{I_c}^* x \right\|^2 : x \in \mathbb{C}^n, \|x\| = \|x_0\| \right\}. \tag{6}$$

Current initialization methods, (2), (3) and (6) are all about finding the leading eigenvector, which can be efficiently solved by power method. We illustrate the Algorithm 1 for computing (2) as an example.

Algorithm 1. The spectral method

Input: $A, b, \|x_0\|$, threshold value ϵ.
Initialization: x_1

  1: **for** $k = 1, 2, \cdots$ **do**
  2:      $x'_{k+1} \leftarrow A \operatorname{diag}(b^2) A^* x_k$
  3:      $x_{k+1} \leftarrow x'_k / \|x'_{k+1}\|$
  4:      **if** $\|x_{k+1} - x_k\| \leq \epsilon$, **break**
  5: **end for**
Output: $x_{\text{spec}} = x_{k+1} \|x_0\| / \|x_{k+1}\|$.

---

3 Algorithm

3.1 Inverse Power Method

Related work show that the null vector method has the best numerical performance compared with spectral method and the truncated spectral method [15]. However, several drawbacks remains. An important step in the null vector is setting a threshold value for picking out *weak* vectors, and the problem of how to choose the proper threshold value has not been solved yet. Moreover, the selected *weak* vectors are treated without indistinguishably, the accuracy could be improved if proper weights are added upon these vectors. Based on these considerations, our method, the inverse power method is proposed as follows:

$$x_{\text{null}} = \arg\max \left\{ \left\| \operatorname{diag}(b^{-\gamma/2}) A^* x \right\|^2 : x \in \mathbb{C}^n, \|x\| = \|x_0\| \right\}. \tag{7}$$

where γ is a positive number.

The inverse power method is based on the following facts:

1. By minimizing the function $f_i(x) = \frac{x^*}{\|x\|} a_i a_i^* \frac{x}{\|x\|}$, one can obtain an arbitrary vector in the orthogonal complement space of a_i.

2. Instead of selecting only a proportion of measuring vectors by comparing b_i, we carefully give various weights to measuring vectors. Specifically, the inverse power method is to minimize a combination of weighted $f_i(x)$:

$$f(x) = \sum_i^m w_i f_i(x). \tag{8}$$

The measurements b_i can also be regarded as the measure of orthogonality between a_i and x_0. For arbitrary two measuring vectors a_i and a_j, if the b_i is smaller than b_j, then x is more orthogonal with a_i than a_j, hence more weights is added upon the function $f_i(x)$. Therefore, it is reasonable to weight more $f_i(x)$ corresponding to smaller b_i. A natural way to satisfy this goal is weighting $f_i(x)$ with simple functions. Here we take the weights $w_i = b_i^{-\gamma}$ with $\gamma \geq 0$, which makes (8) and (7) equivalent. Through numerical implementations, we find that $\gamma > 1$ would ensure relative good performance.

Solving the minimization problem (7) is identical to searching for the eigenvector with the smallest eigenvalue. This can be solved efficiently through the propose inverse power approach presented in Algorithm 2. The core step of this algorithm is solving a linear system of equation, which can be implemented efficiently by the well-known Gauss-Seidel method, Jacobi method or successive over relaxation method.

Algorithm 2. The inverse power method (IPM)

Input: $A, b, \|x_0\|$, threshold value ϵ.
Initialization: x_1
  1: **for** $k = 1, 2, \cdots$ **do**
  2:      $x_k' \leftarrow \left(A \operatorname{diag}(b^{-2}) A^* \right)^{-1} x_k$
  3:      $x_{k+1} \leftarrow x_k' / \|x_k'\|$
  4:      **if** $\|x_{k+1} - x_k\| \leq \epsilon$, **break**
  5: **end for**
Output: $x_{\text{IPM}} = x_k \|x_0\| / \|x_k\|$.

3.2 Iterative Inverse Power Method

After we obtain an estimate x_{IPM} by the inverse power algorithm, the similar analysis about orthogonality can be made upon the residual $x_{\text{res}} = x_0 - x_{\text{IPM}}$. This inspires us to propose an iterative inverse power algorithm to improve the estimate.

Denote $b_{\text{IPM}} = A^* x_{\text{IPM}}$, the residual between the true measurements $A^* x$ and $A^* x_{\text{IPM}}$ can be approximated by $b_{\text{res}} := b - |A^* x_{\text{IPM}}|$. Then the proportion of x_{res} in the orthogonal complement space of a_i can be characterized by $(b_{\text{IPM}})_i^{-\gamma}$. In other words, we can implement the inverse power algorithm upon the b_{res} to approximate x_{res}, which can be use as the search direction for better estimate.

The iterative inverse power method is presented in Algorithm 3. The assignment $x_{\mathrm{IPM}} \leftarrow \mathrm{sign}\,(x_{\mathrm{IPM}}^* x_s)\, x_{\mathrm{IPM}}$ adds a phase factor $e^{i\theta}$ upon x_{IPM}, where $\theta = \arg\min_\theta \left\| e^{i\theta} x_{\mathrm{IPM}} - x_s \right\|$. The step size is restricted to be less than l such that the elements of b_{res} are always positive, hence ensuring the weights used in the inverse power method are always positive. Otherwise, the negative weights will invalidate the inverse power method. The relaxation parameter α controls the amount of each adjustment.

Algorithm 3. The iterative inverse power method (IIPM)

Input: $A, b, \alpha, \|x_0\|, \epsilon$, maximum number of iterations: K
Initialization: $x_s = 0$

1: **for** $k = 1, 2, \cdots, K$ **do**
2:     $b_{\mathrm{res}} \leftarrow b - |A^* x_s|$
3:     $x_{\mathrm{IPM}} \leftarrow \mathrm{IPM}(A, b_{\mathrm{res}}, \|x_0\|, \epsilon)$
4:     $x_{\mathrm{IPM}} \leftarrow \mathrm{sign}\,(x_{\mathrm{IPM}}^* x_s)\, x_{\mathrm{IPM}}$
5:     $l \leftarrow \max\left\{ l \in \mathbb{R}^+ : |a_i^*(x_s + l x_{\mathrm{IPM}})| \le b_i, \quad i = 1, \cdots, m. \right\}$
6:     $x_s \leftarrow x_s + \alpha l x_{\mathrm{IMP}}$
7: **end for**
Output: $x_{\mathrm{IIPM}} = x_s \|x_0\| / \|x_s\|$.

---

4   Numerical Experiments

In this section, we implement several numerical experiments to compare the performance of our algorithms with other initialization algorithms. For comparison, we define the relative error between recovered signal $\hat{x}$ and the true signal x as:

$$\mathrm{RE:} = \frac{\mathrm{dist}\,(\hat{x}, x_0)}{\|x\|^2}, \tag{9}$$

where the function $\mathrm{dist}\,(\hat{x}, x_0) = \min_\theta \left\| e^{i\theta}\hat{x} - x_0 \right\|$.

Figure 1 compares the inverse power method with three initialization schemes mentioned in Sect. 2. The relative errors of the returned initialization estimate under different oversampling rate m/n are presented. The measuring vectors are i.i.d. $\mathcal{N}(0, I_n/2) + i\mathcal{N}(0, I_n/2)$. Obviously, all methods perform better as oversampling rate increases. The spectral and truncated spectral method exhibit generally the worst performance compared with other methods. The null vector method enjoys a better performance than the spectral and truncated spectral method, and it achieves similar performance with the inverse method. However, all the inverse power methods performs better than the null vector method as oversampling rate increases. The inverse power methods with $\gamma = 3$ and $\gamma = 3.5$ have the lowest relative error over all oversampling rate. And interestingly, the inverse power method performs almost the same with $\gamma \ge 2$ when oversampling rate is sufficiently large ($m/n > 25$).

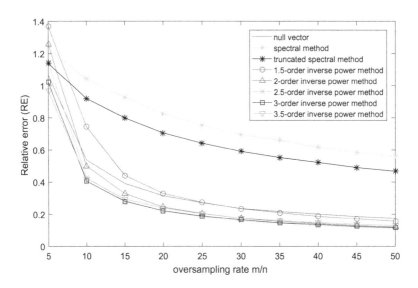

Fig. 1. Relative error of estimates by different initialization schemes under different oversampling rate m/n. $n = 256$, and m/n varies from 5 to 50. The parameter γ of the inverse power method varies from 1.5 to 3.5.

Figure 2 illustrates the effectiveness of the proposed iterative inverse power method. Overall, the iterative inverse power method perform considerably better than the single inverse power method. And better accuracy is achieved as oversampling rate increases. Let α correspond to the step size of each update. Different α can lead to different rates of convergence. Apparently, a larger step size can cause a faster converging rate. It only takes about 10 iterations to converge for $\alpha = 0.9$, while for the $\alpha = 0.1$, dozens of iterations are implemented before converging. However, a larger α can skip the optimum solution, which has been widely discussed in optimization theory [16]. As shown in Fig. 2b, for $\alpha = 0.9$, the relative error is 0.48, much higher than 0.32 for $\alpha = 0.6$, and 0.31 for $\alpha = 0.3$.

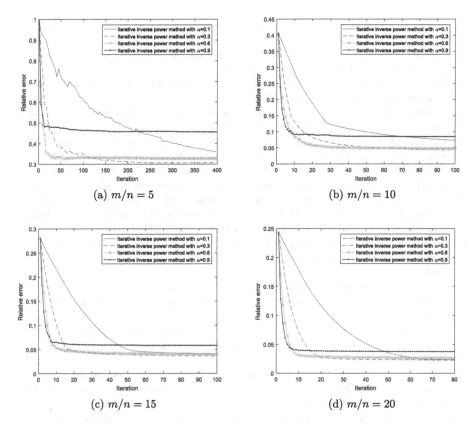

Fig. 2. Relative error for the iterative inverse power method versus iteration count with various step size. α under different oversampling rates.

5   Conclusion

This paper develops a new initialization method, which can efficiently give a more accurate estimate of the original signal for phase retrieval. And through iterative use of the proposed inverse power method, a better performance is achieved. This work is helpful for solving various imaging problems based on phase retrieval.

References

1. Miao, J., Charalambous, P., Kirz, J., Sayre, D.: Extending the methodology of x-ray crystallography to allow imaging of micrometre-sized non-crystalline specimens. Nature **400**(6742), 342 (1999)
2. Shechtman, Y., Eldar, Y.C., Cohen, O., Chapman, H.N., Miao, J., Segev, M.: Phase retrieval with application to optical imaging: a contemporary overview. IEEE Sig. Process. Mag. **32**(3), 87–109 (2015)

3. Stefik, M.: Inferring dna structures from segmentation data. Artif. Intell. **11**(1–2), 85–114 (1978)
4. Fienup, C., Dainty, J.: Phase retrieval and image reconstruction for astronomy. Image Recovery Theory Appl. **231**, 275 (1987)
5. Balan, R., Casazza, P., Edidin, D.: On signal reconstruction without phase. Appl. Comput. Harmonic Anal. **20**(3), 345–356 (2006)
6. Bodmann, B.G., Hammen, N.: Stable phase retrieval with low-redundancy frames. Adv. Comput. Math. **41**(2), 317–331 (2015)
7. Pardalos, P.M., Vavasis, S.A.: Quadratic programming with one negative eigenvalue is NP-hard. J. Glob. Optim. **1**(1), 15–22 (1991)
8. Netrapalli, P., Jain, P., Sanghavi, S.: Phase retrieval using alternating minimization. In: Advances in Neural Information Processing Systems, pp. 2796–2804 (2013)
9. Elser, V.: Phase retrieval by iterated projections. JOSA A **20**(1), 40–55 (2003)
10. Candes, E.J., Li, X., Soltanolkotabi, M.: Phase retrieval via wirtinger flow: theory and algorithms. IEEE Trans. Inf. Theory **61**(4), 1985–2007 (2015)
11. Zhang, H., Liang, Y.: Reshaped wirtinger flow for solving quadratic system of equations. In: Advances in Neural Information Processing Systems, pp. 2622–2630 (2016)
12. Wang, G., Giannakis, G.B., Eldar, Y.C.: Solving systems of random quadratic equations via truncated amplitude flow. IEEE Trans. Inf. Theory **64**, 773–794 (2017)
13. Wang, G., Giannakis, G., Saad, Y., Chen, J.: Solving most systems of random quadratic equations. In: Advances in Neural Information Processing Systems, pp. 1865–1875 (2017)
14. Chen, Y., Candes, E.: Solving random quadratic systems of equations is nearly as easy as solving linear systems. In: Advances in Neural Information Processing Systems, pp. 739–747 (2015)
15. Chen, P., Fannjiang, A., Liu, G.R.: Phase retrieval by linear algebra. SIAM J. Matrix Anal. Appl. **38**(3), 854–868 (2017)
16. Nesterov, Y.: Introductory Lectures on Convex Optimization: A Basic Course, vol. 87. Springer, New York (2013). https://doi.org/10.1007/978-1-4419-8853-9

Robust Discriminative Principal Component Analysis

Xiangxi Xu[1], Zhihui Lai[1(✉)], Yudong Chen[1], and Heng Kong[2]

[1] The College of Computer Science and Software Engineering,
Shenzhen University, Shenzhen 518060, China
lai_zhi_hui@163.com
[2] School of Medicine, Shenzhen University, Shenzhen 518060, China

Abstract. Least square regression (LSR) and principal component analysis (PCA) are two representative dimensionality reduction algorithms in the fields of machine learning. In this paper, we propose a novel method to jointly learn projections from the subspaces derived from the modified LSR and PCA. To implement simultaneous feature learning, we design a novel joint regression learning model by imposing two orthogonal constraints. Therefore, the learned projections can preserve the minimum reconstruction error and the discriminative information in the low-dimensional subspaces. Besides, since the traditional LSR and PCA are sensitive to the outliers, we utilize the robust $L_{2,1}$-norm as the metric of loss function to improve the model's robustness. A simple iterative algorithm is proposed to solve the proposed framework. Experiments on face databases show the promising performance of our method.

Keywords: Regression framework · Subspace learning · Robustness

1 Introduction

In pattern recognition tasks, subspace learning is a key technique that can reduce the features of the patterns and simultaneously improve the classification performance. Subspace learning methods aim to learn a transformation matrix to project the original high-dimensional data into low-dimensional subspaces so that the redundant information can be eliminated and the important information can be preserved. It is well known that the principal component analysis (PCA) [1, 2] is a classical unsupervised method for dimensionality reduction. PCA aims to guarantee minimal information loss by constructing the linear combination of all original features. However, PCA does not make full use of the label information and lack robustness.

To improve the robustness of PCA, a number of extensions of PCA have been proposed [3–5]. The robust principal component analysis (RPCA) [6–8] uses non-greedy L_1-norm maximization strategy to get a robust solution. Except for the L_1-norm-based PCA, the $L_{2,1}$-norm-based methods also attract great attentions [9], including the optimal mean robust principal component analysis (OMRPCA) [10, 11] and joint sparse principal component analysis (JSPCA) [12]. Although the existing extensions of PCA can effectively solve the problem of robustness, they do not consider the label

© Springer Nature Switzerland AG 2018
J. Zhou et al. (Eds.): CCBR 2018, LNCS 10996, pp. 231–238, 2018.
https://doi.org/10.1007/978-3-319-97909-0_25

information of databases so that the effectiveness of these methods for classification will be degraded.

In contrast to the PCA-based methods, the supervised methods, such as the least square regression (LSR) [13] and the low-rank linear regression (LRLR) [14], utilize label information to obtain discriminative projections. LRLR adds a low-rank constraint on the traditional LSR model for discovering global information from the data. However, LRLR uses Frobenius norm as the distance metric and is difficult to be solved with the non-convex constraint.

Currently, how to integrate the discriminative information into the model of minimum reconstruction error is the research hotspot. Inspired by LSR, we relaxed the traditional PCA model by adding discriminative information with general least square regression. Specifically, we first relax the minimum reconstruction error model of PCA by imposing one projection matrix into orthogonal constraint. Then the model will inherit the discriminative information from the ridge regression to the relaxed PCA model. Thus, this model not only solves the problem of insufficient number of projections in LSR, but also enhances the robustness of PCA. In brief, this paper proposes a novel regression framework to jointly learn the projections from the subspaces derived from LSR and PCA. The main contributions of this paper are described as follows:

(1) We construct a jointly regression framework based on PCA and LSR by imposing two orthogonal constraints. The key is to learn a novel projection matrix, so that this model has both the discriminant and reconstructive ability in the learning steps.
(2) Instead of using L_1-norm or L_2-norm, we adopt the robust $L_{2,1}$-norm as the main metric of distance, which effectively improve the robustness to noise of our proposed model.

2   Related Works

In this section, we simply review the traditional LSR and PCA. The training sample set is denoted by $X = [x_1, x_2, \ldots, x_i, \ldots, x_n] \in R^{m \times n}$, where m is the dimension of sample and n is the number of sample. Besides, $Y = [y_1, y_2, \ldots, y_i, \ldots, y_n] \in R^{c \times n}$ denotes the label matrix, where c is the number of classes.

The $L_{2,1}$-norm of matrix X is defined as:

$$\|X\|_{2,1} = \sum_{i=1}^{m} \|x^i\|_2 . \tag{1}$$

where x^i is the i-th row of X and $\|\bullet\|_2$ is L_2-norm.

2.1   Least Square Regression

Least square regression (LSR) has been well discussed in recent years because of its simplicity and effectiveness. The traditional LSR regresses the data matrix to the label matrix for discovering discriminative information between different classes. The objective function of LSR is as follows:

$$\min_{W} \sum_{i=1}^{n} \|y_i - Wx_i\|_2^2. \tag{2}$$

where $W \in R^{c \times d}$ is weight matrix. However, the traditional LSR is sensitive to outliers since it uses L_2-norm as main metric.

2.2 Principal Component Analysis

Principal component analysis (PCA) focuses on maximizing the covariance of dataset. Alternatively, PCA also try to minimizing the reconstruction error. Suppose data matrix X is centralized, the objective function of PCA can be written as:

$$\min_{Q} \sum_{i=1}^{n} \|x_i - Q^T Q x_i\|_2^2. \quad \text{s.t.} \quad Q Q^T = I_d \tag{3}$$

where $Q \in R^{d \times m}$ is projection matrix and d is desired dimension of low-dimensional features.

3 Jointly Learning Framework for RDPCA

3.1 Robust Discriminative Principal Component Analysis

In order to use the global structure of data and preserve discriminative information in the low-dimensional subspaces, we modify the classical PCA algorithm by introducing the ridge regression, making this model has discriminant information, also has the ability of flexible feature extraction. The regression model of PCA is as follows:

$$\min_{A,B,P} \alpha \sum_{i=1}^{n} \|y_i^T - x_i^T AB^T\|_{2,1} + (1 - \alpha) \sum_{i=1}^{n} \|x_i^T - x_i^T AP^T\|_{2,1}. \tag{4}$$
$$\text{s.t.} \quad B^T B = I_d, \ P^T P = I_d$$

where $A \in R^{m \times d}$ can be regarded as a projection matrix, and both $B \in R^{c \times d}$ and $P \in R^{m \times d}$ are the orthogonal matrices and $\alpha > 0$ is the balance parameter. We use the $L_{2,1}$-norm on these two terms in (4) so that this model can guarantee the robustness to noise. In particular, we can obtain enough projections since the number of projections in A can be set to arbitrary. By this way, this model not only solves the small-class problem, but also can jointly learn the global and discriminative information and preserve it in the optimal subspaces spanned by matrix A. That means the matrix A can inherit the discriminative information from the first term and can be of strong further reconstruction ability in modified regression.

The matrix form of RDPCA is presented as follows:

$$\min_{A,B,P} \alpha \|Y^T - X^T AB^T\|_{2,1} + (1-\alpha)\|X^T - X^T AP^T\|_{2,1}.$$
$$\text{s.t.} \quad B^T B = I_d, \ P^T P = I_d \tag{5}$$

In next subsection, we design an iterative algorithm to solve (5).

3.2 Iterative Algorithm

We can expand model (5) as follows:

$$\min_{A,B,P} \alpha\|Y^T - X^T AB^T\|_{2,1} + (1-\alpha)\|X^T - X^T AP^T\|_{2,1}$$
$$= \min_{A,B,P} \alpha tr((Y^T - X^T AB^T)^T W_1 (Y^T - X^T AB^T))$$
$$+ (1-\alpha)tr((X^T - X^T AP^T)^T W_2(X^T - X^T AP^T)). \tag{6}$$
$$\text{s.t.} \quad B^T B = I_d, \ P^T P = I_d$$

where

$$W_1 = \frac{1}{2\|(Y^T - X^T AB^T)^i\|_2}, \quad W_2 = \frac{1}{2\|(X^T - X^T AP^T)^i\|_2}. \tag{7}$$

and $(Y^T - X^T AB^T)^i$ and $(X^T - X^T AP^T)^i$ is the i-th row of $Y^T - X^T AB^T$ and $X^T - X^T AP^T$, respectively.

For fixed B and P, taking partial derivative with respect to A to be zero, we can derive

$$A = (\alpha XW_1 X^T + (1-\alpha)XW_2 X^T)^{-1}(\alpha XW_1 Y^T B + (1-\alpha)XW_2 X^T P). \tag{8}$$

For fixed A and P, we can derive following maximization problem

$$\max_B tr(XW_1 Y^T AB^T). \quad \text{s.t.} \quad B^T B = I_d \tag{9}$$

According to Theorem 4 in [15], with Singular Value Decomposition (SVD) of $XW_1 Y^T A = \tilde{U}\tilde{D}\tilde{V}^T$

$$B = \tilde{U}\tilde{V}^T. \tag{10}$$

Similarly, for fixed A and B, we can derive following maximization problem

$$\max_P tr(XW_2 X^T AP^T). \quad \text{s.t.} \, P^T P = I_d \tag{11}$$

With SVD of $XW_2 X^T A = \widehat{U}\widehat{D}\widehat{V}^T$,

$$P = \widehat{U}\widehat{V}^T . \qquad (12)$$

From the above formulation, the algorithm steps of our method are summarized in Algorithm 1.

Algorithm 1. Robust Discriminative Principal Component Analysis algorithm

---

Input: Training data X, iteration number T, parameter α.
Step 1: Initialize $P \in R^{m \times d}$ as orthogonal matrix, W_1, W_2 as identity matrix.
Step 2: For $j = 1 : T$ do

        Given B and P, compute the matrix A by solving (8);
        Given A and P, compute the matrix B by solving (10);
        Given A and B, compute the matrix P by solving (12);
        Update W_1, W_2 by using (7);
Output: the projection matrix A.

---

4 Experiment

In this section, we will perform a set of experiments to evaluate the proposed methods, and the compared dimensionality reduction algorithms include the unsupervised method PCA, its variants JSPCA, the supervised method LDA [16, 17], LRLR, and the regularized label relaxation linear regression (RLR) [18]. We use three datasets AR, FERET and CMU PIE to verify the robustness and effectiveness of the proposed method.

4.1 Data Sets Details

The **AR** face database [19] contains 120 individuals (55 women and 65 men), and these images were divided into two parts, including different facial changes. In our experiments, 20 images of each individual were selected. And the pixels of each image are normalized to 50×40. Specifically, we randomly selected *TrainN* (*TrainN* = 5, 6) data points of each individual as training samples and the rest as test samples. The **FERET** dataset [20] consists of 1400 images which are categorized into 200 classes (7 images per class). These images are related to changes in facial expression, pose and light condition. And we resized the pixels of each images to 40×40. For FERET dataset, we set *TrainN* (*TrainN* = 3) data points of each class as training data. The **CMU PIE** dataset [21] consists of 41368 face images which are divided into 68 individuals. We selected 1632 images of 68 individuals (24 images per individual) and set *TrainN* = 6, 7. For experiments, each image is cropped to 32×32 pixels.

Table 1. Best average recognition rate (%) and corresponding standard deviation on AR database.

Method	PCA	LDA	LRLR	JSPCA	RLR	Ours
TrainN = 5	84.97 ± 7.49	96.62 ± 7.77	96.4 ± 7.46	84.97 ± 7.49	93.31 ± 16.51	**97.23 ± 7.42**
TrainN = 6	87.98 ± 7.03	97.67 ± 6.43	97.47 ± 6.14	87.98 ± 7.03	96.00 ± 15.59	**97.98 ± 6.61**

Table 2. Best average recognition rate (%) and corresponding standard deviation on FERET database.

Method	PCA	LDA	LRLR	JSPCA	RLR	Ours
TrainN = 3	72.32 ± 3.80	81.01 ± 2.84	80.16 ± 3.07	72.32 ± 3.80	69.04 ± 7.09	**81.61 ± 5.42**

Table 3. Best average recognition rate (%) and corresponding standard deviation on CMU PIE database.

Method	PCA	LDA	LRLR	JSPCA	RLR	Ours
TrainN = 6	79.03 ± 7.93	90.52 ± 4.69	90.62 ± 5.17	79.03 ± 7.93	89.41 ± 12.30	**90.91 ± 6.77**
TrainN = 7	83.84 ± 7.85	**92.61 ± 3.75**	92.61 ± 4.14	83.84 ± 7.85	91.66 ± 11.21	92.43 ± 6.02

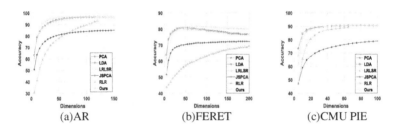

(a)AR   (b)FERET   (c)CMU PIE

Fig. 1. The accuracy rates (%) versus the dimensions of different methods on three databases.

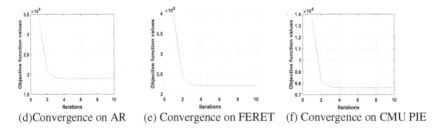

(d)Convergence on AR   (e) Convergence on FERET   (f) Convergence on CMU PIE

Fig. 2. The objective function values versus iteration number on three databases.

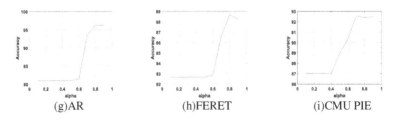

(g)AR   (h)FERET   (i)CMU PIE

Fig. 3. Sensitivity to α on three databases.

4.2 Experimental Results Comparison

In this section, we show that the performance of our proposed method to compare with the different methods. Figure 3(g)–(i) indicate that our method can obtain good performance on three databases with $0.7 \leq \alpha \leq 0.9$. So we set the parameter to be 0.9 and the maximum iteration to be 10 in our algorithm.

Figure 1(a)–(c) show that the accuracy rates of six methods on three databases. With the increasing number of the dimensions, the accuracy of the proposed method is increases steadily on AR data set. On FERET data set, when the dimension increases to 60 or more, the accuracy rate of our approach begins to be significantly higher than the other five methods. The accuracy rates of different methods are not distinct on CMU PIE data set. But from another point of view, our method achieves the best average recognition rate 90.91% when the dimension is 80 and the sample training number is 6. According to Fig. 2(d)–(f), the convergence curves versus iteration number of the proposed method on the three databases can prove that the method is convergent.

To further demonstrate the best performance of each method, the best average recognition rate and corresponding dimension are also selected as shown in Tables 1, 2, and 3. From Table 1, we can find that the performance of our approach in the case of 5 or 6 training samples is better than any other method. From Table 2, we know that our approach achieves the best average recognition rate 81.61% when the training number is 3. Thus, compared to other five methods, this method has been improved by 1%–12% on all three databases.

5 Conclusion

In this paper, a robust jointly learning framework is presented by integrating the generalized ridge regression into minimized reconstruction error with $L_{2,1}$-norm on loss function as the measurement. The constructed regression model can not only make full use of the discriminative information of LSR but also improve the robustness of PCA. More importantly, the orthogonal matrices are imposed to fit the regressed term in order to learning the discriminant subspace. Thus, we can learn the optimal discriminant subspace preserving the global discriminative information and reconstruction property. The experimental results suggest that our method increases the effectiveness and the robustness of the model compared with other five algorithms.

Acknowledgments. This work was supported in part by the Natural Science Foundation of China (Grant 61573248, Grant 61773328, Grant 61773328 and Grant 61703283), Research Grant of The Hong Kong Polytechnic University (Project Code:G-UA2B), China Postdoctoral Science Foundation (Project 2016M590812 and Project 2017T100645), the Guangdong Natural Science Foundation (Project 2017A030313367 and Project 2017A030310067), the Guangdong medical scientific and technological research funding under grant A2017251, Shenzhen Municipal Science and Technology Innovation Council (No. JCYJ20170302153434048, No. JCYJ20160429182058044 and No. JCYJ20160429182058044).

References

1. Abdi, H., Williams, L.J.: Principal component analysis. Wiley Interdiscip. Rev. Comput. Stat. **2**, 433–459 (2010)
2. Jolliffe, I.T.: Principal Component Analysis, vol. 87, pp. 41–64. Springer, Berlin (2010). https://doi.org/10.1007/b98835
3. Zhou, Z., Jin, Z.: Double nuclear norm-based robust principal component analysis for image disocclusion and object detection. Neurocomputing **205**, 481–489 (2016)
4. Lai, Z., Xu, Y., Chen, Q., Yang, J., Zhang, D.: Multilinear sparse principal component analysis. IEEE Trans. Neural Netw. Learn. Syst. **25**, 1942–1950 (2014)
5. Zhang, F., Yang, J., Qian, J., Xu, Y.: Nuclear norm-based 2-DPCA for extracting features from images. IEEE Trans. Neural Netw. Learn. Syst. **26**, 2247–2260 (2015)
6. Brooks, J.P., Boone, E.L.: A pure L1-norm principal component analysis. Comput. Stat. Data Anal. **61**, 83 (2013)
7. Nie, F., Huang, H., Ding, C.H.Q., Luo, D., Wang, H.: Robust principal component analysis with non-greedy l1-norm maximization. Presented at the IJCAI Proceedings-International Joint Conference on Artificial Intelligence (2011)
8. Kwak, N.: Principal component analysis based on L1-norm maximization. IEEE Trans. Pattern Anal. Mach. Intell. **30**, 1672–1680 (2008)
9. Ding, C., Zhou, D., He, X., Zha, H.: R1-PCA: rotational invariant L1-norm principal component analysis for robust subspace factorization. In: Proceedings of the 23rd International Conference on Machine Learning, pp. 281–288 (2006)
10. Shi, X., Nie, F., Lai, Z., Guo, Z.: Robust principal component analysis via optimal mean by joint $\ell 2,1$ and Schatten p-norms minimization. Neurocomputing **283**, 205–213 (2018)
11. Nie, F., Yuan, J., Huang, H.: Optimal mean robust principal component analysis. In: Proceedings of the 31st International Conference on Machine Learning, pp. 1062–1070 (2014)
12. Yi, S., Lai, Z., He, Z., Cheung, Y.M., Liu, Y.: Joint sparse principal component analysis. Pattern Recognit. **61**, 524–536 (2016)
13. Nie, F., Huang, H., Cai, X., Ding, C.: Efficient and robust feature selection via joint L2,1-norms minimization. In: Advances in Neural Information Processing Systems, pp. 1813–1821 (2010)
14. Cai, X., Ding, C., Nie, F., Huang, H.: On the equivalent of low-rank linear regressions and linear discriminant analysis based regressions. In: Proceedings of the 19th ACM SIGKDD International Conference on Knowledge Discovery and Data Mining, pp. 1124–1132. ACM (2013)
15. Zou, H., Hastie, T., Tibshirani, R., Url, S.: Sparse principal component analysis. J. Comput. Graph. Stat. **15**, 265–286 (2006)
16. Yang, J., Yang, J.Y.: Why can LDA be performed in PCA transformed space? Pattern Recognit. **36**, 563–566 (2003)
17. Zheng, W.S., Lai, J.H., Li, S.Z.: 1D-LDA vs. 2D-LDA: when is vector-based linear discriminant analysis better than matrix-based? Pattern Recognit. **41**, 2156–2172 (2008)
18. Fang, X., Xu, Y., Li, X., Lai, Z., Wong, W.K., Fang, B.: Regularized label relaxation linear regression. IEEE Trans. Neural Netw. Learn. Syst. **PP**, 1–13 (2017)
19. Martinez, A.M.: The AR face database. CVC Technical Report 24 (1998)
20. Jonathon Phillips, P., Moon, H., Rizvi, S.A., Rauss, P.J.: The FERET evaluation methodology for face-recognition algorithms. IEEE Trans. Pattern Anal. Mach. Intell. **22**, 1090–1104 (2000)
21. Sim, T., Baker, S., Bsat, M.: The CMU pose, illumination, and expression database. IEEE Trans. Pattern Anal. Mach. Intell. **25**, 1615–1618 (2003)

Guided Learning: A New Paradigm for Multi-task Classification

Jingru Fu[1], Lei Zhang[1(✉)], Bob Zhang[2], and Wei Jia[3]

[1] College of Communication Engineering, Chongqing University, Chongqing, China
{jrfu,leizhang}@cqu.edu.cn
[2] Department of Computer and Information Science, University of Macau,
Macau, China
bobzhang@umac.mo
[3] School of Computer and Information, Hefei University of Technology, Hefei, China
china.jiawei@139.com

Abstract. A prevailing problem in many machine learning tasks is that the training and test data have different distribution (non i.i.d). Previous methods to solve this problem are called Transfer Learning (TL) or Domain Adaptation (DA), which belong to one stage models. In this paper, we propose a new, simple but effective paradigm, Guided Learning (GL), for multi-stage progressive training. This new paradigm is motivated by the "tutor guides student" learning mode in human world. Further, under the framework of GL, a Guided Subspace Learning (GSL) method is proposed for domain disparity reduction, which aims to learn an optimal, invariant and discriminative subspace through the guided learning strategy. Extensive experiments on various databases show that our method outperforms many state-of-the-art TL/DA methods.

Keywords: Guided Learning · Subspace Learning · Domain disparity

1 Introduction

Conventional machine learning algorithms are based on the assumption that the training and test data lie in the same feature space with the same distribution. However, this assumption may not hold in many real-world scenarios. Especially in the field of computer vision owing to various factors such as different camera devices, illuminations, background, etc. Fig. 1 shows some images of different distributions. When the disparity exists between the training and test data, the classification accuracy dropped dramatically [5]. However, retraining a new classifier often requires a large amount of labeled training data of the same distribution (i.i.d), which consumes a lot of human resources and is not realistic with the explosive growth of unlabeled data. TL/DA methods have been used to solve this problem [9]. They aim to transfer well-learned knowledge from the source domain (training set) to the target domain (test set). In this paper, we introduce a new paradigm, Guided Learning (GL), for solving such domain mismatch problem.

© Springer Nature Switzerland AG 2018
J. Zhou et al. (Eds.): CCBR 2018, LNCS 10996, pp. 239–246, 2018.
https://doi.org/10.1007/978-3-319-97909-0_26

Fig. 1. Some examples from different domains. (a) 4DA: Each column represents the data of Amazon, DSLR, Caltech and Webcam, respectively. (b) MSRC (left) and VOC2007 (right). (c) CMU PIE: The first two rows indicate different illuminations and poses, the last row indicates different expressions and glass occlusion.

Conventional TL/DA methods can be divided into classifier-based methods and representation-based methods [9,10]. The classifier-based methods tend to solve the domain disparity problem by adapting the existing classifiers to the data with different distributions, such as A-SVM [16]. However, they may not utilize the intrinsic information of the data, and it strongly depends on the specific classifier. Further, the representation-based methods tend to learn a better representation for classification, such as RDALR [4], TSL [11], LTSL [10], LSDT [17] and DTSL [15]. However, most of them only consider the domain adaptation at the data level, which ignore the global information of domains. SA [2] and CORAL [12] stand in another perspective, which tend to align the first-order and second-order statistical global features (e.g. PCA subspace and feature for domain discrepancy reduction at subspace level). Additionally, the TL/DA tends to find a classifier or transformation in one stage, which may not work when domain disparity is large.

Therefore, we propose a new GL paradigm for domain disparity reduction through a progressive, guided, and multi-stage strategy. The GL paradigm is relevant but different from TL/DA methods that it is established upon the main idea of "tutor guides student" mode in human world. Tutor-students' teaching mode is general route in human learning process. In general, the tutor not only transfers expert knowledge to the students at a time, but to progressively guide the students achieving a certain learning purpose through the tutor's learning experience. Therefore, considering the domain difference between source and target domains, we propose a Guided Subspace Learning (GSL) method, which tends to progressively learn an optimal target subspace guided by source domain. The key contributions of this work are three-folds:

(1) Inspired by the "tutor guides student" learning mode in human world, we propose a new learning paradigm called Guided Learning (GL), which can achieve knowledge transfer in a progressive guided manner.
(2) Under the GL framework, we propose a Guided Subspace Learning (GSL) method for solving domain mismatch. Compared with the TL/DA methods, the concept of progressive guiding in GL makes the model more robust.

(3) The GSL method can simultaneously eliminate domain disparity at data level and subspace level. Finally, an optimal, invariant and discriminative target subspace can be achieved through subspace, data and label guidance.

2   Related Work

According to the objective of this paper, we present a overview of TL/DA methods from data and subspace level, respectively.

2.1   Data Level Approach

As mentioned before, this type of methods learn better feature representation from the data level. RDALR [4] presented a low-rank reconstruction constraint to reduce the domain shift, which can capture the intrinsic relationship in data. It assumes that the transformed source samples can be linearly reconstructed by target samples. TSL [11] solved the problem by minimizing Bregman divergence between the distribution of domains in a common subspace. LTSL [10] also used the reconstruction matrix and derived a generalized framework. LSDT [17] further presented sparse reconstruction constraint and generalized model into a kernel-based linear/nolinear framework. DTSL [15] imposed low-rank and sparse constraints on the reconstruction matrix to guarantee the global and local property. Then, it obtained a linear classifier by learning a non-negative label relaxation matrix. Obviously, those approaches heavily depend on the well-designed reconstruction matrices and sensitive to noise.

2.2   Subspace Level Approach

It is not enough to get robust representation for classification by only exploiting the data level information of two domains. Subspace level approach can align the statistical features of two domains. SA [2] seeks a domain invariant feature space by learning a linear mapping which aligns subspaces spanned by eigenvectors (obtained by PCA). This kind of statistical features have global domain information, so that the subspace level approaches are more robust to noise and outliers that are irrelevant to the target domain. It is worth mentioning that SA can be explained by the manifold learning perspective. SDA [13] considered the distribution difference in the subspace, and proved that SA can be extended to GFK [3] in the case of an infinite subspaces distribution alignment.

3   Proposed Method

3.1   Mathematical Notation

We first clarify the definition of terminologies. Given the source domain $S = \{X_s, y_s\}$ and target domain $T = \{X_t, y_t\}$, where $X_s \in \mathbb{R}^{D \times n_s}$ and $X_t \in \mathbb{R}^{D \times n_t}$ are samples, y_s and y_t are labels (note that y_t is only used during testing step). D is the dimensionality of the original samples, and n_s and n_t indicate the number of samples in source and target domain, respectively. Let $P_s \in \mathbb{R}^{D \times d}$ and $P_t \in \mathbb{R}^{D \times d}$ be the projection of the source domain and target domain, respectively, where d is the dimensionality of the invariant subspace. Define $Z \in \mathbb{R}^{n_s \times n_t}$ as the reconstruction matrix.

3.2   Problem Formulation

As mentioned above, GSL can reduce the distribution mismatch by learning a target subspace. To sum up, GSL can be composed of three parts: (1) subspace guidance; (2) data guidance; (3) label guidance.

(1) **Subspace Guidance:** We first guide the target subspace P_t by the source subspace P_s. Similar to SA, we expect that the subspaces of the two domains can be aligned to reduce the domain disparity. It can be easily achieved by minimizing the following Frobenius norm, instead of learning an additional mapping function:

$$\min_{P_s, P_t} \|P_s - P_t\|_F^2 \tag{1}$$

It treats two subspaces equally and may extremely preserve the useful information of the two data sets. Moreover, the subspaces of the two domains are adjusted at the same time, which encourages to seek a better P_t under the guidance of P_s.

(2) **Data Guidance:** Second, we expect to use the intrinsic information of data to guide the learning of P_t. For data guidance, we tend to seek an invariant subspace by forcing the target data linearly combined by source data. For revealing the underlying structure of source and target data, we constrain that each target data can be reconstructed by the neighbors of the source data. Mathematically, we can achieve this purpose by placing a low-rank constraint on the reconstruction matrix Z. Actually, this constraint has been extensively discussed in machine learning field due to its impact on subspace recovery [14]. This can be formulated as:

$$\min_{P_s, P_t, Z} \left\| P_t^T X_t - P_s^T X_s Z \right\|_F^2 + \alpha \|Z\|_* \tag{2}$$

By using term (2) together with (1), an invariant target subspace where the domain disparity has been largely reduced can be obtained.

(3) **Label Guidance:** Although an invariant subspace has been found, the discrimination of such invariant subspace is not enough for classification problems. Additionally, a large amount of label information of source domain is neglected. So, we further introduce label guidance strategy in both domains to improve the subspace discriminability. Firstly, we expect that the learned projections can serve as classifier, which can be achieved by forcing $P_t^T X_t$ close to the pseudo label matrix $\hat{Y}_t \in \mathbb{R}^{d \times n_t}$ ($d \geq c$, and c indicates the number of classes) with category information. Unfortunately, the pseudo label information of the target

domain is not accurate. Therefore, we propose to use the existing classifiers (e.g. SVM) to generate pseudo labels and then learn a discriminative target subspace alternatively, under the label guidance. Inspired by EDA [6], we introduce a relaxation matrix M to alleviate this effect while increasing the robustness of the framework. Secondly, to make full use of the known labels in the source domain and improve the accuracy of this strategy, we define the constructed label matrix $Y = \left[Y_s, \hat{Y}_t\right] \in \mathbb{R}^{d \times n}$ ($n = n_s + n_t$ indicates the total number of samples in both domains) as:

$$Y\{i, j\} = \begin{cases} 1, & if \ x_j \in c_i \\ -1, & otherwise \end{cases} \tag{3}$$

The purpose of label guidance strategy is to seek a discriminative P_t, which also approximates the common subspace between domains, formulated as:

$$\min_{P_t, M} \left\| P_t^T X - Y \circ M \right\|_F^2 \ s.t. \ M \succ 0 \tag{4}$$

where $X = [X_s, X_t] \in \mathbb{R}^{D \times n}$. $M \in \mathbb{R}^{D \times n}$ represents the relaxation matrix. $\circ$ is a hadamard product operator.

We can obtain the following ultimate objection function by incorporating the above three Eqs. (1), (2) and (4) as:

$$\min_{P_s, P_t, M, Z} \beta \left\| P_s - P_t \right\|_F^2 + \left\| P_t^T X_t - P_s^T X_s Z \right\|_F^2 + \alpha \left\| Z \right\|_* + \frac{1}{2} \left\| P_t^T X - Y \circ M \right\|_F^2 \tag{5}$$
$$s.t. \ M \succ 0$$

where β and α are trade-off parameters to balance the constraints. We iteratively update the pseudo labels of target domain data using the learned invariant and discriminative target subspace. Finally, an optimal, invariant, and discriminative target subspace P_t can be achieved in a progressive manner.

3.3 Optimization

It can be seen from problem (5) that four variables are involved when Y is fixed. To solve the problem, an inexact augmented Lagrange multiplier method (IALM) [14] is used. With an auxiliary variable L, the problem (5) can be converted into:

$$\min_{P_s, P_t, M, Z, L} \beta \left\| P_s - P_t \right\|_F^2 + \left\| P_t^T X_t - P_s^T X_s Z \right\|_F^2 + \alpha \left\| L \right\|_* + \frac{1}{2} \left\| P_t^T X - Y \circ M \right\|_F^2$$
$$s.t. \ M \succ 0, \ Z = L$$
$$\tag{6}$$

Then, by using variables alternating strategy, we can derive the solution of each variable in IALM algorithm:

$$P_t = (2\beta I + 2X_t X_t^T + XX^T)^{-1}(2\beta P_s + 2X_t Z^T X_s^T P_s + X(Y \circ M)^T) \tag{7}$$

$$P_s = (2\beta I + 2X_s ZZ^T X_s^T)^{-1}(2\beta P_t + 2X_s ZX_t^T P_t) \tag{8}$$

$$Z = (2Xs^T P_s P_s^T X_s + \mu I)^{-1}(2Xs^T P_s P_t^T X_t + \mu(L - Y_1/\mu)) \tag{9}$$

$$L = arg \min_{L} \alpha \|L\|_* + \frac{\mu}{2} \|Z - L + Y_1/\mu\|_F^2 \qquad (10)$$

$$M = arg \min_{M} \frac{1}{2} \|P_t^T X - Y \circ M\|_F^2 \qquad (11)$$

where Y_1 is a Langrange multiplier, $\mu > 0$ is a penalty parameter and I is identity matrix. The optimal solution of formula (10) can be computed via the singular value thresholding (SVT) algorithm [1]. Problem (11) can be similarly solved by [15]. Then multiplier Y_1 and iteration step-size ρ ($\rho > 1$) are updated by:

$$\begin{cases} Y_1 = Y_1 + \mu(Z - L) \\ \mu = min(\rho\mu, \mu_{max}) \end{cases} \qquad (12)$$

Once the guided P_t is obtained through the IALM algorithm, then an existing classifier can be used to get better pseudo-target-labels (also a better $\hat{Y}_t$) based on the optimal representation. To check the convergence, we define $\triangle P_t = \left\|P_t^{(t+1)} - P_t^{(t)}\right\|_F / \left\|P_t^{(t)}\right\|_F$, where t indicates iteration. Convergence is achieved when $\triangle P_t < \varepsilon$, where ε indicates a very small positive number.

4   Experiment

In this section, extensive experiments are conducted to justify the effectiveness of our method. The experiments on three different benchmark DA tasks, including 4DA object data set [3], MSRC-VOC2007 data set [8] and CMU PIE face data set [7]. Some examples are illustrated in Fig. 1.

Experimental Setting: In all experiments, we use SVM to progressively generate pseudo target labels. The dimensionality d of the invariant subspace is set as c (the number of classes) in each data set.

(1) **4DA Data Set:** 4DA consists of Office and Caltech-256. Office contains three real-world object domains, Amazon, Webcam and DSLR. 4DA is formulated with 10 shared categories of the two data sets. We use the same SURF features as [3]. Therefore, 4 domains: A (Amazon), C (Caltech-256), D (DSLR) and W (Webcam) are exploited. By deploying two different domains as the source domain and target domain alternatively, we construct 12 cross-domain tasks.

(2) **MSRC and VOC2007 Data Set:** MSRC contains 4,323 images of 18 classes, which was released by Microsoft Research Cambridge. VOC2007 contains 5011 images of 20 classes. 6 shared semantic classes: aeroplane, bicycle, bird, car, cow, sheep are formulated. Following the experimental setting as [15], two cross-domain tasks are constructed: MSRC vs VOC2007 and VOC2007 vs MSRC.

(3) **CMU PIE Face Data Set:** PIE contains 68 individuals with 41,368 face images of size 32×32. PIE1 (C05, left pose), PIE2 (C07, upward pose), PIE3 (C09, downward pose), PIE4 (C27, frontal pose), PIE5 (C29, right pose). The face images were captured by 13 different poses and 21 different illuminations

Table 1. Accuracy (%) On 3 types data sets. NA denotes no adaptation.

Data Set	Compared transfer learning methods							
	NA	SA	JDA [7]	TSL	RDALR	LTSL	DTSL	GSL
C→A(1)	50.09	48.02	51.46	52.30	52.51	24.11	53.34	**56.68**
C→W(2)	43.05	31.86	41.36	40.34	40.68	22.93	45.76	**47.12**
C→D(3)	47.77	42.68	46.50	49.04	45.22	14.58	**50.96**	49.04
A→C(4)	42.79	34.37	43.90	43.28	43.63	21.36	44.70	**45.24**
A→W(5)	37.03	33.90	33.90	34.58	35.93	18.17	38.31	**39.32**
A→D(6)	37.22	38.85	33.76	38.85	36.94	22.29	39.49	**43.95**
W→C(7)	29.47	30.01	31.17	31.43	28.05	**34.64**	30.28	32.24
W→A(8)	34.15	32.15	36.33	34.66	31.21	**39.46**	34.66	38.94
W→D(9)	80.62	83.44	77.71	79.62	83.44	72.61	82.80	**85.99**
D→C(10)	30.11	32.24	31.43	33.13	32.32	**35.35**	30.72	31.70
D→A(11)	32.05	33.40	38.41	32.57	33.72	**39.35**	33.19	36.95
D→W(12)	72.20	70.51	75.59	72.54	72.54	74.92	76.61	**79.32**
MSRC→VOC2007(1)	37.12	31.76	38.17	32.35	37.45	38.04	38.04	**41.76**
VOC2007→MSRC(2)	55.48	46.02	59.26	43.18	62.33	**67.06**	56.42	61.54
PIE1→PIE4(1)	51.76	42.75	25.14	46.68	41.66	20.01	81.29	**84.77**
PIE4→PIE4(2)	65.88	51.41	33.76	59.15	48.11	52.79	79.71	**83.85**
PIE4→PIE5(3)	51.96	47.92	29.47	45.22	48.84	47.00	71.02	**71.75**
PIE5→PIE4(4)	53.41	43.11	25.38	53.08	44.46	23.61	**66.09**	63.17
Average	47.33	43.02	41.82	45.67	45.50	37.13	52.96	**55.19**

and/or expressions. Alternatively, we constructed 4 cross-domain tasks: PIE1 vs PIE4, PIE4 vs PIE1, PIE4 vs PIE5, and PIE5 vs PIE4.

Specifically, the experimental results on the three datasets are shown in Table 1, from which we can observe that our GSL method outperforms other TL/DA methods in most tasks. The average classification performance of GSL shows significant improvement than others.

5   Conclusion

We firstly propose a new learning paradigm called Guided Learning (GL), which is inspired by the "tutor guides student" learning mode in human world. In order to solve the problem of domain mismatch in multi-task classification, we further proposed a Guided Subspace Learning (GSL) method, which aims to progressively seek an optimal target subspace through the GL paradigm. The proposed GSL is imposed the optimality, invariance, and discrimination by proposing three strategies, including subspace guidance, data guidance and label guidance. Notably, the label guidance strategy is constructed by formulating label relaxation and progressive target pseudo target label pre-computing method. The proposed GL provides a new learning mechanism for multi-task classification as TL/DA methods do. Experimental results demonstrate that our method outperforms many state-of-the-art TL/DA methods.

Acknowledgements. This work was supported by the National Science Fund of China under Grants (61771079).

References

1. Jian Feng Cai, C., Emmanuel, J.S., Shen, Z.: A singular value thresholding algorithm for matrix completion. SIAM J. Optim. **20**(4), 1956–1982 (2008)
2. Fernando, B., Habrard, A., Sebban, M., Tuytelaars, T.: Unsupervised visual domain adaptation using subspace alignment. In: IEEE ICCV, pp. 2960–2967 (2014)
3. Gong, B., Shi, Y., Sha, F., Grauman, K.: Geodesic flow kernel for unsupervised domain adaptation. In: IEEE CVPR, pp. 2066–2073 (2012)
4. Hong Jhuo, I, Liu, D., Lee, D.T., Chang, S.F.: Robust visual domain adaptation with low-rank reconstruction. In: CVPR, pp. 2168–2175 (2012)
5. Kan, M., Junting, W., Shan, S., Chen, X.: Domain adaptation for face recognition: targetize source domain bridged by common subspace. IJCV **109**(1–2), 94–109 (2014)
6. Lei, Z., Zhang, D.: Robust visual knowledge transfer via extreme learning machine-based domain adaptation. IEEE Trans. IP **25**(10), 4959–4973 (2016)
7. Long, M., Wang, J., Ding, G., Sun, J., Yu P.S.: Transfer feature learning with joint distribution adaptation. In: IEEE ICCV, pp. 2200–2207 (2014)
8. Long, M., Wang, J., Ding, G., Sun, J., Yu, P.S.: Transfer joint matching for unsupervised domain adaptation. In: IEEE Conference on Computer Vision and Pattern Recognition, pp. 1410–1417 (2014)
9. Pan, S.J., Yang, Q.: A survey on transfer learning. IEEE Trans. Knowl. Data Eng. **22**(10), 1345–1359 (2010)
10. Shao, M., Kit, D., Yun, F.: Generalized transfer subspace learning through low-rank constraint. IJCV **109**(1–2), 74–93 (2014)
11. Si, S., Tao, D., Geng, B.: Bregman divergence-based regularization for transfer subspace learning. IEEE Trans. Knowl. Data Eng. **22**(7), 929–942 (2010)
12. Sun, B., Feng, J., Saenko, K.: Correlation alignment for unsupervised domain adaptation. In: Csurka, G. (ed.) Domain Adaptation in Computer Vision Applications. ACVPR, pp. 153–171. Springer, Cham (2017). https://doi.org/10.1007/978-3-319-58347-1_8
13. Sun, B., Saenko, K.: Subspace distribution alignment for unsupervised domain adaptation. In: BMVC, pp. 24.1–24.10 (2015)
14. Wright, J., Ganesh, A., Rao, S., Ma, Y.: Robust principal component analysis: exact recovery of corrupted low-rank matrices. J. ACM **87**(4), 20:3–20:56 (2009)
15. Xu, Y., Fang, X., Wu, J., Li, X., Zhang, D.: Discriminative transfer subspace learning via low-rank and sparse representation. IEEE Trans. IP **25**(2), 850–863 (2016)
16. Yang, J., Yan, R., Hauptmann, A.G.: Cross-domain video concept detection using adaptive SVMS. In: ACM International Conference on Multimedia, pp. 188–197 (2007)
17. Zhang, L., Zuo, W., Zhang, D.: LSDT: latent sparse domain transfer learning for visual adaptation. IEEE Trans. IP **25**(3), 1177–1191 (2016)

An Image Fusion Algorithm Based on Modified Regional Consistency and Similarity Weighting

Tingting Yang[✉] and Peiyu Fang

Beijing University of Posts and Telecommunications, Beijing, China
muyi1024b@163.com

Abstract. We propose an image fusion algorithm based on modified regional consistency and similarity weighting to fuse two multi-focus images with strict registration of the same scene. The algorithm decomposes source image with the shift-invariant discrete wavelet transform (SIDWT) and obtain high frequency components and low frequency component. The regional energy consistency is used in high frequency fusion. The saliency map of multi-focus images is calculated with spectral residual (SR), and combine the similarity weighting method to fuse low frequency coefficient. The simulation results show that the improved algorithm is an effective image fusion algorithm. In terms of visual effects, fusion image keeps details and advances the vagueness. Compared with fusion algorithms based on regional consistency and similarity weighting, its objective evaluation indicators, such as standard deviation and mutual information are also improved.

Keywords: Multi-focus image fusion · SIDWT · Regional energy consistency Similarity weighting · Spectral residual (SR)

1 Introduction

When photograph a scene with an optical sensor, it is hard to image objects of diverse distances clearly due to focal length scope limitation [1]. Multi-focus image fusion technology blends multiple images focusing on different objects. It can make full use of the redundant and complementary information existing in focused images, obtain a more comprehensive and accurate description of the scene. This kind of technologies are extensively used in digital imaging, computer vision, automatic target recognition and other fields [2]. Generally, images are blended at multiple resolution mainly based on pyramid decomposition [3] and wavelet transform [4]. Compared with pyramid decomposition, the wavelet transform is more widely applied in image processing field owing to directivity and non-redundancy. An image is filtered by N layer wavelet transform to get 3 N directional high frequency images and one low frequency image. High frequency sub-images retain details and edges of diverse resolutions. Low frequency sub-image contains background information. Fusion carries out at different scales, and fusion rules determine the quality of blending image. Traditional method takes average value of coefficients. fusion image preserves the basic characteristics of objects in focus. However, its overall visual effect is plain and with blurred details and edges. Burt [5] proposes a similarity weighting method that compares the similarity of

© Springer Nature Switzerland AG 2018
J. Zhou et al. (Eds.): CCBR 2018, LNCS 10996, pp. 247–254, 2018.
https://doi.org/10.1007/978-3-319-97909-0_27

processing images with the set threshold to select fusion rules. This algorithm is not only simple with a small amount calculation, but also preserves more details and edges. Nevertheless, the false contour of blended image is obvious. Wang [6] puts forward the region consistency method that fuses according to number of regional maximum value falls in every source image. This method takes maximum value in pixel centered region as the image feature description, which highlights regional characteristics while weakens local characteristics. Fused image basically eliminates false contour, but some details are missing too.

In view of shortcomings in above fusion methods, this paper decomposes source images with the shift-invariant discrete wavelet transform (SIDWT) and gets high frequency components and low frequency component. The high and low frequency coefficients have emphasis on different features, thus should be carried out with diverse rules. In high frequency part, we improve regional consistency method. In low frequency part, we introduce the spectral residual [7] (SR) to calculate the saliency maps of undecomposed images, and combine the similarity weighting method to get fused coefficient. The simulation results show that fusion image of the proposed method keeps details of source images and improves the vague phenomena. Compared with fusion algorithms based on regional consistency and similarity weighting, its objective evaluation indicators, such as standard deviation and mutual information are advanced.

2 Related Technology

2.1 SIDWT-Based Image Fusion

Owing to down-sampling and non-translation invariance, 2-D discrete wavelet transform is easy to introduce false information such as ringing and aliasing effects. The shift-invariant discrete wavelet transform (SIDWT) is proposed in literature [8] to overcome these shortcomings. It divides 1-D signal into scale sequence and wavelet sequences at each scale. 2-D signal can be decomposed by continuous 1-D decomposition in row and column [9]. After N layer filtering, image is decomposed into a scale sequence (low frequency) and 3 N wavelet sequences of different resolutions (high frequency), and each sequence has the same size as original image.

The convolution results of upper sequences and reconstruction filters are added as scale sequence of lower layer. The convolution and addition process are repeated at each layer until the downmost scale sequence is obtained, that is, the original input signal is reconstructed and the SIDWT inverse transform has been accomplished.

In this paper, the input images are decomposed into wavelet expressions by SIDWT, got fused wavelet coefficients with certain rules, obtained final fusion image by SIDWT inverse transform. The wavelet base selects Haar wavelet with translation invariance.

2.2   SR-Based Saliency Detection

Based on information theory, Barlow [10] proposes effective coding hypothesis which divides image information into two parts: salient part (salient objects) and redundant part (background information). Itti [11] puts forward the visual attention system inspired by early visual system of primate. This system mainly focuses on salient part of the whole image, and extracts saliency map by overall consideration of brightness, color and direction features. Hou [7] proposes the spectral residual method (SR) which is a completely different model from the visual attention system. SR mainly focuses on redundant part of the image. The original logarithmic amplitude spectrum subtracts background imformation, which is smoothing logarithmic amplitude spectrum, is considered as salient object in frequency domain [12]. SR model is with less calculations. Its steps are as follows.

1. An image is transformed into frequency domain with 2-D Fourier transform to calculate amplitude and phase.
2. The smoothing logarithmic amplitude is computed as background imformation.
3. The original logarithmic amplitude subtracts redundant part is the salient objects.
4. The saliency map at spatial domain is obtained by Fourier inverse transform.

The more remarkable position in an image has a greater value in its saliency map. In Fig. 1, The left half of picture b and the right half of picture d are detected as salient regions, which are consistent with the focused areas of original images.

(a)   (b)   (c)   (d)

Fig. 1. (a) Left focus image of "cup". (b) the saliency map of (a) calculated by SR. (c) Right focus image of "cup". (d) the saliency map of (c) calculated by SR.

3   Image Fusion Algorithm

3.1   High Frequency Component Fusion

After SIDWT decomposition, each layer gets three high frequency components representing the horizontal, vertical and diagonal direction information of the input signal respectively. The high frequency component pixels change fast, and larger absolute value of coefficient means more details and edges at this position. Regional energy reflects the uniformity of image texture. We take coefficient from image which larger region energy values in an area mostly derive from as fusion coefficient. This kind of fusion rules retain directional information and get better overall effects. The regional energy consistency fusion steps are as follows.

1. Calculate the regional energy of two images to be blended.

$$E(i,j) = \sum_{i \in J} \sum_{j \in K} I(i,j)^2. \tag{1}$$

$E(i,j)$ is regional energy in $3 * 3$ window at position (i,j).

2. Compare regional energy value at every pixel.

$$\begin{cases} E_A(i,j) > E_B(i,j), A_h(i,j) = 1 \\ E_A(i,j) \le E_B(i,j), B_h(i,j) = 1 \end{cases}. \tag{2}$$

If $E_A(i,j)$ is larger than $E_B(i,j)$, $A_h(i,j)$ is 1. otherwise, $B_h(i,j)$ is 1.

3. Count the number of bigger energy values in pixel centered area. The window is generally $N * N$, in this article $N = 5$.

$$\begin{cases} Ca(i,j) = \sum_{m \in J} \sum_{n \in K} w(m,n) A_h(i,j) \\ Cb(i,j) = \sum_{m \in J} \sum_{n \in K} w(m,n) B_h(i,j) \end{cases}. \tag{3}$$

w is a $N * N$ matrix of value 1. Ca and Cb record number of bigger energy values in every pixel centered area that stem from sub-images A and B.

4. Compare the number of larger energy values in every pixel centered area in order to determine fusion coefficient.

$$\begin{aligned} &\text{if } Ca(i,j) > Cb(i,j) \ T(i,j) = A(i,j) \\ &\text{else} \quad T(i,j) = B(i,j) \end{aligned}. \tag{4}$$

$T(i,j)$ is fused coefficient in position (i,j).

The advantage of improved regional consistency is that its fusion coefficient stems from image with more bigger energy values in an area, in consideration of local and regional characteristics comprehensively, has balanced image details and uniformity.

3.2   Low Frequency Component Fusion

After SIDWT decomposition, the uppermost layer obtains a low frequency component similar to source image. The low frequency component pixels change slowly, mainly include background information. When calculate low frequency saliency map, we take the saliency map of multi-focus image without wavelet decomposition instead, because their focused objects are consistent and with the same size. Besides, source image is clearer and has more salient information than filtered sub-image. The low frequency fusion steps are as follows.

1. The SR method is used to compute saliency map SF of source multi-focus images.
2. $S(X,p)$ is the regional saliency of image X in position p. w is a $3 * 3$ matrix of value 1.

$$S(X,p) = \sum_{q \in Q} w(q) \cdot SF^2(X,q). \qquad (5)$$

3. The similarity R changes from 0 to 1. The correlation degree of two source multi-focus images SA and SB is high at position where R is large.

$$R(p) = \frac{2 \sum_{q \in Q} w(q) \cdot SF(SA,q)SF(SB,q)}{S(SA,p) + S(SB,p)}. \qquad (6)$$

4. If R is not more than a certain threshold (in this paper is 0.75), two sub-images A and B are not relevant. We select coefficient with larger regional saliency as fused coefficient. Otherwise, two sub-images are relevant, the weighted average value of coefficients is used as fused coefficient.

$$\begin{array}{l} \text{if } R(p) < = T \; w_{min} = 0, w_{max} = 1 \\ \text{else } w_{min} = \frac{1}{2} - \frac{1}{2}[\frac{1-R(p)}{1-T}], w_{max} = 1 - w_{min} \\ \text{if } S(SA,p) > S(SB,p) \; w(A,p) = w_{max}, w(B,p) = w_{min} \\ \text{else } w(B,p) = w_{max}, w(A,p) = w_{min} \end{array} \qquad (7)$$

The low frequency fusion coefficient is:

$$T(p) = w(A,p) \cdot A(p) + w(B,p) \cdot B(p). \qquad (8)$$

3.3   Multi-focus Image Fusion Algorithm

1. Two multi-focus images are decomposed into 3 N high frequency sub-images and 1 low frequency sub-image by SIDWT.
2. The high frequency coefficient is selected based on regional energy consistency.
3. The low frequency coefficient is determined according to the similarity weighting and saliency map calculated by SR.
4. The fusion image is obtained by SIDWT inverse transform.

4   Simulation Results and Analysis

We select three group multi-focus images "Cup", "Clock" and "Flower", one is left focus image and the other is right focus image, for simulation experiments, and compare fused images got from three existing algorithms and proposed algorithm.

4.1   Subjective Evaluation

Figure 2(c) preserves the basic features of focused images, but its overall visual effect is general and the details and edges are blurred. As for partial enlarged maps, Fig. 3(a) has distinct boundary of left and right objects, but the false contour [13] of the letters is obvious too. Figure 3(b) basically eliminates the false contour of blended image, but some details are lost. In contrast, the detail information in Fig. 3(c) is clearer, and its false contour phenomenon is better than Fig. 3(a).

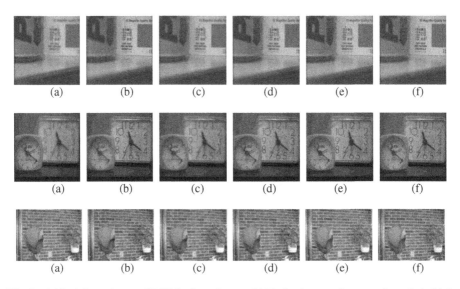

Fig. 2. (a) Left focus image. (b) Right focus image. (c) Fusion image of mean value rule in high and low frequency sub-images. (d) Fusion image of similarity weighting rule in high and low frequency sub-images. (e) Fusion image of regional consistency rule in high and low frequency sub-images. (f) Fusion image of proposed algorithm. (Multi-focus images are decomposed by 3 layers of SIDWT.)

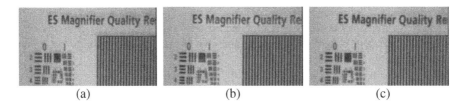

Fig. 3. (a, b and c) are the magnifying "Cup" images of Fig. 2 (d, e and f) in the same region respectively.

4.2 Objective Evaluation

In the evaluation of algorithms, we not only need to compare subjective observation of fusion images, but also need to measure their objective evaluation indicators [14]. In this paper, we calculate their non-reference evaluation indicators average gradient (AG), information entropy (EN), standard deviation (SD), and reference evaluation indicators mutual information (MI), structural similarity (SSIM) (MI and SSIM are mean values of two multi-focus images and fusion image calculated respectively). The greater value of these indicators, the more details and higher quality fusion image is. We can see from Table 1, the AG, EN, SSIM values of proposed method are larger than or between similarity weighting [5] image and regional consistency [6] image. The values of SD and MI are larger than other methods. It shows that proposed algorithm improves performance based on similarity weighting and regional consistency methods.

Table 1. Evaluation indexes of several fused images

Images	Fusion methods	AG	EN	SD	MI	SSIM
Cup	Average method	4.5082	6.8408	44.1810	1.9984	0.9083
	similarity weighting [5]	6.4173	7.2328	45.4676	1.6010	0.8881
	Regional consistency [6]	6.3149	7.1759	45.6327	1.5830	0.8811
	Proposed method	6.4125	7.1899	45.6753	1.6103	0.8844
Clock	Average method	3.3383	6.9705	39.3549	2.4323	0.9389
	Similarity weighting [5]	4.4476	7.0068	40.1173	2.4197	0.9108
	Regional consistency [6]	4.5321	7.0025	40.2322	2.4343	0.9012
	Proposed method	4.6016	7.0188	40.6137	2.5326	0.9081
Flower	Average method	6.2217	7.0982	35.2440	1.8427	0.9679
	Similarity weighting [5]	7.0982	7.1582	37.2677	1.8625	0.9561
	Regional consistency [6]	8.0231	7.1595	37.7223	1.8158	0.9449
	Proposed method	8.0727	7.1830	38.1175	2.0064	0.9471

5 Conclusion

We propose an image fusion algorithm based on improved regional consistency and similarity weighting methods. Using the shift-invariant discrete wavelet transform (SIDWT) to decompose multi-focus image and obtain high and low frequency sub-images. The high frequency coefficient is obtained according to regional energy consistency. we calculate the saliency map of multi-focus images with spectral residual (SR), and combine the similarity weighting method to fuse low frequency coefficient. The simulation results show that fusion image preserves source image details and makes the blurred phenomenon better. Compared with existing algorithms, the objective evaluation indicators, such as standard deviation and mutual information, are also improved. It shows that the algorithm improves performance of image fusion algorithm based on region consistency and similarity weighting.

References

1. Zheng, J.N.: Multi Focus Image Fusion Method. Chongqing University, Chongqing (2016)
2. Varshney, P.K.: Multisensor data fusion. Electron. Commun. Eng. **9**(6), 245–253 (1997)
3. Toet, A.: Image fusion by a ratio of low-pass pyramid. Pattern Recogn. Lett. **9**(4), 245–253 (1989)
4. Li, S., Kwok, J.T., Wang, Y.: Using the discrete wavelet frame transform to merge landsat TM and SPOT panchromatic images. Inf. Fusion **3**, 17–23 (2002)
5. Burt, P.J., Kolczynski, R.J.: Enhanced image capture through fusion. In: Proceedings of the International Conference on Computer Vision. DBLP, pp. 173–182 (1993)
6. Wang, J., Wang, G.H., Wang, Q.L.: Multi focus image fusion algorithm based on region consistency. Ordnance Autom. **32**(04), 55–57 (2013)
7. Hou, X.D., Zhang, L.: Saliency detection: a spectral residual approach. In: IEEE Conference on Computer Vision and Pattern Recognition, pp. 1–8 (2007)
8. Rockinger, O.: Image sequence fusion using a shift-invariant wavelet transform. In: Proceedings of the International Conference on Image Processing. IEEE, 2002:288 (1997)
9. Yu, L.S., Wen, G.J., Li, Z.Y.: Remote sensing image fusion algorithm based on SIDWT. Comput. Eng. **37**(17), 197–199 (2011)
10. Barlow, H.B.: Possible principles underlying the transformation of sensory messages. In: Rosenbluth, W.A. (ed.) Sensory Communication, pp. 217–234. MIT Press, Cambridge, MA (1961)
11. Itti, L., Koch, C., Niebur, E.: A model of salient-based visual attention for rapid scene analysis. In: IEEE Computer Society (1998)
12. Gao, H.R., Pan, C.: Image fusion of visual saliency detection and pyramid transform. Comput. Sci. Explor. **9**(04), 491–500 (2015)
13. Wang, H.M., Chen, L.H., Li, Y.J., Zhang, K.: An image fusion algorithm based on salient features. J. Northwest. Polytechnical Univ. **28**(04), 486–490 (2010)
14. Zhang, W.: Objective image quality assessment algorithm and its application. China University of Mining and Technology (2016)

Face

Discriminative Weighted Low-Rank Collaborative Representation Classifier for Robust Face Recognition

Xielian Hou[⊠], Caikou Chen[⊠], Shengwei Zhou, and Jingshan Li

College of Information Engineering, Yangzhou University, Yangzhou, China
xielhou@163.com, yzcck@126.com, 15605527305@163.com,
lijingshan123@163.com

Abstract. Recently, low-rank collaborative representation classification (LCRC) has proven to have good performance under controlled conditions. However, this algorithm stipulates that each singular value of the kernel norm is equal, which limits its ability and flexibility to deal with practical problems. Moreover, training samples and test samples may be damaged due to occlusion or disguise; this factor may reduce the face recognition rate. This paper presents a novel robust face recognition based on discriminative weighted low-rank collaborative representation (WDLCRC). Based on the LCRC, we add the constraint of structural inconsistency and assign the singular values with different weights by adaptively weighting the kernel norm. It is proved through experiments that the recognition rate of WDLCRC on AR database and CMU PIE database is higher than that of SRC, CRC and LCRC algorithms.

Keywords: Face recognition · Low-rank collaborative representation
Inconsistent structure · Adaptive weighting

1 Introduction

Automatic face recognition has received significant attention in the field of pattern recognition and computer vision in the past decades. The effective representation and classification techniques for face images play an important role in face recognition. Numerous methods for face representation and classification have been proposed so far. Over the years, extensive research has been devoted to the study of representation based classification methods (RBC). The main idea behind RBC is to model a test sample as a linear combination of training samples and obtain its label by minimizing the reconstruction error. Many RBC methods have been developed. Among them, the most representative is Sparse Representation Based Classification method (SRC) [1], which has shown interesting results in face recognition in recent years. SRC represents a testing sample as a sparse linear combination of training samples from all classes and classifies it to the class which has the minimal representation residual to it. Although SRC has been proven to be powerful in many applications, especially face recognition, its nature is not still clearly revealed and it is still computationally expensive. To address these drawbacks, some efforts have been made on the role of sparsity in face recognition. Zhang et al. [2]

J. Zhou et al. (Eds.): CCBR 2018, LNCS 10996, pp. 257–264, 2018.
https://doi.org/10.1007/978-3-319-97909-0_28

has shown that the collaborative representation mechanism is more important than the l_1-norm constraint in improving the performance of face recognition. They propose a collaborative representation classification method (CRC) which uses l_2-norm instead of l_1-norm as regularization to represent the query sample collaboratively by samples from all the classes. More importantly, they demonstrate theoretically and experimentally that the l_2-norm constraint for CRC can lead to similar recognition result to SRC but with much less computational cost. Additionally, it has been demonstrated that if the test sample is noisy duo to occlusion, pose, illumination, and expression, SRC and CRC can show powerful robustness. However, when training samples are corrupted and not well aligned, their performance will be degraded.

In practical applications, both training and test samples such as face images may often be contaminated by noise, the above SRC and CRC might not achieve promising performance. To address this problem, Lu et al. [3] proposed a low-rank constrained collaborative representation classifier (LCRC). LCRC integrate a low-rank constraint on the representation coefficient matrix into the CRC framework, which can simultaneously minimize the class-specific reconstruction error and rank of representation coefficient matrix.

Compared with SRC and CRC, LCRC achieve promising results for applications with both corrupted training and testing samples. Although its success as aforementioned, LCRC still has certain drawbacks. LCRC recover the final clean representation matrix through imposing a low-rank constraint on the representation matrix. Since solving for low-rank minimization directly is NP-hard and is not easy to solve, the optimization problem is often relaxed by minimizing the nuclear norm of a matrix which is a convex relaxation of the matrix rank minimization. This method is referred as to nuclear norm minimization (NNM). NNM does not consider the priori information on the singular values of the real data matrix; all singular values are to be regarded equally [6]. Clearly, the existing NNM methods ignore the significant priori knowledge on the singular values of the real data matrix, which might result in a degraded LCRC. Moreover, different classes of face samples may have similarities, so the LCRC algorithm cannot provide enough identification information [4].

In order to solve the above problem, this paper proposes a robust face recognition method based on discriminative weighted constrained low-rank collaborative representation classifier (WDLCRC). WDLCRC replace the original nuclear norm with weighted nuclear norm. The imposed weights will improve the representation capability of the original nuclear norm. And the WDLCRC method adds a regular term to the LCRC to make the data matrix as independent as possible. The experimental part of this paper will verify that this algorithm has good robustness and recognition ability.

2 Related Work

2.1 Low-Rank Collaborative Representation

The low-rank collaborative representation is to add a low-rank constraint on the basis of the collaborative representation to capture a global sample data structure; it has strong robustness to the input noise, pushes the meaningful coefficient into the target subclass, and reduces the rank of the coefficient matrix to improve the recognition ability [3]. The objective function is:

$$\arg \min_{\Lambda}\{\|\Lambda\|_* + \lambda\|\Lambda\|_2\}$$
$$s.t. \mathbf{Y} = \mathbf{X}\Lambda \tag{1}$$

Where $\mathbf{X}$ is the training sample, $\mathbf{Y}$ is the test sample, Λ is the low-rank matrix, λ is a scalar that balances the low- rank and the local, and $\|.\|_*$ is the nuclear norm which is used to relax the low-rank operation. But in the real world, face images usually have noise. Therefore, the test sample matrix can be rewritten as: $\mathbf{Y} = \mathbf{X}\Lambda + \mathbf{E}$, where $\mathbf{E}$ is the error matrix. So, the objective function can be rewritten as:

$$\arg \min_{\Lambda,\mathbf{E}}\{\|\Lambda\|_* + \lambda\|\Lambda\|_2 + \beta\|\mathbf{E}\|_1\}$$
$$s.t. \mathbf{Y} = \mathbf{X}\Lambda + \mathbf{E} \tag{2}$$

Where β is the penalty parameter. We can use the linearized alternating direction method with adaptive penalty (LADMAP) [5] to solve (2) optimization problems.

2.2 Weighted Nuclear Norm Minimization

Since the traditional nuclear norm minimization (NNM) limits the ability and flexibility to deal with practical problems, L. Zhang et al. proposed weighted nuclear norm minimization (WNNM) to improve flexibility. However, the weight vector itself also introduces more parameters in the model, so the correct weight vector setting plays an important role in the success of the WNNM model [6].

In order to enhance the sparseness of sparse coding, Candes et al. [7] proposed an impactful reweighting mechanism for adaptive adjustment weights. The formula is as follows:

$$w_i^{l+1} = \frac{C}{|x_i^l| + \varepsilon} \tag{3}$$

Where x_i^l is the i-th sparse coding coefficient of the l-th iteration, w_i^{l+1} is the corresponding regularization parameter for the $(l + 1)$-th iteration, ε is a small positive number to avoid tending to zero, C is a compromise constant. This reweighting method has proven to be very similar to the l_0-norm, and the model has achieved advantageous capability in compressive sensing.

3   WDLCRC

Although low-rank collaborative representation (LCRC) is an effective face recognition algorithm, it limits the ability and flexibility to deal with practical problems, and human faces have similarities, the algorithm cannot provide enough identification information. Therefore, this paper proposes robust face recognition based on discriminative weighted low-rank cooperative representation. We assume that there is a training set $\mathbf{X} = [\mathbf{X}_1, \mathbf{X}_2 \ldots, \mathbf{X}_t]$ for t classes, test sample $\mathbf{Y} = [\mathbf{y}_1, \mathbf{y}_2 \ldots, \mathbf{y}_n]$. Using $\mathbf{X}$ as a dictionary, then a test sample $\mathbf{y}_i$ can be approximated by a linear combination of training samples $\mathbf{X}:\mathbf{y}_i = \mathbf{X}\boldsymbol{\alpha}_i$; Where $\boldsymbol{\alpha}_i$ is the coefficient vector of $\mathbf{y}_i$, and its matrix is as follows:$\mathbf{Y} = \mathbf{X}\boldsymbol{\Lambda}$, where $\boldsymbol{\Lambda} = [\boldsymbol{\alpha}_1, \boldsymbol{\alpha}_2 \ldots, \boldsymbol{\alpha}_n]$ is a representation matrix of $\mathbf{Y}$. Inspired by [4, 6, 8], we weight the kernel norm and added the regularization term $\left\| \mathbf{Y}_j^{\mathrm{T}} \mathbf{Y}_i \right\|$ on the basis of LCRC to improve flexibility and enhance independence between samples after recovery. The new objective function is as follows:

$$\min_{\boldsymbol{\Lambda}_i, \mathbf{E}_i} \|\boldsymbol{\Lambda}_i\|_{w.*} + \lambda\|\boldsymbol{\Lambda}_i\|_2 + \beta\|\mathbf{E}_i\|_1 + \eta \sum_{j \neq i} \left\| (\mathbf{X}_j\boldsymbol{\Lambda}_j)^{\mathrm{T}} \mathbf{X}_i\boldsymbol{\Lambda}_i \right\|$$
$$s.t. \mathbf{Y}_i = \mathbf{X}_i\boldsymbol{\Lambda}_i + \mathbf{E}_i, i = 1, 2 \ldots, n \tag{4}$$

In order to solve the optimization problem of formula (4), we first introduce the auxiliary variable $\mathbf{W}_i$ to make its objective function separable, and then the objective function can be rewritten as:

$$\min_{\boldsymbol{\Lambda}_i, \mathbf{E}_i} \|\boldsymbol{\Lambda}_i\|_{w.*} + \lambda\|\mathbf{W}_i\|_2 + \beta\|\mathbf{E}_i\|_1 + \eta \sum_{j \neq i} \left\| (\mathbf{X}_j\boldsymbol{\Lambda}_j)^{\mathrm{T}} \mathbf{X}_i\mathbf{W}_i \right\|_{\mathrm{F}}^2$$
$$s.t. \mathbf{Y}_i = \mathbf{X}_i\boldsymbol{\Lambda}_i + \mathbf{E}_i, \boldsymbol{\Lambda}_i = \mathbf{W}_i, i = 1, 2 \ldots, n \tag{5}$$

In this paper, we use linearized alternating direction method with adaptive penalty (LADMAP) to solve the (5) optimization problem, and the corresponding augmented Lagrange function can be expressed as follows:

$$\mathbf{L} = \|\boldsymbol{\Lambda}_i\|_{w.*} + \lambda\|\mathbf{W}_i\|_2 + \beta\|\mathbf{E}_i\|_1 + \eta \sum_{j \neq i} \left\| (\mathbf{X}_j\boldsymbol{\Lambda}_j)^{\mathrm{T}} \mathbf{X}_i\mathbf{W}_i \right\|_{\mathrm{F}}^2$$
$$+ <\mathbf{T}_1, \mathbf{Y}_i - \mathbf{X}_i\boldsymbol{\Lambda}_i - \mathbf{E}_i> + <\mathbf{T}_2, \boldsymbol{\Lambda}_i - \mathbf{W}_i> + \frac{\mu}{2}(\|\mathbf{Y}_i - \mathbf{X}_i\boldsymbol{\Lambda}_i - \mathbf{E}_i\|_{\mathrm{F}}^2 + \|\boldsymbol{\Lambda}_i - \mathbf{W}_i\|_{\mathrm{F}}^2) \tag{6}$$

Where $\mathbf{T}_1, \mathbf{T}_2$ are the Lagrange factors and $\mu > 0$ is the penalty parameter. After simple algebraic operations, (6) can be converted to:

$$\mathbf{L} = \|\boldsymbol{\Lambda}_i\|_{w.*} + \lambda\|\mathbf{W}_i\|_2 + \beta\|\mathbf{E}_i\|_1 + \eta \sum_{j \neq i} \left\| (\mathbf{X}_j\boldsymbol{\Lambda}_j)^{\mathrm{T}} \mathbf{X}_i\mathbf{W}_i \right\|_{\mathrm{F}}^2$$
$$+ h(\boldsymbol{\Lambda}_i, \mathbf{W}_i, \mathbf{E}_i, \mathbf{T}_1, \mathbf{T}_2, \mu) - \frac{1}{2\mu}(\|\mathbf{T}_1\|_{\mathrm{F}}^2 + \|\mathbf{T}_1\|_{\mathrm{F}}^2) \tag{7}$$

Where $h(\Lambda_i, \mathbf{W}_i, \mathbf{E}_i, \mathbf{T}_1, \mathbf{T}_2, \mu) = \frac{\mu}{2}\left(\left\|\mathbf{Y}_i - \mathbf{X}_i\Lambda_i - \mathbf{E}_i + \frac{\mathbf{T}_1}{\mu}\right\|_F^2 + \left\|\Lambda_i - \mathbf{W}_i + \frac{\mathbf{T}_2}{\mu}\right\|_F^2\right).$

We can use the alternating direction method [9] to minimize Eq. (7). Let's discuss how to update the variable in (6) after each iteration:

A. Update Λ_i: We can fix the variables except Λ_i to solve the optimization problem of (7):

$$\Lambda_i^{k+1} = \arg\min_{\Lambda_i} \|\Lambda_i\|_{w.*} + <\nabla\Lambda h(\Lambda_i^k, \mathbf{W}_i^k, \mathbf{E}_i^k, \mathbf{T}_{1,k}, \mathbf{T}_{2,k}, \mu_k), \Lambda_i - \Lambda_i^k>$$

$$+ \frac{\mu_k L}{2}\|\Lambda_i - \Lambda_i^k\|_F^2$$

$$= \arg\min_{\Lambda_i} \|\Lambda_i\|_{w.*} + \frac{\mu_k L}{2}\left\|\Lambda_i - \left(\Lambda_i^k + \mathbf{X}_i^T\frac{\mathbf{Y}_i - \mathbf{X}_i\Lambda_i^k - \mathbf{E}_i^k + \frac{\mathbf{T}_{1,k}}{\mu_k}}{L} - \frac{\Lambda_i^k - \mathbf{W}_i^k + \frac{\mathbf{T}_{2,k}}{\mu_k}}{L}\right)\right\|_F^2 \quad (8)$$

$$= \Theta_{(\mu L)^{-1}}\left(\Lambda_i^k + \mathbf{X}_i^T\frac{\mathbf{Y}_i - \mathbf{X}_i\Lambda_i^k - \mathbf{E}_i^k + \frac{\mathbf{T}_{1,k}}{\mu_k}}{L} - \frac{\Lambda_i^k - \mathbf{W}_i^k + \frac{\mathbf{T}_{2,k}}{\mu_k}}{L}\right)$$

Where Θ is the singular value threshold operator.

B. Update $\mathbf{W}_i$: We can fix $\Lambda_i, \mathbf{E}_i$ to update auxiliary variables $\mathbf{W}_i$:

$$\mathbf{W}_i^{k+1} = (2\eta\sum_{j\neq i}(\mathbf{X}_j\Lambda_j^{k+1})^T\mathbf{X}_j\Lambda_j^{k+1}\mathbf{X}_i^T\mathbf{X}_i + \mu_k)^{-1}(\mu_k\Lambda_i^{k+1} - \mathbf{T}_{2,k} - 2\lambda\mathbf{W}_i) \quad (9)$$

C. Update $\mathbf{E}_i$: We can fix two variables except $\mathbf{E}_i$ to minimize (7):

$$\mathbf{E}_i^{k+1} = \arg\min_{\mathbf{E}_i} \beta\|\mathbf{E}_i\|_1 + \frac{\mu_k}{2}\left\|\mathbf{Y}_i - \mathbf{X}_i\Lambda_i^{k+1} - \mathbf{E}_i + \frac{\mathbf{T}_{1,k}}{\mu_k}\right\|_F^2 \quad (10)$$

4 Experiment

4.1 AR Database

The AR database [10] contains over 4000 frontal images of 126 people. There are 26 face images with different changes in each class. We divide the 26 images into two parts. Each part contains 13 images, of which 3 images wear glasses, 3 images with scarves, and the remaining 7 images have lights and expressions change, so it is called clean face images. In the experiment, we selected 120 classes of face images. All images are 165 × 120 pixels. We first convert the image to a gray scale image and crop it to 50 × 40 pixels. Some images in the AR database are shown in Fig. 1:

Fig. 1. Image of the first person in the AR database

In order to prove the effectiveness of our algorithm, we use images with both clean and occluded images as the training set. There are three situations that need to be tested:

(1) Sunglasses: In the first part, we chose 7 clean samples and 3 glasses-based samples as the training set, the second part of the 7 clean samples and 3 glasses-based samples as the test set.
(2) Scarf: We selected 7 clean samples and 3 scarves as the training set in the first part, 7 clean samples and 3 scarves as the test set in the second part.
(3) Sunglasses + scarf: we choose samples of wearing glasses and samples of scarves as training set. That is to say, we choose 7 clean samples, 3 glasses wearing samples and 3 samples of scarves as training set, and the remaining samples as test set.

The recognition rates of different algorithms on the AR database are shown in Table 1:

Table 1. Recognition rates of different algorithms on AR database

AR	Sunglass	Scarf	Sunglass+ Scarf
Our method	0.8275	0.8335	0.8067
LCRC	0.7796	0.7956	0.7532
CRC	0.7525	0.7325	0.7218
SRC	0.7508	0.7192	0.7357

From the experimental results in Table 1, we can see that the improved method proposed in this paper has better robustness against the presence of occlusion in training samples. Compared with SRC and CRC, the recognition rate of the proposed algorithm can be increased by 6%. Compared with LCRC, the recognition effect is also improved to a certain extent. It can be seen that the algorithm proposed in this paper is superior to other algorithms for face recognition in the case of occlusion.

4.2 CMU PIE Database

The CMU PIE [11] database consists of 68 people with more than 40,000 face images. Each person's face image was obtained in 43 different light conditions through 13 different poses and 4 different expressions. In the experiment, each image will be uniformly cropped to 32 × 32 pixels. All images can be divided into 4 subsets, subset 1: sample 35–42; subset 2: sample 10, 11, 13, 22, 23, 27, 28, 29, 30, 45; subset 3: sample 8, 9, 12, 14, 15, 16, 17, 18, 21, 24; Subset 4: sample 2,3, 6, 7, 19, 20, 46, 7, 48, 49. The partial images in the 4 subsets are shown in Fig. 2:

Subset1   Subset2   Subset3   Subset4

Fig. 2. Image of the first person in the CMU PIE database

As shown in Table 2, we can intuitively see the recognition rate of different algorithms under different lighting conditions:

Table 2. Recognition rates of different algorithms on CMU PIE database

CMU PIE	Subset 1	Subset 2	Subset 3
Our method	0.9491	0.8395	0.8271
LCRC	0.9122	0.8053	0.7985
CRC	0.8926	0.7632	0.7382
SRC	0.9103	0.7703	0.7971

We compare our method with LCRC, SRC, and CRC. From Table 2 we can see that our proposed algorithm obtains higher recognition rate, and it is better than other algorithms in all sessions. It can be seen that the method proposed in this paper is less affected by illumination and has better robustness.

4.3 WDLCRC vs PCAnet

In order to verify the effectiveness of our proposed algorithm, we compare the proposed algorithm with the PCAnet algorithm [12]. We perform experiments on the AR and CMU PIE databases, using frontal lighting and neural representations of face images as training sets. The test set is the lighting change used to identify. We compared the code runtime and recognition rate to verify that our proposed algorithm has similar performance to the deep learning algorithm.

From Table 3, we can see that the recognition rate of our algorithm is almost equal to that of PCAnet, but from the point of view of code running time, our algorithm is much lower than PCAnet. On the AR database, the running time of WDLCRC is 1/3 of PCAnet. On the CMU PIE database, the running time of WDLCRC is 1/2 of PCAnet. Therefore, our proposed algorithm can obtain similar experimental results with advanced deep learning algorithms.

Table 3. Comparison between WDLCRC and PCAnet under different conditions

Face database	AR database		CMU PIE database	
Algorithm	Recognition rate	Code runtime(s)	Recognition rate	Code runtime(s)
WDLCRC	98.68%	3037.34	99.56%	1538.67
PCAnet	98.50%	9136.35	98.70%	2525.11

5 Conclusion

In the real world, different types of faces have similarities, and each singular value of the nuclear norm has a clear physical meaning. In order to solve the above problems, this paper proposes robust face recognition based on discriminative weighted low-rank cooperative representation. It adds a regular item and an adaptive weighted kernel norm based on the LCRC to enhance the independence of data and the flexibility to deal with practical problems. Compared with SRC, CRC and LCRC, our algorithm is more effective. However, our downside is that we do not have more verification on different face databases.

References

1. Wright, J., Yang, A.Y., Ganesh, A., Sastry, S., Ma, Y.: Robust face recognition via sparse Representation. IEEE Trans. Pattern Anal. Mach. Intell. **31**(2), 210–227 (2009)
2. Zhang, L., Yang, M., Feng, X.: Spare representation or collaborative representation: which helps face recognition? In: Proceedings of International Conference on Computer Vision, Barcelona, Spain, pp. 471–478 (2011)
3. Lu, T., Guan, Y., Chen, D., Xiong, Z., He, W.: Low-rank constrained collaborative representation for robust face recognition. IEEE (2017)
4. Wei, C.-P., Chen, C.-F., Fank Wang, Y.-C.: Robust face recognition with structurally incoherent low-rank matrix decomposition. In: IEEE Transactions On Image Processing, vol. 23, no. 8, August 2014
5. Lin, Z., Liu, R., Su, Z.: Linearized alternating direction method with adaptive penalty for low-rank representation. In: Proceedings of Neural Information Processing Systems, Granada, Spain, pp. 1–9 (2011)
6. Gu, S., Xie, Q., Meng, D., Zuo, W., Feng, X., Zhang, L.: Weighted nuclear norm miniminzation and its applications to low level vision. Int. J. Comput. Vis. 1–26 (2016)
7. Cand'es, E.J., Li, X., Ma, Y., Wright, J.: Robust principal component analysis? J. ACM **58** (3), 11 (2011)
8. Ramirez, P.S., Sapiro, G.: Classification and clustering via dictionary learning with structured incoherence and shared features. In: Proceedings of the IEEE Conference on Computer Vision and Pattern Recognition (CVPR), pp. 3501–3508, June 2010
9. Yang, J., Zhang, Y.: Alternating direction algorithms for l_1-problems in compressive sensing. SIAM J. Sci. Comput. **33**(1), 250–278 (2011)
10. Martinez,A., Benavente, R.: The AR face database. CVC Technical Report, vol. 24 (1998)
11. Gross, R., Matthews, I., Cohn, J., Kanade, T., Baker, S.: Multi-PIE. Image Vis. Comput. **28** (5), 807–813 (2010)
12. Chan, T.H., Jia, K., Gao, S., Lu, J., Zeng, Z., Ma, Y.: Pcanet: a simple deep learning baseline for image classification? IEEE Trans. Image Process. **24**(12), 5017–5032 (2015)

Face Expression Recognition Using Gabor Features and a Novel Weber Local Descriptor

Jucheng Yang[✉], Meng Li, Lingchao Zhang, Shujie Han,
Xiaojing Wang, and Jie Wang

College of Computer Science and Information Engineering,
Tianjin University of Science and Technology, Tianjin, China
jcyang@tust.edu.cn

Abstract. This paper presents a novel fusion approach for facial expression recognition. The novelty of this paper lies in: (i) Gabor wavelets are introduced for image representation, which describes well local spatial scale characteristics and orientation selectivity of image textures. Gabor features are robust to variations due to illumination and noise. Furthermore, we reduce the dimensionality of Gabor feature vector, in order to reduce computation cost and improve discriminative power for feature extraction. (ii) The paper proposes Multi-orientation Symmetric Local Graph Structure (MSLGS) to calculate feature value for replacing differential excitation of Weber Local Descriptor (WLD), which captures more discriminative local images details. The orientation of original WLD also is extended by bringing more gradient direction, thus it can obtain more precise image description to spatial structure information. The comparative experimental results illustrated that the algorithm could achieve a superior performance with high accuracy.

Keywords: Facial expression recognition · Gabor feature infusion
Weber Local Descriptor · Multi-orientation Symmetric Local Graph Structure
ROC curve

1 Introduction

Facial expression recognition (FER) has been a trending research field in Human-Computer Interaction [1]. Facial expression reveals human emotion states that helps to understand people's opinions and intentions.

In general, face expression feature extraction methods can be divided into several types: the first is called geometric approaches [2] that extracts features by distance changes, shape and size proportion of key points on face. Facial Action Coding System encodes facial muscles movements as basic Action Units to distinguish different emotions [3]. The second use holistic features of entire image that is much prone to interfered by complex illumination, postures-variant, partial occlusions, and so on. The third approaches focus on facial movement characteristics, among of which, optical flow reflects faces motions by dynamic image sequences, but it is less vulnerable to illumination, and higher computation cost limit its application. Recently, Weber Local Descriptor (WLD) and Local Graph Structure (LGS) descriptors have become popular

© Springer Nature Switzerland AG 2018
J. Zhou et al. (Eds.): CCBR 2018, LNCS 10996, pp. 265–274, 2018.
https://doi.org/10.1007/978-3-319-97909-0_29

since they are effective and more stable to local image texture changes. In 2011, Abusham firstly proposed LGS to extract robust features [4]. In 2014, Mohd et al. proposed Symmetrical Local Graph Structure (SLGS) that made up the defect of asymmetrical LGS [5]. Orthogonal Symmetric Local Graph Structure (OSLGS) introduced difference of Gaussians for image representation [6]. Whereas, LGS-based approaches above have an inherent problem that neglect directional information in image. Though WLD presents local orientation features of image [7], it just places emphasis on contrast information on target pixel. Fang et al. introduced Weber Local Gradient Pattern (WLGP) [8] that added the gradient in horizontal and diagonal directions, but it lacked gradient changes that cause poor stability. Weber Local Circle Gradient Pattern (WLCGP) [9] calculated spatial relationship among neighboring pixels that confined to the change of adjacent pixels.

Despite great progress has been made in FER, it still takes many challenges: owing to small between-class difference under different expression for same person, and big in-class difference under same emotion for different person, recognition accuracy and real-time requirement should be further strengthen. And external interference need be weaken, such as angle offset, illumination. Besides, deep learning requires amounts of training data to learn feature, such large datasets are hard to get and are computationally expensive in actual application. Compared with deep learning, the proposed method has an advantage in resolving small sample problem. This paper propose a novel fusion approach for FER, which enhances image details and effectively reduce noise.

The structure of this paper is listed as follows. Section 2 reviews the related theory. Section 3 presents the proposed approach based on Gabor features and WLD-improved fusion. Section 4 shows the detailed experiments and analyses. Finally, conclusions can be drawn in Sect. 5.

2 Related Theory

2.1 Weber Local Descriptor (WLD)

Chen et al. firstly proposed WLD inspired by Weber's Law. The law says that the distinction only can be perceived when the ratio of stimulus variation and stimulus itself reaches a threshold, as shown in formula (1):

$$\frac{\Delta I}{I} = k \tag{1}$$

where I is initial stimulus intensity, ΔI denotes increment threshold, k is an invariant constant signifying the proportion.

g_0	g_1	g_2
g_7	g_c	g_3
g_6	g_5	g_4

Fig. 1. A 3×3 filter window of WLD operator.

As is seen in Fig. 1, WLD operator uses 3×3 filter to calculate gray changes of current pixel. And it has empirically proved not only effective but also efficient. WLD consists of differential excitation and orientation two parts. The differential excitation describes intensity changes among central pixel and neighboring pixels, which can be calculated as Eq. (2):

$$WLD(x_c, y_c) = \arctan \left[\sum_{i=0}^{P-1} \left(\frac{g_i - g_c}{g_c} \right) \right] \tag{2}$$

where P represents the number of neighbor pixels, $g_i(i = 0, 1, \ldots, p - 1)$ denotes gray value of neighbor pixel, g_c is gray value of center pixel (x_c, y_c). arctan function keeps output at a reasonable range when input pixel value becomes too large or too small.

WLD's orientation part expresses gradient changes of pixels in image. It can be expressed as the ratio of the change in horizontal direction to that in vertical direction, which is described by Eq. (3):

$$\theta(x_c, y_c) = arctan \left(\frac{g_7 - g_3}{g_5 - g_1} \right) \tag{3}$$

After combining differential excitation with orientation two components, WLD features are constructed as a 2D concatenated histogram.

2.2   LGS and SLGS

LGS utilizes graph theory to describe gray difference of neighbor pixels and is encoded as a binary pattern. It constructs a graph to explore the relationship determined by target pixel and surrounding 5 pixels. The calculation process of LGS as follows: at the left side of target pixel, the comparison follows an anticlockwise direction starting from the target pixel, if the pixel gray value of vertex that an arrow points to is greater than previous vertex, assign 1 on the edge connected the two vertices, else assign 0 to the edge. The process carries on at the right side of target pixel, but pixel values are compared clockwise. Lastly, LGS value will be gained for target pixel after an 8-digit binary number is converted into a decimal number. LGS is illustrated in Fig. 2, where gray value of target pixel is assumed as 27.

LGS (10101001)=1×2⁷+0×2⁶+1×2⁵+0×2⁴+1×2³+0×2²+0×2¹+1×2⁰=169

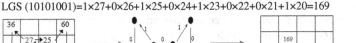

Fig. 2. Local Graph Structure (LGS) operator.

Fig. 3. SLGS operator.

Compared to LGS, SLGS utilizes a symmetric structure to keep a balance of weights, where the left and the right side of target pixel contains 3 pixels. SLGS operator is depicted in Fig. 3. SLGS operator only exploits gradient information in horizontal direction, as a result, it lacks the representative ability to spatial structure.

3 Proposed Method

The framework of FER system based on the proposed method is illustrated in Fig. 4. Its main steps include: image preprocessing, feature extraction using Gabor Features and a novel WLD operator, image classification using k-Nearest Neighbor classifier.

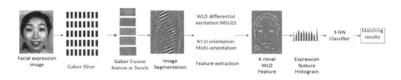

Fig. 4. The framework of the proposed FER system.

3.1 Gabor Feature

Gabor wavelet filter is known as a linear filter, which has been successfully applied for FER. Gabor kernels are similar to 2D receptive fields of simple neuron cells, which could describe spatial localization and frequency properties of facial image. Thus Gabor features strengthens local texture details of key regions on face, and are robust to illumination variations. The simplified Gabor filter is shown in formula (4):

$$G(k, x, y, \theta) = \frac{\|k_{u,v}\|^2}{\sigma^2} e^{-\frac{\|k_{u,v}\|^2 (x^2 + y^2)}{2\sigma^2}} \left(e^{i k_{u,v} (x \cos\theta + y \sin\theta)} - e^{\frac{-\sigma^2}{2}} \right) \tag{4}$$

where (x, y) represents central pixel position in the spatial domain, θ denotes the orientation of Gabor kernel. Rotate $k_{u,v}$ can obtain u orientation and v scale. $\| \ \|$ is a norm operator, σ is spatial aspect ratio of width to length in a Gaussian window. In this paper, we use empirical parameters: $v \in \{0, 1, \cdots, 4\}$, $u \in \{0, 1, 2, \cdots, 7\}$, $\theta = \frac{u\pi}{8}$, $\sigma = 2\pi$. To highlight effective amplitudes of Gabor signals and reduce dimension of Gabor feature vector, Gabor features are fused at 5-scale and 8-orientation by Eq. (5), where $G_{u,v}(x, y)$ denotes Gabor feature image corresponding to 8 orientation Gabor feature at each scale, $MG_v(x, y)$ is mean fusion pixel value of v-scale. Figure 5 shows fusion process with Gabor feature of one facial expression image.

$$MG_v(x, y) = \frac{\sum_{u=0}^{7} G_{u,v}(x, y)}{8} \quad v \in \{0, 1, \cdots, 4\} \tag{5}$$

Fig. 5. Gabor feature fusion image with 8-orientation at each scale.

3.2 The Novel Weber Local Descriptor

Though WLD and LGS have achieved good recognition performance, they still exist some shortages: WLD descriptor ignores the relation among neighboring pixels within a neighborhood; The novelty of LGS is that introduces the pixel intensity changes among neighboring pixels, but big weights assignment center on the left side of target pixel, leading to final LGS value is determined by the part, and LGS is sensitive to local texture changes. To resolve the defects above, this paper proposes a Multi-orientation Symmetrical Local Graph Structure (MSLGS) that constructs a symmetrical graph structure in 4 directions.

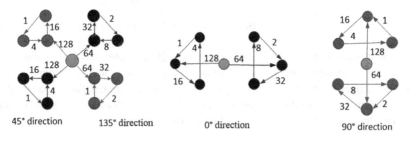

Fig. 6. Multi-orientation Symmetrical Local Graph Structure (MSLGS).

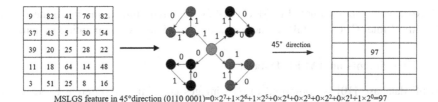

MSLGS feature in 45°direction (0110 0001)=0×2⁷+1×2⁶+1×2⁵+0×2⁴+0×2³+0×2²+0×2¹+1×2⁰=97

Fig. 7. The demonstration of MSLGS operator in 45° direction.

As illustrated in Fig. 6, MSLGS calculates feature value respectively in 0°, 45°, 90°, and 135° direction in a 5 × 5 filter window. Figure 7 illustrates calculation process in 45° direction of MSLGS, where target pixel is depicted in gray color. The calculation method of feature value in one direction is same as that in 45° direction. Comparison on the left and above of target pixel follows counterclockwise, and at the right and below of target pixel follows clockwise. Note that the structure of MSLGS in 0° and 90° direction is different from other algorithms, there are 4 pixels very close to target pixel and are given more weights, to emphasize their influence on target pixel.

Finally, MSLGS algorithm can obtain 4 feature values in total. The greater feature value in one direction, the larger difference of pixel gray values. So this paper chooses the biggest feature value as the differential excitation of new WLD, since it reflects the most representative features of image details.

The orientation of original WLD only describe gradient information in horizontal and vertical direction. This paper adds gradient information in 45° direction and 135° direction on the basis of WLD's orientation, then choose the biggest ratio as final orientation of WLD by Eqs. (6–8), as direction corresponding to the bigger ratio dominates direction of texture changes. By introducing more gradient direction for target pixel, the new method captures more discriminative features of image details. The orientation of proposed algorithm can be defined as follows:

$$\theta(0°, 90°) = \arctan(\frac{g_7 + g_{15} - g_3 - g_{11}}{g_5 + g_{13} - g_1 - g_9}) \tag{6}$$

$$\theta(45°, 135°) = \arctan(\frac{g_6 + g_{14} - g_2 - g_{10}}{g_4 + g_{12} - g_0 - g_8}) \tag{7}$$

$$\theta(x_c, y_c) = \max[\theta(0°, 90°), \theta(45°, 135°)] \tag{8}$$

where θ represents dominant orientations. Then a 2D concatenated histogram is constructed for FER, where differential excitations are quantified into 6 dominant intervals and θ are mapped to 8 intervals. The proposed algorithm makes fully use of spatial structure information based on graph structure. The main advantage of paper is that it can extract texture direction features of facial expression image.

4   Experiments

All experiments are conducted in MATLAB 2016a environment, and performed on a PC with i7 Intel CPU, 8.0 GB memory and 64 bit, windows 10 operating system.

4.1   Experiments on JAFFE Database

JAFFE database [10] is composed of 213 images containing 7 different expressions from 10 Japanese females, each person has 7 expressions: disgust, fear, happy, sad, surprise and neutral, respectively. All images are cropped and resized to 224 × 224.

An appropriate partition mode contributes to improve recognition performance, we firstly determine the optimal block manner. In this part, 7 images including each expression from the same person are used for training and the remaining for testing. As seen in Table 1, the optimal block mode is 2 × 4 and applied in all experiments.

Table 1. Recognition rate under different block manners on JAFFE database.

Block manner	2×2	2×4	3×3	4×2	4×4
Recognition rate (%)	91.14	92.77	91.60	91.84	90.68

4.1.1 Recognition Performance Comparison of Different Methods

To validate the effectiveness of the method proposed, in this paper, some experiments are conducted compared with some typical relevant algorithms: LGS, SLGS, WLD, OSLWGS, and ours. N images (N = 9, 10, 11, 12, 13,14) are selected randomly for each person are used for training, the N images at least include 7 facial expressions from the same individual, while the rest images on JAFFE database are used for testing. We run this experiment for three times and take the mean value as final facial recognition results. Figure 8 shows experimental results with other methods based on different training sample number, where the horizontal axis denotes training samples number N, the vertical axis denotes the recognition performance with N increasing.

Figure 8 indicates that recognition rate of each algorithm has improved accordingly as the training samples numbers N increases. When N equals to 14, the recognition rate is above 90% for all algorithms, especially, the recognition rate of the proposed approach is the best as high as 100%. Experimental results illustrate that the proposed approach outperforms other relevant methods for JAFFE database.

4.1.2 Experimental Evaluation Comparison with Other Methods

Receiver Operating Characteristic (ROC) curves are drawn between the proposed method and some other methods in Fig. 9, the Equal Error Rate (EER) is used to evaluate the matching accuracy, it is a value that the false reject rate equals to the false accept rate. The smaller value of EER is, the better matching accuracy of algorithm has. In this experiment, $2 \times (10 \times (10 - 1) \times 20) = 3600$ imposter versus $2 \times (10 \times 20) = 400$ genuine matches respectively are implemented for evaluation.

The matching results of different methods are shown in Fig. 9, the EER rate of SLGS, WLD, MOWSLGS, OSLWGS are 4.00%, 3.72%, 1.83%, 1.05% respectively.

Note that the area inside ROC curve of the proposed method is the smallest among above methods. It can be concluded that our method has achieved the best matching performance on JAFFE database, with the smallest EER equaling to 0.87%.

4.2 Experiments on CK+ Database

The Extended Cohn-Kanade dataset (CK+) [11] is challenging for FER due to a large number of images. CK+ dataset includes 593 sequences of 123 subjects with 7 emotions: namely, anger, disgust, contempt, fear, happiness, sadness and surprise. The last 4 peak images from each expression sequence, 6 expressions (except for contempt) from 40 subjects are used in the experiment. N image (N = 1, 2, 3) of each expression for per person are used as training and the rest is used as testing. Recognition results are obtained with by 4-fold cross-validation to ensure testing set is different in every time. Each image is cropped and resized to 280×320.

Image sub-block experiments are carried out for CK+ database, where N is set to 2. Note that the dimension of feature vector cannot be divided by 3, hence we no longer set any partition including the length of sub-block image with size of 3. As shown in Table 2, the best performance can be achieved when block mode is 4×2. So the optical image block mode is used to explore recognition effect of different methods.

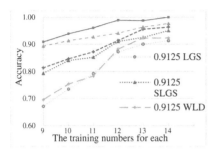

Fig. 8. Experiments on JAFFE database.

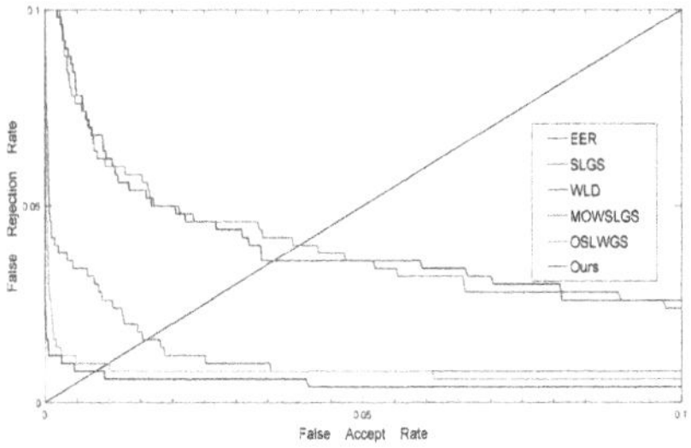

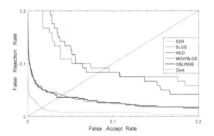

Fig. 9. The ROC curves on JAFFE database.

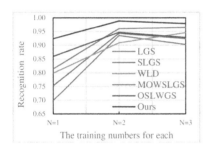

Fig. 10. Experiments on CK+ database.

Fig. 11. The ROC curves for CK+ database.

Table 2. Recognition rate under different block manners on CK+ database.

Block manner	1×1	2×2	2×4	4×2	2×5	5×2
Recognition rate (%)	92.29	95.00	97.71	98.83	94.79	92.92

4.2.1 Recognition Performance Comparison of Different Methods

In order to prove the validity of the presented method for FER, experiments are carried out on CK+ database. Figure 10 illustrates the recognition performance of different relevant approaches. When N equals to 2, the recognition rate of our method is as high as 98.83%. Note that the proposed method acquires the best recognition effects for all cases. By analysis, our method achieved the superior performance than other relevant methods due to its powerful representation ability to texture features.

4.2.2   Experimental Evaluation Comparison with Other Methods

In this subsection, ROC curves are applied to evaluate the effectiveness of our algorithm. $2 \times (40 \times (40 - 1) \times 24) = 74880$ imposter matches versus $2 \times (40 \times 24)$ = 1920 genuine matches respectively are implemented for evaluation. The ROC curves obtained using above algorithms and our method are illustrated in Fig. 11, whose EER is 9.30%, 8.16%, 4.00%, 3.44%, 1.78%, respectively. ROC curve of our method appears at the bottom in the figure, and EER is the smallest, which proves the effectiveness of proposed method for FER and verifies the innovation in this paper.

5   Conclusion

Motivated by WLD and LGS, this paper proposes a novel feature extraction algorithm combining Gabor features and WLD-improved fusion for FER. The main advantages of paper have: (1) Gabor filter has frequency characteristics and orientation selectivity, and is insensitive to illumination variation. (2) MSLGS not only reflect the location distance away from target pixel has an influence on weight, but also keep a balance on weight distribution. In summary, the proposed method describes more orientation features and captures more useful spatial information in image, thus enhancing the ability to extract image features. Experimental results in two databases illustrate that the proposed method has achieved a favorable performance.

In the future study, we will further improve the recognition rate and speed of algorithm, and extend and apply it in facial expression detection and analysis.

Acknowledgments. This paper was supported by the National Natural Science Foundation of China under Grant No. 61502338, No. 61502339 and No. 61702367.

References

1. Goyal, S.J., Upadhyay, A.K., Jadon, R.S., Goyal, R.: Real-life facial expression recognition systems: a review. In: Satapathy, S.C., Bhateja, V., Das, S. (eds.) Smart Computing and Informatics. SIST, vol. 77, pp. 311–331. Springer, Singapore (2018). https://doi.org/10.1007/978-981-10-5544-7_31
2. Fernandes, J.D.A., Matos, L.N., Aragão, M.G.D.S.: Geometrical approaches for facial expression recognition using support vector machines. In: 29th SIBGRAPI Conference on Graphics, Patterns and Images, pp. 347–354. IEEE Press (2017)
3. Facial Action Coding System. https://en.wikipedia.org/wiki/Facial_Action_Coding_System
4. Abusham, E.E.A., Bashir, H.K.: Face recognition using local graph structure (LGS). In: Jacko, J.A. (ed.) HCI 2011. LNCS, vol. 6762, pp. 169–175. Springer, Heidelberg (2011). https://doi.org/10.1007/978-3-642-21605-3_19
5. Abdullah, M.F.A., Sayeed, M.S., Muthu, K.S., et al.: Face recognition with symmetric local graph structure (SLGS). Expert Syst. Appl. **41**(14), 6131–6137 (2014)
6. Tao, G., Zhao, X., Chen, T., et al.: Image feature representation with orthogonal symmetric local weber graph structure. Neurocomputing **240**, 70–83 (2017)
7. Chen, J., Shan, S., He, C., et al.: WLD: a robust local image descriptor. IEEE Trans. Pattern Anal. Mach. Intell. **32**(9), 1705–1720 (2010)

8. Fang, S., Yang, J., Liu, N., Chen, Y.: Weber local gradient pattern (WLGP) method for face recognition. Biometric Recognition. LNCS, vol. 9428, pp. 186–192. Springer, Cham (2015). https://doi.org/10.1007/978-3-319-25417-3_23
9. Fang, S., Yang, J., Liu, N., et al.: Face recognition using weber local circle gradient pattern method. Multimedia Tools Appl. **77**(12), 1–16 (2017)
10. The Japanese Female Facial Expression Database. http://www.kasrl.org/jaffe.html
11. Cohn-Kanade (CK and CK+) database. http://www.consortium.ri.cmu.edu

Face Synthesis for Eyeglass-Robust Face Recognition

Jianzhu Guo[1,2], Xiangyu Zhu[1,2(✉)], Zhen Lei[1,2], and Stan Z. Li[1,2]

[1] CBSR&NLPR, Institute of Automation, Chinese Academy of Sciences,
Beijing, China
{jianzhu.guo,xiangyu.zhu,zlei,szli}@nlpr.ia.ac.cn
[2] University of Chinese Academy of Sciences, Beijing, China

Abstract. In the application of face recognition, eyeglasses could significantly degrade the recognition accuracy. A feasible method is to collect large-scale face images with eyeglasses for training deep learning methods. However, it is difficult to collect the images with and without glasses of the same identity, so that it is difficult to optimize the intra-variations caused by eyeglasses. In this paper, we propose to address this problem in a virtual synthesis manner. The high-fidelity face images with eyeglasses are synthesized based on 3D face model and 3D eyeglasses. Models based on deep learning methods are then trained on the synthesized eyeglass face dataset, achieving better performance than previous ones. Experiments on the real face database validate the effectiveness of our synthesized data for improving eyeglass face recognition performance.

Keywords: Face recognition · 3D eyeglass fitting
Face image synthesis

1 Introduction

In recent years, deep learning based face recognition systems [1–4] have achieved great success, such as Labeled Faces in the Wild (LFW) [5], YouTube Faces DB (YFD) [6], and MegaFace [7].

However, in practical applications, there are still extra factors affecting the face recognition performance, e.g., facial expression, poses, occlusions etc. Eyeglasses, especially black-framed eyeglasses significantly degrade the face recognition accuracy (see Table 4). There are three common categories of eyeglasses: thin eyeglasses, thick eyeglasses, and sunglasses. In this work, we mainly focus on the category of thick black-framed eyeglasses, since the effects of thin eyeglasses are tiny, while the impact of sunglasses are too high because of serious identity information loss in face texture.

The main contributions of this work include: (1) A eyeglass face dataset named MeGlass, including about $1.7K$ identities, is collected and cleaned for eyeglass face recognition evaluation. It will be made public on https://github.com/cleardusk/MeGlass. (2) A virtual eyeglass face image synthesis method is

© Springer Nature Switzerland AG 2018
J. Zhou et al. (Eds.): CCBR 2018, LNCS 10996, pp. 275–284, 2018.
https://doi.org/10.1007/978-3-319-97909-0_30

proposed. An eyeglass face training database named MsCeleb-Eyeglass is generated, which helps improve the robustness to eyeglass. (3) A novel metric learning method is proposed to further improves the face recognition performance, which is designed to adequately utilize the synthetic training data.

The rest of this paper is organized as follows. Section 2 reviews several related works. Our proposed methods are described in Sect. 3. The dataset description is in Sect. 4. Extensive experiments are conducted in Sect. 5 to validate the effectiveness of our synthetic training data and loss function. Section 6 summarizes this paper.

2   Related Work

Automatic Eyeglasses Removal. Eyeglasses removal is another method to reduce the effect of eyeglasses on face recognition accuracy. Several previous works [8–11] have studied on automatic eyeglasses removal. Saito et al. [8] constructed a non-eyeglasses PCA subspace using a group of face images without eyeglasses, one new face image was then projected on it to remove eyeglasses. Wu et al. [9] proposed an intelligent image editing and face synthesis system for automatic eyeglasses removal, in which eyeglasses region was first detected and localized, then the corrupted region was synthesized adopting a statistical analysis and synthesis approach. Park et al. [11] proposed a recursive process of PCA reconstruction and error compensation to further eliminate the traces of thick eyeglasses. However, these works did not study the quantitative effects of eyeglasses removal on face recognition performance.

Virtual Try-on. Eyeglass face image synthesis is similar to virtual eyeglass try-on. Recently, eyeglasses try-on has drawn attentions in academic community. Niswar et al. [14] first reconstructed 3D head model from single image, 3D eyeglasses were next fitted on it, but it lacked the rendering and blending process compared with our synthesis method. Yuan et al. [12] proposed a interactive real time virtual 3D eyeglasses try-on system. Zhang et al. [13] firstly took the refraction effect of corrective lenses into consideration. They presented a system for trying on prescription eyeglasses, which could produce a more real look of wearing eyeglasses.

Synthetic Images for Training. Recently, synthetic images generated from 3D models have been studied in computer vision [15–18]. These works adopted 3D models to render images for training object detectors and viewpoint classifiers. Because of the limited number of 3D models, they tweaked the rendering parameters to generate more synthetic samples to maximize the model usage.

3   Proposed Method

3.1   Eyeglass Image Synthesis

We describe the details of eyeglass face synthesis in this section. To generate faces with eyeglasses, we estimate the positions of the 3D eyeglasses based on the fitted 3D face model and then render the 3D eyeglasses on the original face images. The whole pipeline of our eyeglass faces synthesis is shown in Fig. 2. Firstly, we reconstruct the 3D face model based on pose adaptive 3DMM fitting method [19], which is robust to pose. Secondly, the 3D eyeglass is fitted on the reconstructed 3D face model. The fitting is based on the corresponding anchor points on the 3D eyeglass and 3D fitted face model, where the indices of these anchor points are annotated beforehand. Then z-buffer algorithm and Phong illumination model are adopted for rendering, and the rendered eyeglass image is blended on the original image to generate the final synthetic result (Fig. 1).

The 3D eyeglass fitting problem is formed as Eq. 1, where f is the scale factor, Pr is the orthographic projection matrix, p_g is the anchor points on 3D eyeglass, p_f is the anchor points on reconstructed 3D face model, R is the 3×3 rotation matrix determined by pitch(α), yaw(β), and roll(γ) and t_{3d} is the translation vector.

$$\arg \min_{f, Pr, R, t_{3d}} ||f * Pr * R * (p_g + t_{3d}) - p_f||, \tag{1}$$

Although the amount of images of MsCeleb is large, the model may overfit during training if the patterns of synthetic eyeglasses are simple. To increase the diversity of our synthetic eyeglass face images, we inject randomness into two steps of our pipeline: 3D eyeglass preparation and rendering. For 3D eyeglasses,

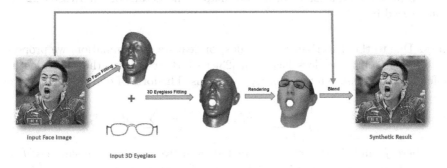

Fig. 1. Four pairs of origin-synthesis images selected from MsCeleb.

Fig. 2. The pipeline of eyeglass synthesis.

we prepare four kinds of eyeglasses with different shapes and randomly select one as input. For eyeglass rendering, we explore three sets of parameters: light condition, pitch angle and vertical transition of eyeglass. For the light condition, the energies and directions are randomly sampled. Furthermore, to simulate the real situations of eyeglass wearing, we add small perturbations to the pitch angle ($[-1.5, 0.8]$) and vertical transition ($[1, 2]$ pixel). Finally, we put together the synthetic eyeglass face images with original images as our training datasets.

Table 1. Our ResNet-22 network structure. Conv3.x, Conv4.x and Conv5.x indicates convolution units which may contain multiple convolution layers and residual blocks are shown in double-column brackets. E.g., $[3 \times 3, 128] \times 3$ denotes 3 cascaded convolution layers 128 feature maps with filters of size 3×3, and S2 denotes stride 2. The last layer is global pooling.

Layers	22-layer CNN
Conv1.x	$[5 \times 5, 32] \times 1$, S2
Conv2.x	$[3 \times 3, 64] \times 1$, S1
Conv3.x	$\begin{bmatrix} 3 \times 3, 128 \\ 3 \times 3, 128 \end{bmatrix} \times 3$, S2
Conv4.x	$\begin{bmatrix} 3 \times 3, 256 \\ 3 \times 3, 226 \end{bmatrix} \times 4$, S2
Conv5.x	$\begin{bmatrix} 3 \times 3, 512 \\ 3 \times 3, 512 \end{bmatrix} \times 3$, S2
Global Pooling	512

3.2 Network and Loss

Network. We adapt a 22 layers residual network architecture based on [21] to fit our task. The original ResNet is designed for ImageNet [22], the input image size is 224×224, while ours is 120×120. Therefore, we substitute the original 7×7 convolution in first layer with 5×5 and stack one 3×3 convolution layer to preserve dimensions of feature maps. The details of our ResNet-22 are summarized in Table 1.

Loss. Due to the disturbance of eyeglass on feature discrimination, we propose the Mining-Contrasive loss based on [23] to further enlarge the inter-identity differences and reduce intra-identity variations. The form of our proposed loss is in Eq. 2.

$$L_{mc} = -\frac{1}{2|\mathcal{P}|} \sum_{(i,j) \in \mathcal{P}} d(f_i, f_j) + \frac{1}{2|\mathcal{N}|} \sum_{(i,j) \in \mathcal{N}} d(f_i, f_j). \tag{2}$$

Where f_i and f_j are vectors extracted from two input image samples, $\mathcal{P}$ is hard positive samples set, $\mathcal{N}$ is hard negative samples set, $d(f_i, f_j) = \frac{f_i \cdot f_j}{\|f_i\|_2 \|f_j\|_2}$ is cosine similarity between extracted vectors.

Gradual Sampling. Besides, we employ the gradual process into data sampling to make the model fit the synthetic training images in a gentle manner. In naive sampling, the probability of eyeglass face image of each identity is fixed at 0.5. It means that we just brutally mix MsCeleb and MsCeleb-Eyeglass datasets. We then generalize the sampling probability as $p = \lambda \cdot n + p_0$, where n is the number of iterations, λ is the slope coefficient determining the gradual process, p_0 is the initialized probability value.

Table 2. Summary of dataset description. G and NG indicate eyeglass and non-eyeglass respectively. Mixture means the MsCeleb and MsCeleb-Eyeglass.

Dataset	Identity	Images	G	NG
MeGlass	1,710	47,917	14,832	33,085
Testing set	1,710	6,840	3,420	3,420
Training set (MsCeleb)	78,765	5,001,877	–	–
Training set (Mixture)	78,765	10,003,754	–	–

Fig. 3. Sample images of our testing set. For each identity, we show two faces with and without eyeglasses.

4 Dataset Description

In this section, we describe our dataset in detail and the summary is shown in Table 2.

4.1 Testing Set

We select real face images with eyeglass from MegaFace [7] to form the MeGlass dataset. We first apply an attribute classifier to classify the eyeglass and non-eyeglass face images automatically. After that, we select the required face images manually from the attribute-labeled face images. Our MeGlass dataset contains 14,832 face images with eyeglasses and 33,085 images without eyeglasses, from 1,710 subjects.

To be consistent with the evaluation protocol (in Sect. 4.3), we select two faces with eyeglasses and two faces without eyeglasses from each identity to build our testing set and the total number of images is 6, 840. Figure 3 shows some examples of testing set with and without eyeglasses.

4.2   Training Set

Two types of training set are adopted, one is only the MsCeleb and the other is the mixture of MsCeleb with synthetic MsCeleb-Eyeglass. Our MsCeleb clean list has 78, 765 identities and 5, 001, 877 images, which is slightly modified from [20]. For each image, we synthesize a eyeglass face image using the method proposed in Sect. 3.1. Therefore, there are totally 10, 003, 754 images from 78, 765 subjects in the mixture training set.

4.3   Evaluation Protocol

In order to examine the effect of eyeglass on face recognition thoroughly, we propose four testing protocols to evaluate different methods.

(I)   All gallery and probe images are without eyeglasses. There are two non-eyeglass face images per person in gallery and probe sets, respectively.

(II)   All gallery and probe images are with eyeglasses. There are two eyeglasses face images per person in gallery and probe sets, respectively.

(III)   All gallery images are without eyeglasses, and all probe images are with eyeglasses. There are two non-eyeglass face images per person in gallery set and there are two eyeglass face images per person in probe set.

(IV)   Gallery images contain both eyeglass images and non-eyeglass images, so as probe images. There are four face images (including two non-eyeglass and two eyeglass face images) per person for gallery and probe sets.

5   Experiments

Firstly, we evaluate the impact of eyeglasses on face recognition. Second, several experiments are conducted to study the effect of synthetic training data and proposed loss. In experiments, two losses including the classification loss A-Softmax and the metric learning based contrastive loss are investigated. Totally there are four deep learning models are trained based on different losses and training sets. Table 3 lists the four deep face models. For ResNet-22-A, we apply A-Softmax loss to learn the model from original MsCeleb dataset. We then finetune the model on MsCeleb dataset using contrastive loss to obtain ResNet-22-B. We also finetune the ResNet-22-A model on MsCeleb and its synthetic eyeglasses database to obtain ResNet-22-C. The ResNet-22-D is finetuned from base model ResNet-22-A using gradual sampling strategy with the slope coefficient λ of 0.00001 and p_0 of 0.

5.1   Experiments Settings

Our experiments are based Caffe [24] framework and Tesla M40 GPU. All face images are resized to size 120×120, then being normalized by subtracting 127.5 and being divided by 128. We use SGD with a mini-batch size of 128 to optimize the network, with the weight decay of 0.0005 and momentum of 0.9. Based on these configurations, the training speed can reach about 260 images per second on single GPU and the inference speed is about 1.5 ms per face image.

Table 3. The configuration settings of different models. ResNet-22-B, ResNet-22-C and ResNet-22-D are all finetuned from ResNet-22-A. GS indicates gradual sampling.

Model	Training data	Loss	Strategy
ResNet-22-A	MsCeleb	A-Softmax [4]	–
ResNet-22-B	MsCeleb	Mining-Contrasive	Finetune
ResNet-22-C	Mixture	Mining-Contrasive	Finetune
ResNet-22-D	Mixture	Mining-Contrasive	Finetune + GS

Table 4. Recognition performance (%) of ResNet-22-A following protocols I-IV.

Protocol	TPR@FAR $= 10^{-4}$	TPR@FAR $= 10^{-5}$	TPR@FAR $= 10^{-6}$	Rank1
I	96.14	91.49	84.68	98.48
II	94.09	86.55	69.21	96.90
III	88.13	74.72	59.34	95.61
IV	78.17	60.25	41.36	92.31

5.2   Effect of Eyeglass on Face Recognition

In this experiment, we use the original MsCeleb database only as the training set to examine the robustness of traditional deep learning model to eyeglasses.

Table 4 shows the results of ResNet-A model tested on four protocols. From the results, one can see that the ResNet-A model achieves high recognition accuracy on protocol I, which is without eyeglass occlusion. However, its performance degrades significantly on protocols II-IV, where eyeglasses occlusion occurs in gallery or probe set, especially for the TPR at low FAR. It indicates that the performance of deep learning model is sensitive to eyeglasses occlusion.

5.3   Effectiveness of Synthetic Data and Proposed Loss

For comparison, we further train deep face model, ResNet-C, using the mixture of the original MsCeleb and its synthesized eyeglasses version MsCeleb-Eyeglass. Tables 5 and 6 show the comparison results of ResNet-B and ResNet-C following four protocols. It can be seen that using our synthesized eyeglass face images, it

Table 5. Recognition performance (%) of ResNet-22-B following protocols I-IV.

Protocol	TPR@FAR $= 10^{-4}$	TPR@FAR $= 10^{-5}$	TPR@FAR $= 10^{-6}$	Rank1
I	96.61	91.26	87.02	98.60
II	94.91	87.87	73.27	97.08
III	89.55	76.86	62.56	96.02
IV	81.96	65.68	46.71	94.18

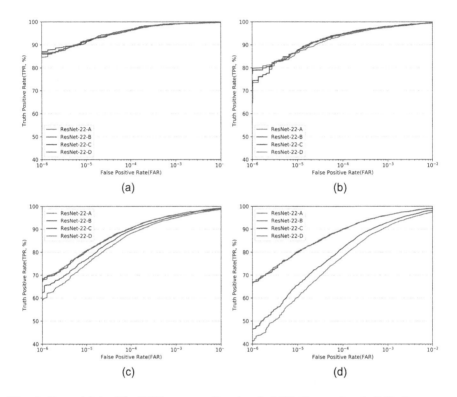

Fig. 4. From (a) to (d): ROC curves of protocols I-IV. For protocols I-II, the curves are almost the same. While for protocols III-IV, ResNet-22-C and ResNet-D models outperform the other two. Especially in protocol IV, they outperform by a large margin (better view on electronic version).

significantly improves the face recognition performance following protocol III-IV, especially at low FAR. It enhances about 20% when FAR $= 10^{-6}$ on protocol IV, which is the hardest case in four configurations, indicating the effectiveness of virtual face synthesis data for the robustness improvement of face deep model. Moreover, with the face synthesis data, the proposed loss function with gradual sampling, model ResNet-22-D achieves the best results on four protocols (Table 7).

Table 6. Recognition performance (%) of ResNet-22-C following protocols I-IV.

Protocol	TPR@FAR $= 10^{-4}$	TPR@FAR $= 10^{-5}$	TPR@FAR $= 10^{-6}$	Rank1
I	96.20	91.58	85.94	98.19
II	94.80	87.31	78.89	96.73
III	90.35	80.40	67.93	96.67
IV	89.94	79.88	66.82	96.67

Table 7. Recognition performance (%) of ResNet-22-D following protocols I-IV.

Protocol	TPR@FAR $= 10^{-4}$	TPR@FAR $= 10^{-5}$	TPR@FAR $= 10^{-6}$	Rank1
I	96.37	91.99	86.37	98.30
II	94.68	87.54	78.68	96.78
III	90.54	80.71	68.10	96.75
IV	90.14	80.32	66.92	96.73

Finally, we also plot the ROC curves for four protocols in Fig. 4 to further validate the effectiveness of our synthetic training dataset and proposed loss function.

6   Conclusion

In this paper, we propose a novel framework to improve the robustness of face recognition with eyeglasses. We synthesize face images with eyeglasses as training data based on 3D face reconstruction and propose a novel loss function to address this eyeglass robustness problem. Experiment results demonstrate that our proposed framework is rather effective. In future works, the virtual-synthesis method may be extended to alleviate the impact of other factors on the robustness of face recognition encountered in real life application.

Acknowledgments. This work was supported by the Chinese National Natural Science Foundation Projects #61473291, #61572536, #61572501, #61573356, the National Key Research and Development Plan (Grant No. 2016YFC0801002), and AuthenMetric R&D Funds.

References

1. Taigman, Y., Yang, M., Ranzato, M.A., Wolf, L.: Deepface: closing the gap to human-level performance in face verification. In: CVPR (2014)
2. Sun, Y., Wang, X., Tang, X.: Deep learning face representation from predicting 10,000 classes. In: CVPR (2014)
3. Schroff, F., Kalenichenko, D., Philbin, J.: Facenet: a unified embedding for face recognition and clustering. In: CVPR (2015)

4. Liu, W., Wen, Y., Yu, Z., Li, M., Raj, B., Song, L.: Sphereface: deep hypersphere embedding for face recognition. In: CVPR (2017)
5. Huang, G.B., Ramesh, M., Berg, T., Learned-Miller, E.: Labeled faces in the wild: a database for studying face recognition in unconstrained environments. Technical report (2007)
6. Wolf, L., Hassner, T., Maoz, I.: Face recognition in unconstrained videos with matched background similarity. In: CVPR (2011)
7. Kemelmacher-Shlizerman, I., Seitz, S.M., Miller, D., Brossard, E.: The megaface benchmark: 1 million faces for recognition at scale. In: CVPR (2016)
8. Saito, Y., Kenmochi, Y., Kotani, K.: Estimation of eyeglassless facial images using principal component analysis. In: ICIP (1999)
9. Wu, C., Liu, C., Shum, H.Y., Xy, Y.Q., Zhang, Z.: Automatic eyeglasses removal from face images. TPAMI **26**, 322–336 (2004)
10. Du, C., Su, G.: Eyeglasses removal from facial images. PR **26**, 2215–2220 (2005)
11. Park, J.S., Oh, Y.H., Ahn, S.C., Lee, S.W.: Glasses removal from facial image using recursive error compensation. TPAMI **27**, 805–811 (2005)
12. Yuan, X., Tang, D., Liu, Y., Ling, Q., Fang, L.: From 2D to 3D. TCSVT **27** (2017)
13. Zhang, Q., Guo, Y., Laffont, P.Y., Martin, T., Gross, M.: A virtual try-on system for prescription eyeglasses. IEEE COMPUT GRAPH **37**, 84–93 (2017)
14. Niswar, A., Khan, I.R., Farbiz, F.: Virtual try-on of eyeglasses using 3D model of the head. In: VRCAI (2011)
15. Su, H., Qi, C.R., Li, Y., Guibas, L.J.: Render for CNN: Viewpoint estimation in images using CNNs trained with rendered 3d model views. In: ICCV (2015)
16. Massa, F., Russell, B.C., Aubry, M.: Deep exemplar 2D–3D detection by adapting from real to rendered views. In: CVPR (2016)
17. Stark, M., Goesele, M., Schiele, B.: Back to the future: learning shape models from 3D CAD data. In: BMVC (2010)
18. Liebelt, J., Schmid, C.: Multi-view object class detection with a 3D geometric model. In: CVPR (2010)
19. Zhu, X., Lei, Z., Yan, J., Yi, D., Li, S.Z.: High-fidelity pose and expression normalization for face recognition in the wild. In: CVPR (2016)
20. Wu, X., He, R., Sun, Z., Tan, T.: A light CNN for deep face representation with noisy labels. arXiv preprint arXiv:1511.02683 (2015)
21. He, K., Zhang, X., Ren, S., Sun, J.: Deep residual learning for image recognition. CVPR (2016)
22. Deng, J., Dong, W., Socher, R., Li, L.J., Li, K., Fei-Fei, L.: Imagenet: a large-scale hierarchical image database. In: CVPR (2009)
23. Sun, Y., Chen, Y., Wang, X., Tang, X.: Deep learning face representation by joint identification-verification. In: NIPS (2014)
24. Jia, Y., Shelhamer, E., Donahue, J., et al.: Caffe: convolutional architecture for fast feature embedding. In: ACM Multimedia (2014)

Single Shot Attention-Based Face Detector

Chubin Zhuang[1,2], Shifeng Zhang[1,2], Xiangyu Zhu[1,2], Zhen Lei[1,2(✉)], and Stan Z. Li[1,2]

[1] CBSR&NLPR, Institute of Automation, Chinese Academy of Sciences, Beijing, China
{chubin.zhuang,shifeng.zhang,xiangyu.zhu,zlei,szli}@nlpr.ia.ac.cn
[2] University of Chinese Academy of Sciences, Beijing, China

Abstract. Although face detection has taken a big step forward with the development of anchor based face detector, the issue of effective detection of faces with different scales still remains. To solve this problem, we present an one-stage face detector, named Single Shot Attention-Based Face Detector (AFD), which enables accurate detection of multi-scale faces with high efficiency, especially for small faces. Specifically, AFD consists of two inter-connected modules, namely attention proposal module (APM) and face detection module (FDM). The former aims to generate the attention region and coarsely refine the anchors. The latter takes the output from APM as input and further improve the detection results. We obtain state-of-the-art results on common face detection benchmarks, *i.e.* FDDB and WIDER FACE, and can run at 20 FPS on a Nvidia Titan X (Pascal) for VGA-resolution images.

Keywords: Face detection · Attention mechanism · Single shot

1 Introduction

Face detection is a fundamental and essential step for many face related applications, *e.g.* face recognition [1,2] and face alignment [3,4]. Since the pioneering work of Viola-Jones [5], face detection has achieved significant progress in the past few decades, especially the CNN [6] based detector. However, there are still some challenging problems: (1) The large variation of faces in cluttered backgrounds requires detectors to be more robust and accurate; (2) The large search space of possible faces further imposes a serious challenge of trade-off between accuracy and efficiency, especially for small faces.

To address these problems, recent CNN based face detectors can be divided into two categories. One is cascade based methods, such as CascadeCNN [7] and MTCNN [8]. The other is anchor based methods [9,10]. However, these two kinds of methods focus on different aspects. The former can well handle faces with diverse scales, but tends to be much time-consuming when the number of faces is large. While the latter's speed is invariant to the object number, but the

© Springer Nature Switzerland AG 2018
J. Zhou et al. (Eds.): CCBR 2018, LNCS 10996, pp. 285–293, 2018.
https://doi.org/10.1007/978-3-319-97909-0_31

performance will drop dramatically as the objects getting smaller as indicated in [11]. Therefore, efficient detection of multi-scale faces is still one of the critical issues that remains to be settled.

To solve these two conflicting issues, our core idea is introducing attention mechanism to detection and leveraging feature fusion of different layers as RefineDet [12] so as to highlight the possible facial regions and enrich the feature information to promote the performance of detection. Specifically, we present an effective face detector called Single Shot Attention-Based Face Detector (AFD), which consists of two inter-connected modules, respectively attention proposal module (APM) and face detection module (FDM). The former aims to generate the attention region and coarsely refine the anchors. The latter takes attention maps as input and dot-multiply them with the feature maps to highlight the features from the facial region. Then the feature maps from the high-level layers are integrated into the low-level layers to increase the richness of feature information and output the final detection results.

Due to the attention mechanism in APM and the fusion of features in different layers in FDM, our face detector can well address the dramatic deterioration problem of anchor based detectors as faces getting smaller, especially for small faces. Consequently, for VGA-resolution images, our face detector can run at 20 FPS on a NVIDIA Titan X (Pascal) GPU in inference. Besides, we comprehensively evaluate this detector and demonstrate state-of-the-art detection performance on several common face detection benchmark datasets, including the FDDB [13] and WIDER FACE [14]. For clarity, the main contribution of this work can be summarized as three-fold:

- We propose an attention mechanism to enhance the robustness and performance of detectors.
- We leverage feature fusion in different detection layers to enrich the feature information.
- We achieve state-of-the-art performance on common face detection benchmarks and keep the efficiency.

2   Related Work

Face detection has attracted large research attention in past few decades, which can be roughly divided into two categories. One is hand-craft based detectors, and the other is built on CNN. This section briefly reviews these two methods.

Hand-Craft Based Methods. Following the milestone work of Viola-Jones face detector [5], most early methods pay attention to designing robust features [15] and training effective classifiers [16]. Besides, the deformable part model [17] is introduced into face detection task by [18] and achieves remarkable performance. However, these detectors highly depend on non-robust hand-craft features, thus they are efficient but not accurate enough for the large visual variation of faces.

CNN Based Methods. Recent years have witnessed the advance of CNN based detectors. CascadeCNN [7] employs a cascade structure to detect face in a coarse to fine way. MTCNN [8] proposes an architecture to address both detection and landmark alignment jointly. Besides, the anchor based methods originated from Faster-RCNN [19] structure have achieved great progress in past few years. Jiang et al. [20] apply Faster R-CNN framework in face detection and achieves promising results. SSD [9] introduces multi-scale mechanism to anchor designing. S³FD [10] proposes anchor matching strategy to improve the recall rate of small faces. FPN [21] proposes a top-down structure to use high-level semantic feature maps at different scales. FAN [22] introduces anchor-level attention to improve the detection performance. RefineDet [12] develops a single-shot inter-connected architecture to improve the performance of detector while maintain the high efficiency.

Generally, the hand-craft based methods tend to be efficient but less accurate. While the CNN based methods dominate the performance but present less efficiency. Notably, our proposed AFD is able to achieve state-of-the-art performance and keep the high efficiency.

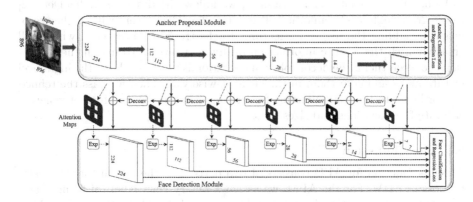

Fig. 1. The framework of AFD. We only display the layers used for detection. The parallelograms denote the attention maps associated with different feature layers and the white rectangles represent the possible facial regions.

3   Single Shot Attention-Based Face Detector

This section introduces the details of AFD. It includes three components: the overall network architecture, loss function and some implementation details.

3.1   Overall Network Architecture

Anchor-based object detection frameworks with reasonable design of anchors in different layers have proven to be effective to handle faces with different scales [9]. As illustrated in Fig. 1, the architecture of AFD uses the same extended

VGG16 backbone and anchor design strategy as [10], which can generate feature maps at different layers and anchors with equal-proportion interval. Besides, the attention proposal module and face detection module is added on this backbone to get the final results.

Attention Proposal Module (APM). We use the APM to roughly predict the locations and scores of anchors from different layers as the attention supervision information, and construct the attention maps which indicate the possible facial regions based on these supervision information. Then these hierarchical attention maps are sent to FDM to highlight the potential face areas. Besides, we also leverage the predicted information of different anchors in APM to coarsely refine the anchors as [12], which provides better initialization for the detection in the FDM.

Face Detection Module (FDM). After obtaining these attention maps, we feed the attention maps to an exponential operation to rescale the value of score from 1 to e and only take the maximum score for the overlapping parts, which will not only highlight the detection information, but also maintain more context messages. Then these attention maps are dot-multiplied with the feature maps to highlight the facial regions. Besides, we follow the design in RefineDet [12] to integrate high-level semantic features into low-level layers with higher resolution by adding the high-level features to the transferred features, which will greatly enrich the feature information of different layers. To match the dimensions between them, the deconvolution operation is used to enlarge the high-level feature maps and sum them in the element-wise way. Then we pass the refined anchor boxes to the corresponding feature maps in the FDM to further generate accurate face locations and sizes.

3.2 Loss Function

The loss function for AFD consists of two parts, *i.e.*, the loss in the APM and the loss in FDM. For the APM, we assign a binary class label (of being a face or not) to each anchor and regress its location and size. After that, we send the anchors with positive confidence higher than threshold to the FDM to further predict the locations and sizes of faces. The loss function is defined as:

$$L(p_i, x_i, c_i, t_i) = \frac{1}{N_{apm}} \left(\sum_i L_b(p_i, l_i^*) + \sum_i l_i^* L_r(x_i, g_i^*) \right)$$

$$+ \frac{1}{N_{fdm}} \left(\sum_i L_b(c_i, l_i^*) + \sum_i l_i^* L_r(t_i, g_i^*) \right). \quad (1)$$

where i is the index of anchor in a batch, l_i^* is the ground truth class label of anchor i, g_i^* is the ground truth location and size of anchor i. p_i and x_i are the predicted confidence and coordinates of anchor i in the APM. c_i and t_i are the predicted class and coordinates of the bounding box in the FDM. N_{apm} and N_{fdm} are the numbers of positive anchors in the APM and FDM. The binary classification loss L_b is the softmax loss over two classes (face vs. background) confidences. We use the smooth L_1 loss as the regression loss L_r.

3.3 Training and Implementation Details

This subsection introduces the training dataset, anchor setting strategy, hard negative mining and other implementation details.

Training Dataset. Our AFD is trained end-to-end on 12,880 images from the WIDER FACE [14] training set. To increase the robustness of training data, each training image is sequentially processed by color distortion, random cropping, horizontal flipping and scale transformation, and finally gets a 896×896 square sub-image from original image.

Anchor Setting Strategy. We tile the anchors scaled from 16 to 512 pixels at different detection layers as [10], and set the corresponding stride size to be a quarter of the anchor size, which gradually doubled from 4 to 128 pixels. During training, we firstly match each face to the anchor with the best jaccard overlap, and then match anchors to any faces with jaccard overlap higher than 0.45.

Hard Negative Mining. After anchor matching step, the positive and negative training samples are extremely imbalance because most of the anchors are negative, which will make training process slow and unstable. Thus we sort these samples by the loss values and choose the top ones to make sure that the ratio between negatives and positives is almost 3:1.

Other Implementation Details. We initialize the parameters of the base layers from the pre-trained VGG16, and the other additional layers are randomly initialized with the "xavier" method. We fine-tune the model using SGD with 0.9 momentum, 0.0005 weight decay and batch size 12. The maximum number of iteration is 120k and we use 10^{-3} learning rate for the first 80k iterations, and continue training for 20k iterations with 10^{-4} and 10^{-5}. Our method is implemented in Caffe [23].

4 Experiments

In this section, we first analyze our model in an ablative way, then evaluate our model on the common face detection benchmarks and introduce its runtime efficiency.

4.1 Model Analysis

We evaluate our model on the FDDB dataset by extensive experiments, the experiments are carried out on the same settings, except for specified changes to the components. Firstly, we redesign the network by directly using the regularly paved anchors instead of the refined ones from the APM. Secondly, we cut off the feature fusion part in FDM, and only use the independent feature maps from different layers to detect faces. Finally, we ablate the attention proposal part.

According to Table 1, some promising conclusions can be summed up. Firstly, we find that mAP is reduced from 98.5% to 97.9%, which indicates that the refined anchor in APM can help promote the performance of detector. Secondly, cutting off the feature fusion part in FDM will deteriorate the performance (*i.e.*, 0.9%). Finally, the attention map can help the FDM highlight the features from facial region and improve the performance by 0.7%.

Table 1. Ablative results on FDDB (True positive rate at 1,000 false positives).

Component	AFD			
Attention?	√	√	√	
Feature fusion?	√	√		
Anchor Refined?	√			
Accuracy (mAP)	98.5	97.9	97.0	96.3

4.2   Evaluation on Benchmark

We evaluate our AFD model on the common face detection benchmarks, including Face Detection Data Set and Benchmark (FDDB) [13] and WIDER FACE [14].

FDDB Dataset. It consists of 5,171 faces in 2,845 images. Considering that FDDB uses ellipse face annotation while our model outputs rectangle bounding box. For a more fair comparison, we train an elliptical regressor to transform our predicted bounding boxes to bounding ellipses. As illustrated in Fig. 2, our model achieves state-of-the-art performance.

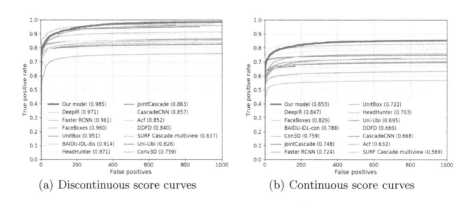

(a) Discontinuous score curves   (b) Continuous score curves

Fig. 2. Evaluation on the FDDB dataset

WIDER FACE Dataset. It has 32,203 images and labels 393,703 faces with a high degree of variability in scale, pose and occlusion. These images are divided into three levels (Easy, Medium and Hard) according to the difficulties of the detection. Our model is trained only on the training set and tested on the validation and test set against recent face detection methods. As shown in Fig. 3, our model achieves state-of-the-art performance across the three subsets, *i.e.*, on validation set, 0.953 (Easy), 0.943 (Medium) and 0.882 (Hard) and 0.946(Easy), 0.938 (Medium) and 0.878 (Hard) on test set.

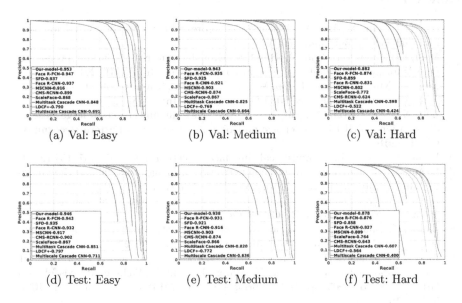

(a) Val: Easy   (b) Val: Medium   (c) Val: Hard

(d) Test: Easy   (e) Test: Medium   (f) Test: Hard

Fig. 3. Precision-recall curves on WIDER FACE validation and test sets

4.3 Runtime Efficiency

Despite great performance, the speed of our algorithm is not compromised. The computational cost is tested on a Titan X (Pascal) and cuDNN v6.0. For a VGA-resolution image using a single GPU, our face detector can run at 20 FPS, which keeps the efficiency and owns higher accuracy.

5 Conclusion

In this paper, we present a single shot attention-based face detector, which consists of two inter-connected modules, *i.e.*, the APM and the FDM. The APM generates the attention region and coarsely refines the anchors. The FDM takes attention maps as input and dot-multiply them with the feature maps to highlight the features from the facial region. Then the feature maps from the high-level layers are integrated into the low-level layers to enrich the feature information and output the final detection results. The whole net is trained end-to-end fashion and tested on common face detection benchmarks, which achieves state-of-the-art performance and keeps high efficiency.

Acknowledgments. This work was supported by the Chinese National Natural Science Foundation Projects #61473291, #61572536, #61572501, #61573356, the National Key Research and Development Plan (Grant No. 2016YFC0801002), and AuthenMetric R&D Funds.

References

1. Luan, T., Yin, X., Liu, X.: Disentangled representation learning GAN for pose-invariant face recognition. In: CVPR (2017)
2. Masi, I., Chang, F.J., Choi, J., Harel, S., Kim, J., Kim, K.G.: Learning pose-aware models for pose-invariant face recognition in the wild. In: PAMI (2018)
3. Xing, J., Niu, Z., Huang, J., Hu, W., Xi, Z., Yan, S.: Towards robust and accurate multi-view and partially-occluded face alignment. In: PAMI (2018)
4. Zhu, X., Lei, Z., Liu, X., Shi, H., Li, S.Z.: Face alignment across large poses: a 3D solution. In: IEEE Conference on Computer Vision and Pattern Recognition, CVPR (2016)
5. Viola, P., Jones, M.J.: Robust real-time face detection. IJCV **57**, 137–154 (2004)
6. Lecun, Y., Bengio, Y.: Convolutional networks for images, speech, and time series. In: The Handbook of Brain Theory and Neural Networks (1995)
7. Li, H., Lin, Z., Shen, X., Brandt, J., Hua, G.: A convolutional neural network cascade for face detection. In: CVPR (2015)
8. Zhang, K., Zhang, Z., Li, Z., Qiao, Y.: Joint face detection and alignment using multitask cascaded convolutional networks. Sig. Process. Lett. **23**, 1499–1503 (2016)
9. Liu, W., Anguelov, D., Erhan, D., Szegedy, C., Reed, S., Fu, C.Y.: SSD: single shot multibox detector. In: Leibe, B., Matas, J., Sebe, N., Welling, M. (eds.) ECCV 2016. LNCS, vol. 9905, pp. 21–37. Springer, Cham (2016). https://doi.org/10.1007/978-3-319-46448-0_2
10. Zhang, S., Zhu, X., Lei, Z., Shi, H., Wang, X., Li, S.Z.: S³FD: single shot scale-invariant face detector. In: ICCV (2017)
11. Huang, J., Guadarrama, S., Murphy, K., Rathod, V., Sun, C., Zhu, M., et al.: Speed/accuracy trade-offs for modern convolutional object detectors. In: CVPR (2017)
12. Zhang, S., Wen, L., Bian, X., Lei, Z., Li, S.Z.: Single-shot refinement neural network for object detection. In: CVPR (2018)
13. Jain, V., Learned-Miller, E.: FDDB: a benchmark for face detection in unconstrained settings. UMass Amherst Technical report (2010)
14. Yang, S., Luo, P., Loy, C.C., Tang, X.: Wider face: a face detection benchmark. In: CVPR (2016)
15. Huang, C., Ai, H., Li, Y., Lao, S.: High-performance rotation invariant multiview face detection. In: PAMI (2007)
16. Li, S.Z., Zhu, L., Zhang, Z.Q., Blake, A., Zhang, H.J., Shum, H.: Statistical learning of multi-view face detection. In: Heyden, A., Sparr, G., Nielsen, M., Johansen, P. (eds.) ECCV 2002. LNCS, vol. 2353, pp. 67–81. Springer, Heidelberg (2002). https://doi.org/10.1007/3-540-47979-1_5
17. Felzenszwalb, P., Mcallester, D., Ramanan, D.: A discriminatively trained, multiscale, deformable part model. In: CVPR (2008)
18. Yan, J., Zhang, X., Lei, Z., Li, S.Z.: Face detection by structural models. Image Vis. Comput. **32**, 790–799 (2014)
19. Ren, S., He, K., Girshick, R., Sun, J.: Faster R-CNN: towards real-time object detection with region proposal networks. NIPS (2015)

20. Jiang, H., Learned-Miller, E.: Face detection with the faster R-CNN. In: Automatic Face and Gesture Recognition (2017)
21. Lin, T.Y., Dollar, P., Girshick, R., He, K., Hariharan, B., Belongie, S.: Feature pyramid networks for object detection. In: CVPR (2017)
22. Wang, J., Yuan, Y., Yu, G.: Face attention network: an effective face detector for the occluded faces. arXiv: 1711.07246 (2017)
23. Jia, Y., et al.: Caffe: convolutional architecture for fast feature embedding. In: ACMMM (2014)

Local Directional Amplitude Feature for Illumination Normalization with Application to Face Recognition

Chitung Yip, Haifeng Hu$^{(\boxtimes)}$, and Zhihong Chen

School of Electronics and Information Technology,
Sun Yat-Sen University, Guangzhou, China
huhaif@mail.sysu.edu.cn

Abstract. Face recognition under variant illumination conditions has been one of the major research topics in the development of face recognition systems. In this paper we analyze the strength and the weakness of different types of approaches, and design an illumination robust feature by combining the directional and amplitude information as an optimal solution to the problem. We first extract and process the direction and amplitude information of the pixel changes, and then fuse them into a comprehensive feature. We conducted our experiments on CMU-PIE database and Extended Yale B database, and all the results have shown the effectiveness of our approach.

Keywords: Illumination-invariant face recognition
Direction and amplitude · Local gravity · Weberface

1 Introduction

The face recognition robust to different variations including illumination, occlusion and pose have been a popular topic in the field of computer vision and biometrics. Among these, the condition of illumination is one of the most common challenges for face recognition systems. The changes of angles of lighting can result in different shades on human face that would seriously affect the feature extraction. To cope with these problems, a wide range of methods have been proposed. These methods were based on different principles and theories, but generally fall in three basic categories.

The first one is **preprocessing**, which seeks to compensate the illumination changes with conventional image processing techniques including multi-scale retinex (MSR) [8] and discrete cosine transform (DCT) [4].

The second category involves the **modeling** of human faces. This category includes two types of modeling techniques: 3-D face modeling and illumination modeling. The illumination cone demonstrated by Belhumeur and Kriegman in [2], and the low dimensional linear subspace developed by Baseri and Jacob in [1] are all examples of this category.

© Springer Nature Switzerland AG 2018
J. Zhou et al. (Eds.): CCBR 2018, LNCS 10996, pp. 294–301, 2018.
https://doi.org/10.1007/978-3-319-97909-0_32

The third category, which is also the one our method falls into, is to seek an **illumination invariant feature representation**. Zhang et al. [12] developed "Gradientface", using the gradient of pixel intensity as an illumination invariant feature representation. In [9] a similar approach is presented, only using local gravitational force angle instead of gradients to represent the direction of pixelwise intensity change, and it received promising results. Wang et al. [11] followed a different idea. They utilized the amplitude of change around single pixels. Builing upon the weber law presented in [3], they developed "weberface" that use the ratio of the variation of pixel to the pixel intensity as a invariant feature.

All of these methods mentioned above have their own strength as well as shortcomings. The directional based approaches such as [12] and [9] ignores the difference between discernable facial attributions (eyes, mouth, nose) and other irrelevant details. The information regarding the amplitude of pixel intensity change is also lost in the process. As for amplitude oriented methods such as Weberface [11], the use of gaussian smoothing filter in the preprocess stage will result in the loss of details, which will affect the accuracy in the recognition stage. Therefore it is an intuitive thought to combine the strength of both methods, and produce the best balance between them. Based on the previous considerations, we present local directional amplitude feature (LDAF).

2   Proposed Method

In this section, we introduce the method of extracting our LDAF. Our method is composed of two major parts. The first is local force direction (LFD), inspired by [9], to extract the directional information of the pixel changes. The other is local amplitude ratio (LAR), inspired by [11], to extract the major facial attributions by applying weber's law locally on each pixel. In order to exploit the advantages of these two types of methods, we fuse them in a linear form, adjusted by their corresponding weights, which can be tuned according to the real application.

2.1   Local Force Direction Feature Representation

Motivated by [9], we take local gravitational force as an indicator of the direction of the pixel changes, and develop the directional part of our scheme. The local gravitational force between two adjacent pixels is:

$$F_{12} = G\frac{I_1 I_2}{r^2} \tag{1}$$

in which I_1 and I_2 are the intensity of the two adjacent pixels, and r is the distance between the two pixels, which will be set as 1 if the two pixels are horizontally or vertically adjacent, and $\sqrt{2}$ if they are orthogonally adjacent.

Now let us consider a 3×3 window, as shown in Fig. 1. Each of the 8 surrounding pixels exerts gravitational force on the center pixel. If we decompose the force on the center pixel on direction X and Y, we get:

$$F_{cj_x} = F_{cj} \times \cos\theta_{cj} \; F_{cj_y} = F_{cj} \times \sin\theta_{cj} \tag{2}$$

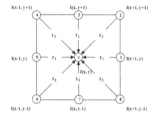

Fig. 1. Local gravity exerted on the center pixel in a 3×3 window

in which F_{cj_x} denotes the gravitational forced exerted on the center pixel by the surrounding pixel p_j $(1 \leq j \leq 8)$, θ_{cj} denotes the angle between the center pixel and the j-th pixel. In this way, the total force exerted on the center pixel can be expressed as:

$$F_x = \sum_{j=1}^{8}(F_{cj} \times \cos\theta_{cj}) \quad F_y = \sum_{j=1}^{8}(F_{cj} \times \sin\theta_{cj}) \tag{3}$$

Therefore, we can get the direction of the local gravitational force (LFD) as:

$$LFD = \arctan(\frac{\sum_{j=1}^{8}(F_{cj} \times \sin\theta_{cj})}{\sum_{j=1}^{8}(F_{cj} \times \cos\theta_{cj})}) \tag{4}$$

We adopt the Lambertian reflectance model, that the intensity of a pixel can be seen as the product of two parts, reflectance and illuminance:

$$I_i = R_i \times L_i \tag{5}$$

It has been proven in [9] that α is determined exclusively by the reflectance, which means that α is illumination invariant. Then we can apply this model to the 3×3 window in Fig. 1, and obtain the local force direction on each pixel:

$$LFD = \arctan(\frac{-\frac{I_2}{\sqrt{2}} - I_3 - \frac{I_4}{2\sqrt{2}} + \frac{I_6}{2\sqrt{2}} + I_7 + \frac{I_8}{2\sqrt{2}}}{-I_1 - \frac{I_2}{2\sqrt{2}} + \frac{I_4}{2\sqrt{2}} + I_5 + \frac{I_6}{2\sqrt{2}} - \frac{I_8}{2\sqrt{2}}}) \tag{6}$$

2.2   Local Amplitude Ratio Based on Weber Law

Following the spirit of weber law, we develop the amplitude part of our illumination invariant feature. If we denotes the difference of a pixel with its surrounding pixels as ΔI and the pixel itself as I, then by their ratio $k = \Delta I/I$ we can determine if the area around the pixel is a perceptual feature such as the edges of nose and eyes. In this way we can utilize the amplitude of the change of pixel in the image as an illumination invariant feature.

The Local Amplitude Ratio (LAR) of a center pixel and its 8 surrounding pixels in a 3 × 3 window can be expressed as:

$$LAR = \arctan(\alpha \sum_{i=1}^{8} \frac{I_c - I_i}{I_c + \lambda}) \tag{7}$$

where I_c denotes the intensity of the center pixel, while I_i denotes the intensity of the eight surrounding pixels. α is a parameter for magnifying the difference between the adjacent pixels. $\lambda = 0.01$ is added to the denominator in case I_c is too small and results in calculation error during devision. arctangent function is adopted in case the output gets too large.

2.3 Local Directional Amplitude Feature

Having obtained LFD and LAR, we can begin constructing our LDAF. First we preprocess the input facial image before the feature extraction process. As shown in (7), laplacian operator has been applied to obtain LAR, which, however, is sensitive to to noisy pixels. Therefore Gaussian smoothing is applied to the original facial image I beforehand:

$$I' = I * G(x, y, \sigma) \tag{8}$$

$$G(x, y, \sigma) = \frac{1}{2\pi\sigma^2} exp(-\frac{x^2 + y^2}{2\sigma}) \tag{9}$$

where I is the original image, and I' is the processed image after Gaussian smoothing. G denotes the Gaussian kernel, and σ is the standard deviation. $*$ denotes convolution operation.

In order to exploit the merits of both LFD and LAR, we linearly combine these two features, controlling their portion through their corresponding weights, and form our Local Directional Amplitude Feature (LDAF)

$$LDAF = w_1 LFD + w_2 LAR$$
$$(w_1 + w_2 = 1) \tag{10}$$

With such a combination, we are able to exploit the merits of both the LFD and LAR. Just like the samples shown in Fig. 2, the extracted feature face depicted both the details and the facial attributions clearly.

3 Experiments

In this section we conduct extensive experiments on two of the most widely used databases: CMU-PIE [10] and Extended Yale B [5]. In the following part, we will introduce our implementation on these two databases separately, introducing the experiment setup first, and then presenting our results. In order to examine the superiority of our method, we conduct the same experiments on some of the methods presented in the literature for comparison.

3.1   Experiments on CMU-PIE

Experiment Setup. The illumination subset of CMU-PIE database (Pose27, 1428 images) consists of 68 subjects under 21 different illuminations. All the images have been properly aligned and cropped to 128*128. In our experiment we choose all of the images of the 68 subjects under each illumination as gallery, and the rest 20 illuminations as probe. We use l_2 norm as the similarity measure. We calculate the l_2 norm of gallary and probes under each illumination, and find the probe most similar to the gallery as the result of the 21 rank 1 recognition. After extensive experiments, we have found the best set of parameters for our model: $\alpha = 5, \sigma = 0.75, w_1 = 0.6, w_2 = 0.4$. When these conditions are satisfied, our model yields the highest recognition rate. The sample face of the first subject in the CMU-PIE database in shown in Fig. 2.

Results on CMU-PIE. In order to examine the effectiveness of our model, we compare our method with some of the state-of-art approaches in the literature,

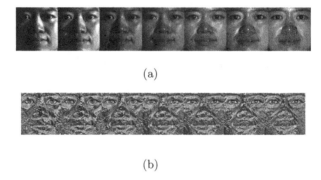

(a)

(b)

Fig. 2. (a) Original images from CMU-PIE (b) Samples of LDAF face from CMU-PIE

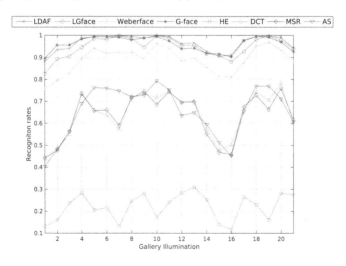

Fig. 3. Recognition rates versus gallery illuminations on CMU-PIE

namely, LG-face [9], Weberface [11], G-face [12], HE [6], DCT [4], MSR [8] and AS [7]. All algorithms are fine-tuned accrording to their own papers. The recognition rates on every one of the 21 illuminations in the gallery is shown in Fig. 3. As we can see, the LDAF remains the top under most of the illumination conditions. The average recognition rate of our method also excels among all the methods, as shown in Table 1. Notably, LDAF has not only shown remarkable recognition rate on the average, but also shown great stability across illumination, swaying within a margin of only 10%.

Table 1. Recognition Rate for Different Methods on CMU-PIE

Method	LG-face	Weberface	G-face	HE	DCT	MSR	AS	**LDAF**
Accuracy	94.73	88.81	96.08	22.01	63.86	63.44	65.50	**96.54**

3.2 Experiments on Extended Yale B

Experiment Setup. The Extended Yale B database contains image of 38 subjects under 64 different illumination conditions. The whole database is divided into 5 subsets according to the angle of illumination: Subset 1 (illumination angle 0° to 12°, 7 images per subject), Subset 2 (illumination angle 13° to 25°, 12 images per subject), Subset 3 (illumination angle 26° to 50°, 12 images per subject), Subset 4 (illumination angle 51° to 77°), and Subset 5 (illumination angle greater than 78°, 19 images per subject). In Subset 1, the images with the illumination condition "A+000E+00" have the best illumination and are taken as the gallery, all the rest images in 5 subsets are used as probes. We conduct our rank 1 recognition experiment on 5 subsets separately. After extensive experiments, we discovered the optimal parameters for this dataset: $\alpha = 2, \sigma = 1, w_1 = 0.6, w_2 = 0.4$. Some samples of our LDAF images on Extended Yale B is shown in Fig. 4.

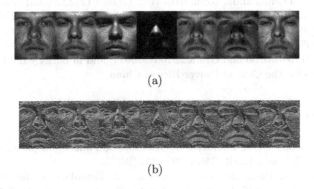

(a)

(b)

Fig. 4. (a) Original images from Extended Yale B (b) Samples of LDAF face from Extended Yale B

Table 2. Recognition Rate for Different Methods on Extended Yale B

Methods	S1	S2	S3	S4	S5	Average
LG-face	97.78	100	94.19	91.12	86.45	93.95
Weberface	74.74	98.73	73.73	80.73	80.39	81.67
G-face	98.48	100	94.19	84.41	86.81	92.78
HE	60.60	28.53	68.18	13.20	47.05	31.24
DCT	93.94	94.95	61.36	44.15	39.93	66.85
MSR	51.57	49.27	45.20	11.25	16.75	34.79
LDAF	97.92	100	94.53	94.87	94.48	96.36

Results on Extended Yale B. Similar to the experiments on CMU-PIE, we also compare our method with the previous methods in the literature. The recognition rates on all 5 subsets and the average rates are shown in Table 2. The results have once again shown the superiority of our method: LDAF has not only shown outstanding accuracy on every subset, but are also stable across all the subsets, especially on Subset 4 and 5 which are the most challenging subsets due to the large illumination angles.

4   Conclusion

In this paper we have proposed a new illumination invariant feature called Local Directional Amplitude Feature for illumination robust face recognition tasks. Our method is able to utilize both the directional information and the amplitude information of the local pixel changes, and reaches a balance between the emphasis on discernible facial features and the preservation of details. Extensive experiments have been carried out on some of the most classic databases to prove the merits of our method.

Acknowledgement. This work was supported in part by the National Natural Science Foundation of China under Grant 61673402, Grant 61273270, and Grant 60802069, in part by the Natural Science Foundation of Guangdong under Grant 2017A030311029, Grant 2016B010109002, Grant 2015B090912001, Grant 2016B010123005, and Grant 2017B090909005, in part by the Science and Technology Program of Guangzhou under Grant 201704020180 and Grant 201604020024, and in part by the Fundamental Research Funds for the Central Universities of China.

References

1. Basri, R., Jacobs, D.W.: Lambertian reflectance and linear subspaces. IEEE Trans. Pattern Anal. Mach. Intell. **25**(2), 218–233 (2003)
2. Belhumeur, P.N., Hespanha, J.P., Kriegman, D.J.: Eigenfaces vs. fisherfaces: recognition using class specific linear projection. IEEE Trans. Pattern Anal. Mach. Intell. **19**(7), 711–720 (1997). https://doi.org/10.1109/34.598228

3. Chen, J., et al.: WLD: a robust local image descriptor. IEEE Trans. Pattern Anal. Mach. Intell. **32**(9), 1705–1720 (2010). https://doi.org/10.1109/TPAMI.2009.155
4. Chen, W., Er, M.J., Wu, S.: Illumination compensation and normalization for robust face recognition using discrete cosine transform in logarithm domain. IEEE Trans. Syst. Man Cybern. B Cybern. **36**(2), 458–466 (2006)
5. Georghiades, A.S., Belhumeur, P.N., Kriegman, D.J.: From few to many: illumination cone models for face recognition under variable lighting and pose. IEEE Trans. Pattern Anal. Mach. Intell. **23**(6), 643–660 (2001)
6. Gonzalez, R.: Digital Image Processing. Pearson Education, London (2009). https://books.google.com/books?id=a62xQ2r_f8wC
7. Gross, R., Brajovic, V.: An image preprocessing algorithm for illumination invariant face recognition. In: Kittler, J., Nixon, M.S. (eds.) AVBPA 2003. LNCS, vol. 2688, pp. 10–18. Springer, Heidelberg (2003). https://doi.org/10.1007/3-540-44887-X_2
8. Jobson, D.J., Rahman, Z., Woodell, G.A.: A multiscale retinex for bridging the gap between color images and the human observation of scenes. IEEE Trans. Image Process. **6**(7), 965–976 (1997)
9. Roy, H., Bhattacharjee, D.: Local-gravity-face (lg-face) for illumination-invariant and heterogeneous face recognition. IEEE Trans. Inf. Forensics Secur. **11**(7), 1412–1424 (2016). https://doi.org/10.1109/TIFS.2016.2530043
10. Sim, T., Baker, S., Bsat, M.: The CMU pose, illumination, and expression (pie) database. In: Proceedings of Fifth IEEE International Conference on Automatic Face Gesture Recognition, pp. 46–51 (2002). https://doi.org/10.1109/AFGR.2002.1004130
11. Wang, B., Li, W., Yang, W., Liao, Q.: Illumination normalization based on weber's law with application to face recognition. IEEE Signal Process. Lett. **18**(8), 462–465 (2011). https://doi.org/10.1109/LSP.2011.2158998
12. Zhang, T., Tang, Y.Y., Fang, B., Shang, Z., Liu, X.: Face recognition under varying illumination using gradientfaces. IEEE Trans. Image Process. **18**(11), 2599–2606 (2009). https://doi.org/10.1109/TIP.2009.2028255

Facial Expression Bilinear Encoding Model

Haifeng Zhang[1,3(✉)], Wen Su[1,2,3], and Zengfu Wang[1,2,3(✉)]

[1] University of Science and Technology of China, Hefei, China
{hfz,wensu}@mail.ustc.edu.cn, zfwang@ustc.edu.cn
[2] Institute of Intelligent Machines, Chinese Academy of Sciences, Hefei, China
[3] National Engineering Laboratory for Speech and Language Information Processing, Hefei, China

Abstract. Facial expressions are generated by contractions of facial muscles. The contractions lead to variations in the appearance of facial parts. It has been proved that the features from different facial parts can improve the accuracy of facial expression recognition. In this paper, we propose a bilinear encoding model for facial expression recognition. Our system uses the still facial expression images as inputs and employs the bilinear convolutional networks to capture the features in the appearance of facial parts. It detects crucial facial parts and extracts the appearance features simultaneously with end-to-end learning. To verify the performance of our system, we have made experiments on two popular expression databases: CK+ and Oulu-CASIA. The experimental results show that the proposed method achieves comparable or better performance compared with the state-of-the-art methods for facial expression recognition.

Keywords: Facial expression recognition · Facial parts
Appearance features · Bilinear encoding

1 Introduction

Facial expression recognition (FER) is an important research topic in the field of pattern recognition and computer vision, as it is desired in a wide range of applications in human-computer interaction (HCI) and health care. Over the last 10 years, even though a number of researches on facial expression recognition have been made, it is still a challenging problem. One of the key problems is how to extract facial expression specific features and avoid the influence of illumination, location, pose, and viewpoint etc.

Studies in psychology have shown that facial expressions are generated by contractions of facial muscles. The contractions result in temporally deformed facial features such as eyelids, eye brows, nose, lips and skin texture, often revealed by wrinkles and bulges. These facial parts contain the most descriptive information for representing expressions. It has been proved that extraction of facial features by dividing the face region into several parts can achieve better accuracy. This is primarily due to part-based methods focus on the feature

© Springer Nature Switzerland AG 2018
J. Zhou et al. (Eds.): CCBR 2018, LNCS 10996, pp. 302–310, 2018.
https://doi.org/10.1007/978-3-319-97909-0_33

changes in the crucial regions of the face, and their invariance to position and pose of the face. Thus, in the past decade, a lot of part-based features extraction methods have been proposed. Zhong *et al.* [1] divided the face into 64 sub regions and explored the common facial patches which are active for most expressions and special facial patches which are active for specific expressions. And they used features of several facial patches to classify facial expressions. Happy *et al.* [2] proposed a novel framework for expression recognition by using appearance features of selected facial patches. A few prominent facial patches which are active during emotion elicitation are extracted depending on the position of facial landmarks. These active patches are further processed to obtain the salient patches containing discriminative features for classification of each pair of expressions, thereby selecting different facial patches as salient for different pair of expression classes. Liu *et al.* [3] incorporated a deformable parts learning component into 3D CNN framework. It can detect specific facial action parts under the structured spatial constraints, and obtain the discriminative part-based representation simultaneously. Perveen *et al.* [4] divided the face into expressive salient regions. Deep CNN based feature extraction was implemented for extracting features from each region and then inputed into the SVM. However, these methods need to localize crucial facial parts firstly and model the appearance conditioned on their detected locations. It usually require quite accurate and reliable detection as well as tracking of the facial landmarks, it is sometimes difficult to achieve in many practical situations. Moreover, separating the face into different parts can be time-consuming and computationally expensive. Sometimes, the parts selected may not be optimal for the facial expression recognition task.

In this paper, We focus on facial expression recognition in still images. Learning and extracting features from static images are more suitable for applications. To avoid the problems mentioned above, we propose a facial expression bilinear encoding model (FEBE). It is based on the idea of bilinear convolutional networks (bilinear CNNs) [5], and it has been provided that bilinear CNNs combine both part-based models and appearance models. FEBE can detect crucial facial parts automatically and extract the appearance features on their detected locations simultaneously. In the experiments, we apply FEBE on two popular expression databases, CK+ [6] and Oulu-CASIA [7]. We show that FEBE has a good performance in facial expression recognition, and the recognition accuracy is even better than that of some methods which utilize dynamic information. The remainder of this paper is organized as follows, Sect. 2 details the proposed facial expression bilinear encoding model. In Sect. 3, the experiments we have performed to evaluate the performance of FEBE are presented and compared with several recent facial expression recognition methods. The conclusions are presented in Sect. 4.

2   Proposed Method

In this section, we detail the components and architecture of FEBE. An overview of the proposed FEBE is illustrated in Fig. 1.

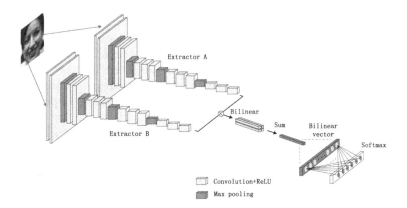

Fig. 1. An overview of the proposed facial expression bilinear encoding model. Two VGG-16 based extractors extract features from the same facial expression image. A facial expression descriptor is produced with bilinear encoding model and is used as the input of softmax classifier.

2.1   Feature Extractors

Considering the advantages of CNNs, the feature extractors in this paper are based on VGG-16. We consider a partial network of it with initial parameters obtained from pre-trained model on ImageNet dataset truncated at the last convolutional layer (conv5_3), followed by non-linearity (ReLU) and max pooling as feature extractor. This CNNs based extractor can extractor high-level features from raw images. However, previous work has shown that without the part localization, CNNs typically don't perform as well since there is a tremendous variation in appearance due to different poses or positions of the face. In order to combine the CNN based extractor with a detector that localizes various parts of the face, in this paper, we introduce two feature extractors. One of the feature extractors can be considered as a part detector which extracts position information and the other can be considered as a local feature extractor which extracts appearance information. These two extractors are similar to the two pathways in the human visual cortex: the ventral stream (which performs object identification and recognition) and the dorsal stream (which processing the object's spatial location relative to the viewer).

2.2   Bilinear Encoding

A bilinear encoding model $\mathcal{B}$ for image classification consists of a quadruple $\mathcal{B} = (f_A, f_B, \mathcal{P}, \mathcal{C})$. where f_A and f_B are feature extract functions, $\mathcal{P}$ is the pooling function and $\mathcal{C}$ is the classification function. The feature function is a mapping $f : \mathcal{L} \times \mathcal{I} \to \mathbb{R}^{(hw) \times c}$, which takes an image $\mathcal{I}$, a location $\mathcal{L}$ and outputs a feature of size $(hw) \times c$, where h, w and c are height, width and channels of feature maps respectively. For each location, we extract features $f_A(l, I)$ and $f_B(l, I)$. They contain both appearance and location information.

These two features are then combined at each location using outer product: $bilinear(l, I, f_A, f_B) = f_A(l, I)^T \otimes f_B(l, I)$, where $l \in \mathcal{L}$, $I \in \mathcal{I}$. In other words, multiplication is performed on features from each channel at each location on the input image. Here, $bilinear(l, I, f_A, f_B)$ is an appearance representation of the input facial expression image at location l. The pooling function $\mathcal{P}$ in this work aggregates the bilinear feature across all locations in the image by sum all of them, i.e,

$$\phi(I) = \sum_{l \in \mathcal{L}} bilinear(l, I, f_A, f_B) = \sum_{l \in \mathcal{L}} f_A(l, I)^T \otimes f_B(l, I), \phi(I) \in \mathbb{R}^d$$

where $\phi(I)$ is a global image representation of the input facial expression image. d denotes the encoded feature dimensions.

2.3   Facial Expression Bilinear Encoding Model

In facial expression bilinear encoding model (FEBE), two VGG-16 based extractors (mentioned in 2.1) serve as f_A and f_B. In our experiment, the two extractors extract features from the same facial expression image whose size is 64×64, and resulting in a $2 \times 2 \times 512$ outputs (2×2 and 512 denote the spatial dimensions and the channel of feature maps respectively). After we get the outputs from the two extractors, we produce a facial expression descriptor ($x = \phi(I)$) with bilinear encoding. The facial expression descriptor can be normalized to provide additional invariance. In this work, we perform power normalization $y = sign(x)\sqrt{|x|}$, followed by l_2 normalization $z = y/\|y\|_2$. Then, the final facial expression descriptor can be used with a softmax classification function.

Table 1. Comparisons of different methods on the CK+ database.

Method	Classes	Feature	Strategy	Accuracy
HOG 3D [10]	7	Dynamic	10 folds	91.44%
TMS [11]	6	Dynamic	4 folds	91.89%
3DCNN-DAP [3]	7	Dynamic	15 folds	92.40%
Inception [12]	6	Static	5 folds	93.20%
Happy et al. [2]	6	Static	10 folds	94.09%
STM-ExpLet [13]	7	Dynamic	10 folds	94.19%
IACNN [14]	7	Static	8 flods	95.37%
DTAGN [15]	7	Dynamic	10 folds	97.25%
PPDN [16]	6	Static	10 folds	97.30%
PHRNN-MSCNN [17]	7	Dynamic	10 folds	98.50%
FEBE	7	Static	10 folds	**94.30%**

In FEBE, the bilinear encoding model captures pairwise correlations between the feature channels at each location and can model part-feature interactions. In our experiment, the spatial dimensions of the features obtained from two feature extractors are 2×2, that means the features maps are divided into 4 locations, i.e. the input image is divided into 4 parts. Every channel of the features extracted from an facial expression image at each location l interacts with other channels, thus leading to a powerful feature representation (bilinear features) for the input image. Then, the pooling function aggregates the bilinear features across all the 4 locations in the feature maps, the final representation of the input facial expression image contains all the location information and appearance features. We can consider that our bilinear encoding model is proposed to model two-factor variations, i.e. part location and appearance. If one of the networks is a part detector of face and the other a local feature extractor. Therefore, it bridges the gap between appearance models and part-based CNN models.

Table 2. Confusion matrix of FEBE on the CK+ database. The labels in the leftmost column and on the top represent the ground truth and prediction results, respectively.

	An	Co	Di	Fe	Ha	Sa	Su
An	**90.37%**	2.22%	0%	0%	0%	7.41%	0%
Co	11.11%	**66.67%**	0%	5.56%	0%	11.11%	5.56%
Di	0%	0%	**96.61%**	0%	0%	3.39%	0%
Fe	0%	2.67	0%	**90.67%**	6.67%	0%	0%
Ha	0%	0%	0%	0%	**100%**	0%	0%
Sa	7.14%	0%	0%	0%	0%	**92.86%**	0%
Su	0%	2.01%	0%	0%	0%	0%	**97.99%**

3   Experiments

3.1   Implementation

Since the research object of facial expression recognition is human face, but most of the facial expression database is a face image containing background. So it is necessary to preprocess to detect and cut only the face region. In this paper, face alignment is conducted to reduce variation in face scale and in-plane rotation on each facial image based on the facial landmarks detected with a Supervised Descent Method (SDM) [8]. The detected face are cropped and rescaled to 64×64. To avoid over-fitting, two types of data augmentation strategies are adopted: rotate and flip horizontal. First, each preprocessed training image is rotated at angles of $-15°, -10°, -5°, 5°, 10°, 15°$. Then, they are flipped horizontally. Finally, there are 14 possible samples in one image.

For boosting the performance of FEBE, we train it in two steps. Firstly, we pretrain FEBE on the Facial Expression Recognition (FER2013) database [9] with 40 epochs. Optimizing the softmax loss using stochastic gradient decent with a batch size of 200, momentum of 0.9. The learning rate and weight decay are 0.01, 0.005 for the feature extractors. We adjust them as 0.1, 0.0001 for the last layer. Then we fine-tune on each training set to further improve the performance of FEBE. In this stage, we change the learning rate for the feature extractor and the last layer from 0.01 and 0.1 to 0.001 and 0.01, respectively.

Table 3. Comparisons of different methods on the Oulu-CASIA database.

Method	Classes	Feature	Strategy	Accuracy
HOG 3D [10]	6	Dynamic	10 folds	70.63%
AdaLBP [7]	6	Dynamic	10 folds	73.54%
STM-ExpLet [13]	6	Dynamic	10 folds	74.59%
IL-CNN [18]	6	Static	10 folds	77.29%
DTAGN [15]	6	Dynamic	10 folds	81.86%
PPDN [16]	6	Static	10 folds	84.59%
PHRNN-MSCNN [17]	6	Dynamic	10 folds	86.25%
FEBE	6	Static	10 folds	**79.02%**

3.2 Experimental Results

In all databases, we report the results using 10-fold cross validation protocol. In order to ensure the generalization ability of classifiers, the database separated in ten groups without subject overlap between the groups. For each run, nine groups are used for training and the remaining is employed to testing. The performance of the proposed FEBE is compared with several methods evaluated on two databases. Moreover, the confusion matrices are reported.

Table 4. Confusion matrix of FEBE on the Oulu-CASIA database. The labels in the leftmost column and on the top represent the ground truth and prediction results, respectively.

	An	Di	Fe	Ha	Sa	Su
An	**74.17%**	8.75%	5.42%	0%	11.67%	0%
Di	21.25%	**71.25%**	1.25%	0%	6.25%	0%
Fe	8.75%	2.50%	**70.00%**	11.25%	1.25%	6.25%
Ha	3.75%	0%	4.58%	**89.17%**	2.50%	0%
Sa	15%	5%	0%	1.25%	**78.75%**	0%
Su	0%	0%	7.50%	0%	1.67%	**90.83%**

Results on the CK+ database. The CK+ database [6] consists of 593 sequences collected from 123 different subjects. Each image sequence starts with a neutral facial expression and ends with a peak facial expression. Among these videos, only 327 sequences from 118 subjects are annotated with six basic facial emotions, i.e. Angry (An), Disgust (Di), Fear (Fe), Happy (Ha), Sadness (Sa), and Surprise (Su) and one non basic expression Contempt (Co). In this work, the last three frames per sequence are considered for training and testing. Thus, the CK+ database contains 981 images for our experiments. The results are reported as the average score of the ten runs and the comparison results are presented in Table 1. FEBE achieves an average recognition accuracy of 94.30% on the CK+ database for the seven expressions. Table 2 is the confusion matrix of the proposed FEBE on the CK+ database.

Results on the Oulu-CASIA database. The Oulu-CASIA database [7] consists of 480 sequences collected from 80 different subjects. Each sequence begins with a neutral emotion, ends with a peak of the emotion. All sequences have been labeled with six basic emotions. The last three frames of each sequence is selected for training and testing. Hence, there are 1440 images totally. The results are also reported as the average of 10 runs and the comparison results are presented in Table 3. FEBE achieves an average recognition accuracy of 79.02% on the Oulu-CASIA database for the six basic expressions. The confusion matrix of the proposed FEBE model is reported in Table 4.

As showed in Tables 1 and 3, FEBE achieves better or at least comparable performance compared to the state-of-the-art methods. Note that, some of the state-of-the-art methods utilized dynamic features extracted from image sequences. The proposed FEBE takes only raw static images, which is more favorable for online applications or snapshots where per frame labels are preferred.

4   Conclusions

In this paper, we propose a facial expression bilinear encoding model (FEBE). This model captures pairwise correlations between the feature channels and can model part-feature interactions. It can detect crucial facial parts and extract the appearance features on their detected locations simultaneously. It is a concise and end-to-end trainable model. We have demonstrated that the proposed FEBE achieves comparable or better performance compared with the state-of-the-art. It provides a general model for the task of facial expression recognition.

Acknowledgements. This work was supported by the National Natural Science Foundation of China (No. 61472393).

References

1. Zhong, L., Liu, Q., Yang, P., Liu, B., Huang, J., Metaxas, D.N.: Learning active facial patches for expression analysis. In: Proceedings of the IEEE Conference on Computer Vision and Pattern Recognition, pp. 2562–2569 (2012)
2. Happy, S.L., Routray, A.: Automatic facial expression recognition using features of salient facial patches. IEEE Trans. Affect. Comput. **6**(1), 1–12 (2015)
3. Liu, M., Li, S., Shan, S., Wang, R., Chen, X.: Deeply learning deformable facial action parts model for dynamic expression analysis. In: Proceedings of the IEEE Asian Conference on Computer Vision, pp. 143–157 (2014)
4. Perveen, N., Singh, D., Mohan, C.K.: Spontaneous facial expression recognition: a part based approach. In: Proceedings of the IEEE Conference on Machine Learning and Applications, pp. 819–824 (2016)
5. Lin, T.Y., RoyChowdhury, A., Maji, S.: Bilinear convolutional neural networks for fine-grained visual recognition. IEEE Trans. Pattern Anal. Mach. Intell. **40**(6), 1309–1322 (2017)
6. Lucey, P., Cohn, J.F., Kanade, T., Saragih, J., Ambadar, Z., Matthews, I.: The extended Cohn-Kanade dataset (CK+): a complete dataset for action unit and emotion-specified expression. In: IEEE Conference on Computer Vision and Pattern Recognition Workshops, pp. 94–101 (2010)
7. Zhao, G., Huang, X., Taini, M., Li, S.Z., PietikaInen, M.: Facial expression recognition from near-infrared videos. Image Vis. Comput. **29**(9), 607–619 (2011)
8. Xiong, X., De la Torre, F.: Supervised descent method and its applications to face alignment. In: Proceedings of the IEEE Conference on Computer Vision and Pattern Recognition, pp. 532–539 (2013)
9. Goodfellow, I.J., et al.: Challenges in representation learning: a report on three machine learning contests. In: Proceedings of the IEEE International Conference on Neural Information Processing, pp. 117–124 (2013)
10. Klaser, A., Marszalek, M., Schmid, C.: A spatio-temporal descriptor based on 3d-gradients. In: BMVC 2008–19th British Machine Vision Conference, pp. 275–1 (2008)
11. Jain, S., Hu, C., Aggarwal, J.K.: Facial expression recognition with temporal modeling of shapes. In: Proceedings of the IEEE International Conference on Computer Vision Workshops, pp. 1642–1649 (2011)
12. Mollahosseini, A., Chan, D., Mahoor, M.H.: Going deeper in facial expression recognition using deep neural networks. In: Proceedings of the IEEE Winter Conference on Applications of Computer Vision, pp. 1–10 (2016)
13. Liu, M., Shan, S., Wang, R., Chen, X.: Learning expressionlets on spatio-temporal manifold for dynamic facial expression recognition. In: Proceedings of the IEEE Conference on Computer Vision and Pattern Recognition, pp. 1749–1756 (2014)
14. Meng, Z., Liu, P., Cai, J., Han, S., Tong, Y.: Identity-aware convolutional neural network for facial expression recognition. In: Proceedings of the IEEE International Conference on Automatic Face & Gesture Recognition, pp. 558–565 (2017)
15. Jung, H., Lee, S., Yim, J., Park, S., Kim, J.: Joint fine-tuning in deep neural networks for facial expression recognition. In: Proceedings of the IEEE International Conference on Computer Vision, pp. 2983–2991 (2015)
16. Zhao, X., et al.: Peak-piloted deep network for facial expression recognition. In: Proceedings of the IEEE European Conference on Computer Vision, pp. 425–442 (2016)

17. Zhang, K., Huang, Y., Du, Y., Wang, L.: Facial expression recognition based on deep evolutional spatial-temporal networks. IEEE Trans. Image Process. **26**(9), 4193–4203 (2017)
18. Cai, J., Meng, Z., Khan, A.S., Li, Z., Tong, Y.: Island loss for learning discriminative features in facial expression recognition. arXiv:1710.03144

Face Clustering Utilizing Scalable Sparse Subspace Clustering and the Image Gradient Feature Descriptor

Mingkang Liu[1,2,3,4], Qi Li[1,2,3,4(✉)], Zhenan Sun[1,2,3,4(✉)], and Qiyao Deng[1,2,3,4]

[1] Center for Research on Intelligent Perception and Computing (CRIPAC),
Beijing, China
{mingkang.liu,qiyao.deng}@cripac.ia.ac.cn
[2] National Laboratory of Pattern Recognition (NLPR), Beijing, China
{qli,znsun}@nlpr.ia.ac.cn
[3] Institute of Automation, Chinese Academy of Sciences (CASIA), Beijing, China
[4] Center for Excellence in Brain Science and Intelligence Technology (CEBSIT),
CAS, Beijing, China

Abstract. Face clustering is an important topic in computer vision. It aims to put together facial images that belong to the same person. Spectral clustering-based algorithms are often used for accurate face clustering. However, a big occlusion matrix is usually needed to deal with the noise and sparse outlying terms, which makes the sparse coding process computationally expensive. Thus spectral clustering-based algorithms are difficult to extend to large scale datasets. In this paper, we use the image gradient feature descriptor and scalable Sparse Subspace Clustering algorithm for large scale and high accuracy face clustering. Within the image gradient feature descriptor, the scalable Sparse Subspace Clustering algorithm can be used in large scale face datasets without sacrificing clustering performance. Experimental results show that our algorithm is robust to illumination, occlusion, and achieves a relatively high clustering accuracy on the Extended Yale B and AR datasets.

Keywords: Face clustering · Scalable sparse subspace clustering
Image gradient feature descriptor

1 Introduction

With the development of Internet, the problem of image organization and management has become an important issue. Naturally, most Internet images contain human faces. To better understand and manage face images, face clustering becomes an essential task. Face clustering aims to group faces which refer to the same people together. It has many applications, such as a preprocessing step for face retrieval and face tagging. Many face clustering algorithms have been reported in recent years [1–3]. Although great progress has been achieved, face clustering algorithms still suffer from large variations in illumination, expression

J. Zhou et al. (Eds.): CCBR 2018, LNCS 10996, pp. 311–320, 2018.
https://doi.org/10.1007/978-3-319-97909-0_34

and occlusion, *etc.* Spectral clustering-based algorithms can handle noise and outliers in data samples and thus have drawn much attention in recent years for face clustering. Methods such as Enhanced Sparse Subspace Clustering, Conditional Pairing Clustering, and Subspace Clustering based on Orthogonal Matching Pursuit are recent novel face clustering approaches. The application showed that these methods not only have computational efficiency, but also achieve the best balance between accuracy and efficiency [4–7]. Besides, the method named sorted local gradient pattern and color image inpainting algorithm are highly discriminative and robust [8,9].

The first step of spectral clustering-based algorithms is to construct an affinity matrix, and then Normalized Cuts [10] is employed to segment the data samples into different clusters. Various spectral clustering-based algorithms have been proposed based on sparse and low-rank representation. The main difference of these algorithms is construction of the affinity matrix. Sparse Subspace Clustering algorithm [11,12] uses the l_1 norm regularization on the coefficient matrix to find the sparsest representation of each data sample. Low-Rank Representation algorithm [13–15] employs nuclear norm to seek the lowest rank representation of all data samples. Least Squares Regression algorithm [16] encourages l_2 norm regularization on the coefficient matrix to obtain a block diagonal solution. In particular, Sparse Subspace Clustering algorithm is well supported by theoretical analysis and achieves state-of-the-art results on many publicly available datasets [17].

There are still some issues to be further addressed for clustering various face images when using spectral clustering-based algorithms. Most of the spectral clustering-based algorithms are difficult to extend to large scale datasets because of the sparse outlying term represented by a variable matrix [E] is in the objective function, seen in Eq. (8). In addition, for the noise item, its complexity is determined by the feature dimension. For example, if the dimensionality of features used in Sparse Subspace Clustering algorithm is 4096, then an extra 4096×4096 noise matrix is needed. Such a big noise term will make the sparse coding process computationally expensive and sometimes even prohibitive when the dimensionality of features is high. While the clustering accuracy will be down dramatically without the noise and sparse outlying terms. What's more, the ability to cope with various illumination and occlusion for spectral clustering-based algorithms still needs to be improved.

Feature descriptors provide a possible solution to deal with the above problems. A low dimensional yet powerful feature descriptor is very helpful for face clustering. Recent studies have shown that the image gradient feature descriptor is widely used in many applications: face recognition, face alignment, visual tracking [18–20]. Compared with pixel based methods, the image gradient feature descriptor is less sensitive to variations of illumination and occlusion. The dimensionality of the image gradient feature descriptor is lower compared with other frequently used feature descriptors. In this paper, we propose a scalable Sparse Subspace Clustering algorithm for face clustering utilizing the image gradient feature descriptor. Our algorithm achieves a satisfying clustering accuracy and can be applied to large scale face datasets.

The main contributions of our work are summarized as follows.

(1) We proposed a scalable Sparse Subspace Clustering algorithm for face clustering utilizing the image gradient feature descriptor. Our algorithm achieves a better clustering performance than other spectral clustering-based algorithms. Besides, the computational cost of our algorithm is low, which provides a promising solution for large scale and high accuracy face clustering problem.
(2) The image gradient feature descriptor is first introduced to cluster large scale face datasets. Different feature descriptors are compared for face clustering. Experimental results show that image gradient feature descriptor is very simple but very competitive compared with other feature descriptors, e.g., HOG, LBP and Gabor.

2 Image Gradient Based Subspace Clustering Algorithm

2.1 Image Gradient Feature Descriptor

Given a face image $I_i \in \mathbb{R}^{w \times h}$, we compute the gradient and the corresponding gradient orientation:

$$\Phi_i = \arctan \frac{H_y * I_i}{H_x * I_i}, \tag{1}$$

where H_x and H_y are the differential filters along the horizontal and vertical face image axis respectively, $H_x * I_i \in \mathbb{R}^{w \times h}$ and $H_y * I_i \in \mathbb{R}^{w \times h}$ denote the horizontal and vertical convolution of the face image. We write Φ_i in lexicographic order and stack it as a m dimensional vector ϕ_i, then we have the image gradient feature descriptor as follows:

$$f(\phi_i) = \frac{1}{\sqrt{m}} \left[\cos(\phi_i)^T + j \sin(\phi_i)^T \right]^T, \tag{2}$$

where

$$\cos(\phi_i) = [\cos(\phi_i(1)), ..., \cos(\phi_i(m))]^T,$$
$$\sin(\phi_i) = [\sin(\phi_i(1)), ..., \sin(\phi_i(m))]^T.$$

Next, we will illustrate that the image gradient feature descriptor is a simple yet powerful feature descriptors to measure image similarity and thus it is useful for face clustering. With the image gradient feature descriptor, the correlation of two face images can be expressed as:

$$c(f_i, f_j) = f_i^T f_j = \frac{1}{m} \sum\nolimits_{k=1}^{m} \cos(\Delta\phi_{ij}(k)), \tag{3}$$

where $\Delta\phi_{ij} = \phi_i - \phi_j$ is the difference of the feature descriptor between face image I_i and I_j. The difference of two face images can be written as:

$$d^2(f_i, f_j) = \frac{1}{2}\|f_i - f_j\|_2^2 = 1 - \frac{1}{m} \sum\nolimits_{k=1}^{m} \cos(\Delta\phi_{ij}(k)). \tag{4}$$

Definition 1. *If two images I_i and I_j are dissimilar, then $\Delta\phi_{ij}(k) \sim U[0, 2\pi]$.*

Definition 1 has already been verified by [20]. From Eqs. (3) and (4), we can see that if two face images are similar to each other, then $c \to 1$, $d \to 0$. Note that similar feature descriptor has also been used in [20,21]. This feature descriptor is robust to outliers and there is no need to add the noise term in the sparse coding process.

2.2   Scalable Sparse Subspace Clustering

We denote the i-th face image as vector $y_i \in \mathbb{R}^m$ ($m = w \times h$) by stacking its columns. Then the dataset of n face images can be represented as a matrix $Y = [y_1, ... y_n] \in \mathbb{R}^{m \times n}$. According to [22], y_i can be represented by a linear combination of other images:

$$y_i = Yx_i, \quad x_{ii} = 0, \tag{5}$$

where $x_i = [x_{i1}, ..., x_{in}]^T \in \mathbb{R}^{n \times 1}$, $x_{ii} = 0$ avoids writing a face image as a linear combination of itself. Because the solution is not unique, l_0 norm is used as a constraint to seek the sparse solution of Eq. (5). Considering the non-convexity of l_0 norm, l_1 norm is replaced with the l_0 norm and Eq. (5) becomes:

$$\min \|x_i\|_1 \quad s.t. \quad y_i = Yx_i, \quad x_{ii} = 0. \tag{6}$$

We rewrite Eq. (6) in matrix form:

$$\min \|X\|_1 \quad s.t. \quad Y = YX, \quad \text{diag}(X) = 0. \tag{7}$$

In order to deal with the corrupted or occluded face images, the noise term is usually added in Eq. (7):

$$\min \|X\|_1 + \|E\|_1 \quad s.t. \quad Y = YX + E, \quad \text{diag}(X) = 0. \tag{8}$$

Eq. (8) is first proposed in [11,12]. However, the noise term prohibits this algorithm using in large scale face datasets.

If we remove the noise term from Eq. (8) directly, the clustering performance will decrease dramatically. Fortunately, the powerful image gradient feature descriptor provides an opportunity to remedy this drawback. With the image gradient feature descriptor, there is no need to use the noise term. Based on the above analysis, the proposed scalable Sparse Subspace Clustering (sSSC) is formulated as:

$$\min \|X\|_1 \quad s.t. \quad Y = YA, \quad A = X - \text{diag}(X). \tag{9}$$

Augmented Lagrange Multiplier method is used to solve this problem. The augmented Lagrangian function of Eq. (9) is defined by:

$$\begin{aligned}
\mathcal{L}(A, X, \Delta_1, \Delta_2) &= \min \|X\|_1 + tr\left(\Delta_1^T(Y - YA)\right) \\
&+ tr\left(\Delta_2^T(A - (X - \text{diag}(X)))\right) \\
&+ \tfrac{\mu}{2}\left(\|Y - YA\|_F^2 + \|A - (X - \text{diag}(X))\|_F^2\right),
\end{aligned} \tag{10}$$

where Δ_1^T, Δ_2^T are the Lagrangian multipliers, tr denotes the trace operator of a matrix, μ is the penalty term. Eq. (10) can be minimized through an alternative strategy with respect to A and X by fixing the other variables and then we update Δ_1^T, Δ_2^T and μ as the following forms:

$$A^{k+1} = \arg\min_A \ \mathcal{L}_{\mu^k}(A, X^k, \Delta_1^k, \Delta_2^k), \tag{11}$$

$$X^{k+1} = \arg\min_X \ \mathcal{L}_{\mu^k}(A^{k+1}, X, \Delta_1^k, \Delta_2^k), \tag{12}$$

$$\Delta_1^{k+1} = \Delta_1^k + \mu^k\left(Y - YA^{k+1}\right), \tag{13}$$

$$\Delta_2^{k+1} = \Delta_2^k + \mu^k\left(A^{k+1} - C^{k+1}\right), \tag{14}$$

$$\mu^{k+1} = \rho\mu^k. \tag{15}$$

Eq. (11) can be solved by computing the derivative of $\mathcal{L}$ with respect to A and setting it to zero:

$$A^{k+1} = \left(\mu\left(Y^TY + I\right)\right) \left(\mu Y^TY + \mu\left(C - \text{diag}\left(\text{C}\right)\right) + \Delta_1 - \Delta_2\right). \tag{16}$$

Eq. (12) can be solved by the soft threshold method:

$$X^{k+1} = J - \text{diag}\left(J\right)$$
$$J = \mathcal{S}_{\frac{1}{\mu}}\left(A^{k+1} + \frac{\Delta_2^k}{\mu}\right), \tag{17}$$

where $\mathcal{S}$ is the soft-thresholding operator. After obtaining the representation parameter, we define the affinity matrix as $\left(|X| + |X^T|\right)/2$. Then Normalized Cuts [10] is used to segment the image datasets. In summary, given face images, we extracted the image gradient feature descriptor (IG). Then we put the feature vectors to the scalable Sparse Subspace Clustering algorithm (sSSC) to cluster the face images.

3 Experiments

Experiments are conducted on two datasets: the Extended Yale B and the AR datasets. The Extended Yale B [23] dataset consists of 2,414 frontal face images from 38 subjects under various lighting conditions. The cropped and normalized 192×168 face images are captured under various controlled lighting conditions [24]. The AR dataset consists of over 4,000 face images from 126 subjects. For each subject, 26 face images are taken in two separate sessions. These images suffer from different facial expressions (neutral, smile, anger, and scream), illumination variations (left light on, right light on, and all side lights on), and occlusion by sunglasses or scarf.

The clustering result is evaluated by the **error rate**:

$$error = 1 - \frac{\sum_{i=1}^n \delta\left(y_i, map(s_i)\right)}{n}$$

where y_i and s_i is the obtained cluster label and the ground truth label, δ is the delta function, $map(s_i)$ is the permutation function that maps each cluster label s_i to the equivalent label in y. All of the experiments are implemented using MATLAB on a Intel Core i7-2600 3.40 GHZ machine with 16 GB memory.

3.1   Experimental Results on the Extended Yale B Dataset

The first 10 subjects of Extended Yale B dataset are used to validate the clustering accuracy of our algorithm. Different feature descriptors are extracted from the original cropped images (192×168) and then sent to the sSSC algorithm for face clustering. Similar to other sparse representation algorithms for data processing, we use l_2 norm to normalize all of the feature descriptors. Because of the high dimensional feature descriptors, PCA is used to project all of the feature descriptors to $k \times 6$, where k is the number of subspaces (here is the number of person). The parameter μ is tuned empirically to have the best clustering results across all of the 10 subjects. The compared feature descriptors are listed as follows.

Local Binary Patterns (LBP) [25]: The standard uniform LBP operator $\text{LBP}_{8,2}^{U2}$ is used with the MATLAB source code from [25,26]. Cell size of 8×8 is used to form a local histogram of 59 uniform patterns. Histograms of all the cells are combined to represent the whole image, resulting a 29736 ($192/8 \times 168/8 \times 59$) dimensional feature descriptor. Gabor Energy Filters (Gabor) [27]: For the Gabor feature descriptor, similar to [28], a filter bank of 5 scales and 8 orientations are used. We also down-sample the obtained feature descriptor by a factor of 16. Then the combined 40 filters result in a 80640 ($192 \times 168 \times 40/16$) dimensional feature descriptor. Histogram of the Oriented Gradient (HOG) [29]: For the HOG feature descriptor, we use the toolbox from [30]. The Spatial bin size is 8×8. Four different normalizations are computed using adjacent histograms, resulting in a 9×4 length vector for each region. Thus a total number of 18144 ($192/8 \times 168/8 \times 36$) dimensional feature descriptor is extracted from the cropped image.

The clustering accuracy of different feature descriptors is shown in Fig. 1. From Fig. 1, we can see that image gradient feature descriptor achieves the best clustering performance. Besides, LBP feature descriptor performs better than HOG and Gabor feature descriptors. This may be because LBP feature descriptor is more robust to illumination changes than HOG and Gabor feature descriptors. Although HOG feature descriptor also utilizes image gradient information, the quantization process may lose some useful information and lead to a poor performance on face clustering task.

Besides, we also compare our algorithm with other subspace clustering algorithms. The compared algorithms are: Sparse Subspace Clustering algorithm (SSC) [11], Low-rank Recovery algorithm (LRR) [14] and Least Squares Regression algorithm (LSR) [16]. In order to have a fair comparison, we test all of the algorithms (including our algorithm) on the down-samples images of resolution 48×42 without performing PCA projection. All of the parameters are tuned

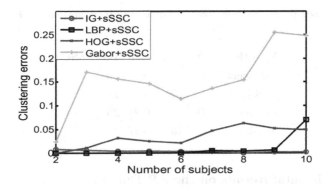

Fig. 1. Clustering errors of different feature descriptors on the Extended Yale B dataset (the less, the better). IG: image gradient feature descriptor, HOG: HOG feature descriptor, LBP: LBP feature descriptor, Gabor: Gabor feature descriptor.

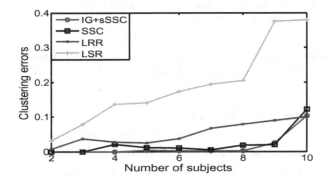

Fig. 2. Clustering errors of different algorithms on the Extended Yale B dataset (the less, the better). LBP, Gabor and HOG feature descriptors have poor clustering performances on the down-sampled images. So we haven't reported their clustering accuracy.

carefully across the 10 subjects to have the best clustering accuracy. The clustering accuracy of different algorithms is shown in Fig. 2. From Fig. 2, we can see that our algorithm has the lowest clustering error among all of the compared algorithms. This result further validates that our algorithm is robust to illumination changes.

The computational time of different algorithms are listed in Table 1. As shown in Table 1, the computational time of our algorithm is lower compared with SSC, LRR. This advantage is exaggerated when the number of subjects becomes large. Although the computational time of LSR is much lower, its clustering accuracy is also much lower than other algorithms. Compared with other algorithms, our algorithm achieves a satisfying clustering results while still maintaining the low computational cost.

Table 1. The computational time (sec.) of different algorithms on the Extended Yale B dataset.

Algorithm	SSC	LRR	LSR	IG+sSSC
2 subjects	22	6	0.02	**4**
5 subjects	46	26	0.08	**14**
8 subjects	71	68	0.24	**29**
10 subjects	117	135	0.27	**43**

3.2 Experimental Results on the AR Dataset

In this experiment, we evaluate the robustness of our algorithm on the AR dataset with different occlusions. A subset of 50 male and 50 female subjects are selected for this experiment. It contains two separate sessions. In each session, each subject has 7 face images with different facial variations, 3 face images with sunglasses occlusion and 3 face images with scarf occlusion. All of the images are resized to a resolution of 32×32.

Table 2. Clustering errors of different algorithms on the AR dataset (the less, the better). The clustering performance of LSR, LRR and SSC, CIL2 and rCIL2 is reported in [31].

Algorithm	Session 1		Session 2	
	Sunglasses	Scarf	Sunglasses	Scarf
IG+sSSC	**0.200**	**0.182**	**0.184**	**0.178**
LSR	0.218	0.284	0.200	0.274
LRR	0.228	0.278	0.204	0.254
SSC	0.562	0.594	0.722	0.598
rCIL2	0.148	0.216	0.136	0.188
CIL2	0.188	0.246	0.146	0.210

Because of the limited speed of LRR and SSC algorithms, we can't cluster all of the images at a time. So two sessions are used separately which is the same experimental setting as [31]. The first 2 normal face images and 3 face images with sunglasses of each subject are used for sunglasses occlusion. The first 2 normal face images and 3 face images with scarf of each subject are used for scarf occlusion. The clustering accuracy of different algorithms is shown in Table 2. From Table 2 we can see that the clustering accuracy of our algorithm is better than SSC, LSR and LRR algorithms. Our algorithm performs better than [31] for scarf occlusion. While for sunglasses occlusion, [31] performs better than our algorithm. The possible reason is that there are limited number of face images for each subject. If the number of images per subject is increased, both SSC and our algorithm can achieve a better clustering performance.

4 Conclusions

In this paper, we have proposed an efficient scalable face clustering algorithm utilizing the image gradient feature descriptor. Our algorithm has the advantage of relatively low computational cost and high clustering accuracy, which provides a promising solution for large scale face clustering problem.

References

1. Vretos, N., Solachidis, V., Pitas, I.: A mutual information based face clustering algorithm for movie content analysis. Image Vis. Comput. **29**(10), 693–705 (2011)
2. Wu, B., Zhang, Y., Hu, B.-G., Ji, Q.: Constrained clustering and its application to face clustering in videos. In: IEEE Conference on Computer Vision and Pattern Recognition, pp. 3507–3514 (2013)
3. Xiao, S., Tan, M., Xu, D.: Weighted block-sparse low rank representation for face clustering in videos. In: Fleet, D., Pajdla, T., Schiele, B., Tuytelaars, T. (eds.) ECCV 2014. LNCS, vol. 8694, pp. 123–138. Springer, Cham (2014). https://doi.org/10.1007/978-3-319-10599-4_9
4. Ren, J., Zhao, S., Yang, K., Zhao, B.N.: A novel and robust face clustering method via adaptive difference dictionary, pp. 627–632 (2017)
5. Shi, Y., Otto, C., Jain, A.K.: Face clustering: representation and pairwise constraints. IEEE Trans. Inf. Forensics Secur. **13**(7), 1626–1640 (2018)
6. You, C., Robinson, D.P., Vidal, R.: Scalable sparse subspace clustering by orthogonal matching pursuit, pp. 3918–3927 (2017)
7. Javed, S., Mahmood, A., Bouwmans, T., Jung, S.K.: Backgroundcforeground modeling based on spatiotemporal sparse subspace clustering. IEEE Trans. Image Process. **26**(12), 5840–5854 (2017)
8. Song, T., Xin, L., Gao, C., Zhang, G., Zhang, T.: Grayscale-inversion and rotation invariant texture description using sorted local gradient pattern. IEEE Signal Process. Lett. **25**(5), 625–629 (2018)
9. Jurio, A., Paternain, D., Fernandez, J., De Miguel, L., Bustince, H.: Image in painting using colour and gradient features. In: Joint 17th World Congress of International Fuzzy Systems Association and 9th International Conference on Soft Computing and Intelligent Systems, pp. 1–6 (2017)
10. Shi, J., Malik, J.: Normalized cuts and image segmentation. IEEE Trans. Pattern Anal. Mach. Intell. **22**(8), 888–905 (2000)
11. Elhamifar, E., Vidal, R.: Sparse subspace clustering: algorithm, theory, and applications. IEEE Trans. Pattern Anal. Mach. Intell. **35**(11), 2765–2781 (2013)
12. Elhamifar, E., Vidal, R.: Sparse subspace clustering. In: IEEE Conference on Computer Vision and Pattern Recognition, pp. 2790–2797 (2009)
13. Liu, G., Yan, S.: Latent low-rank representation for subspace segmentation and feature extraction. In: IEEE International Conference on Computer Vision, pp. 1615–1622 (2011)
14. Liu, G., Lin, Z., Yan, S., Sun, J., Yu, Y., Ma, Y.: Robust recovery of subspace structures by low-rank representation. IEEE Trans. Pattern Anal. Mach. Intell. **35**(1), 171–184 (2013)
15. Favaro, P., Vidal, R., Ravichandran, A.: A closed form solution to robust subspace estimation and clustering. In: IEEE Conference on Computer Vision and Pattern Recognition, pp. 1801–1807 (2011)

16. Lu, C.-Y., Min, H., Zhao, Z.-Q., Zhu, L., Huang, D.-S., Yan, S.: Robust and efficient subspace segmentation via least squares regression. In: Fitzgibbon, A., Lazebnik, S., Perona, P., Sato, Y., Schmid, C. (eds.) ECCV 2012. LNCS, vol. 7578, pp. 347–360. Springer, Heidelberg (2012). https://doi.org/10.1007/978-3-642-33786-4_26
17. Patel, V.M., Van Nguyen, H., Vidal, R.: Latent space sparse subspace clustering. In: IEEE International Conference on Computer Vision, pp. 225–232 (2013)
18. Tzimiropoulos, G., Zafeiriou, S., Pantic, M.: Sparse representations of image gradient orientations for visual recognition and tracking. In: IEEE Conference on Computer Vision and Pattern Recognition Workshops, pp. 26–33 (2011)
19. Tzimiropoulos, G., Zafeiriou, S., Pantic, M.: Robust and efficient parametric face alignment. In: EEE International Conference on Computer Vision, pp. 1847–1854 (2011)
20. Tzimiropoulos, G., Zafeiriou, S., Pantic, M.: Subspace learning from image gradient orientations. IEEE Trans. Pattern Anal. Mach. Intell. 34(12), 2454–2466 (2012)
21. Cootes, T., Taylor, C.: On representing edge structure for model matching. In: IEEE Conference on Computer Vision and Pattern Recognition, pp. 1114–1119 (2001)
22. Wright, J., Yang, A.Y., Ganesh, A., Sastry, S.S., Ma, Y.: Robust face recognition via sparse representation. IEEE Trans. Pattern Anal. Mach. Intell. 31(2), 210–227 (2009)
23. Georghiades, A.S., Belhumeur, P.N., Kriegman, D.: From few to many: illumination cone models for face recognition under variable lighting and pose. IEEE Trans. Pattern Anal. Mach. Intell. 23(6), 643–660 (2001)
24. Lee, K.-C., Ho, J., Kriegman, D.: Acquiring linear subspaces for face recognition under variable lighting. IEEE Trans. Pattern Anal. Mach. Intell. 27(5), 684–698 (2005)
25. Ahonen, T., Hadid, A., Pietikainen, M.: Face description with local binary patterns: application to face recognition. IEEE Trans. Pattern Anal. Mach. Intell. 28(12), 2037–2041 (2006)
26. Heikkil, M., Ahonen, T.: A general local binary pattern (lbp) implementation for matlab. http://www.cse.oulu.fi/CMV/Downloads/LBPMatlab/
27. Liu, C., Wechsler, H.: Gabor feature based classification using the enhanced fisher linear discriminant model for face recognition. IEEE Trans. Image Process. 11(4), 467–476 (2002)
28. Yang, M., Zhang, L.: Gabor feature based sparse representation for face recognition with gabor occlusion dictionary. In: Daniilidis, K., Maragos, P., Paragios, N. (eds.) ECCV 2010. LNCS, vol. 6316, pp. 448–461. Springer, Heidelberg (2010). https://doi.org/10.1007/978-3-642-15567-3_33
29. Dalal, N., Triggs, B.: Histograms of oriented gradients for human detection. In: IEEE Conference on Computer Vision and Pattern Recognition, pp. 886–893 (2005)
30. Dollár, P.: Piotr's Image and Video Matlab Toolbox (PMT). http://vision.ucsd.edu/~pdollar/toolbox/doc/index.html
31. Lu, C., Tang, J., Lin, M., Lin, L., Yan, S., Lin, Z.: Correntropy induced l2 graph for robust subspace clustering. In: IEEE International Conference on Computer Vision, pp. 1801–1808

Fusing Multiple Deep Features
for Face Anti-spoofing

Yan Tang, Xing Wang, Xi Jia, and Linlin Shen[✉]

Computer Vision Institute, School of Computer Science and Software Engineering,
Shenzhen University, Shenzhen 518060, China
{tangyan2016,jiaxi}@email.szu.edu.cn, wangdaxing10@126.com,
llshen@szu.edu.cn

Abstract. With the growing deployment of face recognition system in recent years, face anti-spoofing has become increasingly important, due to the increasing number of spoofing attacks via printed photos or replayed videos. Motivated by the powerful representation ability of deep learning, in this paper we propose to use CNNs (Convolutional Neural Networks) to learn multiple deep features from different cues of the face images for anti-spoofing. We integrate temporal features, color based features and patch based local features for spoof detection. We evaluate our approach extensively on publicly available databases like CASIA FASD, REPLAY-MOBILE and OULU-NPU. The experimental results show that our approach can achieve much better performance than state-of-the-art methods. Specifically, 2.22% of EER (Equal Error Rate) on the CASIA FASD, 3.2% of ACER (Average Classification Error Rate) on the OULU-NPU (protocol 1) and 0.00% of ACER on the REPLAY-MOBILE database are achieved.

Keywords: Deep convolutional neural networks · Face anti-spoofing Multiple features

1 Introduction

With the advancement of computer vision technologies, face recognition has been widely used in various applications such as access control and login system. As printed photos and replay videos of a user can easily spoof the face recognition system, approaches capable of detecting these spoof attacks are highly demanded.

To decide whether the faces presented before the camera are live person, or those spoof attacks, a number of approaches have been proposed in the literature. The main cues widely used are the depth information, the color texture information and the motion information. As majority of the attacks use printed photos or replayed videos, depth information could be a useful clue since live faces are 3D but the spoof faces are 2D. Wang et al. [11] combined the depth information and the textual information for face anti-spoofing. They used LBP (Local Binary Pattern) feature to represent the depth image captured by a Kinect and used a CNN (Convolutional Neural Network) to learn the texture information from the RGB image. This method needs an extra depth camera, which is usually not available for many applications. Instead of using the depth sensor

© Springer Nature Switzerland AG 2018
J. Zhou et al. (Eds.): CCBR 2018, LNCS 10996, pp. 321–330, 2018.
https://doi.org/10.1007/978-3-319-97909-0_35

like [11], the work presented in [9] adopted the CNN to estimate the depth information and then fused such depth information with the appearance information extracted from the face regions to distinguish between the spoof and the genuine faces. Besides the depth information, color texture or motion information has also been widely applied for face liveness detection [10, 13, 14]. Boulkenafet et al. [10] used different color spaces (HSV and YCbCr) to explore the color texture information and extracted LBP features from each space channel. The LBP features from all space channels were concatenated and then fed into the SVM (Support Vector Machine) for classification. An EER of 3.2% was obtained on the CASIA dataset. In contrast to the color texture information extracted from the static images, methods using motion cues tried to explore the temporal information of the genuine faces. Feng et al. [13] utilized the dense flow to capture the motion and designed optical flow based face motion and scene motion features. They also proposed a so called shearlet-based image quality feature, and then fused all the three features using a neural network for classification. Pan et al. [14] proposed a real-time liveness detection approach against photograph spoofing in face recognition by recognizing spontaneous eye blinks.

Motivated by the fact that CNN can learn features with high discriminative ability, recently many methods [8, 15] tried to use CNN for face anti-spoofing. Yang et al. [8] trained a CNN network with five convolutional layers and three fully-connected layers. Both single frame and multiple frames were input to the network to learn the spatial features and the spatial-temporal features, respectively, and an EER of 4.64% was reported on the CASIA dataset. Li et al. [15] fine-tuned the pre-trained VGG-face, and used the learned deep features to identify spoof attacks. An EER of 4.5% was achieved on the CASIA dataset.

While the existing methods explore various information for face antis-spoofing, most of them apply only single cue of the face. Although several methods [11, 13] indeed explored multiple cues of the face for anti-spoofing, they only adopted hand-crafted features. In this paper we propose to use CNNs to learn multiple deep features from different cues of the face to integrate different complementary information. Experiments show that our approach can outperform state-of-the-art approaches.

Below we detail the proposed method in Sect. 2. Then we present the experimental results in Sect. 3. And in Sect. 4 some conclusions are drawn.

2   The Proposed Method

In this paper, we aim to exploit three types of information, i.e. the temporal information, the color information and local information, for face anti-spoofing. As shown in Fig. 1, the face detector proposed in [2] is firstly applied to detect and crop the face from a given image. Then we use CNNs to learn three deep features from different cues of the face. Specifically, we learned temporal feature from the image sequences, the color based feature from different color spaces and the patch based local feature from the local patches. Each CNN learning process is supervised by a binary softmax classifier. Considering all the multiple features are complementary to another, we further propose a strategy to integrate all of the features: the class probabilities output by the softmax function of each CNN are concatenated as a class probability vector, which is then fed into SVM for classification.

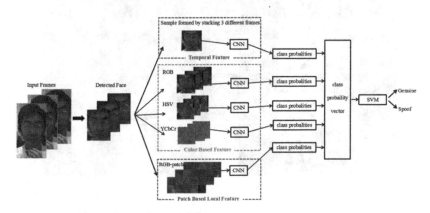

Fig. 1. The proposed multiple deep feature method.

2.1 Multiple Deep Features

Temporal Feature. Here we introduce a strategy to exploit the temporal information between image frames in the video sequence. Specifically, we first convert three color images at different temporal positions into three gray images, and then stack the gray images as a whole sample and feed the stacked volume into the CNN. Figure 2 shows an example volume stacked by three gray images.

Fig. 2. A volume stacked by three gray images in the CASIA database.

Color Based Feature. It was demonstrated in [12] that the color information in the HSV and YCbCr color spaces were more discriminative than that in the RGB space for face anti-spoofing. But [12] used hand-crafted features (i.e. LBP features) to encode these color information. Here we use CNN to learn high-level color-based features from the RGB, HSV and YCbCr color spaces, respectively. For the HSV (or YCbCr) color space, we first convert the RGB image into the HSV (or YCbCr) color space and then feed the converted image into the CNNs for feature learning. Figure 3 shows an example face with different color spaces i.e. RGB, HSV and YCbCr.

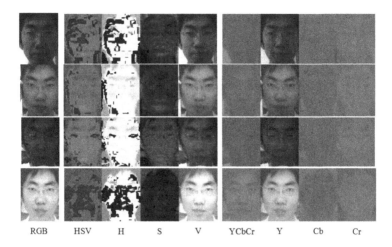

RGB HSV H S V YCbCr Y Cb Cr

Fig. 3. Sample images of different color spaces i.e. RGB, HSV and YCbCr. The first row shows the genuine face images. The second row shows the warped print photo face images. The third row shows the cut print photo face images. The last row shows the replay video face images. All sample images are sampled from the CASIA database. (Color figure online)

Patch Based Local Feature. While the temporal and color features are mainly learnt from the whole face images, important local information could be missing. In order to exploit the local information, we divided the face image into a number of patches with the same size for local feature representation. A set of ten patches with size 96×96 are randomly cropped from training faces and then used to train the network. Figure 4 shows a set of patches cropped from an example face.

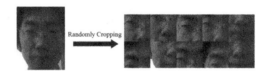

Randomly Cropping

Fig. 4. Samples of face patches in the CASIA database.

2.2 Network Architecture

In our work, we employ the 18-layer residual network (ResNet) [16] as the CNN. However, the last 1000-unit softmax layer (originally designed to predict 1000 classes) is replaced by a 2-unit softmax layer, which assigns a score for genuine and spoof classes. A brief illustration of the network architecture is shown in Fig. 5. The network consists of seventeen convolutional (conv) layers and one fully-connected (fc) layer. The orange, green, dark green and red rectangles represent the convolutional layer, max pooling layer, average pooling layer and fully-connected layer, respectively. The purple rectangle represents BatchNorm (BN) and ReLU layers. As shown in Fig. 6, the light blue rectangle represents residual blocks 1 (RB1), and the dark blue rectangle represents residual blocks 2 (RB2).

Fig. 5. The network architecture. (Color figure online)

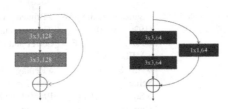

Fig. 6. Left: the residual block 1, Right: the residual block 2. (Color figure online)

2.3 SVM Classification with Integration of Multiple Deep Features

Different features capture different characteristics of the face and are complementary to each other. So we perform the classification with the integration of all multiple features. As shown in Fig. 1, each CNN can output a probability of whether the given face belongs to the genuine class or the spoof class. Then the class probabilities output by the softmax function of each CNN are concatenated as a class probability vector and then fed into SVM for classification. Given a video with N frames, N class probability vectors can be generated, then the video can be classified using the average of these class probability vectors.

3   Experiments

3.1   Datasets and Protocol

In this paper, the experiments were conducted on three databases, i.e.CASIA FASD, OULU-NPU and REPLAY-MOBILE databases, whose details are summarized in Table 1.

Table 1. The summary of three face spoof databases.

Database	Subjects	Videos (live, spoof)	Acquisition device	Spoof type	Year of release
CASIA FASD [4]	50	(150,450)	o USB camera (640 × 480, 480 × 640) o Sony NEX-5 camera (1920 × 1080).	o Warped photo o Cut photo o Replay video	2012
REPLAY-MOBILE [6]	40	(390,640)	o Smartphone o Tablet (720 × 1280)	o Printed photo o Mattescreen (displayed photo and video)	2016
OULU-NPU [5]	55	(1980,3960)	o Samsung Galaxy S6 (1920 × 1080) o HTC Desire EYE o MEIZU X5 o ASUS Zenfone Selfie o Sony XPERIA C5 Ultra Dual o OPPO N3	o Printed photo (Canon imagePRESS C6011 and PIXMA iX6550) o Replay video (19" Dell UltraSharp 1905FP and Macbook 13" laptop)	2017

CASIA FASD Database. The CASIA FASD (face anti-spoofing database) [4] contains 600 genuine and spoof videos of 50 subjects, 12 videos (3 genuine and 9 spoof) were captured for each subject. This database consists of three imaging qualities and attacks, i.e. the warped photo attack, the cut photo attack (hides behind the cut photo and blink, another intact photo is up-down moved behind the cut one) and video attack. In [4], they design 7 testing scenarios, i.e. three imaging qualities, three fake face types and overall data (all data are used). In our experiments, we use all the videos (overall scenarios). The training and the test set consist of 20 subjects (60 live videos and 180 attack videos) and 30 subjects (90 live videos and 270 attack videos), respectively. As shown in Fig. 7, we detected and aligned faces in the video with the detector from MTCNN [2] and cropped them to 256 × 256. The same face alignment and cropping way also applied to the following two databases.

REPLAY-MOBILE Database. The REPLAY-MOBILE database [6] consists of 1190 videos of 40 subjects, i.e. 16 attack videos for each subject. This database has five different mobile scenarios, including the background of the scene that is uniform or complex, lighting conditions. Real client accesses were recorded under five different lighting conditions (controlled, adverse, direct, lateral and diffuse) [6]. In our experiments, we use 120 genuine videos and 192 spoof videos for training. The development set contains 160 real videos and 256 attack videos, and there are 110 live videos and 192 fake videos in the test set.

OULU-NPU Database. The OULU-NPU database [5] consists of 5940 real access and attack videos of 55 subjects (15 female and 40 male). The attacks contain both print and video-replay attacks. Furthermore, the print and video-replay attacks were produced using two different printers and display devices. We use 4950 genuine and spoof videos

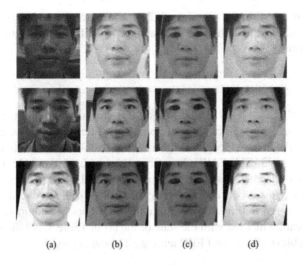

(a)   (b)   (c)   (d)

Fig. 7. Example images with different qualities of the CASIA FASD database. (a) genuine face image. (b) warped print photo attack. (c) cut print photo attack. (d) video attack.

in the public set [5] for testing. This database has three sessions with different illumination conditions, six different smartphones and four kinds of attacks, which has 90 videos for each client. The database is divided into three disjoint subsets, i.e. training set (20 users), development set (15 users) and testing set (20 users). In our experiments, two protocols were employed to evaluate the robustness of the proposed algorithm, i.e. protocol 1 for illumination variation and protocol 2 for presentation attack instruments (PAI) variation.

3.2 Performance Metrics

FAR (False Acceptance Rate) [3] is the ratio of the number of false acceptances and the number of negative samples. FRR (False Rejection Rate) is the ratio of the number of false rejections and the number of positive samples. The EER is the point in the ROC curve where the FAR equals the FRR. In our experiment, the results of CASIA-FASD are reported in EER. The Replay-mobile and OULU-NPU database are reported using the standardized ISO/IEC 30107-3 metrics [18], i.e. APCER (Attack Presentation Classification Error Rate) and BPCER (Bona Fide Presentation Classification Error Rate). The ACER (Average Classification Error Rate) is half of the sum of the APCER and the BPCER.

3.3 Experimental Settings

As the number of samples in publicly available datasets is very limited, CNN could easily over-fit when trained from scratch. So we fine-tune the ResNet-18 [16] model pre-trained on the ImageNet database. The proposed framework is implemented using the Caffe toolbox [19]. Size of input images is 256×256. The network is trained with a mini-batch size of 64. In the training of CNN, the learning rate is 0.0001; the decay rate is 0.0005; and the momentum during training is 0.9. These parameters are constant in our experiments.

3.4   Results

We first use the CASIA-FASD dataset to test the performance of different features, i.e. the temporal feature, the color based features in three different color space (RGB, HSV, and YCbCr), the patch based local feature, and their fusion. Table 2 details the EERs of different features on CASIA-FASD. It can be observed from the table that when only single feature is used, patch based local feature achieves the best performance, i.e. EER of 2.59%. After we fuse all different features, the EER is further reduced to 2.22%. This validates the proposed multiple deep feature method. Then we compare the proposed multiple deep feature method with the state of the art in Table 3. As shown in Table 3, our approach achieves the lowest EER among all of the approaches.

Table 2.   Performance of different features on the CASUA-FASD database.

Feature type	EER (%)
Temporal Feature	5.56
Color based feature (RGB)	3.33
Color based feature (HSV)	4.44
Color based feature (YCbCr)	3.33
Patch based local feature	2.59
Fusion	**2.22**

Table 3.   Performance comparison with the state of the art on the CASIA-FASD database.

Method	EER (%)
DOG [4]	17.00
IDA + SVM [1]	12.90
Color texture [12]	6.20
MUlti-cues integration + NN [13]	5.83
CNN [8]	4.64
DPCNN [15]	4.50
CSURF [17]	2.80
Patch and Depth [9]	2.67
Our method	**2.22**

Tables 4 and 5 lists the results of the proposed approach and the other methods on the REPLAY-MOBILE and the OULU-NPU databases, respectively. For the REPLAY-MOBILE database, our approach achieves much better performance than IQM and Gabor, i.e. no error was recorded. For the OULU-NPU dataset, the ACER on protocol 1 and 2 for our proposed method are 3.2% and 2.4%, respectively, which are much better than that of CPqD and GRADIANT. Overall, with the above experiments we can demonstrate the superiority of the proposed approach over the other methods.

Table 4. Performance comparison with the state of the art on the REPLAY-MOBILE database.

Method	Test (%)		
	APCER	BPCER	ACER
IQM [6]	19.87	7.40	13.64
Gabor [6]	7.91	11.15	9.53
Our method	**0.00**	**0.00**	**0.00**

Table 5. Performance comparison with the state of the art on the OULU-NPU database.

Protocol	Method	Dev (%)	Test (%)		
		EER	APCER	BPCER	ACER
1	Boulkenafet [5]	4.7	5.8	21.3	13.5
	CPqD [7]	0.6	**2.9**	10.8	6.9
	GRADIANT_extra [7]	0.7	7.1	5.8	6.5
	Our method	**0.56**	3.1	**3.3**	**3.2**
2	Boulkenafet [5]	4.1	22.5	6.7	14.6
	GRADIANT_extra [7]	0.7	6.9	2.5	4.7
	GRADIANT [7]	0.9	3.1	1.9	2.5
	Our method	**0.37**	**2.5**	**2.2**	**2.4**

4   Conclusions

In this paper, we proposed to employ the CNNs to learn discriminative multiple deep features from different cues of the face for face anti-spoofing. Because theses multiple features are complementary to each other, we further presented a strategy to integrate all the multiple features to boost the performance. We evaluated the proposed approach in three public databases and the experimental results demonstrated that the proposed approach can outperform the state of the art for face anti-spoofing. Regarding to the future work, we will conduct more cross-dataset experiments to investigate the generalization ability of the proposed method.

Acknowledgments. The work is supported by Natural Science Foundation of China under grands No. 61672357 and U1713214.

References

1. Wen, D., Han, H., Jain, A.K.: Face spoof detection with image distortion analysis. IEEE Trans. Inf. Forensics Secur. **10**(4), 746–761 (2015)
2. Zhang, K., Zhang, Z., Li, Z., Qiao, Y.: Joint face detection and alignment using multitask cascaded convolutional networks. IEEE Signal Process. Lett. **23**(10), 1499–1503 (2016)
3. Bengio, S., Mariéthoz, J.: A statistical significance test for person authentication. In: The Speaker and Language Recognition Workshop (Odyssey), pp. 237–244, Toledo (2004)
4. Zhang, Z., Yan, J., Liu, S., Lei, Z., Yi, D., Li, S. Z.: A Face antispoofing database with diverse attacks. In: IAPR International Conference on Biometrics, pp. 26–31 (2012)
5. Boulkenafet, Z., Komulainen, J., Li, L., Feng, X., Hadid, A.: OULU-NPU: a mobile face presentation attack database with real-world variations. In: IEEE International Conference on Automatic Face and Gesture Recognition, pp. 612–618 (2017)
6. Costa-Pazo, A., Bhattacharjee, S., Vazquez-Fernandez, E., Marcel, S.: The replay-mobile face presentation-attack database. In: Biometrics Special Interest Group (2016)
7. Boulkenafet, Z., Komulainen, J., Akhtar, Z., Benlamoudi, A., Samai, D., Bekhouche, S., et al.: A competition on generalized software-based face presentation attack detection in mobile scenarios. In: IEEE International Joint Conference on Biometrics (2017)
8. Yang, J., Lei, Z., Li, S.Z.: Learn convolutional neural network for face anti-spoofing. Comput. Sci. **9218**, 373–384 (2014)
9. Atoum, Y., Liu, Y., Jourabloo, A., Liu, X.: Face Anti-spoofing using patch and depth-based CNNs. In: IEEE International Joint Conference on Biometrics (2018)
10. Boulkenafet, Z., Komulainen, J., Hadid, A.: Face spoofing detection using colour texture analysis. IEEE Trans. Inf. Forensics Secur. **11**(8), 1818–1830 (2016)
11. Wang, Y., Nian, F., Li, T., Meng, Z., Wang, K.: Robust face anti-spoofing with depth information. J. Vis. Commun. Image Represent. **49**, 332–337 (2017)
12. Boulkenafet, Z., Komulainen, J., Hadid, A.: Face anti-spoofing based on colour texture analysis. In: IEEE International Conference on Image Processing, pp. 2636–2640 (2015)
13. Feng, L., Po, L.M., Li, Y., Xu, X., Yuan, F., Cheung, C.H., et al.: Integration of image quality and motion cues for face anti-spoofing. J. Vis. Commun. Image Represent. **38**(2), 451–460 (2016)
14. Pan, G., Sun, L., Wu, Z., Lao, S.: Eyeblink-based anti-spoofing in face recognition from a generic webcamera. In: IEEE International Conference on Computer Vision, pp. 1–8 (2007)
15. Li, L., Feng, X., Boulkenafet, Z., Xia, Z., Li, M., Hadid, A.: An original face anti-spoofing approach using partial convolutional neural network. In: International Conference on Image Processing Theory TOOLS and Applications, pp. 1–6. IEEE (2017)
16. He, K., Zhang, X., Ren, S., Sun, J.: Deep residual learning for image recognition. In: Computer Vision and Pattern Recognition, pp. 770–778 (2016)
17. Boulkenafet, Z., Komulainen, J., Hadid, A.: Face antispoofing using speeded-up robust features and fisher vector encoding. IEEE Sig. Process. Lett. **24**, 141–145 (2017)
18. ISO/IEC JTC 1/SC 37 Biometrics. Information technology - Biometric Presentation attack detection - Part 1: Framework. International Organization for Standardization (2016)
19. Jia, Y., Shelhamer, E., Donahue, J., Karayev, S., Long, J., Girshick, R., et al.: Caffe: convolutional architecture for fast feature embedding. In: 22nd ACM International Conference on Multimedia, pp. 675–678. ACM (2014)

Sensitive Information of Deep Learning Based Face Anti-spoofing Algorithms

Yukun Ma, Lifang Wu$^{(\boxtimes)}$, and Meng Jian

Faculty of Information Technology, Beijing University of Technology,
Beijing 100124, China
yukuner@126.com, lfwu@bjut.edu.cn, Jianmeng648@163.com

Abstract. Face anti-spoofing based on deep learning achieved good accuracy recently. However, deep learning model has no explicit mathematical presentation. Therefore, it is not clear about how the model works effectively. In this paper, we estimate the regions in face image, which are sensitive in deep learning based anti-spoofing algorithms. We first generate the adversarial examples from two different gradient-based methods. Then we analyze the distribution of the gradient and perturbations on the adversarial examples. And next we obtain the sensitive regions and evaluate the contribution of these regions to classification performance. By analyzing the sensitive regions, it could be observed that the CNN based anti-spoofing algorithms are sensitive to rich detailed regions and illumination. These observations are helpful to design an effective face anti-spoofing algorithm.

Keywords: Face anti-spoofing · Sensitive regions · Gradient
Convolutional neural networks · Adversarial example

1 Introduction

Face anti-spoofing is a critical technology in face based identification system. In the past decade, several methods on this problem have been proposed using various features, such as color texture [1], local shade [2] and optical flow [3] etc. These features are handcrafted and low-level, and the performance is limited. With the development of deep learning, face anti-spoofing based on Convolutional Neural Networks (CNN) achieved good performance [4, 5].

Despite the good performance, CNN is self-learning and without explicit mathematical expressions. Therefore, it is not clear that how it works. For face anti-spoofing task, what kind of information it will focus on is not clear. If we could find out this information, it will be helpful to design a more secure face identification system.

In this paper, we explore this problem from the perspective of adversarial example. The conception of adversarial example was proposed in 2013 by Szegedy C, which means that, applying a certain hardly perceptible perturbation on an image could make the network misclassify it [6]. In face anti-spoofing, which is a two-category problem, adversarial example sets up a bridge between genuine face and spoofing. And the distribution of perturbation can reflect the difference between the two classes in perspective of CNN.

© Springer Nature Switzerland AG 2018
J. Zhou et al. (Eds.): CCBR 2018, LNCS 10996, pp. 331–339, 2018.
https://doi.org/10.1007/978-3-319-97909-0_36

In this paper, we estimate the regions in face image, which are sensitive to deep learning based anti-spoofing algorithms. We first generate adversarial examples with two different gradient-based methods. Then we analyze the distribution of the gradient and perturbations on the adversarial examples. And next we obtain the sensitive regions and evaluate the contribution of these regions to classification performance. By analyzing the sensitive regions, it could be observed that the CNN based anti-spoofing algorithms are sensitive to rich detailed regions and illumination. These observations are helpful to design an effective face anti-spoofing algorithm.

The rest of paper is organized as follows. Section 2 of this paper analyzes neural networks. Section 3 generates the adversarial examples based on the gradient of CNN. Section 4 gives the experiment results and analysis. Finally, the paper is concluded in Sect. 5.

2   Analysis of Simplified Neural Networks

Deep neural networks can learn features that is more abstract through overlaying multiple nonlinear layers [7]. Neural cells are connected with different weights and biases that are learned by minimizing the loss function. The model training is conducted by back-propagating stochastic gradient descent [8]. Simplifying neural networks is helpful for us to understand the model theoretically.

Suppose that the input of CNN is a gray-scale image with only two pixels a_1 and a_2. The input vector is $X = (x_1, x_2)$, where x_i is the value of pixel a_i. Suppose a simple neural network implements a nonlinear function as follows:

$$F : [-20, 20]^2 \to [0, 1]$$

$$F(X) = sigmoid(w_1 \times x_1 + w_2 \times x_2 + b)$$

Where $sigmoid(x) = 1/(1 + e^{-x})$ is the typical activation function in neural networks. w_1 and w_2 are weights, and b is bias. Weights and bias are determined in training stage. The network classifies the input according to the value of $F(X)$. If $F(X) > 0.5$, it is classified as 1, otherwise it is 0.

Due to the different weights of each x_i, the gradient in each direction are not equal for a given input. Suppose $w_1 = 1$, $w_2 = 0.3$, and $b = 0$. If $X = (-2, 5)$, then the gradient is:

$$grad\, F\big|_{X=(-2,5)} = \left[\frac{\partial F(X)}{\partial x_1}, \frac{\partial F(X)}{\partial x_2}\right] = (0.2350, 0.0705) \tag{1}$$

$\frac{\partial F(X)}{\partial x_1}$ is greater than $\frac{\partial F(X)}{\partial x_2}$. It means that x_1 is more likely than x_2 to change the output F. In another word, the output of the network is more sensitive to x_1.

To a general neural network classifier for face anti-spoofing, the input is an color image of size $m \times n$, which can be represented as a $m \times n \times 3$ vector $X = (x_{1,1,1}, \cdots, x_{1,n,1}; \cdots, x_{m,n,1}; \cdots, x_{m,n,3})$, $x_{i,j,k} \in [0, 255]$. Because the function $F(X)$ is unknown, in order to analyze the effect of each pixel to output, we define the saliency map as gradient value $S = \nabla F(X)$:

$$S(X) = \nabla F(X) = \left(\frac{\partial F(X)}{\partial x_{1,1,1}}, \cdots, \frac{\partial F(X)}{\partial x_{m,n,3}} \right) \Bigg|_{x_{i,j,k}} \qquad (2)$$

Figure 1 shows the saliency map of a neural network classifier for R component in an input image. Abscissa axis in Fig. 1 is the width and height of input image $m \times n$ (28 × 28 in this paper). Vertical coordinates is the gradient vector of input image for output value, which is named as saliency map. We can see that the gradient amplitude on each pixel is very different, and pixels in the image have different effects on the output value. The greater the gradient amplitude is, the greater the effect of this pixel on the output is. For the input image X, changes on pixels that the gradient is 0 have nearly no effect on output. Therefore, the pixels with great gradient belong to the sensitive region for face anti-spoofing task.

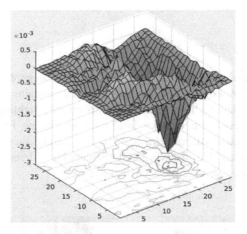

Fig. 1. The saliency map of R component in input image to the output of the neural networks. The size of the image is 28 × 28, and the vertical coordinate represents the saliency values.

3 Generate the Adversarial Examples

We introduce the concept of adversarial examples to analyze the relation of two classes. In 2013, Szegedy C found that, applying a certain hardly perceptible perturbation on an image could make the network misclassified [6]. This is named as the adversarial example. In face anti-spoofing task, which is a two-category problem, adversarial example adds certain perturbation on fake image to make the classifier believe it as genuine face. In other words, adversarial example sets up a bridge between genuine face and spoofing. And the distribution of perturbation can reflect the difference between the two classes in perspective of CNN.

At present, several methods to generate an adversarial example have been proposed [9–11]. In these methods, DeepFool [10] and method with minimum perturbation dimensions [11] are proposed based on the gradient value. DeepFool sets the perturbation on x_i dimension as formula (3), and it generates adversarial example by iteration until deceive the classifier successfully.

$$r_*(x_i) = -\frac{f(x_i)}{\|\nabla f(x_i)\|_2^2} \nabla f(x_i) \tag{3}$$

From formula (3) we can see that perturbations are greater on the dimensions that have greater gradient. Therefore, DeepFool is more effective and the resulted adversarial examples have smaller average distortion.

In 2018, Y. Ma proposed another method to generate adversarial examples with minimum perturbation dimensions [11], and perturbation is concentrated on a few dimensions with largest gradient. This method modifies only 1.36% on average of input dimensions to generate adversarial examples for spoofing the classifier.

In this paper, we generate adversarial examples based on above two methods as our analysis basis.

4   Experiments

Our experiment is conducted on Print Attack [12] face anti-spoofing dataset, which is released in 2011. The Print-Attack Replay Database contains 200 video clips of printed-photo attack attempts from 50 clients, under different lighting conditions. It also contains 200 real-access attempt videos from the same clients. Figure 2 shows some examples in Print Attack database. (a) and (b) are genuine faces and photo attacks respectively. We can see that, there is hardly perceptible difference between genuine faces and photo attacks, so the task is challenging.

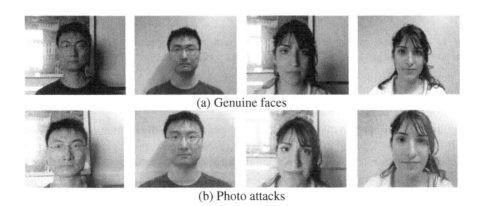

(a) Genuine faces

(b) Photo attacks

Fig. 2. Examples of Print Attack database

The CNN used for classification includes four convolutional layers and a softmax layer. The first two convolutional layers are followed by pooling layer. Network outputs two classes: genuine/fake. The details of the CNN model are presented in Table 1.

Table 1. Network architecture of face-spoofing detection classifier

Type	Filter size/Stride, Padding	Output size	Parameters
Input		$28 \times 28 \times 3$	
Conv1	$3 \times 3 \times 3/1,0$	$26 \times 26 \times 20$	540
Pool1	$2 \times 2/2$	$13 \times 13 \times 20$	
Conv2	$4 \times 4 \times 20/1,0$	$10 \times 10 \times 30$	9.6 k
Pool2	$2 \times 2/2$	$5 \times 5 \times 30$	
Conv3	$4 \times 4 \times 40/1,0$	$2 \times 2 \times 40$	25.6 k
Conv4	$2 \times 2 \times 40/1,0$	$1 \times 1 \times 50$	8 k
Softmax		2	100

We extract every frame of the video as the input of CNN classifier after face detection. Figure 3 shows an example of face detection results. Finally, we get total 72806 training images and 48451 testing images. The train CNN can get 1.72% HTER (Half Error Rate).

Fig. 3. Example of face detection result

Then we generate the adversarial examples of the testing images with DeepFool method and method with minimum perturbation dimensions. Figure 4 shows some clean examples, adversarial examples and corresponding perturbations. From the first row to the last row, they are clean examples, gradient of clean examples, adversarial examples with DeepFool method, perturbations with DeepFool method, adversarial examples with minimum perturbation dimensions, perturbations with minimum dimensions respectively.

In order to find the exact region that CNN is sensitive to, we calculate the average map of perturbations for all testing images, as shown in Fig. 5. From the average map, we can see that, perturbations are concentrated on right cheek. It means that right cheek is the region of interest for this CNN classifier, and the information contained in this region influences the final judgment result greatly.

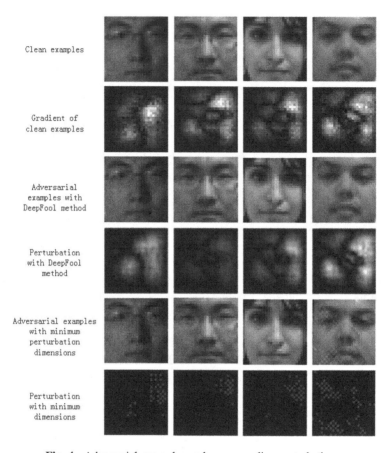

Clean examples

Gradient of clean examples

Adversarial examples with DeepFool method

Perturbation with DeepFool method

Adversarial examples with minimum perturbation dimensions

Perturbation with minimum dimensions

Fig. 4. Adversarial examples and corresponding perturbations.

(a)   (b)

Fig. 5. Average map of perturbations for all testing images. (a) DeepFool method (b) Method with minimum perturbation dimensions

To verify this conclusion, we choose several sub-regions on face like Fig. 6, and instead the other area with average face, as shown in Fig. 7. Among them, *A–E* regions account for 15.31% of the full image, and *F–G* regions is half of region *A*. Additionally, average face is the average of all training face image. In test, the network classifies the average face as genuine.

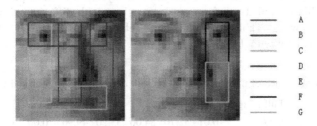

Fig. 6. Several sub-regions on face

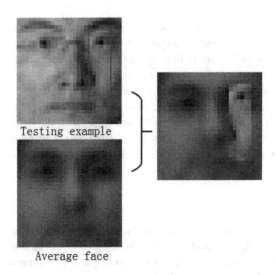

Fig. 7. Diagram of the operation to sample.

Table 2. Performance comparison with different sub-regions and full image

	Full image	A	B	C	D	E	F	G
FRR (%)	0.69	1.05	8.28	22.58	17.93	57.48	0.54	3.99
FAR (%)	2.74	19.43	33.45	41.59	6.06	67.58	20.71	29.81
HTER (%)	1.71	10.24	20.86	32.04	12.0	62.53	10.62	16.90

Table 2 compares the performance with different sub-regions and full image. Seen from Table 2, performance on full image is best. What's more, sub-region A achieves 10.24% HTER with 15.31% of full image, and the remaining 85% face region does not disturb it nearly. Sub-region F achieves 10.62% HTER which is close to sub-region A's, and F only accounts for the upper half region of A.

In order to validate our finding further, we design another CNN network with different structure. It contains five convolutional layers, and more parameters than network in Table 1. And its performance comparison with different sub-regions and full image are shown in Table 3. Among them, sub-region A and F can achieve lower HTER, which is tally with Table 2.

Table 3. Performance of the second network with different sub-regions and full image

	Full image	A	B	C	D	E	F	G
FRR (%)	0.57	0.01	32.70	84.06	33.20	49.96	0.60	0.14
FAR (%)	3.88	17.23	53.63	54.90	10.15	78.70	17.37	34.63
HTER (%)	2.23	8.62	43.16	69.48	21.68	64.33	8.99	17.39

In conclusion, we believe that, the network classifier aiming to face anti-spoofing is most sensitive to the area around right eye. The possible reason is that this area contains more high-frequency information like eyelash, eyeball, eye orbit and so on. Print attacks has less such information due to secondary imaging.

Another question that need to explain is why right eye is more sensitive than left eye. Because face has natural symmetry, two eyes should contribute equally in ideal condition. We analyze the database carefully and notice that, the light irradiate from left to right in most face images, as shown in Fig. 2 (first and third lines). In addition, the area has some rise and fall, and includes rich light and shadow information.

5   Conclusion

Face anti-spoofing based on Convolutional Neural Networks has achieved good performance, but the working principle inside is unknown yet. In this paper, we try to explore it based on gradient and adversarial examples. We generate the adversarial examples with DeepFool and method with minimum perturbation dimensions, which are both based on gradient, and find that most perturbations are concentrated on a certain region. That means that the network classifier is more sensitive to that region. Then we select several sub-regions to combine with average face, and test the HTER. The results show that region around right eye can have highest accuracy, and mainly dominates the judgement. This region contains more high-frequency information, light and shadow information, so we consider that Convolutional Neural Networks classifier for face anti-spoofing is focus on high-frequency information, light and shadow information. This discovery will be helpful to design a more secure face identification system.

References

1. Boulkenafet, Z., Komulainen, J., Hadid, A.: Face spoofing detection using colour texture analysis. IEEE Trans. Inf. Forensics Secur. **11**(8), 1818–1830 (2017)
2. Maatta, J., Hadid, A., Pietikainen, M.: Face spoofing detection from single images using texture and local shape analysis. IET Biometrics **1**(1), 3–10 (2012)
3. Wu, L., Xu, Y., Jian, M., Cai, W., Yan, C., Ma, Y.: Motion analysis based cross-database voting for face spoofing detection. In: Zhou, J., et al. (eds.) CCBR 2017. LNCS, vol. 10568, pp. 528–536. Springer, Cham (2017). https://doi.org/10.1007/978-3-319-69923-3_57
4. Li, L., Feng, X., Boulkenafet, Z., et al.: An original face anti-spoofing approach using partial convolutional neural network. In: International Conference on Image Processing Theory TOOLS and Applications, pp. 1–6. IEEE (2017)
5. Lucena, O., Junior, A., Moia, V., Souza, R., Valle, E., Lotufo, R.: Transfer learning using convolutional neural networks for face anti-spoofing. In: Karray, F., Campilho, A., Cheriet, F. (eds.) ICIAR 2017. LNCS, vol. 10317, pp. 27–34. Springer, Cham (2017). https://doi.org/10.1007/978-3-319-59876-5_4
6. Szegedy, C., Zaremba, W., Sutskever, I., Bruna, J., Erhan, D., Goodfellow, I.J., Fergus, R.: Intriguing properties of neural networks. In: ICLR, abs/1312.6199 (2014)
7. Yin, B., Wang, W., Wang, L.: Review of Deep Learning. J. Beijing Univ. Technol. **1**, 48–59 (2015)
8. Rumelhart, D.E., Hinton, G.E., Williams, R.J.: Learning representations by back-propagating errors. Readings Cogn. Sci. **323**(6088), 399–421 (1988)
9. Goodfellow, I.J., Shlens, J., Szegedy, C.: Explaining and harnessing adversarial examples. In: ICML, pp. 1–10 (2015)
10. Moosavidezfooli, S.M., Fawzi, A., Frossard, P.: DeepFool: a simple and accurate method to fool deep neural networks. Computer Vision and Pattern Recognition. IEEE, pp. 2574–2582 (2016)
11. Ma, Y., Wu, L., Jian, M., Liu, F., Yang, Z.: Approach to generate adversarial examples for face-spoofing detection. J. Softw. http://www.jos.org.cn/jos/ch/reader/view_abstract.aspx?file_no=5568
12. Anjos, A., Marcel, S.: Counter-measures to photo attacks in face recognition: a public database and a baseline. In: International Joint Conference on Biometrics, pp. 1–7. IEEE (2011)

Weighted Softmax Loss for Face Recognition via Cosine Distance

Hu Zhang$^{(\boxtimes)}$, Xianliang Wang, and Zhixiang He

Beijing Hisign Corp., Ltd., Hanwei International Square, Area 4, no. 186, West Road, 4th South Ring Road, Fengtai District, Beijing 100160, China
{zhanghu, wangxianliang, hezhixiang}@hisign.com.cn

Abstract. Softmax loss is commonly used to train convolutional neural networks (CNNs), but it treats all samples equally. Focal loss focus on training hard samples and takes the probability as the measurement of whether the sample is easy or hard one. In this paper, we use cosine distance of features and the corresponding centers as weight and propose weighted softmax loss (called C-Softmax). Unlike focal loss, we give greater weight to easy samples. Experiment results show that the proposed C-Softmax loss can train many well known models like ResNet, ResNeXt, DenseNet and Inception V3, and the performance of the proposed loss is better than softmax loss and focal loss.

Keywords: Face recognition · Focal loss · Softmax loss · C-Softmax loss

1 Introduction

Over the past few years, due to the success of convolutional neural networks, the accuracy of face recognition has improved greatly. Although there are many new loss functions [1–5], the most commonly used one is still softmax loss, which mainly optimizes the inter-class difference, and gives same weight to all samples. Although most training samples are easy samples in face recognition, there are still hard samples. These hard samples may degrade the generalization performance of the model. Focal loss [6] is proposed for dense object detection, it down-weights the loss assigned to easy samples, and focuses on training hard samples in order to prevent the vast number of easy samples from overwhelming the model during training. Although its performance is better, it is difficult to apply to face recognition, because most of the time, the number of training samples of one subject is not large. Meanwhile, we think it is unreasonable to measure the difficulty of training samples by probability. One main difference between face recognition and detection is the variation of one person is small (although there are still changes in pose, expression and illuminations), and thus we can obtain the feature's centers of each subject. We think it is more reasonable to use the angle between features and its corresponding centers than probability to measure whether it is easy sample or hard one. We also think it may degrade the generalization performance of the model when focus on training hard samples, so we give greater weight to those easy samples. In this paper, we use cosine distance of features and its corresponding centers as the weight and propose a new loss function called C-Softmax loss.

J. Zhou et al. (Eds.): CCBR 2018, LNCS 10996, pp. 340–348, 2018.
https://doi.org/10.1007/978-3-319-97909-0_37

The advantages of C-Softmax loss is as follows: 1. It is easier to convergence than L-Softmax [4] and A-Softmax [5]. When training data has too many subjects, the convergence of L-Softmax and A-Softmax will be more difficult than softmax loss, and thus they used a learning strategy. The proposed loss is based on softmax loss, so it is easy to convergence. 2. It does not need any pre-trained model. Both COCO loss [7] and NormFace [8] use a pre-trained model and fine tune the model by their loss. We use softmax loss in the first few epochs to get the rough centers, which could not be considered as the pre-trained model, because the total number of training epoch remains unchanged, and the performance of the model is poor at this time. 3. It does not need to design pair selection procedure like triplet loss [2] and contrastive loss [3].

Although C-Softmax has many advantages, it still faces some problems. One main problem is it has to maintain feature centers like center loss [1], and we update feature centers the same way center loss does. Another problem is we have to train the model by softmax in the first few epochs, and decrease the number of epoch by C-Softmax loss, so as to keep the total number of training epoch unchanged.

2 Related Work

Given an input image x_i with label y_i, original softmax loss function is defined as:

$$Ls = -\frac{1}{m}\sum_{i=1}^{m}\log(\frac{e^{W_{y_i}^T f(x_i) + b_{y_i}}}{\sum_{j=1}^{n} e^{W_j^T f(x_i) + b_j}})\tag{1}$$

where m is the batch size, n is the number of training class, $f(x_i)$ is the feature, $W \in R^{n \times d}$ and $b \in R^n$ are the weight and bias of the fully-connected layer before softmax loss, W_j is the j-th column of W and d is the feature dimension.

Focal loss [6] is proposed for dense object detection. It is used to handle extreme imbalance between foreground and background classes. The α-balanced variant of the focal loss is defined as:

$$FL(p_t) = -\alpha_t(1 - p_t)^\gamma \log(p_t)\tag{2}$$

$$p_t = \begin{cases} p_i & \text{if } y_i = 1 \\ 1 - p_i & \text{otherwise} \end{cases}\tag{3}$$

$$\alpha_t = \begin{cases} \alpha & \text{if } y_i = 1 \\ 1 - \alpha & \text{otherwise} \end{cases}\tag{4}$$

where $\alpha \in [0, 1]$ is a weighting factor, $p_i \in [0, 1]$ is the model's estimated probability for the class with label $y_i = 1$, γ is set to 2 in the paper.

We can apply focal loss to face recognition. But the performance is worse than softmax loss. We think the reason is that it is unreasonable to use probability to measure the degree of difficulty of samples, and it may degrade the performance when focus on training hard samples. Inspired by focal loss, we modified softmax loss and proposed weighted Softmax loss via Cosine Distance (C-Softmax) to train deep models for face recognition.

3 Proposed C-Softmax Loss

Given two vectors $f \in R^d$ and $C \in R^d$, the cosine distance of them is:

$$d = \frac{f \cdot c^T}{\|f\|_2 \|c\|_2} \tag{5}$$

The range of the cosine distance is $[-1, 1]$. The greater the distance, the more similar these two vectors is. The proposed C-Softmax loss is defined as:

$$CS_i = -w_i^r \times \log(p_i) \tag{6}$$

where w_i is the modified cosine distance of the current features f_i and the corresponding centers c_i. γ is set to 2, so there is no hyper-parameter in C-Softmax loss. As the angle between the feature and its corresponding center is greater than $90°$, the weight is negative, so w_i is defined as follows to keep its monotony.

$$w_i = \begin{cases} d & \text{if } d \geq 10^{-6} \\ 10^{-6} & \text{otherwise} \end{cases} \tag{7}$$

We do not use α-balanced variant of C-Softmax loss in order to keep it concise. If all the weights are 1, then C-Softmax loss becomes softmax loss. If the weight of hard examples are greater than easy ones, C-Softmax loss is more like focal loss.

4 Results and Analysis

4.1 Experiment Details

Experiment Settings: We implement the proposed loss using PyTorch [11] framework. The face landmarks are detected by MTCNN [12]. The aligned face images are of size 112 * 96. The weight decay is $5e^{-4}$. The batch size is 256 and we use stochastic gradient descent to train the model. The learning rate begins with 0.1 and is divided by 10 at 11, 16 and 19 epochs, and finishes at 20 epochs. There are three ways to obtain the centers. 1 initialize the centers randomly and train the model by C-Softmax from the beginning. 2 fine tune the model by C-Softmax loss from a pre-trained model and the corresponding centers. 3 train the model by Softmax for a few epochs and by C-Softmax for the remaining epochs. For the first one, the centers could not be 0 because the cos distance between vector **0** and any vector is 0, result in C-Softmax loss always be 0. When the centers is initialized improper (cosine distance of the features and its centers is negative), the performance of C-Softmax loss will be bad. We will get the best performance with the second way, but it will consume twice as much time (train by softmax and fine tune by C-Softmax). We choose the third way. The feature's centers are more stable when the epochs trained by softmax loss increases and the epochs trained by C-Softmax decreases as the total number of training epochs is fixed. We found the performance is the best when trained with softmax for 3 epochs. So we set all centers to be 0 at the beginning, train the model by softmax loss for 3 epochs, and update the centers like center loss. We use C-Softmax loss to train the model from epoch 4, the training finishes at 20 epochs.

Network Structure: We compare the performance of different loss functions with four network structures. model-A is the same as [5]. model-B has Batch Normalization (BN) [13] layer after FC1 layer. Model-C has BN layer after each convolution layer and FC1 layer. Model-D uses RReLU [14] instead of PReLU [15] as activation function, and it has BN layer after each convolution layer and FC1 layer.

Training: We use CASIA-WebFace [9] to train our CNN models. CASIA-WebFace has 494414 face images belonging to 10575 different individuals. In [16] they reported 17 overlapped identities between CASIA-WebFace and LFW [10], and 42 overlapped identities between CASIA-WebFace and MegaFace [17] set1. We checked their result and found 3 mismatched overlapped identities, meanwhile we also found another 5 overlapped identities, so there are totally 19 overlapped identities between CASIA-WebFace and LFW. We removed all these 61 identities, and use the remaining 447020 images from 10541 identities to train the model.

Evaluation: We extract the features from the output of the FC1 layer, and if there is BN layer after FC1 layer, we thus use the output of BN layer as the features instead. Features from the original image and its horizontally flipped one are extracted, and then merged by element-wise mean as the representation. The dimension of the feature is 512. We use LFW [10] and MegaFace [17] set1 for evaluation. We follow the unrestricted with labeled outside data protocol [18] on both datasets. We also evaluate the performance through BLUFR protocols [19], it is more challenging and generalized for LFW because it utilize all 13233 images while the standard evaluation protocol only evaluated on 6000 image pairs.

4.2 Experiment Results

The 3 to 5 columns in Table 1 show the performance of different network structures trained with A-Softmax loss [5], softmax loss, center loss [1], focal loss [6] and the proposed C-Softmax loss. We can see that the performance of A-Softmax with model-A and model-B are both good, but when BN layer is added after convolution layer, DIR@FAR = 1% drops from 82.03% to 75.99%. Although it increases to 80.61% when use RReLU (model-D), the performance is still lower than the original model.

When BN layer is added after FC1 layer (changed from model-A to model-B), and trained with softmax loss, focal loss and center loss, the performance of DIR@ FAR = 1% increase greatly. The performance are further improved when BN layer is added after each convolution layer (model-C). When we replace PReLU with RReLU, the performance of these three loss all decrease (model-D). Although focal loss outperforms softmax loss in dense object detection [6], its performance is worse than softmax loss in face recognition.

Although the performance of the C-Softmax loss is not very good to train model-A, it works quite well with other three model structures. DIR@FAR = 1% increases to 86.17% when trained model-D, and it outperforms the performance of model-B trained with A-Softmax loss, which is 82.03%. Meanwhile, C-Softmax loss outperforms both focal loss and softmax loss when trained with same model (except model-A), and the improvement is obvious. The improvement benefits from not only the cosine distance instead of probability as the measurement of easy or hard samples, but also gives greater weight to easy samples than hard samples. We ignored some difficult samples, but the generalization performance of the model was improved. If the proportion of hard samples in the training datasets is low, and we focus on training them, it may degrade the generalization performance of the model, like focal loss used in face recognition. Otherwise we should give greater weight to hard samples and focus on training them, like focal loss used in object detection [6].

As is analyzed in [13], the distributions of features trained by softmax changed significantly over time without BN layer, both in mean and variance, and the features are not necessarily discriminative [5]. On the contrary, A-Softmax can learn discriminative features [5]. Focal loss and C-Softmax loss are both based on softmax loss, so the features are not as discriminative as A-Softmax loss. This is why the performance

Table 1. Performance (%) comparison for different loss functions with different structures on LFW and MegaFace dataset.

Model	Loss	LFW			MegaFace	
		Acc.	VR@FAR = 0.1%	DIR@FAR = 1%	Rank-1	VR@FAR = 10^{-6}
Model-A	A-Softmax loss	**99.12**	**97.7**	**81.75**	**62.77**	**72.48**
	Softmax loss	97.55	87.6	59.82	49.79	55.48
	Center loss	98.01	91.7	68.96	59.42	67.74
	Focal loss	97.38	84.87	58.05	49.25	54.45
	C-Softmax loss	97	82.93	63.29	47.53	52.79
Model-B	A-Softmax loss	**99.2**	**97.56**	**82.03**	**64.81**	**75.97**
	Softmax loss	98.61	93.53	75.43	61.82	73.65
	Center loss	98.5	93.53	76.55	62.2	75.17
	Focal loss	98.32	92.27	72.6	60.45	72.31
	C-Softmax loss	98.78	93.6	80.93	61.93	74.11
Model-C	A-Softmax loss	**99.16**	96.67	75.99	58.93	68.18
	Softmax loss	98.57	95.5	77.41	64.46	78.01
	Center loss	98.62	95.73	77.81	64.59	78.85
	Focal loss	98.36	94	75.93	63.26	76.27
	C-Softmax loss	99.1	**96.93**	**83.17**	**65.41**	**79.67**
Model-D	A-Softmax loss	99.15	96.47	80.61	63.48	74.93
	Softmax loss	98.38	89.43	76.05	63.13	74.51
	Center loss	98.48	94.1	76.65	63.5	74.54
	Focal loss	98.33	90.33	71.72	61.01	71.56
	C-Softmax loss	**99.2**	**98.2**	**86.17**	**68.66**	**83.15**

of model-A trained by softmax loss, focal loss and C-Softmax loss are poor. BN layer makes the distribution of the features more stable as training progresses and reduces the internal covariate shift [13], so the performance of the model trained by softmax loss, focal loss and C-Softmax loss improved greatly when BN layer is added, and the features are necessarily discriminative. At this time, BN layer may affect discriminant performance of A-Softmax loss.

From the above analysis we can also see that no loss function can work quite well with all structures. A-Softmax is more suitable for models without BN layer after convolution layer, while others are more suitable for models with it. A-Softmax and C-Softmax are more suitable for models with RReLU layer, while others are more suitable for models with PReLU layer. And we should train model with the most suitable loss function, so as to get best performance.

Table 2 list the accurate of different methods on LFW. Some methods use their own dataset, like FaceNet [2]; some methods trained on MS-Celeb-1 M [20], like SeqFace [21], ArcFace [22]; some methods trained on CASIA-WebFace [9], like LGM [23], NormFace [8]. We have the following observations. First, the performance of the methods trained on large datasets (The number of images is more than 1M) are quite good. Second, the performance will be further improved with more layers. The number of layers of SeqFace [21], SeqFace [21] and Ring Loss [24] are all greater than or equal to 64 layer, and their accurate are very high. Third, the performance of the proposed method is equal or better than LGM [23], NormFace [8] and AM-Softmax [16] when trained on the same dataset (Strictly speaking, the training images we used is the least). Generally speaking, we obtain state of the art performance by using the least number of training images.

Table 2. Detailed information and verification accuracy (%) of different methods on LFW

Method	Images	Networks	Layers	Acc. on LFW
FaceNet [2]	200M	1	–	99.63
CosFace [25]	5M	1	64	99.73
SeqFace [21]	4M+	1	64	99.83
ArcFace [22]	3.8M	1	100	99.83
Ring loss [24]	3.5M	1	64	99.52
Baidu [26]	1.2M	10	9	99.77
Center loss [1]	0.7M	1	27	99.28
SphereFace [5]	0.49M	1	64	99.42
LGM [23]	0.49M	1	27	99.2
NormFace [8]	0.49M	1	27	99.19
AM-Softmax [16]	0.44M	1	20	99.17
Proposed	0.44M	1	20	99.2

The last two columns in Table 1 show rank-1 identification accuracy with 1 M distractors and verification TAR for 10^{-6} FAR of various loss functions on MegaFace set1. C-Softmax outperforms the other loss functions and gets the best result when trained with the most suitable model.

To make our experiment more convincing, we also trained simplified Inception V3 [27], DenseNet [28], ResNeXt [29] with softmax loss, center loss [1], focal loss [6] and C-Softmax loss. The depth of Inception V3 is 37. The depth of ResNeXt is 29 with cardinality = 32 and bottleneck width = 4d. The depth of DenseNet is 21 with growth rate = 32, dense blocks = 4 while each have 2 layers. Table 3 lists the results. C-Softmax loss outperforms other loss functions and gets the best result with all these models.

Table 3. Performance (%) on LFW dataset with other well known models

Model	Loss	Acc.	VR@FAR = 0.1%	DIR@FAR = 1%
Inception V3	Softmax loss	98.45	92.56	71.38
	Center loss	**98.8**	94.77	71.35
	Focal loss	98.22	92.4	68.67
	C-Softmax loss	98.65	**97.47**	**76.62**
DenseNet	Softmax loss	97.33	86.87	60.74
	Center loss	97.51	85.93	64.16
	Focal loss	97.41	86.53	59.76
	C-Softmax loss	**98.17**	**93.73**	**71.29**
ResNeXt	Softmax loss	98.53	92.67	71.83
	Center loss	98.58	93.77	74.07
	Focal loss loss	98.17	91.4	69.18
	C-Softmax loss	**99**	**97.3**	**80.71**

5 Conclusion

Inspired by focal loss, we proposed a new loss function called C-Softmax loss in this paper. Firstly, we use the cosine distance of the features and the corresponding centers as the measurement of whether the sample is easy or hard, and add it as the modulating factor to the softmax loss. Secondly, we give greater weight to easy samples than hard samples in training phase. There is no hyper-parameter in the proposed loss. The results show that the proposed loss function provides a significant and consistent boost over softmax loss and focal loss, and can be used to train other well known models like ResNet, ResNeXt, DenseNet and Inception V3.

References

1. Wen, Y., Zhang, K., Li, Z., Qiao, Y.: A discriminative feature learning approach for deep face recognition. In: Leibe, B., Matas, J., Sebe, N., Welling, M. (eds.) ECCV 2016. LNCS, vol. 9911, pp. 499–515. Springer, Cham (2016). https://doi.org/10.1007/978-3-319-46478-7_31
2. Schroff, F., Kalenichenko, D., Philbin, J.: FaceNet: a unified embedding for face recognition and clustering. In: IEEE Conference on Computer Vision and Pattern Recognition, pp. 815–823 (2015)

3. Hadsell, R., Chopra, S., Lecun, Y.: Dimensionality reduction by learning an invariant mapping. In: 2006 IEEE Computer Society Conference on Computer Vision and Pattern Recognition, pp. 1735–1742 (2006)
4. Liu, W., Wen, Y., Yu, Z., Yang, M.: Large-margin softmax loss for convolutional neural networks. In: ICML, pp. 507–516 (2016)
5. Liu, W., Wen, Y., Yu, Z., Li, M., Raj, B., Song, L.: SphereFace: deep hypersphere embedding for face recognition. In: IEEE Conference on Computer Vision and Pattern Recognition, pp. 212–220 (2017)
6. Lin, T.Y., Goyal, P., Girshick, R., He, K., Dollár, P.: Focal loss for dense object detection. arXiv preprint arXiv:1708 (2017)
7. Liu, Y., Li, H., Wang, X.: Rethinking feature discrimination and polymerization for large-scale recognition. arXiv preprint arXiv:1710.00870 (2017)
8. Wang, F., Xiang, X., Cheng, J., Yuille, A.L.: NormFace: L2 hypersphere embedding for face verification. arXiv preprint arXiv:1704.06369 (2017)
9. Yi, D., Lei, Z., Liao, S., Li, S.Z.: Learning face representation from scratch. arXiv preprint arXiv:1411.7923 (2014)
10. Huang, G.B., Mattar, M., Berg, T., Learned-Miller, E.: Labeled faces in the wild: a database for studying face recognition in unconstrained environments. Technical report, University of Massachusetts (2007)
11. Paszke, A., Gross, S., Chintala, S., Chanan, G.: PyTorch: tensors and dynamic neural networks in Python with strong GPU acceleration (2017)
12. Zhang, K., Zhang, Z., Li, Z., Qiao, Y.: Joint face detection and alignment using multitask cascaded convolutional networks. IEEE Sig. Process. Lett. **23**, 1499–1503 (2016)
13. Ioffe, S., Szegedy, C.: Batch normalization: accelerating deep network training by reducing internal covariate shift. arXiv preprint arXiv:1502.03167 (2015)
14. Xu, B., Wang, N., Chen, T., Li, M.: Empirical evaluation of rectified activations in convolutional network. arXiv preprint arXiv:1505.00853 (2015)
15. He, K., Zhang, X., Ren, S., Sun, J.: Delving deep into rectifiers: surpassing human-level performance on ImageNet classification. In: Proceedings of the IEEE International Conference on Computer Vision, pp. 1026–1034 (2015)
16. Wang, F., Liu, W., Liu, H., Cheng, J.: Additive margin softmax for face verification. arXiv preprint arXiv:1801.05599 (2018)
17. Kemelmachershlizerman, I., Seitz, S.M., Miller, D., Brossard, E.: The MegaFace benchmark: 1 million faces for recognition at scale. In: Proceedings of the IEEE Conference on Computer Vision and Pattern Recognition, pp. 4873–4882 (2016)
18. Huang, G.B., Learned-Miller, E.: Labeled faces in the wild: updates and new reporting procedures. Technical report, Department of Computer Science, University of Massachusetts Amherst, Amherst (2014)
19. Liao, S., Lei, Z., Yi, D., Li, S.Z.: A benchmark study of large-scale unconstrained face recognition. In: 2014 IEEE International Joint Conference on Biometrics (IJCB), pp. 1–8 (2014)
20. Guo, Y., Zhang, L., Hu, Y., He, X., Gao, J.: MS-Celeb-1M: a dataset and benchmark for large-scale face recognition. In: Leibe, B., Matas, J., Sebe, N., Welling, M. (eds.) ECCV 2016. LNCS, vol. 9907, pp. 87–102. Springer, Cham (2016). https://doi.org/10.1007/978-3-319-46487-9_6
21. Hu, W., Huang, Y., Zhang, F., Li, R., Li, W., Yuan, G.: SeqFace: make full use of sequence information for face recognition. arXiv preprint arXiv:1803.06524 (2018)
22. Deng, J., Guo, J., Zafeiriou, S.: ArcFace: additive angular margin loss for deep face recognition. arXiv preprint arXiv:1801.07698 (2018)

23. Wan, W., Zhong, Y., Li, T., Chen, J.: Rethinking feature distribution for loss functions in image classification. arXiv preprint arXiv:1803.02988 (2018)
24. Zheng, Y., Pal, D.K., Savvides, M.: Ring loss: convex feature normalization for face recognition. arXiv preprint arXiv:1803.00130 (2018)
25. Wang, H., et al.: CosFace: large margin cosine loss for deep face recognition. arXiv preprint arXiv:1801.09414 (2018)
26. Liu, J., Deng, Y., Bai, T., Wei, Z., Huang, C.: Targeting ultimate accuracy: face recognition via deep embedding. arXiv preprint arXiv:1506.07310 (2015)
27. Szegedy, C., Vanhoucke, V., Ioffe, S., Shlens, J., Wojna, Z.: Rethinking the inception architecture for computer vision. In: Proceedings of the IEEE Conference on Computer Vision and Pattern Recognition, pp. 2818–2826 (2015)
28. Huang, G., Liu, Z., Weinberger, K.Q., Laurens, V.D.M.: Densely connected convolutional networks. In: Proceedings of the IEEE Conference on Computer Vision and Pattern Recognition, vol. 1 (2017)
29. Xie, S., Girshick, R., Dollár, P., Tu, Z., He, K.: Aggregated residual transformations for deep neural networks. In: 2017 IEEE Conference on Computer Vision and Pattern Recognition, pp. 5987–5995 (2017)

Improving Large Pose Face Alignment by Regressing 2D and 3D Landmarks Simultaneously and Visibility Refinement

Xu Luo, Pengfei Li, Fuxuan Chen, and Qijun Zhao[✉]

National Key Laboratory of Fundamental Science on Synthetic Vision,
College of Computer Science, Sichuan University, Chengdu, China
qjzhao@scu.edu.cn

Abstract. This paper proposes an improved method for large pose face alignment. Unlike existing methods, the proposed method regresses both 2D and 3D coordinates of facial landmarks simultaneously. It first computes a coarse estimation of the landmarks via a shape regression network (SRN) whose input is only the input image. It then refines the landmarks with another SRN whose input consists of three components: the transformed image, the visible landmark heatmap and the feature map from the first SRN. These components are constructed by a transformation module based on the current estimates of 3D and 2D landmarks. By effectively exploring the 3D property of faces for constraining 2D landmarks and refining their visibility, the proposed method can better align faces under large poses. Extensive experiments on three public databases demonstrate the superiority of the proposed method in large pose face alignment.

Keywords: Face alignment · 3D/2D facial landmarks
Cascaded shape regression · Visible landmark heatmap

1 Introduction

Face alignment, also known as facial landmarks detection, aims at detecting facial key points (such as eye-corners, nose tip, and mouth corners) on face images, which is fundamental to many face-related tasks, e.g., expression recognition, 3D face reconstruction and face recognition. The last decade has witnessed significant progresses in face alignment. With the introduction of cascaded regression [1], many state-of-the-art face alignment methods achieve high precision in detecting the landmarks in frontal and near-frontal (i.e., yaw rotation angles are within ±60°) face images. However, they may still fail in challenging large pose face alignment, due to self-occlusion and unreliable features around invisible landmarks on the face images.

Many recent methods [2–6] use convolutional neural networks (CNN) to learn more effective features rather than using hand-crafted features for detecting

© Springer Nature Switzerland AG 2018
J. Zhou et al. (Eds.): CCBR 2018, LNCS 10996, pp. 349–357, 2018.
https://doi.org/10.1007/978-3-319-97909-0_38

facial landmarks. Some other recent methods resort to 3D face models [7–9] to improve the robustness of facial landmarks detection to large pose variations, from which 2D-based methods suffer. Such 3D-based methods generally fit a 3D morphable face model (3DMM) [11] to the input 2D face image and infer landmarks from the reconstructed 3D face via 3D-to-2D projection. Despite the significant progresses made by CNN-based methods [2–6] and 3D-based methods [7–10], large pose face alignment is still a challenging problem.

In this paper, we propose an improved method to solve the large pose facial landmarks detection problem. Instead of fitting a 3DMM, we directly regress 3D landmarks based on CNN to refine 2D landmarks. It imposes a strong shape constraint to the 2D landmarks. To exclude unreliable features around invisible landmarks, we estimate the visibility of the landmarks based on the obtained 3D coordinates, and generate a visible landmark heatmap that can facilitate the extraction of pose-robust features. Evaluation results on three public benchmark databases with comparison to state-of-the-art methods prove the effectiveness of our proposed method.

2 Related Work

Many methods utilize 3D face alignment to refine 2D face alignment for large pose faces considering the limitation of 2D-based methods in dealing with self-occlusion. Zhu et al. [9] proposed a method called 3D Dense Face Alignment (3DDFA), which generated PNCC map from the obtained 3D face shape and stacked it with the input image as the input to the next stage. Although having well advanced the state-of-the-art of face alignment, like most existing 3D-based methods [7,8], it still has difficulties in dealing with near profile faces because it does not explicitly consider invisible landmarks. Chen et al. [10] refined 2D face landmarks by using 3D landmarks that were regressed from hand-crafted features. These 3D-based methods, regressing either 3DMM parameters or 3D coordinates, compute 2D landmarks via projecting the obtained 3D landmarks onto 2D images. In this paper, instead, we regress directly both 3D and 2D coordinates of the landmarks with learned features, and use the 3D landmarks as a strong shape constraint to refine the 2D landmarks.

Various types of feature maps have been used to assure focusing on the region of interest and extracting more robust features. DAN [5] aims at detecting visible facial contour points and utilizes landmark heatmaps to constrain the region of interest from which features are extracted. However, the heatmaps in DAN do not consider the visibility of landmarks, and would thus lead to unreliable features around invisible landmarks. The PNCC feature maps [9] are obtained by projecting 3D face shapes onto 2D plane via z-buffering. The Z-Buffer representation is, however, not differentiable, preventing end-to-end training. In our work, we utilize the regressed 3D landmarks to estimate the visibility of each landmark and generate heatmaps based on the visible landmarks. This way, we can better ensure that more robust features are learned.

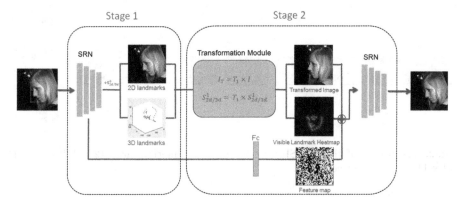

Fig. 1. The main steps in our proposed method, which regresses the landmarks in two stages. The first stage coarsely estimates the residual of 2D and 3D landmarks with respect to the landmarks' initial estimates (i.e., the mean locations in frontal view). The second stage refines the estimated 2D and 3D landmarks by taking the transformed image (I_T), the visible landmark heatmap and the feature map from the prior stage as input, which are generated by the transformation module. In practice, the second stage can be repeated, resulting in a deeper cascade structure, though we implement only two stages in this paper.

3 Proposed Method

3.1 Overview

Figure 1 shows the main steps in our proposed method, which consists of two stages. In the first stage, a Shape Regression Network (SRN) is employed to generate coarse estimates of both 2D and 3D landmarks for the input face image. Unlike general 3D-based face alignment methods that need to fit a 3DMM, we directly regress 3D landmarks and their corresponding semantically consistent 2D landmarks.

In the second stage, another SRN is deployed to refine the estimated 3D and 2D landmarks. To fully explore the knowledge obtained in the first stage, we combine the information from three different sources to form the input of the SRN, specifically, the transformed input image, the heatmap of currently estimated visible 2D landmarks, and a feature map from the first stage SRN. In the transformation module, the transformation applied to the input image as well as the 2D landmarks, and the visibility of 2D landmarks are computed.

3.2 Shape Regression Network

As shown in Fig. 2, the structure of SRN is inspired by the VGG network [12]. While the SRNs in the two stages share similar structure, they differ in their inputs: The input of the first SRN is the original input image; but the input of the second SRN is a combination of the transformed input image, visible landmark

Fig. 2. The inputs of the two SRN in our proposed method are $112 \times 112 \times 1$ and $112 \times 112 \times 3$, respectively.

heatmap and a feature map from the first SRN. These three components are generated in the transformation module and stacked across channel. Each SRN regresses simultaneously 2D and 3D shape ΔS_{2d} and ΔS_{3d}, which are used to update the current estimates of 2D landmarks S_{2d} and 3D landmarks S_{3d}.

3.3   Transformation Module

The transformation module generates the input for the second SRN based on the output of the first SRN. Specifically, it transforms the input image as well as its 2D landmarks to a canonical frontal view via an affine transformation. The parameters involved in the transformation (denoted by T) are estimated by minimizing the error between the transformed 2D landmarks and the mean 2D landmarks on frontal face images ($\hat{S}_{2d}^F$):

$$\arg \min_{T} ||\hat{S}_{2d}^F - T \times S_{2d}||_2^2. \tag{1}$$

with the computed affine transformation, the original input face image and its 2D landmarks are transformed accordingly with bilinear interpolation.

Since the transformed image is used as input to the second SRN, its regressed shape residuals should be transformed back to the coordinate system of the original input image. Hence, the refined 2D/3D landmarks in the second stage are computed as follows,

$$S_{2d/3d}^2 = T_2^{-1} \times (T_2 \times S_{2d/3d}^1 + \Delta S_{2d/3d}^2) \tag{2}$$

where $\Delta S_{2d/3d}^2$ is the output of the SRN of stage 2, T_2^{-1} is the inverse of transform T_2.

Note that the visibility of the landmarks is not considered so far. Fortunately, the estimated 3D landmarks can be used to determine the visibility. Let M denote the weak perspective projection matrix from 3D to 2D. We compute it by minimizing the fitting error between the 3D and 2D landmarks. Given the 3D landmarks and the 3D-to-2D projection matrix, we can compute the visibility of the corresponding 2D landmarks. More detail will be given in the next subsection.

3.4   Visible Landmark Heatmap

To utilize landmark heatmap to improve the quality of extracted features especially for large pose faces, we need to estimate the visibility of each facial landmark based on the corresponding 3D and 2D landmarks. The computation of visibility is proposed in [7]:

$$v = sign(\overrightarrow{N_i} \cdot (\frac{m1}{||m1||} \times \frac{m2}{||m2||})) \tag{3}$$

where $m1$ and $m2$ are, respectively, first row vector and second row vector of the 3D-to-2D projection matrix M, $\overrightarrow{N_i}$ is the normal vector at the landmark i in 3D space, and $sign$ denotes the sign function. Thus, if v is positive, the landmark is visible; otherwise invisible.

After estimating the visibility of each landmark, we utilize the visible landmarks to generate visible landmark heatmap. Landmark heatmap is an image whose pixel intensity has an inverse relationship with the distance between the pixel location and nearest landmark location. The visible landmark heatmap can be computed by

$$H(x,y) = \frac{1}{1 + min_{s_i \in T_k \times S_{2d}^k}||(x,y) - s_i||_2} \tag{4}$$

where $H(x,y)$ is the intensity of pixel (x,y) in visible landmark heatmap image, $T_k \times S_{2d}^k$ are transformed visible landmarks at regression stage k, s_i is the nearest visible landmark of pixel (x,y).

3.5   Feature Map

The feature map is an image generated by a fully connected layer, whose input is the convolutional feature map of the last pooling layer in SRN. The output size of the fully connected layer is $12,544$, and the output is reshaped to an image ($112 \times 112 \times 1$). The feature map as a complement to the input facial image and visible landmark heatmap transfers the learned information of prior stage to later stage.

3.6   Loss Function

At each stage, we learn to minimize the 2D and 3D landmarks location error normalized by facial bounding box diagonal lengths. Therefore, our loss function can be written as

$$L = \frac{||T_k^{-1}(T_k S_{2d}^{k-1} + \Delta S_{2d}^{k-1}) - S_{2d}^*||}{d_{2d}} + \frac{||T_k^{-1}(T_k S_{3d}^{k-1} + \Delta S_{3d}^{k-1}) - S_{3d}^*||}{d_{3d}} \tag{5}$$

where S_{2d}^* and S_{3d}^* are ground truth 2D and 3D landmarks, d_{2d} and d_{3d} are the diagonal lengths of the 2D and 3D facial bounding boxes respectively. Note that in the first SRN the input is original face image. Therefore, the loss function of the first stage does not include the transformation T or its inverse T^{-1}.

4   Experiments

4.1   Implementation Details

We train our model with the 300W-LP database [9], which contains 61,225 images of front, middle-front and challenging profile faces together with their 68 ground truth 3D landmarks and their corresponding semantically consistent 2D landmarks. To increase the data diversity, we do data augmentation for the training data by applying mirror, rotation, translation and scaling.

While our model consists of two stages, we first pre-train the first stage, and then train both stages together in an end-to-end manner. We use Adam stochastic optimization [14] to optimize our loss with a learning rate of 0.001 and mini batch size of 64. The method is implemented with Tensorflow 1.4.0. The obtained model can run at 35 fps on a computer with one GeForce GTX 1050Ti.

4.2   Experimental Results

We compare our method with some state-of-the-art methods on three databases: AFLW- 2000-3D [9], Menpo-3D [15], and 300W-Testset-3D [16]. In the experiments, we use the facial bounding boxes generated from ground truth landmarks, and the mean frontal face shape as the initial face shape $S^0_{2d/3d}$.

Table 1. Mean error normalized by bounding box diagonal length on AFLW2000-3D database.

Method	$[0°, 30°]$	$[30°, 60°]$	$[60°, 90°]$	Mean
RCPR (300W-LP) [17]	4.26	5.96	13.18	7.80
ESR (300W-LP) [18]	4.60	6.7	12.67	7.99
SDM (300W-LP) [19]	3.67	4.94	9.76	6.12
3DDFA [9]	3.78	4.54	7.93	5.42
3DDFA+SDM [9]	3.43	4.24	7.17	4.94
Chen et al. [10]	3.20	5.48	6.12	4.93
3D-FAN [6]	3.38	4.46	5.59	4.47
Ours (heatmap)	2.97	3.93	5.18	4.02
Ours (visible-heatmap)	**2.97**	**3.85**	**5.09**	**3.97**

Table 2. Mean error normalized by bounding box diagonal length on AFLW2000-3D database (Only visible landmarks are considered).

Method	$[0°, 30°]$	$[30°, 60°]$	$[60°, 90°]$	Mean
DAN [5]	3.07	4.01	8.16	5.08
Ours	**2.92**	**3.36**	**4.12**	**3.46**

AFLW2000-3D is a challenging large pose database containing 2,000 facial images and their annotated ground truth 68 semantic landmarks. We categorize the face images in AFLW2000-3D into three view groups $[0°, 30°], [30°, 60°], [60°, 90°]$ according to their yaw rotation angles. The resulting three groups contain $1, 312, 390$ and 298 images, respectively. Table 1 shows the landmark localization errors of the proposed method and the counterpart methods. Obviously, our method achieves the lowest error. In Table 1, we also report the performance of our method when conventional heatmap rather than the visibility-refined heatmap is used. The increased error proves the importance of considering the landmark visibility. Table 2 further compares our method with the latest DAN method. Note that only visible landmarks are considered here for the sake of fair comparison. Again, our method performs better.

Menpo-3D contains 8,955 challenging images with varying illuminations, poses and occlusions. 300W-Testset-3D contains 600 in-the-wild images. We compare our method with Chen et al. [10] and 3D-FAN [6] on these two databases. The results are shown in Table 3, which again demonstrate the superiority of our method in robustly detecting facial landmarks under challenging conditions. Figure 3 shows the landmarks detected by our method on some example images.

Table 3. Mean error normalized by bounding box diagonal length on Menpo-3D and 300W-Testset-3D databases.

Method	300W-Testset-3D	Menpo-3D
Chen et al. [10]	3.38	4.46
3D-FAN [6]	2.83	3.70
Ours	**2.77**	**3.35**

Fig. 3. Landmark detection results of our method on images from AFLW2000-3D (first row), 300W-Testset-3D (second row) and Menpo-3D (third row). Green and red dots show the visible and invisible landmarks, respectively. (Color figure online)

5   Conclusions

In this paper, we propose an improved large pose face alignment method that can locate 2D and 3D facial landmarks simultaneously. Our proposed method effectively explores the 3D property of faces to refine the detected 2D landmarks. Unlike existing methods, our proposed method simultaneously estimates the 2D and 3D coordinates of the facial landmarks, and regularizes the landmark heatmap with the landmark visibility that is determined based on the 3D coordinates. Extensive experiments on challenging databases show that our method is superior to the compared existing methods in challenging large pose face alignment.

Acknowledgements. This work is supported by the National Key Research and Development Program of China (2017YFB0802300) and the National Natural Science Foundation of China (61773270).

References

1. Zhou, S., Comaniciu, D.: Shape regression machine. Inf. Process. Med. Imaging **45**(84), 13–25 (2007)
2. Sun, Y., Wang, X., Tang, X.: Deep convolutional network cascade for facial point detection. In: CVPR, pp. 3476–3483 (2013)
3. Zhang, Z., Luo, P., Loy, C.C., Tang, X.: Facial landmark detection by deep multi-task learning. In: Fleet, D., Pajdla, T., Schiele, B., Tuytelaars, T. (eds.) ECCV 2014. LNCS, vol. 8694, pp. 94–108. Springer, Cham (2014). https://doi.org/10.1007/978-3-319-10599-4_7
4. Zhu, S., Li, C., Chen, CL., Tang, X.: Face alignment by coarse-to-fine shape searching. In: CVPR, pp. 4998–5006 (2015)
5. Kowalski, M., Naruniec, J., Trzcinski, T.: Deep alignment network: a convolutional neural network for robust face alignment. In: CVPRW, pp. 2034–2043 (2017)
6. Bulat, A., Tzimiropoulos, G.: How far are we from solving the 2D&3D face alignment problem? (and a dataset of 230,000 3D facial landmarks). In: ICCV, pp. 1021–1030 (2017)
7. Jourabloo, A., Liu, X.: Pose-invariant 3D face alignment. In: ICCV, pp. 3694–3702 (2015)
8. Liu, F., Zeng, D., Zhao, Q., Liu, X.: Joint face alignment and 3D Face reconstruction. In: Leibe, B., Matas, J., Sebe, N., Welling, M. (eds.) ECCV 2016. LNCS, vol. 9909, pp. 545–560. Springer, Cham (2016). https://doi.org/10.1007/978-3-319-46454-1_33
9. Zhu, X., Lei, Z., Liu, X., Shi, H., Li, S.: Face alignment across large poses: a 3D solution. In: CVPR, pp. 146–155 (2016)
10. Chen, F., Liu, F., Zhao, Q.: Robust multi-view face alignment based on cascaded 2D/3D face shape regression. In: You, Z., et al. (eds.) CCBR 2016. LNCS, vol. 9967, pp. 40–49. Springer, Cham (2016). https://doi.org/10.1007/978-3-319-46654-5_5
11. Blanz, V., Vetter, T.: Face recognition based on fitting a 3D morphable model. IEEE Trans. Pattern Anal. Mach. Intell. **25**(9), 1063–1074 (2003)
12. Simonyan, K., Zisserman, A.: Very deep convolutional networks for large-scale image recognition. arXiv preprint, pp. 1409–1556 (2014)

13. Tuzel, O., Marks, T.K., Tambe, S.: Robust face alignment using a mixture of invariant experts. In: Leibe, B., Matas, J., Sebe, N., Welling, M. (eds.) ECCV 2016. LNCS, vol. 9909, pp. 825–841. Springer, Cham (2016). https://doi.org/10.1007/978-3-319-46454-1_50
14. Kingma, D., Adam, J.: A method for stochastic optimization. In: International Conference on Learning Representations, pp. 1–13 (2014)
15. Zafeiriou, S., Trigeorgis, G., Chrysos, G., Deng, J., Shen, J.: The menpo facial landmark localisation challenge: a step closer to the solution. In: CVPRW, pp. 2116–2125 (2017)
16. Sagonas, C., Tzimiropoulos, G., Zafeiriou, S., Pantic, M.: 300 faces in-the-wild challenge: the first facial landmark localization challenge. In: ICCVW, pp. 397–403 (2013)
17. Burgos-Artizzu, X., Perona, P., Dollar, P.: Robust face landmark estimation under occlusion. In: ICCV, pp. 1513–1520 (2013)
18. Cao, X., Wei, Y., Wen, F., Sun, J.: Face alignment by explicit shape regression. Int. J. Comput. Vis. **107**(2), 177–190 (2014)
19. Xiong, X., Torre, F.: Supervised descent method and its applications to face alignment. In: CVPR, pp. 532–539 (2013)

RGB-D Face Recognition: A Comparative Study of Representative Fusion Schemes

Jiyun Cui[1,2], Hu Han[1(✉)], Shiguang Shan[1,2], and Xilin Chen[1,2]

[1] Key Laboratory of Intelligent Information Processing of Chinese Academy of Sciences (CAS), Institute of Computing Technology, CAS, Beijing 100190, China
`jiyun.cui@vipl.ict.ac.cn`, {`hanhu,sgshan,xlchen`}`@ict.ac.cn`
[2] University of Chinese Academy of Sciences, Beijing 100049, China

Abstract. RGB-D face recognition (FR) has drawn increasing attention in recent years with the advances of new RGB-D sensing technologies, and the decrease in sensor price. While a number of multi-modality fusion methods are available in face recognition, there is not known conclusion how the RGB and depth should be fused. We provide a comparative study of four representative fusion schemes in RGB-D face recognition, covering signal-level, feature-level, score-level fusions, and a hybrid fusion we designed for RGB-D face recognition. The proposed method achieves state-of-the-art performance on two large RGB-D datasets. A number of insights are provided based on the experimental evaluations.

Keywords: RGB-D face recognition · Signal-level fusion
Feature-level fusion · Score-level fusion · Hybrid fusion

1 Introduction

While significant progress has been made for visible light face recognition in past five years, face recognition under bad environmental illumination, large head pose and big expression variations remains challenging using only visible light face images. With the popularity of RGB-D sensors such as RealSense and Kinect, apart from visible light face image, it becomes easy to obtain near-infrared (NIR) and depth information of human face. While visible face images represent texture information, depth modality provides face space information such as shape and surface normal. Multi-modal face recognition using both color and depth images has been found to be more robust in unconstrained environment. Studies on RGB-D face recognition aims to design representation and fusion approaches which can explore the complementary information from both modalities as much as possible [10, 21].

In review of published modality fusion methods, the fusion schemes can be grouped into two main categories: feature-level fusion methods and score-level fusion methods. Feature-level fusion methods usually learn modality-specific features first, which were fused to form a combined feature representation. Score-level fusion methods compute per-modality similarity scores first, and then fuse

© Springer Nature Switzerland AG 2018
J. Zhou et al. (Eds.): CCBR 2018, LNCS 10996, pp. 358–366, 2018.
https://doi.org/10.1007/978-3-319-97909-0_39

the scores via particular rules, e.g., a sum rule. In this paper, we provide a comparative study of four fusion scheme using the RGB-D two modalities information, apart from the above two fusion strategies, we also consider the signal-level fusion methods which combine the raw color and depth images and the hybrid fusion strategy consisting of two or more fusion schemes.

The contributions of the paper are two-fold: (i) four representative fusion strategies are summarized in RGB-D face recognition covering signal-level, feature-level, score-level, and hybrid fusions; (ii) individual fusion schemes are fully evaluated on two large-scale RGB-D datasets (Lock3DFace and our dataset) and a number of insights are provided.

2 Related Work

RGB-D multi-modal face recognition has been studied for many years. [1] proposed to extract HOG features from entropy/saliency maps calculated from RGB and depth images and then trained a Random Decision Forest (RDF) classifier for matching. [2] fused both the entropy map based match score and attribute based match scores of depth image for face recognition. [3] built a 12-layer Deep Convolutional Neural Network (CNN) consisting of six modules, in which three loss modules were added after the second, fourth and sixth network modules, respectively. In each loss module, in addition to using softmax loss for identification, contrastive loss was utilized for verification purpose. [10] proposed an approach to learn complementary features and common features from RGB-D face images during the training phase. During testing, this method extracted modal-specific features for per-modality matching, and used a score-level fusion to compute the final matching score.

Besides the fusion schemes used in RGB-D face recognitioin, there are also a number of studies on how to fuse the RGB and depth in other tasks, such as object recognition [4,6,8], scene recognition [5,9], and person re-identification [7]. [4] proposed a pair of deep residual networks for RGB and depth data to explore the sharable and modal-specific features. The input data of depth modal is surface normals instead of depth image. [5] proposed an approach that combines RGB and depth modalities from multiple sources, the depth modality has two streams networks which are transfered from RGB pre-trained modal and direct training. The extracted features of multiple modalities were added as a fusion features for recognition. [7] proposed a RGB-D based approach for person re-identification, in which, the anthropometric feature vectors were extracted in a fusion layer consisting of the depth-specific part, the sharable part and the RGB-specific part. [8] proposed an approach that combines convolutional and recursive neural networks (RNN) in which RNN worked as a fusion part to get the final features from RGB and depth. [9] proposed a novel discriminative multi-modal feature fusion method which also used two CNN steams for handling color and depth, respectively.

3 Fusion Schemes in RGB-D Face Recognition

We group the fusion schemes for RGB-D face recognition into four categories: signal-level fusion, feature-level fusion, score-level fusion and hybrid fusion. The details of each scheme are summarized below.

3.1 Signal-Level Fuison

The signal-level fusion method operates directly on the raw RGB and depth images. Since RGB images are treated as three-channel input data of the network, we can also concatenate RGB and depth into a four-channel input data for signal-level fusion. Apart from such a four-channel fusion method, we also explore other signal-level RGB-D fusion methods such as sum or average of the corresponding pixels in RGB and depth images. In these methods, the depth modality data is copied to a three-channel format to keep consistent with the RGB three-channel format. Figure 1(a) shows a general diagram of the signal-level fusion for RGB-D face recognition.

3.2 Feature-Level Fusion

The feature-level fusion is to fuse the features extracted from RGB and depth modality network and then fed into the classification layers. In feature-level fusion, the fusion can be in the form of feature concatenated or sum or average of the feature map, or projections from two modalities' feature maps. In this paper, our experiments are all based on ResNet [15] modal, the feature vector of the first fully connected layer is used as the features. With feature-level fusion, we usually get a single feature vector representing the RGB-D face images. Figure 1(b) shows a general diagram of the feature-level fusion for RGB-D face recognition.

3.3 Score-Level Fusion

Score-level fusion was thoroughly discussed in [13] for multi-biometric systems, i.e., face, fingerprint, etc. Here, we focus on the fusion of the matching scores by RGB and depth, respectively. A straightforward strategy is to calculate the average score of the two modalities' scores. Such an average fusion can be formulated in a more general format, i.e., a weighted sum of the two score, $S = \omega \cdot S_{RGB} + (1 - \omega) \cdot S_D$ where ω and $1 - \omega$ are the weights for the RGB and depth, respectively, which can be determined empirically based on the performance of each modality ($\omega = 0.5$ in our experiments). Figure 1(c) shows a general diagram of the score-level fusion for RGB-D face recognition.

3.4 Hybrid Fusion

In real applications, multiple fusion strategies might be jointly used, i.e., a hybrid fusion consisting of more than two of the above fusion schemes. We propose a

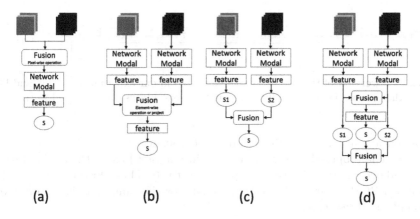

Fig. 1. The diagrams of the four representative fusion schemes for RGB-D face recognition: (a) signal-level fusion, (b) feature-level fusion, (c) score-level fusion, (d) hybrid fusion.

hybrid fusion consisting of both feature-level fusion and score-level fusion (see Fig. 1(d)). In particular, the feature-level fusion part aims to learn a joint feature representation from both RGB and depth. The score-level fusion part takes into account three matching scores obtained using RGB feature, depth feature, and the joint feature. Finally, a score-level fusion is applied with a weighed sum rule $S = \frac{\alpha \cdot S_{RGB} + \beta \cdot S_D + \gamma \cdot S_C}{\alpha + \beta + \gamma}$, where α, β and γ balance the importances of individual features, and are determined empirically ($\alpha = \beta = \gamma = 1$ in our experiments).

4   Implementation Details

4.1   Network Training

We use a ResNet-80 network as the backbone network[1] for our RGB-D face recognition experiments (see Fig. 2). Our ResNet-80 was pre-trained using a large RGB face dataset compiled from multiple public-domain datasets, such as MS Celeb [14], etc. We then finetune the pre-trained model under various RGB-D fusion schemes. The learning rate is set to 0.001.

In signal-level fusion (Fig. 1(a)), the fusion operation was performed ahead of the first of convolution layer of ResNet-80. We consider pixel-wise operations such as pixel-wise sum and average, which comes up a three-channel data. The concatenation operation generates a six-channel input data. In this situation, we revise the first convolution layer and train this layer from scratch. In score-level fusion, two ResNet-80 modals are separately trained using RGB and depth modalities, respectively. In feature-level fusion, a fully connect layer is used to

---

[1] We also tried AlexNet [18], GoogLeNet [17], and VGG-16 [19], but the best performance of the three model for RGB and depth fusion is 96.8%, which is lower than our ResNet-80 (98.7%). So we only report the results using our ResNet-80.

Fig. 2. An overview of the ResNet-80 network used in our experiments. Conv. and FC denote the convolutional and fully convolution layers, blocks are explained in [15].

get a concatenation of the RGB and depth features, followed by a single loss function. The proposed hybrid fusion contains an joint loss for the feature fusion layer, and two losses for RGB and depth respectively. Thus, three features (RGB, depth and RGB-D) are extracted. The final score is computed via a score-level fusion of the three scores.

4.2   The Preprocessing of the RGB-D Images

We use an open-source face recognition engine to detect the face and keypoint landmark[2] from RGB, and normalize the detected faces to 256×256. For depth image, we follow a preprocessing pipeline in [10]. We also use a bilateral filter [12] to suppress the noises in depth.

5   Experiments

5.1   Datasets and Evaluation Metrics

We provide experiments on two large-scale RGB-D datasets: Lock3DFace [11] and our RGB-D dataset [10]. Lock3DFace consists of 5,711 video sequences of 509 subjects with variations in head pose, expression, occlusion, etc. We extract 33,780 RGB-D images from the video sequences and randomly select 22,798 RGB-D images of 340 subjects for training, the remaining of 169 subjects for testing. Our RGB-D dataset contains about 845K RGB-D images of 742 subjects captured by RealSense II with variable of head pose and illumination. About 580K RGB-D images of 500 subjects are randomly selected for training and the remaining 280K RGB-D images of 242 subjects are used for testing.

We perform face identification on the two databases, and report the rank-1 identification accuracy. For each subject in the testing dataset, one frontal RGB-D image is used as gallery, and the remaining RGB-D images are used as probe. Cosine distance is used to mesure the similarity between two features.

5.2   Overall Performance and Analysis

We report the rank-1 identification accuracy by the four representative fusion schemes in Table 1. As a comparison, we also provide the unimodal face recognition accuracy, i.e., using RGB alone and using depth alone as the baselines. On

---

[2] https://github.com/seetaface/SeetaFaceEngine.

Table 1. The overall performance of the representative RGB-D fusion schemes in terms of the rank-1 identification accuracy and the average feature extraction time per RGB-D image.

Fusion schemes	Method	Datasets		Time (s)
		Our dataset	Lock3DFace	
Unimodality	RGB alone	97.14%	97.30%	0.012
	Depth alone	94.33%	74.45%	0.012
Signal-level fusion	Pixel-wise max	92.27%	90.35%	0.021
	Pixel-wise sum	96.54%	97.38%	0.013
	Concatenation	92.65%	79.32%	0.013
Feature-level fusion	Element-wise max	97.66%	**97.86%**	0.030
	Element-wise sum	98.90%	97.60%	0.033
	Concatenation	99.03%	97.74%	0.026
Score-level fusion	Weighted sum	98.67%	97.43%	0.024
Hybrid fusion	Use at least 2 of the above fusions	**99.05%**	97.53%	0.033

our RGB-D dataset collected by RealSense II, all the fusion methods except for the signal-level fusion can improve the face recognition by a large margin. The hybrid fusion method achieves the highest recognition accuracy among the four types of fusion methods. However, on Lock3DFace, the improvement by hybrid fusion becomes slightly smaller than using feature-level fusion. We think the main reason is that the depth captured by Kinect II is much worse than using RealSense II (see Table 1). Among the three methods in signal-level fusion, the pixel-wise sum operation is better than the other two signal-level fusion methods, but still does not show improved performance than the baseline results using RGB alone. The possible reason is that the three signal-level operations are not able to properly make use of the information in the color and depth images. Feature-level, score-level and hybrid fusions all are found to be helpful in improving face recognition accuracy than unimodality face recognition, and feature-level and hybrid fusions are slightly better than score-level fusion. In addition, the feature-level fusion and hybrid fusion report very similar rank-1 accuracies on our dataset (see an example of the top-5 matched gallery images in Fig. 3). This is consistent with previous studies where multiple feature descriptors are fused for improving classification accuracies. These results suggest that RGB and depth may not share the same network weights during feature learning. The observations on the Lock3DFace dataset is similar, except that the feature-level fusion becomes slightly better than hybrid fusion. The main reason is that each video in Lock3DFace was recorded with almost a still subject, leading to near-duplicated video frames, and thus reducing the effective training data samples during network learning. We also provide evaluations on EURE-COM [16], but since this dataset is very small, we directly use the model trained on our dataset. The rank-1 identification accuracies of using RGB and depth alone are 94.41% and 58.74%, respectively, and the fusion does not improve the accuracy. The main reasons are: (i) the race difference between our dataset and EURECOM and (ii) the device difference between RealSense and Kinect.

We also profile the average feature extraction time of individual fusion schemes on a Titan Xp GPU. While signal-level fusion does not incur additional computation cost, the other three fusion schemes have 2–3 times higher computation cost in feature extraction. This is understandable because RGB and depth are handled via separate subnetworks by the other three fusion schemes. Still, they are able to process images in real time (30fps), and should meet the requirement of general applications.

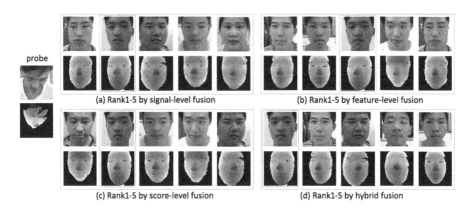

Fig. 3. The top1-5 matches by the four representative fusion methods. (a) top-5 matched gallery using signal-level fusion; (b) top-5 matched gallery using feature-level fusion; (c) top-5 matched gallery using score-level fusion; (d) top-5 matched gallery using hybrid fusion. The gallery images marked with red boxes are the correct mated gallery images for the probe.

6   Conclusions

We provide a comparative study of four representative fusion strategies covering signal-level fusion, feature-level fusion, score-level fusion, and hybrid fusion on two large-scale RGB-D databases. While signal-level fusion should retain the most amount of information in theory, the four-channel or pixel-wise fusion of RGB and depth signals does not show better performance than the feature-level or score-level fusion. Furthermore, the proposed fusion approach, a hybrid fusion scheme, achieves the best accuracy on our RGB-D dataset which is more challenging than Lock3DFace in terms of pose and illumination vairations. These motivate us to investigate new network architectures so that the signal-level fusion could better leverage the information of RGB-D to improve face recognition accuracy. In addition, we are going to study 3D reconstruction based method [20] for RGB-D face recognition.

Acknowledgement. This research was supported in part by the Natural Science Foundation of China (grants 61732004, and 61672496), External Cooperation Program of Chinese Academy of Sciences (CAS) (grant GJHZ1843), and Youth Innovation Promotion Association CAS (2018135).

References

1. Goswami, G., Bharadwaj, S., Vatsa, M., Singh, R.: On RGB-D face recognition using kinect. In: Proceedings of BTAS, pp. 1–6 (2013)
2. Goswami, G., Vatsa, M., Singh, R.: RGB-D face recognition with texture and attribute features. IEEE Trans. Inf. Forensics Secur. **9**(10), 1629–1640 (2014)
3. Lee, Y., Chen, J., Tseng, C., Lai, S.: Accurate and robust face recognition from RGB-D images with a deep learning approach. In: Proceedings of BMVC, pp. 123.1–123.14 (2016)
4. Wang, Z., Lu, J., Lin, R., Feng, J., Zhou, J.: Correlated and individual multi-modal deep learning for RGB-D object recognition, in arXiv:1604.01655 (2016)
5. Song, X., Jiang, S., Herranz, L.: Combining models from multiple sources for RGB-D scene recognition. In: Proceedings of IJCAI, pp. 4523–4529 (2017)
6. Eitel, A., Springenberg, J., Spinello, L., Riedmiller, M., Burgard, W.: Multimodal deep learning for robust RGB-D object recognition. In: Proceedings of IROS, pp. 681–687 (2015)
7. Ren, L., Lu, J., Feng, J., Zhou, J.: Multi-modal uniform deep learning for RGB-D person re-identificaiton. Pattern Recogn. **72**(12), 446–457 (2017)
8. Socher, R., Huval, B., Bath, B.: Convolutional-recursive deep learning for 3D object classification. In: Proceedings of NIPS, pp. 665–673 (2012)
9. Zhu, H., Weibel, J., Lu, S.: Discriminative multi-modal feature fusion for RGBD indoor scene recognition. In: Proceedings of CVPR, pp. 2969–2976 (2016)
10. Zhang, H., Han, H., Cui, J., Shan, S., Chen, X.: RGB-D face recognition via deep complementary and common feature learning. In: Proceedings of FG, pp. 1–8 (2018)
11. Zhang, J., Huang, D., Wang, Y., Sun, J.: Lock3DFace: a large-scale database of low-cost kinect 3D faces. In: Proceedings of ICB, pp. 1–8 (2016)
12. Tomasi, C., Manduchi, R.: Bilateral filtering for gray and color images. In: Proceedings of ICCV, pp. 839–846 (1998)
13. Jain, A.K., Nandakumar, K., Ross, A.: Score normalization in multimodal biometric systems. Pattern Recogn. **38**(12), 2270–2285 (2005)
14. Guo, Y., Zhang, L., Hu, Y., He, X., Gao, J.: MS-Celeb-1M: a dataset and benchmark for large-scale face recognition. In: Proceedings of ECCV (2016)
15. He, K., Zhang, X., Ren, S., Sun, J.: Deep residual learning for image recognition, in arXiv:1512.03385 (2015)
16. Min, R., Kose, N., Dugelay, J.: KinectFaceDB: a kinect database for face recognition. IEEE Trans. SMC Syst. **44**(11), 1534–1548 (2014)
17. Ioffe, S., Szegedy, C.: Batch normalization: accelerating deep network training by reducing internal covariate shift. In: Proceedings of ICML, pp. 448–456 (2015)
18. Krizhevsky, A., Sutskever, I., Hinton, G.: ImageNet classification with deep convolutional neural networks. In: Proceedings of NIPS, pp. 1097–1105 (2012)
19. Simonyan, K., Zisserman, A.: Very deep convolutional networks for large-scale image recognition, in arXiv:1409.1556 (2015)

20. Han, H., Jain, A.K.: 3D face texture modeling from uncalibrated frontal and profile images. In: Proceedings of BTAS, pp. 223–230 (2012)
21. Cui, J., Zhang, H., Han, H., Shan, S., Chen, X.: Improving 2D face recognition via discriminative face depth estimation. In: Proceedings of ICB, pp. 1–8 (2018)

An ICA-Based Other-Race Effect Elimination for Facial Expression Recognition

Mingliang Xue[1], Xiaodong Duan[1(✉)], Wanquan Liu[2], and Yuehai Wang[3]

[1] Dalian Key Lab of Digital Technology for National Culture, College of Computer Science and Engineering, Dalian Minzu University, Dalian 116600, Liaoning, China
duanxd_dlnu@126.com
[2] Department of Computing, Curtin University, Kent Street, Perth, WA 6102, Australia
[3] School of Electronic Information Engineering, North China University of Technology, Beijing 100144, China

Abstract. Other-race effect affects the performance of multi-race facial expression recognition significantly. Though this phenomenon has been noticed by psychologists and computer vision researchers for decades, few work has been done to eliminate this influence caused by other-race effect. This work proposes an ICA-based other-race effect elimination method for 3D facial expression recognition. Firstly, the local depth features are extracted from 3D face point clouds, and then independent component analysis is used to project the features into a subspace in which the feature components are mutually independent. Second, a mutual information based feature selection method is adopted to determine race-sensitive features. Finally, the features after race-sensitive information elimination are utilized to conduct facial expression recognition. The proposed method is evaluated on BU-3DFE database, and the results reveal that the proposed method is effective to other-race effect elimination and could improve the multi-race facial expression recognition performance.

Keywords: Other-race effect · Facial expression recognition
Feature selection

1 Introduction

Enabling computers to recognize human expressions has been a popular research topic for decades, due to its application potentials in human computer interaction, robotics, and psychological studies. In multi-race or multi-ethnicity situation, facial expression recognition performance is significantly affected by racial

This work is supported by National Natural Science Foundation of China (Grant No.61672132), Science and Technology Foundation of Liaoning Province of China (Grant No.20170520234), CERNET next generation Internet technical innovation project (Grant No. NGII20170419 and Grant No. NGII20170631).

© Springer Nature Switzerland AG 2018
J. Zhou et al. (Eds.): CCBR 2018, LNCS 10996, pp. 367–376, 2018.
https://doi.org/10.1007/978-3-319-97909-0_40

or ethnical information lurking in face images. Psychological studies [1] have revealed the existence of other-race effect (ORE) in human face perception and processing, i.e. the facial features of other-race are more difficult to be memorized and recognized than that of own-race. It has been proved that the existence of ORE will not only obstruct the inter-race or inter-culture communication [2], but also cause the difficulties to facial expression recognition algorithms [3]. In fact, human face conveys various kinds of demographic information, including race, age, gender etc., which usually mix together with each other and cause difficulties to face-based biometric recognition tasks. Until now, there are very few work focuses on how to remove or depress the influence caused by other-race effect to facial expression recognition, though it has been noticed by computer vision community for quite long a time.

The concept of other-race effect was first proposed by Feingold [4] in 1914, which means human has better ability in recognizing the faces of own race than that of other races. It has been an active research interest in psychological study ever since the first report [1] was published in 1969. The studies on ORE attempt to prove the universality of the human face perception and interpret this phenomenon in social cognition. Human facial expression plays a crucial role in social communication since it provides an effective way to express intentions and convey emotions. Hence, the influence caused by other-race effect to facial expression understanding and recognition has attracted many psychological researchers' attention. Many works [5–7] have been done to verify the existence of ORE in facial expression recognition and explore the generating neuromechanism of ORE. Though the generating reason and mechanism of ORE are still unclear, the pioneer studies in psychological field shed lights on the investigation of ORE in computer vision models.

This paper attempts to eliminate other-race effect from 3D facial expression recognition by removing the race-sensitive features from face images. The 3D facial expression images are used to conduct this work because they are not only invariant to illumination changes and pose variations, but also rich in shape and deformation [8]. Firstly, the extracted local depth features of 3D faces are projected into a subspace constructed by independent component analysis (ICA), in which the projected features are mutually independent. Secondly, a feature learning algorithm is wrapped with race classification to obtain the race-sensitive features. These race-sensitive features are then discarded, and the rest features without race information are used to conduct facial expression recognition. We evaluate the proposed method on BU-3DFE database [9]. The experimental results show that the multi-race facial expression recognition performance could be improved significantly with the proposed other-race effect elimination method.

2   Related Works

The diversity of the facial expression features among different races is the essential reason why the other-race effect exists expression recognition. Ever since

Darwin's seminal works [10], the universality of facial expressions of emotion has remained one of the most controversial opinions in the biological and social sciences. The *universality hypothesis* claims that all the humans from different cultures and races use the same facial movements to communicate six basic internal emotions [11,12]. Based on this hypothesis, Ekman [13] proposed facial action coding system (FACS) to analyze facial features of emotions, and defined six prototypic expressions (happy, surprise, fear, disgust, anger, and sad). This universality hypothesis based six prototypic expression definition by Ekman has been widely adopted in facial expression recognition researches. However, the recent studies reveal the facial expression variations among different race or cultures, which refute the assumed expression universality. The work [14] proved that the individuals of different races use various expressions to communicate same emotions. Another work [15] analyzed the basic expressions and facial action units of Caucasians and Asians by clustering, and pointed out that the six prototypic expressions are not universal. These studies suggest that facial expression feature varies among different races. In order to reveal the mechanism of other-race effect and eliminate its influence to expression recognition, it is important to determine what kind of facial features are highly related to race, and then figure out how these race-sensitive features affect facial expression recognition in computational models.

The other-race effect was first observed and studied by psychologists, which focused on the factors that may cause the effect. The progress in the psychological investigation has inspired the computer vision researchers to study the other-race effect from the computational perspective. In order to explore the mechanism of ORE in face image based recognition tasks, several computational models have been proposed. O'Toole et al. [16] reviewed the studies which focus on the other-race effect in face recognition algorithm from the perspective of feature learning. This survey paper discussed the contribution of training data and feature learning strategy to other-race effect generation, and proposed the conditions on which other-race effect could be simulated based on computational models. Another work [17] verified other-race effect in facial expression recognition using the Caucasian and East Asian individuals' expression images in BU-3DFE database. The facial depth features are extracted to represent expressions for each race group, and cross-validation results show that the performance of 3D facial expression recognition is affected by other-race effect significantly. Meanwhile, Fu et al. [2] studied facial race information caused influence to multi-race facial feature analysis, and argued that other-race effect in face recognition and facial expression recognition is mainly caused by training data. In order to solve the issues rendered by other-race effect, it is worth to construct a training database with equal samples from all the races or embed imbalanced learning into biometric recognition framework. In [5], the authors design a computational model EMPATH [18] based on neural network to encode the varieties of the facial expression perception between two cultural groups, the results show that 'expression dialect' exists between different cultural groups, which causes the own-group recognition advantage.

The works mentioned above focused on either the existence verification of other-race effect in computational facial expression recognition or the conditions to simulate other-race effect in computer vision models. To the best of our knowledge, there are no work which seeks to eliminate the other-race effect in facial expression recognition except Fu et al. [2] points out that imbalanced learning may help to alleviate the influence. Hence, inspired by the idea of blind signal source separation, this paper proposed an ICA-based other-race elimination method, which tries to decompose the information contained in face images into independent components. A race-sensitive facial feature component selection is then designed using entropy-based evaluation. The race-sensitive features are filtered out according to its relevance score, and finally the expression are conducted using the de-race features. The experimental results show that the proposed method could depress the influence caused by other-race effect and improve the performance of facial expression recognition in multi-race situation.

3   Other-Race Effect Elimination Method

Facial race information is the internal demographical features of faces, which always affect the computational recognition tasks. Unlike the pose and illumination variations, the external factors could be constrained when capturing images of faces. The facial race information co-exists with the target features, i.e. facial expression features in this work. Hence, it is necessary to separate facial expression and race features during feature learning stage. Inspired by the application in blind signal source separation, independent component analysis is embed in facial expression feature extraction to isolate race information out from expression images. Actually, independent component analysis has been applied to face recognition and facial expression recognition for decades, in which ICA is mainly to learn a subspace for face image representation. However, this paper attempts to use ICA to identify what kind of features are related to facial race information, which facilitates the following race information elimination. The expression features will not be affected if the race-sensitive features are removed, because the components in the feature space obtained by ICA are independent to each other.

3.1   ICA-Based Facial Feature Extraction and Decomposition

Human face is a non-convex 3D object which usually deformed non-rigidly according to different expressions. In order to represent facial expression sufficiently, various kinds of features [19–21] have been proposed to encode 3D facial expression features. The raw scan of faces are encoded in a 3D point cloud. This work use grid-fitting to obtain a smooth facial surface based on the given face point cloud and then detected 30 facial landmarks to extract local depth features. Finally, each 3D face is represented by the local depth features around the 30 landmarks. For more details of feature extraction, please check paper [22].

For facial expression recognition, the other-race effect could be depressed if the race-sensitive features could be identified and removed. However, human facial feature is affected by various kinds of information, including race, gender, age etc., which usually mixed together in extracted facial features. Hence, eliminating any of these features may cause the loss of useful expression information, which is obviously unhelpful to improve the recognition performance. Hence, this work proposes to decompose facial features into statistically independent bases and then use their linear combination to represent facial expression. The decomposition could decorrelate the mixed information and facilitates the race-sensitive feature elimination. Suppose there are n faces $x_i (i = 1, 2, ..., n)$ in the training set that could be observed, and human face shape are affected by m factors $s_j (j = 1, 2, ..., m)$ that are mutually and statistically independent. That is to say, the factors that affect facial features are assumed to be independent, and facial features could be represented by the linear combination of these factors as follows,

$$X = AS, \tag{1}$$

where $X = [x_1, x_2.., x_n]^T$ is the observed training images, $S = [s_1, s_2.., s_m]^T$ is the matrix composed by the independent factors, and A is an $n \times m$ matrix. Actually, Eq. (1) is the basic model of ICA, which describes how the observed face x_i are composed by the independent factor s_j. Normally, the independent factor s_j could not be observed and the mixing matrix A is unknown, the only information we have is the training images. Hence, facial features decomposition is to estimate mixing matrix A and independent component s_j using the observed training face images. However, it is unfeasible to obtain the independent component s_j from training images X, since the mixing matrix A is unknown. An alternative method is to seek a demixing matrix W using ICA, and independent components $\hat{S}$ could be obtained by $\hat{S} = WX$, in which the $\hat{S}$ is as close to the real independent factors S. Once the demixing matrix are obtained, the training images could be projected into ICA subspace and the facial features could be represented based on the independent components. This problem could be solved by fastICA algorithm [23]. Using the demixing matrix W, the independent components or basis could be estimated as follows,

$$U = WX = WAS \tag{2}$$

$$W = A^{-1} \tag{3}$$

where $U = [u_1, u_2.., u_M]^T$ is the estimated independent basis, each u_k represents one statistically independent basis. Given a face images f, it could be represented by a linear combination of U,

$$f = a_1 u_1 + a_2 u_2 + ... + a_M u_M \tag{4}$$

where a_k is the projection coefficients.

3.2   Race-Sensitive Feature Identification

Once the face images are represented in ICA subspace, the facial features could be considered as mutually independent. The other-race effect could be depressed by filtering the race-sensitive features out. In this work, we proposed a race-sensitive feature identification method by feature selection for race classification. The selected features which yields the best race classification performance are considered as race-sensitive features. In multi-race facial expression recognition, the training data have the labels of race and expression. The training data X for expression recognition are split into two subset for race classification, denoted as $X_{r-train}$ and X_{r-test}. The race-sensitive features could be identified by a forward feature learning process, during which the relevance and redundancy among the features are considered. Since the race label r in the training set $X_{r-train}$ and the feature set $F = \{f_1, f_2, \cdots, f_i, \cdots, f_N\}$ are known, the mutual information between feature f_i and the race r could be calculated to measure the relevance by

$$I(f_i, r) = \int \int p(f_i, r) log \frac{p(f_i, r)}{p(f_i)P(r)} df_i dr, \tag{5}$$

where $p(f_i)$ and $p(r)$ is the probability distribution of feature f_i and race r, and $p(f_i, r)$ is the joint probability distribution of feature f_i and race r. Normally, information redundancy exists among the features, which could be measured by mutual information between feature f_i and f_j as follows,

$$I(f_i, f_j) = \int \int p(f_i, f_j) log \frac{p(f_i, f_j)}{p(x_i)p(f_j)} df_i df_j. \tag{6}$$

It can be seen that that combination of most relevant features does not necessarily form the optimal feature set, due to the redundancy existing among the features. Therefore, the feature learning criterion is define as follows:

$$max \frac{\frac{1}{|F|} \sum_{f_i \in F} I(f_i; r)}{\frac{1}{|F|^2} \sum_{f_i, f_j \in F} I(f_i; f_j)} \tag{7}$$

where $|F|$ is the size of the depth feature set F. The most relevant features to target races, which also have the least mutual redundancy, could be achieved simultaneously by maximizing this feature learning criterion.

Table 1. The Race distribution of BU-3DFE database.

Race	Number of individuals	Number of 3D faces
White	51	1224
East-Asian	24	576
Black	9	216
Hispanic-Latino	8	192
Indian	6	144
Middle-East Asian	2	48

3.3   Other-Race Effect Elimination

In Sect. 3.2, the optimal race-sensitive features can be determined one by one by an incremental algorithm according to the criterion in Eq. (7). Denoting the original facial expression set S and the optimal race-sensitive feature set S^*, the feature set $S_{deORE} = S - S^*$ is used for facial expression recognition in the proposed method. The features belong to this set have the weakest relationship with race information, which are supposed to alleviate the influence caused by other-race effect. When the face samples are represented by the features in S_{deORE}, a wrapper which works with a nearest-neighbour classifier is used to conduct expression classification using Linear Discriminant Analysis (LDA) projection. In the learning process, the features which can reduce the classification error most is added to the final feature set in each iteration. This selection operation is repeated until the classification error stop decreasing or all the candidate features have been chosen. The features which belong to the final feature set S_{opt} are insensitively to race variations and could achieve the best expression recognition performance. Thus, they are considered as the best features for other-race effect elimination.

4   Experimental Results

4.1   Experiment Setup

The proposed method is evaluated base on the BU-3DFE database [9], which is originally created for the purpose of 3D facial expression recognition. This database contains 3D faces of 100 individuals. Each subject shows the 6 prototypic expressions with 4 different intensity. As shown in Table 1, the subjects of BU-3DFE database belong to 6 different races. In order to evaluate other-race effect in multi-race facial expression recognition, the images of subjects from Black, Hispanic-Latino, Indian, and Middle-East Asian are combined together as the training data, and the 48 White subjects are used for testing. This setup also meet the commonly used person-independent setup for facial expression recognition. The experiments are then accordingly performed, and the average results are reported.

4.2   Evaluation of the Proposed Method

In order to evaluate the effectiveness of the propose method, the local depth features of the 3D face images are extracted and then ICA is applied to construct a subspace in which the features are mutually independent. The race-sensitive features are then determined using mutual information based feature selection and removed from the ICA subspace. Finally, the features after elimination are used to conduct facial expression recognition. For comparison, the expression recognition performance of the ICA features before removing race information is also obtained. As shown in Fig. 1, the recognition rates obtained based on the features before and after other-race effect elimination are plotted. It can be seen

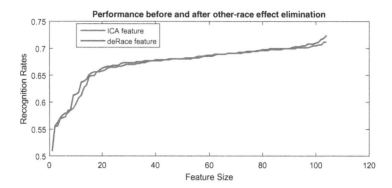

Fig. 1. Recognition performance comparison before and after other-race effect elimination. ICA features and deRace features mean the features before and after race-sensitive feature elimination.

that the recognition performance based on the features after other-race effect elimination is better than that of ICA features before race information removing. The confusion matrix of the recognition has been illustrated in Fig. 2(a) and (b). The comparison of these two figures show that the recognition rates of expression anger, disgust, fear, sad and happy are improved significantly by eliminating race-sensitive features. The average recognition rate is improve from 69% to 72%. This improvement suggest that the proposed method is effective in other-race effect elimination.

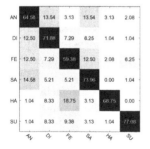

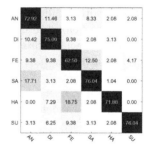

(a) ICA features based recognition.   (b) The deORE feature based recognition.

Fig. 2. The confusion matrix of multi-race facial expression recognition before(a) and after(b) other-race effect elimination evaluation.

5   Conclusion

This paper proposes an ICA-based other-race effect elimination method for facial expression recognition. It has been noticed by psychological and computer vision researchers that other-race effect influence the performance of facial expression recognition. Hence, this work tries to depress or eliminate the other-race effect by removing the race-sensitive features from face images. After feature extraction, the facial features are projected into ICA subspace in which the feature component are statistically independent. The race-sensitive features are then identified by feature selection aiming at race classification. Finally, the features after race information removing are used to conduct facial expression recognition. The experimental results show that the proposed method is effective to other-race effect elimination and improve the performance of multi-race facial expression recognition.

References

1. Malpass, R.S., Kravitz, J.: Recognition for faces of own and other race. J. Pers. Soc. Psychol. **13**(4), 330 (1969)
2. Fu, S., He, H., Hou, Z.G.: Learning race from face: a survey. IEEE Trans. Pattern Anal. Mach. Intell. **36**(12), 2483–2509 (2014)
3. Phillips, P.J., Jiang, F., Narvekar, A., Ayyad, J., O'Toole, A.J.: An other-race effect for face recognition algorithms. ACM Trans. Appl. Percept. (TAP) **8**(2), 14 (2011)
4. Feingold, G.A.: The influence of environment on identification of persons and things. J. Am. Inst. Crim. Law Criminol. **5**(1), 39–51 (1914)
5. Dailey, M.N., Joyce, C., Lyons, M.J., Kamachi, M., Ishi, H., Gyoba, J., Cottrell, G.W.: Evidence and a computational explanation of cultural differences in facial expression recognition. Emotion **10**(6), 874 (2010)
6. Craig, B.M., Jing, Z., Lipp, O.V.: Facial race and sex cues have a comparable influence on emotion recognition in chinese and australian participants. Attention Percept. Psychophysics **1**, 1–12 (2017)
7. Yan, X., Andrews, T.J., Jenkins, R., Young, A.W.: Cross-cultural differences and similarities underlying other-race effects for facial identity and expression. Q. J. Experimental Psychol. **69**(7), 1247–1254 (2016)
8. Zhen, Q., Huang, D., Wang, Y., Chen, L.: Muscular movement model based automatic 3D facial expression recognition. In: He, X., Luo, S., Tao, D., Xu, C., Yang, J., Hasan, M.A. (eds.) MMM 2015. LNCS, vol. 8935, pp. 522–533. Springer, Cham (2015). https://doi.org/10.1007/978-3-319-14445-0_45
9. Yin, L., Wei, X., Sun, Y., Wang, J., Rosato, M.J.: A 3D facial expression database for facial behavior research. In: 7th International Conference on Automatic Face and Gesture Recognition (FGR 2006), pp. 211–216. IEEE (2006)
10. Darwin, C., Rachman, I.J.: The Expression of Emotions in Man and Animals. Julian Friedmann (1979)
11. Ekman, P., Sorenson, E.R., Friesen, W.V.: Pan-cultural elements in facial displays of emotion. Science **164**(3875), 86–88 (1969)
12. Susskind, J.M., Lee, D.H., Cusi, A., Feiman, R., Grabski, W., Anderson, A.K.: Expressing fear enhances sensory acquisition. Nature Neurosci. **11**(2), 843–850 (2008)
13. Ekman, P., Friesen, W.V.: Facial action coding system (FACS): a technique for the measurement of facial actions. Rivista Di Psichiatria **47**(2), 126–38 (1978)
14. Jack, R.E., Blais, C., Scheepers, C., Schyns, P.G., Caldara, R.: Cultural confusions show that facial expressions are not universal. Curr. Biol. **19**(18), 1543–8 (2009)

15. Jack, R.E., Garrod, O.G.B., Yu, H., Caldara, R., Schyns, P.G.: Facial expressions of emotion are not culturally universal. Proc. Nat. Acad. Sci. U.S.A. **109**(19), 7241–7244 (2012)
16. Natu, V., O'Toole, A.J.: Neural perspectives on the other-race effect. Vis. Cognit. **21**(9–10), 1121–1137 (2013)
17. Xue, M., et al.: A computational other-race-effect analysis for 3D facial expression recognition. In: You, Z., et al. (eds.) CCBR 2016. LNCS, vol. 9967, pp. 483–493. Springer, Cham (2016). https://doi.org/10.1007/978-3-319-46654-5_53
18. Dailey, M.N., Cottrell, G.W., Padgett, C., Adolphs, R.: Empath: a neural network that categorizes facial expressions. J. Cognit. Neurosci. **14**(8), 1158–1173 (2014)
19. Zhen, Q., Huang, D., Wang, Y., Chen, L.: Muscular movement model-based automatic 3D/4D facial expression recognition. IEEE Trans. Multimed. **18**(7), 1438–1450 (2016)
20. Li, H., Sun, J., Xu, Z., Chen, L.: Multimodal 2D+3D facial expression recognition with deep fusion convolutional neural network. IEEE Trans. Multimed. **19**(12), 2816–2831 (2017)
21. Li, H., Sun, J., Chen, L.: Location-sensitive sparse representation of deep normal patterns for expression-robust 3D face recognition. In: 2017 IEEE International Joint Conference on Biometrics (IJCB), pp. 234–242. IEEE (2017)
22. Xue, M., Mian, A., Liu, W., Li, L.: Fully automatic 3D facial expression recognition using local depth features. In: IEEE Winter Conference on Applications of Computer Vision, pp. 1096–1103. IEEE (2014)
23. Hyvarinen, A.: Fast and robust fixed-point algorithms for independent component analysis. IEEE Trans. Neural Netw. **10**(3), 626–34 (1999)

ClusterFace: Clustering-Driven Deep Face Recognition

Lingjiang Xie[1], Cuican Yu[2], Huibin Li[2(✉)], and Jihua Zhu[1]

[1] School of Software Engineering, Xi'an Jiaotong University, Xi'an, China
sowhatxie@stu.xjtu.edu.cn, zhujh@xjtu.edu.cn
[2] School of Mathematics and Statistics, Xi'an Jiaotong University, Xi'an, China
ccy2017@stu.xjtu.edu.cn, huibinli@xjtu.edu.cn

Abstract. Recent years, image-based 2D face recognition has achieved human-level performance with the big breakthrough of deep learning paradigm. However, almost all of the existing deep face recognition methods depend on millions and millions of labeled 2D face images from different individual for supervised deep learning. In this case, face labelling becomes the pain point of deep face recognition. To solve this issue, we propose a novel clustering driven unsupervised deep face recognition framework, namely *ClusterFace*. In particular, our framework firstly assume that we already have a well-trained deep face model and a large number of face images without any labels. Then, all these face images are represented by this deep face model and then unsupervised clustered into different clusters using a certain clustering algorithm. Finally, these clustering-based face labelling results are employed to train a new deep CNN model for face recognition. Experimental results demonstrated that the proposed framework with a simple Mini-batch K-Means clustering algorithm can achieve surprising state-of-the-art performance (99.41%) on the LFW dataset. We also presented an intuitional explanation the reason of achieving good performance of our framework and also demonstrated its robustness to the choice of the number of clusters and the amount of unlabeled face images.

Keywords: Deep face recognition · Face clustering
Mini-batch K-Means

1 Introduction

In the past few years, with the big breakthrough of deep learning and big data paradigm, image-based 2D face recognition methods have surpassed the human-level performance in most real application scenarios such as the LFW benchmark [1,2]. 2D face recognition and verification solutions have been widely used in our daily life such as cell phone unlocking, online payment, various access control systems and so on.

© Springer Nature Switzerland AG 2018
J. Zhou et al. (Eds.): CCBR 2018, LNCS 10996, pp. 377–386, 2018.
https://doi.org/10.1007/978-3-319-97909-0_41

Table 1. An overview of 2D face datasets. *Label indicates that whether labelling images involves human efforts.

Dataset	Year	Identities	Images	Label*	Public
FaceBook [3]	2014	4,030	4.4M	Yes	No
CelebFaces+ [6]	2014	10,177	202,599	Yes	Yes
CASIA-WebFace [7]	2014	10,575	494,414	Yes	Yes
VGGFace [8]	2015	2,622	2.6M	Yes	Yes
Google [4]	2015	8M	200M	Yes	No
MegaFace [9]	2016	690,572	4.7M	Yes	Yes
MS-Celeb-1M [5]	2016	100,000	10M	Yes	Yes
VGGFace2 [10]	2018	9,131	3.31M	Yes	Yes

As a typical pattern recognition and image categorization problem, image-based 2D face recognition can be well-solved by the deep convolutional neural network (CNN) methodology. However, this kind of supervised strategy requires a large number of labelled face images, which need a lot of efforts by our humans. As shown in Table 1, a group of large 2D face dataset have been collected and used to train deep CNN models in the academic community from the year 2014 to 2018. Some of them are collected by big companies such as FaceBook [3], Google [4] and Microsoft [5]. The number of face identities of these datasets are vary from thousands to millions and the number of face images are up to 200 millions. Even some semi-automatic human-machine interactive face annotation methods have been used to label these datasets, the final data cleaning is still a very time consuming work. Once these datasets have been well collected and the data labels have been carefully annotated, they are used to train a deep CNN model for deep face recognition. For example, the FaceBook dataset [3] was used to train the DeepFace model, which can close the gap to human-level performance in face verification. The CASIA-WebFace [7] have been widely used to train deep face models [7,11,12], and reporting more than 99% accuracy on the LFW benchmark. VGGFace2 [10] was used to train a deep face model to evaluate the performance of cross-age face verification.

As introduced above, all these existing deep face recognition approaches used a large number of manual labelled face images to train their deep CNN models. However, in practical application, manually labelling a large set of images is impracticable for many different application scenarios. Consequently, the potential value of large amounts of un-labelled images cannot be well exploited. To solve this problem, in this paper, we propose an unsupervised framework for deep face recognition. In particular, our framework firstly assume that we already have a well-trained deep face model and a large number of face images without any label. Then, all these face images are represented by this deep face model and then unsupervised clustered into different clusters using a certain clustering algorithm. Finally, these clustering-based face labelling results are employed to train a new deep CNN model for face recognition. To the best of our knowledge, this is the first work using clustering-based face labelling scheme for deep face recognition. Our experimental results demonstrated that this clustering-driven face recognition method is quite efficient and can achieve 99.41% accuracy on the LFW dataset in face verification.

The reminder of this paper is organized as follows. Section 2 introduces the related works. Section 3 describes the details of the proposed clustering-based deep face recognition framework. In Sect. 4, we will present and discuss the experimental results and Sect. 5 concludes the paper.

2 Related Work

CNN Strucuture. Recent face recognition methods tend to learn image features using deep CNN architectures. This is because of the extraordinary success of famous CNN architectures, such as VGGNet [13], GoogleNet [14] and ResNet [15]. In particular, the residual module proposed in ResNet deepens the network and avoids the vanishing gradient problem which is beneficial for the optimization of model parameters. The idea is applied by recent state-of-the-arts such as SphereFace [11] and CosFace [16]. DeepVisage [12] employs a 22-layer network with 11 residual modules and achieves competitive results on LFW benchmark.

Loss Functions. In the field of face recognition, the aim of loss functions is to learn discriminative deep features. Contrastive loss [17] and triplet loss [4] learn better feature embedding by increasing Euclidean margin. Center loss [18] learns the centers for deep features of each identity and uses them to reduce intra-class variance. L-Softmax [19] and A-Softmax [11] increase angular margins by adding angular constraints. The difference is that A-softmax normalizes the weights.

Face Clustering. Face clustering is a challenging problem especially when both the number of face images and the number of identities are very large. The main difficulty of the challenge is that there is no universally agreed methodology for face representation and clustering results evaluation. [20] proposed a semi-supervised method which is based on hidden Markov random field model that represents the dependencies of cluster labels and tracklet association between video frames. [21] proposed an efficient and scalable unsupervised algorithm for face clustering leveraging an approximate nearest neighbor.

Datasets. As a data-driven model, face recognition methods based on deep CNN require a large amount of training data. Large-scale datasets of human face images [5,10] also play an important role in face recognition. However, manually labelling such a large scale face images is a time-consuming work. To deal with this problem, we propose a novel clustering-based deep face recognition framework. To the best of our knowledge, this is the first approach which uses automatically labelled face images for deep face recognition.

3   Clustering-Driven Deep Face Recognition

The pipeline of our proposed clustering-driven deep face recognition method is described in Fig. 1.

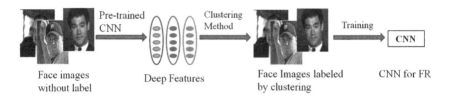

Fig. 1. The pipeline of the proposed clustering-driven deep face recognition approach. Firstly, a set of un-labelled face images are fed to a pre-trained deep face model to extract deep features. Then, a clustering algorithm is used to cluster these face images based on these deep features. Finally, these clustering-based labelled face images are used to train a new deep CNN model for the final face recognition.

3.1   Deep Face Representation

The purpose of this step is to extract deep features of un-labelled face images. Theoretically, any feature extractor method can be used for face representation. Since face representation plays an important role in face clustering, we suggest to use a pre-trained deep CNN model such as LResNet34E-IR used in [22]. This CNN model uses improved residual unit with a BN-Conv-BN-PReLu-Conv-BN structure and its first convolutional layer uses conv7 × 7 with stride = 2.

3.2   Clustering-Based Face Labelling

Clustering-based face labelling gives the same label to those face images belonging to the same identity, but use an unsupervised clustering algorithm instead of precise human manual labelling. Deep features are used as input of the clustering algorithm. [23] suggested that intrinsic distribution of the dataset may hinder the performance of the clustering. Thus, choosing proper clustering algorithm is the key issue to achieve good clustering performance.

In this paper, we suggest to use the Mini-batch K-Means [23] algorithm for face clustering. The K-Means algorithm minimizes over a set X of examples $x \in \mathbb{R}^m$ the following objective function:

$$\min \sum_{x \in X} \|f(C, x) - x\|^2 \tag{1}$$

The Optimization problem is to find the set C of cluster centers $c \in \mathbb{R}^m$, with $|C| = k$. Here $f(C, x)$ returns the nearest cluster center $c \in C$ to x using Euclidean distance. For efficient clustering of large scale dataset, the idea of stochastic gradient descent (SGD) is applied in K-Means, namely Mini-batch

K-Means (MBKM) algorithm. It takes samples from the dataset randomly and then cluster them using the K-Means algorithm. The centroids are then updated accordingly. Since only a small number of face samples are selected for clustering at each time, the computation time is faster than K-Means. The detail procedures of the Mini-batch K-Means algorithm is described in [23]. Notice that the number of clusters and the noise caused by the clustering may impact the performance of our proposed method. We conducted exploratory experiments to investigation their impacts which will be detailed in Sect. 4.

3.3 Clustering-Driven Deep Face Recognition

The aim of this step is to perform clustering-driven deep face recognition. That is, the clustering results of the previous step is used to train a new deep CNN model for face recognition. To evaluate the effectiveness of our clustering-based deep face recognition framework, we use the same deep CNN architecture as in Sphereface [11]. As shown in Table 2, a 36-layer deep CNN with two kinds of main structures: the convolutional layers and the residual learning blocks are used. Meanwhile, the A-softmax loss function firstly proposed in [11] is used to train the deep model.

Table 2. The CNN architecture of our deep face model, which is similar to the deep model used in [11].

Conv1.x	Conv2.x	Conv3.x	Conv4.x	FC1
$[3 \times 3, 64] \times 1, S2$	$[3 \times 3, 128] \times 1, S2$	$[3 \times 3, 256] \times 1, S2$	$[3 \times 3, 512] \times 1, S2$	
$\begin{bmatrix} 3 \times 3, 64 \\ 3 \times 3, 64 \end{bmatrix} \times 2$	$\begin{bmatrix} 3 \times 3, 128 \\ 3 \times 3, 128 \end{bmatrix} \times 4$	$\begin{bmatrix} 3 \times 3, 256 \\ 3 \times 3, 256 \end{bmatrix} \times 8$	$\begin{bmatrix} 3 \times 3, 512 \\ 3 \times 3, 512 \end{bmatrix} \times 2$	512

4 Experiments

4.1 Database and Preprocessing

To evaluate the effectiveness of our proposed clustering-based face recognition framework, we used three un-labelled datasets to train the deep face model. (1) The widely used CASIA-WebFace dataset [7] which contains about 0.49M face images with 10,575 identities. (2) The VGGFace2 dataset [10] which contains 3.3M face images from 9,131 identities. (3) The refined version of MS-Celeb-1M dataset [5] from [22] which contains 3.8M face images of 8.5 K identities. Notice that, all the labels of these face images are omitted and the clustered labels achieved by the Mini-batch K-Means algorithm are used as the ground truth labels. In the testing stage, we used the LFW dataset to evaluate the performance of our clustering-driven deep face model. It contains 13,233 face images from 5749 different identities. We follow the unrestricted with labeled outside data protocol. That is, the performance is evaluated on 6,000 pairs of face images in the face verification scenario.

For face preprocessing, we use the MTCNN [24] for face detection and landmark detection. Five landmarks including nose tip, two eye centers and two mouth corners are detected. Then these landmarks are adopted to perform a similarity transformation for face alignment. Finally, all face images are cropped and resized to the size of 112×112 before fed into the deep CNN model. When used for training, all face images are horizontally flipped for data augmentation.

4.2 Experimental Settings

Clustering Numbers. The cluster numbers are selected as the identity numbers of corresponding datasets.

Network Training. We use the PyTorch to implement the CNN architecture. A-softmax [11] loss with the parameter m (angular margin) set to 4 is adopted. To optimize the model parameters, we apply SGD algorithm with the batch size of 256 on one GTX 1080Ti GPU. For the case of training in clustered CASIA-WebFace dataset, we initialize the learning rate as 0.1 for 4 epochs and decrease it with a factor of 0.1 in the 4th epoch and the 7th epoch. We stop the training after 10 epochs. When training on the other two datasets, we set the initial learning rate as 0.01 and degenerates it with the factor of 0.5 every 10 epochs. The experiments are stopped after 40 epochs.

Network Testing. In the testing stage, the final representation of a testing face image is obtained by concatenating its original face features and its horizontally flipped features. The cosine distance of normalized deep features is computed as the similarity score. Finally, the face verification is conducted by thresholding the scores.

4.3 Experiments on the LFW Dataset

Table 3 shows the face verification results on the LFW dataset. As shown in the table, our proposed clustering-based deep face recognition framework achieves accuracy of 99.04% based on the CASIA-WebFace. In addition, we also find that when training larger volume of unlabelled images using our framework, the performance can be persistently increased under the same deep CNN architecture. That is, from 99.04% to 99.41% when using refined MS-Celeb-1M as the training dataset. It should be notice that all the labels of training face images are automatically achieved by the unsupervised clustering algorithm, which is totally different from all the other methods which used the manually labelled face labels for deep model training. Thus, we believe that this finding is very important for the following studies for deep face recognition.

4.4 Discussion

The Number of Clusters. As we know, the number of clusters is the key parameter for the Mini-batch K-Means algorithm adopted in our experiments. Here, we conduct experiments to explore the impact of the initial number of clusters. In particular, we perform face clustering on the CASIA-WebFace dataset using different cluster numbers. Note that the correct number of clusters is 10575. Different clustering results are used to train the deep CNN model and test their performance on the LFW dataset. Table 4 shows the results. We list the Fowlkes-Mallows index (FMI) [25] of the Mini-batch K-Means algorithm for face clustering under different numbers of clusters. The experimental results show that even using an estimated number of clusters, such as 10,000, our framework can still achieve stable face verification performance. That is, 98.92% vs. 99.04%. This indicates that our framework is robust to the variation of the number of clusters. In practice, if the number of face identities is unknown for a given unlabelled face dataset, we can also use an estimated number approximates to a proper range as the clustering number.

Table 3. Comparing the face verification accuracy on the LFW dataset.

Method	Training data size	Label	#Model	ACC%
DeepFace [3]	4M	Yes	3	97.35
FaceNet [4]	200M	Yes	1	99.63
CenterFace [18]	0.7M	Yes	1	99.28
VGGFace [8]	2.6M	Yes	1	98.95
CASIA-WebFace [7]	0.49M	Yes	1	97.73
SphereFace [11]	0.49M	Yes	1	99.42
Proposed Framework	0.49M	No	1	99.04
Proposed Framework	3.3M	No	1	99.33
Proposed Framework	3.8M	No	1	99.41

Table 4. The effect of the number of clusters for our proposed framework. The Fowlkes-Mallows index (FMI) is used to evaluate the face clustering results.

Number of Clusters	9,000	10,000	10,575	11,000	11,500
Accuracy	98.51%	98.92%	99.04%	98.90%	98.46%
FMI	0.2256	0.3280	0.3508	0.3327	0.2043

The Numbers of Noise Labels. To explain the surprise results that there are many face images are incorrectly labelled by our clustering algorithm, while a very high face verification performance can be achieved by our framework, we conducted an experiment to investigate the tendency of face verification accuracy degradation with respect to the noise images in the training face images.

In particular, we substituted training images in CASIA-WebFace with different levels of noise face images. The noise face images are randomly selected from the MS-Celeb-1M. For convenience, we directly apply the images and their original labels to train the deep CNN model. Figure 2 shows the experimental results. We can see that the performance is quite stable with the levels of noise images. When 40% of noise images are merged into the original dataset, the performance only drops about 2% compared with all the training face images used in the original dataset. This is the reason why our proposed clustering-based deep face recognition framework can achieve state-of-the-art performance.

The Choice of Pre-trained Models. To verify the ability of generalization of our proposed framework, we choose three pre-trained models: AlexNet [26], VGG-16 [13] and SE-LRResNet50E-IR [22] to extract deep features of CASIA-WebFace dataset for face clustering. Table 5 shows the results of the experiments. These two pre-trained models:VGG-16 and LResNet50E-IR, which are trained by face images, get the very similar performance of 98.93% and 99.04% respectively. In order to cope with different usage scenarios, we can try different pre-trained models to achieve competitive performance.

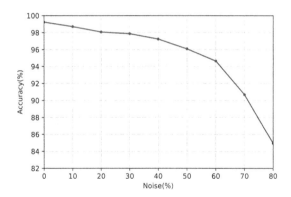

Fig. 2. The effect of incorrect labelled face images to a deep face recognition approach.

Table 5. The effect of incorrect labelled face images to a deep face recognition approach.

Pre-trained Models	AlexNet	VGG-16	SE-LRestNet50E-IR
Accuracy	98.56%	98.93%	99.04%

5 Conclusion

In this paper, we propose a novel clustering based deep face recognition framework, namely *ClusterFace*. The main feature of our framework is that our deep face model is trained by using a set of face images automatically labelled by a simple Mini-batch K-Means clustering algorithm. By applying clustering, millions and millions of unlabelled images are available to improve the performance of deep CNN face models. Experimental results demonstrated that the proposed framework can achieve surprise accuracy (99.41%) for face verification on the LFW dataset. In addition, further experiments indicate that deep CNN model achieves comparable results if the noise ratio is lower enough. With this property, adopting effective clustering algorithms and pre-trained models in the process of model training is considered to be practical and plausible.

References

1. Huang, G.B., Ramesh, M., Berg, T., Learned-Miller, E.: Labeled faces in the wild: A database for studying face recognition in unconstrained environments. Technical report, University of Massachusetts (2007)
2. Learned-Miller, E., Huang G.B.: Labeled faces in the wild: Updates and new reporting procedures. Technical report, University of Massachusetts (2014)
3. Taigman, Y., Yang, M., Ranzato, M., Wolf, L.: Deepface: closing the gap to human-level performance in face verification. In: CVPR (2014)
4. Schroff, F., Kalenichenko, D., Philbin, J.: Facenet: a unified embedding for face recognition and clustering. In: CVPR (2015)
5. Guo, Y., Zhang, L., Hu, Y., He, X., Gao, J.: MS-Celeb-1M: a dataset and benchmark for large-scale face recognition. In: Leibe, B., Matas, J., Sebe, N., Welling, M. (eds.) ECCV 2016. LNCS, vol. 9907, pp. 87–102. Springer, Cham (2016). https://doi.org/10.1007/978-3-319-46487-9_6
6. Sun, Y., Wang, X., Tang, X.: Deep learning face representation from predicting 10,000 classes. In: CVPR (2014)
7. Yi, D., Lei, Z., Liao, S., Li, S.Z.: Learning face representation from scratch. Computer Science (2014)
8. Parkhi, O.M., Vedaldi, A., Zisserman, A.: Deep face recognition. In: BMVC (2015)
9. Kemelmacher, I., Shlizerman, Seitz, S.M., Miller, D., Brossard, E.: The megaface benchmark: 1 million faces for recognition at scale. In: CVPR (2016)
10. Cao, Q., Shen, L., Xie, W., Parkhi, O.M., Zisserman, A.: VGGFace2: A dataset for recognising faces across pose and age. CoRR (2017)
11. Liu, W., Wen, Y., Yu, Z., Li, M., Raj, B., Song, L.: Sphereface: deep hypersphere embedding for face recognition. In: CVPR (2017)
12. Hasnat, M.A., Bohné, J., Milgram, J., Gentric, S., Chen, L.: Deepvisage: making face recognition simple yet with powerful generalization skills. In: IEEE International Conference on Computer Vision Workshops (2017)
13. Simonyan, K., Zisserman, A.: Very deep convolutional networks for large-scale image recognition. Computer Science (2014)
14. Szegedy, C., Liu, W., Jia, Y., Sermanet, P., Reed, S.E., Anguelov, D., Erhan, D., Vanhoucke, V., Rabinovich, A.: Going deeper with convolutions. In: CVPR (2015)

15. He, K., Zhang, X., Ren, S., Sun, J.: Deep residual learning for image recognition. In: CVPR (2016)
16. Wang, H., Wang, Y., Zhou, Z., Ji, X., Li, Z., Gong, D., Zhou, J., Liu, W.: Cosface: large margin cosine loss for deep face recognition. In: CVPR (2018)
17. Hadsell, R., Chopra, S., LeCun, Y.: Dimensionality reduction by learning an invariant mapping. In: CVPR (2006)
18. Wen, Y., Zhang, K., Li, Z., Qiao, Y.: A discriminative feature learning approach for deep face recognition. In: Leibe, B., Matas, J., Sebe, N., Welling, M. (eds.) ECCV 2016. LNCS, vol. 9911, pp. 499–515. Springer, Cham (2016). https://doi.org/10.1007/978-3-319-46478-7_31
19. Liu, W., Wen, Y., Yu, Z., Yang, M.: Large-margin softmax loss for convolutional neural networks. In: ICML (2016)
20. Wu, B., Lyu, S., Hu, B., Ji, Q.: Simultaneous clustering and tracklet linking for multi-face tracking in videos. In: ICCV (2013)
21. Otto, C., Wang, D., Jain, A.K.: Clustering millions of faces by identity. In: IEEE Transactions on Pattern Analysis and Machine Intelligence (2018)
22. Deng, J., Guo, J., Zafeiriou, S.: Arcface: Additive angular margin loss for deep face recognition. CoRR (2018)
23. Sculley, D.: Web-scale k-means clustering. In: International Conference on World Wide Web (2010)
24. Zhang, K., Zhang, Z., Li, Z., Qiao, Y.: Joint face detection and alignment using multitask cascaded convolutional networks. IEEE Signal Process. Lett. **23**, 1499–1503 (2016)
25. Fowlkes, E.B., Mallows, C.L.: A method for comparing two hierarchical clusterings. Publ. Am. Stat. Assoc. **78**, 553–569 (1983)
26. Alex, K., Ilya, S., Hinton, G.E.: Imagenet classification with deep convolutional neural networks. In: NIPS (2012)

Sketch Synthesized Face Recognition with Deep Learning Models

Wei Shao, Zhicheng Chen, Guangben Lu, Xiaokang Tu,
and Yuchun Fang$^{(\boxtimes)}$

School of Computer Engineering and Science, Shanghai University,
Shanghai, China
ycfang@shu.edu.cn

Abstract. Sketch face recognition is of great significance in the field of criminal investigation, Internet search and management. In this paper, we explore the feature presentation of sketch synthesized face images with several deep learning models. In order to complete the matching of heterogeneous images, we propose a modified face synthesis technology that combines sketches and face templates into a human face portrait. Through experiments, we investigate the essential problem of the degree of synthetic with respect to face recognition. Several state-of-the-art Deep Neural Network (DNN) models in face recognition are transferred in feature extraction of sketch synthesized face images. Experiments show that the proposed synthetic method is effective working with the DNN models in sketch face recognition.

Keywords: Heterogeneous face recognition · Sketch face recognition
CNNs · Face synthesis

1 Introduction

The research on face recognition originated in the late 19th century [2]. Until now, face recognition is still one of the core contents of computer vision research. In the early times, methods such as subspace and binary coding were used in feature extraction. Later, researchers focused on finding a sparse representation [3]. Recently, deep learning becomes dominant in face recognition research. The current face recognition is applied more and more in industry. For the controllable face recognition has been well developed, the center of gravity of the face recognition gradually shifts to an uncontrollable situation.

Heterogeneous face recognition technology refers to the matching of faces in different data sources. As an important field of heterogeneous face recognition, sketch face recognition involves two different styles of images, namely sketches and photos. Sketch face recognition has many important roles. In the field of criminal investigation, draft sketches created by forensic sketch artist can be used to identify the suspects. In the field of comics, sketch face recognition helps to achieve retrieval. In addition, through sketched face recognition, it is possible to tag the sketch information on the Internet for statistics and management. However, the accuracy of the current sketch face recognition technology has not yet reached the level that can be applied to the

© Springer Nature Switzerland AG 2018
J. Zhou et al. (Eds.): CCBR 2018, LNCS 10996, pp. 387–398, 2018.
https://doi.org/10.1007/978-3-319-97909-0_42

criminal investigation, so the technology has not yet been popularized. Therefore, sketch face recognition still has a long way to go. At present, sketch face recognition mainly includes three methods: synthesis, projection, and feature-based.

The idea of the synthesis method is to transform the sketches and photographs into one another, and then uses a common recognition algorithm to identify them [13, 17]. Tang et al. [4] used the PCA method to perform linear mapping synthesis. They also proposed a nonlinear method by using a multiscale Markov Random Fields (MRF) model [5, 20]. While Gao et al. [6, 7] used an embedded hidden Markov model (E-HMM) and selective ensemble strategy to fit the nonlinear relationship of a photo-sketch pair, Liong and Erin [15] used CNN to learn a type of nonlinear relationship between sketches and photos. Some synthesis methods laid emphasis on efficiency such as the Offline random sampling method [21].

The projection method is to find the lower dimensional common subspace of sketches and photos, where different styles of paintings become recognizable. Tang [4, 5, 8] pioneered the use of linear transformation to extract common linear features in sketches and photos as common subspace. Liu et al. [9] used a nonlinear kernel classifier to map sketches and photos to a common subspace. Pereira [18] proposed to fit both sketch and infrared images. Klare [19] proposed a more general projection method to fit on many different occasions.

The feature-based approach is to find a feature descriptor that allows it to have stability for different styles of paintings and needs to be differentiated [10]. The most widely used feature descriptors are: SIFT, Gabor, HOG, and MLBPs [22, 23]. Zhang et al. used a tree method to reduce the gap between different modal when extracting features [14]. Roy et al. [16] took a local gradient checksum as a local feature and had a great achievement, especially when meeting blur or noise.

This paper proposes a new synthesis method for sketch face recognition. Existing sketch face synthesis methods is basically either converting photos into complete sketches or converting sketches into complete photos. Differently, we combine the sketch with specific face template in a certain proportion with face morph. Specifically, after using Delaunay to divide the face into many triangular areas, we use affine transformation to synthesized the corresponding area of sketch and photo with certain proportion. On one hand, this method maintains the correspondence of the geometric area, on the other hand, the complexity of the algorithm is acceptable. The synthesis method in this paper is highly efficient and easy to implement. Besides, we also investigate the generalization ability of the benchmark DNN models [1, 11, 12] in representing the synthesized image.

Figure 1 illustrates the proposed sketch synthesis and recognition algorithm. In region one there are the sketches of the "suspects" and the face templates of photos. After face detection, facial feature point location, and Delaunay preprocessing, the suspect's sketches and face template are synthesized in the region three. In region two there is the photo library and the face template of sketches. Similarly, each photo in the photo library is synthesized with the face template of sketches. Finally, all the synthesized images are input to the DNN models to obtain feature representation. In the feature space, a distance measure is used to compare the image similarity to get the final ranking result.

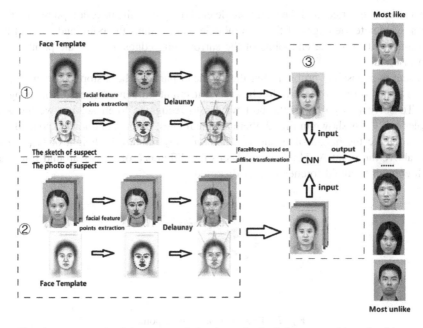

Fig. 1. Framework of the proposed sketch synthesized face recognition algorithm.

2   Face Synthesis

As described, there are three major methods for sketch face synthesis. In the past, face synthesis is basically a transformation between face and sketch. In this paper, we propose an innovative method to combine faces and sketches according to a certain degree of integration to reduce the gap between the two styles of photos. Besides, this method of synthesis means that in addition to the sketch and the face template of photos' synthesis, each photo in the photo library also needs to be synthesized with the face template of sketches in order to achieve unity of style.

2.1   Delaunay Triangulation

In order to combine the corresponding areas of the sketch and photo, that is, to maintain the geometric correspondence of the image, we use the Delaunay triangulation algorithm to achieve this aim. The triangulation of the human face is to connect the facial feature points into a triangulation network.

Delaunay triangulation has three methods: triangulation growth, incremental insertion, and divide-conquer. The incremental insertion method is simple to implement, requires small memory, and performs better in practical applications, but the time complexity is relatively high. Considering there are only 68 facial feature points, we choose this method since its time complexity is not very high.

The main idea of the incremental insertion method is to first construct a large triangle, repeatedly add one vertex at a time, and retriangulate the affected parts. Each time a point is inserted, and the edges are deleted that affect the insertion point. In other words, we delete the edges of the circumcircle that contains the point and connect the insertion point to all the endpoints of the surrounding edges until all the points have been inserted.

There is a possible problem that the forehead part can be distorted for the facial feature points do not cover the forehead, and it might influence the result of recognition. To solve this problem, the best way is to recognize forehead, but we adopt a simpler one. As is shown in Fig. 2, there are the highest point A and lowest point B. Y_A and Y_B denote the height of A and B. Then we only remain the height of $(Y_A - Y_B)$ units above the point A. This method keeps the difference of shapes around forehead small enough to avoid forehead being distorted.

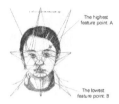

Fig. 2. Two marginal feature points.

2.2   Synthesis Method Based on Affine Transformation

After triangulation, we can get multiple triangular areas as the example shown in Fig. 3. We keep Region I as the shape of the original piece of a triangle area, while use Region II to denote the changes of the shape of Region I. The sketches and average face on the left side which obtains an untreated Region I are preprocessed with the Delaunay algorithm. The degree of combination α determines the shape of the synthesized triangle. Then the two images of Region I are mapped to Region II by the affine transformation. Finally, the two regions of Region II are merged to obtain Region III based on α.

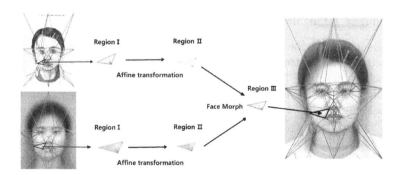

Fig. 3. Illustration of affine transformation and synthesis.

The above Region I conversion to Region II is implemented by the affine transformation. An affine map is the composition of two functions: a translation map and a linear map to denoting scaling, rotating, translating and mirroring. The quantities are constant before and after affine transform, such as parallelism or collinearity between points, the convexity of sets, ratios of lengths along a line. These properties minimize the impact of the affine transformation on the facial features and adapt to the different shapes and sizes of the corresponding regions of the sketch and the photo. At the same time, the affine transformation contains matrix operations, which greatly accelerates the speed. Therefore, the affine transformation is chosen for synthesis in this paper.

The affine process can be represented by matrix notations. The matrix X is a certain triangular region of the human face. The matrix Y is the result of X mapping according to the shape of the synthesized region. Z is the final triangle region that is composed of two Y_S in α. We denote $Y = f(X)$ as the mapping function and $Z = G(Y_1, Y_2)$ as the synthesis function.

Since by the affine transformation is linear as in Eq. (1), where a and b are coefficients. Apparently, it can also be written as Eq. (2), where M is a coefficient matrix. In Eq. (2), both $F(X)$ and M are unknown. Let one of the vertices of the synthesized region Y be vector P, and the corresponding two vertex vectors in the original region X are P_0 and P_1. We can derive a vertex in Y with Eq. (3). The degree of combination parameter α affects the morphed face through Eq. (3). The point pairs (X_i, Y_i) of triangle region's three vertices can be obtained by Eq. (3), where $i \in \{1, 2, 3\}$. In this way, the matrix M can be obtained, eliminating an unknown number. Then, for each point p_i within X, the corresponding position $F(p_i)$ in Y can be calculated by Eq. (2). The mapping process in the above figure can be represented by $R_2 = F(R_1)$, where R_1 denotes RegionI and R_2 denotes RegionII. Finally, Z is a simple combination of Y_1 and Y_2, namely $G(Y_1, Y_2)$, as in Eq. (4), where Y_1 comes from the sketch and Y_2 comes from the template of photos. In Eq. (4), α denotes the degree of combination parameter. It affects the positions of triangle regions' vertices in the synthesized face by Eq. (3). It also affects the positions of the points inside the triangle regions of the synthesized face by Eq. (4).

$$F(X) = a \times X + b \tag{1}$$

$$F(X) = M \times \left[X^T, 1\right]^T \tag{2}$$

$$P = \alpha \times P_0 + (1 - \alpha) \times P_1 \tag{3}$$

$$G(Y_1, Y_2) = \alpha \times Y_1 + (1 - \alpha) \times Y_2 \tag{4}$$

The realization of the synthesis method is summarized in Fig. 4.

Algorithm 1:Face Synthesis

Input : sketch image, template image, α
Output : morphed face image
1 : get feature points of input image by face Detect algorithm
2 : get Triangle regions of input image by Delaunay
3 : repeat
        1 : choose a piece of Triangle region X
        2 : get 3 Points P[1...3] of morphed region by Equation (3)
        3 : calculate M by P[1...3] and Equation (2)
        4 : calculate F(P[1...n]) by Equation (2) where P[1...n] denote
points within X
        5: calculate G(Y1, Y2) by Equation (4)
        6: add G(Y1, Y2) to morphed face image
4: until no piece to choose
5: return morphed face image

Fig. 4. Algorithm of face synthesis.

3 Face Recognition with DNN Models

Several DNN models are used to extract the feature representations for the synthesized face images. It is interesting to verify the representation ability of these benchmark models in sketch face recognition.

The DNN models usually extract different features based on the convolution kernels in the convolution layer and the pooled layers to eliminate overfitting. Assume that a face photo is 100×100 in size. If the number of neurons in the next hidden layer is $1e6$, $1e12$ is required in the case of full connection. This kind of parameter scale is impossible to train. To improve the algorithm, we can take local connections. Each neuron only connects with 10×10 partial images. This requires $1e8$ parameters. Although many optimizations have been made, the size of the parameters is still very large. The sharing of weights can greatly reduce the parameter scale. That is, each neuron connects only one 10×10 partial image, and all 10×10 neurons share the parameters of this one neuron. This only requires 100 parameters. Through continuous alternation, the final result is output using the full connection when the feature is reduced to a very small scale. Although the parameters are few, they still produce good results.

In order to achieve accurate sketch face recognition results, three popular models adopted in this paper are SeetaFace [11], VGGFace [12] and FaceNet [1]. VGGFace takes smaller convolution kernel (3×3) instead of the traditional one. Meanwhile, it applies smaller pooling kernels (2×2). For this two features, the model becomes deeper and wider, and the increase of calculation becomes slower. Face Net consists of a Batch (a input layer), a deep CNN, L_2 (used to normalize), which result in the face embedding. SeetaFace contains three key parts, among which the SeetaFace Identification uses a convolutional neural network to extract the features. The Fast Normalization Layer is introduced to speed up the convergence process and improve the generalization ability. As the benchmark algorithm in face recognition, their performance is compared in Table 1.

Table 1. SeetaFace, FaceNet, VGGFace comparison table

Methods	LFW accurancy	Parameter scale (M)
SeetaFace [11]	0.986	–
VGGFace [12]	0.973	134.2
FaceNet [1]	0.996	26(NNS1), 4.3(NNS2)

It's easy to find that these face recognition systems all perform well in LFW, and all of them use CNN as a basement. That is the reason why we choose these face recognition systems. To choose the most promising ones for sketch face recognition.

4 Experiment

4.1 Database

The database used in this experiment is the CUHK database [5], the CUHK database is established for the study of sketch face synthesis and recognition. It contains a total of 606 face photos, of which 188 are from the University of Hong Kong, China, 123 from the AR database, and 295 from the XM2VTS database. Each photograph in CUHK has a corresponding sketch. This article uses the database of the University of Hong Kong. Figure 5 shows the average faces generated in this database, which are used as templates for synthesis.

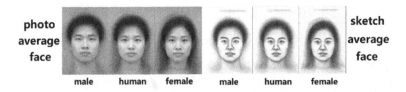

Fig. 5. Average face generation result.

4.2 The Result of Face Synthesis

By taking the average face as the simplest template, we observe the influence of synthesis parameter by their visual effect. From the synthesis results shown in Fig. 6, it can be found that the larger the α, the closer to the original, and the smaller the α, the closer to the average face. It can also be seen that there are slight differences in the two synthesis directions, which is due to the need to take into account both styles of photographs. The content of the follow-up experiment is to choose the right α to achieve the best recognition effect.

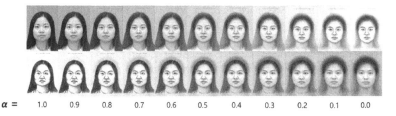

$\alpha =$ 1.0   0.9   0.8   0.7   0.6   0.5   0.4   0.3   0.2   0.1   0.0

Fig. 6. Synthetic result, first line: photo and average face synthesis, second line: sketch and average face synthesis.

4.3   Verification Experiments

For each picture in the database, we synthesized it using the method mentioned above, and generate the result using gender-insensitive and gender-sensitive average faces with different α. Then we use the SeetaFace feature to calculate the synthesized photos-sketches similarities of the above results, normalize the data and draw the corresponding histograms. The gender-insensitive, $\alpha = 0.8$ one is shown as an example in Fig. 7. The left half in the Fig. 7 shows the distribution of similarities between synthesized photos and sketches of different person, and the distribution of similarities between synthesized photos and sketches of the same person. Then, we use normal distribution and Gaussian kernel distribution to estimate their probability density curve and the result is shown in the right half of Fig. 7. The curve can be used to find the best threshold to differentiate the photos mentioned above.

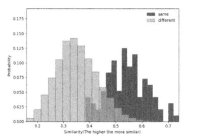
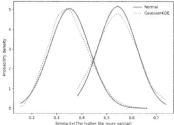

Fig. 7. Similarity histogram (left), probability density plot (right).

We use a simple method to get the ROC curve: for each histogram mentioned above, choose different threshold and calculate the True Positive Rate and the False Positive Rate, finally, connect the points to a line. The results of the experiments using the gender-insensitive average face for synthesis are shown on the left of Fig. 8. The results of the experiments using the gender-specific average face for synthesis are shown on the right of Fig. 8. Based on the results, we can draw the conclusion that the best value α is between 0.6 and 0.8.

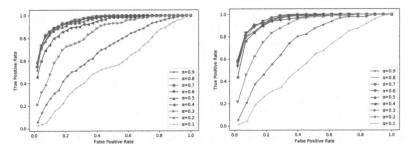

Fig. 8. ROC curve that uses gender-insensitive average face (left), uses gender-specific average face (right).

4.4 Identification Experiments

The identification experiments are evaluated with the Cumulative Match Curve (CMC) to compare three DNN models as shown in Fig. 9, in which each CMC curve has chosen the α with the highest accuracy. Seetaface performs the best, which proves its adaptability and transferability in heterogeneous recognition. Hence, we choose SeetaFace feature in the experiments hereafter.

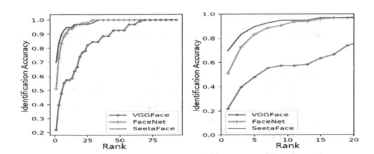

Fig. 9. CMC curves that use VGGFace, FaceNet, SeetaFace feature.

With the identification experiment, we also explore the influence of templates in synthesis in identification experiments. As shown in Fig. 10, the Cumulative Match Curve (CMC) is plotted for the SeetaFace feature for different α. The first and the third graph of the Fig. 10 show the correct rate of α of 20%, 40%, 60% and 80%. It can be found that the synthesis in the range of 40% to 80% has a good effect. The second and the fourth graph of Fig. 10 shows the specific results after amplification. It can be found that the synthesis effect is the best in the range of 60% to 70%. Since the average face can be divided into gender-specific and gender-insensitive, the experiment proves that the gender-specific average face gains better result. Therefore, when the gender is known, the gender-specific average face should be selected as a face template, and if the gender is unknown, the gender-insensitive average face should be selected as a template for synthesis.

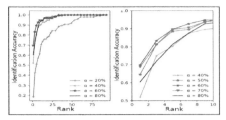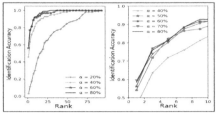

Fig. 10. CMC curves that use gender-specific average face (left) and gender-insensitive average face (right).

In Table 2, we compare the identification results of synthetic face recognition algorithms. It can be observed that the result obtained with the proposed method is by par with or better than the benchmark methods. This shows the effectiveness of the proposed synthesis method and the adaptability of the DNN models. However, the results with simple distance measurement still are not as good as those methods with class label enhanced models, which reported results of over 90% at rank 1 [16, 18, 19]. Moreover, we believe that the performance of DNN models can be further improved after pre-training with large labeled sketch databases. Even so, our experiments shown the strong generalization ability of the DNN models in sketch synthesized face recognition.

Table 2. Rank in our opinion and hits relationship table

Rank	1	2	3	4	5	6	7	8
Geometry [4]	30	37	45	48	53	59	62	66
Eigenface [4]	31	43	48	55	61	63	65	65
SketchTransform [4]	71	78	81	84	88	90	94	94
MSMRF+LDA [16]	96	–	–	–	–	–	–	
SIFT+MLBP [16]	98	–	–	–	–	–	–	
MCCA [16]	99	–	–	–	–	–	–	
I S V [18]	96	–	–	–	–	–	–	
D-RS [19]	96	–	–	–	–	–	–	
Ours	70	76	83	88	90	92	93	94

5   Conclusion

In this paper, a new synthesis method is proposed for sketch face recognition. Two types of face modal are affine-transformed according to adjustable proportion and the control parameters are selected through experiments. In addition, we propose using variable templates to make sketch face recognition more flexible and take full advantage of the available semantic information. Under the premise that the known appearance feature is a priori condition, a related template can be generated. The more the amount of information contained in the template is, the more accurate the matching is. This flexibility allows it to adapt to a variety of applications, that is, in different situations, we only need to adjust the template. The synthesized images are used in face recognition by taking DNN models for feature extraction. Though no pre-training is performed, the results are already over the benchmarks with only distance matching.

We believe that with enough data for pre-training and label-enhanced learning, more promising results can be obtained, so enlarging the dataset scale of the experiment will be the next step of our work.

Acknowledgements. The work is funded by the Shanghai Undergraduate Student Innovation Project, the National Natural Science Foundation of China (No. 61170155) and the Shanghai Innovation Action Plan Project (No. 16511101200).

References

1. Schroff, F., Kalenichenko, D., Philbin, J.: FaceNet: a unified embedding for face recognition and clustering, pp. 815–823 (2015)
2. Galton, F.: Personal identification and description. J. Anthropol. Inst. Great Br. Irel. **18**(973), 177–191 (1889)
3. Wagner, A., et al.: Toward a practical face recognition system: robust alignment and illumination by sparse representation. IEEE Trans. Pattern Anal. Mach. Intell. **34**(2), 372–386 (2012)
4. Tang, X., Wang, X.: Face sketch recognition. IEEE Trans. Circ. Syst. Video Technol. **14**(1), 50–57 (2004)
5. Wang, X., Tang, X.: Face photo-sketch synthesis and recognition. In: IEEE International Conference on Computer Vision, p. 687. IEEE Computer Society (2003)
6. Gao, X., et al.: Face sketch synthesis algorithm based on E-HMM and selective ensemble. IEEE Trans. Circ. Syst. Video Technol. **18**(4), 487–496 (2008)
7. Xiao, B., et al.: A new approach for face recognition by sketches in photos. Signal Process. **89**(8), 1576–1588 (2009)
8. Tang, X., Wang, X.: Face photo recognition using sketch. In: 2002 Proceedings of the IEEE International Conference on Image Processing, vol. 1, pp. I-257–I-260 (2002)
9. Liu, Q., et al.: A nonlinear approach for face sketch synthesis and recognition. In: IEEE Computer Society Conference on Computer Vision and Pattern Recognition, pp. 1005–1010. IEEE Computer Society (2005)
10. Hu, Y.: Research on sketch-based cross-modal face retrieval framework. Beijing University of Posts and Telecommunications (2017)
11. Liu, X., et al.: VIPLFaceNet: an open source deep face recognition SDK. Front. Comput. Sci. **11**(2), 208–218 (2017)
12. Parkhi, O.M., Vedaldi, A., Zisserman, A.: Deep face recognition. In: British Machine Vision Conference, pp. 41.1–41.12 (2015)
13. Wang, N., et al.: A comprehensive survey to face hallucination. Int. J. Comput. Vis. **106**(1), 9–30 (2014)
14. Zhang, W., Wang, X., Tang, X.: Coupled information-theoretic encoding for face photo-sketch recognition. In: IEEE Conference on Computer Vision and Pattern Recognition, pp. 513–520. IEEE Computer Society (2011)
15. Liong, V.E., et al.: Deep coupled metric learning for cross-modal matching. IEEE Trans. Multimed. **19**(6), 1234–1244 (2017)

16. Roy, H., Bhattacharjee, D.: Face sketch-photo recognition using local gradient checksum: LGCS. Int. J. Mach. Learn. Cybern. **8**, 1–13 (2016)
17. Gao, X., et al.: Face sketch–photo synthesis and retrieval using sparse representation. IEEE Trans. Circ. Syst. Video Technol. **22**(8), 1213–1226 (2012)
18. De Freitas Pereira, T., Marcel, S.: Heterogeneous face recognition using inter-session variability modelling. In: Computer Vision and Pattern Recognition Workshops, pp. 179–186. IEEE (2016)
19. Klare, B.F., Jain, A.K.: Heterogeneous face recognition using kernel prototype similarities. IEEE Trans. Pattern Anal. Mach. Intell. **35**(6), 1410–1422 (2013)
20. Zhang, W., Wang, X., Tang, X.: Lighting and Pose Robust Face Sketch Synthesis. In: Daniilidis, K., Maragos, P., Paragios, N. (eds.) ECCV 2010. LNCS, vol. 6316, pp. 420–433. Springer, Heidelberg (2010). https://doi.org/10.1007/978-3-642-15567-3_31
21. Wang, N., Gao, X., Li, J.: random sampling for fast face sketch synthesis. Pattern Recogn. **76**, 215–227 (2017)
22. Klare, B.F., et al.: Matching composite sketches to face photos: a component-based approach. IEEE Trans. Inf. Forensics Secur. **8**(1), 191–204 (2013)
23. Klare, B., Li, Z., Jain, A.K.: Matching forensic sketches to mug shot photos. IEEE Trans. Pattern Anal. Mach. Intell. **33**(3), 639–646 (2011)

Face Anti-spoofing to 3D Masks by Combining Texture and Geometry Features

Yan Wang, Song Chen, Weixin Li, Di Huang$^{(\boxtimes)}$, and Yuhong Wang

IRIP Lab, School of Computer Science and Engineering,
Beihang University, Beijing 100191, China
dhuang@buaa.edu.cn

Abstract. Anti-spoofing has become more important in face recognition systems. This paper proposes a novel approach to resist 3D face mask attacks, which jointly uses texture and shape features. Different from existing methods where depth information by extra equipments is required, we reconstruct geometry cues from RGB images through 3D Morphable Model. The hand-crafted features as well as the deep ones are then extracted to comprehensively represent texture and shape differences between real and fake faces and finally fused for decision making. The experiments are carried out on the 3D-MAD dataset and the competitive results indicate the effectiveness.

Keywords: Face anti-spoofing · 3D face reconstruction
Deep learning

1 Introduction

Face recognition (FR), with its wide applications in various fields, e.g., security and business, has received tremendous attention over the past decades. For most existing FR systems, despite their satisfactory accuracies, the vulnerability to Spoofing Attacks (SA) still remains a serious problem, which tends to impede further pervasion of FR techniques. In general, there are three means of SA, where attackers attempt to gain access by presenting fake faces of authorized users using printed photos, recorded videos and 3D face masks. Currently, it is not so hard to launch such attacks as face data are easily acquired and the copies, in particular images and videos, are of a relatively low cost. Therefore, face anti-spoofing is of great significance within the community.

In the literature, a number of methods have been proposed to deal with photo and video based SA [3,23,24,29], and very good results have been reported. However, compared to 2D image and video data, 3D masks can mimic genuine faces with much better appearance and geometry properties, thus making face anti-spoofing more challenging. To the best of our knowledge, existing studies on 3D face mask anti-spoofing are basically texture-based [1,9,21,27]. Although they

© Springer Nature Switzerland AG 2018
J. Zhou et al. (Eds.): CCBR 2018, LNCS 10996, pp. 399–408, 2018.
https://doi.org/10.1007/978-3-319-97909-0_43

show promising results, their performance is likely to degrade in the presence of some variations, such as illumination conditions and mask materials. To solve this issue, researchers try to employ additional auxiliary cues, including heart rate signals [20] and 3D depth/geometry features [15]. Unfortunately, these methods often rely on special acquisition sensors that cannot be conveniently mounted on popular end devices, e.g., smart phones and tablet PCs, and inevitably increase the expenditure in hardware, both of which limit them in real-world scenarios.

In this paper, we propose a novel approach to 3D face mask anti-spoofing by fusing texture and shape features. In contrast to current solutions that capture depth information by extra equipments, we reconstruct depth cues from RGB images through 3D Morphable Model (3DMM). A feature set, including both the hand-crafted and deep ones, is then built to comprehensively represent the texture and geometry differences between real and fake faces. The selected features are finally integrated for decision making. The experiments are conducted on 3D-MAD [7] and the results demonstrate the effectiveness of reconstructed depth images as well as its complementary to original RGB data. Besides, our method proves very competent at detecting 3D mask attacks.

2   Related Work

Early face anti-spoofing methods mainly handle image and video attacks, and according to the features used, they can be roughly classified into three groups, i.e., motion-based, image quality based, and texture-based.

Motion-based methods make use of the movement of organs and muscles to distinguish the genuine faces from the fake ones, and relative motions, such as eye blinking, mouth opening, and head rotating, can be detected in continuous video frames. Bharadwaj et al. [4] present a method to amplify motions, which improves the SA detection rate. In [30], a CNN-LSTM architecture is proposed to learn more powerful features to detect false faces. However, these methods tend to take a long time to capture stable live characteristics, because the human physiological rhythm ranges from 0.2 to 0.5 Hz [4]. In addition, these methods are vulnerable to replay video attacks.

Image quality based methods focus on surface reflectivity, arguing the reflectivity of human skin is different from that of other materials used in attacks. Angelopou et al. [2] measure the reflectivity distribution of real skins under visible spectrum, and find out that with the increase of wavelength, reflectivity decreases. [6,22] show that the reflectance at the wavelength of 850 nm is high and that of 1400 nm is low. Such methods are theoretically sound, but they require well controlled lighting condition and the materials that are similar to skin may incur trouble.

Texture based methods emphasize the texture difference between real and fake faces since the surface characteristics of artificial pigment and human skin are different. For instance, global image blur occurs in print-attacks. Maata et al. [21] model the difference between real and fake faces by LBP features, highlighting the importance of micro-textures. In [9], Galbally et al. investigate more texture features of LBP, DoG and HOG. Agarwal et al. [1] exploit block-wise Haralick texture features from redundant discrete wavelet transformed images. Li et al. [19] apply Convolutional Neural Network (CNN) to generate more discriminative features from still images and then feed them to SVM for classification. Shao et al. [27] further take dynamic clues into consideration and conduct deep convolutional dynamic texture learning.

Recently, with the development of 3D printing technologies, 3D mask based SA becomes popular and anti-spoofing is more challenging. The methods to image and video attacks aforementioned are preliminarily discussed but not qualified. In this case, geometric attributes of 3D facial shapes are important to supplement those in the 2D modality. In [8], Erdogmus and Marcel extract LBP from depth images, and its credit is combined with that of LBP histograms of RGB images in SVM and LDA based classifiers. [27] highlights the CNN based motion difference between the shapes of genuine faces and fake masks, which is jointly used with that in the texture channel for prediction. But as we state, such shape features are dependent on additional sensors and there is also some room to ameliorate the overall performance.

3 Method

3.1 Framework

The framework of our proposed method is illustrated in Fig. 1. As shown in the figure, we use both the texture and shape modalities for 3D face mask anti-spoofing. The textures come from the original RGB images, while the shapes are recovered using a 3D morphable model. For both the two modalities, we extract a set of features, including the traditional hand-crafted ones, i.e. LBP histograms and normal vectors, as well as the deep ones, i.e., the CNN features computed by the VGG-16 models. MKL is adopted to integrate the contributions of the traditional features, while softmax is used to combine the deep learned ones, deciding whether a given face in front of the camera is genuine or fake.

3.2 3D Face Reconstruction

Instead of using the depth maps acquired by additional sensors, we employ 3DMM to recover a 3D face model from a given 2D face image.

In 3DMM, a face is represented by vectors $S, T \in \mathbf{R}^{3N}$, providing the x, y, z components of the shape coordinates and the corresponding RGB color values respectively, where N is the number of the mesh vertices. A 3DMM thus contains two PCA models, one for the shape and the other for the texture. Each PCA model

$$M := (\overline{v}, \sigma, V) \tag{1}$$

consists of the mean of the meshes $\overline{v} \in R^{3N}$(3D coordinates or 2D pixel values), a set of principal components $V = [v_1, ..., v_{n-1}] \in R^{3N \times (n-1)}$ and the standard

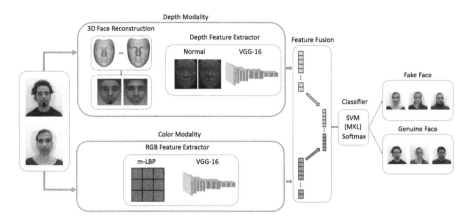

Fig. 1. Framework of the proposed method.

deviations $\sigma \in R^{n-1}$, in which n is the number of scans used to build the model. The shape of 3D face can be further generated by

$$S = \overline{v} + \sum_{i}^{M} \alpha_i \sigma_i v_i \tag{2}$$

For the shape, $M \leq n - 1$ is the number of selected principal components and $\alpha \in R^M$ denotes the coefficients, i.e. the coordinates of the 3D face instance in the shape space. The generation process for the texture is similar.

For computation efficiency, we use a low-resolution (3,448 vertices) shape-only model (sfm-shape-3,448 from an open-source library named EOS [14]). Given an input face image and its landmarks (localized using the dlib library), we find its PCA shape coefficients α by minimizing the cost function:

$$\mathbb{E} = \sum_{i=1}^{3N} \frac{(y_{2D,i} - y_i)^2}{2\sigma_{2D}^2} + ||\alpha||_2^2 \tag{3}$$

where N is the number of landmarks, y denotes the 2D landmarks, σ_{2D}^2 is an optional variance for these landmark points, and y_{2D} are the 2D projection of the 3DMM shape. Refer to [14] for more details. Some recovered depth maps are illustrated in the middle row in Fig. 2.

3.3 Feature Extraction

When the depth map is reconstructed, a given face has the information both in the RGB and D channels. We then calculate a number of features to capture the possible differences between real and fake faces. The features are introduced in the following.

LBP Features. LBP is a widely used hand-crafted texture descriptor, and it has shown success in many face analysis tasks [10–13] . In our study, an LBP variant, namely Modified LBP (MLBP), is used to encode texture features. Instead of sampling from surrounding pixels in original LBP, MLBP uses the mean values of neighboring blocks, and proves more efficient in face anti-spoofing [23]. In this work, we divide the whole face image into 3 × 3 non-overlapping blocks, and for each block, a 59-bin histogram is computed, resulting a 531-bin feature.

Normal Features. To better highlight the face shape attributes, normal values of all the vertices in the range image are calculated. As in [16–18], three normal component maps in the x, y and z directions are produced. All the values are concatenated to a 3D matrix, and this matrix is squeezed to form a feature vector of a dimension of 10,344 (3448 × 3).

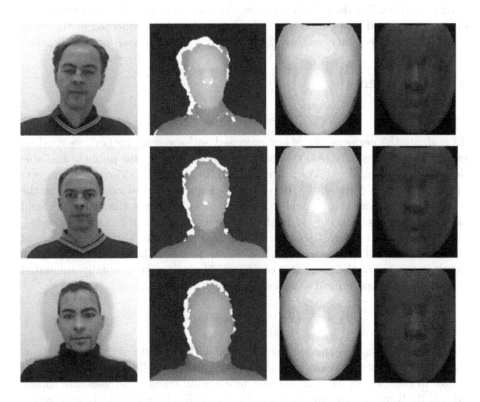

Fig. 2. Illustration of original RGB images, real depth images captured by the Kinect sensor, reconstructed depth images from 3DMM, and normal maps computed on the recovered depth images, in the three sessions of the same subject.

CNN Features. Deep learning features are also extracted both from the texture and shape modalities. To balance efficiency and precision, we choose VGG-16 [28] as the base architecture. For each modality, input images go through an individual network. There are 13 convolution layers and 5 max pooling layers, where the kernel size of each convolution layer is 3×3, and that of the max pooling layer is 2×2. The stride is 1, and the activation functions are ReLu. Two fully connected layers behind generate a 4,096-d feature vector.

3.4   Fusion and Classification

Finally, the features in the two modalities are combined to decide whether a face is fake or genuine. For hand-crafted features, we adopt SVM with SimpleMKL [26]. MKL makes use of a pre-defined set of kernels and learns an optimal linear or non-linear combination of kernels, which is claimed to be superior to the single kernel solutions. For deep CNN features, the feature maps at the last conv layer of the texture and shape model are concatenated and the squeezed feature map is fed into the fully connected layer, followed by a softmax layer for classification.

4   Experiments

4.1   Dataset

To evaluate the performance of our proposed anti-spoofing method, we conduct experiments on the 3D-MAD database. As far as we know, the publicly available dataset with 3D mask attacks is very limited. In 3D-MAD, videos of 17 subjects are made by the Microsoft Kinect sensor under controlled conditions, in the frontal-view and with a neutral expression. A subject has three sessions, and each session contains 5 videos. In the first two sessions, real faces are recorded, and in the third session, the mask attacks are captured. All the videos are of the same length of 300 frames (in total 76,500 frames). The color image and the depth image are of the same size of 640×480 pixels with manually annotated eye positions. Some typical samples are presented in Fig. 2.

4.2   Setting

Protocol. To compare the proposed method with the state of the art, we adopt the standard protocol, namely Leave-One-Out Cross-Validation (LOOCV), as in [8]. In each video, we take one out of every 30 frames and generate totally 10 still RGB images for our experiments. For each fold, a subject is selected for test while the other 16 subjects are randomly divided into two equal parts as the training and development set respectively. The experiment is repeated 17 times so that all the subjects appear in test. We report the average accuracies of 2D features, 3D features, and some of their combinations.

Parameters. The normal and LBP features are respectively compacted to 200 and 100 using PCA before classification. In MKL, the Polynomial kernels with the degree of 1 and 3 are adopted for normal vectors and the RBF kernels with the gamma value of 0.8 and 1 are used for LBP histograms.

For RGB images, the VGG-16 model is pre-trained on ImageNet [5], and for depth images, the model is pre-trained on the FRGC dataset [25]. In the VGG-16 models in both modalities, we employ the Cross-Entropy loss and SGD is used for optimization. Each training process has 25 epochs, and the learning rate is set to 0.01. The learning rate is multiplied by 0.1 every 5 epochs. The weight decay is set to 0.0001 and the batch size is set to 32.

4.3   Results

The accuracies of texture features, shape features, and some of their fusions in terms of EER and AUC are displayed in Table 1. From this table, we can find that, the recovered shape information is useful in 3D face mask anti-spoofing. Based on shallow normal features, the EER of the depth channel is 6.37%, which is largely boosted to 0.90% by deep CNN features, highlighting a better discriminative power. Meanwhile, we can also notice that the reconstructed depth map presents a good complementarity to the original texture image, evidenced by their fusion result that is superior to that of either single modality. By combining the deep texture and shape features, we make correct predictions on all the test samples. Figure 3 shows the ROC curves when we integrate texture and shape clues.

In Table 2, we compare our top results to the state of the art ones reported on the 3D-MAD database. The scores in [8, 20, 27, 28] are based on texture features, and the one in [24] is based on the original depth data. On the other side, [8, 28] make use of static information, while [20, 24, 28] also consider dynamic cues. We can see that the proposed method that integrates the deep features of the RGB and recovered depth data reaches the best performance.

Table 1. Accuracies of different texture features, shape features, and some of their combinations on the 3D-MAD database.

	Features	EER (%)	AUC (%)
Hand-crafted	MLBP-Texture	6.37	98.58
	Normal-Depth	11.93	94.97
	Fusion	2.65	99.66
Deep	CNN-Texture	0.90	99.80
	CNN-Depth	6.92	84.44
	Fusion	0.00	100.00

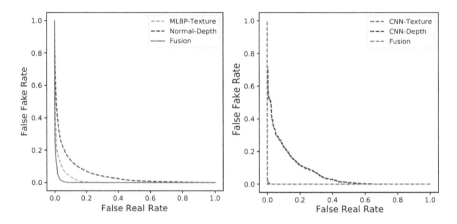

Fig. 3. ROC curves of hand-crafted features (left) and deep learning features (right) on 3D-MAD.

Table 2. Comparison with the state-of-art methods on the 3DMAD dataset.

Method	EER (%)	AUC (%)
MS LBP [8]	5.25	98.65
fc CNN [28]	3.24	98.36
LBP-TOP [24]	1.35	99.92
Optical Flow [27]	10.87	94.21
rPPG [20]	8.59	96.81
Dynamic texture [27]	0.56	99.99
Ours (CNN fusion)	0.00	100

5   Conclusion

In this paper, we propose an effective method for 3D face mask anti-spoofing. It makes use of both texture and shape features, but instead of launching the additional sensor, our depth maps are recovered from original RGB images through 3DMM. Both the hand-crafted and deep features are investigated to capture differences between the real faces and the fake ones. Experiments are conducted on the 3D-MAD dataset, and the results show that reconstructed depth maps are indeed useful and they provide complementary information to improve the overall performance.

Acknowledgment. This work is supported by the National Natural Science Foundation of China (No. 61673033).

References

1. Agarwal, A., Singh, R., Vatsa, M.: Face anti-spoofing using Haralick features. In: IEEE International Conference on Biometrics Theory, Applications and Systems, pp. 1–6 (2016)
2. Angelopoulou, E.: Understanding the color of human skin. In: SPIE Human Vision and Electronic, Imaging, pp. 243–251 (2001)
3. Atoum, Y., Liu, Y., Jourabloo, A., Liu, X.: Face anti-spoofing using patch and depth-based CNNs. In: IEEE International Joint Conference on Biometrics, pp. 319–328 (2017)
4. Bharadwaj, S., Dhamecha, T.I., Vatsa, M., Singh, R.: Computationally efficient face spoofing detection with motion magnification. In: IEEE Conference on Computer Vision and Pattern Recognition Workshops, pp. 105–110 (2013)
5. Deng, J., Dong, W., Socher, R., Li, L.-J., Li, K., Fei-Fei, L.: Imagenet: a large-scale hierarchical image database. In: IEEE Conference on Computer Vision and Pattern Recognition, pp. 248–255 (2009)
6. Dowdall, J., Pavlidis, I., Bebis, G.: Face detection in the near-IR spectrum. Image Vis. Comput. 21(7), 565–578 (2003)
7. Erdogmus, N., Marcel, S.: Spoofing in 2D face recognition with 3D masks and anti-spoofing with kinect. In: IEEE International Conference on Biometrics: Theory, Applications and Systems, pp. 1–6 (2013)
8. Erdogmus, N., Marcel, S.: Spoofing face recognition with 3d masks. IEEE Trans. Inf. Forensics Secur. 9(7), 1084–1097 (2014)
9. Galbally, J., Marcel, S., Fierrez, J.: Image quality assessment for fake biometric detection: application to iris, fingerprint, and face recognition. IEEE Trans. Image Process. 23(2), 710–724 (2014)
10. Huang, D., Ardabilian, M., Wang, Y., Chen, L.: 3-d face recognition using eLBP-based facial description and local feature hybrid matching. Trans. Inf. Forensics Secur. 7(5), 1551–1565 (2012)
11. Huang, D., Ouji, K., Ardabilian, M., Wang, Y., Chen, L.: 3D face recognition based on local shape patterns and sparse representation classifier. In: Lee, K.-T., Tsai, W.-H., Liao, H.-Y.M., Chen, T., Hsieh, J.-W., Tseng, C.-C. (eds.) MMM 2011. LNCS, vol. 6523, pp. 206–216. Springer, Heidelberg (2011). https://doi.org/10.1007/978-3-642-17832-0_20
12. Huang, D., Shan, C., Ardabilian, M., Wang, Y., Chen, L.: Local binary patterns and its application to facial image analysis: a survey. IEEE Trans. Syst. Man Cybern. Part C Appl. Rev. 41(6), 765–781 (2011)
13. Huang, D., Wang, Y., Wang, Y.: A robust method for near infrared face recognition based on extended local binary pattern. In: Bebis, G., et al. (eds.) ISVC 2007. LNCS, vol. 4842, pp. 437–446. Springer, Heidelberg (2007). https://doi.org/10.1007/978-3-540-76856-2_43
14. Huber, P., Hu, G., Tena, R., Mortazavian, P., Koppen, W.P., Christmas, W.J., Rätsch, M., Kittler, J.: A multiresolution 3D morphable face model and fitting framework. In: International Joint Conference on Computer Vision, Imaging and Computer Graphics Theory and Applications (2016)
15. Lagorio, A., Tistarelli, M., Cadoni, M., Fookes, C., Sridharan, S.: Liveness detection based on 3D face shape analysis. In: IEEE International Workshop on Biometrics and Forensics, pp. 1–4 (2013)
16. Li, H., Huang, D., Chen, L., Wang, Y., Morvan, J.-M.: A group of facial normal descriptors for recognizing 3D identical twins. In: IEEE International Conference on Biometrics: Theory, Applications and Systems, pp. 271–277. IEEE (2012)

17. Li, H., Huang, D., Morvan, J.-M., Chen, L.: Learning weighted sparse representation of encoded facial normal information for expression-robust 3D face recognition. In: IEEE International Joint Conference on Biometrics, pp. 1–7. IEEE (2011)

18. Li, H., Huang, D., Morvan, J.-M., Chen, L., Wang, Y.: Expression-robust 3D face recognition via weighted sparse representation of multi-scale and multi-component local normal patterns. Neurocomputing **133**, 179–193 (2014)

19. Li, L., Feng, X., Boulkenafet, Z., Xia, Z., Li, M., Hadid, A.: An original face anti-spoofing approach using partial convolutional neural network. In: IEEE International Conference on Image Processing Theory, Tools and Applications, pp. 1–6 (2017)

20. Liu, S., Yuen, P.C., Zhang, S., Zhao, G.: 3D Mask face anti-spoofing with remote photoplethysmography. In: Leibe, B., Matas, J., Sebe, N., Welling, M. (eds.) ECCV 2016. LNCS, vol. 9911, pp. 85–100. Springer, Cham (2016). https://doi.org/10.1007/978-3-319-46478-7_6

21. Maatta, J., Hadid, A., Pietikainen, M.: Face spoofing detection from single images using micro-texture analysis. In: IEEE International Joint Conference on Biometrics, pp. 1–7 (2011)

22. Pavlidis, I., Symosek, P.: The imaging issue in an automatic face/disguise detection system. In: IEEE Workshop on Computer Vision Beyond the Visible Spectrum: Methods and Applications, pp. 15–24 (2000)

23. de Freitas Pereira, T., Anjos, A., De Martino, J.M., Marcel, S.: *LBP - TOP* based countermeasure against face spoofing attacks. In: Park, J.-I., Kim, J. (eds.) ACCV 2012. LNCS, vol. 7728, pp. 121–132. Springer, Heidelberg (2013). https://doi.org/10.1007/978-3-642-37410-4_11

24. De Freitas, T., Pereira, J.K., Anjos, A., Martino, J.M.D., Hadid, A., Pietikäinen, M., Marcel, S.: Face liveness detection using dynamic texture. EURASIP J. Image Video Process. **2014**(1), 2 (2014)

25. Phillips, P.J., et al.: Overview of the face recognition grand challenge. In: IEEE Conference on Computer Vision and Pattern Recognition, pp. 947–954 (2005)

26. Rakotomamonjy, A., Bach, F.R., Canu, S., Grandvalet, Y.: Simplemkl. J. Mach. Learn. Res. **9**(3), 2491–2521 (2008)

27. Shao, R., Lan, X., Yuen, P.C.: Deep convolutional dynamic texture learning with adaptive channel-discriminability for 3D mask face anti-spoofing. In: IEEE International Joint Conference on Biometrics, pp. 748–755 (2017)

28. Simonyan, K., Zisserman, A.: Very deep convolutional networks for large-scale image recognition. arXiv preprint arXiv:1409.1556 (2014)

29. Wen, D., Han, H., Jain, A.K.: Face spoof detection with image distortion analysis. IEEE Trans. Inf. Forensics Secur. **10**(4), 746–761 (2015)

30. Xu, Z., Li, S., Deng, W.: Learning temporal features using LSTM-CNN architecture for face anti-spoofing. In: IAPR Asian Conference on Pattern Recognition, pp. 141–145 (2016)

An Illumination Augmentation Approach for Robust Face Recognition

Zhanxiang Feng[1], Xiaohua Xie[2,3], Jianhuang Lai[2,3(✉)], and Rui Huang[2]

[1] School of Electronics and Information Technology,
Sun Yat-sen University, Guangzhou, China
fengzhx@mail2.sysu.edu.cn
[2] School of Data and Computer Science, Sun Yat-sen University, Guangzhou, China
{xiexiaoh6,stsljh}@mail.sysu.edu.cn
[3] Guangdong Key Laboratory of Machine Intelligence and Advanced Computing,
Ministry of Education, Guangzhou, China

Abstract. Deep learning has achieved great success in face recognition and significantly improved the performance of the existing face recognition systems. However, the performance of deep network-based methods degrades dramatically when the training data is insufficient to cover the intra-class variations, e.g., illumination. To solve this problem, we propose an illumination augmentation approach to augment the training set by constructing new training images with additional illumination components. The proposed approach first utilizes an external benchmark to generate several illumination templates. Then we combine the generated templates with the training images to simulate different illumination conditions. Finally, we conduct color correction by using the singular value decomposition (SVD) algorithm to confirm that the color of the augmented image is consistent with the input image. Experimental results demonstrate that the proposed illumination augmentation approach is effective for improving the performance of the existing deep networks.

Keywords: Face recognition · Deep learning
Illumination augmentation

1 Introduction

Face recognition has been a hot research topic in the past decades and attracted considerable research attention. In recent years, with the development of deep learning techniques and the emergences of large-scale face datasets, deep network-based methods have significantly advanced face recognition techniques [1–3]. Applications of face recognition are emerging in video surveillance, social security, company attendance, and identity authentication.

Although deep models have proved their effectiveness in improving the performance of face recognition techniques, most of the existing face recognition systems are trained with large-scale datasets. In some applications, each person

© Springer Nature Switzerland AG 2018
J. Zhou et al. (Eds.): CCBR 2018, LNCS 10996, pp. 409–417, 2018.
https://doi.org/10.1007/978-3-319-97909-0_44

contains only 1–2 samples, and the training data may be inadequate to cover the changing illumination, pose, and image quality. Particularly, the performance of the existing deep networks will decrease dramatically when dealing with extreme lighting condition. Therefore, the topic of learning robust deep representations with insufficient training samples will be worthwhile for face recognition.

A natural idea is to augment the training data and generate additional training samples. Some recent works have focused on synthesizing novel face images with changing poses, attributes, and identities by GAN (generative adversarial network) [4–6]. Learning deep networks with the synthesized face images improves the performance of deep networks to some specific problem. However, the generalizability of GAN-based approaches to other datasets is under study. Besides, controlling the facial details and ID of the generated image by GAN is extremely difficult. Furthermore, the training process of the GAN models is time-consuming, and the labeling of face image attributes is costly.

In this paper, we focus on improving the performance of face recognition systems using the data augmentation technique. We propose to perform illumination augmentation to increase the diversity of the training data. Firstly, we generate different reference illumination templates from other datasets. For each training sample, our approach simulates different illumination conditions using the pre-defined illumination templates. Eventually, we utilize the singular value decomposition (SVD) algorithm to transform the output image to the color subspace which is consistent with the input image. Furthermore, we construct a new dataset by collecting images stored in the second-generation ID cards and images captured in the realistic surveillance environment. We also build a testing set which comprises of images captured in the railway station. Experiments demonstrate that the proposed illumination augmentation approach is effective for improving the performance of deep network-based face recognition models.

2   Related Works

Deep networks have achieved remarkable success in face recognition and dramatically improved the performance of the state-of-the-art methods [1–3]. Taigman et al. [1] proposed a pioneer CNN model named DeepFace which outperformed traditional face recognition methods and closely approached human-level performance. Sun et al. [2] proposed a DeepID network which employed identification and verification supervisory signals to improve the recognition performance. Schroff et al. [3] proposed a network named FaceNet which adopted triplet loss to enforce a margin between distances of intra-class samples and those of inter-class samples.

3   Proposed Method

3.1   Overall Framework

Figure 1 demonstrates the overall framework of the proposed illumination augmentation approach. We first perform Gaussian filtering on the reference images

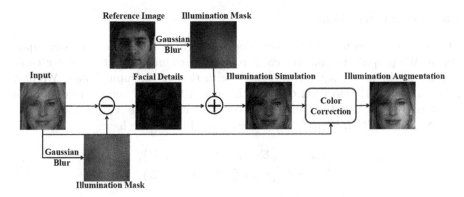

Fig. 1. Proposed framework. We first simulate different illumination situations using the reference images from an external dataset and then perform color correction to obtain the illumination augmentation output.

from an external benchmark to extract the reference illumination masks. Then, we extract the facial details of the input image by subtracting the illumination mask of the input. After that, we combine the facial details of the input image with the reference illumination masks to generate face images with different illumination situations. Eventually, we perform color correction to make sure that the color components of the augmented image is consistent with the input image.

3.2   Illumination Variation Simulation

We perform Gaussian filtering with a large blur kernel on the reference image and input image to extract the corresponding illumination mask. Denote the input image and the reference image as X_i and X_r, we can compute the illumination masks X_i^m and X_r^m as follows:

$$X_i^m = X_i * \mathcal{G},$$
$$X_r^m = X_r * \mathcal{G}, \tag{1}$$

where $\mathcal{G}$ denotes the function of Gaussian filtering and can be defined as follows:

$$\mathcal{G} = \frac{1}{2\pi\sigma^2}e^{-\frac{x^2+y^2}{2\sigma^2}}. \tag{2}$$

We can obtain the facial details of the input image by subtracting the illumination mask. Denote X_i^d as the facial details, the computation is as follows:

$$X_i^d = X_i - X_i^m. \tag{3}$$

Then we combine the facial details with the reference illumination mask to simulate different illumination conditions X_i^v, which is formulated as follows:

$$X_i^v = X_i^d + X_r^m. \tag{4}$$

3.3   Color Correction

The color components of the simulated image may be different to the input image. We propose to conduct color correction to ensure that the color components of the final output is consistent with that of the input image. We first perform SVD [11] algorithm on each channel of both the input image and the simulated output to extract their color components. Denote $\boldsymbol{X}_{iA}, A = \{R, G, B\}$ and $\boldsymbol{X}_{iA}^{v}, A = \{R, G, B\}$ as input and simulated image, we have:

$$\begin{aligned} \boldsymbol{X}_{iA} &= U_{iA}\Sigma_{iA}V_{iA}, A = \{R, G, B\}, \\ \boldsymbol{X}_{iA}^{v} &= U_{iA}^{v}\Sigma_{iA}^{v}V_{iA}^{v}, A = \{R, G, B\}. \end{aligned} \tag{5}$$

Note that Σ_{iA} and Σ_{iA}^{v} contains the color components of the input and simulated image, we can correct the color condition of the simulated image according to the input image by replacing Σ_{iA}^{v} with Σ_{iA}. Denote $\boldsymbol{X}_{oA}$ as the augmented output, then we have:

$$\boldsymbol{X}_{oA} = U_{iA}^{s}\Sigma_{iA}V_{iA}^{s}, A = \{R, G, B\} \tag{6}$$

4   Experiment

4.1   Experimental Settings

Training Set. We utilize CASIA-WebFace [7], a popular public face dataset, to train the baseline model. CASIA-WebFace contains 494,414 samples of 10,575 subjects detected from the Internet.

We also construct a domestic dataset for training a stronger model for the domestic face recognition. The domestic training dataset contains 864,652 samples of 386,847 subjects. Most of the subjects contain only 2–3 images, of which one image is from the second-generation ID cards and other images are from the surveillance videos. Training a robust model for the domestic dataset is challenging because of the lack of training sample for each person.

Testing Set. We evaluate the performance of the proposed illumination augmentation approach on the LFW dataset [8]. The LFW dataset contains 13,233 images of 5,749 subjects captured in the unconstrained environment. The LFW dataset is now the most popular benchmark for face recognition. We adopt the standard verification protocol to conduct fair comparison with other methods.

We also construct a domestic testing set to evaluate the performance of the face recognition models under realistic surveillance environment. The domestic testing dataset contains 3,722 prob images of 39 subjects captured in a railway station. The challenges include illumination, pose, and occlusion. For testing, we conduct matching between the domestic testing dataset and a gallery set comprised of 10,039 images captured in the second-generation ID cards.

Implementation Details. We select 20 images from the CMU-PIE [9] dataset to generate reference illumination templates. For each training sample, we randomly select 2 reference templates and obtain 2 illumination augmentation

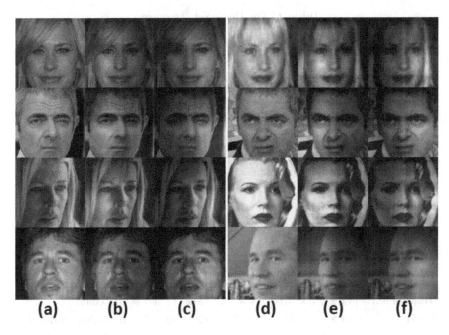

Fig. 2. Illumination augmentation results on CASIA-WebFace. (b) and (c) are the augmented images of (a), while (e) and (f) are the augmented images of (d).

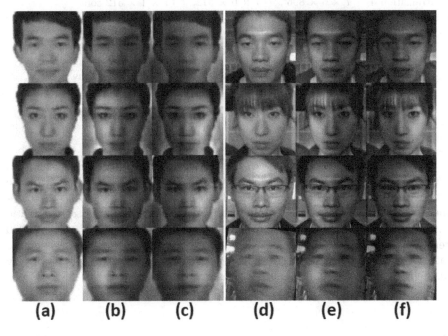

Fig. 3. Illumination augmentation results on the domestic training set. (b) and (c) are the augmented images of (a), while (e) and (f) are the augmented images of (d).

Table 1. The DenseNet structure

Layer name	Input size	Output size	Parameters
Conv1a	$112 \times 96 \times 3$	$112 \times 96 \times 64$	$3 \times 3 \times 64$ conv
Conv1b	$112 \times 96 \times 64$	$112 \times 96 \times 128$	$3 \times 3 \times 128$ conv
Pool1	$112 \times 96 \times 128$	$56 \times 48 \times 128$	2×2 max pooling, stride 2
Dense Block 1	$56 \times 48 \times 128$	$56 \times 48 \times 320$	$\begin{bmatrix} 1 \times 1\,conv \\ 3 \times 3\,conv \end{bmatrix} \times 3$
Transition 1	$56 \times 48 \times 320$	$56 \times 48 \times 128$	$1 \times 1 \times 128$ conv
Pool2	$56 \times 48 \times 128$	$28 \times 24 \times 128$	2×2 max pooling, stride 2
Dense Block 2	$28 \times 24 \times 128$	$28 \times 24 \times 384$	$\begin{bmatrix} 1 \times 1\,conv \\ 3 \times 3\,conv \end{bmatrix} \times 4$
Transition 2	$28 \times 24 \times 384$	$28 \times 24 \times 256$	$1 \times 1 \times 256$ conv
Pool3	$28 \times 24 \times 256$	$14 \times 12 \times 256$	2×2 max pooling, stride 2
Dense Block 3	$14 \times 12 \times 256$	$14 \times 12 \times 576$	$\begin{bmatrix} 1 \times 1\,conv \\ 3 \times 3\,conv \end{bmatrix} \times 5$
Transition 3	$14 \times 12 \times 576$	$14 \times 12 \times 512$	$1 \times 1 \times 512$ conv
Pool4	$14 \times 12 \times 512$	$7 \times 6 \times 512$	2×2 max pooling, stride 2
Dense Block 4	$7 \times 6 \times 512$	$7 \times 6 \times 896$	$\begin{bmatrix} 1 \times 1\,conv \\ 3 \times 3\,conv \end{bmatrix} \times 6$
Transition 4	$7 \times 6 \times 896$	$7 \times 6 \times 512$	$1 \times 1 \times 512$ conv
Pool5	$7 \times 6 \times 512$	$4 \times 3 \times 512$	2×2 max pooling, stride 2
Dense Block 5	$4 \times 3 \times 512$	$4 \times 3 \times 896$	$\begin{bmatrix} 1 \times 1\,conv \\ 3 \times 3\,conv \end{bmatrix} \times 6$
Transition 5	$4 \times 3 \times 896$	$4 \times 3 \times 1024$	$1 \times 1 \times 1024$ conv
Pool6	$4 \times 3 \times 1024$	$1 \times 1 \times 1024$	2×2 Global pooling
fc7	$1 \times 1 \times 1024$	10,575	Full connection

results. Our training process is two step. First we train a baseline model with CASIA-WebFace using the DenseNet [10] structure. Table 1 demonstrates the details of the network. Then we utilize the triplet loss [3] to fine-tune the baseline model with the domestic training set. For the first step, we set the batch size as 128, the learning rate as 0.1 and will be decreased by half every 40,000 iterations, and the weight decay as 5×10^{-4}. For the second step, we set the batch size as 120, the learning rate as 0.01 and will be decreased by half every 40,000 iterations, and the weight decay as 5×10^{-4}.

4.2   Qualitative Evaluation of Illumination Augmentation

Figures 2 and 3 demonstrate the illumination augmentation results on CASIA-WebFace and the domestic training set. We can see that the illumination augmentation approach manage to add additional illumination variations to the input image without changing the facial details for both CASIA-WebFace and the domestic training set. Our approach is proved to be adaptive to any training sample with changing illumination, pose, and image quality.

4.3   Quantitative Evaluation of Illumination Augmentation

Evaluation on LFW. Table 2 demonstrates the quantitative evaluation of the proposed illumination augmentation (IA) approach on the LFW dataset. We compare our method with DeepFace [1], DeepID2+ [2], and FaceNet [3]. The experimental results verify that the proposed IA approach is effective for improving the performance of the existing deep models. Implementing the proposed network with the augmented training samples results in an improvement of 0.27% verification accuracy. We also notice that the verification accuracy of the proposed approach outperforms DeepFace and DeepID2+. Note that with the same training samples, the accuracy of our method is higher than that of FaceNet. Consequently, our method is competitive against the state-of-the-art methods.

Evaluation on the Domestic Testing Set. Table 3 demonstrates the evaluation results on the domestic testing set. We can see that training deep models

Table 2. Evaluation on LFW

Method	DeepFace [1]	DeepID2+ [2]	FaceNet [3]	FaceNet [3]	Proposed	Proposed (IA)
Number of samples	4M	-	0.49M	200M	0.49M	0.49M
Verification accuracy	97.35%	98.70%	98.3%	99.63%	98.45%	98.72%

Table 3. Evaluation on the domestic testing set

Method	Training set	Number of samples	Accuracy
FaceNet (Softmax)	CASIA-WebFace	0.49M	57.1%
FaceNet (Triplet)	Domestic set	0.12M	74.7%
FaceNet (Triplet)	Domestic set	0.86M	81.7%
Proposed (Softmax)	CASIA-WebFace	0.49M	65.66%
Proposed (Triplet)	Domestic set	0.12M	76.7%
Proposed (Triplet+IA)	Domestic set	0.12M	80.91%
Proposed (Triplet)	Domestic set	0.86M	85.43%
Proposed (Triplet+IA)	Domestic set	0.86M	89.45%

with the domestic training set is beneficial to improving the recognition accuracy on the test set captured in the realistic surveillance environment. Compared with the deep models trained with CASIA-WebFace, an improvement of 24.6% is obtained for FaceNet trained with the domestic training set. Similarly, an improvement of 19.77% is also observed for the proposed network. With more training data, the performance of deep networks continue to improve. As the number of training data increases from 0.12M to 0.86M, we can see a performance gain of 7% for FaceNet and 8.73% for our network. Furthermore, we notice that the proposed IA approach is effective for improving the performance of deep networks with the domestic dataset. With IA approach, an improvement of 4.02% is observed for the proposed network. Note that the performance of the proposed network trained with CASIA-WebFace outperforms that of FaceNet with a margin of 8.56%. Consequently, our method achieves better generalizablity than FaceNet.

5   Conclusion

In this paper, we study the topic of data augmentation for face recognition and propose an illumination augmentation (IA) method. We first simulate different illumination conditions from the external benchmark and then perform color correction to obtain the augmented training samples with additional illumination variations while preserving the facial details. The IA approach is suitable for any face image with changing illumination, pose, and image quality. To further improve the performance of the deep networks towards robust face recognition under realistic environment, we construct a domestic training set together with a domestic testing set. Experimental results on the LFW and the domestic testing set verify the effectiveness of the proposed approach.

Acknowledgments. This project was supported by the NSFC (U1611461, 61573387, 61672544) and Tip-top Scientific and Technical Innovative Youth Talents of Guangdong special support program (NO. 2016TQ03X263).

References

1. Taigman, Y., Yang, M., Ranzato, M.A., Wolf, L.: DeepFace: closing the gap to human-level performance in face verification. In: Proceedings of the IEEE Conference on Computer Vision and Pattern Recognition, pp. 1701–1708 (2014)
2. Sun, Y., Wang, X., Tang, X.: Deeply learned face representations are sparse, selective, and robust. In: Proceedings of the IEEE Conference on Computer Vision and Pattern Recognition, pp. 2892–2900 (2015)
3. Schroff, F., Kalenichenko, D., Philbin, J.: FaceNet: a unified embedding for face recognition and clustering. In: Proceedings of the IEEE Conference on Computer Vision and Pattern Recognition, pp. 815–823 (2015)
4. Yin, W., Fu, Y., Sigal, L., Xue, X.: Semi-latent GAN: learning to generate and modify facial images from attributes. arXiv preprint arXiv:1704.02166

5. Bao, J., Chen, D., Wen, F., Li, H., Hua, G.: CVAE-GAN: fine-grained image generation through asymmetric training. In: Proceedings of the IEEE International Conference on Computer Vision, pp. 2745–2754 (2017)
6. Tran, L., Yin, X., Liu, X.: Disentangled representation learning GAN for pose-invariant face recognition. In: Proceedings of the IEEE Conference on Computer Vision and Pattern Recognition, pp. 1415–1424 (2017)
7. Yi, D., Lei, Z., Liao, S., Li, S.Z.: Learning face representation from scratch. arXiv preprint arXiv:1411.7923
8. Huang, G.B., Ramesh, M., Berg, T., Learned-Miller, E.: Labeled faces in the wild: a database for studying face recognition in unconstrained environments. Technical report 07–49, University of Massachusetts, Amherst (2007)
9. Sim, T., Baker, S., Bsat, M.: The CMU pose, illumination, and expression (PIE) database. In: Proceedings of the Fifth IEEE International Conference on Automatic Face and Gesture Recognition, pp. 53–58 (2002)
10. Huang, G., Liu, Z., Weinberger, K.Q., van der Maaten, L.: Densely connected convolutional networks. In: Proceedings of the IEEE Conference on Computer Vision and Pattern Recognition, pp. 4700–4708 (2017)
11. Demirel, H., Anbarjafari, G.: Pose invariant face recognition using probability distribution functions in different color channels. IEEE Sig. Process. Lett. 537–540 (2008)

Robust Face Recognition with Deeply Normalized Depth Images

Ziqing Feng and Qijun Zhao$^{(\boxtimes)}$

National Key Laboratory of Fundamental Science on Synthetic Vision,
College of Computer Science, Sichuan University, Chengdu, China
`qjzhao@scu.edu.cn`

Abstract. Depth information has been proven useful for face recognition. However, existing depth-image-based face recognition methods still suffer from noisy depth values and varying poses and expressions. In this paper, we propose a novel method for normalizing facial depth images to frontal pose and neutral expression and extracting robust features from the normalized depth images. The method is implemented via two deep convolutional neural networks (DCNN), normalization network (Net_N) and feature extraction network (Net_F). Given a facial depth image, Net_N first converts it to an HHA image, from which the 3D face is reconstructed via a DCNN. Net_N then generates a pose-and-expression normalized (PEN) depth image from the reconstructed 3D face. The PEN depth image is finally passed to Net_F, which extracts a robust feature representation via another DCNN for face recognition. Our preliminary evaluation results demonstrate the superiority of the proposed method in recognizing faces of arbitrary poses and expressions with depth images.

Keywords: Depth images · Face recognition
Pose and expression normalization

1 Introduction

Face recognition can be implemented using different modalities of face data, such as RGB images (2D) [1], depth images (2.5D) [2] and shapes (3D) [3]. Since the advent of low-cost depth sensors (e.g., Kinect and RealSense), depth information has been increasingly used in many applications, including face recognition, semantic segmentation, and robot navigation, etc. It appears that depth images contain rich information that is worth human beings to explore.

RGB-image-based face recognition technology has developed rapidly in the past decade thanks to the emerging deep learning techniques [4]. However, depth-image-based face recognition still confronts many challenging problems, e.g., noisy depth values, occlusion, pose and expression variations. Some researchers [2] propose to fuse multiple frames of depth images to improve the precision. Other researchers directly transform depth images to 3D point clouds with an assumed camera model [5], and rotate the faces to frontal pose and complete

ⓒ Springer Nature Switzerland AG 2018
J. Zhou et al. (Eds.): CCBR 2018, LNCS 10996, pp. 418–427, 2018.
https://doi.org/10.1007/978-3-319-97909-0_45

the invisible areas on the faces via symmetric filling [6]. Although these methods achieve promising results on several benchmark databases, none of them can well cope with facial depth images with both noise in depth values and variations in pose and expression, which frequently occur in real-world applications.

This paper aims to improve the depth-image-based face recognition accuracy particularly on noisy data with varying poses and expressions. To this end, we propose a deep learning (DL) based facial depth image normalization approach. Given a facial depth image of arbitrary view and expression, we first reconstruct its 3D face (represented by a 3D morphable model (3DMM) [8]) via regressing its 3DMM-based shape and expression parameters, then generate a pose-and-expression-normalized (PEN) depth image for the face, and finally use the PEN depth image for face recognition. Preliminary evaluation results show that our proposed method is more robust to depth noise and pose and expression variations than counterpart methods, and thus obtains better face recognition accuracy.

The rest of this paper is organized as follows. Section 2 reviews related work on depth-image-based face recognition. Section 3 introduces in detail our proposed method, and Sect. 4 reports the experimental results. Section 5 finally concludes the paper.

2   Related Work

Existing depth-image-based face recognition methods can be roughly divided into two categories depending on whether 3D faces (as point clouds) are used. Methods in the first category either assume that 3D faces are available during acquisition [6,7] or reconstruct 3D faces from depth images or videos [5,10]. With the 3D faces, Li et al. [6] and Sang et al. [10] correct the facial pose to frontal, and further preprocess the obtained frontal facial depth images by symmetric filling and smooth resampling. They do not explicitly process varying facial expressions, but require multiple depth images per subject with different expressions in the gallery. Zhang et al. [5] directly match the 3D faces by using the iterative closest point algorithm. However, they have to capture videos of 3D faces so that higher-precision 3D faces can be reconstructed to assure good face recognition accuracy. Unlike these methods, our proposed method reconstructs 3D faces from only single depth images, and can remove both pose and expression variations on the faces, resulting in depth images with frontal pose and neutral expression, which are preferred by face recognition systems.

Methods in the second category directly work on depth images, and focus on devising effective feature descriptors and classifiers. A variety of hand-crafted descriptors have been introduced for depth-image-based face recognition, such as local binary patterns [11], local quantized patterns [12], and bag of dense derivative depth patterns [13]. After feature descriptors are extracted from depth images, different classifiers like support vector machines [14] and nearest neighbor classifiers [15] are applied to recognize the faces in the depth images. These methods often suffer from noisy depth values or varying poses and expressions.

In this paper, instead of employing hand-crafted feature descriptors, we adopt a deep convolutional neural network (DCNN) to extract features from the normalized facial depth images.

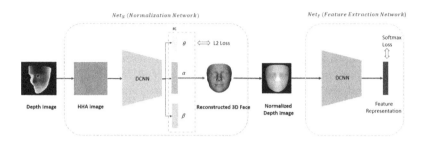

Fig. 1. Flowchart of our proposed face recognition method using deeply normalized depth images. DCNN denotes deep convolutional neural network. FC denotes fully-connected layer. θ, α and β are, respectively, pose, shape and expression parameters of the face in the input depth image.

3   Proposed Method

3.1   Overview

As shown in Fig. 1, our proposed method consists of two main components, normalization network (Net_N) and feature extraction network (Net_F). Given a facial depth image with arbitrary pose and expression, Net_N first converts it to an HHA image [16] which represents horizontal disparity, height over ground, and the angle between the local surface normal and gravity direction at each pixel, from which the 3D face is reconstructed as pose, shape and expression parameters defined by the 3D morphable model (3DMM). Net_N then generates from the obtained 3DMM shape parameters a pose-and-expression normalized (PEN) facial depth image that has frontal pose and neutral expression. During this normalization process, invisible facial regions are completed, and noisy depth values can also be regularized, resulting in higher-precision complete facial depth images. Robust features are finally extracted from the normalized depth images by Net_F, which is trained for face recognition purpose.

3.2   Normalization Network

Data Transformation. Motivated by RGB-D semantic segmentation methods [16], we transform depth images to HHA images. While depth images, as single-channel images, record only the depth values of pixels, HHA images represent pixels in three channels, including horizontal disparity, height over ground, and the angle between local surface normal and gravity direction. Therefore, HHA images convey more geometric information, which is beneficial to the reconstruction of 3D face shapes. In this paper, we employ the method in [16] for this data transformation from depth images to HHA images.

3D Face Reconstruction. Let $S = [x_1, y_1, z_1, \cdots, x_n, y_n, z_n]^T$ be a 3D face shape of n vertices, where (x_i, y_i, z_i) are coordinates of the ith vertex and 'T' denotes the transpose operator. Following the 3DMM definition, we represent 3D face shapes as

$$S = \bar{S} + \Sigma_{k=1}^{K} \alpha_k S_k + \Sigma_{l=1}^{L} \beta_l S_l^{Exp}, \tag{1}$$

where $\bar{S}$ is the mean 3D face shape, $\{S_k | k = 1, 2, \cdots, K\}$ and $\{S_l^{Exp} | l = 1, 2, \cdots, L\}$ are the shape and expression bases, respectively. In this paper, we employ the shape bases ($K = 199$) provided by BFM [8] and a simplified version of the expression bases ($L = 29$) provided by FaceWarehouse [17].

A facial depth image is a projection of a 3D face onto 2D plane, in which the pixel values are the depth values of the corresponding 3D face vertices. In this paper, we use a weak perspective projection to approximate this 3D-to-2D projection, which is defined by scaling, rotation and translation parameters. We call these parameters (totally seven parameters) together as pose parameters.

Given a facial depth image, the goal of the 3D face reconstruction network is to estimate the aforementioned 199-dim shape parameters, 29-dim expression parameters and 7-dim pose parameters, denoted as α, β and θ, respectively. To this end, we implement a deep convolutional neural network (DCNN) to regress the parameters from the HHA image constructed from the input depth image. Specifically, we employ the SphereFace network [1] as the base network whose last fully-connected (FC) layer is adapted to output a 235-dim vector corresponding to the parameters to be estimated.

Normalized Depth Image Generation. With the reconstructed 3D face, we next generate a facial depth image of frontal pose and neutral expression. This is fulfilled by first generating a frontal 3D face with neutral expression via substituting the reconstructed shape parameters to the 3DMM in Eq. (1) (while setting the expression parameters to zero), and then applying a pre-specified 3D-to-2D projection to the 3D face. In this paper, we fit weak perspective projections to the frontal depth images and their corresponding frontal 3D faces in the training dataset based on their annotated facial landmarks, and the resulting mean weak perspective projection is used here. We call the obtained depth images as *deeply normalized depth images*.

3.3 Feature Extraction Network

Feature extraction network takes the deeply normalized depth image as input and extracts from it a robust feature representation, for face recognition. In this paper, we implement a feature extraction network based on the LightCNN model [18]. LightCNN is a well-known model in the field of 2D face recognition for its simple but effective network structure.

3.4   Implementation Detail

Loss Functions. Two loss functions are used in training the proposed depth-image-based face recognition method. One is an $L2$ loss defined over the normalization network, measuring the mean squared error between the estimated values and the ground truth values of the 3DMM parameters. Note that the pose, shape and expression parameters are separately normalized such that their values are of similar order of magnitude.

The other is an identification loss (i.e., softmax loss) defined over the feature extraction network. Minimization of this identification loss aims to enable the feature extraction network to generate feature representations that are effective in distinguishing different persons based on their facial depth images.

Training Data. The normalization network and the feature extraction network are sequentially trained with $L2$ loss and softmax loss, respectively. The training data are from three sources, the 300W-LP dataset, the Lock3DFace database, and the FRGC database. The 300W-LP dataset is used to pre-train the normalization network, the Lock3DFace is used to fine-tune the pre-trained normalization network, and the FRGC network is used to fine-tune the original LightCNN model. Faces in the depth images from these databases are detected, and the cropped face regions are resized to 128×128 pixels.

The 300W-LP dataset [19] contains RGB images with varying poses and expressions of $3,837$ subjects as well as their corresponding ground truth 3DMM parameters. We generate depth images from the 3D faces of these subjects defined by the 3DMM parameters. The data of $3,717$ subjects are randomly chosen to pre-train the normalization network. To further augment the training data, we down-sample the depth images, add noise to them, and simulate occlusion on them. Finally, we obtain around 40 depth images per subject.

The Lock3DFace database [5] consists of RGB and depth images of 509 subjects with variations in pose, expression, illumination and occlusion. After excluding some very low quality data, we have 446 subjects. We choose 280 of these subjects, and calculate the ground truth shape parameter values for each subject based on his/her RGB images by using the method in [21], which can estimate the shape parameters from a set of RGB images. As a result, all the depth images of one subject share the same shape parameters. As for the computation of the ground truth expression and pose parameter values of a depth image, we employ the method in [22] to fit 3DMM to the RGB image corresponding to the depth image.

The FRGC database [20] contains high-precision 3D faces of 466 subjects. We generate depth images from these 3D faces, and use the depth images to fine-tune the original LightCNN model. It is worth mentioning that in the following experiments we fine-tune the LightCNN model only using the FRGC database, though the recognition experiments are done on the Lock3DFace database.

4   Experimental Results

4.1   Evaluation Protocols

We evaluate the proposed method from two aspects: the accuracy of 3D face reconstruction and the accuracy of face recognition. For 3D face reconstruction accuracy evaluation, the data of 120 subjects in 300W-LP are used. These subjects are different from the subjects in training dataset. We assess the 3D face reconstruction accuracy by measuring the difference between the reconstructed 3D face shape and its ground truth in terms of root mean squared error (RMSE). Given the estimated and ground truth 3DMM parameters of a test sample, the parameters are first substituted into Eq. (1) to generate the corresponding 3D face shapes, and the RMSE on the test set is then calculated by

$$\text{RMSE} = \frac{1}{N_T} \sum_{j=1}^{N_T} (\|S_j^* - \hat{S}_j\|/n), \tag{2}$$

where S_j^* and $\hat{S}_j$ are the ground truth and estimated 3D face shapes of the jth test sample, n is the number of vertices in the 3D face shapes, and N_T is the total number of test samples.

As for face recognition accuracy evaluation, we do face identification experiments by using the data of the remaining 166 subjects in the Lock3DFace database as test data. In the experiments, the gallery is composed by one frontal facial depth image with neutral expression of each of the test subjects, and the probe includes two parts: depth images of frontal pose and different expressions (denoted as *Probe_Set_1*) and depth images of different poses (denoted as *Probe_Set_2*). We calculate the similarity between gallery and probe depth images based on the *cosine* distance between their feature representations extracted by our proposed method. We report the face recognition accuracy in terms of Rank-1 identification rate.

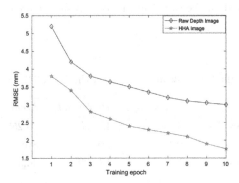

Fig. 2. Reconstruction accuracy in terms of RMSE w.r.t. the number of epochs. HHA images obtain obviously better reconstruction accuracy than raw depth images.

4.2   3D Face Reconstruction Accuracy

Figure 2 gives the 3D face reconstruction accuracy (in terms of RMSE) with respect to the number of training epochs of our proposed method on the test data in 300W-LP. In order to show the effectiveness of HHA images, we report the results of using raw depth images as the input to the 3D face reconstruction DCNN. As can be seen, HHA images achieve obviously lower reconstruction errors than raw depth images. Figure 3 shows some example reconstruction results.

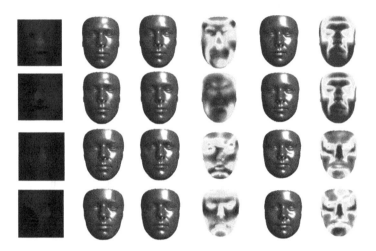

Fig. 3. Reconstruction results of some depth images. Each row is for one depth image. From left to right columns: Input raw probe images, ground truth 3D faces, reconstructed 3D faces using HHA images and the corresponding error maps, and reconstructed 3D faces using raw depth images and the corresponding error maps. Errors increase as the color changes from dark blue to dark red in the error maps. Note that occlusions are simulated on the test depth images. (Color figure online)

Table 1. Rank-1 identification rates on the Lock3DFace database.

	$Probe\_Set\_1$	$Probe\_Set\_2$	$Mean$
Raw depth	62%	10.5%	36.25%
Ours	**92%**	**80%**	**86%**
Baseline [5]	74.12%	18.63%	46.38%

4.3 Face Recognition Accuracy

Face recognition accuracy is presented in Table 1 in terms of rank-1 identification rate. From these results, the following observations can be made. (i) When recognizing frontal faces with varying expressions, our proposed method improves the accuracy by 30% compared with using the raw depth images. This proves the effectiveness of our method in removing expression-induced deformation in depth images. (ii) As for depth images of arbitrary poses, our method makes a more substantial improvement. A possible reason is that our method can well generate the frontal view depth images while recovering the invisible regions. (iii) On average, our proposed method significantly advances the state-of-the-art performance on the Lock3DFace database, thanks to the effective normalization of the depth images in favor of face recognition. See Fig. 4 for the recognition results of some probe depth images.

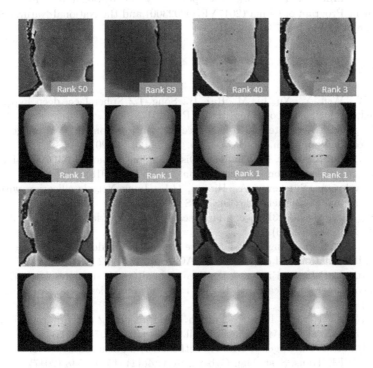

Fig. 4. Recognition results of some probe depth images. Each column is for a probe depth image. From top to bottom rows: Input raw probe depth images, Deeply normalized probe depth images, Corresponding gallery depth images, Deeply normalized gallery depth images. The ranks at which the corresponding gallery depth images are hit are shown on the right bottom of the probe depth images.

5   Conclusions

This paper has proposed a novel method for depth-to-depth face recognition. It employs a deep neural network to reconstruct 3D faces from single depth images under arbitrary poses and expressions, and then generates pose-and-expression normalized facial depth images. This way, factors like noisy depth values and varying poses and expressions that may distract face recognition are suppressed. The proposed method then utilizes another deep neural network to extract robust features from the deeply normalized depth images. Experimental results demonstrate the effectiveness of the proposed method in recognizing faces of arbitrary poses and expressions. In the future, we are going to evaluate the proposed method on more benchmarks, and further improve the method by better preserving the identity information during depth image normalization.

Acknowledgements. This work is supported by the National Key Research and Development Program of China (2017YFB0802300) and the National Natural Science Foundation of China (61773270).

References

1. Liu, W., Wen, Y., Yu, Li, M., Raj, B., Song, L.: Sphereface: deep hypersphere embedding for face recognition. In: CVPR (2017)
2. Lee Y., et al.: Accurate and robust face recognition from RGB-D images with a deep learning approach. In: BMVC, pp. 123.1–123.14 (2016)
3. Liu, F., Zhu, R., Zeng, D., Zhao, Q.: Disentangling features in 3D face shapes for joint face reconstruction and recognition. In: CVPR (2018)
4. Krizhevsky, A., Sutskever, A., Hinton, G.E.: ImageNet classification with deep convolutional neural networks. In: NIPS (2012)
5. Zhang, J., et al.: Lock3DFace: a large-scale database of low-cost Kinect 3D faces. In: ICB, pp. 1–8 (2016)
6. Li, B.Y.L., et al.: Using Kinect for face recognition under varying poses, expressions, illumination and disguise. In: WACV, pp. 186–192 (2013)
7. Berretti, S., Pala, P., Bimbo, A.D.: Face recognition by super-resolved 3D models from consumer depth cameras. IEEE Trans. Inf. Forensics Secur. **9**(9), 1436–1449 (2014)
8. Blanz, V., Vetter, T.: Face recognition based on fitting a 3D morphable model. IEEE Trans. Pattern Anal. Mach. Intell. **25**(9), 1063–1074 (2003)
9. Min, R., Kose, N., Dugelay, J.L.: KinectFaceDB: a kinect database for face recognition. IEEE Trans. Syst. Man Cybern. Syst. **4**(11), 1534–1548 (2017)
10. Sang, G., Li, J., Zhao, Q.: Pose-invariant face recognition via RGB-D images. In: CIN, pp. 1–9 (2015)
11. Aissaoui, A., Martinet, J., Djeraba, C.: DLBP: a novel descriptor for depth image based face recognition. In: ICIP, pp. 298–302 (2017)
12. Mantecon, T., Del-Bianco, C.R., Jauregizar, F.: Depth-based face recognition using local quantized patterns adapted for range data. In: ICIP, pp. 293–297 (2015)
13. Mantecon, T., et al.: Visual face recognition using bag of dense derivative depth patterns. IEEE Signal Process. Lett. **23**(6), 771–775 (2016)

14. Olegs, N., Kamal, N., Modris, G., Thomas, B.M.: RGB-D-T based face recognition. In: ICPR (2014)
15. Goswami, G., et al.: On RGB-D face recognition using Kinect. In: BTAS, pp. 1–6 (2014)
16. Gupta, S., Girshick, R., Arbeláez, P., Malik, J.: Learning rich features from RGB-D images for object detection and segmentation. In: Fleet, D., Pajdla, T., Schiele, B., Tuytelaars, T. (eds.) ECCV 2014. LNCS, vol. 8695, pp. 345–360. Springer, Cham (2014). https://doi.org/10.1007/978-3-319-10584-0_23
17. Cao, C., et al.: FaceWarehouse: a 3D facial expression database for visual computing. IEEE Trans. Vis. Comput. Graph. **20**(3), 413–425 (2014)
18. Wu, X., He, R., Sun, Z.: A lightened CNN for deep face representation. In: CVPR (2015)
19. Zhu, X., Lei, Z., Liu, X., Shi, H., Li, S.: Face alignment across large poses: a 3D solution. In: CVPR, pp. 146–155 (2016)
20. Phillips, P., et al.: Overview of the face recognition grand challenge. In: CVPR, pp. 947–954 (2005)
21. Tian, W., Liu, F., Zhao, Q.: Landmark-based 3D face reconstruction from an arbitrary number of unconstrained images. In: FGW (2018)
22. Zhu, X., et al.: High-fidelity pose and expression normalization for face recognition in the wild. In: CVPR, pp. 787–796 (2015)

MobileFaceNets: Efficient CNNs for Accurate Real-Time Face Verification on Mobile Devices

Sheng Chen[1,2(✉)], Yang Liu[2], Xiang Gao[2], and Zhen Han[1]

[1] School of Computer and Information Technology, Beijing Jiaotong University,
Beijing, China
sheng.chen@watchdata.com, zhan@bjtu.edu.cn
[2] Research Institute, Watchdata Inc., Beijing, China
{yang.liu.yj,xiang.gao}@watchdata.com

Abstract. We present a class of extremely efficient CNN models, MobileFaceNets, which use less than 1 million parameters and are specifically tailored for high-accuracy real-time face verification on mobile and embedded devices. We first make a simple analysis on the weakness of common mobile networks for face verification. The weakness has been well overcome by our specifically designed MobileFaceNets. Under the same experimental conditions, our MobileFaceNets achieve significantly superior accuracy as well as more than 2 times actual speedup over MobileNetV2. After trained by ArcFace loss on the refined MS-Celeb-1 M, our single MobileFaceNet of 4.0 MB size achieves 99.55% accuracy on LFW and 92.59% TAR@FAR1e-6 on MegaFace, which is even comparable to state-of-the-art big CNN models of hundreds MB size. The fastest one of MobileFaceNets has an actual inference time of 18 ms on a mobile phone. For face verification, MobileFaceNets achieve significantly improved efficiency over previous state-of-the-art mobile CNNs.

Keywords: Mobile network · Face verification · Face recognition
Convolutional neural network · Deep learning

1 Introduction

Face verification is an important identity authentication technology used in more and more mobile and embedded applications such as device unlock, application login, mobile payment and so on. Some mobile applications equipped with face verification technology, for example, smartphone unlock, need to run offline. To achieve user-friendliness with limited computation resources, the face verification models deployed locally on mobile devices are expected to be not only accurate but also small and fast. However, modern high-accuracy face verification models are built upon deep and big convolutional neural networks (CNNs) which are supervised by novel loss functions during training stage. The big CNN models requiring high computational resources are not suitable for many mobile and embedded applications. Several highly efficient neural network architectures, for example, MobileNetV1 [1], ShuffleNet [2], and MobileNetV2 [3], have been proposed for common visual recognition tasks rather than face verification in recent years. It is a straight-forward way to use these common

J. Zhou et al. (Eds.): CCBR 2018, LNCS 10996, pp. 428–438, 2018.
https://doi.org/10.1007/978-3-319-97909-0_46

CNNs unchanged for face verification, which only achieves very inferior accuracy compared with state-of-the-art results according to our experiments (see Table 2).

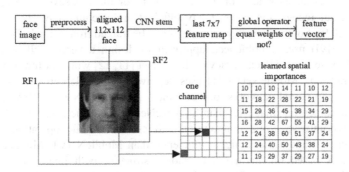

Fig. 1. A typical face feature embedding CNN and the receptive field (RF). The last 7×7 feature map is denoted as FMap-end. RF1 and RF2 correspond to the corner unit and the center unit in FMap-end respectively. The corner unit should be of less importance than the center unit. When a global depthwise convolution (GDConv) is used as the global operator, for a fixed spatial position, the norm of the weight vector consisted of GDConv weights in all channels can be considered as the spatial importance. We show that GDConv learns very different importances at different spatial positions after training.

In this paper, we make a simple analysis on common mobile networks' weakness for face verification. The weakness has been well overcome by our specifically designed MobileFaceNets, which is a class of extremely efficient CNN models tailored for high-accuracy real-time face verification on mobile and embedded devices. Our MobileFaceNets use less than 1 million parameters. Under the same experimental conditions, our MobileFaceNets achieve significantly superior accuracy as well as more than 2 times actual speedup over MobileNetV2. After trained on the refined MS-Celeb-1 M [4] by ArcFace [5] loss from scratch, our single MobileFaceNet model of 4.0 MB size achieves 99.55% face verification accuracy (see Table 3) on LFW [6] and 92.59% TAR@FAR10-6 (see Table 4) on MegaFace Challenge 1 [7], which is even comparable to state-of-the-art big CNN models of hundreds MB size. Note that many existing techniques such as pruning [37], low-bit quantization [29], and knowledge distillation [16] are able to improve MobileFaceNets' efficiency additionally, but these are not included in the scope of this paper.

The major contributions of this paper are summarized as follows: (1) After the last (non-global) convolutional layer of a face feature embedding CNN, we use a global depthwise convolution layer rather than a global average pooling layer or a fully connected layer to output a discriminative feature vector. The advantage of this choice is also analyzed in both theory and experiment. (2) We carefully design a class of face feature embedding CNNs, namely MobileFaceNets, with extreme efficiency on mobile and embedded devices. (3) Our experiments on LFW, AgeDB ([8]), and MegaFace show that our MobileFaceNets achieve significantly improved efficiency over previous state-of-the-art mobile CNNs for face verification.

2 Related Work

Tuning deep neural architectures to strike an optimal balance between accuracy and performance has been an area of active research for the last several years [3]. For common visual recognition tasks, many efficient architectures have been proposed recently [1–3, 9]. Some efficient architectures can be trained from scratch. For example, SqueezeNet ([9]) uses a bottleneck approach to design a very small network and achieves AlexNet-level [10] accuracy on ImageNet [11, 12] with 50x fewer parameters (i.e., 1.25 million). MobileNetV1 [1] uses depthwise separable convolutions to build lightweight deep neural networks, one of which, i.e., MobileNet-160 (0.5x), achieves 4% better accuracy on ImageNet than SqueezeNet at about the same size. ShuffleNet [2] utilizes pointwise group convolution and channel shuffle operation to reduce computation cost and achieve higher efficiency than MobileNetV1. MobileNetV2 [3] architecture is based on an inverted residual structure with linear bottleneck and improves the state-of-the-art performance of mobile models on multiple tasks and benchmarks. The mobile NASNet [13] model, which is an architectural search result with reinforcement learning, has much more complex structure and much more actual inference time on mobile devices than MobileNetV1, ShuffleNet, and MobileNetV2. However, these lightweight basic architectures are not so accurate for face verification when trained from scratch (see Table 2).

Accurate lightweight architectures specifically designed for face verification have been rarely researched. [14] presents a light CNN framework to learn a compact embedding on the large-scale face data, in which the Light CNN-29 model achieves 99.33% face verification accuracy on LFW with 12.6 million parameters. Compared with MobileNetV1, Light CNN-29 is not lightweight for mobile and embedded platform. Light CNN-4 and Light CNN-9 are much less accurate than Light CNN-29. [15] proposes ShiftFaceNet based on ShiftNet-C model with 0.78 million parameters, which only achieves 96.0% face verification accuracy on LFW. In [5], an improved version of MobileNetV1, namely LMobileNetE, achieves comparable face verification accuracy to state-of-the-art big models. But LMobileNetE is actually a big model of 112 MB model size, rather than a lightweight model. All above models are trained from scratch.

Another approach for obtaining lightweight face verification models is compressing pretrained networks by knowledge distillation [16]. In [17], a compact student network (denoted as MobileID) trained by distilling knowledge from the teacher network DeepID2 + [33] achieves 97.32% accuracy on LFW with 4.0 MB model size. In [1], several small MobileNetV1 models for face verification are trained by distilling knowledge from the pretrained FaceNet [18] model and only face verification accuracy on the authors' private test dataset are reported. Regardless of the small student models' accuracy on public test datasets, our MobileFaceNets achieve comparable accuracy to the strong teacher model FaceNet on LFW (see Table 3) and MegaFace (see Table 4).

3 Approach

In this section, we will describe our approach towards extremely efficient CNN models for accurate real-time face verification on mobile devices, which overcome the weakness of common mobile networks for face verification. To make our results totally reproducible, we use ArcFace loss to train all face verification models on public datasets, following the experimental settings in [5].

3.1 The Weakness of Common Mobile Networks for Face Verification

There is a global average pooling layer in most recent state-of-the-art mobile networks proposed for common visual recognition tasks, for example, MobileNetV1, ShuffleNet, and MobileNetV2. For face verification and recognition, some researchers ([5, 14], etc.) have observed that CNNs with global average pooling layers are less accurate than those without global average pooling. However, no theoretical analysis for this phenomenon has been given. Here we make a simple analysis on this phenomenon in the theory of receptive field [19].

A typical deep face verification pipeline includes preprocessing face images, extracting face features by a trained deep model, and matching two faces by their features' similarity or distance. Following the preprocessing method in [5, 20–22], we use MTCNN [23] to detect faces and five facial landmarks in images. Then we align the faces by similarity transformation according to the five landmarks. The aligned face images are of size 112×112, and each pixel in RGB images is normalized by subtracting 127.5 then divided by 128. Finally, a face feature embedding CNN maps each aligned face to a feature vector, as shown in Fig. 1. Without loss of generality, we use MobileNetV2 as the face feature embedding CNN in the following discussion. To preserve the same output feature map sizes as the original network with 224×224 input, we use the setting of stride = 1 in the first convolutional layer instead of stride = 2, where the latter setting leads to very poor accuracy. So, before the global average pooling layer, the output feature map of the last convolutional layer, denoted as FMap-end for convenience, is of spatial resolution 7×7. Although the theoretical receptive fields of the corner units and the central units of FMap-end are of the same size, they are at different positions of the input image. The receptive fields' center of FMap-end's corner units is in the A typical deep face verification pipeline includes preprocessing face images, extracting face features by a trained deep model, and matching two faces by their features' similarity or distance. Following the preprocessing method in [5, 20–22], we use MTCNN [23] to detect faces and five facial landmarks in images. Then we align the faces by similarity transformation according to the five landmarks. The aligned face images are of size 112×112, and each pixel in RGB images is normalized by subtracting 127.5 then divided by 128. Finally, a face feature embedding CNN maps each aligned face to a feature vector, as shown in Fig. 1. Without loss of generality, we use MobileNetV2 as the face feature embedding CNN in the following discussion. To preserve the same output feature map sizes as the original network with 224×224 input, we use the setting of stride = 1 in the first convolutional layer instead of stride = 2, where the latter setting leads to very poor accuracy. So, before the global average pooling layer, the output feature map of the last convolutional layer, denoted as FMap-end for convenience, is of spatial resolution 7×7. Although the theoretical receptive fields of the corner units and the central units of FMap-end are of the same size, they are at different positions of the input image. The receptive fields' center of FMap-end's corner units is in the corner of the input image and the receptive fields' center of FM-end's central units are in the center of the input image, as shown in Fig. 1. According to [24], pixels at the center of a receptive field have a much larger impact on an output and the distribution of impact within a receptive field on the output is nearly Gaussian. The effective receptive field [24] sizes of FMap-end's corner units are much smaller than the ones of FMap-end's central units. When the input image is an aligned face, a corner unit of FMap-end carries less information of the face than a central unit. Therefore, different units of FMap-end are of different importance for extracting a face feature vector.

In MobileNetV2, the flattened FMap-end is unsuitable to be directly used as a face feature vector since it is of a too high dimension 62720. It is a natural choice to use the output of the global average pooling (denoted as GAPool) layer as a face feature vector, which achieves inferior verification accuracy in many researchers' experiments [5, 14] as well as ours (see Table 2). The global average pooling layer treats all units of FMap-end with equal importance, which is unreasonable according to the above analysis. Another popular choice is to replace the global average pooling layer with a fully connected layer to project FMap-end to a compact face feature vector, which adds large number of parameters to the whole model. Even when the face feature vector is of a low dimension 128, the fully connected layer after FMap-end will bring additional 8 million parameters to MobileNetV2. We do not consider this choice since small model size is one of our pursuits.

3.2 Global Depthwise Convolution

To treat different units of FMap-end with different importance, we replace the global average pooling layer with a global depthwise convolution layer (denoted as GDConv). A GDConv layer is a depthwise convolution (c.f. [1, 25]) layer with kernel size equaling the input size, pad = 0, and stride = 1. The output for global depthwise convolution layer is computed as:

$$G_m = \sum_{i,j} K_{i,j,m} \cdot F_{i,j,m} \tag{1}$$

where F is the input feature map of size $W \times H \times M$, K is the depthwise convolution kernel of size $W \times H \times M$, G is the output of size $1 \times 1 \times M$, the m_{th} channel in G has only one element G_m, (i,j) denotes the spatial position in F and K, and m denotes the channel index.

Global depthwise convolution has a computational cost of:

$$W \cdot H \cdot M \tag{2}$$

When used after FMap-end in MobileNetV2 for face feature embedding, the global depthwise convolution layer of kernel size $7 \times 7 \times 1280$ outputs a 1280-dimensional face feature vector with a computational cost of 62720 MAdds (i.e., the number of operations measured by multiply-adds, c.f. [3]) and 62720 parameters. Let MobileNetV2-GDConv denote MobileNetV2 with global depthwise convolution layer. When both MobileNetV2 and MobileNetV2-GDConv are trained on CIASIA-Webface [26] for face verification by ArcFace loss, the latter achieves significantly better accuracy on LFW and AgeDB (see Table 2). Global depthwise convolution layer is an efficient structure for our design of MobileFaceNets.

Table 1. MobileFaceNet architecture for feature embedding. We use almost the same notations as MobileNetV2 [3]. Each line describes a sequence of operators, repeated n times. All layers in the same sequence have the same number c of output channels. The first layer of each sequence has a stride s and all others use stride 1. All spatial convolutions in the bottlenecks use 3×3 kernels. The expansion factor t is always applied to the input size. GDConv7 $\times$ 7 denotes GDConv of 7×7 kernels.

Input	Operator	t	c	n	s
$112^2 \times 3$	conv3 $\times$ 3	–	64	1	2
$56^2 \times 64$	depthwise conv3 $\times$ 3	–	64	1	1
$56^2 \times 64$	bottleneck	2	64	5	2
$28^2 \times 64$	bottleneck	4	128	1	2
$14^2 \times 128$	bottleneck	2	128	6	1
$14^2 \times 128$	bottleneck	4	128	1	2
$7^2 \times 128$	bottleneck	2	128	2	1
$7^2 \times 128$	conv1x1	–	512	1	1
$7^2 \times 512$	linear GDConv7 $\times$ 7	–	512	1	1
$1^2 \times 512$	linear conv1 $\times$ 1	–	128	1	1

3.3 MobileFaceNet Architectures

Now we describe our MobileFaceNet architectures in detail. The residual [38] bottlenecks proposed in MobileNetV2 [3] are used as our main building blocks. For convenience, we use the same conceptions as those in [3]. The detailed structure of our primary MobileFaceNet architecture is shown in Table 1. Particularly, expansion factors for bottlenecks in our architecture are much smaller than those in MobileNetV2. We use PReLU [27] as the non-linearity, which is slightly better for face verification than using ReLU (see Table 2). In addition, we use a fast downsampling strategy at the beginning of our network, an early dimension-reduction strategy at the last several convolutional layers, and a linear 1×1 convolution layer following a linear global depthwise convolution layer as the feature output layer. Batch normalization [28] is utilized during training and batch normalization folding (c.f. Sect. 3.2 of [29]) is applied before deploying.

Our primary MobileFaceNet network has a computational cost of 221 million MAdds and uses 0.99 million parameters. We further tailor our primary architecture as follows. To reduce computational cost, we change input resolution from 112×112 to 112×96 or 96×96. To reduce the number of parameters, we remove the linear 1×1 convolution layer after the linear GDConv layer from MobileFaceNet, the resulting network of which is called MobileFaceNet-M. From MobileFaceNet-M, removing the 1×1 convolution layer before the linear GDConv layer produces the smallest network called MobileFaceNet-S. These MobileFaceNet networks' effectiveness is demonstrated by the experiments in the next section.

4   Experiments

In this section, we will first describe the training settings of our MobileFaceNet models and our baseline models. Then we will compare the performance of our trained face verification models with some previous published face verification models, including several state-of-the-art big models.

4.1   Training Settings and Accuracy Comparison on LFW and AgeDB

We use MobileNetV1, ShuffleNet, and MobileNetV2 (with stride = 1 for the first convolutional layers of them since the setting of stride = 2 leads to very poor accuracy) as our baseline models. All MobileFaceNet models and baseline models are trained on CASIA-Webface dataset from scratch by ArcFace loss, for a fair performance comparison among them. We set the weight decay parameter to be 4e−5, except the weight decay parameter of the last layers after the global operator (GDConv or GAPool) being 4e−4. We use SGD with momentum 0.9 to optimize models and the batch size is 512. The learning rate begins with 0.1 and is divided by 10 at the 36K, 52K and 58K iterations. The training is finished at 60K iterations. Then, the face verification accuracy on LFW and AgeDB-30 is compared in Table 2.

Table 2. Performance comparison among mobile models trained on CASIA-Webface. In the last column, we report actual inference time in milliseconds (ms) on a Qualcomm Snapdragon 820 CPU of a mobile phone with 4 threads (using NCNN [30] inference framework).

Network	LFW	AgeDB-30	Params	Speed
MobileNetV1	98.63%	88.95%	3.2 M	60 ms
ShuffleNet (1×, g = 3)	98.70%	89.27%	**0.83 M**	27 ms
MobileNetV2	98.58%	88.81%	2.1 M	49 ms
MobileNetV2-GDConv	98.88%	90.67%	2.1 M	50 ms
MobileFaceNet	**99.28%**	**93.05%**	**0.99 M**	24 ms
MobileFaceNet (112 × 96)	99.18%	92.96%	0.99 M	21 ms
MobileFaceNet (96 × 96)	99.08%	92.63%	0.99 M	**18 ms**
MobileFaceNet-M	99.18%	92.67%	0.92 M	24 ms
MobileFaceNet-S	99.00%	92.48%	**0.84 M**	23 ms
MobileFaceNet (ReLU)	99.15%	92.83%	0.98 M	23 ms
MobileFaceNet (expansion factor × 2)	99.10%	92.81%	1.1 M	27 ms

As shown in Table 2, compared with the baseline models of common mobile networks, our MobileFaceNets achieve significantly better accuracy with faster inference speed. Our primary MobileFaceNet achieves the best accuracy and MobileFaceNet with a lower input resolution of 96 × 96 has the fastest inference speed. Note that our MobileFaceNets are more efficient than those with larger expansion factor such as MobileFaceNet (expansion factor × 2) and MobileNetV2-GDConv.

To pursue ultimate performance, MobileFaceNet, MobileFaceNet (112 × 96), and MobileFaceNet (96 × 96) are also trained by ArcFace loss on the cleaned training set of MS-Celeb-1 M database [5] with 3.8M images from 85K subjects. The accuracy of our primary MobileFaceNet is boosted to 99.55% and 96.07% on LFW and AgeDB-30, respectively. The three trained models' accuracy on LFW is compared with previous published face verification models in Table 3.

Table 3. Performance comparison with previous published face verification models on LFW.

Method	Training data	#Net	Model size	LFW Acc.
Deep Face [31]	4 M	3	–	97.35%
DeepFR [32]	2.6 M	1	0.5 GB	98.95%
DeepID2+ [33]	0.3 M	25	–	99,47%
Center Face [34]	0.7 M	1	105 MB	99.28%
DCFL [35]	4.7 M	1	–	99.55%
SphereFace [20]	0.49 M	1	–	99.47%
CosFace [22]	5 M	1	–	99.73%
ArcFace (LResNet100E-IR) [5]	3.8 M	1	250 MB	**99.83%**
FaceNet [18]	200 M	1	30 MB	99.63%
ArcFace (LMobileNetE) [5]	3.8 M	1	112 MB	99.50%
Light CNN-29 [14]	4 M	1	50 MB	99.33%
MobileID [17]	–	1	4.0 MB	97.32%
ShiftFaceNet [15]	–	1	**3.1 MB**	96.00%
MobileFaceNet	3.8 M	1	**4.0 MB**	99.55%
MobileFaceNet (112 × 96)	3.8 M	1	**4.0 MB**	99.53%
MobileFaceNet (96 × 96)	3.8 M	1	**4.0 MB**	99.52%

4.2 Evaluation on MegaFace Challenge1

In this paper, we use the Facescrub [36] dataset as the probe set to evaluate the verification performance of our primary MobileFaceNet on Megaface Challenge 1. Table 4 summarizes the results of our models trained on two protocols of MegaFace where the training dataset is regarded as small if it has less than 0.5 million images, large otherwise. Our primary MobileFaceNet shows comparable accuracy for the verification task on both the protocols.

Table 4. Face verification evaluation on Megafce Challenge 1. "VR" refers to face verification TAR (True Accepted Rate) under 10^{-6} FAR (False Accepted Rate). MobileFaceNet (R) are evaluated on the refined version of MegaFace dataset (c.f. [5]).

Method	VR (large protocol)	VR (small protocol)
SIAT MMLAB [34]	87.27%	76.72%
DeepSense V2	95.99%	82.85%
SphereFace-Small [20]	–	90.04%
Google-FaceNet v8 [18]	86.47%	–
Vocord-deepVo V3	94.96%	–
CosFace (3-patch) [22]	97.96%	**92.22%**
iBUG_DeepInsight (ArcFace [5])	**98.48%**	–
MobileFaceNet	90.16%	85.76%
MobileFaceNet (R)	92.59%	88.09%

5   Conclusion

We proposed a class of face feature embedding CNNs, namely MobileFaceNets, with extreme efficiency for real-time face verification on mobile and embedded devices. Our experiments show that MobileFaceNets achieve significantly improved efficiency over previous state-of-the-art mobile CNNs for face verification.

Acknowledgements. We thank Jia Guo for helpful discussion, and thank Yang Wang, Lian Li, Licang Qin, Yan Gao, Hua Chen, and Min Zhao for application development.

References

1. Howard, A.G., Zhu, M., Chen, B., Kalenichenko, D., Wang, W., Weyand, T., et al.: Mobilenets: Efficient convolutional neural networks for mobile vision applications. CoRR, abs/1704.04861 (2017)
2. Zhang, X., Zhou, X., Lin, M., Sun, J.: Shufflenet: An extremely efficient convolutional neural network for mobile devices. CoRR, abs/1707.01083 (2017)
3. Sandler, M., Howard, A., Zhu, M., Zhmoginov, A., Chen, L.C.: MobileNetV2: Inverted Residuals and Linear Bottlenecks. CoRR, abs/1801.04381 (2018)
4. Guo, Y., Zhang, L., Hu, Y., He, X., Gao, J.: Ms-celeb-1 m: A dataset and benchmark for large-scale face recognition, arXiv preprint (2016). arXiv:1607.08221
5. Deng, J., Guo, J., Zafeiriou, S.: ArcFace: Additive Angular Margin Loss for Deep Face Recognition. arXiv preprint (2018). arXiv:1801.07698
6. Huang, G.B., Ramesh, M., Berg, T., et al.: Labeled faces in the wild: a database for studying face recognition in unconstrained environments (2007)
7. Kemelmacher-Shlizerman, I., Seitz, S.M., Miller, D., Brossard, E.: The megaface benchmark: 1 million faces for recognition at scale. In: CVPR (2016)
8. Moschoglou, S., Papaioannou, A., Sagonas, C., Deng, J., Kotsia, I., Zafeiriou, S.: AgeDB: The first manually collected in-the-wild age database. In: CVPRW (2017)

9. Iandola, F.N., Han, S., Moskewicz, M.W., Ashraf, K., Dally, W.J., Keutzer, K.: Squeezenet: Alexnet-level accuracy with 50x fewer parameters and 0.5 MB model size, arXiv preprint (2016). arXiv:1602.07360

10. Krizhevsky, A., Sutskever, I., Hinton, G.E.: Imagenet classification with deep convolutional neural networks. In: NIPS (2012)

11. Deng, J., Dong, W., Socher, R., Li, L.J., Li, K., Fei-Fei, L.: ImageNet: a large-scale hierarchical image database. In: CVPR. IEEE (2009)

12. Russakovsky, O., Deng, J., Su, H., et al.: Imagenet large scale visual recognition challenge. Int. J. Comput. Vis. 115, 211–252 (2015)

13. Zoph, B., Vasudevan, V., Shlens, J., Le, Q.V.: Learning transferable architectures for scalable image recognition, arXiv preprint (2017). arXiv:1707.07012

14. Wu, X., He, R., Sun, Z., Tan, T.: A light cnn for deep face representation with noisy labels, arXiv preprint (2016). arXiv:1511.02683

15. Wu, B., Wan, A., Yue, X., Jin, P., Zhao, S., Golmant, N., et al.: Shift: A Zero FLOP, Zero Parameter Alternative to Spatial Convolutions, arXiv preprint (2017). arXiv:1711.08141

16. Hinton, G. E., Vinyals, O., Dean, J.: Distilling the knowledge in a neural network (2015). arXiv:1503.02531

17. Luo, P., Zhu, Z., Liu, Z., Wang, X., Tang, X., Luo, P., et al.: Face Model Compression by Distilling Knowledge from Neurons. In: AAAI (2016)

18. Schroff, F., Kalenichenko, D., Philbin, J.: Facenet: a unified embedding for face recognition and clustering. In: CVPR (2015)

19. Long, J., Zhang, N., Darrell, T.: Do convnets learn correspondence? Adv. Neural. Inf. Process. Syst. 2, 1601–1609 (2014)

20. Liu, W., Wen, Y., Yu, Z., Li, M., Raj, B., Song, L.: Sphereface: deep hypersphere embedding for face recognition. In: CVPR (2017)

21. Wang, F., Cheng, J., Liu, W., Liu, H.: Additive margin softmax for face verification. IEEE Signal Proc. Lett. 25(7), 926–930 (2018)

22. Wang, H., Wang, Y., Zhou, Z., Ji, X., Gong, D., Zhou, J., et al.: CosFace: Large Margin Cosine Loss for Deep Face Recognition (2018). arXiv:1801.0941

23. Zhang, K., Zhang, Z., Li, Z., Qiao, Y.: Joint face detection and alignment using multi-task cascaded convolutional networks. IEEE Signal Proc. Lett. 23(10), 1499–1503 (2016)

24. Luo, W., Li, Y., Urtasun, R., Zemel, R.: Understanding the effective receptive field in deep convolutional neural networks. In: NIPS (2016)

25. Chollet, F.: Xception: Deep learning with depthwise separable convolutions, arXiv preprint (2016). arXiv:1610.02357

26. Yi, D., Lei, Z., Liao, S., Li, S.Z.: Learning face representation from scratch, arXiv preprint (2014). arXiv:1411.7923

27. He, K., Zhang, X., Ren, S., Sun, J.: Delving deep into rectifiers: surpassing human-level performance on imagenet classification. In: CVPR (2015)

28. Ioffe, S., Szegedy, C.: Batch normalization: accelerating deep network training by reducing internal covariate shift. In: International Conference on Machine Learning (2015)

29. Jacob, B., Kligys, S., Chen, B., Zhu, M., Tang, M., Howard, A., et al.: Quantization and Training of Neural Networks for Efficient Integer-Arithmetic-Only Inference, arXiv preprint (2017). arXiv:1712.05877

30. NCNN: a high-performance neural network inference framework optimized for the mobile platform, Apr 20 2018. https://github.com/Tencent/ncnn

31. Taigman, Y., Yang, M., Ranzato, M., et al.: DeepFace: closing the gap to human-level performance in face verification. In: CVPR (2014)

32. Parkhi, O.M., Vedaldi, A., Zisserman, A., et al.: Deep face recognition. In: BMVC, vol. 1, p. 6 (2015)

33. Sun, Y., Wang, X., Tang, X.: Deeply learned face representations are sparse, selective, and robust. In: Computer Vision and Pattern Recognition, pp. 2892–2900 (2015)
34. Wen, Y., Zhang, K., Li, Z., Qiao, Y.: A discriminative feature learning approach for deep face recognition. In: Leibe, B., Matas, J., Sebe, N., Welling, M. (eds.) ECCV 2016. LNCS, vol. 9911, pp. 499–515. Springer, Cham (2016). https://doi.org/10.1007/978-3-319-46478-7_31
35. Deng, W., Chen, B., Fang, Y., Hu, J.: Deep Correlation Feature Learning for Face Verification in the Wild. IEEE Signal Proc. Lett. **24**(12), 1877–1881 (2017)
36. Ng, H.W., Winkler, S.: A data-driven approach to cleaning large face datasets. In: IEEE International Conference on Image Processing (ICIP), pp. 343–347 (2014)
37. Han, S., Mao, H., Dally, W.J.: Deep compression: Compressing deep neural network with pruning, trained quantization and Huffman coding, CoRR, abs/1510.00149 (2015)
38. He, K., Zhang, X., Ren, S., Sun, J.: Deep residual learning for image recognition. In: CVPR (2016)

Eye-Based Biometrics

Gabor Filtering and Adaptive Optimization Neural Network for Iris Double Recognition

Shuai Liu[1,2], Yuanning Liu[1,3], Xiaodong Zhu[1,3(✉)], Zhen Liu[3,4],
Guang Huo[5], Tong Ding[1,2], and Kuo Zhang[1,3]

[1] Key Laboratory of Symbolic Computation and Knowledge Engineering
of Ministry of Education, Jilin University, Changchun 130012, China
zhuxd@jlu.edu.cn
[2] College of Software, Jilin University, Changchun 130012, China
[3] College of Computer Science and Technology,
Jilin University, Changchun 130012, China
[4] Graduate School of Engineering, Nagasaki Institute of Applied Science,
Nagasaki 851-0193, Japan
[5] College of Information Engineering,
Northeast Electric Power University, Jilin 132012, China

Abstract. The iris image is greatly affected by the collection environment, so, the outputs of different iris categories in the distance recognition algorithm may similar. Neural network recognition algorithm can improve the results distinction, but the same neural network structure has a great difference in the recognition effect of different iris libraries. They all may reduce the accuracy of iris recognition. This paper proposes an iris double recognition algorithm based on Gabor filtering and adaptive optimization neural network. Gabor filtering is used to extract iris features. Hamming distance is used to eliminate most of different categories in the first recognition. The BP neural network that connection weights are optimized by immune particle swarm optimization algorithm is used for the second recognition. The results that the proposed algorithm compares with many algorithms in different iris libraries show that the proposed algorithm can effectively improve iris recognition accuracy.

Keywords: Iris double recognition · Gabor filtering
Adaptive optimization neural network · Hamming distance
Immune particle swarm optimization

1 Introduction

The key steps of iris recognition are feature extraction and recognition [1]. In the one-to-more iris recognition (discriminate iris category from multiple categories), Gabor filtering is always used to extract features. Hamming or other distance algorithms are used to recognize iris category [2]. However, iris collection environment change greatly, distance algorithms may not accurately differentiate iris category. The recognition algorithm based on neural network [3] can improve accuracy. However, neural network structure and adjustment methods are complex, fixed neural network structure may not well in different iris libraries.

© Springer Nature Switzerland AG 2018
J. Zhou et al. (Eds.): CCBR 2018, LNCS 10996, pp. 441–449, 2018.
https://doi.org/10.1007/978-3-319-97909-0_47

Aiming at multiple category iris recognition of frontal captured iris image, this paper proposes an iris double recognition algorithm based on Gabor filtering and adaptive optimization neural network. Use Gabor filtering to extract iris feature. In the first recognition, iris features are converted to a binary feature code and do one-to-more recognition by Hamming distance, which can reach purpose of eliminate most different iris categories and narrow recognition range. The iris that can not confirm category need to do second recognition. Use BP neural network which connection weights are adaptive optimized for different iris libraries by using immune particle swarm optimization (IPSO) algorithm, which can increase applicability of neural network structure in iris recognition and the ability of parameters jump out of local optimum. Enter values of response amplitude nodes into BP neural network for one-to-one recognition in the second recognition.

2   Iris Double Recognition

In this paper, iris library for comparison is named template iris library, of which the iris is template iris. And iris used to test iris category is named test iris. Iris double recognition flowchart as shown in Fig. 1.

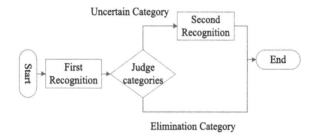

Fig. 1. Iris double recognition flowchart

2.1   Gabor Filtering and Iris Image Processing

Gabor filtering expression as shown in Eq. 1 [4].

$$\varphi_{m,n} = \frac{\left\| \vec{k}_{m,n} \right\|}{2\pi\sigma^2} e^{\left(\frac{\left\| \vec{k}_{m,n} \right\|^2 \left\| \vec{z} \right\|^2}{2\sigma^2} \right)} \times \left(j \vec{k}_{m,n} \times \vec{z} \right) \tag{1}$$

σ is the standard deviation of Gaussian function. $\vec{k}_{m,n} = k_n e^{(i\varphi_m)}$, $k_n = k_{max}/f^v$, $\phi_m = \pi m/16$. ϕ and k_v represent Gabor filtering direction and frequency. $\sigma = 2\pi$. k_{max} is the maximum frequency. f^v is frequency difference between two adjacent Gabor filtering, $v = 1, 2, 3...m$. Construct m different scales. In direction, ϕ is divided into n copies from $0°$ to $360°$.

The iris image needs to be processed before recognition [5]. Through quality evaluation, localization, normalization and enhancement, iris area is mapped into a rectangle of 512 × 64 dimensions. Cut a 256 × 32 dimensions strongest texture region from the upper left corner as iris recognition area. The images in iris image processing process are shown in Fig. 2.

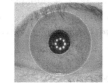  

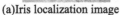

(a)Iris localization image   (b)Normalized and enhanced iris   (c)Recognition area

Fig. 2. Iris processing process

2.2 First Recognition

In the first recognition, $k_{\max} = 0.5\pi, f^v = \sqrt{2}$, m set to 5, n set to 8. The Gabor filtering group with 40 filters is used to do first recognition. Use Gabor filtering group to process iris recognition area, then form 40 Gabor images, numbered G_1–G_{40}. For each 256 × 32 dimensions Gabor image, divide it into 8 × 4 sub-graphs of 32 × 8 dimensions, numbered B_1–B_{32}.

Calculate each sub-graph average amplitude value, and set feature code by using over-threshold judgment method. Set determination threshold P. If amplitude value is smaller than determination threshold, the feature code of this sub-graph is set to 0. If amplitude is bigger than or equal to determination threshold, the feature code of this sub-graph is set to 1. Iris features can be formed 1280 (32 × 40) bit binary feature code. Calculate the Hamming distance HD between test feature code and each template feature code. The formula for calculating HD is shown in Eq. 2.

$$HD = \frac{1}{1280} \times \sum_{i=1}^{1280} \left[\frac{1 + \text{sgn}(AT_{n-i} - M_1)}{2}\right] \oplus \left[\frac{1 + \text{sgn}(BT_{n-i} - M_1)}{2}\right] \quad n = 1, 2, \ldots, 40 \quad i = 1, 2, \ldots, 32 \quad (2)$$

AT_{n-i} denotes the average amplitude value of the i-th sub-graph of the n-th Gabor image in test iris. BT_{n-i} denotes the average amplitude value of the i-th sub-graph of the n-th Gabor image in template iris. The value of determination threshold P depends on the specific iris library. The usual value range is [0.2, 0.5].

Set feature threshold M, the value range is [0.4, 0.7]. Template iris whose HD is larger than feature threshold belongs to elimination category (test iris is not belong to any template iris category), and template iris whose HD is smaller than M belongs to uncertain category. Template iris of uncertain category need to be second recognition.

The role of first recognition is to eliminate different categories in the template iris library as much as possible, narrow the scope of second recognition.

2.3   Second Recognition

Second recognition use BP neural network for one-to-one accurate recognition. Set a three-layer neural network with nodes of 64, 16, 1. The excitation function of hidden layer and output layer use tanh function [6].

Specific process:

1. Calculate average response amplitudes of 64 sub-graphs of 32×4 dimensions of test iris and template iris, respectively. Calculate the difference between test iris response amplitude L_i and template iris response amplitude M_i, numbered as C_1–C_{64}. Input them into neural network. Each node inputs is shown as Eq. 3.

$$C_i = L_i - M_i \qquad i = 1, 2, 3, \ldots, 64 \tag{3}$$

2. Calculate each node input value G_t in the hidden layer, as Eq. 4.

$$G_t = \sum_{i=1}^{64} \omega_{t-i} \times C_i \quad t = 1, 2, \ldots, 16 \tag{4}$$

ω_{i-t} represents the i-th connection weight of the t-th node connecting hidden layer from the input layer. Each node output value Y_t in the hidden layer is shown as Eq. 5:

$$Y_t = \frac{1 - e^{-2 \times G_t}}{1 + e^{-2 \times G_t}} \qquad t = 1, 2, \ldots, 16 \tag{5}$$

3. Calculate each node input value R in the hidden layer, as Eq. 6.

$$R = \sum_{t=1}^{16} \omega_t \times Y_t \tag{6}$$

ω_t represents the t-th connection weight connecting output layer from the hidden layer. Each node output value S in the output layer is shown as Eq. 7.

$$S = \frac{1 - e^{-2 \times R}}{1 + e^{-2 \times R}} \tag{7}$$

According to the value of S to determine whether test iris and template iris are the same category or not. According to tanh function definition, the more similar of two irises, S closer to 1.

The role of second recognition is perform more accurate analysis of categories that cannot be identified in the first recognition to confirm test iris category.

2.4 Connection Weights Adaptive Optimization

This paper use adaptive optimization neural network which composed of immune particle swarm optimization(IPSO) [7, 8] and BP neural network to adaptive optimize connection weights for different iris libraries and then improve the applicability of neural network structure.

For one specific iris library, select M iris images as reference irises. For each reference iris there select P iris of the same category as reference iris, Q iris of different categories from reference iris, a total of $M \times (P+Q)$ iris as training iris. Particle swarm optimization algorithm uses 30 particles with an initial velocity range of $[-50,50]$. Each particle contains a set of connection weights that need to be trained. The initial individual best $pBest$ of the particle is set to initial value, and global initial best $gBest$ is set to 0. Using neural network output S to calculate affinity. Reference iris as antigen, training iris as antibody. Equation 8 shows that use neural network output S to calculate the affinity U between the i-th reference iris and the t-th training iris.

$$U = 1/(1+S) \tag{8}$$

Because the same category has high affinity and different categories have low affinity [9], the fitness function of PSO is shown in Eq. 9.

$$F = \frac{1}{M} \sum_{i=1}^{M} \frac{\frac{1}{P} \sum_{t_1=1}^{P} U_{t_1}}{\frac{1}{Q} \sum_{t_2=1}^{Q} U_{t_2}} \tag{9}$$

U_{t_1} indicates the affinity between the i-th reference iris and the t_1-th the same category training iris. U_{t_2} indicates the affinity between the i-th reference iris and the t_2-th different categories training iris. The fitness F is an average of the sum of ratios of the same category average affinity of the M reference iris to different categories average affinity. If new F is greater than original F, new $pBest$ is set to connection weights corresponding to new F, and weights of the connection with the largest F value in 30 particles is set to new $gBest$. After determining new $pBest$ and $gBest$, evolve particles.

$$v_i^d = \omega \times v_i^d + c_1 \times rand_1^d \times \left(pBest_i^d - x_i^d\right) + c_2 \times rand_2^d \times \left(gBest^d - x_i^d\right) \tag{10}$$

$$x_i^d = x_i^d + v_i^d \tag{11}$$

ω is inertia weight, set 0.729. c_1 and c_2 are acceleration factors, set 1.49445 [10]. x_i^d is the value of d-th parameter in i-th group, v_i^d is the speed of d-th parameter in i-th group. $pBest_i^d$ is the historical best for d-th parameter in i-th group, and $gBest^d$ is the best for d-th parameter in 30 groups. $rand_1^d$ and $rand_2^d$ are random numbers in the range of $[0,1]$. After 300 iterations, the final $gBest$ is used as connection weights for neural network at the time of recognition. Neural network structure and connection weights adaptive optimization process are shown in Fig. 3.

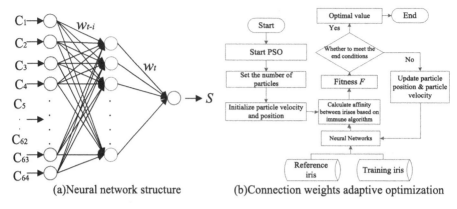

(a)Neural network structure   (b)Connection weights adaptive optimization

Fig. 3. Neural network structure and connection weights adaptive optimization

3 Experiment and Analysis

The irises used in the recognition experiment are different from irises used in training connection weights. Through comparisons of the same category (inter matching) and different categories (outer matching), use correct recognition rate (CRR), equal error rate (EER) and ROC curve [11] to evaluate algorithms. EER is the value of false rejection rate (FRR) is equal to false acceptance rate (FAR).

The irises selected from CASIA-Iris-Lamp iris library of Chinese Academy of Sciences [12] and the JLU-4.0 [13] iris library of Jilin University are used to test. The comparisons of this paper algorithm (Evolutionary + Double) are as follows:

1. Use conjugate gradient method [14] to optimize connection weights. Observe the influence of optimization algorithm on iris recognition. (Gradient + Double)
2. Use deep learning architecture [15] to replace BP neural network. Observe the effect of neural network in iris recognition. (Deep Learning + Double)
3. Secondary iris recognition method based on local texture [16]. Observe the effect of other double recognition algorithms. (Local Feature + Secondary)
4. The iris recognition algorithm based on Zernike moment phase feature [17]. Compare with a phase model algorithm. (Zernike)
5. The iris recognition algorithm based on cross-spectral matching [18]. Compare with a spatial domain algorithm. (Cross-spectral)

The number of irises, categories and match count in each iris library are shown in Table 1. Each algorithm CRR, EER are shown in Table 2.

Table 1. The number of matches within each iris library

Iris	Category	Sample	Total	Inter matching	Outer matching	Total match
JLU	150	200	30000	56324	102235	158559
CASIA	411	40	16440	31652	86532	118184

Table 2. CRR and EER of each algorithm

| | JLU-4.0 | | CASIA-Iris-Lamp | |
	CRR	EER	CRR	EER
Gradient + Double	98.75%	1.12%	98.01%	1.68%
Deep Learning + Double	94.98%	2.67%	96.47%	2.44%
Local Feature + Double	99.12%	0.75%	98.87%	0.98%
Zernike	97.79%	1.83%	98.43%	1.34%
Cross-spectral matching	98.11%	1.49%	97.88%	1.76%
Evolutionary + Double	**99.72%**	**0.37%**	**99.37%**	**0.54%**

The ROC curves of JLU-4.0 and CASIA-Iris-Lamp are shown in Fig. 4.

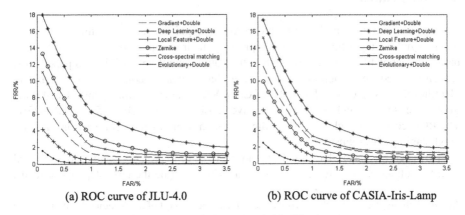

(a) ROC curve of JLU-4.0   (b) ROC curve of CASIA-Iris-Lamp

Fig. 4. ROC curve of each iris libraries

Gradient learning algorithm considers convergence, but IPSO considers the final recognition effect to prevent the final connection weights from falling into a local optimal. IPSO is to search for parameters that can improve the accuracy of iris recognition by expanding the optimal search range as much as possible and jumping out of the original framework. Improve the ability of global search capability.

Deep learning requires the support of large amounts of data, but current iris library is difficult to meet requirement. This paper only imitate deep learning architecture to establish a simple model for experiments, which also led to inability to play advantages of deep learning. CRR relatively is low. However, data for training neural networks is less. According to immune algorithm concept, set the affinity in the search space, the effect of the search interval is reflected and adjust search space in time. Use a small amount of data to maximize search.

Compare with Zernike moment phase feature and cross-spectral matching algorithm, spatial domain and phase model algorithms are affected by environment and there may be interference from noise and redundancy, making a fixed threshold is difficult to accurately do iris recognition in large quantities. On the basis of narrowing recognition range in the first recognition, there add a second recognition, through neural network optimized by IPSO to achieve more accurate recognition, which effectively prevent fixed thresholds restrictions on multiple categories recognition, improve the accuracy. In addition, IPSO also helps neural network to better adapt to irises shot in different environments and make relevant adjustments in time. Improve the applicability of fixed neural network structures for different iris libraries. This is also the advantage compared to other types of double recognition.

In all experiments, this paper algorithm has the highest CRR, the lowest EER, and the ROC curve is closest to the axis, which show good robustness and stability.

4   Conclusions

Aiming at improving applicability and correct recognition rate of multiple categories iris recognition algorithm, this paper propose an iris double recognition algorithm based on Gabor filtering and adaptive optimization neural network in this paper. First recognition reduce recognition range, after that, second recognition can accurately identifies the iris category. The CRR of CASIA-Iris-Lamp iris library and JLU-4.0 iris library are 99.37% and 99.72%, respectively. EER respectively: 0.54% and 0.37%. The ROC curve is the closest to coordinate axis in many method comparisons and has good stability and robustness.

However, this paper does not deal with the issue of iris rotation, and it does not deal with the influence of image noise and light, which will be the next steps work focus.

Acknowledgments. The authors would like to thank the support of the National Natural Science Foundation of China (NSFC) under Grant No. 61471181. Natural Science Foundation of Jilin Province under Grant No. 20140101194JC, 20150101056JC. Science and technology project of the Jilin Provincial Education Department under Grant No. JJKH20180448KJ.

References

1. Xing-guang, L., Zhe-nan, S., Tie-niu, T.: Overview of iris image quality-assessment. J. J. Image Graph. **19**(6), 813–824 (2014)
2. Liu, S., Liu, Y., Zhu, X., Huo, G., Cui, J., Chen, Y.: Iris recognition based on adaptive gabor filter. In: Zhou, J., Wang, Y., Sun, Z., Xu, Y., Shen, L., Feng, J., Shan, S., Qiao, Yu., Guo, Z., Yu, S. (eds.) CCBR 2017. LNCS, vol. 10568, pp. 383–390. Springer, Cham (2017). https://doi.org/10.1007/978-3-319-69923-3_41
3. Shuai, L., Yuan-ning, L., Xiao-dong, Z., et al.: Iris double recognition based on modified evolutionary neural network. J. Electron. Imaging **26**(6), 063023 (2017)
4. Fei, H., Yuan-ning, L., Xiao-dong, Z., et al.: Score level fusion scheme based on adaptive local Gabor features for face-iris-fingerprint multimodal biometric. J. Electron. Imaging **23**(3), 033019 (2014)

5. Zhi-ming, L.: Research on iris liveness detection algorithm based on convolutional neural network. J. Comput. Eng. **42**(5), 239–243 (2016)
6. Abdelkawy, M.A., Bhrawy, A.H., Zerrad, E., et al.: Application of tanh method to complex coupled nonlinear evolution equation. J Acta Phys. Pol. A **129**(3), 278–283 (2016)
7. Sheng, L., Qian, S.Q., Ye, Y.Q.: An improved immune algorithm for optimizing the pulse width modulation control sequence of inverters. J. Eng. Optim. **49**(9), 1463–1482 (2017)
8. Qi, B., Kairui, Z., Xinmin, W., et al.: System identification method for small unmanned helicopter based on improved particle swarm optimization. J. Bionic Eng. **13**(3), 504–514 (2016)
9. Liang, X., Huang, M., Ning, T.: Flexible job shop scheduling based on improved hybrid immune algorithm. J. Ambient Intell. Hum. Comput. **9**(1), 165–171 (2018)
10. Dongfeng, W., Li, M., Wenjie, Z.: Improved bare bones particle swarm optimization with adaptive search center. J. Chin. J. Comput. **39**(12), 2652–2667 (2016)
11. Guang, H., Yuan-ning, L., Xiao-dong, Z., et al.: Face-iris multimodal biometric scheme based on feature level fusion. J. Electron. Imaging **24**(6), 063020 (2015)
12. CASIA Iris Image Database. http://www.cbsr.ia.ac.cn/china/Iris%20Databases%20CH.asp
13. JLU Iris Image Database. http://www.jlucomputer.com/Irisdb.php
14. Xiuyan, L., Qian, H., Jianming, W., et al.: ERT image reconstruction based on improved CG method. Chin. J. Sci. Instrum. **37**(7), 1673–1679 (2016)
15. Fei, H., Ye, H., Han, W., et al.: Deep learning architecture for iris recognition based on optimal Gabor filters and deep belief network. J. Electron. Imaging **26**(2), 023005 (2017)
16. Huo, G., Liu, Y., Zhu, X., et al.: Secondary iris recognition method based on local energy-orientation feature. J. Electron. Imaging **24**(1), 013033 (2015)
17. Tan, C.W., Kumar, A.: Accurate iris recognition at a distance using stabilized iris encoding and zernike moments phase features. J. IEEE Trans. Image Process. **23**(9), 3962–3974 (2014). A Publication of the IEEE Signal Processing Society
18. Nalla, P.R., Kumar, A.: Toward more accurate iris recognition using cross-spectral matching. J. IEEE Trans. Image Process. **26**(1), 208–221 (2016). A Publication of the IEEE Signal Processing Society

Efficient Method for Locating Optic Disc in Diabetic Retinopathy Images

Aili Han[1], Anran Yang[1], and Feilin Han[2(✉)]

[1] Department of Computer Science and Technology,
Shandong University, Weihai 264209, China
[2] College of Computer Science and Technology,
Zhejiang University, Hangzhou 310027, China
hanfeilin@zju.edu.cn

Abstract. Diabetic retinopathy has no obvious symptoms at early stage, which leads to missing the best time for treatment. We apply image processing techniques to early diagnosis of diabetic retinopathy and present an efficient method of locating optic disc in fundus images. We first normalize the images in color, brightness, and exposure distribution to weaken the interference of pigment difference, uneven brightness and low contrast, and then extract the regions of interest in fundus images by the convolution of fundus images with a binary mask template to eliminate the influence of background on the accuracy of locating OD and decrease the computation amount. Next, we convert ROI into three grayscale images, in which the grayscale one from G channel is selected to locate OD since it is with the highest contrast and most original information. Finally, we create a universal template of optic disc for diabetic retinopathy images and design a fast method of locating OD in fundus images based on the OD template. The similarity between the OD template and the overlaid patch in fundus images is computed by means of correlation matching or standard correlation matching, and the position with maximal similarity is regarded as the center of OD. Experimental results demonstrate that our method is efficient and has a certain prospect of clinical application.

Keywords: Image processing · Image detection · Computer-aided diagnose
Diabetic retinopathy

1 Introduction

Diabetes mellitus has become a kind of diseases with high incidence, which are prone to develop retinopathy. Diabetic retinopathy has no obvious symptoms at the early stage, which is usually found after visual impairment. This leads to missing the best time for treatment. Therefore, it is necessary for early computer-aided diagnosis and prevention of diabetic retinopathy. In this paper, we discuss the method of applying image processing techniques to detect diabetic retinopathy in fundus images to provide valuable information for early treatment and reduce the blindness rate.

The fundus images contain three important physiological structures: macula, blood vessel and optic disc (OD). Determining the precise location of OD can help the early diagnosis of retinopathy. Zheng et al. [1] proposed a method of locating OD based on

© Springer Nature Switzerland AG 2018
J. Zhou et al. (Eds.): CCBR 2018, LNCS 10996, pp. 450–458, 2018.
https://doi.org/10.1007/978-3-319-97909-0_48

the directional local-contrast filtering and the local blood vessel density, which locates OD after determining the center of macula. Ke et al. [2] presented a method of locating OD based on human visual attention mechanism, which computes saliency map for fundus images since OD is the salient part in fundus images. Xiao et al. [3] proposed a method of locating OD based on structural features of color fundus images, which first uses the least-squares parabolic fitting method to get the initial location of OD and then takes the sliding-window scanning method for the precise location of OD in fundus images.

We discuss the fast method of locating OD in fundus images for computer-aided diagnosis of diabetic retinopathy in this paper. We first extract the regions of interest (ROI) in fundus images and normalize them to weaken the interference of noises and low-contrast in fundus images on the accuracy of locating OD and the diagnosis results of diabetic retinopathy. And then, we create a universal OD template for diabetic retinopathy images and design a fast method of locating OD in fundus images based on the OD template. Our method is efficient and has a certain prospect of clinical application.

2 Related Work

Determining the position of OD in fundus images can help for the computer-aided diagnosis of fundus diseases. Zheng et al. [1] proposed a method of locating OD based on the directional local-contrast filtering and the local blood vessel density in 2014. They first detect the candidate region of macula according to the characteristics of macular region being gradually darkening from edge region to center region in the images, and then locate the position of macula based on the characteristics of macular area being without vessel or only a small amount of micro vessel. The location of OD is determined according to that of macula because the relative location between OD and macula is fixed. This method can improve the accuracy of locating OD.

Ke et al. [2] presented a method of locating OD based on human visual attention mechanism in 2015, which computes saliency map for fundus images since OD is the salient part in fundus images. They first convert fundus images into binary ones by means of the OSTU threshold segmentation algorithm to obtain ROI and carry out the circular corrosion and morphology open operations to narrow the boundaries of ROI, which weaken the interference of the boundary lines between the black background and the foreground in fundus images and reduce the computation amount. And then, they normalize the images to reduce the difference between images. Next, they generate the feature maps with different scales. By the Gauss filtering and continuous down sampling, the features are extracted at 9 different scales to construct the Gauss Pyramid. The single-scale feature map is obtained by the linear center-periphery difference. And then, the feature maps at different scales are normalized. The feature maps are combined into 3 descriptors of feature saliency, i.e., the descriptors of gray features, color features, and direction features. The integrated saliency map is from the three saliency maps of single feature, and the maximal values in the integrated saliency map correspond to the location of OD.

Xiao et al. [3] proposed a method of locating OD based on structural features of color fundus images in 2016. The method first extracts the veins in fundus images and uses the least-squares parabolic fitting method to get the initial location of OD based on structural characteristics of venous vessels. And then, it takes the sliding-window scanning method for the precise location of OD. Through analyzing the fundus images, they find that the shape of the upper and lower veins around OD area is similar to a parabola and that the pole of the parabola is the intersection of the two veins, which falls in the OD region. Based on this, they determine the initial location of OD by using structural features of venous vessels. The green channel is selected for subsequent processing, and the veins are extracted in the preprocessing image by means of low-hat operation and OSTU binary segmentation algorithm. The coordinate system is set up to fit the veins in fundus images. In order to make the fitted curve reflect the trend of data, the least-square fitting method is used to minimize the square sum of residuals of all points. They use two criteria to evaluate the fitting results. The results are regarded as the effective ones only when the two evaluations are both satisfied. The effective fitting results are used to obtain the initial coordinates of OD. Finally, the gray window scanning method is used to accurately locate OD according to the characteristic of OD being with high brightness in the region around OD.

Locating OD in fundus images has significance in the computer-aided diagnose of retinopathy. There are many methods for the detection, locating and segmentation of OD. Some can better locate OD but the accuracy depends on that of vessel segmentation; some have higher accuracy but the accuracy depends on the selected training set; some focus on balancing the speed against the accuracy. In this paper, we design an OD template for diabetic retinopathy images and propose a fast method of locating OD in fundus images based on the OD template, which is effective and has a certain prospect of clinical application.

3 Method for Locating OD in Diabetic Retinopathy Images

The equipment used in image acquisition and the imaging environment affect the quality of images, such as uneven brightness, low contrast. The factors of brightness and contrast have an impact on the results of locating OD in fundus images. Therefore, we first preprocess the images by means of image normalization to weaken the interference of uneven brightness and low contrast. And then, we extract ROI and process grayscale in fundus images. Finally, we create a universal OD template for diabetic retinopathy images and use the OD template to locate OD in fundus images.

3.1 Image Normalization

We carry out the normalizations of color, brightness, and exposure distribution to reduce the influence of natural pigment difference in fundus images of different patients and the error from image acquisition. We have tried several normalization methods, including the brightness normalization, the histogram equalization, the HSV channel normalization based on statistics, the normalization based on proportional operators.

The experimental results demonstrate that the normalization method based on proportional operators is the best one for diabetic retinopathy images.

Let $I_i(x, y)$ be the *RGB* image, where $i = 1, 2, \ldots n$. The normalization method based on proportional operators first converts the *RGB* image into the *HSV* one, and then computes the average pixel-values $\bar{H}_i$, $\bar{S}_i$, $\bar{V}_i$ in *H*, *S*, *V* channels, respectively. The pixel-values H_i, S_i, V_i in *H*, *S*, *V* channels are computed as follows.

$$H_i(x, y) = H_i(x, y) * \frac{\sum_{i=1 \sim n} \bar{H}_i}{n \bar{H}_i} \qquad (1)$$

$$S_i(x, y) = S_i(x, y) * \frac{\sum_{i=1 \sim n} \bar{S}_i}{n \bar{S}_i} \qquad (2)$$

$$V_i(x, y) = V_i(x, y) * \frac{\sum_{i=1 \sim n} \bar{V}_i}{n \bar{V}_i} \qquad (3)$$

The normalized pixel-values in *H*, *S*, *V* channels are merged together, which are then converted into the *RGB* color space. The experimental results demonstrate that this method can preserve the color information in fundus images and reduce the color difference between fundus images, as shown in Fig. 1.

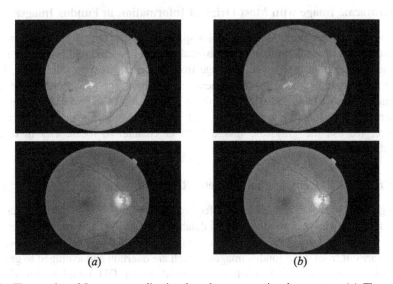

(a)   (b)

Fig. 1. The results of Image normalization based on proportional operators. (a) The original fundus images; (b) The images after normalization.

3.2   ROI Extraction

ROI extraction is to reduce the interference of black background in fundus images and decrease the computation amount. We use a binary mask to extract ROI in fundus images. The color fundus images are first converted into the gray ones, and then it is converted into the binary ones. The threshold value is determined by the pixel-values obtained from the unsupervised method. Thus, we obtain a binary mask template, in which each pixel-value in background is 0, and that in ROI is 1. ROI is extracted by the convolution of fundus images with the binary mask template, as shown in Fig. 2.

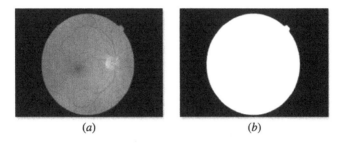

(a)   *(b)*

Fig. 2.   ROI extraction. (*a*) A fundus image; (*b*) The binary mask template.

3.3   Grayscale Image with Most Original Information in Fundus Images

Fundus images are represented in *RGB* color space. We extract the pixel-values in *R*, *G*, *B* channels and convert them into three grayscale images, as shown in Fig. 3. Extensive experiments show that the grayscale image from *R* channel is with salient OD, lower contrast and contains the most brightness information, the grayscale image from *B* channel is almost dark and with the lowest contrast, and the grayscale image from *G* channel is with the highest contrast and retains the most original information. Therefore, we use the grayscale image from *G* channel to locate OD in diabetic retinopathy images.

3.4   Creating OD Template for Diabetic Retinopathy Images

Locating OD in fundus images need an effective OD template. We select some standard fundus images from the fundus image database MESSIDOR, including the same number of right-eye images and left-eye images. The OD regions with the size of 140*140 are cut from these fundus images, which are overlain and averaged to generate an OD sub-image. The OD sub-image is used as an OD template for diabetic retinopathy images, as shown in Fig. 4.

3.5   Locating OD in Fundus Images Based on OD Template

Let $I(x, y)$ be a fundus image and $T(x, y)$ be the OD template for diabetic retinopathy images. The OD template is slid on the fundus image from left to right and from top to

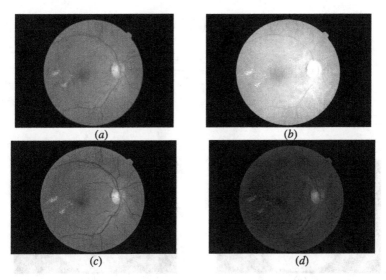

Fig. 3. The grayscale images from fundus images. (*a*) The original color fundus image; (*b*) The grayscale image from *R* channel. (*c*) The grayscale image from *G* channel. (*d*) The grayscale image from *B* channel.

Fig. 4. An OD template with the size of 140*140 for diabetic retinopathy images

bottom. At each position of movement, the similarity between the OD template and the overlaid patch in the fundus image is computed, which is stored in the result matrix *R*. The position with maximal similarity is the approximate center of OD.

We match the fundus image with the OD template by means of the OpenCV function *matchTemplate*. We have tried different matching schemes including square difference matching, standard square difference matching, correlation matching, standard correlation matching, correlation coefficient matching, and standard correlation coefficient matching. The experimental results demonstrate that correlation matching and standard correlation matching are with higher accuracy than other matching methods for diabetic retinopathy images, as shown in Fig. 5. The similarity for correlation matching and standard correlation matching are computed according to the following formulas (4) and (5), respectively.

$$R_1(x,y) = \sum_{x',y'} T(x',y') \cdot I(x+x',y+y') \tag{4}$$

$$R_2(x,y) = \frac{\sum_{x',y'} T(x',y') \cdot I(x+x',y+y')}{\sqrt{\sum_{x',y'} T(x',y')^2 \cdot \sum_{x',y'} I(x+x',y+y')^2}} \tag{5}$$

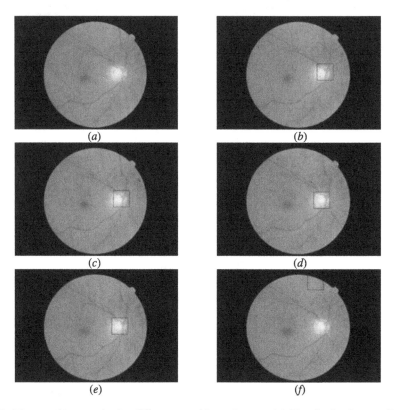

Fig. 5. The matching results by different matching schemes. (*a*) The fundus image; (*b*) The matching result by square difference matching; (*c*) The matching result by standard square difference matching; (*d*) The matching result by correlation matching; (*e*) The matching result by standard correlation matching; (*f*) The matching result by correlation coefficient matching. Extensive experiments demonstrate that correlation matching and standard correlation matching are with higher accuracy than other matching methods for diabetic retinopathy images.

4 Experimental Results

We test our method on the largest and publicly available fundus image database MES-SIDOR. This database consist of 1200 fundus images in TIFF format, which are from three different ophthalmic institutions. The resolutions are $1440 \times 960, 2240 \times 1488$ and 2304×1536, respectively. The MESSIDOR database gives the symptoms of diabetic retinopathy at different stages and macular edema, which is the common database of fundus images.

We do the experiments of locating OD in 379 fundus images with a resolution of 1440×960 in the MESSIDOR database. The original data are divided into 4 datasets, each includes 100 or 79 fundus images. The number of images in which OD is correctly detected and the accuracy rate are shown in Table 1.

Table 1. The results of locating OD in 4 datasets of fundus images.

Datasets	The number of correct detection	The total number of fundus images	Accuracy rate
Base21	93	100	93%
Base22	91	100	91%
Base23	89	100	89%
Base24	71	79	89.9%

5 Conclusion

Image processing techniques can be used in clinical diagnosis. The analysis of fundus images contributes to early screening and treatment of ophthalmology diseases. In this paper, we discuss a fast method of locating OD in diabetic retinopathy images. We first preprocess fundus images to reduce the difference of fundus images caused by various factors, and then create an OD template for diabetic retinopathy images, which are used to match fundus images. Our work can help the subsequent detection and diagnose of ophthalmology diseases. Presently, many researchers made great contributions to computer-aided diagnosis systems. They proposed some efficient and fast algorithms for locating, segmentation, detection and recognition, but the accuracy and efficiency need to be improved, which will be addressed in our future work.

Acknowledgments. This work is supported by the Natural Science Foundation of Shandong Province of China under Grant No. ZR2016FM20.

References

1. Zheng, S., Chen, J., Pan, L., et al.: A novel automatic detection method for macula center and optic disk in retinal images. J. Electron. Inf. Technol. **36**(11), 2586–2592 (2014)
2. Ke, X., Jiang, W., Zhu, J.: Fast locating and segmentation of optic disk in fundus image based on visual attention. Sci. Technol. Eng. **15**(35), 47–53 (2015)

3. Xiao, Z., Shao, Y., Zhang, F., et al.: Optic disc localization in color fundus images based on fundus structure feature. Chin. J. Biomed. Eng. **35**(3), 257–263 (2016)
4. Salazar-Gonzalez, A.G., Kaba, D., Li, Y.M., et al.: Segmentation of the blood vessels and optic disk in retinal images. IEEE J. Biomed. Health Inform. **18**(6), 1874–1886 (2014)
5. Foracchia, M., Grisan, E., Ruggeri, A.: Detection of optic disc in retinal images by means of a geometrical model of vessel structure. IEEE Trans. Med. Imaging **23**(10), 1189–1195 (2004)
6. Lalonde, M., Beaulieu, M., Gagnon, L.: Fast and robust optic disc detection using pyramidal decomposition and Hausdorff-based template matching. IEEE Trans. Med. Imaging **20**(11), 1193–1200 (2001)

Research on Security of Public Security Iris Application

Li Li[1,2(✉)], Shengguang Li[1,2], Shiwei Zhao[1,2], and Lin Tan[1,2]

[1] First Research Institute of the Ministry of Public Security of PRC, Beijing 100048, China
13426026933@163.com, lishengg@163.com, 13671230231@163.com,
kelvin3497@163.com
[2] Key Laboratory of Internet of Things Application Technology of the Ministry of Public
Security of PRC, Beijing 100048, China

Abstract. Combined with the security problems encountered in the public security iris application, this paper makes a comprehensive analysis of these security problems from two aspects of iris acquisition and iris verification. And using the current academic research results, combined with the practical application requirements, the iris template encryption, the original image encryption, transmission encryption, equipment authentication and other technical means are used to construct the security system of the public security iris application and ensure the public security iris application in an all-round way. Finally, the application of the research results in actual use is introduced.

Keywords: Public security · Iris application · Security threat · Iris verification
Hash value

1 Introduction

With the development of the times and the progress of science and technology, the application of iris recognition technology in public security organs is becoming increasingly urgent. Some applications have been carried out in some areas. The Public Security Bureau of Beijing city started the construction of the iris database of key personnel in 2016, and carried out a pilot trial. In 2017, the Xinjiang Uygur Autonomous Region began to collect various biometric information including iris. This paper will analyze the security threats faced by the public security iris application, and put forward the safety protection measures.

2 Security Threat

The public security iris application is composed of two parts: Iris acquisition and iris verification. Iris acquisition includes identity verification, iris image acquisition, iris original image storage, iris feature extraction, iris feature storage and so on. Iris verification is the core function of the public security iris application. By extracting the iris features and matching the iris features stored in the database, the identification is

J. Zhou et al. (Eds.): CCBR 2018, LNCS 10996, pp. 459–467, 2018.
https://doi.org/10.1007/978-3-319-97909-0_49

completed [1]. In the two processes of iris acquisition and iris verification, the system is in a state of interaction with the outside world, and is very vulnerable to external attacks [2].

2.1 Threat of Acquisition Process

There are 6 kinds of attacks which are easy to be attacked in the iris acquisition process.

AT1: Fake biometric [3, 4]. The attacker passed the system's examination of the organism itself by means of deception, such as fake identity cards. So as to complete the collection of false iris information of individuals.

AT2: Illegal equipment. Attackers use illegal iris collection devices to access the network, causing data leakage, data packet replay, denial of service, virus infection and other threats.

AT3: Transmission attack. When the iris collection end transmits the data to the server side, the attacker can get the iris information. On the other hand, tampering and forgery of iris information can also be sent to the background database.

AT4: Original image database attack. Attacking the original database of iris, such as modifying, deleting, increasing some data, etc.

AT5: Override feature extractor. It generates the iris feature template needed by attackers and saves them to the iris feature template database (Fig. 1).

AT6: Tampering template. It mainly attacks on the iris feature template database, such as modifying, deleting, increasing some data, etc.

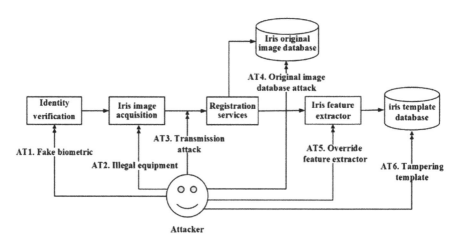

Fig. 1. Threats in the process of iris acquisition.

2.2 Threat of Verification Process

There are 5 kinds of attacks which are vulnerable to the iris verification process.

VT1: Illegal equipment. Attackers use illegal iris verification devices to access the network, causing data leakage, data packet replay, denial of service, virus infection and other threats.

VT2: Override feature extractor. It generates the iris feature template required by attackers, and submits it to the backstage for authentication.

VT3: Transmission attack. When the iris verification end transmits the data to the server side, the attacker can get the iris information. On the other hand, tampering and forgery of iris information can also be sent to the backstage for authentication.

VT4: Tamper with verification results. The result of iris verification is two valued output, and is easy to be tampered into an attacker's desired results (Fig. 2).

VT5: Tampering template. It mainly attacks the iris feature template database in verification, such as modifying, deleting, increasing some data, etc.

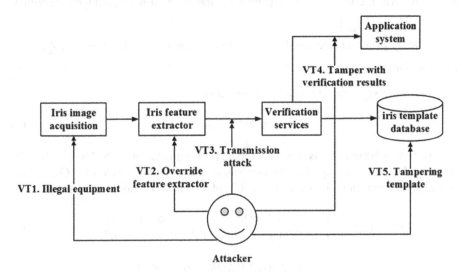

Fig. 2. Threats in the process of iris verification.

3   Security Protection

3.1   Iris Feature Template Encryption

Juels and Wattenberg proposed the Fuzzy Commitment scheme [5] in 1999. It is a typical key binding scheme which combines error correcting code technology with biometrics. The algorithm is simple and efficient, and it is suitable for protecting binary iris feature template [6].

In this paper, the Fuzzy Commitment scheme is improved. An iris template encryption model which is compatible with iris templates of several mainstream iris manufacturers in China is designed. It is in line with the actual situation of public security iris application. The concrete realization process is as follows.

(1) Parameter definition:

- M: Vendor code set, $\{M_1, M_2, \ldots, M_n\}$;
- w_m: A set of iris feature templates extracted from a manufacturer's algorithm, $\{w_{m1}, w_{m2}, \ldots, w_{mn}\}$;
- N: Iris feature length set, $\{N_1, N_2, \ldots, N_n\}$;
- K: A uniform random key set with a length of L ($L \leq N$), $\{K_1, K_2, \ldots, K_n\}$;
- δ: The key K is processed by some error correcting code to get N bit binary string set, $\{\delta_1, \delta_2, \ldots, \delta_n\}$;
- ε_m: Binding information set of key and iris feature template, $\{\varepsilon_{m1}, \varepsilon_{m2}, \ldots, \varepsilon_{mn}\}$;
- w'_m: A verifying iris feature template set extracted by a manufacturer's algorithm, $\{w'_{m1}, w'_{m2}, \ldots, w'_{mn}\}$;
- δ': Binary string set calculated when the template is validated, $\{\delta'_1, \delta'_2, \ldots, \delta'_n\}$.

(2) Encryption process:

Computing key template binding information:

$$\varepsilon_{mn} = \delta_n \text{ XOR } w_{mn}. \tag{1}$$

The SM3 algorithm [7] is used to compute the hash value of the δ_n, $\text{Hash}(\delta_n)$ can be obtained. During the computing, the Boolean function is used as below (2) (3), and the permutation function is shown below (4) (5), of which X, Y, and Z are 32 words:

$$FF_j(X, Y, Z) = \begin{cases} X \text{ XOR } Y \text{ XOR } Z, & 0 \leq j \leq 15 \\ (X \wedge Y) \vee (X \wedge Z) \vee (Y \wedge Z), & 16 \leq j \leq 63 \end{cases}. \tag{2}$$

$$GG_j(X, Y, Z) = \begin{cases} X \text{ XOR } Y \text{ XOR } Z, & 0 \leq j \leq 15 \\ (X \wedge Y) \vee (X \wedge Z), & 16 \leq j \leq 63 \end{cases}. \tag{3}$$

$$P_0(X) = X \text{ XOR}(X \lll 9) \text{ XOR } (X \lll 17). \tag{4}$$

$$P_1(X) = X \text{ XOR}(X \lll 15) \text{ XOR } (X \lll 23). \tag{5}$$

After that, ε_{mn} and $\text{Hash}(\delta_n)$ are stored in the M_n vendor specific template database.

(3) Verification process:

The following calculations were performed using ε_{mn} and the verifying iris feature template w'_{mn}.

$$\delta'_n = \varepsilon_{mn} \text{ XOR } w'_{mn}. \tag{6}$$

To bring the formula (1) into the formula (6) can be obtained:

$$\delta'_n = \delta_n \; XOR \; w_{mn} \; XOR \; w'_{mn} = \delta_n \; XOR \; (w_{mn} \; XOR \; w'_{mn})$$

And then, the SM3 algorithm is used to compute the hash value of the δ'_n, $\text{Hash}(\delta'_n)$ can be obtained.

When Hamming distance between w_{mn} and w'_{mn} does not exceed the error correction range of error correcting codes, δ'_n and δ_n can be considered as consistent. Then we can verify whether authentication is successful by verifying whether the hash value is equal to $\text{Hash}(\delta_n)$ and $\text{Hash}(\delta'_n)$.

This algorithm is proposed for AT6 and VT5. It is simple and efficient, and the key is not stored in the database, only the hash value of the key is stored, which can effectively avoid the risk of key disclosure.

At present, many biometric template protection algorithms are studying how to combine biometrics and cryptography to protect biometrics template safety. However, the contradiction between the accuracy required by cryptography and the ambiguity inherent in biometric features has become the biggest obstacle to the combination of the two. In this paper, the algorithm uses the error correcting code technology to form a balance between the two, so that it can be applied to the actual combat platform.

3.2 Fragmented Storage of Iris Original Image

Hundreds of billions of iris original images need to be stored in the public security iris application, and the SeaweedFS file storage server based on Linux is used to store the iris original image. These iris original images are not directly involved in iris verification. Only when the iris feature template library is invalid, the new iris feature template is generated, and the real time requirement of iris original image reading is not high. But iris original image is related to the privacy of the public, and its confidentiality is very high.

For AT4, this paper proposes a way of image segmentation and block encryption to store original image. That is, not a complete picture is stored on the picture file storage server, but it is cut into an encrypted file fragment [8] which even the system administrator can't identify. It effectively guarantees the privacy of the data. After the image file is segmented and encrypted, an index that points to the fragment of the file can be generated at the same time, and a complete original image of the iris can be synthesized according to the index.

3.3 Data Transmission Encryption

The application of public security iris includes two kinds of transmission data, iris image data and text data. Compared with text data, iris images have the characteristics of large data volume, high redundancy, and generally store data in two-dimensional array [9]. Comprehensive security, operation efficiency and other factors, this paper uses the SM4 algorithm to protect the transmission data, effectively resisting the three kinds of threats such as AT3, VT3 and VT4.

The packet length of the SM4 algorithm is 128 bits, and the key length is 128 bits [10]. When we use SM4 algorithm to encrypt iris images, we first transform 2-D data into one-dimensional data [11], and then encrypt one dimension data in groups of 128 bits. After the encryption operation, the original iris image becomes the information similar to the random noise of the channel, which can't be recognized by the network eavesdropper who does not know the key, and can effectively protect the iris image data in the transmission.

At the same time, in order to ensure the integrity of the iris image data, the SM3 algorithm is used to perform hash operation on the iris image, and the summary value obtained by the hash operation is passed together with the iris image cipher text to the public security iris application background. The background calculates the hash value with the received image file, and compares it with the hash value passed by the front end. Whether the image file is tampered with in the transmission process is judged by judging whether the hash value is equal or not.

3.4   Terminal Equipment Authentication

For AT2 and VT1, this paper proposes a device authentication method. When the device is used for the first time, it will need to be audited by the administrator. After the device is down, it needs to send messages to identify it.

When the terminal device is first connected, the device will be audited by the administrator. The information is submitted to the administrator, such as device information, user information, serial number and so on. After the audit is passed, the PIN code is allocated for the device, and the information of the device is recorded to the background database.

When the terminal device is reconnected after each power failure, equipment authentication is necessary [12]. The device authentication message when the terminal device is powered up includes the product serial number, the local time stamp, the authentication code $Hash_{auth}$ and the IP address of the current operation. The authentication code is obtained by using SM3 algorithm to hash the string composed of serial number, PIN code and local timestamp (Fig. 3).

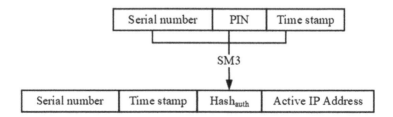

Fig. 3.   Device authentication code message

After receiving the authentication message in the public security iris application background, according to the serial number field of the device authentication message, find the device description file in the background, read the PIN code from it, make up the string together with the serial number and time stamp received, and use the SM3 algorithm to obtain the correct authentication code $Hash_{rec}$. Comparing $Hash_{rec}$ and $Hash_{auth}$, if $Hash_{rec}$ and $Hash_{auth}$ are identical, the device is identified as a legitimate device, otherwise it is identified as an illegal device (Fig. 4).

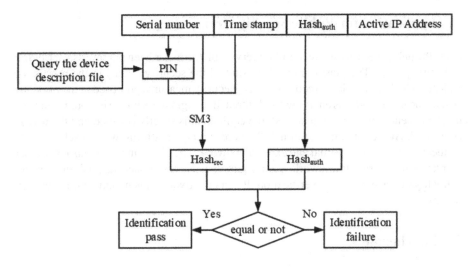

Fig. 4. Equipment authentication process

3.5 Other Means of Protection

For AT1, using identity card photo and face comparison technique, we compare and identify the face of the field face with the identity card at the scene, and judge whether it is the same person, Strengthen the identity review of the organism itself.

For VT2, the attack at this level is rather difficult [13]. AT5, because the feature extraction in the acquisition process is completed in the background, and the attack difficulty is more difficult than VT2.

In addition, the public security iris application uses role based access control (RBAC) to connect access rights to roles, and to connect users with access rights by assigning appropriate roles to users [14]. Roles are set according to different duties and responsibilities. Users can get all the privileges that the role owns by playing a role. It can transform between multiple roles and play different roles. You can also add or delete a role according to the needs of access control, so as to achieve flexible access control [15].

At the same time, the front-end acquisition and verification equipment of the public security iris application is widely distributed throughout the prisons, airports, checkpoints and other places. It is deployed in the public security information network, and is also deployed in other networks, even with the use of mobile network. In view of the actual demand of cross network, the network isolation switching technology [16] is adopted. "Isolation" means that the trusted internal network and the untrusted external network are logically or physically separated so that they can't communicate directly. "Switching" refers to the ability to provide secure communication data exchange between internal and external networks through the third party system. The technology of network isolation exchange provides a security [17] for the deployment and use of inter network devices and data exchange between networks in public security iris application.

4   Application for Public Security Iris

Now, the public security iris recognition service platform has been put into use in Beijing and other places. The platform has fully studied the security threats in the process of collection and verification. According to the security measures proposed in the previous article, the iris template is encrypted and stored, the original iris image is stored in pieces, the data is encrypted and transmitted, the equipment is strictly certified and the user is controlled. At the same time, through the border access platform, we can achieve data connectivity between internal and external network. The platform has set up a whole set of platform security framework from equipment access, image acquisition, feature extraction, data storage and verification. It can effectively prevent and control security threats.

5   Conclusion

Iris recognition technology is becoming more and more widely used in the public security industry because of its high recognition rate, non-contact, and good fraud prevention. And the security problems that followed have also been paid much attention to. This paper systematically analyzes various threats of security in the process of collecting and verifying of the public security iris application. In view of these security threats, combined with the characteristics of the public security industry, the security of iris application is guaranteed by using the security measures such as iris feature template encryption, original image encryption, transmission encryption, and equipment authentication and so on. We will continue to focus on the security threats of iris recognition technology, and further develop and improve the security protection measures of public security iris applications.

Acknowledgment. This work was supported by Beijing Municipal Science and Technology Project: Z171100004417022, Science and Technology Project of the Ministry of Public Security: 2017GABJC35.

References

1. Zheng, F., Askar, R., Wang, R.Y., Li, L.T.: Overview of biometric recognition technology. J. Inf. Secur. Res. **2**(1), 12–26 (2016)
2. Huo, H.W., Xia, T.N., Feng, J.: Security analysis on biometrics system. Stand. Res. **4**, 48–51 (2013)

3. Ratha, N.K., Connell, J.H., Bolle, R.M.: An analysis of minutiae matching strength. In: Bigun, J., Smeraldi, F. (eds.) AVBPA 2001. LNCS, vol. 2091, pp. 223–228. Springer, Heidelberg (2001). https://doi.org/10.1007/3-540-45344-X_32
4. Ao, S., Ma, J., Tang, S.L.: Safety analysis and reflection on biometrics system. Microcomput. Inf. **23**(1–2), 288–290 (2007)
5. Juels, A., Wattenberg, M.: A fuzzy commitment scheme. In: Proceedings of the 6th ACM Conference on Computer and Communications Security (CCCS), pp. 28 – 36. ACM, New York (1999)
6. Li, P., Tian, J., Yang, X., Shi, P., Zhang, Y.Y.: Biometric template protection. J. Softw. **20**(6), 1553–1573 (2009)
7. Sheng, Y.Z.: Cryptanalysis of SM3 Cryptographic Hash Algorithm. DongHua University, Shanghai (2013)
8. Xu, S.W., Qin, X.L.: Data security analysis and measures based on cloud storage. J. Beijing Electr. Sci. Technol. Inst. **22**(2), 15–19 (2014)
9. Huang, X.S.: Research progress of digital image security technology. J. East China Jiaotong Univ. **23**(1), 82–86 (2006)
10. Wang, C.G., Qiao, S.S., Hei, Y.: Low complexity implementation of block cipher SM4 algorithm. Comput. Eng. **39**(7), 177–180 (2013)
11. Song, G.Q.: Research on Digital Image Encryption Technology. National University of Defense Technology, Changsha (2007)
12. Qian, K.F., Wang, P., Wang, H.W.: Research of device authentication mechanism in EPA. Comput. Eng. Des. **28**(24), 5877–5902 (2007)
13. Qi, Y.F., Huo, Y.L., Zhang, J.S.: Techniques and security on biometrics system. Microcomput. Inf. **24**(6–3), 30–34 (2008)
14. Li, M.K., Yu, X.X.: Role based access control technology and its application. Appl. Res. Comput. **10**, 44–47 (2000)
15. Chang, J.: The Design of Multi-domain and Multi-level Secure Access Control Model. Hebei University of Science and Technology, Hebei (2015)
16. Bai, X.S.: Research on network security isolation and information exchange technology. Silicon valley **1**, 66 (2010)
17. Wang, S.Q.: Systematic analysis of network security isolation and information exchange technology. Inf. Commun. **3**, 211–212 (2012)

Hybrid Fusion Framework
for Iris Recognition Systems

He Zhang[1,2], Jing Liu[1(✉)], Zhiguo Zeng[3], Qianli Zhou[3], Shengguang Li[4],
Xingguang Li[1], and Hui Zhang[1]

[1] Beijing IrisKing Co., Ltd., Beijing, China
liujing@irisking.com
[2] Beihang University of China, Beijing, China
[3] Beijing Municipal Public Security Bureau, Beijing, China
[4] First Research Institute of The Ministry of Public Security of PRC, Beijing, China

Abstract. Due to the advantages in uniqueness, convenience and non-contact, iris recognition is widely deployed for automatic identity authentication. Instead of a single signature, multiple templates are registered in real-world applications for the diversity of gallery samples, resulting in great enhanced user experience. In this paper, we exploit the connection among the multiple registration data and then make efforts to give a more comprehensive decision based on them. A novel hybrid fusion framework is proposed to fuse information at groups in feature and score levels. Specifically, the gallery samples are firstly divided into groups to balance the abundance and the robustness of information. Afterwards, hierarchical fusion is performed at the groups, which is actually the procedure of information mapping and reducing. The experimental results demonstrate the effectiveness and generalization ability of the proposed hybrid fusion framework.

Keywords: Iris recognition · Hybrid fusion · Feature level fusion
Score level fusion

1 Introduction

Biometric identification is revolutionizing the security world by authenticating individuals through the modalities of face, fingerprint, iris and so on. Compared with traditional passwords or cards, biometrics is stable, unique and difficult to cheat. Due to the uniqueness and stability of texture patterns, iris is one of the most reliable biometric traits [1–3]. However, the robustness and the accuracy of a single-matching system are usually unsatisfactory because of the great differences between the enrollment and the verification situations. Therefore, real-world applications generally take more than one samples for enrollment to enrich the gallery space and decrease the significant variance of gallery and probe samples. Based on the multiple gallery samples, there are various fusion approaches to make the final decision.

© Springer Nature Switzerland AG 2018
J. Zhou et al. (Eds.): CCBR 2018, LNCS 10996, pp. 468–475, 2018.
https://doi.org/10.1007/978-3-319-97909-0_50

According to the fusion information, fusion systems can be divided into feature-level, score-level, and decision-level categories [4–6]. Feature level fusion reduces the features into a new feature vector [2,3]. [12] proposed a feature level approach based on Markov formulation for heterogeneous image sequences. Score level fusion combines the respective scores matched between the probe and the multiple gallery samples. The scores contain gratified information to discriminate inter and intra, fusing them is straitforward but effective [6,7]. This strategy can be additionally applied in multi-mode systems, e.g., the fusion of iris and palmprint [5], face and iris [8,9]. Decision level fusion integrates the results from each systems to decide whether to accept or reject. Qian Tao *et al.* applied threshold-optimized decision level fusion to biometrics, which improves the system performance effectively [10]. Different fusion levels have their own advantages and limitations. Specifically, as the fusion level upgrades, less information can be utilized but the robustness to noises increases. Therefore, choosing a suitable fusion algorithm is of great significance to practical systems.

In this paper, we focus on the strategy of multi-registration templates which is commonly used in real-world application, and propose a novel hybrid framework to fuse the information more effectively. As stated above, single-level fusion methods suffer their own limitations in flexibility and generalization ability. We believe in a hierarchical framework can map and reduce information in different fusion stages, resulting in combined advantages. First, multiple registration templates are divided into groups for better robustness. Since noises cannot pollute all samples, grouping registration templates can effectively avoid the negative influence of outliers. After then, feature level fusion is applied to each group of samples. It will eliminate fragile feature codes and provide a more accurate fusion feature by strengthening the stable patterns, especially for heterogeneous iris images. Finally, given a probe feature vector, it will compare with not only the enrollment features but also the mapped fusion features. Score level fusion takes the above matching scores in a block into consideration and give the more comprehensive decision. The experimental results demonstrate that the proposed hybrid fusion approach has satisfactory performance and satisfying accuracy.

The remainder of this paper is organized as follows. Section 2 introduces the details of the proposed hybrid fusion framework. The experimental results are illustrated in Sect. 3.2. Section 4 draws the final conclusion.

2 Hybrid Fusion for Iris Recognition

2.1 Framework

Before the hybrid fusion, iris images are preprocessed by quality assessment, iris segmentation, normalization and coding [12,13]. Quality assessment is applied to select ideal images for better recognition performance. Adaboostcascade iris detector and "Pulling and pushing" model is applied to segment the iris. The iris feature is coded by ordinal measures (OM) [14]. "1" represents the next region is brighter than the current region, otherwise it will be encoded by "0". Thus, binary strings which denote iris features are yielded.

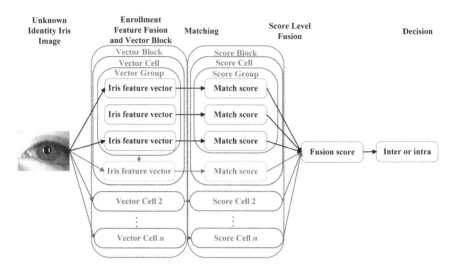

Fig. 1. The flowchart of the proposed method.

Due to the differences between registration and the verification circumstances, iris images sometimes are captured in uncontrolled scenarios with low-quality. Single-matching systems may be interfered by random noise. Multiple templates are enrolled in real-word applications to enhance user experience. A novel hybrid fusion framework is proposed in this section to find a nature but comprehensive way to map and reduce registered information. Its flowchart is shown in Fig. 1.

First, the enrollment features are divided into vector **groups** in consideration of outliers. Feature level fusion is then performed at the groups to generate a more accurate and reliable fused feature by strengthening the stable patterns, especially for heterogeneous iris images. It will eliminate the fragile feature patterns as well as enrich the gallery feature space. Groups and their corresponding fused features form a vector **cell**. n ($n = 1, 2...$) vector cells make up a vector **block**. Probe set matches with each vector in the block to generate a match score block. The matching method is based on Hamming Distance. At last, score level fusion integrates all the information in a score block to give a comprehensive score. If the fusion score is larger than the preset threshold, the unknown individual is classified as intra class and vice versa.

2.2 Division into Groups

Since iris features are inevitably polluted by noises, e.g., eyelash occlusion and lens flare, the registration samples are divided into groups. The outliers can be estimated to a certain extent by the subsequent group fusions, while they will not make negative influence to the other groups. In our implementation, each three features of the same individual are grouped, and other numbers for grouping have similar experimental results.

2.3   Fusion at Feature Level

For the purposes of strengthening stable patterns [2], decreasing heterogenous variances [12] and so on, different fusion algorithms can be integrated into our framework, resulting in its great generalization ability. According to the preceding sections, iris features are represented by binary values ("0" or "1"). For simplicity in the description of our hybrid framework, the mode method is selected to fuse each values over three enrollment features here. Three enrollment features $F_1 = [a_{11}, a_{12},, \ldots, a_{1m}], F_2 = [a_{21}, a_{22},, \ldots, a_{2m}], F_3 = [a_{31}, a_{32},, \ldots, a_{3m}]$, are fused to obtain the fusion feature $F_f = [a_{f1}, a_{f2}, \ldots, a_{fm}]$. a_{fi} is calculated as:

$$a_{fi} = Mode(a_{1i}, a_{2i}, a_{3i}), \tag{1}$$

where Mode represents the mode of the array. The mode is the value that is repeated most often in the array. For example, if $F_1 = [0, 1, 1], F_2 = [1, 0, 1], F_3 = [1, 1, 0], a_{f1} = Mode(0, 1, 1) = 1, F_f = [1, 1, 1]$. Feature fusion will suppress the random noise and weaken the influence of outliers. Therefore, more accurate fusion features are provided.

2.4   Fusion at Score Level

Generally, score level fusion is regarded as a simple but effect solution to multi-registration systems. The proposed framework takes it to reduce the augmented information which is obtained by mapping features. The probe set will match with registration blocks to yield score blocks. Fusion at score level combines the scores from one score block into a comprehensive result. Our framework is flexible for diverse score level fusion methods. Some methods are introduced in this section.

Triangular Norms-Based Score Level Fusion. Triangular norms (t-norms) are widely used in data conjunction. T-norm $T(S_1, S_2)$ mapping S_1, S_2 in $[0, 1]$ to $[0, 1]$ must be commutative, monotonic and associative, while subjecting to $T(S_1, 1) = S_1$. The frequently-used t-norms are given as follows:

(a) Einstein product: $\frac{S_1 S_2}{(2-(S_1+S_2-S_1 S_2))}$,
(b) Hamacher: $\frac{S_1 S_2}{S_1+S_2-S_1 S_2}$,
(c) Yager ($p > 0$): $max(1 - ((1 - S_1)^p + (1 - S_2)^p)^{1/p}, 0)$,
(d) Schweizer & Sklar ($p > 0$): $(max(S_1^p + S_2^p - 1, 0))^{1/p}$,
(e) Frank ($p > 0$): $log_p(1 + \frac{(p^{S_1}-1)(p^{S_2}-1)}{p-1})$.

As mentioned above, there are $4n$ scores in a score block. Matching scores must be in the $[0, 1]$ interval. If not, normalization is demanded. If $n = 1$, the fusion score is calculated as follow:

$$S = T(T(T(S_1, S_2), S_3), S_f), \tag{2}$$

where S_1, S_2, S_3 and S_f are the matching scores. Since T-norms are commutative and associative, the order of integration is insignificant.

Sum Rule-Based Score Level Fusion. Given a set of normalized scores $(S_1, S_2, \ldots, S_m)$, sum rule calculates the summation of the scores with different weights to integrate the information. The formula of sum rule is expressed as

$$S = \omega_1 S_1 + \omega_2 S_2 + \omega_3 S_3 + \cdots + \omega_m S_m, \tag{3}$$

where $\omega_1, \omega_2, \ldots, \omega_m$ are the weights. m is the number of scores. Different weights will be applied for the optimal results of the scores from different systems.

Support Vector Machines-Based Score Level Fusion. Support vector machines (SVM), as a classical machine learning method, is to find an optimal hyperplane dividing the data into two classes with maximized margin between the two classes. In our implementation, scores in a block are regarded as a score vector. Training data consists of score vectors belonging to inter and intra class. Given the probe set, the trained model will yield probability scores that whether the vector belongs to intra class or inter class.

3   Experiments

3.1   Databases and Evaluation Metrics

Two databases are used for the experimental evaluation of the proposed framework. One is called DBA database, which was collected by ourselves. We randomly selected a subset that contained 186 subjects with 13,091 iris images in total. Iris region of part images are interfered by reflection and glasses. Another database is CASIA-IrisV4-Distance [14]. We selected a subset of the database that contained 142 subjects with 5,134 iris images. Images in two database are divided into probe set and gallery set, respectively.

Receiver operator characteristic (ROC) curve is introduced as the evaluation method. The ordinate represents the false acceptance rate (FAR), and the abscissa represents the false rejection rate (FRR).

$$FRR = \frac{NFR}{NGRA} \times 100\%, \tag{4}$$

$$FRR = \frac{NFR}{NGRA} \times 100\%, \tag{5}$$

where NGRA, NIRA, NFR, NFA represent the total number of intra and inter class, the number of false rejection and false acceptance, respectively.

3.2   Experiments Results

Three experiments are conducted in this section.

(1) Influence of n: n denotes the cell number in a block, and its influence to the proposed framework is evaluated in this experiment. Mode rule and Max rule are selected as the feature and the score level fusion methods respectively.

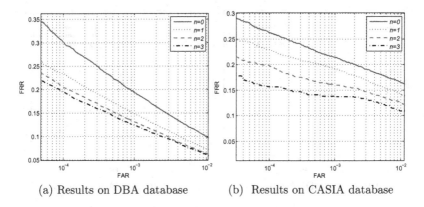

(a) Results on DBA database   (b) Results on CASIA database

Fig. 2. ROC curves of the hybrid framework with $n = 0, 1, 2, 3$.

The results is provided in Fig. 2. It can be found that the gallery space can be enriched and lower FRR is obviously obtained with the increase of n. Similar results can be obtained by using other fusion methods.

(2) Evaluation of the proposed framework: In this section, we compared the ROC curves of score level fusion, feature level fusion and the proposed hybrid fusion. For the simplicity of illustration, $n = 1$, mode rule and Max rule are used. Figure 3 reports the ROC curves on DBA database and CASIA database, respectively. It can be seen that the feature fusion commonly performs better than the score fusion. It meets the general opinion that features imply more information details than the matching scores. Thus fusion at feature level can offer more accurate fusion information at a fine granularity. Further, the hybrid framework is shown to obtain more satisfactory performance by combining the score level fusion. It exploits the connection among the score block, making each matching score contributes to the final decision. This experiment effectively validates the contributions of the proposed hybrid fusion framework.

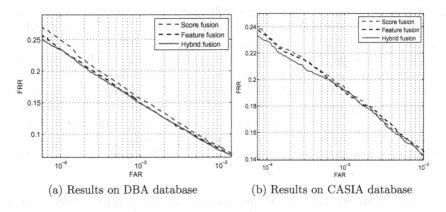

(a) Results on DBA database   (b) Results on CASIA database

Fig. 3. Performance of score fusion, feature fusion and hybrid fusion methods.

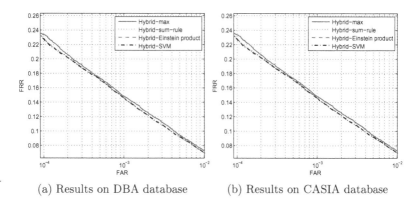

(a) Results on DBA database   (b) Results on CASIA database

Fig. 4. Performance of the hybrid methods using max, sum-rule, Einstein product and SVM.

(3) Comparison of integrating different score-level fusion methods: The proposed hybrid fusion framework is flexible for diverse feature and score level fusion methods. However, due to the limit of space, only the integrations of different score level fusion approaches are evaluated in this section. The max fusion, sum-rule fusion method [7], Einstein product and SVM are selected for comparison. The equal weights are used in sum-rule, since the enrolled data in experiments is acquired by the same system. SVM applies the polynomial kernel function. It can be seen from Fig. 4 that the integrations of sum-rule, Einstein product and SVM are superior to the max-fusion one. It is supposed that suitable fusion approaches can further enhance the recognition e.g., super resolution fusion methods in low resolution connditions.

4   Conclusions

In this paper, we simulate the real-world application scenario to propose a novel hybrid fusion method of feature level fusion and score level fusion, which contributes more robust systems. The enrollment features are first divided into vector groups. Afterwards, each vector group is fused at feature level, which obtains a more reliable feature and enriches the gallery space. The fused feature and the corresponding group form a cell. Score level fusion is applied to integrate the matching scores in a block to provide a more comprehensive decision. The hierarchical fusion framework is flexible for diverse feature and score level fusion methods. The experimental results indicate that FRR decreases as n increases. The proposed hybrid fusion framework is superior to merely feature or score level fusion in system performance, stability and generalization ability. At last, the experiments demonstrate that promising score level fusion methods can further increase the precision of recognition.

Acknowledgement. This work is supported by the Natural Science Foundation of China (61503365).

References

1. Li, H., Sun, Z., Zhang, M., Wang, L., Xiao, L., Tan, T.: A brief survey on recent progress in iris recognition. In: Sun, Z., Shan, S., Sang, H., Zhou, J., Wang, Y., Yuan, W. (eds.) CCBR 2014. LNCS, vol. 8833, pp. 288–300. Springer, Cham (2014). https://doi.org/10.1007/978-3-319-12484-1_33
2. Hollingsworth, K., Bowyer, K., Flynn, P.: All iris code bits are not created equal. In: IEEE International Conference on Biometrics Theory, Applications, and Systems 2007, pp. 1–6. IEEE Press (2007)
3. Nguyen, K., Fookes, C., Sridharan, S.: Robust mean super-resolution for less cooperative NIR iris recognition at a distance and on the move. In: Symposium on Information and Communication Technology, SOICT 2010, pp. 122–127. Symposium on Information & Communication Technology Press, Hanoi (2010)
4. Grover, J., Hanmandlu, M.: Hybrid fusion of score level and adaptive fuzzy decision level fusions for the finger-knuckle-print based authentication. J. Appl. Soft Comput. **31**, 1–13 (2015)
5. Madane, M., Sudeep Thepade, D.: Score level fusion based bimodal biometric identification using Thepade's sorted n-ary block truncation coding with variod proportions of iris and palmprint traits. J. Proc. Comput. Sci. **79**, 466–473 (2016)
6. Hanmandlu, M., Grover, J., Gureja, A., Gupta, H.: Score level fusion of multimodal biometrics using triangular norms. J. Pattern Recogn. Lett. **32**, 1843–1850 (2011)
7. He, M., et al.: Performance evaluation of score level fusion in multimodal biometric systems. J. Pattern Recogn. **43**, 1789–1800 (2010)
8. Sim, H., Asmuni, H., Hassan, R., Othman, R.: Multimodal biometrics: weighted score level fusion based on non-ideal iris and face images. J. Expert Syst. Appl. **41**, 5390–5404 (2014)
9. Miao, D., Zhang, M., Sun, Z., Tan, T., He, Z.: Bin-based classifier fusion of iris and face biometrics. J. Neurocomput. **224**, 105–118 (2017)
10. Tao, Q., Veldhuis, R.: Threshold-optimized decision-level fusion and its application to biometrics. J. Pattern Recogn. **42**, 823–836 (2009)
11. Dong, W., Sun, Z., Tan, T.: Iris matching based on personalized weight map. J. IEEE Trans. Pattern Anal. Mach. Intell. **33**, 1744–1757 (2011)
12. Liu, N., Liu, J., Sun, Z., Tan, T.: A code-level approach to heterogeneous iris recognition. J. IEEE Trans. Inf. Forensics Secur. **12**, 2373–2386 (2017)
13. Sun, Z., Tan, T.: Ordinal measures for iris recognition. J. IEEE Trans. Pattern Anal. Mach. Intell. **31**, 2211–2226 (2009)
14. CASIA-Dataset. http://biometrics.idealtest.org/

Design of a Long Distance Zoom Lens for Iris Recognition

Xiaoyu Lv(✉), Wenzhe Liao, Kaijun Yi, and Junxiong Gao

Wuhan Hongshi Technologies Co., LTD, Wuhan 430200, China
{Xiaoyu.Lv,Wenzhe.Liao,Kaijun.Yi,
Junxiong.Gao}@hongshi-tech.com

Abstract. This paper presents a zoom lens for iris recognition to solve the problem of narrow working range with fixed size of iris image. The lens with a wide and long working range and high resolution images with the same iris size in different work distance was designed. An 2.6× long distance zoom lens was designed which includes 35 ∼ 91 mm focal length, work distance from 750 mm to 1910 mm, less than 0.5% distortion, 3.5 working F number, 9.5 mm image diameter, 780 nm ∼ 890 nm wavelength of operating spectrum. At 166 lp/mm, the lens can capture iris image over all field of view with MTF > 0.3.

Keywords: Zoom lens · Iris recognition · Wide and long working range

1 Introduction

Nowadays, iris recognition is becoming the most widely used technology at security industry. Compared to other biometric modalities, iris is more stable, unique and is contactless use. While the commonly prime lens for iris recognition has short work distance and narrow work range [1], the usability of iris recognition is not good.

Prime lens was used in most iris recognition modules. The work range of this kind of modules is narrow, and it needs to reduce the resolution using modified blur algorithm to enhance usability of use. The shortcoming of prime lens is obvious. While blurred iris images can make the range of working distance broaden ostensibly, iris image quality decreases dramatically. Products using this approach are flexible and efficient of use; however their safety is seriously compromised.

Traditional zoom lens need zoom and focus. Zoom lens changes the focal length of lens, and focus changes the back focal length of lens. Normally, zoom lens was designed at a fixed object distance or infinity. When using this lens, the first step is zoom, and then using focus to get the best image plane. It would take two steps to capture high-quality images. And if we use traditional zoom lens for iris capture, it is difficult to guarantee high resolution image with enough pixels for iris size quickly.

X. Lv—F1-1201, No. 999 Gaoxin Avenue, East Lake High-Tech Development Zon, Wuhan, Hubei Province.

© Springer Nature Switzerland AG 2018
J. Zhou et al. (Eds.): CCBR 2018, LNCS 10996, pp. 476–485, 2018.
https://doi.org/10.1007/978-3-319-97909-0_51

There is a new technology: one piece of liquid lens is used in iris lenses which are used in iris recognition device [2]. This kind of lens can provide a wide working range, but have some weakness which cannot be overcome. First, the liquid lens is unstable. The curvature of liquid lens is affected by temperature and gravity. Second, the driving is not easy. It needs more than 40 V voltage to adjust the liquid lens curvature. At last, with different work distance the image of view by liquid lens is always changed. When we use them for iris capture, this lens can't guarantee enough pixels for iris recognition. So the working range is not broad enough.

This paper presents a long distance zoom lens to obtain practical wide and long working range with a fixed size of iris image for iris recognition. This lens can be used to improve the image quality and working in some special place, like security check channel and high-speed intersection.

2 The Optical Principle

2.1 Optical Principle of Lens System

A ray model is built by geometrical optics which demonstrates the imaging procedure of lens from object plane to image plane [3]. The lens system is shown in Fig. 1 where $y, -x - f, f' + x', f'$ and $-y'$ is respectively the object height, object distance, image distance, focal length and image height. The relationship between them could be described by Newton formula [3]:

$$l = -x - f \tag{1}$$

$$-f = f' \tag{2}$$

$$y/y' = (l - f')/f' \tag{3}$$

$$f' = l/[(y/y') + 1] \tag{4}$$

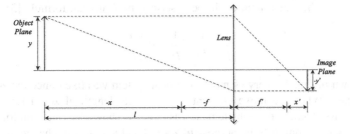

Fig. 1. Optical principle of the lens system.

2.2   Introduction for Zoom Lens

A zoom lens is a mechanical assembly of lens elements for which the focal length (and thus angle of view) can be varied, as opposed to a fixed focal length lens which called prime lens. A true zoom lens, also called a parfocal lens, is one that maintains focus when its focal length changes [4].

2.3   Optical Principle of Zoom Lens

A zoom lens model is built by geometrical optics which demonstrates in Fig. 2. The lens system is shown in Fig. 2, φ_1 φ_2 φ_3 φ_4 is four elements of a zoom lens which respectively denote.

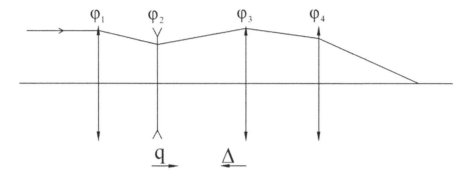

Fig. 2. A simple zoom system

In the zoom process, φ_3 and φ_4 would move a small shift. The distance of this small shift we call it q and Δ in Fig. 2. In this situation, the focal length changes following the q and Δ.

When constructing a new lens by combining two lens with known focal length, the focal length is f_1 and f_2, the distance of two lens is d, and the new lens focal length is f. The relationship between them could be described by Gaussian formula [3]:

$$\frac{1}{f} = \frac{1}{f_1} + \frac{1}{f_2} - d\frac{1}{f_1}\frac{1}{f_2} \qquad (5)$$

As shown in Fig. 1, every element of optical system was fixed once the zoom lens was designed. When we move element φ_2, the focal length of zoom lens changes. Because the focal length of each element was fixed, as shown by Gaussian formula (5), the only way to accomplish the purpose of zoom focal length is to change the space of specific parts. But the position of the image would remove following the change of the different elements, this not an zoom lens but a varifocal lens, so an extra element was needed to keep the position of image fixed, this is the compensatory element in zoom lens [3].

In conclusion, there should be three parts in zoom lens: fixed element, zoom element, compensatory element. We call two fixed elements φ_1 and φ_4, φ_1 is the front fixed element, φ_4 is the back fixed element. And we call two moving elements φ_2, φ_2 is the zoom element, and φ_3 is the compensatory element.

2.4   The Conditions for Zoom Lens Design

A perfect zoom lens should meet the following three conditions.

1. Change the focal length evenly and designed the corresponding work distance;
2. The size of image is stable during the zoom process;
3. The imaging quality meets the requirements.

3   Requirements of a Wide Working Range Iris Lens

3.1   The International Standard for Iris Image

According to international standard ISO/IEC29794-6 [5] and the government standard GB/T20979-2007, the requirements of iris recognition image quality standard is shown as Table 1.

Table 1. Iris image quality standard.

Image quality standard	Evaluation value	Pixels across iris diameter	Conclusion
Poor	0–25	50–100	Unacceptable
Low	26–50	100–149	Marginal
Medium	51–75	150–199	Acceptable
High	76–100	200 or more	Good

3.2   Illumination Requirements for Iris Recognition

Considering particularity of iris, the diffuse reflectivity of an iris connects with its albedo which is dependent on illumination wavelength. In NIR band of $700 \sim 850$ nm illumination, the unique pattern of iris can be presented.

According to literature [2], the reflectivity and transmissivity of iris in different wavelength of illumination is shown in Table 2.

Table 2. The reflectivity and transmissivity of iris in different wavelength.

Wavelength (nm)	Reflectivity (%)	Transmissivity (%)	Absorptivity (%)	Absorption coefficient
440	8	4	88	2.75
488	17	20	63	1.25
632	19	24	57	1.07
749	28	40	31	0.45
850	34	48	16	0.22

According to the results given in Table 2, 850 nm wavelength has the highest reflectivity and the lowest absorption coefficient. So we choose a LED chip product with wavelength 850 nm span of 30 nm as the illumination to design iris system [2].

3.3   Appropriate CMOS Chip

In order to make iris recognition device small and compact, small size of CMOS is needed in iris recognition. So we select a 1/4 inch monochrome CMOS sensor with good quantum efficiency at 850 nm. Table 3 shows the key parameters [6].

Table 3. Key parameters of CMOS chip.

Parameters	Typical value
Optical format	1/2.7 inch
Active pixels	1920(H) × 1080(V)
Pixel size	3.0 μm × 3.0 μm

3.4   Long Distance of Iris Recognition

According to test, it is found that too close work distance such as 30 cm always gives the user a feeling of pressure and discomfort. And since the iris size is too small, far work distance for iris recognition is very difficult. In this paper, 750 mm ∼ 1910 mm was designed, which is very powerful to improve the usability of iris recognition.

4   Optical Lens Design

4.1   Design Requirements of Iris Lens

With above analysis, the design specification of wide and long working range iris lens can be obtained. It is essential that at least 200 pixels are needed to cross an iris diameter at the working distance of 750–1910 mm to ensure the quality of iris image. The regular iris diameter is 12 mm. Suppose there are 200 pixels cross an iris diameter in object plane with working distance 450 mm, so y = 12/200 = 0.06 mm. The corresponding image plane y' equal to 0.003 mm (the pixels size). According to geometrical optics formulas (1) ∼ (4), we can gain that the focal length of the appropriate is 35–91 mm. Then the design requirements of iris lens are shown in Table 4.

Table 4. Design requirements of iris lens.

Technical parameters	Target value
Focus length	35 mm–91 mm
Ratio of zoom	2.6×
Image diameter	6.6 mm
Wavelength	780 nm–890 nm
Distortion	<0.5%
MTF/lp·mm^{-1}	166
F number	3.5

4.2 Structure Type of Iris Lens

The initiating structure was choose by requirements. According to literature [7], a zoom lens is selected as the initial structure. The focal length is 33 mm, F# 4.5. The structure of the initial structure is shown in Fig. 3.

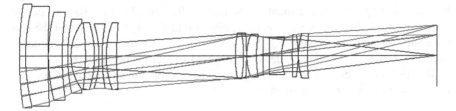

Fig. 3. The initial structure of three separation modified objective.

Next, classify the lens to four elements ready to design zoom lens through optical design software. We should note that the structure of elements must be simple and each lens is suitable for zoom.

4.3 Optimization

Optical design software is used to optimize the initial structure, to normalize focal length, setting the image size 6.6 mm, setting the wavelength 750–890 nm, setting the variable and constraint condition. And building the merit function: First, setting two multi-configuration. Setting the thickness of lens in each elements as variable. Second, adding the operand to fixed focal length to what we need in merit function, the purpose is to keep the focal length constant in the process of optimization. Finally, adding more configuration in optical design software editor.

As previously stated, this lens design in different work distance, the work distance matches the focal length to make sure the number of pixels across iris diameter is 200. The specific relationship between focal length and work distance can be calculated by formula [6] is shown in Table 5.

$$WD = f \times [D/(N \times P) + 1] \qquad (6)$$

WD is the work distance, f is the focal length, D is the iris diameter, N is the number of pixels of iris diameter and P is the size of pixel.

Table 5. Relationship between focal length and work distance

Focal length	Work distance
35 mm	735 mm
57 mm	1428 mm
68 mm	1579 mm
79 mm	1659 mm
91 mm	1911 mm

Adjust the distance between lens, specification of optical glass and radius of lens surface again and again. Then a good zoom lens for iris recognition is given.

4.4 Optimized Results

In the final optimized design, zoom lens with focus length of 35 mm ∼ 91 mm meets the wide working range requirement of 750 mm to 1910 mm. Figure 4 shows a design of wide working distance of iris lens in preview. From Fig. 4, it is found that the lens has a wide object distance. And Fig. 5 shows the detail structure of the lens elements. From Fig. 5, we can see this iris lens is composed of four elements lenses.

By this lens, we can capture iris images with high resolution and enough pixels in a long work distance for iris recognition.

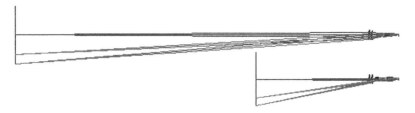

Fig. 4. The preview of nearest and farthest working distance.

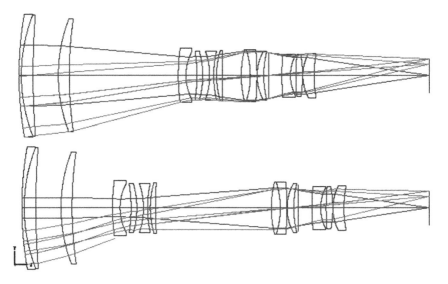

Fig. 5. The detail structure of designed iris lens.

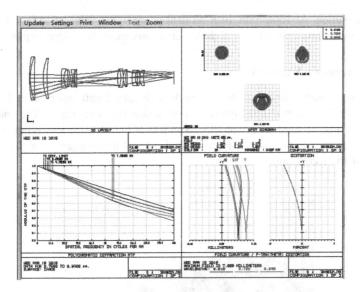

Fig. 6. The optical aberration chart at working distance of 750 mm. From left to right, up to bottom, these four charts are MTF chart at 166lp/mm, spot diagram, field curvature and distortion.

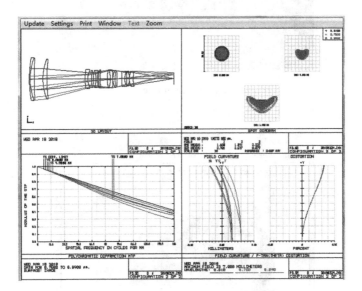

Fig. 7. The optical aberration chart at working distance of 1910 mm. From left to right, up to bottom, these four charts are MTF chart at 166lp/mm, spot diagram, field curvature and distortion.

Figures 6 and 7 show that this lens can acquire good image quality with all field of view at working distance of 750 mm and 1910 mm. The spot diagram shows that RMS radius are less than 3 μm which is the size of a CMOS pixel, so it perfectly matches the

CMOS resolution. At 160lp/mm, over all field of view, the valve of MTF > 0.3. And the distortion is less than 0.5%. All these parameters meet the design requirements.

4.5   Performance Simulation

The real image performance can be simulation with optical software design. There is a iris image which is captured by high resolution optical system at Fig. 8. The real image performance had be simulation with this zoom lens at Fig. 9, if the lens is not good, the simulation image will be obscure. Figure 9 indicate that the lens can get high definition images for iris recognition.

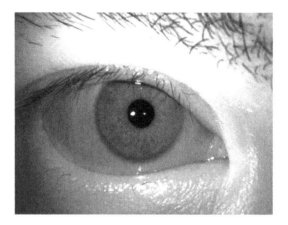

Fig. 8. Iris image

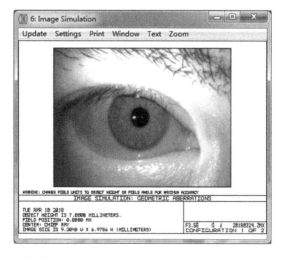

Fig. 9. Simulation performance with this zoom lens

5   Conclusion

This paper presents a lens with zoom ratio 2.6× and long distance for iris recognition. The lens has a focal length of 35 mm ~ 91 mm and a working range from 750 mm to 1910 mm. The lens can match 1/2.7 in. CMOS image sensor perfectly and can produce iris image with high resolution and fixed size. This lens can be deployed to improve the usability of iris recognition. Other than that, it also has great market potential for machine vision industry.

References

1. Burge, M.J., Bowyer, K.W. (eds.).: Handbook of Iris Recognition. Springer, London (2013). https://doi.org/10.1007/978-1-4471-4402-1
2. Liao, W., Yi, K., Gao, J., Lv, X., Wang, J.: Design of a wide working range lens for iris recognition. In: You, Z., et al. (eds.) CCBR 2016. LNCS, vol. 9967, pp. 339–348. Springer, Cham (2016). https://doi.org/10.1007/978-3-319-46654-5_37
3. Yu, D., Tan, H.: Engineering Optics. China Machine Press, China (2006)
4. Cavanagh, Roger (29 May 2003). "Parfrocal Lenses". Archived from the original on 07 October 2007. Accessed 18 Nov 2007
5. Iris Image Quality Standard, SC 37 N 3331. ISO/IEC 29794-6 Annex A (2009)
6. 1/2.7-Inch Digital Image Sensor. http://www.onsemi.cn/pub/Collateral/AR0238-D.PDF
7. Laikin, M.: Lens Design, Forth Edition. China Machine Press, China (2011)

Efficient Near-Infrared Eye Detection Utilizing Appearance Features

Qi Wang, Ying Lian, Ting Sun, Yuna Chu, and Xiangde Zhang[✉]

College of Sciences, Northeastern University,
No. 3-11 Wenhua Road, Heping District, Shenyang 110819, Liaoning, China
wangqimath@126.com, lianying1211@126.com, sunflowerting78@gmail.com,
chuyunamath@163.com, zhangxiangde@mail.neu.edu.cn

Abstract. Eye detection has been a critical problem for iris recognition, face recognition and some other applications. However, the unconstrained scene brings a lot of challenging problems to eye detection such as occlusion, rotation, blur and complex background etc. In this paper, we propose a novel eye detection algorithm for near-infrared image. We put forward four factors, which are IVSF, PLG, DRDF and IOSF to represent eye region features. The method is mainly composed of two steps. Firstly, candidate positions are generated. Secondly, a multi-strategy fusion method is designed to confirm final eye position. The experimental results demonstrate that the proposed algorithm is accurate and fast compared with some existing methods.

Keywords: Eye detection · Unconstrained scene
Near-infrared face image · Multi-strategy fusion

1 Introduction

Eye detection plays an important role in many computer vision problems, such as iris recognition [1], face recognition [2], eye gazing [3,4] and some other applications [5].

Some eye detection methods follow the face detection process [6,7]. When a face is detected from an image, the eye region can be easily located according to relative position [8,9]. However, this strategy requires accurate face extraction. The other strategies detect eye region directly [15,16]. It is also a challenging task due to the undetermined image acquisition environment and cooperation problems. Specifically, uneven illumination, arbitrary head pose, wearing eyeglasses and complex background requires the algorithm insensitive to intensity-level, scale and rotation. Currently, many existing eye detection methods can not deal well with eyeglasses problem [9]. Actually, both spectacle-frames and light spots may change the facial intensity distribution and bring occlusion problems.

X. Zhang—Professor with the Department of Mathematics, College of Sciences, Northeastern University, Heping District, Shenyang, Liaoning Province, P.R. China.

© Springer Nature Switzerland AG 2018
J. Zhou et al. (Eds.): CCBR 2018, LNCS 10996, pp. 486–496, 2018.
https://doi.org/10.1007/978-3-319-97909-0_52

To our knowledge, the existing methods can be further divided into three categories:

(1) Shape matching based methods: Coots [10] presented the Active Shape Model (ASM) and the Active Appearance Model (AAM) which both start from a given initial shape, then match shape and update parameter until meeting the stopping condition.
(2) Intensity integral projection based methods: Researchers did many relative researches based on this idea, such as in [11,12]. For those images interfered by noise, Zhou and Geng [13] put forward the Generalized Integral Projection Function (GPF) to improve the robustness.
(3) Features representation based data-driven methods: Common algorithms extracted features to represent eye and then used massive samples to train classifiers, such as Haar-AdaBoost [14] and SVM [17]. Compared to prior two types of methods, it archieves more accurate and robust performance.

This paper presents a novel eye detection method. Here, we combine a variety of features including spots in pupil, facial intensity distribution information to estimate eye positions. Then, a weight calculation function and symmetry based monocular location estimation algorithm are put forward to improve the detection accuracy. Experimental results indicate that the proposed method is more robust to challenge cases such as eyeglasses and obstacles, and faster than other algorithms.

2   Image Preprocessing

Integral projection function (IPF) [18] which projects a 2-D image to 1-D vector, illustrated in Fig. 1. It can reflect the intensity distribution in a specific direction.

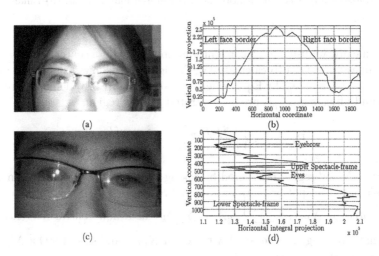

Fig. 1. Examples of integral projection. (a) The example of vertical integral projection. (b) The result of vertical integral projection. (c)The example of horizontal integral projection. (d) The result of horizontal integral projection.

In the near-infrared face image, the overall gray-level of background is generally lower than that of face. Thus, we can get rid of part of background and confine the range of eye detection area with size of $M' \times N'$ based on the IPF.

3   Generating Candidate Eye Regions

In this section, a generating strategy for candidate eye regions is presented using the intensity and gradient information of eye region. Then, we design different candidate weight initialization methods according to the count of candidates.

Horizontal integral projection is used to roughly locate the candidate eye regions. The local minimums of this projection, whose gray intensities are less than average intensity, are generally eyebrows, dark upper spectacle-frames and eyes. Let $X_{TBD} = [x_1, x_2, ..., x_p]$ be the horizontal coordinates of local minimums.

Intensity Variation Sensitive Factor: The intensity variation sensitive factor (IVSF) is formulated as the pixels with high intensities, which are surrounded by low-intensities.

(a)   (b)

Fig. 2. Horizontal axis coarse positioning. (a) Filtered matrix I_{spot}. (b) Binary image B_{spot}.

Specifically, we use a 5×5 convolution template whose center value is 1, and other values are $-1/24$ to calculate IVSF. Figure 2(a) shows the filtered matrix I_{spot}. Image is binarized by Eq. 1, where $\alpha = 0.55$. Figure 2(b) demonstrates that foreground objects of B_{spot} are concentrated at eyes region.

$$B_{spot_{i,j}} = \begin{cases} 1 \; if \; B_{spot_{i,j}} > \alpha \max(I_{spot}) \\ 0 \; otherwise \end{cases} \qquad (1)$$

A $80 \times N'$ subregion is selected by taking x_k as a central reference line, and then calculate the spot area A_k in every subregion. A rough horizontal location is calculated by $X_{POS} = \sum_{k=1}^{p} \left[x_k A_k \middle/ \sum_{k=1}^{p} A_k \right]$ as a new central reference line. After that, ROI region is selected with center X_{POS} and size of $600 \times N'$ image I_{loc} as shown in Fig. 3(a).

According to observations, there are light spots in pupil regions in most of images. Since the spots have higher intensities than pupil, the spot boundaries

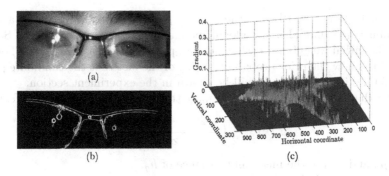

Fig. 3. The selection of eye candidate positions based on PLG. (a) The result image I_{loc} through horizontal coarse positioning. (b) Eye contour $B_{eyeglasses}$ after thresholding. (c) The Sobel Gradient I_{grad}.

have large gradient values. We calculate Sobel gradient I_{grad} of image I_{loc} as shown in Fig. 3(c) for fast localization. Due to Pixels with Large Gradient (PLG) generally have strong edges, the spots on lens, dark spectacle-frames and naris may be PLG. We extract the eyeglasses and spots by binary I_{grad} (threshold is 0.005). Figure 3(b) illustrates the binary image $B_{eyeglasses}$ after removing small responses.

Then, we use a higher threshold 0.06 to acquire the binary image B_{grad}'. The intersection of B_{grad}' and $B_{eyeglasses}$ is used to remove most of non-spots and morphological dilation is used to filled the hole. Then a binary images B_{TBD} is obtained. Let r_0 be the count of connected regions in B_{TBD}. If $r_0 > 2$, g_k is defined as the maximum PLG in each connected region C_k:

$$g_k = \max(C_k \odot I_{grad}), k = 1, 2, \cdots, r_0 \quad r_0 \geq 2 \tag{2}$$

where, $\odot$ is dot product of matrix. Similarly, the maximum intensity variation sensitive factor i_k in each connected region is:

$$i_k = \begin{cases} \max(C_k \odot I_{spot}), k = 1, 2, \cdots, r_0 & r_0 > 2 \\ \max(C_k' \odot I_{spot}), k = 1, 2, \cdots, r_0 & r_0 < 2 \end{cases} \tag{3}$$

If $r_0 = 2$, we just use g_k to generate the candidate points, initialize weights and omit i_k. If $r_0 < 2$, we recalculate the connected regions with the filtered matrix I_{spot}, and just use i_k to initialize weight. A threshold $\alpha = 0.45$ is adopted to binarize the filtered matrix by Eq. 1 and get the binary image B_{spot}'. Similarly, the image B_{TBD} is the result of the intersection of $B_{eyeglasses}$ and B_{spot}'. i_k is calculated according to Eq. 3.

Let (a_k, b_k) be the position with maximum gradient in each connected region. If the position of $g_k(i_k)$ is non-unique, just the position with minimum g_k is selected.

$$P_{TBD} = \begin{cases} \{(a_k, b_k) | (a_k, b_k) = \arg\min(g_k), k = 1, 2, \cdots, r_0\} & r_0 \geq 2 \\ \{(a_k, b_k) | (a_k, b_k) = \arg\min(i_k), k = 1, 2, \cdots, r_0\} & r_0 < 2 \end{cases} \tag{4}$$

In our experiment, PLG of the spot in pupil is probably not only a local maximum value, but also the global maximum with high probability. So we assign the initial weights for each candidate point on the basis of $g_k(i_k)$. For g_k, we need to know the prior probability $h_g(k)$ of the fact that the candidate point $P_{TBD}(k)$ lies in eye region. It will be shown in the experiment section.

After that, we use the Eq. 5 to calculate the initial weight of gradient feature:

$$\omega_g(k) = \frac{1}{2}\left(\frac{e^{h_g(k)-\mu_g} - e^{-\mu_g}}{\sigma_g}\right) \tag{5}$$

where μ_g and σ_g are the mean and variance of h_g.

The weight $\omega_i(k)$ is defined as:

$$\omega_i(k) = \frac{1}{2}\left(\frac{e^{h_i(k)-\mu_i} - e^{-\mu_i}}{\sigma_i}\right) \tag{6}$$

where h_i is the prior probability under the feature of filtered matrix, μ_i and σ_i are the mean and variance of h_i.

Hence, the weights $\omega_0(k)$ of candidate point $P_{TBD}(k)$ are defined as:

$$\omega_0(k) = \begin{cases} \omega_g(k) + \omega_i(k) & r > 2 \\ \omega_g(k) & r = 2 \\ \omega_i(k) & r < 2 \end{cases} \tag{7}$$

Let r be the count of candidate points. If $r > 5$, just the first five candidate points are retained. And the weights of fifth candidate points are initialized to be 0. The schematic diagram of this section is shown in Fig. 4(a).

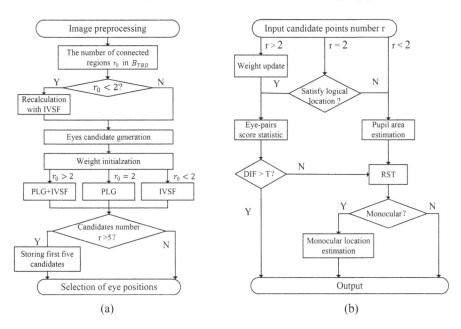

(a)   (b)

Fig. 4. Schematic diagrams. (a) Eye candidates generation. (b) Eye positions selection.

4   Selecting Eye Positions

To accelerate detection speed and improve detection accuracy, we adopt multi-strategy fusion method to select eye position which is designed according to candidates amount.

In detail, if $r > 2$, we choose Weight Update Algorithm and Eye-pairs Score Statistic. If $r = 2$ and the two eye candidate points accord with the determination criterion of eye location $|a_1 - a_2| < 80$, $|b_1 - b_2| > N'/3$, Eye-pairs Score Statistic is used. Otherwise, the area of pupil is estimated and RST is used to select eye positions. The whole process is illustrated in Fig. 4(b).

4.1   Weight Update Algorithm and Pupil Area Estimation Based on Dark Region Distribution Factor

Dark Region Distribution Factor: Dark region distribution factor (DRDF) is defined as the distribution of low-intensity pixels of local image. Based on observation, low-intensity pixels emerge on zonal distribution in local image of spectacle-frames while mainly concentrated to pupil in eyes local image. Therefore, we use DRDF to update weights of candidate points and estimate the pupil area.

Fig. 5. Eye selection based on DRDF. (a) Weight sort result of candidate points. (b) The local image R_m and R_s of eye region. (c) The local image R_m and R_s of upper spectacle-frame region.

Figure 5(a) shows the ω_0 ranking result of candidate points. Firstly, we regard $(a_k + 30, b_k)$ as the center and crop a rectangular region R_m which is 60×70 to avoid the effects of eyelash. Then we fill light spots and normalize $R_m(k)$. After that, centering on $(a_k + 26, b_k)$ and cropping a smaller local region $R_s(k)$ which is 52×60. As shown in Fig. 5(b and c), R_m includes the shadow area and R_s does not. The count of low-intensity pixels is less in shadow area of local eye region than those in local spectacle-frames region due to the different distribution. Therefore, we calculate the number of low-intensity pixels in R_m and R_s respectively. $A_m(k)$ is defined as the number of pixels whose intensity values are less than 0.2 in $R_m(k)$. $A_s(k)$ is defined as the largest connected region area in binary image of $R_s(k)$. The difference between $A_m(k)$ and $A_s(k)$ is $DIF_p(k) = A_m(k) - A_s(k)$. Apparently, $DIF_p(k)$ is inversely related to the possibility of eye region. We take DRDF to update weight $\omega_0(k)$:

$$\omega_p(k) = \frac{1}{2} \left(\frac{e^{h_p(k) - \mu_p} - e^{-\mu_p}}{\sigma_p} \right) \tag{8}$$

where μ_p and σ_p are the mean and variance of h_p. The calculation for prior probability $h_g(k)$ will be shown in the experiment section in detail. Therefore, the updated weight of candidate point is defined as:

$$\omega_1(k) = \omega_0(k) + \omega_p(k) \tag{9}$$

In addition, we can estimate the area of pupil in eye region by A_s, the pupil area $A_p = 1.5A_s$. A_p is applied for the radius estimation of RST and the final scores calculation of algorithm is based on symmetry.

4.2 Eye Detection Based on RST

According to the intensity and circular symmetry of pupil, we use RST [15] to locate the pupil coarsely. However, the RST has poor timeliness. Thus, to raise the speed of detection, we scale the local image depending on the result of pupil area A_p before RST:

$$r_p = \sqrt{\frac{A_p}{\pi}}, \ k_{scale} = \min\left(1, \frac{r_{\min}}{r_p}\right), \ r_{TBD} = k_{scale}r_p \tag{10}$$

where, k_{scale} is the scale factor, $r_{\min} = 6$ is the minimum radius. r_{TBD} is the estimated radius after scaling. The range of radius is $[r_{TBD} - 3, r_{TBD} + 3]$.

4.3 Eye-Pairs Score Statistic and Monocular Location Estimation Algorithm Based on Inter-ocular Symmetry Factor

Inter-ocular Symmetry Factor: Inter-ocular symmetry factor (IOSF) is defined as the symmetry of vertical gray integration projection distribution between the two eyes. It is used to determine the position of eyes.

Supposed that (a_i, b_i) and (a_j, b_j) are two candidate points, the horizontal distance and the vertical distance between them are $X_{DIS} = |a_i - a_j|$, $Y_{DIS} = |b_i - b_j|$ which have to satisfy the following conditions:

$$Y_{DIS} > N/3 \ and \ \begin{cases} X_{DIS} > 50 + (Y_{DIS} - 200)/10 \ \ if \ Y_{DIS} > 300 \\ X_{DIS} > 50 \ \ otherwise \end{cases} \tag{11}$$

If the conditions are not satisfied, the difference $DIF = +\infty$. We obtain the line between two eyes according to Eq. 12:

$$a = \left\lfloor \frac{(b - b_i)(a_j - a_i)}{(b_j - b_i) + a_i} \right\rfloor, \ b = [min(b_i, b_j), \ max(b_i, b_j)] \tag{12}$$

The line is moved vertically on image until it intersects with the image border. The shadow parallelogram is shown in Fig. 6(a). This figure illustrates the scanned region. Figure 6(b) describes the result of vertical integral projection $IPF_h{}'$ of this parallelogram. It indicates that vertical integral projection $IPF_h{}'$ is horizontally symmetric if the two candidate points are correctly chosen. Based on center axis (the red line in Fig. 6(b)), we make the difference of left and right sides of integral projection and get the summation. As shown in Fig. 6(c), considering face rotation, we move the two sides projection curves rightward, and compare with the initial curve in the other side. The final difference DIF is the minimum in 20 comparison results:

$$DIF = \min \left(\frac{2 \left| \sum_{k=1+q}^{\lfloor Y_{DIS}/2 \rfloor - p} IPF_h{'}(k) - \sum_{k=\lfloor Y_{DIS}/2 \rfloor + 1 + p}^{2\lfloor Y_{DIS}/2 \rfloor - q} IPF_h{'}(k) \right|}{Y_{DIS}} \right) \quad (13)$$

where, $p = 0, 1, \cdots 9; q = 0, 1, \cdots 9; pq = 0; T = 0.4$. If $DIF > T$, it can not satisfy the symmetry requirement of eyes. If $DIF \leq T$, The final score is defined as Eq. 14:

$$Score_{i,j} = \begin{cases} \frac{Y_{DIS}(\omega_1(i)\omega_1(j)+C)}{X_{DIS}DIF(|A_{pup}(i)-A_{pup}(j)|+1)} & if \; DIF < T \\ -\infty & otherwise \end{cases} \quad (14)$$

$C = 0.001$ is the penalty term of candidate points whose weight is 0. We obtain a couple of candidate points which has the maximum score.

The algorithm requires the two eyes should be included in the candidate points list. That is why we can not delete exclude too much points but update the weights of all candidate points. When it is unsatisfied with above conditions, RST is used to make a further detection.

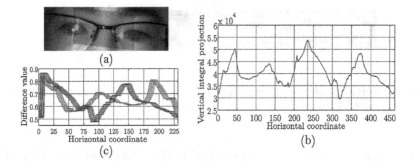

Fig. 6. The selection of eyes based on symmetry. (a) The calculation of vertical integral projection area. (b) The result of vertical integral projection. (c) The segmentation and move approach of projection curve. (Color figure online)

5   Experimental Result

The experiments were operated on a desktop computer with 8 cores and 8 threads of i7@3.60 GHz CPU. A self-built Mobile Iris Image Database (MIID) with hand-labeled ground truth is used in our experiment. The images on MIID are captured by an altered cell phone with near-infrared camera. The database totally contains 7823 images with resolution of 1920×1080. These are from 8 subjects, in which 3816 images are captured with eyeglasses and 4007 without eyeglasses. In the caputuring process, each person holds the cell phone by himself. The imaging distance from eye to the camera is between 15 cm and 30 cm adjusted by user. And MIID includes various types of challenging circumstances, such as occlusion, glasses, rotation, blur, complex background, and so on.

Similar to Jung [16], the detection result is determined to be positive if the distance from detected box center and hand-labeled iris center is less than 50 pixels. And Recall, Precision, Time are selected as our performance evaluation criterias, where $Recall = TP/(TP+FN), Precision = TP/(TP+FP)$, TP, FN and FP is True Positive, False Negative and False Positive for short separately.

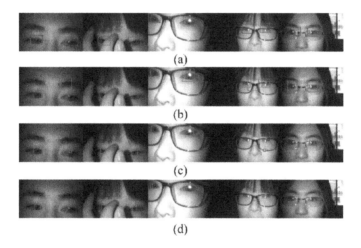

Fig. 7. Detection results of different methods. (a) the proposed method, (b) Haar-AdaBoost, (c) RST, (d) EC+EV.

The proposed method is compared with Haar-AdaBoost [14], RST [15], EC+EV [16]. Figure 7 shows some detection results of different methods. And the detailed performances are displayed in Table 1. According to this table, the proposed method can obtain high detection recall and precision especially st a almost real-time speed. Moreover, our method is more robust to various challenging problems, especially to eyeglasses.

We also evaluate the effectiveness of three features, IVSF, PLG and DRDF. Some related results are displayed in Table 2. The prior probability is used to calculate the weight. Firstly, $g_k(i_k)$ and candidate position $P_{TBD}(k)$ are corresponding one by one. We sort $g_k(i_k)$ in a descending order to get the result of $r_g(k)(r_i(k))$. When $r_g(k) = 1, 2, 3, 4$, the prior probability $h_g(k)$ is shown in the first row of Table 2, which represents the candidate positions $P_{TBD}(k)$ in

Table 1. Detection performance of different methods.

Method	Recall (%)	Precision (%)	Time (s/image)
The proposed method	98.21	98.42	0.058
Haar-AdaBoost	76.90	92.76	0.139
RST	84.84	86.56	3.342
EC+EV	56.16	89.94	1.703

eye region. The result indicates that $h_g(k)(h_i(k))$ decreases as the reduction in $r_g(k)(r_i(k))$. The probability is very small when $r_g(k) = 4$ and $r_i(k) = 4$. Therefore, we only reserve the top five ones if the number of candidate points is large. Similarly, We sort feature $DIF_p(k)$ in ascending order to get the result $r_p(k)$. The third row of Table 2 shows the prior probability $h_p(k)$.

Table 2. The prior probability of three features.

	$r_g(k) = 1$	$r_g(k) = 2$	$r_g(k) = 3$	$r_g(k) = 4$
$h_g(k)\,\|\omega_g(k)$	91.3% 1.2	68.5% 0.8	29.4% 0.3	9.0% 0.1
	$r_i(k) = 1$	$r_i(k) = 2$	$r_i(k) = 3$	$r_i(k) = 4$
$h_i(k)\,\|\omega_i(k)$	94.7% 1.1	76.8% 0.8	21.0% 0.2	7.4% 0.1
	$r_p(k) = 1$	$r_p(k) = 2$	$r_p(k) = 3$	$r_p(k) = 4$
$h_p(k)\,\|\omega_p(k)$	87.1% 1.1	78.1% 0.9	25.2% 0.2	4.0% 0

6 Conclusion

To detect eyes effectively in an unconstrained scene, we propose a novel eye detection algorithm. The main contributions are as follows: (1) generating eye candidates by IVSF and PLG; (2) selecting eye candidates based on presented DRDF, IOSF and RST; (3) multi-strategy fusion method to achieve robust eye detection in various unconstrained scenes. The experimental results show the proposed eye detection algorithm is fast, accurate and robust to challenging problems of occlusion, rotation, blur, complex background and eyeglasses, etc.

Acknowledgement. This research is supported by National Natural Science Funds of China, No. 61703088, the Doctoral Scientific Research Foundation of Liaoning Province, No. 20170520326 and "the Fundamental Research Funds for the Central Universities", N160503003.

References

1. Daugman, J.: High confidence visual recognition of persons by a test of statistical independence. IEEE Trans. Pattern Anal. Mach. Intell. **15**(1), 1148–1161 (1993)
2. Singh, A.K., Joshi, P., Nandi, G.C.: Face recognition with liveness detection using eye and mouth movement. In: International Conference on Signal Propagation and Computer Technology, pp. 592–597 (2014)
3. Zhu, Z., Ji, Q.: Robust real-time eye detection and tracking under variable lighting conditions and various face orientations. Comput. Vis. Image Underst. **98**(1), 124–154 (2005)
4. Gou, C., Wu, Y., Wang, K., Wang, K., Wang, F.Y., Ji, Q.: A joint cascaded framework for simultaneous eye detection and eye state estimation. Pattern Recogn. **67**(1), 23–31 (2017)
5. Mandal, B., Li, L., Wang, G., Lin, J.: Towards detection of bus driver fatigue based on robust visual analysis of eye state. IEEE Trans. Intell. Transp. Syst. **18**(1), 1–13 (2017)
6. Wang, P., Green, M.B., Ji, Q., Wayman, J.: Automatic eye detection and its validation. IEEE Comput. Soc. Conf. Comput. Vis. Pattern Recogn. Workshops **3**(1), 164 (2006)
7. Sirohey, S.A., Rosenfeld, A.: Eye detection in a face image using linear and non-linear filters. Pattern Recogn. **34**(7), 1367–1391 (2001)
8. Song, J., Chi, Z., Liu, J.: A robust eye detection method using combined binary edge and intensity information. Pattern Recogn. **39**(6), 1110–1125 (2006)
9. Peng, K.: A robust algorithm for eye detection on gray intensiry face without spectacles. J. Comput. Sci. Technol. **5**(3), 127–132 (2005)
10. Cootes, T.F., Taylor, C.J., Cooper, D.H.: Active shape models-their trainingand application. Comput. Vis. Image Underst. **61**(1), 38–59 (1995)
11. Dieckmann, U., Plankensteiner, P., Schamburger, R., Fröba, B., Meller, S.: SESAM: a biometric person identification system using sensor fusion. In: Bigün, J., Chollet, G., Borgefors, G. (eds.) AVBPA 1997. LNCS, vol. 1206, pp. 301–310. Springer, Heidelberg (1997). https://doi.org/10.1007/BFb0016009
12. Sobottka, K., Pitas, I.: A fully automatic approach to facial feature detection and tracking. In: Bigün, J., Chollet, G., Borgefors, G. (eds.) AVBPA 1997. LNCS, vol. 1206, pp. 77–84. Springer, Heidelberg (1997). https://doi.org/10.1007/BFb0015982
13. Zhou, Z.H., Geng, X.: Projection functions for eye detection. Pattern Recogn. **37**(5), 1049–1056 (2004)
14. Viola, P.A., Jones, M.J.: Rapid object detection using a boosted cascade of simple features. Proc. IEEE Int. Conf. Comput. Vis. Pattern Recogn. **1**(2), 511–518 (2001)
15. Loy, G., Zelinsky, A.: Fast radial symmetry for detecting points of interest. IEEE Trans. Pattern Anal. Mach. Intell. **25**(8), 959–973 (2003)
16. Jung, Y., Kim, D., Son, B., Kim, J.: An eye detection method robust to eyeglasses for mobile iris recognition. Expert Syst. Appl. Int. J. **67**(C), 178–188 (2017)
17. Chen, S., Liu, C.: Eye detection using discriminatory haar features and a new efficient SVM. Image Vis. Comput. **33**(1), 68–77 (2015)
18. Zhang, L., Lenders, P.: Knowledge-based eye detection for human face recognition. Int. Conf. Knowl. Based Intell. Eng. Syst. Allied Technol. **1**(1), 117–120 (2000)

Attention Detection by Learning Hierarchy Feature Fusion on Eye Movement

Bing Liu[1($\boxtimes$)], Peilin Jiang[2], Fei Wang[3], Xuetao Zhang[3], Haifan Hao[1], and Shanglin Bai[1]

[1] The Software Engineering School, Xi'an Jiaotong University, Xi'an, China
1246449316@qq.com, 457764906@qq.com, 947994255@qq.com
[2] The Software Engineering School,
National Engineering Laboratory for Visual Information Processing
and Application, Xi'an Jiaotong University, Xi'an, China
pljiang@xjtu.edu.cn
[3] The Electric and Information Engineering School, Xi'an Jiaotong University,
Xi'an, China
{wfx, zhangxt}@xjtu.edu.cn

Abstract. Human concentration state detection using the eye movement information is now a popular research topic in computer vision, especially the detection of driver fatigue and advertising analysis. In this paper we analyze eye movement styles on a person's concentration state through watching different video clips. We propose a novel method including the fusion features of eye event data and raw eye movement to detect attention. Firstly, we use the logistic regression algorithm to conduct the new feature by eye movement event data, and use wavelet and approximate entropy algorithm to conduct the new feature by raw eye movement data. Secondly, we train attention detection model using these new merged features. In order to avoid the problem caused by insufficient samples, crossing method is used to train the model to ensure its accuracy. Our model achieves a satisfying 95.25% accuracy.

Keywords: Attention · Eye movement data · Logistic regression
Wavelet · Entropy · Learning

1 Introduction

In the field of attention detection based on video, eye movement data tracking graphs obtained by eye tracker can intuitively show the changes of saccade path over time. Randomly select two eye movement data tracking graphs of a movie trailer and a pharmaceutical advertising (see Fig. 1):

From Fig. 1, it is very easy to find that there is a significant difference in the saccade path between positive and negative samples when people watch a movie trailer and an advertising video. The saccade point regularly moves among the main characters when people are watching positive samples. When people are watching negative sample, however, the saccade point irregularly moves among the entire screen.

© Springer Nature Switzerland AG 2018
J. Zhou et al. (Eds.): CCBR 2018, LNCS 10996, pp. 497–503, 2018.
https://doi.org/10.1007/978-3-319-97909-0_53

Fig. 1. Sample of eye movement data tracking graphs on two kinds of video. The upper graph indicates the interesting video (movie trailer) and the bottom graph indicates the non-interesting video (advertisement).

These differences indicate that there is a clear difference in eye movement data between people watching videos and advertisements, and we can utilize eye movement data to analyze people's attention when they are watching videos. We can use the learning hierarchy feature fusion on eye movement to study the changes of all eye movement data because people's eye movement data is significantly different, when people watches videos under difference concentration states including attention and inattention. The analytical algorithm flow diagram is indicated in Fig. 2. From Fig. 2, it can be clearly seen that attention detection by learning hierarchy feature fusion on eye movement is obviously effective.

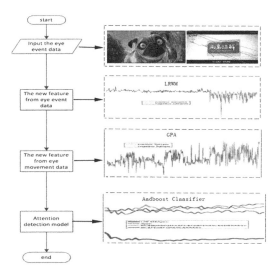

Fig. 2. Flow diagram

Many studies have shown that the movement of the eye can reflect the individual's cognitive process, and different eye movement indicators can reflect different processes. For example, in the study of eye movement for reading, Yan [1] proposes that the indicator of saccade's distance reflects the efficiency of reading and the difficulty of processing materials. In the study of advertising psychology [2], eye movement indicators commonly used fixation time, the number of fixation, saccades, pupil diameter and so on. Roshovgen [3] studies the effect of recurring advertisements on people's attention. The duration to look at the text is four times of the pattern when the ad is repeated 1–3 times, the ad's fixation duration will be reduced by 50%. Xu [4] collects experimental materials, which clips of the current hit TV series will be implanted with advertising clips and analyzes eye movement to show that advertising implanted by combination of screen and lines or pure screen can be seen by the audience. A lot of research studies the driver's attention, commonly used indicators including fixation duration, saccades duration, saccades distance and so on [5]; some scholars uses pupil changes as an indicator to evaluate the driver's visual load [6] and Mita [7] uses the blink rate to judge the driver's fatigue state.

2   Material and Experiment Design

In experiment we have prepared short videos which may catch attention or not. Stimulus materials include 25 movie trailers that most people like and 11 videos ad that most people do not like. The total duration of these stimulus materials is 104 min. Each participant has been experimented twice, the first time to watch 25 movie trailers, the second time 11 ads. Twenty individuals have participated in the experiment. All participants give their informed consent. The requirements for participation are to adjust their position, which eye tracker can accurately capture their eyes. To ensure good eye tracking results, the participants are asked to watch an hour each time and fill in the questionnaire.

3   Intent Eye Movement Data Analysis

3.1   Data Collection

We have used the eye tracker to collect two levels of data, the original data and event data. The original data refers to the eye movement information of each frame when the subject is watching the stimulus material, including the position of the pupil, the diameter of the pupil, the position of the eye, the position of the gaze etc. The event data refers to fixation event, saccades event and blink events including when to start and end these events, when the experimenter is watching the stimulus material, these data reflects people's concentration state. Therefore, we use the event statistics data and raw eye movement data with time series information for analysis.

3.2   Extraction and Fusion of the Event Data

The event data has many characteristics (totally 64 characteristics for two eyes), we have used weighted logistic regression to intent feature extraction and fusion, which logistic regression coefficients represent weights.

The fusion feature is able to intuitively distinguish between positive and negative samples. The fusion data of positive and negative samples can be seen Fig. 3.

From Fig. 3, it can be clearly seen that the new fusion feature positive samples are larger than negative samples. Therefore, the new fusion feature can be used as feature of training samples.

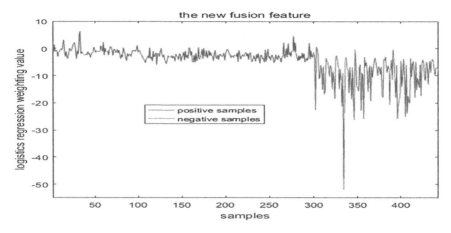

Fig. 3. The fusion data of positive and negative samples

3.3   Extraction and Fusion of the Raw Eye Movement Data

The raw eye movement data has four characteristics including pupil position, pupil diameter, gaze position and eye position. Firstly, we adopt wavelet decomposition deals with these features, and then calculate the approximate entropy of these data. Approximate entropy (ApEn) is used to quantify the complexity or irregularity of a signal and describes the rate of producing new information. Sample results processed by wavelet decomposition are shown in Figs. 4 and 5.

From Figs. 4 and 5, it is found that the positive and negative samples still retain the saccade path of eye-tracking after wavelet decomposition. Therefore, this method can be used for eye movement data processing. The fusion data of positive and negative samples see Fig. 6.

From Fig. 6, It can be seen that the positive and negative samples of the new fusion feature are not significantly different, but to a certain extent can reflect the difference between positive and negative samples. Therefore, the new fusion feature can be used to train the model together with the previous features.

Actually, when these subjects watch the stimulus materials that are marked interest, the shortest fixation duration and average fixation duration are longer than watching the stimulating materials that are marked non-interest, but Fixation Dispersion Maximum value is less than watching the stimulating materials that are marked non-interest. The reason for the results is that when watching the stimulating materials of interest, the fixation point is focused on the interested characters and changes with the characters, while when watching the stimulating materials of non-interest, the fixation point is scattered, which not interesting focus. Therefore, there are many features that reflect the degree of concentration including the event data and the fusion features. Next, we will use different features for model training.

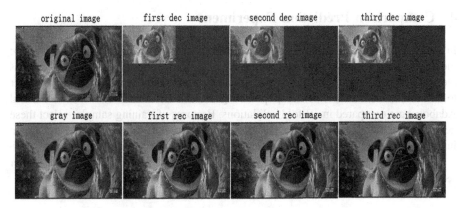

Fig. 4. Wavelet decomposition and reconstruction of positive samples

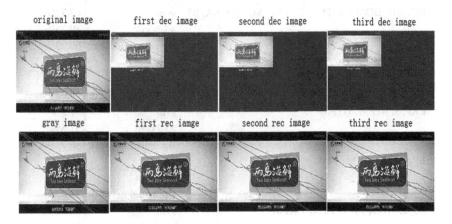

Fig. 5. Wavelet decomposition and reconstruction of negative samples

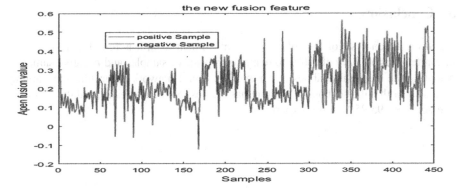

Fig. 6. The fusion data of positive and negative samples

4   Comparison Prediction Experiment

In the previous experiments, the new features built by the event data and the raw eye movement data are processed to describe the attention action. In this part, we discuss the practical prediction methods to find out attention from the row video data. In order to determine the classifier, three popular algorithms, BP neural network, SVM, and Adaboost are compared in 10-fold validations. Features of training samples select these new fusion features and common eye movement features (Feature symbols are shown in appendix). The average accuracy can be found in Table 1 using classifiers.

From Table 1, it can be observed that the Adaboost algorithm performed better using the fusion features than others.

Table 1. Attention prediction accuracy results

Feature	Classifier	Accuracy
BC, BD, BDMAX, FC, FD, FDe, SL, SD, SA, SV	svm	67.71%
	adaboost	80.75%
	Bp neural network	69.93%
BC, FDe, FDA, SC, SA, SV	svm	67.72%
	adaboost	81.45%
	Bp neural network	69.92%
LRFM, ReFM, DTFM	svm	91.2%
	adaboost	91.5%
	Bp neural network	86.71%
EPA, GPA, PDA, PPA	svm	83.07%
	adaboost	82%
	Bp neural network	72.03%
EPA, GPA, PDA, PPA, LRFM	svm	94.36%
	adaboost	**95.25%**
	Bp neural network	89.51%

5   Conclusion

Based on the analysis of the collected eye movement data, it is found that these new fusion features are very effective to distinguish positive samples and negative samples. Adopting the classical adaboost, svm and BP neural network algorithm, the training results show that the adaboost algorithm has the best prediction result, and the accuracy rate achieved 95.25% in our experiment.

Appendix

Feature Symbol

Feature	Blinks count	Bduration	Max duration	Fixation count
Symbol	BC	BD	BDMAX	FC
Feature	Fduration	Fduration avg	Fdeviation	Slength
Symbol	FD	FDA	FDe	SL
Feature	Scount	Sduration	Samplitude	Svelocity
Symbol	SC	SD	SA	SV
Feature	LR coef	Relief weight	DT weight	Eye position
Symbol	LRFM	ReFM	DTFM	EPA
Feature	Gaze position	Pupil position	Pupil diameter	
Symbol	GPA	PDA	PPA	

References

1. Yan, G., Bai, X.: Research and Development Trend of Eye Movement in Advertising Psychology. Tianjin Normal University (2004). (in Chinese)
2. Yan, G., et al.: A review of the main eye movement indicators in reading. Adv. Psychol. Sci. **21**(004), 589–605 (2013). (in Chinese)
3. Duchowski, A.T.: Eye Tracking Methodology: Theory and Practice. Springer, London (2003). https://doi.org/10.1007/978-1-4471-3750-4
4. Xu, W.: The tracking effect assessment by eye tracker in movie and television play implanted by advertising. Shanghai Jiaotong University (2016). (in Chinese)
5. Kliegl, R., Grabner, E., Rolfs, M.: Length frequency predictability effects of words on eye movement in reading. Eur. J. Cognit. Psychol. **16**(1), 262–284 (2001)
6. Du, Z., Pan, X., Guo, X.: Study on the application of traffic safety evaluation indicator in import and export of highway tunnel. J. Tongji Univ. (Natural Science Edition) **36**(3), 325–329 (2008). (in Chinese)
7. Stato, S.: Does fatigue exist in a quantitative measurement of eye movement. Ergonomics **35**(5), 607–615 (1992)

Emerging Biometrics

An Efficient 3D Ear Recognition System Based on Indexing

Qinping Zhu and Zhichun Mu[(✉)]

School of Automation and Electrical Engineering,
University of Science and Technology Beijing, Beijing 10083, China
mu@ies.ustb.edu.cn

Abstract. We propose a system for time-efficient 3D ear biometrics. The system is composed of two primary components, namely: (1) an ear shape-based index; and (2) categorization using the index. We built an index tree by using the shape feature computed from measures of circularity, rectangularity, ellipticity, and triangularity, based on ear segmentation results and then perform a nearest neighbor search to obtain a gallery of ear images that are closest in shape to the probe subjects. For the categorization component, separate index trees are built out of the gallery of ear images by using a reduced depth feature space for each image. We utilize an indexing technique to perform a range query in a reduced depth feature space for ears that are closest in shape to the probe subject. Experiments on the benchmark database demonstrate that the proposed approach is more efficient compared to the state-of-the-art 3D ear biometric system.

Keywords: Ear biometrics · 3D ear segmentation
3D ear database categorization · Indexing · KD tree · Pyramid technique

1 Introduction

Ear recognition is a novel biometric technology with many advantages and unique features, including high user acceptability and naturalness, that has attracted more and more attention recently [1]. Currently, ear recognition is being widely used in public security, law enforcement and video surveillance. Anthropometric theory has established that ear structure does not change significantly between 7 and 70 years old for a specific individual. At the same time, there are no two individuals whose ears are completely identical even if they are twins [1]. Ears are thus special objects, distinctive to each other, and without long-term change. Additionally, the 3D shape characteristics of ears are not influenced by illumination, glasses, facial hair, makeup, or variations in facial expression. This has made 3D ear recognition an increasingly attractive topic of research over recent years.

In an automated segmentation method that locates ear pits and uses an active contour algorithm on both color and depth images, Yan and Bowyer [2] have developed a 3D ear shape matching technique that is based on an improved iterative closest point (ICP) approach. In [3], Chen and Bhanu propose a two-step iterative closest point (ICP)-based approach for matching 3D ear images. First of all, the ICP algorithm is used to coarsely align the helix of a test ear image with a model ear image. Then, the ICP

© Springer Nature Switzerland AG 2018
J. Zhou et al. (Eds.): CCBR 2018, LNCS 10996, pp. 507–516, 2018.
https://doi.org/10.1007/978-3-319-97909-0_54

algorithm works iteratively to obtain the best final alignment between the two ear images. As a further development, in [4] Chen and Bhanu put forward a 3D ear recognition algorithm that is based on a local surface patch representation, a helix/antihelix representation, and a modified ICP method. In [5, 6], Zhou et al. proposed a general technique for 3D object recognition that uses local and holistic feature matching. First of all, a boundary box is constructed around the ear region on a 3D profile face image. 3D ear matching is then performed separately using extracted local and holistic features. Finally, the results of the local and holistic matching are fused using a matching score fusion technique. In [7], Maity and Abdel-Mottaleb presented a time efficient ear recognition system. Here, the ear region is first of all accurately segmented using ear contour landmark localization, a flexible mixture model and an active contour algorithm. Then a reduced gallery is obtained through indexing that is based on the shape features. After this, a more reduced gallery is obtained by building a separate indexing tree based on depth information. Finally, a similarity measure method is used for the actual ear recognition.

In this paper, we propose using a global feature in 3D ear images: the shape obtained from ear segmentation results. The motivation for using the ear shape is that it provides an original feature that can help to improve the efficiency of 3D ear recognition systems. By introducing the ear shape as a feature, a 3D ear gallery set can be represented as a KD-tree. The KD-tree can then be applied to indexed results to obtain the gallery ear image that is closest in shape to the probe subject. By using this method, we only need to compare the probe subject to a list of gallery ear images that are similar to the shape of the gallery ear image that was closest to the shape of the probe subject in the categorization through indexing stage. Thus, the efficiency can be improved.

In Sect. 2, we describes the indexing technique based on using the ear shape as a feature and how it is applied in 3D ear recognition. In Sect. 3 we present our experimental results and discuss how they prove the stability and effectiveness of the ear recognition system. A conclusion is given in Sect. 4.

2   Approach

In this section, we detail the proposed ear shape representation and indexing approach and how it is applied in 3D ear recognition. First of all, the ear region is segmented by using a corresponding 3D profile image. Then, a KD-tree-based index using the proposed shape feature space, which is itself composed of four shape similarity measures, is used to obtain a nearest neighbor gallery image of the probe subject. After this, 3D depth features are extracted. Lastly, a novel approach to ear categorization through indexing is proposed. This is able to perform a range query using a list of ear images similar to the shape of the original gallery ear image that was closest to the shape of the probe subject. A block diagram for the approach is shown in In this section, we detail the proposed ear shape representation and indexing approach and how it is applied in 3D ear recognition. First of all, the ear region is segmented by using a corresponding 3D profile image. Then, a KD-tree-based index using the proposed shape feature space, which is itself composed of four shape similarity measures, is used to obtain a nearest neighbor gallery image of the probe subject. After this, 3D depth features are extracted.

Lastly, a novel approach to ear categorization through indexing is proposed. This is able to perform a range query using a list of ear images similar to the shape of the original gallery ear image that was closest to the shape of the probe subject. A block diagram for the approach is shown in Fig. 1.

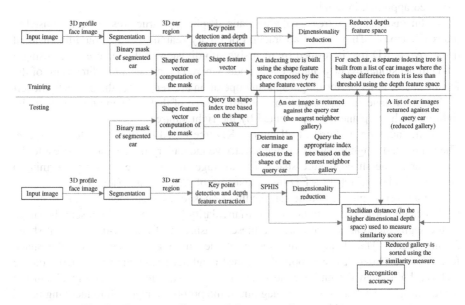

Fig. 1. The system diagram of the proposed recognition system

2.1   Ear Data Segmentation

The ear images used in this paper are segmented from profile face images utilizing an ear segmentation approach [7] that is based on ear landmark localization [8] and a snake algorithm [9]. This algorithm demonstrates an impressive ability to recognize ears from an input image. For the 3D ear database in the University of Notre Dame (UND) Collection J2, with a specified pixel error rate of 5%, we achieved a 96.44% segmentation accuracy. When the pixel error rate was relaxed to 10%, the segmentation accuracy rose to 98.91%.

2.2   Shape-Based Indexing

For efficient ear recognition, Maity and Abdel-Mottaleb have proposed an approach to indexing that uses shape-based categorization. First of all, a set of gallery ears is categorized into four shape classes: round; rectangular; oval; and triangular. These classes are based on maximum ear shape similarity. After this, one or more classes of gallery ear images are obtained using the shape index value of the probe ear [7]. Once this has been done, the probe subject is only queried in a reduced depth feature space generated by just a part of the gallery ear images. As the majority of ear recognition systems need to relate a probe subject to a feature space that is generated by an entire gallery [4–6], the run-time for this approach is less than it is for most ear recognition systems. Inspired by this, we also propose using an ear shape indexing approach. For a given probe subject, our own approach can obtain the gallery ear image closest to its shape. The result obtained by doing this can then guide the selection of the list of ear images that is similar to the shape of the probe subject. We will now describe the proposed approach in detail.

K-dimensional (KD) trees [10] are balanced split data structures that can be used to index a database. They are an abstraction of binary search trees for multidimensional databases. A KD-tree is formed by recursive sub-division of the feature space using a (D-1) dimensional hyper-plane at every node, where D represents the dimension of the feature space. After performing a splitting operation at every node, the points to the left of this hyperplane are represented by the left subtree of that node and the points to the right of the hyperplane are represented by the right subtree.

While indexing, we first of all build a KD-tree based on the shape feature space. Then, a nearest neighbor query is able to retrieve the gallery image that is closest to the probe ear in the shape feature space. The average time complexity for performing a nearest neighbor search in a KD-tree consisting of N nodes is $O(\log(N))$.

For a given segmented probe ear, the first step is to calculate measures of circularity [11], rectangularity [12], ellipticity, and triangularity [13]. Next, to represent the shape of the segmented ear, we concatenate these measures to form a 4-dimensional shape feature vector. The shape feature vector of the entire gallery constructs the shape feature space. After this, we apply the nearest neighbor search algorithm based on the KD-tree built from the entire gallery and use the shape feature space to obtain the nearest neighbor gallery image. A diagram of the proposed approach to indexing based on shape is shown in Fig. 2.

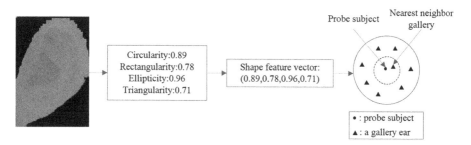

Fig. 2. Proposed approach to indexing based on shape

2.3   3D Feature Extraction

In this section, we explain the 3D feature extraction. Following the method described in [7], we: (1) localize a set of key points that contain salient surface information; (2) compute the Surface Patch Histogram of Indexed Shape (SPHIS) descriptor of these key points [5, 6], which turns out to be a descriptor of 258 elements representing each of the key points; (3) compute the minimum number of robust key points on the segmented ears for the entire gallery, which is kp key points, meaning that the depth feature vector for every 3D ear image contains $258kp$ elements; (4) use principal component analysis (PCA) [14] to reduce the dimensionality of the depth feature vectors for each ear image.

2.4   Categorization Through Indexing

Traditionally ear categorization through indexing [7] uses the depth feature vector to build separate index trees for each shape category (see Sect. 2.2) after the preprocessing step. Later, for a given probe subject, three types of indexing technique are applied to the reduced depth feature space generated by the shape category of the probe ear image. These three types of indexing technique are: a range query based on the KD-tree [10]; the pyramid technique [15]; and the extended pyramid technique [16]. However, the four shape categories (as per Sect. 2.2) cannot be obtained directly using our proposed approach, so the traditional approach to ear categorization through indexing is difficult to use in this case.

Instead, for recognition of the probe subject, we propose a novel technique for ear categorization through indexing. After the preprocessing step described above, we separately build the index tree from the list of gallery ear images by using the reduced depth feature space for each gallery ear image, where the shape difference (the Euclidean distance in the shape feature space) between the list of gallery ear images and the gallery ear image is less than threshold H. We then use the three types of indexing technique set out in [7] in the reduced depth feature space that corresponds to the gallery ear where the shape difference from the probe subject is less than the shape difference between any other gallery ear and the probe subject.

3   Experimental Results

Experiments were conducted on the UND Collection J2 dataset with 1800 images of 415 subjects. Some of the subjects have only two face profile images in the database. Thus, we randomly selected one image per person to compose a gallery set and another per person to compose a probe set, thereby including all of the subjects in the benchmark database. In the training phase, the shape feature vectors of the binary ear masks that were obtained after segmentation were used to build an index tree (see Sect. 2.2). Then, for each of the gallery images separately, we built a feature space using the SPHIS descriptors (see Sect. 2.3). Using the 3D key point selection technique outlined in [7], we computed the minimum number of robust key points on the segmented ears for the entire gallery. This turned out to be 35 key points. Each of the key points was represented by a descriptor of 258 elements (see Sect. 2.3). So, the depth feature vector for every 3D ear image contained $258 \times 35 = 9030$ elements. To reduce redundancy in the depth feature vector, we applied PCA [14] to reduce the depth feature vector of each ear image to a 500-dimensional depth feature vector. Finally, for each of the gallery images separately, the depth feature vectors generated by the H nearest neighbor in the shape feature space were used to build the index tree.

To evaluate the performance of the proposed approach to shape-based indexing, we used an index tree-based nearest neighbor query to index the 3D ear scans. The query image from the probe set was first of all segmented, then the shape feature vector was calculated using the shape similarity technique presented in Sect. 2.2. Based on the shape feature vector, the query image was used to perform a nearest neighbor query on the index tree built from the shape feature space generated by the entire gallery. The index tree then returned a gallery 3D ear image in response to the query image. The average time taken per nearest neighbor query was about 0.00010 s.

To evaluate the performance when indexing the biometrics database with depth features by using algorithms based on balanced and unbalanced split data structures, we used the KD-tree and the pyramid technique, separately, to index the 3D ear scans across multiple lists of ear images. We first of all followed the method described above to obtain a gallery 3D ear image in response to the query image. Then a list of 3D ear images whose shape difference to the gallery 3D ear image was less than the threshold H was determined. This was labeled the reduced gallery. Euclidean distance in higher dimensional depth feature space (the SPHIS descriptors without dimensionality reduction) was used to perform a sequential search on the reduced gallery of 3D ear images to find the best possible match. If the best possible matched ear was of the same subject we considered it to be a rank-one recognition.

To evaluate the robustness of the retrieval performance using the proposed approach, we conducted recognition without categorizing the database. The average calculation time to perform recognition through sequential search of the entire gallery template was about 0.023 s. The results for recognition accuracy and computation time when performing recognition after indexing the database with different amounts of search depth feature space reduction and according to different shape differences are given in Figs. 3 and 4, respectively. The average computation time per query for the proposed approach was only 0.0011 s with a 50% search space reduction where the shape difference threshold was specified as 0.01. For both recognition accuracy and computation time with the shape difference threshold H being set to the same value. To obtain the optimal shape difference threshold, we performed an experiment to compare the recognition accuracy and average computation time per query when using our approach and when using the most efficient state-of-the-art technique [7]. To do this we ran the 3D ear recognition approach proposed in [7] on the same platform, which was a Windows® 7 operating system with an Intel® Core™ i5 processor running a Matlab® implementation. Table 1 shows a comparison between the identification performance achieved by the proposed approach with different amounts of search space reduction and a shape difference threshold set to 0.04 and the recognition accuracy achieved by the state-of-the-art technique at different amounts of search space reduction. Table 2 shows a comparison of the computation time for each of the approaches. For both comparisons we again used the UND Collection J2 database. The results in Tables 1 and 2 and Figs. 3 and 4 demonstrate the superiority and robustness of our approach for shape difference thresholds H of between 0.04 and 0.06 when compared to the state-of-the-art technique. For maximum computational efficiency, the optimal shape difference threshold was found to be 0.04.

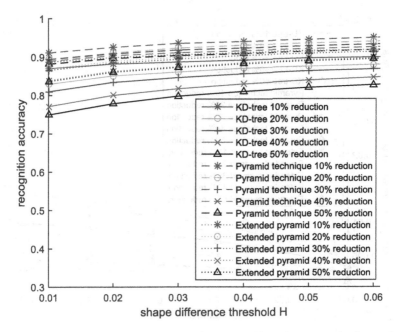

Fig. 3. Recognition accuracy according to different search depth space reduction and shape differences

Table 1. Comparison of recognition accuracy at different search space reductions.

Indexing algorithm	10% reduction	20% reduction	30% reduction	40% reduction	50% reduction
This work (Maity and Abdel-Mottaleb [7])					
KD-tree	**89.27%** (89.26%)	**86.99%** (86.74%)	**85.54%** (85.25%)	**82.89%** (82.71%)	**80.96%** (80.81%)
Pyramid technique	**93.98%** (93.97%)	**93.01%** (92.77%)	**92.29%** (92.19%)	**91.57%** (91.50%)	**90.84%** (90.78%)
Extended pyramid	**91.11%** (91.10%)	**90.84%** (90.62%)	**90.36%** (90.00%)	**88.43%** (88.25%)	**88.19%** (87.91%)

We directly compare our proposed system to a range of other rank-one state-of-the-art efficient ear recognition systems. Table 3 shows a comparison between the recognition performance achieved by our approach without any search space reduction using the optimal shape difference threshold and the recognition accuracy of the other techniques for the UND Collection J2 database. Note that, for [4], we used the UND Collection F database, which is a subset of Collection J2. This was because the probe and gallery ear images used in [4] consist of a single 3D ear model for each of the 302 subjects. Our proposed 3D ear biometric system achieved a rank-one recognition rate of 98.5% for the 415 subjects in the J2 database.

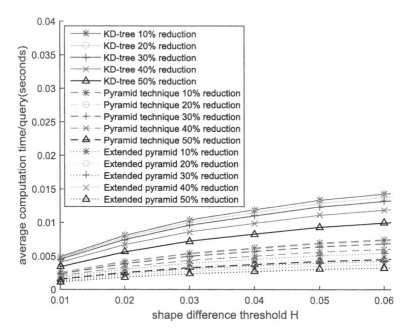

Fig. 4. Average computation time/query (seconds) according to different search depth space reduction and shape differences

Table 2. Comparison of average computation time/query (seconds) at different search space reductions.

Indexing algorithm	10% reduction	20% reduction	30% reduction	40% reduction	50% reduction
This work (Maity and Abdel-Mottaleb [7])					
KD-tree	**0.0119** (0.0171)	**0.0115** (0.0165)	**0.0110** (0.0158)	**0.0099** (0.0142)	**0.0083** (0.0119)
Pyramid technique	**0.0062** (0.0089)	**0.0060** (0.0087)	**0.0057** (0.0082)	**0.0050** (0.0072)	**0.0036** (0.0054)
Extended pyramid	**0.0045** (0.0065)	**0.0040** (0.0058)	**0.0035** (0.0051)	**0.0031** (0.0045)	**0.0027** (0.0039)

Table 3. Comparison of rank-one recognition accuracy and time needed in recognition phase

Method	Rank-one recognition accuracy	Modality of image used
Chen and Bhanu [4]	96.4%	Co-registered 2D+3D
Yan and Bowyer [2]	97.6%	Co-registered 2D+3D
Zhou et al. [6]	98.0%	Only 3D
Prakash and Gupta [17]	98.30%	Co-registered 2D+3D
Maity and Abdel-Mottaleb [7]	98.5%	Only 3D
This work	**98.5%**	Only 3D

4   Conclusion

We have presented a complete, automatic ear biometric system that can accomplish time-efficient identification. Within the system, a novel shape feature vector that concatenates circularity, rectangularity, ellipticity and triangularity measures, was used to robustly index ear shape. This was then used for ear recognition tasks. Our proposed categorization through indexing approach employs the depth features of a list of ear images where the shape difference of a gallery ear image that is similar to the shape of a subject image is less than a certain threshold. Experimental results demonstrated the accuracy and efficiency of our novel 3D ear shape matching approach. We have additionally demonstrated that the proposed approach achieves a significantly higher computational efficiency than other comparable rank-one automatic 3D ear recognition systems.

Future extensions of this work will include the use of an index for general 3D object retrieval and recognition tasks.

References

1. Sun, X., Wang, G., Wang, L., Sun, H., Wei, X.: 3D ear recognition using local salience and principal manifold. Graph. Models **76**(5), 402–412 (2014)
2. Yan, P., Bowyer, K.W.: Biometric recognition using 3D ear shape. IEEE Trans. Pattern Anal. Mach. Intell. **29**(8), 1297–1308 (2007)
3. Chen, H., Bhanu, B.: Contour matching for 3-D ear recognition. In: Proceedings of IEEE Workshop on Applications Computer Vision, January, pp. 123–128 (2005)
4. Chen, H., Bhanu, B.: Human ear recognition in 3D. IEEE Trans. Pattern Anal. Mach. Intell. **29**(4), 718–737 (2007)
5. Zhou, J., Cadavid, S., Abdel-Mottaleb, M.: A computationally efficient approach to 3D ear recognition employing local and holistic features. In: Proceedings of IEEE Computer Society Conference on Computer Vision and Pattern Recognition Workshops (CVPRW), pp. 98–105 (2011)
6. Zhou, J., Cadavid, S., Abdel-Mottaleb, M.: An efficient 3-D ear recognition system employing local and holistic features. IEEE Trans. Inf. Forensics Secur. **7**(3), 978–991 (2012)
7. Maity, S., Abdel-Mottable, M.: 3D segmentation and classification through indexing. IEEE Trans. Inf. Forensics Secur. **10**(2), 423–435 (2015)
8. Lei, J., Zhou, J., Abdel-Mottaleb, M., You, X.: Detection, localization and pose classification of ear in 3D face profile images. In: Proceedings of 20th IEEE International Conference on Image Processing, pp. 4200–4204 (2013)
9. Kass, M., Witkin, A., Terzopoulos, D.: Snakes: active contour models. Int. J. Comput. Vis. **1**(4), 321–331 (1988)
10. Bentley, J.L.: Multidimensional binary search trees used for associative searching. Commun. ACM **18**(9), 509–517 (1975)
11. Žunić, J., Hirota, K., Rosin, P.L.: A Hu moment invariant as a shape circularity measure. Pattern Recognit. **43**(1), 47–57 (2010)
12. Rosin, P.L.: Measuring rectangularity. Mach. Vis. Appl. **11**(4), 191–196 (1999)
13. Rosin, P.: Measuring shape: ellipticity, rectangularity, and triangularity. Mach. Vis. Appl. **14**(3), 172–184 (2003)

14. Jolliffe, I.: Principal Component Analysis. Wiley, Hoboken (2005)
15. Berchtold, S., Böhm, C., Kriegal, H.-P.: The pyramid-technique: towards breaking the curse of dimensionality. ACM SIGMOD Rec. **27**(2), 142–153 (1998)
16. Battiato, S., Cantone, D., Catalano, D., Cincotti, G., Hofri, M.: An efficient algorithm for the approximate median selection problem. In: Bongiovanni, G., Petreschi, R., Gambosi, G. (eds.) CIAC 2000. LNCS, vol. 1767, pp. 226–238. Springer, Heidelberg (2000). https://doi.org/10.1007/3-540-46521-9_19
17. Prakash, S., Gupta, P.: Human recognition using 3D ear images. Neurocomputing **140**, 317–325 (2014)

Actual Radiation Patterns-Oriented Non-deterministic Optical Wireless Channel Characterization

Jupeng Ding[1(✉)], Chih-Lin I[2], Ruiyue Xie[1], Huicheng Lai[1], and Chi Zhang[1]

[1] College of Information Science and Engineering, Xinjiang University, Urumqi 830046, China
jupeng7778@163.com
[2] Green Communication Research Center, China Mobile Research Institute, Beijing 100053, China

Abstract. In optical wireless communication channel characterization, Monte Carlo-based non-deterministic modeling scheme has been widely adopted due to its simplicity and efficiency. Currently, this scheme is only applicable to characterize the optical sources with Lambertain radiation pattern. For flexibly modeling practical non-Lambertain source radiation patterns, the modified edition of above stochastic modeling scheme is systematically proposed in this paper. Numerical results prove that the modified scheme is capable of presenting various non-Lambertain sources with symmetric radiation pattern (e.g. LEDs LUXEON®Rebel from Lumileds Philips) at high accuracy while at significantly reduced computational complexity. As compared with the existing deterministic modeling scheme, the power deviation ratio of impulse response is less than 0.60% for the second order reflection while less than 13.8% for the third order reflection

Keywords: Source radiation pattern · Non-deterministic · Ray tracing Optical wireless · Visible light communications · Channel characterization

1 Introduction

In recent years, optical wireless communications (OWC) has gained renewed interest and investigation due to the aggressive development and application of solid state sources e.g. light emitting diodes (LEDs) around the world [1–3].

To a large extent, the LEDs in OWC systems play a similar role as the antennas in traditional radio frequency wireless systems. At the current stage, some key properties of actual LEDs must be carefully described following the guideline of antennas engineering. Out of all, the radiation property is of top importance in most cases [4, 5]. During OWC modeling and system design, the LEDs are usually described as Lambertian sources following cosine radiation patterns [1, 4]. This pattern fundamentally determines the multipath channel characteristic and coverage performance.

© Springer Nature Switzerland AG 2018
J. Zhou et al. (Eds.): CCBR 2018, LNCS 10996, pp. 517–527, 2018.
https://doi.org/10.1007/978-3-319-97909-0_55

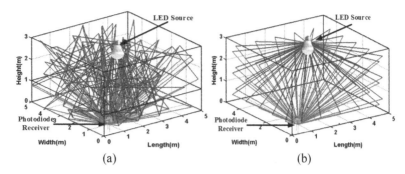

Fig. 1. A typical indoor scenario with optical multipath propagation of (a) non-deterministic modeling scheme, (b) conventional deterministic modeling scheme.

Specifically, the OWC channel modeling schemes include: deterministic and Monte Carlo-based non-deterministic modeling schemes, as shown in Fig. 1. As for deterministic modeling scheme, the respective adaptability can be conveniently accomplished so long as the explicit mathematical expression of concerned radiation pattern is provided. Correspondingly, the basic channel characteristics difference under distinct source radiation patterns is illustrated in [2]. On the other side, the Monte Carlo ray tracing modeling scheme is more superior than the former in efficiency and simplicity. In order to enhance applicability to various cases, this paper proposes an alternative random directions generation method which is suitable for flexible source radiation patterns, including non-Lambertain pattern and Lambertain pattern. Furthermore, the finally derived time/frequency characteristics for the typical receiver positions are respectively compared with the reported work from deterministic OWC channel modeling scheme, and the relevant accuracy is discussed as well.

The remainder of this paper is organized as follows. In Sect. 2, besides the conventional Lambertain radiation pattern and the relevant stochastic representation, the actual radiation patterns are presented. In Sect. 3, the original ray directions statistics for modeling variable radiation patterns are discussed, and the derived channel time/frequency responses are compared with the counterparts obtained via the conventional deterministic modeling scheme. Conclusion is given in Sect. 4.

2   Source Radiation Patterns

2.1   Stochastic Representation of Lambertian Source Radiation Patterns and Channel Impulse Response

In conventional infrared light based OWC, the source is usually assumed to emit a Lambertian pattern. This assumption is approximately valid in some particular circumstances. For instance, the transmitter uses a cluster of laser diodes (LDs) whose output is passed through a translucent plastic diffuser [7, 8].

In conventional OWC modeling, the angular output power of an optical source is typically modeled by a generalized Lambertian pattern having uniaxial symmetry. This means its intensity is proportional to the viewing angle:

$$I(\theta) = \frac{(m+1)}{2\pi} \cos^m(\theta). \tag{1}$$

where $I(\theta)$ is radiant intensity in units of Candelas, and θ is the spherical polar angle off normal axis (degrees). The index m is related to $\theta_{1/2}$, the source semiangle at half intensity, by $m = n(2)/n(\cos \phi_{1/2}$ [5, 7, 8]. In [6, 8], it has been shown that Lambertian sources have the broadest angular characteristics compared with any other sources. In fact, the radiant intensity distribution from a Lambertian source has a circular profile when plotted in polar coordinates. The 3D radiation pattern and the normalized 2D cross section of a generalized Lambertian source are shown in Fig. 2(a) and (c), respectively.

Unlike the deterministic modeling scheme in [8], the noteworthy overhead of dividing inner surfaces of indoor scenario into numerous reflective elements is avoided in the Monte Carlo-based non-deterministic modeling scheme thanks to its stochastic nature, as seen in Fig. 1(a). The basic principle of this stochastic modeling scheme is randomly identifying one original ray direction according to the source radiation pattern, and then one ray in this direction is emitted and traced from the source position until it strikes at the nearest point of the environmental surface. Then, similarly this point i.e. reflection position works as a secondary source to emit a new ray carrying the left power decided by the reflectivity of the struck surface. Generally, this reflection source can also be modeled as a Lambertian source, as previously given in Fig. 2(a) and (c).

When identifying the original ray direction for one source, it is important to delineate what coordinate system is being utilized. Depending on the application, some coordinate systems may be more advantageous than the others. Figure 2(a) includes what is commonly called antenna coordinates. And any unity direction vector R of ray from the concerned source can be represented by the angles θ and ϕ. The azimuth ϕ is the angle between the projection of R onto the x-y axis and x axis while θ is the angle subtended from the z axis to the ray direction. Correspondingly, the unit direction vector R can be represented as:

$$R = (\sin(\theta)\cos(\phi), \sin(\theta)\sin(\phi), \cos(\theta)). \tag{2}$$

with the magnitude of R is set to unity.

For constructing the connection between the original ray directions and the source radiation pattern, first of all, the probability of θ less than certain angle $\Theta \in [0, \pi/2]$ can be mathematically expressed through the radiation pattern:

$$P(\theta \leq \Theta) = \int_0^{2\pi} d\phi \int_0^{\Theta} I(\theta)\sin(\theta)d\theta. \tag{3}$$

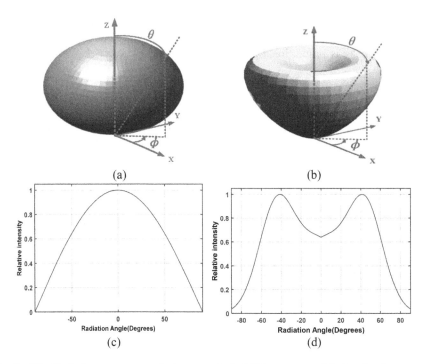

Fig. 2. 3D Radiation patterns of three typical LED sources: (a) Lambertian m = 1, (b) LUXEON®Rebel from Lumileds Philips; respective 2D cross sections are illustrated in (c), (d) [3, 6].

Thanks to the simplicity and symmetry of the expression of the Lambertian pattern, the compact solution of this double integration can be easily obtained by [3]:

$$P(\theta \leq \Theta) = 1 - \cos^{m+1}(\Theta). \tag{4}$$

Equivalently, in Cartesian coordinate system, the probability of that projection of unity vector R in z axis larger than certain value $Z \in [0, 1]$ can be derived as:

$$P(z \geq Z) = P(\theta \leq \Theta) = 1 - \cos^{m+1}(\Theta) = 1 - Z^{m+1}. \tag{5}$$

Then the complementary set of the above probability i.e. the distribution function of z can be tightly expressed as:

$$F(Z) = P(z \leq Z) = 1 - P(z \geq Z) = Z^{m+1}. \tag{6}$$

Once let $F(z) = u$, since the inverse function $F^{-1}(z)$ of $F(z)$ exists, z can be explicitly given by uniform random number $u \in [0, 1]$ as [3]:

$$z = \sqrt[m+1]{u}. \tag{7}$$

Simultaneously, since the direction vector R is set to unity and z can also be written by $z = \cos(\theta)$, its projection on the x-y plane can also be found as:

$$r = \sin(\theta) = \sqrt{1 - z^2}. \tag{8}$$

On the other side, since the radiation pattern of the Lambertian source is symmetric around the z axis, the azimuth can be decided by the other uniform random number $v \in [0, 1]$ as:

$$\phi = 2\pi v. \tag{9}$$

Thus, the left two components of the direction vector R can be randomly identified as [3]:

$$x = r\cos(\phi) = r\cos(2\pi v) = \sqrt{1 - z^2}\cos(2\pi v). \tag{10}$$

and

$$y = r\sin(\phi) = r\sin(2\pi v) = \sqrt{1 - z^2}\sin(2\pi v). \tag{11}$$

During the stated conventional Monte Carlo ray tracing procedure, whenever a new ray direction is required from the local coordinates, a new uniform random number pair is generated for u and v. And then the new direction vector R can be obtained from Eqs. (10), (11) and (7).

2.2   Actual Radiation Patterns

Similar to antennas in radio frequency, the LED source also exhibits directive nature, which means the radiation intensity is not uniform in all directions. The property of radiating more strongly in some directions than in others is called the directivity of the source. For the discussed Lambertain radiation pattern, the maximum intensity still appears in the normal direction of LED source. However, such directivity mode is not consistent with all LED sources. Typically, the maximum intensity of Lower Bound LUXEON®Rebel from Lumileds Philips appears in all direction with certain angle off the normal axis. In Fig. 2(b) and (d), the 3D and 2D radiation pattern of LUXEON®Rebel is illustrated, which is of loose circular cone shape, but partial hollow. This maximum intensity appears in the direction of about 45° off the normal axis. Inherited from [2, 6], the angular distribution of this non-Lambertian pattern can be characterized as:

$$I_{LUX}(\theta) = \sum_i g1_i \exp\left[-\ln 2\left(\frac{|\theta| - g2_i}{g3_i}\right)^2\right]. \tag{12}$$

where $g1_1 = 0.76$, $g2_1 = 0°$, $g3_1 = 29°$, $g1_2 = 1.10$, $g2_2 = 45°$, $g3_2 = 21°$. It can be observed that the compact analytical representation of this pattern is a sum of the modified Gaussian functions as well. Moreover, like the Lambertian case, the intensity is independent of the azimuthal angle which basically dominates its symmetry in the far field.

2.3 Modified Non-deterministic Modeling Scheme Incorporating Flexible Radiation Patterns

For variable actual non-Lambertain source pattern mentioned above, it is quite challenging or even impossible to obtain an explicit formula of $P(\theta \le \Theta)$ like Eq. (4) since their analytical representation is a sum of modified Gaussian functions. Therefore, there is necessity to find alternative method for generating stochastic original ray directions which rigorously match the radiation characteristic of various sources rather than simple cosine function of Lambertian radiation pattern.

For the case of symmetric radiation pattern like LUXEON®Rebel, the radiation intensity is independent of the azimuthal angle which basically dominates its symmetry. Therefore, the azimuth ϕ of its original ray direction can still be acquired via Eq. (9) as conventional Lambertian case. The most challenging portion is the stochastic generation of θ i.e. the spherical polar angle off normal axis. In the proposed non-deterministic modeling scheme, firstly, the maximum intensity value of this pattern should be found among all possible θ as:

$$I_{\max} = \max_{\theta \in [0,\pi/2]} I(\theta). \tag{13}$$

The candidate θ_{cand} can be given by one uniform random number $\delta \in [0, 1]$ as:

$$\theta_{cand} = (\pi/2 - 0)\delta. \tag{14}$$

Following Eq. (14), δ is repeatedly renewed until the following equation is satisfied:

$$I(\theta_{cand}) \ge I_{\max}\xi. \tag{15}$$

Where $\xi \in [0, 1]$ is another uniform random number as well. Then this candidate θ_{cand} is accepted for the current ray:

$$\theta_{acep} = \theta_{cand}. \tag{16}$$

Due to the symmetry of this pattern, for the same ray, the accepted azimuth ϕ_{acep} can be given directly by the third uniform random number $\gamma \in [0, 1]$ as:

$$\phi_{acep} = (2\pi - 0)\gamma. \tag{17}$$

By conversion to Cartesian coordinates from angular coordinates, the projections of generated ray direction on x, y and z axis are given respectively by:

$$x = \sin\left(\theta_{acep}\right)\cos\left(\phi_{acep}\right)$$
$$y = \sin\left(\theta_{acep}\right)\sin\left(\phi_{acep}\right) .$$
$$z = \cos\left(\theta_{acep}\right)$$

(18)

Therefore, at least triple uniform random numbers i.e. δ, ξ and γ are needed for the stochastic generation of each ray direction under symmetric patterns.

3   Numerical Results and Discussion

In this section, the performance of modified non-deterministic scheme is numerically evaluated in representing source radiation pattern and modeling OWC channel characteristics. Table 1 shows the main parameters setting for following simulation analysis.

3.1   Ray Directions Statistics

Intuitively, the more stochastic rays make the source radiation pattern more elaborately represented. From the view of efficiency and computation overhead, the amount of generated rays should be as reduced as possible. The normalized statistics of the generated original ray directions for symmetric patterns are shown at first. In detail, for LUXEON®Rebel case, the statistical histograms of all generated original ray directions are given in Fig. 3. When the amount of generated rays N_{ray} is just 1000, the middle section of the radiation shape cannot be accurately presented, as in Fig. 3(a). Once N_{ray} is further increased to 50000, as plotted in Fig. 3(b), the statistic profile is sufficiently refined which is consistent with the cross section of rigorous LUXEON®Rebel pattern in Fig. 2(d). Meanwhile, since the conventional Lambertian radiation pattern is just one specific case among symmetric patterns, it definitely can be represented by the proposed stochastic presentation scheme. Therefore, the proposed stochastic presentation scheme is capable of flexibly characterizing the various symmetric source patterns.

3.2   Channel Impulse Response

The channel impulse response is vital in quantifying the multipath channel characteristics. The multipath dispersion further causes inter-symbol interference (ISI) of different level to the received signal. Existing work has shown that the various radiation patterns introduce significant influence to the channel characteristics of time domain. Therefore, it is essential to estimate the capability of the modified Monte Carlo ray tracing scheme in generating reliable channel impulse response.

First of all, the adaptability to the typical non-Lambertian symmetric pattern, i.e. LUXEON®Rebel is tested and the separate impulse response components of the central position, i.e. (2.5, 2.5, 0) m, are plotted in Fig. 4(a). Obviously, due to the stochastic nature of the Monte Carlo-based non-deterministic scheme, the slight joggle appears in the response curves from the each order reflection, especially for the second reflection component h2, the third reflection component h3, the fourth reflection component h4 and the left reflection component hleft. Thanks to the efficiency and simplicity of the Monte Carlo ray tracing scheme, up to 20 time reflection is included in the numerical analysis. Intuitively, by comparing with the reported channel impulse response from the deterministic results given in Fig. 4(b) [2], the well consistency can be observed for the comparable h1, h2 and h3 response curves.

More explicitly, under this pattern, due to the symmetry of the described indoor geographical setting, the impulse responses of three key receiver positions are evaluated. Apart from the mentioned central position, the left two positions are located in the side and the corner of the floor. Obviously, a right triangle is surrounded by the three positions. Thanks to the symmetry to the room center, the whole floor can be composed by eight right triangle area of equal size. Therefore, one right triangle area can represent all channel characteristics of the whole receiver plane. In the meantime, the channel characteristic of any position within this triangle can be viewed as a transition among the counterparts of three mentioned key positions [2]. The respective coordinates are: (2.5, 0.1, 0) m and (0.1, 0.1, 0) m. For the central position, the absolute deviations for the h1, h2 and h3 between the comparable modeling schemes are 1.6 nW, 0.1 nW, and 10 nW respectively. The relative deviation ratio is just 0.36%, 0.02%, and 3.63%. And for the side position, the absolute power deviation is about 41.9 nW, 7.7 nW, and 16.8 nW, respectively. Therefore, the relative deviation ratio is restricted to about 6.22%, 1.62%, and 6.08%. The increase in the deviation ratios is mainly due to the lengthened propagation distance of the side position compared to the original central position. When the receiver is relocated to the room corner, the concerned absolute power deviation is about 32.1 nW, 114.5 nW, and 160.6 nW, respectively. Correspondingly, the relative deviation ratio is 6.59%, 24.3%, and 40.2%. Although the deviation ratio to the h2 and h3 is noteworthy, the influence to the total channel impulse response is still limited which can be further reduced by increasing the amount of the emitted rays. Moreover, the work in next subsection will identify that the induced difference in the frequency response is quite slight. Therefore, for the three typical receiver positions, when the ray amount is set to just 50000, the power deviation ratio

Table 1. Parameters for transmission characteristics simulation

Parameters	Value	Parameters	Value
Terminal reflection order	20	Room size	5 m × 5 m × 3 m
FOV of receiver	85°	Height of LED source	3 m
Elevation of receiver	90°	Reflectance of ceiling	0.8
Azimuth of receiver	0°	Reflectance of wall	0.8
Height of receiver	0 m	Reflectance of floor	0.3
Elevation of LED source	−90°	Coordinates of LED source	(2.5, 2.5, 3.0) m
Azimuth of LED source	0°	Coordinates of central receiver position	(2.5, 2.5, 0.0) m
Impulse response time resolution	0.2 ns	Coordinates of side receiver position	(2.5, 0.1, 0.0) m
Detection physical area of receiver	1 cm^2	Coordinates of corner receiver position	(0.1, 0.1, 0.0) m

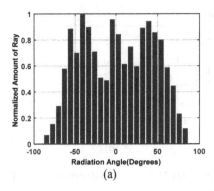
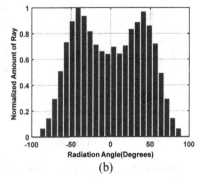

(a)

(b)

Fig. 3. Statistic histogram of original ray directions for LUXEON®Rebel from Lumileds Philips: (a) N_{ray}= 1000, (b) N_{ray}= 50000

Table 2. Comparison of −3 dB transmission bandwidths of different components

	Hsum	H0	H1	H2	H3	H4	Hleft
Modified non-deterministic	7.0	Ideal	101.7	26.1	18.7	14.2	5.6
Conventional deterministic	12.2	Ideal	102.5	25.6	18.3	–	–

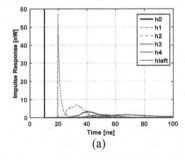
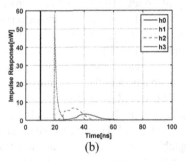

(a)

(b)

Fig. 4. Channel impulse response characteristics: (a) Modified Non-deterministic modeling scheme, (b) conventional deterministic modeling scheme.

of comparable impulse response including up to the third reflection component could be restricted to 0.27%, 0.60%, and 13.8%, respectively. Above analysis identifies that the modified Monte Carlo-based non-deterministic scheme is capable of reliably describing the OWC impulse response characteristics under flexible source radiation patterns.

3.3 Frequency Responses and −3 DB Transmission Bandwidths

Corresponding to the impulse responses of LUXEON®Rebel given in Fig. 4, the frequency responses from the modified Monte Carlo-based non-deterministic modeling

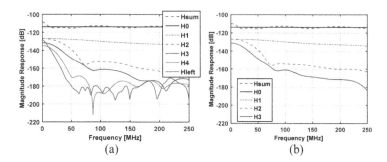

Fig. 5. Channel frequency response characteristics: (a) Modified Non-deterministic modeling scheme, (b) conventional deterministic modeling scheme.

scheme and the conventional deterministic modeling scheme can be observed from Fig. 5. Specifically, the separated frequency response components of the first H1, the second H2, the third H3, the fourth H4 and the left Hleft reflections related to the Fig. 4 (a) are plotted explicitly in Fig. 5(a). On the other side, for the deterministic modeling scheme, the frequency responses of the first H1, the second H2 and the third H3 reflections are given in Fig. 5(b), which is mapped from the channel impulse response from Fig. 4(b). The favourable consistency can be observed from Fig. 5(a) and (b) for the first three order reflections H3. Only perceptible little deviation appears at the frequency of about 210 MHz of the third reflection. Since the most concerned results are the baseband transmission characteristics of various channel components, this limited deviation is acceptable.

Straightforwardly, for −3 dB transmission bandwidths given in Table 2, the comparison is made among different components of the central position from the modified stochastic and the deterministic modeling schemes. The absolute deviation is just 0.8 MHz, 0.5 MHz and 0.4 MHz for the first H1, the second H2, the third H3 reflection, respectively, while the related −3 dB transmission bandwidths are up to about 102 MHz, 26 MHz, and 18 MHz. Therefore, these absolute deviations are within the acceptable range. A significant difference is the −3 dB transmission bandwidths from the total frequency response between the two compared schemes. The related 5.2 MHz deviation is mainly due to the fourth H4, the left Hleft reflections which cannot be affordable in the conventional deterministic modeling scheme.

4   Conclusions

For overcoming the limitation of conventional Monte Carlo-based non-deterministic modeling scheme in characterizing the practical source radiation patterns, a modified scheme with the requisite adaptability is proposed and analyzed. Statistical results show that the non-Lambertian radiation pattern can be stochastically represented. By comparing with the time/frequency channel results from the time-consuming deterministic modeling scheme, the reliability of the efficient modified Monte Carlo ray tracing-based scheme is numerically evaluated. In the view of frequency response, transmission bandwidth deviation ratio is less than 0.8%, 2.0% and 2.2% for the most concerned first, the second and the third reflection components.

Acknowledgments. This work was supported in part by National Natural Science Foundation of China (Grants No. 61561048).

References

1. Miramirkhani, F., Uysal, M.: Channel modeling and characterization for visible light communications. IEEE Photonics J. **7**(6), 1–16 (2015)
2. Ding, J., I, C.L., Xu, Z.: Indoor optical wireless channel characteristics with distinct source radiation patterns. IEEE Photonics J. **8**(1), 1–15 (2016)
3. Lopez´-Hernandez, F.J., Perez-Jimeenez, R., Santamaria, A.: Ray-tracing algorithms for fast calculation of the channel impulse response on diffuse ir wireless indoor channels. Opt. Eng. **39**(10), 2775–2780 (2000)
4. Burton, A., Minh, H.L., Ghassemlooy, Z., Bentley, E., Botella, C.: Experimental demonstration of 50-Mb/s visible light communications using 4×4 MIMO. IEEE Photonics Technol. Lett. **26**(9), 945–948 (2014)
5. Ding, J., Wang, K., Xu, Z.: Accuracy analysis of different modeling schemes in indoorvisible light communications with distributed array sources. In: Proceedings of 2014 9th International Symposium on Communication Systems, Networks Digital Signal Processing, Manchester, pp. 1005–1010, July 2014
6. Moreno, I., Sun, C.-C.: Modeling the radiation pattern of LEDs. Opt. Express **16**(3), 1808–1819 (2008)
7. Jivkova, S.T., Kavehrad, M.: Multispot diffusing configuration for wireless infrared access. IEEE Trans. Commun. **48**(6), 970–978 (2000)
8. Barry, J.R., Kahn, J.M., Krause, W.J., Lee, E., Messerschmitt, D.: Simulation of multipath impulse response for indoor wireless optical channels. IEEE J. Sel. Areas Commun. **11**(3), 367–379 (1993)

Detection of the Toe-off Feature of Planar Shoeprint Based on CNN

Xiangyu Meng, Yunqi Tang$^{(\boxtimes)}$, and Wei Guo$^{(\boxtimes)}$

School of Forensic Science, People's Public Security University of China,
Beijing 10038, China
2016211276@stu.ppsuc.edu.cn, tangyunqi@ppsuc.edu.cn,
gd928@sina.com

Abstract. In Chinese forensic science, a planar footprint can provide police office lots of information, such as sex, age and gait for criminal investigation. The toe-off feature is an important feature of planar shoeprint, which can indicate the gait pattern of the walkers. However, the toe-off features of planar shoeprints are still analyzed artificially by criminal investigators, which is inefficient and subjective. In this research, a novel algorithm for the automatic detection of the toe-off feature is developed. We define the crescent feature in the toe-off feature of planar footprint as a positive sample, and define no such feature as a negative sample. We use CNN to detect them. In order to conduct the research, we take photo of planar shoeprints by the way of criminal scene photography. After performing some pre-processing steps on these pictures, we set up a planar shoeprint database. Experimental results show that the proposed method achieves detection accuracy of 97.0% on our planar shoeprint database.

Keywords: Toe-off feature · Planar shoeprint · Convolutional Neural Network Detection

1 Introduction

In recent years, crime suspects have a growing awareness against investigation. When committing a crime, they destroy evidences and conceal crimes during criminal activities by wearing gloves, cleaning up crime scenes, hiding criminal tools, etc. As a result, we criminal police can only get fewer and fewer traditional physical evidences at crime scenes, like high-quality fingerprints, DNA, etc. Moreover, because of usually covered faces with hoods, masks, etc. and poor resolution of cameras, it is very difficult to get clear facial features of crime suspects from surveillance videos. In recent years, with continuous development of Pattern Recognition technologies, the technology of personal identification through walking postures in surveillance videos is more and more mature [1–5]. Because walking is necessary during suspects' committing a crime, footprints resulted from walking become important trace evidences that frequently appear on crime scenes [6]. Footprints are traces left by feet's pressure on surfaces like the ground during standing, walking, etc. Footprints can be regarded as results of walking, and walking postures in surveillance videos are the process of walking. These two are sure to be interrelated. The feature of footprint gait is the combination of these

© Springer Nature Switzerland AG 2018
J. Zhou et al. (Eds.): CCBR 2018, LNCS 10996, pp. 528–535, 2018.
https://doi.org/10.1007/978-3-319-97909-0_56

two. Footprint gait features refer to the trace characteristics of a person's walking power habit through the foot acting on the object when walking. Although it is a reflection of a behavioral result, we can obtain relevant information about its formation through its analysis. For example, the height, weight and walking posture of the person who created them. According to the law of walking movement, the characteristics of footstep gait can be divided into three phases: Heel strike feature, Mid stance feature, and Toe-off feature.

For above reasons, in order to help public security criminal investigation, we carry out this study. It mainly analyzes and tests Toe-off features of planar shoeprint during walking, and uses Convolutional Neural Network to make a preliminary classification. This lays a good foundation for further research on correlation between Toe-off feature and walking postures in surveillance videos. Its innovation lies in the application of research methods in the field of pattern recognition to traditional criminal technology.

In terms of using computers to automatically classify planar footprint generated by walking, ultimately, it is on basis of its shape. Therefore, the shape with planar footprint characteristics produced by walking is the critical factor for feasibility of the experiment. From videos of planar footprints and walking process, we discover that people with the same walking characteristics have similar Toe-off feature. This trace shape is slightly influenced by the sole pattern, but closely related to walking habits. As shown in the graph, for those whose tiptoe is backward with obvious force downwards when starting to walk, there is a dark crescent shape in the tiptoe of the planar footprint. And people with the walking habit will have this trace feature every time they walk. It also means that the crescent shape feature created by the walking motivational habit has a certain degree of stability. Therefore, it can be used as a basis for identifying criminal suspects (Fig. 1).

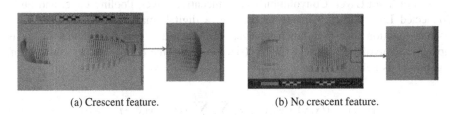

(a) Crescent feature.   (b) No crescent feature.

Fig. 1. The main Toe-off feature of this study

2   Related Works

In the field of public security criminal investigation in China, theories of examining footprints characteristics resulted from walking were originally established and developed on basis of the research on soft earth and snowfields in the north. There is no mature theory to support the study on planar footprint characteristics produced by walking. However, many experienced footprint examination experts, by accurate analyzing planar footprints' characteristics, such as clarity of outline, brightness of color, shape of traces, etc., can deduce footprint maker's walking postures, height, weight and other physical characteristics. This shows that it is feasible to map the walking posture from planar footprint characteristics generated by walking.

But, automation of footprint examination belongs to an interdisciplinary field of criminal technology and information technology. Only few experts have both footprint examination knowledge and high information technology. Meanwhile, due to footprints' ambiguity, uncertainty and complicated changes, etc., all kinds of footprint examination technology is still at the stage of analyzing by artificial observation and judging according to subjective experiences. Footprint examination technology is a professional skill mastered by only a few people.

Therefore, the research on automation inspection of footprint characteristics resulted from walking is still in the initial stage, and there are few related researches to refer and learn directly. Current researches on footprint automatic inspection at home and abroad focus on two main directions: First. use plantar pressure sampling equipment like Footscan to collect enough data of plantar pressure during walking, and try to study walking characteristics through the value of plantar pressure, in order to achieve personal identification [7–9]; second, use some digital image recognition algorithm to extract and classify characteristics of sole pattern in perspective of graphics and images, and try to identify footprints according to sole pattern [10, 11]. Few people use pattern recognition techniques to study footprint gait characteristics [12].

3 Proposed Method

Convolutional Neural Network (CNN) is a feedforward neural network. Recent advances in Convolutional Neural Networks (CNN) have brought significant progress in image classification and other vision tasks. Convolutional Neural Network usually consists of Input Layer, Convolution Layer, Incentive Layer, Pooling Layer and Fully Connected Layer. During image processing, a digital image can be regarded as a discrete function in a two-dimensional space. When a 2 two-dimensional image is input, if a convolution kernel of a * b (size) is given, the corresponding convolution equation is as below:

$$z(x, y) = f(x, y) * w(x, y) = \sum_{t=0}^{t=a} \sum_{h=0}^{h=b} f(t, h) w(x - t, y - h) \tag{1}$$

In the equation, f (x, y) represents the input image; w (x, y) is the convolution kernels. It's also called filter, response function, etc.; a and b show the size of the convolution kernel [13].

The convolution layer of the convolution neural network extracts the different features of the input image by the convolution operation shown above. The excitation layer mainly carries on the nonlinear transformation operation, usually as the activation function through introducing the Rectified linear unit (ReLU). CNN often insert pooling layers periodically between successive convolution layers. Pooling layer is the down sampling of each feature graph. The pooling operation can reduce the eigenvector of convolution layer output while preventing over-fitting. The most common pooling operations are max-pooling and mean-pooling. The fully connected layer is at the back of Convolutional Neural Network structure. It is mainly used for result classification. Each neuron of the fully connected layer is connected with all neurons of the previous layer, so it's called fully connected layer [14].

4   Experiments and Results

4.1   Construction of Experimental Data

We prepared a lot of white paper (about 45 cm in width, about 8 m in length) and pave on the floor tile. Then we found about 320 college students volunteers. Their ages ranged from 17 to 21. At first, we let these volunteers to dip their soles with black ink. Then, they walked on the white paper normally so as to leave their footprints. Everyone left 5 footprints each time and did three times. After that, we selected 3500 footprint samples with good quality from more than 4000 footprint samples to establish the database. According to detail photographing methods of crime scenes, we used Nikon D7000 SLR camera to take photos for the footprints one by one. Photos were taken indoors. As to light conditions, both natural light and fluorescent lamps were used. Then we moved pictures off the camera onto a computer to a computer to set up a planar footprint database. When volunteers left planar footprint by walking, we used Hikvision camera to record videos in three angles: front, 90° and back (Fig. 2).

Fig. 2.   Footprint photographing method at the crime scene.

According to related regulations of taking photos for details of crime scene, we used Photoshop CS6 software to rotate and distort photos of planar footprints. Next, we used MATLAB (R2014a) to modify its size to make it the same with real photos. Then we cut out a rectangular picture of 600 * 600 pixels from each planar footprint area. Depending on whether there was crescent shape trace in the tiptoe area when one started to walk, the samples were divided into two types, positive samples and negative samples. The samples with crescent shape traces were defined as positive samples (Fig. 3).

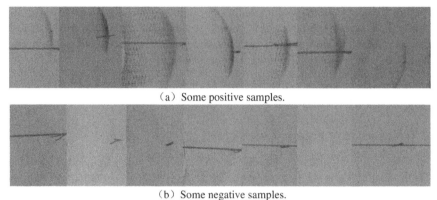

(a) Some positive samples.

(b) Some negative samples.

Fig. 3. Samples.

4.2   Analysis of Experimental Results

Because of a small amount of samples in the database of this research, we used a small CNN under Keras framework. Its network structure chart is shown in Fig. 4 below. Because its network structure is very long vertically, it's divided in the middle and displayed as two parts, one on the left and one on the right. The right part should be below the left part. The whole network has 6 layers with parameters, four Convolution Layers and two Dense Layers.

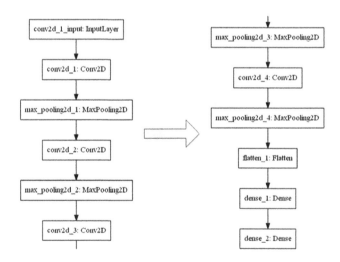

Fig. 4. The network structure of CNN used by this paper.

Figure 5 recorded training and test results of small network model built by ourselves. After 100 times of Iterative training with this small network, the test accuracy could be about 97.0%. Figure 5(a) is a change curve of training accuracy according to quantity of iterations. As can be seen from the graph, it's very fast in narrowing. After only about 40 iterations, the classification accuracy was nearly 90%; after 100 iterations, classification accuracy was about 98.8%. In Fig. 6 below, the training results of our using classic VGG-16 network model under Keras framework. By comparing Figs. 5(a) and 6(a), we can see that VGG-16 network model in this research was not as good as our small network model as to effects. We think it's due to a small amount of database samples. We used only 2000 sample pictures in training (1000 positive samples, 1000 negative samples), 1000 sample picture to verify (500 positive samples, 500 negative samples), and finally 400 sample pictures to test (200 samples, 200 negative samples). Although VGG-16 network model was classic lightweight Convolutional Neural Network model, for such a small database, there were still a lot of network layers and many a parameters to adjust and optimize. It resulted in inadequate training of VGG-16, therefore, its classification effects were not good enough. However, our own small network model has fewer layers and a simple structure, so it has achieved good results in the research.

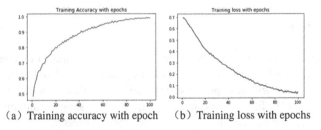

(a) Training accuracy with epoch   (b) Training loss with epochs

Fig. 5. Analysis of training results of small network model under Keras framework.

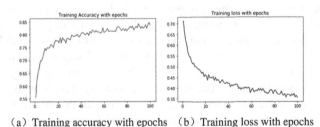

(a) Training accuracy with epochs   (b) Training loss with epochs

Fig. 6. Analysis of VGG-16 network model training results under Keras framework.

Figure 7 is a result analysis graph with Adboost classifier after extracting haar-like characteristics. We extracted Haar-like characteristics from 3000 sample pictures, and then used Adboost training classifier and 400 sample pictures to test. By comparing these figures, we can see that this machine learning method didn't have good effects in this study. After 2000 iterations, the classification test accuracy could only reach 84.3%, and there was still some shortcomings with former methods. We analyzed

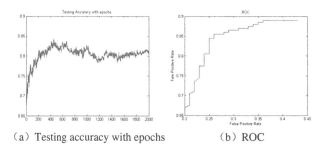

(a) Testing accuracy with epochs   (b) ROC

Fig. 7. Analysis of training results using Adboost classifier after extracting Haar-like features.

causes of this problem. We think that in some cases, characteristics of images selected manually may not be most appropriate. However, by means of Convolutional Neural Network, selecting image features after the computer's automatic learning may be more suitable for the current scene.

5   Conclusion

The study makes a preliminary classification of Toe-off feature of planar footprints through Convolutional Neural Network. Its fast operation speed and high classification precision can be very helpful to public security criminal police in criminal investigating and solving crimes. In future, with increasing quantity of samples and optimization of network structure, we believe its accuracy will improve greatly.

This is just the initial stage of our research on Toe-off feature of planar footprint. Later, our team will divide samples into three categories: inward, middle, and outward, according to the positional relationship between crescent shape in positive samples and the center line. We classify in this way because of following major reasons. According to different directions of tiptoes when walking, characteristics of people's walking can be divided into three categories, namely outward steps (out-toe step), straight steps and inward step (in-toe step). According to probability of scientific statistics, during walking, people with out-toe steps usually create Toe-off feature inwardly. People with pigeon-toed steps usually create Toe-off feature outwardly. People with straight steps usually create Toe-off feature in the middle. Therefore, a further detailed classification of footprint characteristics of crescent shape is helpful for studying the Toe-off directions and walking postures of the footprint maker. Then, they can be connected with crime suspect's' walking postures in surveillance videos. This provides case clues and narrows investigation scope, assisting police in criminal investigation.

Acknowledgments. This work is supported by the National Key Research and Development Program (Grant No. 2017YFC0803506), the Fundamental Research Funds for the Central Universities of China (Grant No. 2018JKF217), the National Natural Science Foundation of China (Grant No. 61503387).

References

1. Castro, F.M., Mata, N.G.: Fisher motion descriptor for multiview gait recognition. Int. J. Pattern Recognit Artif Intell. **31**(01), 1756002 (2016)
2. Mansur, A., Makihara, Y., Aqmar, R., et al.: Gait recognition under speed transition. In: Computer Vision and Pattern Recognition, pp. 249–257. IEEE (2014)
3. Chen, X., Huang, K., Tan, T.: Object Tracking Across Non-overlapping Views by Learning Inter-camera Transfer Models. Elsevier Science Inc., New York (2014)
4. Ma, Y.: Gait recognition using sparse representation. In: IEEE International Conference on Wavelet Analysis and Pattern Recognition, pp. 136–139 (2010)
5. Liu, Z., Malave, L., Sarkar, S.: Studies on silhouette quality and gait recognition. In: Proceedings of the 2004 IEEE Computer Society Conference on Computer Vision and Pattern Recognition, pp. 704–711 (2004)
6. Shi, L., et al.: Footprint 足迹学. People's Public Security University of China, Beijing (2007)
7. Sugimoto, C., Tsuji, M., Lopez, G., et al.: Development of a behavior recognition system using wireless wearable information devices. In: International Symposium on Wireless Pervasive Computing, p. 5. IEEE (2006)
8. Takeda, T., Kuramoto, K., Kobashi, S., et al.: Biometrics personal identification by wearable pressure sensor. In: Fifth International Conference on Emerging Trends in Engineering and Technology, pp. 120–123. IEEE Computer Society (2012)
9. Han, D., Yunqi, T., Wei, G.: Research on the stability of plantar pressure under normal walking condition. In: Tan, T., Li, X., Chen, X., Zhou, J., Yang, J., Cheng, H. (eds.) CCPR 2016. CCIS, vol. 662, pp. 234–242. Springer, Singapore (2016). https://doi.org/10.1007/978-981-10-3002-4_20
10. Jing, M.Q., Ho, W.J., Chen, L.H.: A novel method for shoeprints recognition and classification. In: International Conference on Machine Learning and Cybernetics, pp. 2846–2851. IEEE (2009)
11. Anusudha, K.: Threshold value determination for recognition of partial shoe prints for forensic analysis. Digit. Image Process. **5**(1), 7–13 (2013)
12. Sun, H., Tang, Y., Guo, W.: Research on dig-imprint detection of three-dimensional footprints. In: Zhou, J., et al. (eds.) CCBR 2017. LNCS, vol. 10568, pp. 495–502. Springer, Cham (2017). https://doi.org/10.1007/978-3-319-69923-3_53
13. Sandoval, H., Hattori, T., Kitagawa, S., et al.: A filter of concentric shapes for image recognition and its implementation in a modified DT-CNN. IEICE Trans. Fund. Electron. Commun. Comput. Sci. **95**(9), 2189–2197 (2001)
14. Saatci, E., Tavsanoglu, V.: Multiscale handwritten character recognition using CNN image filters, vol. 3, pp. 2044–2048 (2002)

Identification of the Normal/Abnormal Heart Sounds Based on Energy Features and Xgboost

Ting Li[1($\boxtimes$)], Xing-rong Chen[1], Hong Tang[2], and Xiao-ke Xu[1]

[1] School of Information and Communication Engineering,
Dalian Minzu University, Dalian, China
liting@dlnu.edu.cn
[2] School of Biomedical Engineering,
Dalian University of Technology, Dalian, China

Abstract. A normal/abnormal heart sound identification method was put forward in the paper. The wavelet packet energy features of the heart sounds were extracted in a large database of 1136 recordings and xgboost algorithm was used as the classifier. The feature importance is also evaluated and analyzed. Top 3, 6, 9 and 12 features were used to classify the heart sounds. Experimental results showed that the proposed algorithm can identify the normal and abnormal heart sounds effectively. And the result used top 9 features was as good as that of all features, which can reduce almost half of computation.

Keywords: Heart sounds · Identification · Wavelet packet energy
Xgboost · Feature importance

1 Introduction

Heart disease is the most common overall cause of death for people worldwide. The heart sound reflects the mechanical action of the heart and the cardiovascular system, including the physiology and pathology information of various parts of the heart. Therefore, in all the heart disease detecting methods, heart sound analysis is a non-invasive, economical, easy and efficient method which is widely used to diagnose heart disease and evaluate heart functions during medical check-ups for adults and children.

However, the traditional heart auscultation is over-dependent on the ear sensitivity and the subjective experience of physicians, which can not meet the high accuracy requirement under clinical conditions [1]. In recent years, many features of heart sounds are extracted to describe the heart sound, such as wavelet envelope [2], wavelet-time entropy [3, 7], frequency feature matrix [4] and linear band frequency cepstra [5]. And various classification algorithms have been employed to identify the normal and abnormal heart sounds, such as SVM [2–4], dynamic time warping algorithm [5], adaptive neuro-fuzzy inference system [6, 9], and neural network [8].

However, identification of the normal and abnormal heart sound is still not a straightforward task, with a number of challenges to overcome. The first challenge is the feature extraction and selection to represent the heart sound properties. The features should provide distinguishing quantitative measures to classify the normal and abnormal heart sounds. The second challenge is the construction of the classifiers. Due to the limited

© Springer Nature Switzerland AG 2018
J. Zhou et al. (Eds.): CCBR 2018, LNCS 10996, pp. 536–544, 2018.
https://doi.org/10.1007/978-3-319-97909-0_57

amount of available data, there might be considerable amount of bias if the classifier was not conducted properly. The third challenge is that the database is not big enough. Most of the databases are less than or about 100 recordings.

The aim of this paper is to establish an efficient method to extract the features from pre-processed heart sound signals and identify the normal and abnormal heart sounds. The energy features of the heart sounds using wavelet technology are extracted and xgboost algorithm is used as the classifier. The paper is organized as follows. In Sect. 2, the structure diagram of heart sound identification system is designed, and the basic theories and realization process of the technologies used in this paper are introduced briefly. In Sect. 3, the actual heart sounds (including normal and abnormal heart sounds) are processed according to the proposed feature extraction method and identification method. Feature importance is also evaluated and evaluated. Finally, discussion and conclusion are presented in Sect. 4.

2 Methodology

The normal and abnormal heart sounds identification process we design is shown in Fig. 1, which consists of three parts: preprocessing, feature extraction and identification. In the next sections, the basic theories will be introduced respectively.

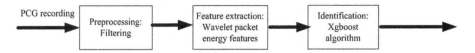

Fig. 1. Structure diagram of heart sound identification process

2.1 Wavelet Packet Decomposition

Wavelet transform (WT) can be used to decompose a signal into sub-bands with low frequency (approximate components) and sub-bands with high frequency (detail components) [10]. Although wavelet analysis has the characteristics of multi-resolution, it only breaks up as an approximation version, that is to say, in the WT, each level is calculated by passing only the previous wavelet approximation coefficients through the discrete-time low and high pass quadrature mirror filters. Wavelet packet decomposition (WPD) proposed by Wicker et al. has solved this problem. In the WPD, it has the same frequency bandwidth in each resolution.

Define sub-space U_j^n as the close packet space of function $u_n(t)$, then the orthogonal wavelet packet is defined as [3]

$$u_{2n}(t) = \sqrt{2} \sum_{k \in Z} h_k u_n(2t - k) \tag{1}$$

$$u_{2n+1}(t) = \sqrt{2} \sum_{k \in Z} g_k u_n(2t - k) \tag{2}$$

where h_k and g_k are the quadrature mirror filters associated with the predefined scaling function and mother wavelet function, respectively. The wavelet packet coefficients are given by:

$$d_{j,n}(k) = \int_{-\infty}^{+\infty} x(t) 2^{\frac{j}{2}} u_n(2^j t - k) dt \qquad (3)$$

where $x(t)$, j, k and n are the signal, scale, band and surge parameter, respectively.

Wavelet packet decomposition is to divide the band into several layers, and to select corresponding sub-band adaptively according to the characteristics of the signal analyzed, which will promote the time-frequency resolution. The structure of the 4-layer wavelet packet decomposition tree is shown in Fig. 2. Moving from top to bottom of Fig. 2, frequencies are divided into small segments. Each layer which emanates down and to the left of a node represents a low-pass filtering operation (h), and to the right a high-pass filtering operation (g). The nodes which have no further nodes emanating down are referred to as terminal nodes, leaves or sub-bands. The other nodes are referred to as non-terminal, or internal nodes. The first layer represents the original signal bandwidth. The other nodes are computed from their father by one application of either the low-pass or high-pass quadrature mirror filters. The bandwidth is 50% decreased with each filtering operation. In the bottom layer, each sub-band is a sixteenth of the original signal bandwidth. Thus, multi-resolution is achieved.

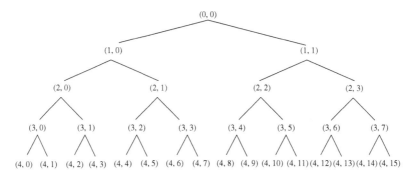

Fig. 2. Tree diagram of wavelet packet decomposition - depth 4

2.2   Extreme Gradient Boosting (Xgboost)

Xgboost [14, 15] is an improved algorithm based on the gradient boosting decision tree and can construct boosted trees efficiently and operate in parallel. This is a machine learning method that has been used by many data researchers, especially in a variety of data competitions and machine learning competitions, reflecting the performance is more superior than other methods.

Xgboost is used for supervised learning problems, where we use the training data (with multiple features) x_i to predict a target variable y_i. As described by Chen and Guestrin [15], Xgboost is an ensemble of K Classification and Regression Trees (CART) $\{T1(x_i, y_i)...TN(x_i, y_i)\}$ where x_i is the given training set of descriptors associated with a molecule to predict the class label, y_i. Given that a CART assigns a real score to each leaf (outcome or target), the prediction scores for individual CART is summed up to get the final score and evaluated through K additive functions, as shown in Eq. 4:

$$\hat{y}_i = \sum_{k=1}^{K} f_k(x_i), f_k \in F \tag{4}$$

where K is the number of trees, f_k is a function in the functional space F, and F is the space of all CART. And the objective function contain two parts: training loss and regularization, as shown in Eq. 5:

$$obj(\theta) = \sum_i l(y_i, \hat{y}_i) + \sum_{k=1}^{K} \Omega(f_k) \tag{5}$$

where l is a differentiable loss function which measures the difference between the predicted $\hat{y}_i$ and the target y_i. Ω is a regularization term which penalizes the complexity of the model to avoid over-fitting.

Since additive training is used, the prediction $\hat{y}_i$ at step t expressed as

$$\hat{y}_i(t) = \sum_{k=1}^{K} f_k(x_i) = \hat{y}_i(t-1) + f_t(x_i) \tag{6}$$

And tree boosting is used to Eq. 5, it can be written as

$$obj(\theta)(t) = \sum_i l(y_i, \hat{y}_i(t-1) + f_t(x_i)) + \Omega(f_t) \tag{7}$$

After a series of improvements and evolutions, Eq. 8 is derived, which is used to score a leaf node during splitting.

$$Gain = \frac{1}{2} \left[\frac{G_L^2}{H_L + \lambda} + \frac{G_R^2}{H_R + \lambda} - \frac{(G_L + G_R)^2}{H_L + H_R + \lambda} \right] - \gamma \tag{8}$$

where the first, second and third term of the equation stands for the score on the left, right and the original leaf respectively. Moreover, the final term, γ, is regularization on the additional leaf.

The most important factor behind the success of the xgboost is its scalability in all scenarios. The scalability of xgboost is due to several important systems and algorithmic optimizations. These innovations include: a new tree learning algorithm for dealing with sparse data; theoretically reasonable weighted quintile sketch program can handle instance weights in approximate tree learning. Parallel and distributed computing makes learning faster, enabling faster model exploration [15]. Although the xgboost is based on the classification and regression tree (CART) and the gradient boosting, xgboost is better than them because it integrates both the advantages.

3   Experimental Results and Discussion

3.1   Data Acquisition

The heart sound data are downloaded from Internet or collected in the authors' lab. The subject laid on his back on an examination bed and was kept under stable conditions. A sensor was placed on mitral site. ECG and heart sounds were recorded synchronously. The bandwidth of heart sounds is about 500 Hz. The aural environment in the lab was controlled to allow recording to be low-noise heart sounds. All heart sound data are preprocessed as follows. First, heart sound signals are filtered by linear low-pass filters whose stop frequency is 2 kHz. Second, heart sound signals are down sampled to 4 kHz. Third, heart sound signals are normalized. There is a total of 1136 heart sound recordings, given as.wav format, lasting from 5 s to 120 s. The recordings were divided into two types: normal and abnormal recordings with a confirmed cardiac diagnosis. The number "1" was used to present abnormal (568 recordings) and "−1" to present normal (568 recordings).

3.2   Feature Extraction Using Wavelet Packet Energy

In this paper, wavelet packet energy features are extracted from a heart sound recording. According to the characteristics of the heart sounds, they are divided into 4 layers, i.e. 16 frequency bands. They are 0–125 Hz, 126–250 Hz, 251–375 Hz, 376–500 Hz, 501–625 Hz, 626–750 Hz, 751–875 Hz, 876–1000 Hz, 1001–1125 Hz, 1126–1250 Hz, 1251–1375 Hz, 1376–1500 Hz, 1501–1625 Hz, 1626–1750 Hz, 1751–1875 Hz, 1876–2000 Hz. According to the general properties of representative normal wavelet family functions (including Daubechis, Coiflets, Symlets and so on) and former work of others [3, 13], Db6 is chosen as the wavelet type. The normal heart sound is shown in Fig. 3 and its wavelet packet energy features are shown in Fig. 4. We can see that after 4-layer decomposition, the energy of normal heart sound is mainly concentrated on the first four frequency bands. The first heart sound mainly exists in the first and second bands, i.e. 0–250 Hz. The second heart sound mainly exists in the first, second and third bands, i.e. 0–375 Hz. The abnormal heart sound is shown in Fig. 5 and its wavelet packet energy features are shown in Fig. 6. We can see that after 4-layer decomposition, the energy of abnormal heart sound is covered almost all the frequency bands.

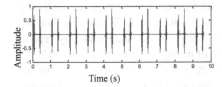

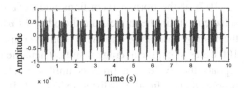

Fig. 3. A normal heart sound

Fig. 5. An abnormal heart sound

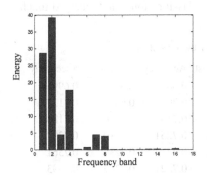

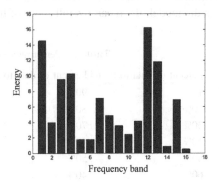

Fig. 4. Energy features of a normal heart sound

Fig. 6. Energy features of an abnormal heart sound

3.3   Identification Results

After extracting the wavelet packet energy features of the heart sounds, xgboost is implemented. In order to test the performance of the proposed method, identification accuracy, sensitivity and specificity are defined below [3]:

$$Accuracy = \frac{TP + TN}{TP + FP + FN + TN} \times 100\% \tag{9}$$

$$Sensitivity = \frac{TP}{TP + FN} \times 100\% \tag{10}$$

$$Specificity = \frac{TN}{FP + TN} \times 100\% \tag{11}$$

where TP is the number of true positives, which means that some subjects with abnormal heart sound are correctly identified as ones with abnormal heart sound; FN is the number of false negatives, which means that some subjects with abnormal heart sound are identified as healthy persons; TN is the number of true negatives, which means that some healthy persons are correctly identified as healthy persons; and FP is the number of false positives, which means that some healthy are identified as patients with abnormal heart sound.

10% of the normal recordings and 10% of the abnormal recordings are randomly selected to train the model, and the other 90% are to test the model. The training data and the testing data are exclusively non-overlapped. This program independently repeats 100 times to get the average results. Then, the rate of training data increases by 10% and repeats the evaluation process until the rate reaches 90%. The performance of the proposed classification is listed in Table 1. It can be found that, with the increasing rate of data to train, the accuracy, sensitivity and specificity all increase. This simulation proves that the proposed features and the model have good stability and are efficient to discriminate the heart sound recordings. To the proposed method, when 70% of data trains the model, the mean overall score of the classification is not changed much.

Table 1. Performance of the classification

Percent of data to train	Percent of data to test	Accuracy	Sensitivity	Specificity
10%	90%	0.6869	0.6742	0.6996
20%	80%	0.7004	0.6871	0.7137
30%	70%	0.7155	0.7126	0.7183
40%	60%	0.7251	0.7210	0.7292
50%	50%	0.7324	0.7286	0.7361
60%	40%	0.7321	0.7249	0.7393
70%	30%	0.7425	0.7382	0.7468
80%	20%	0.7423	0.7353	0.7492
90%	10%	0.7475	0.7442	0.7507

3.4   Feature Importance Evaluation

Xgboost constructs the boosted trees to intelligently obtain the feature scores, thereby indicating the importance of each feature to the training model [16]. The more a feature is used to make key decisions with boosted trees, the higher its score becomes. The algorithm counts out the importance by "gain", "frequency" and "cover". Gain is the main reference factor of the importance of a feature in tree branches. Frequency, which is simple version of gain, is the number of a feature in all constructed trees. Cover is the relative value of feature observation. In this study the feature importance is set by "frequency" because of its simpleness. The importance order of 16 features is shown in Table 2. It is shown that features in low frequency (wp1, 2, 3 and 4) are more important than those in high frequency (wp13, 14,15and 16) and the features in middle frequency (wp9, 10, 11 and 12) are less important. This is because most of the normal heart sounds' energy is concentrated on low frequency, and only abnormal ones have energy on high frequency.

The classification results with top 3, 6, 9, 12 and all features are shown in Table 3. 50% of the data (50% of the normal and abnormal data are selected respectively) are randomly selected to train, and the other 50% are used to test. It can be found that when top 9 features are used, the classification result is approximate with those using more features, which can reduce almost half of computation.

Table 2. The importance order of the features

The importance order of the features							
1	wp2	5	wp7	9	wp13	13	wp15
2	wp4	6	wp8	10	wp16	14	wp12
3	wp1	7	wp6	11	wp14	15	wp9
4	wp3	8	wp5	12	wp11	16	wp10

Table 3. Performance of the classification with different amount features

	Accuracy	Sensitivity	Specificity
Top 3 features	69.10	68.93	69.27
Top 6 features	71.51	71.36	71.66
Top 9 features	72.61	72.40	72.81
Top 12 features	72.53	72.43	72.63
All features (16)	73.24	73.61	72.86

4 Conclusion

In this paper, a normal and abnormal heart sounds identification method is proposed, which is based on wavelet packet energy and xgboost algorithm. The feature importance is also evaluated and analyzed. Top 3, 6, 9 and 12 features were used to classify the heart sounds. Experimental results showed that the proposed algorithm can identify the normal and abnormal heart sounds effectively. And the result used top 9 features was as good as that of all features, which can reduce almost half of computation. Moreover, the identification results of heart sounds also depend on the heart sound data, the selected training samples, the type of wavelet, and the kind of classifier. In future studies, we will focus on extracting more features and choosing more efficient classification methods to acquire better performance.

Acknowledgements. This work was supported in part by the National Natural Science Foundation of China under Grant Nos. 61601081, 61471081; Fundamental Research Funds for the Central Universities under Grant Nos. DC201501056, DCPY2016008, DUT15QY60, DUT16QY13; Dalian Youth Technology Star Project Supporting Plan under Grant No. 2015R091.

References

1. Plett, M.I.: Ultrasonic arterial vibrometry with wavelet based detection and estimation. Ph.D. thesis, University of Washington (2000)
2. Hanbay, D.: An expert system based on least square support vector machines for diagnosis of the valvular heart disease. Expert Syst. Appl. **36**, 4232–4238 (2009)
3. Wang, Y., Li, W., et al.: Identification of the normal and abnormal heart sounds using wavelet-time entropy features based on OMS-WPD. Future Gener. Comput. Syst. **37**, 488–495 (2014)

4. Sun, S.: An innovative intelligent system based on automatic diagnostic feature extraction for diagnosing heart diseases. Knowl. Based Syst. **75**, 224–238 (2015)
5. Chen, X., Ma, Y., et al.: Research on heart sound identification technology. Sci. Chin. Inf. Sci. **55**(2), 281–292 (2012)
6. Sengur, A.: An expert system based on linear discriminant analysis and adaptive neuro-fuzzy inference system to diagnosis heart valve diseases. Expert Syst. Appl. **35**, 214–222 (2008)
7. Avci, E., Turkoglu, I.: An intelligent diagnosis system based on principle component analysis and ANFIS for the heart valve diseases. Expert Syst. Appl. **36**, 2873–2878 (2009)
8. Das, R., Turkoglu, I., et al.: Diagnosis of valvular heart disease through neural networks ensembles. Comput. Methods Programs Biomed. **93**, 185–191 (2009)
9. Harun, U.: Adaptive neuro-fuzzy inference system for diagnosis of the heart valve diseases using wavelet transform with entropy. Neural Comput. Appl. **21**(7), 1617–1628 (2012)
10. Chen, T.H., Han, L.Q., et al.: Research of denoising method of heart sound signals based on wavelet transform. Comput. Simul. **12**(27), 401–405 (2010)
11. Bhatnagar, G., Wu, J., et al.: Fractional dual tree complex wavelet transform and its application to biometric security during communication and transmission. Future Gener. Comput. Syst. **28**(1), 254–267 (2012)
12. Hou, Y., Li, T.: Improvement of BP neural network by LM optimizing algorithm in target identification. J. Detect. Control **30**(1), 53–58 (2008). (in Chinese)
13. Cheng, X., Yang, H.: Analysis and comparison of five kinds of wavelet in processing heart sound signal. J. Nanjing Univ. Posts Telecommun. (Nat. Sci. Ed.) **35**(1), 38–46 (2015). (in Chinese)
14. Friedman, J.H.: Stochastic gradient boosting. Comput. Stat. Data Anal. **38**, 367–378 (2002)
15. Chen, T., Guestrin, C.: Xgboost: a scalable tree boosting system. In: ACM International Conference on Knowledge Discovery and Data Mining (2016)
16. Zheng, H., Yuan, J., Long, C.: Short-term load forecasting using EMD-LSTM neural networks with a Xgboost algorithm for feature importance evaluation. Energies **10**, 1168–1188 (2017)

Muscle Synergy Analysis for Stand-Squat and Squat-Stand Tasks with sEMG Signals

Chao Chen, Farong Gao$^{(\boxtimes)}$, Chunling Sun, and Qiuxuan Wu

School of Automation, Hangzhou Dianzi University, Hangzhou 310018, China
frgao@hdu.edu.cn

Abstract. Human walking is the composite movement of the musculoskeletal system in lower limbs. The interaction mechanism of the different muscle groups in a combination action is of great importance. To this end, under the stand-squat and squat-stand tasks, the problems of the motion model decomposition and the muscle synergy were studied in this paper. Firstly, the envelopes were extracted from acquired and de-noised surface electromyography (sEMG) signals. Secondly, the non-negative matrix factorization (NMF) algorithm was explored to decompose the four synergistic modules and the corresponding activation coefficients under the two tasks. Finally, the relationship between the muscle synergy and the lower limb movement was discussed in normal and fatigue subjects. The results show that muscle participation of each synergistic module is consistent with the physiological function, and exhibit some differences in muscle synergies between normal and fatigue states. This work can help to understand the control strategies of the nervous system in lower extremity motor and have some significance for the evaluation of limb rehabilitation.

Keywords: Lower extremity motor · sEMG signal · Muscle synergy
Envelope · NMF algorithm · Fatigue state

1 Introduction

Human walking movement is performed by the musculoskeletal system. For the body's motor system, on one hand, the skeletons serve as a support and bear the weight of the human body. On the other hand, the muscles, which are mainly composed of muscle fibers, have the function of contraction and relaxation [1]. There is an inseparable and close relationship between skeleton and muscle systems, it is particularly important to explore the mechanical coupling between muscle and skeleton [2].

Surface Electromyography (sEMG) signal is formed by superposition of action potentials on the skin surface with the joint motion and muscle activity [3], which can be applied in fields such as rehabilitation medicine, sports science, pattern recognition, etc. Muscle synergy analyzes movement characteristics and perceptual behavior

This work is supported in part by National Natural Science Foundation of China (U1509203) and Zhejiang Provincial Natural Science Foundation (LY16F030007).

J. Zhou et al. (Eds.): CCBR 2018, LNCS 10996, pp. 545–552, 2018.
https://doi.org/10.1007/978-3-319-97909-0_58

patterns, reveals central nervous system (CNS) motion control strategies to evaluate human motor function by means of sEMG during limb locomotion [4]. The classification algorithms of EMG-based gait recognition were also improved by taking into account the classification accuracy, adaptability, and individual difference [5–7].

In recent years, muscle synergy analysis has been presented in the rehabilitation engineering, clinical medicine etc. Synergetic movement [8] is controlled by the nervous system adaptively recruiting a series of muscle activation commands to control skeletal muscles to perform various motion tasks. Chen et al. [9] investigated the inter-limb and intra-limb muscle coordination mechanism of human hands-and-knees during crawling through sEMG signals. Bejarano et al. [10] used muscle synergies to investigate the muscle organization in rectilinear and curvilinear walking and the variety in different walking condition. NMF algorithm provides a possibility for decomposing complex sEMG data into simpler components to describe the muscles' role in certain task [11]. Lee and Seung theoretically [12] proved the convergence of the NMF algorithm on this basis, and got multiplication iterative rules.

In this paper, the relationship of the motion model and the muscle synergy was analyzed for the tasks in the stand-squat and squat-stand conditions. The study of synergistic structures can help to distinguish the movement pattern and understand the movement mechanism.

2   Principles and Methods

2.1   Envelope Extraction

Filtering refers to removing the noise signals from a specific frequency band and restores as much real information as possible. The commonly method for designing FIR filters is the window function method. Equation (1) is the ideal filter. Assume that the phase-frequency characteristic is $\varphi(\omega) = 0$ and the cut-off frequency ω_c. The window function method is utilized to design FIR low-pass filters as follows.

$$h_d(n) = \frac{1}{2\pi} \int_{-\omega_c}^{\omega_c} H_d(e^{j\omega}) e^{jn\omega} d\omega = \frac{1}{2\pi} \int_{-\omega_c}^{\omega_c} e^{jn\omega} d\omega = \frac{\sin(n\omega_c)}{n\pi} \tag{1}$$

The transfer formula for $h(n)$ is as follows.

$$h(n) = \frac{\sin[(n - M/2)\omega_c]}{(n - M/2)\pi} w(n - M/2), n = 0, 1, \ldots, M \tag{2}$$

In Eq. (2), $h(n)$ is the causal system of frequency response linear phase. The truncation is equivalent to adding a rectangular window function to $h_d(n)$ and window function in $w(n)$. High-pass filter can also be designed in mentioned method. Usually the sEMG is used to extract the muscle activity or envelope information [13].

2.2 NMF Algorithm

The non-negative matrix factorization (NMF) algorithm is used to reduce the high-dimensional random pattern to a low-dimensional random pattern while keeping information as constant as possible. The NMF solution can be written as a standard form of the optimization problem.

$$\begin{cases} \min\limits_{W,H} \frac{1}{2} \|M - WH\|_F^2 \\ \text{s.t. } M \geq 0, W \geq 0, H \geq 0 \end{cases} \tag{3}$$

Where $\|\cdot\|_F^2$ represents the Frobenius norm. The synergy elements reflect the proportion of each muscle's participation, and the activation coefficient of an element is the degree of activation. The non-negative nature of NMF makes the analysis results more in line with physiological phenomena, and it is easy to explain the phenomenon of synergistic meta-activity at the muscle level.

2.3 Muscle Synergy Principles

During the movement of the human body, multiple muscle-skeletal degrees of freedom work together to form control units with coupling and low-dimensional features through the central nervous system [14]. These control units are known as synergy. Synergy produces the movement of the corresponding joints. Based on the muscle synergy theory, the expression of the sEMG signal through the matrix is expressed as follows.

$$M_{N \times T} \approx W_{N \times K} \times H_{K \times T} = \begin{bmatrix} w_1 & w_2 & \cdots & w_K \end{bmatrix} \times \begin{bmatrix} h_1 \\ h_2 \\ \cdots \\ h_K \end{bmatrix} = \sum_{i=1}^{K} w_i h_i \tag{4}$$

In Eq. (4), $M_{N \times T}$ expresses the envelope of the sEMG signal, $W_{N \times K} = [w_{i1}, w_{i2}, \cdots, w_{in}]$ $(i = n)$ denotes the synergistic structure matrix, w_{in} represents the magnitude of the amplitude indicates the muscle contributes in the combined pattern; $H_{K \times T} = [h_{1j}, h_{2j}, \cdots, h_{kj}]$ $(j = t)$ expresses the activation of coefficient matrix, which represents the contribution of each muscle synergy to the overall excitation of a muscle; K is unknown, it can be determined by the size of the matrix of the factor matrix reconstruction and the accuracy of the original matrix. Using the variability accounted for (VAF) [15] as a figure of merit. The coefficient size is measured as shown in Eq. (5).

$$VAF = 1 - \frac{\sum\limits_{i,j} (M - M_r)_{ij}^2}{\sum\limits_{i,j} M_{ij}^2} \tag{5}$$

In which, M represents original matrix, and M_r denotes reconstruction matrix. The VAF parameters range is from 0 to 1 [16]. When the value of the VAF parameter is greater than a certain threshold, it can be considered that muscle synergy in current number can reconstruct the original myoelectric signal.

3   Experiments and Data Processing

3.1   Signal Acquisition

Considering the effects of the movement and measurement in lower limb motion, 6 representative muscles were selected [17]. 7 young men (age: 24 ± 1.5 years, height: 1.68 ± 0.08 m, weight: 65 ± 6.2 kg) were selected with normal gaits and no history of any disease. Before the test, 75% medical alcohol was used to clean the skin. The acquisition module was uniformly placed along the direction of the muscle fibers as shown in Fig. 1. The sEMG signals and its functions are shown in Table 1.

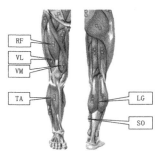

Fig. 1. The distribution of selected muscles

In experiments, the EMG data were acquired by using Delsys's Trigno wireless surface EMG acquisition system. The sampling frequency was set to 2000 Hz. The upper body of the normal group remained upright and completed the stand-squat and squat-stand tasks. After the data of the normal group were collected, the subjects continued to perform the squat motion for several minutes until the muscles in the leg were tired and could no longer be picked up [18].

Table 1. Function of selected muscles of the lower limb

Number	Muscle name	Functions
1	Vastus Medialis (VM)	Extensor of knee joint, hip joint flexion
2	Soleus (SO)	Ankle joint extensor, plantar flexion, standing
3	Tibialis Anterior (TA)	Ankle joint flexor, dorsiflexion of foot
4	Lateral Gastrocnemius (LG)	Extensor of ankle joint, foot swing and support
5	Vastus Lateralis (VL)	Extensor of knee joint, hip flexion
6	Rectus Femoris (RF)	Knee extensor, extension leg, hip flexor, flexor thigh

3.2 Envelope Extraction

In this paper, firstly, a high-pass filter is used to remove noise from the original sEMG. Then average value is removed by full-wave-rectified and disposed by low-pass-filtered. Finally, the maximum value of the channel's muscle envelope signal is normalized. The cut off frequencies are 200 Hz and 4 Hz. The envelopes of the stand-squat and squat-stand are shown in Fig. 2. The horizontal axis represents the number of sampling points and the vertical axis represents the amplitude of the signal.

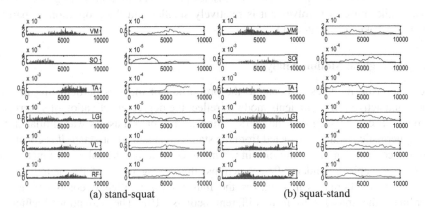

Fig. 2. Envelope extraction in stand-squat (a) and squat-stand (b)

4 Results and Discussion

4.1 Synergies and Activity Coefficients

Based on the NMF method, four synergistic modules can be extracted by reconstructing the original signal according to the Eq. (5). The synergies and activity coefficients of the normal groups are shown in Fig. 3.

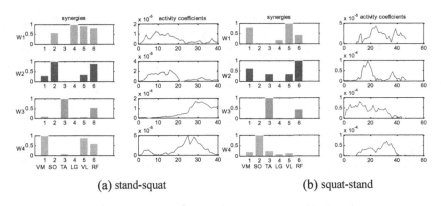

Fig. 3. The synergies and activation coefficients in two tasks

In Fig. 3, four synergies modules (W1, W2, W3, W4) were extracted based on all tasks to reach the 90% VAF standard. The horizontal axis represents the period ratio and the vertical axis represents activation coefficients amplitude. The muscle function of the lower movement meets the human muscle physiological function. Under the motion of stand-squat, the synergistic phenomenon in the modules W1, W2, and W4 are obvious. The LG, VL and RF muscles in the W1 module have a synergistic relationship; muscular participation is weaker in module W3. The same way in the squat-stand, the synergy phenomenon is more obvious in the W1 and W2 modules. From the two tasks, it can be seen that muscles participate in more synergies in stand-squat, while muscles involvement is relatively smaller and the proportion of participation is weaker in squat-stand.

4.2   Synergistic Motion Analysis

The synergistic modules response to the proportion of muscles participating in each block, and activation coefficients modules reflect the degree of activation of synergistic elements. It can be seen that the participation of the main muscles was similar in the four synergistic modules extracted from the stand-squat and squat-stand. It is consistent with the comparison of the muscles in the modules with the physiological functions of muscles in Table 1. Under different actions, the coding mode of the neural control movement is different, which makes the muscles form different combinations and coordinate the muscles to form different actions [19]. The activation coefficients extracted by the above method has a good correspondence in the actual motion categories. The activation coefficient does not fully reflect the fact that it is not completely decoupled. This is consistent with muscle synergy theory [20].

4.3   Synergistic Analysis in Fatigue

In order to further study the influence of fatigue factors on the synergistic structure and activation coefficients. In fatigue, the MF and MPF values also decrease accordingly [21]. The sEMG signals in our experiments can satisfy the characteristics. Synergies and activation coefficients in fatigue for two tasks are shown in Fig. 4.

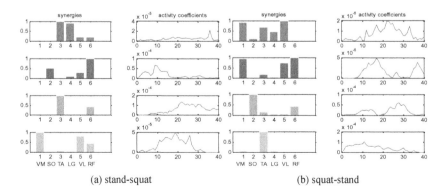

(a) stand-squat   (b) squat-stand

Fig. 4. The synergistic analysis in fatigue of two tasks

The participation of muscles in the modules is consistent with the physiological functions of muscles in Table 1. Comparing the stand-squat and squat-stand tasks of the normal group in Fig. 3 and the fatigue group in Fig. 4, it was found that the difference in W1 is significant. The proportion of LG, VL and RF involved in module W1 is relatively high, while that of the module in the fatigue group is mainly TA and LG. Meanwhile muscle participation in modules W2, W3, and W4 is relatively close. Taking the W2 module as an example, the VM and VL muscles of the normal group are relatively lower in participation, but the fatigue group is actually increased. Corresponding to the participation of other modules, the muscles are changed. In the flexion and extension motion of the lower limb, the muscle synergy mode is embodied as a module with similar functions.

5 Conclusions

Lower limb movement is a complicated movement in which multiple muscles participate in each other. Based on the theory of synergy, this paper extracted the synergies and activity coefficients in stand-squat and squat-stand tasks between the normal group and the fatigue group. It can be seen that muscular participation of each synergistic module is consistent with the physiological action. The synergistic module responds to the movement mechanism, and the interaction between the muscles in module makes up a synergy. In fatigue state, some of the modules involved in the muscles differ from the normal group, while the muscles involved in the overall movement are consistent. The study of synergistic structures can help to distinguish the movement pattern and understand the movement mechanism in human walking.

References

1. Berchtold, M.W., Brinkmeier, H., Müntener, M.: Calcium ion in skeletal muscle: its crucial role for muscle function, plasticity, and disease. Physiol. Rev. **80**, 1215–1225 (2000)
2. Hopkins, P.M.: Skeletal muscle physiology. Continuing Educ. Anaesth. Crit. Care Pain **6**, 1–6 (2006)
3. Pan, L., Zhang, D., Liu, J., Sheng, X., Zhu, X.: Continuous estimation of finger joint angles under different static wrist motions from surface EMG signals. Biomed. Sig. Process. Control **14**, 265–271 (2014)
4. Berger, D.J., D'Avella, A.: Effective force control by muscle synergies. Front. Comput. Neurosci. **8**, 46–57 (2014)
5. Gao, F.R., Wang, J.J., Xi, X.G., She, Q.S., Luo, Z.Z.: Gait recognition for lower extremity ElectroMyoGraphic signals based on PSO-SVM method. J. Electron. Inf. Technol. **37**, 1154–1159 (2015)
6. Wang, J.J., Gao, F.R., Sun, Y., Luo, Z.Z.: Non-uniform characteristics and its recognition effects for walking gait based on sEMG. Chin. J. Sens. Actuators **29**, 384–389 (2016)
7. Li, Y., Gao, F.R., Chen, H.H., Xu, M.H.: Gait recognition based on EMG with different individuals and sample sizes. In: 35th Chinese Control Conference (CCC) on Proceedings, pp. 4068–4072 (2016)

8. Julien, F., François, H.: Between-subject variability of muscle synergies during a complex motor skill. Front. Comput. Neurosci. **6**, 49–58 (2012)
9. Chen, X., Niu, X., Wu, D., Yu, Y., Zhang, X.: Investigation of the intra- and inter-limb muscle coordination of hands-and-knees crawling in human adults by means of muscle synergy analysis. Entropy **19**, 229 (2017)
10. Chia, B.N., et al.: Tuning of muscle synergies during walking along rectilinear and curvilinear trajectories in humans. Ann. Biomed. Eng. **45**, 1–15 (2017)
11. Gizzi, L., Muceli, S., Petzke, F., Falla, D.: Experimental muscle pain impairs the synergistic modular control of neck muscles. PLoS ONE **10**, 399–412 (2015)
12. Yang, S., Mao, Y.: Global minima analysis of Lee and Seung's NMF algorithms. Neural Process. Lett. **38**, 29–51 (2013)
13. D'Alessio, T., Conforto, S.: Extraction of the envelope from surface EMG signals. IEEE Eng. Med. Biol. Mag. Q. Mag. Eng. Med. Biol. Soc. **20**, 55–83 (2001)
14. Steele, K.M., Tresch, M.C., Perreault, E.J.: The number and choice of muscles impact the results of muscle synergy analyses. Front. Comput. Neurosci. **7**, 105–114 (2013)
15. Clark, D.J., Ting, L.H., Zajac, F.E., Neptune, R.R., Kautz, S.A.: Merging of healthy motor modules predicts reduced locomotor performance and muscle coordination complexity post-stroke. J. Neurophysiol. **103**, 844 (2010)
16. Stein, R.B., et al.: Coding of position by simultaneously recorded sensory neurones in the cat dorsal root ganglion. J. Physiol. **560**, 883–896 (2004)
17. Miranda, E.F., Malaguti, C., Marchetti, P.H., Dal, C.S.: Upper and lower limb muscles in patients with COPD: similarities in muscle efficiency but differences in fatigue resistance. Respir. Care **59**, 62–69 (2013)
18. Cifrek, M., Medved, V., Tonković, S., Ostojić, S.: Surface EMG based muscle fatigue evaluation in biomechanics. Clin. Biomech. **24**, 327–340 (2009)
19. Thaler, L., Goodale, M.A.: Neural substrates of visual spatial coding and visual feedback control for hand movements in allocentric and target-directed tasks. Front. Hum. Neurosci. **5**, 92–115 (2011)
20. Tsuji, T., Shima, K., Murakami, Y.: Pattern classification of combined motions based on muscle synergy theory. J. Rob. Soc. Jpn. **28**, 606–613 (2010)
21. Danuta, R.L.: The influence of confounding factors on the relationship between muscle contraction level and MF and MPF values of EMG signal: a review. Int. J. Occup. Saf. Ergon. **22**, 77–91 (2016)

ECG Based Biometric by Superposition Matrix in Unrestricted Status

Gang Zheng[✉], Xiaoxia Sun, Shengzhen Ji, Min Dai, and Ying Sun

TianJin Key Laboratory of Intelligence Computing and Novel
Software Technology, Tianjin University of Technology,
Tianjin 300384, People's Republic of China
kenneth_zheng@vip.163.com, sxx15757118176@163.com,
shulinji@163.com, {daimin,sunying}@tjut.edu.cn

Abstract. The paper proposed an Electrocardiogram (ECG) feature extraction method for biometric. It relied on ECG superposition number matrix built by several single heartbeat ECG data. The target of the study was to find stable features of the ECG signal under unrestricted status for biometric. By matrix segmentation and similarity comparison, the stable feature distribution was gotten, and stable feature sets were also constructed. 13 volunteers' ECG data collected by self-made ECG device in different status were gotten, the collecting period was lasting for half year; 28 healthy individuals' ECG data under calm status were also collected; Besides that, 14 subjects' ECG data in MIT-BIH were also involved in study. From the result of experiments, the average True Positive Rate (TPR) reached 83.21%, 83.93% and 80% on MIT data set, ECG data set in calm status and ECG data in different status respectively. It is also found that along with the increasing amount of ECG single heartbeat used to build superposition matrix, the stable features of one's ECG were gradually revealed and this helped ECG based biometric effectively.

Keywords: ECG biometric · Unrestricted status · Identity authentication
Superposition matrix

1 Introduction

Biometric authentication/identification technology has becoming a hot topic, in the field like, face [1], fingerprint [2], iris [3] and so on. ECG waveform reflects heart electric activities by voltage changing [4]. Since ECG waveform can only exist on living creature, it can hardly be forged, and this character makes it unique to other biometric. The studies of it on biometric have lasting over 20 years. Studies carried out in two directions, one was on ECG fiducial features, and the other was on non-fiducial features [5]. In fiducial features studies, combination of temporal, amplitude, angle between or among peak or valley points of ECG waveform and time length of heartbeat (R-R interval, changeable) were used [6–9]. The biometric accuracy rate was tightly related to the recognition accuracy of peak and valley point on ECG waveform. In non-fiducial features studies, all amplitude value of single or a period of ECG waveform were used. Some frequency features were added [10–13].

© Springer Nature Switzerland AG 2018
J. Zhou et al. (Eds.): CCBR 2018, LNCS 10996, pp. 553–561, 2018.
https://doi.org/10.1007/978-3-319-97909-0_59

Except the previous achievement, there still existed difficulties. Scholars have been very successful in the study of ECG biometric public ECG data or data under calm status, but not under unrestricted status needs further study. For that, stale features which are not affected by different status, are need to be further study.

The paper spent six months to collect ECG data of different people in different status as experimental data continuously. On these ECG data, a feature extraction method based on ECG superposition matrix was proposed to find ECG stable features. From that, ECG biometric accuracy was improved under zero False Positive Rate (FPR) condition.

2   Superposition Matrix Based ECG Feature Extraction

2.1   Data Set Definition

In the paper, $A = \{(X_i, Y_i)\}_{i=1}^n$ was assumed as training set, it was composed of n single periodic ECG signals as input data. Xi stands for i^{th} ECG signal, it was composed of m amplitude value, $X_i = \{x_1^j, x_2^j \cdots, x_m^j\}$, and Yi was test data tag.

2.2   Construction of ECG Superposition Matrix

Firstly, single periodic ECG data Xi was mapped to a two-dimensional matrix E (rows m, columns c), c corresponds to the data resolution of the ECG data, the amplitude of the sample point xc represents the row number of the matrix, m was corresponded to the sample point of ECG data, xm represents the row number of the matrix. If the amplitude of the bth sample point xb of Xi is x, its' corresponding coordinates in the two-dimensional matrix is (x, b), The matrix adds 1 to the corresponding value E(x, b) at (x, b), Such as formula (1).

$$E(x, b) = E(x, b) + 1 \tag{1}$$

By continuously superimposing ECG data, the corresponding distribution features in the matrix are constantly changing, and the distribution characteristics were becoming more and more obviously, the procedure can be seen in Fig. 1.

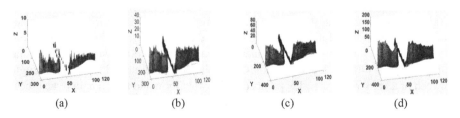

(a)   (b)   (c)   (d)

Fig. 1. Superposition matrix histograms, (a), (b), (c), (d) are three-dimensional images of the ECG superposition matrix constructed with 10, 100, 500, and 1000 single heartbeat ECG signals respectively. The X-axis and Y-axis correspond to the rows and columns of the matrix, and the Z-axis corresponds to the values of the superposition matrix.

2.3   Feature Extraction by Superposition Matrix

(1) Matrix division. Suppose, the ECG template library E is composed of f superposition matrices, $E_1,\ldots, E_f$, E_j represents the jth template matrix in E, $1 \leq j \leq f$. E_j is divided into 3 * 3 sized submatrices e from coordinates (1, 1), as shown formula (2), shown in Fig. 2, the number of that is d, $d = (m * c)/9$, m is the number of row, and c is the number of column

$$
E_j = \begin{bmatrix} e^j_{\frac{m \cdot c}{9} - \frac{c}{3}} & \cdots & e^j_d \\ \vdots & \ddots & \vdots \\ e^j_1 & \cdots & e^j_{\frac{m}{3}} \end{bmatrix} \tag{2}
$$

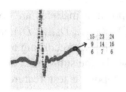

Fig. 2. Matrix diagram

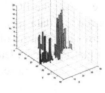

Fig. 3. 3-D schematic diagram of matrix T

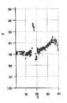

Fig. 4. 2-D schematic diagram of distribution of sub-matrices

(2) Where e^j_d represents the dth 3 * 3 sub-matrix, shown in formula (3).

$$
e^j_d = \begin{bmatrix} E_j(m-2, c-2) & \cdots & E_j(m-2, c) \\ \vdots & \ddots & \vdots \\ E_j(m, c-2) & \cdots & E_j(m, c) \end{bmatrix} \tag{3}
$$

(3) Sub-matrix similarity comparison. Compared the corresponding sub-matrices between template and input ECG data, the result S was shown in formula (4), the threshold Sr is given, and the all-zero matrix T (m/3 rows, c/3 columns) is used to store the sub-matrix comparison results. If S > Sr, the value at the corresponding coordinates in the matrix T is incremented by one, as formula (4). And a three-dimensional schematic diagram of the matrix T is shown in Fig. 3.

$$
\begin{cases} S = \text{Math}\left(e^j_d, e^1_d\right) \\ T\left(\frac{m}{3}, \frac{c}{3}\right) = T\left(\frac{m}{3}, \frac{c}{3}\right) + 1 \quad S > S_r \end{cases} \tag{4}
$$

(4) Stable area extraction. The coordinate information of the point which value is larger than $g/2(g = f - 1)$ was calculated, and the submatrix corresponding to the coordinate point is selected to form a feature set M, as shown in formula (5).

$$M = (\ldots, e_n^1, \ldots) 1 \le n \le d \tag{5}$$

As shown in Fig. 4 the X-axis and the Y-axis respectively correspond to the corresponding coordinates of the sub-matrices satisfying the conditions in the superposition matrix of the electrocardiogram signals. The small squares in the figure represent the sub-matrices satisfying the value greater than g/2 in the matrix T.

2.4   ECG Authentication

The procedure for the ECG authentication method is shown below,

(1) According to the method in Sect. 2.2, the ECG superposition matrices are constructed by ECG signals to form a test data set $D^* = (D_1, D_2, \ldots, D_h, \ldots, D_k)$, and D_h represents the hth ECG superposition matrix of D^*, $1 \le h \le k$. According to the position information of the sub-matrices in the feature set M, the sub-matrix at the same position of the test matrix D_h is extracted to compose a test feature set $M_h = (\ldots d_n^h \ldots)$.
(2) Compute the similarity of sub matrix in M and M_h, shown in formula (6).

$$S = Math(d_n^h, e_n^1) \tag{6}$$

S is similarity, S_r is predefined threshold, if $S > S_r$, d_n^h is matched successfully, otherwise, match is fail.
(3) t was the number of successfully matched sub-matrices in test feature set M_h. l was the number of sub-matrices in training feature set M. If $t > l/2$, the hth sub matrix is authenticated, whereas the authentication was fail.

In the experiment, 10 subjects were selected from self-collected ECG signal data and MIT public dataset randomly, each of which has 1000 heartbeats, each 100 of that constructed an ECG superposition matrix, one matrix of each subject was chose as the template matrix, the remaining matrix were used as for testing. The matrix segmentation and similarity calculation function were identical in authentication method. The similarity between the test matrix and the template sub matrix was calculated by angle cosine, and K-nearest neighbor algorithm was used to determine the label of the sub Matrix, and calculated the similarity coefficients of correct labeled test data. Through observation, the range of the similarity coefficients of the correct matrices was in [0.91, 0.95] on self-collected ECG data, and [0.93, 0.96] on MIT data. After calculating their mathematical expectations separately, S_r is assigned 0.93 and 0.95 on self-collected data and MIT data respectively.

3   Experiment and Analysis

3.1   Data Description

The experimental data used in this paper comes from the MIT-BIH public dataset and the Self-collecting ECG dataset. The sampling rate of the MIT-BIH dataset is 360 Hz, the self-acquired ECG data is collected using laboratory-made ECG signal acquisition device, and its sampling rate is 250 Hz. the Self-collecting ECG datasets were in three groups:

(1)   Self-collecting ECG data set in calm status: 28 healthy persons, (named h1 to h28) aged between 22 and 26 years old. The collection status is calm, and the collection time is 40 min.
(2)   Subjects of MIT-BIH dataset (named M1 to M14)
(3)   Self-collecting ECG signal sets under different emotional status: different emotion status data (pressure and calm, good/poor sleep, healthy/discomfort, hunger/satisfaction) that derived from Zheng Gang's team [14], the volunteers were 19 healthy people (named U1 to U13), aged between 22 and 26 years old. The data collected for each period of time were 4 min each under different emotional status.

There are two experiment schemes in the paper, shown below,

Exp.1: 10 single-period ECG signals are superimposed to construct an ECG signal superposition matrix. 10 matrices of each person were selected as the training set. 20 matrices of each person were selected as the positive sample test set, select 20 matrices from other's test matrices used as a negative sample test set.
Exp.2: 100 single-period ECG signals are superimposed to construct an ECG signal superposition matrix. 10 matrices of each person were selected as the training set. 20 matrices of each person were selected as the positive sample test set, select 20 matrices from other's test matrices used as a negative sample test set.

3.2   Evaluation Standard

True Positive (TP), when test sample is positive, the test result is positive; FN: False Negative (FN), when test sample is positive, the test result is negative; False Positive (FP), when test sample is negative, the test result is positive; True Negative (TN), when test sample is negative, the test result is negative.

TPR: True Positive Rate, shown in formula (7).

$$TPR = TP/(TP + FN) \tag{7}$$

FPR: False Positive Rate, shown in formula (8).

$$FPR = FP/(FP + TN) \tag{8}$$

Since TPR is inversely proportional to FNR, and FPR is inversely proportional to TNR, TPR and FPR are used to measure accuracy in experiments.

3.3   Analysis of Experimental Results

Results of above experiment were shown in Fig. 5, from which, the TPR for authentication using ECG superposition matrix constructed by 100 single periodic ECG signals is much higher than that constructed by 10 single periodic ECG signals, and the FPR is zero.

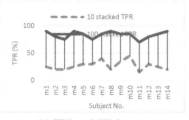

(a) TPR on MIT datasets

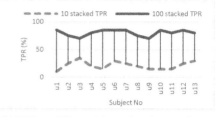

(b) TPR on differential emotional status dataset

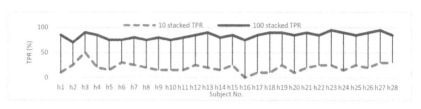

(c) TPR on Self-collecting Dataset in calm status

Fig. 5. TPR on different dataset

Table 1. Average TPR (%) and FPR (%) for authentication on different datasets

Data set	10 stacked TPR	10 stacked FPR	100 stacked TPR	100 stacked FPR
MIT	27.14	2.50	83.21	0.00
calm	20.36	1.61	83.93	0.00
Unrestricted status	21.54	2.69	80.00	0.00

According to Table 1, the features extracted by the ECG superposition matrix constructed with a small amount of ECG signals are very few, the stable characteristics of the ECG signal can't be extracted effectively, and the authentication experiment fails. Under zero FPR, the experiment used ECG superposition matrix constructed by 100 single periodic ECG signals carried out on MIT-BIH data set, self-collecting ECG data set in calm status and self-collecting ECG signal data set in unrestricted status, and the average TPR reached 83.21%, 83.93% and 80% respectively. It proved the effectiveness of the feature extraction method based on the ECG superposition matrix, and can effectively extract the stable characteristics of the ECG signal in unrestricted status and complete the authentication.

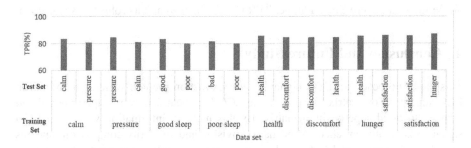

Fig. 6. TPR on different dataset

Table 2. The average TPR (%) of ECG authentication in different status

Training set (mixed data)	Calm/pressure	Good sleep/poor sleep	Health/discomfort	Hunger/satisfaction
Test set (mixed data)				
TPR	85.09	82.82	84.62	85.64

Figure 6 showed that TPR on all status were all around 80%, no matter the training data set or test data set were in different emotional status. And from Table 2, it can be found that if different status data were mixed as training and test data set, the TPR were in same level from 82% to 85%. That was means that different status did little efforts in ECG based biometric.

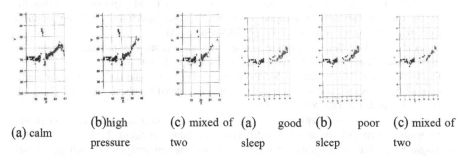

(a) calm   (b)high pressure   (c) mixed of two   (a) good sleep   (b) poor sleep   (c) mixed of two

Fig. 7. Characteristic distribution of ECG data in different emotional status

Fig. 8. Distribution of ECG data in different sleep quality status

Comparing Fig. 7 with Fig. 8, if a single status was used as the training set, the distribution of the stable features is partially different. But if mixed data (calm and high pressure) were used as the training set, the extracted stable features are the intersections of the stable feature distribution in two single status. There was only a small number of differences among different status. The feature extraction method proposed in this paper can negate the doubts about the reliability of ECG biometric under different status. Under the permission of zero FPR, a higher TPR rate is obtained and its robustness was good.

4 Conclusion and Future Study

This paper proposed an ECG signal feature extraction method which was based on ECG superposition matrix. Several single ECG heartbeat data were superimposed and mapped to build superposition matrix. By this method, information volume of ECG signals was greatly enriched. After matrix division and similarity comparison, features of stable distribution of ECG signals were extracted to achieve authentication. On all three experiments, average TPR were all reached over 80%. And furthermore, the experiment result showed that the effectiveness of authentication in different emotional status and sleep quality were slightly different, the average TPR remained at 80%, and most of the features remained stable.

The feature extraction method based on the ECG signal superposition matrix proposed in this paper requires a large number of single heartbeat ECG signals as the training set. Therefore, how to use a small amount of ECG data to extract the stable features of ECG under unrestricted status is the next research step in the future.

Acknowledgment. The paper is supported by TianJin National Science Foundation 16JCYBJC15300 (2016.04-2019.03).

References

1. Ghazi, M.M., Ekenel, H.K.: A comprehensive analysis of deep learning based representation for face recognition. In: Computer Vision and Pattern Recognition Workshops, pp. 102–109 (2016)
2. Ali, M.M.H., Mahale, V.H., Yannawar, P., Gaikwad, A.T.: Fingerprint recognition for person identification and verification based on minutiae matching. IEEE International Conference on Advanced Computing, pp. 332–339 (2016)
3. Garagad, V.G., Iyer, N.C.: A novel technique of iris identification for biometric systems. In: International Conference on Advances in Computing, pp. 973–978 (2014)
4. Ramos, J., Ausín, J.L., Lorido, A.M., Redondo, F., Duque-Carrillo, J.F.: A wireless multi-channel bioimpedance measurement system for personalized healthcare and lifestyle. Stud. Health Technol. Inf. **189**, 59–67 (2013)
5. Odinaka, I., Lai, P.H., Kaplan, A.D., O'Sullivan, J.A., Sirevaag, E.J.: ECG biometric recognition: a comparative analysis. IEEE Trans. Inf. Forensics Secur. **7**, 1812–1814 (2012)
6. Singh, Y.N.: Human recognition using Fisher's discriminant analysis of heartbeat interval features and ECG morphology. Neurocomputing **167**, 322–335 (2015)

7. Hamdi, T., Ben Slimane, A., Ben Khalifa, A.: A novel feature extraction method in ECG biometrics. In: Image Processing, Applications and Systems Conference, pp. 1–5 (2014)
8. Paulet, M.V., Salceanu, A., Salceanu, A.: Automatic recognition of the person by ECG signals characteristics. In: International Symposium on Advanced Topics in Electrical Engineering (ATEE), pp. 281–284 (2015)
9. Choi, H.S., Lee, B., Yoon, S.: Biometric authentication using noisy electrocardiograms acquired by mobile sensors. IEEE Access **4**, 1266–1273 (2016)
10. Zhang, Y., Shi, Y.: A new method for ECG biometric recognition using a hierarchical scheme classifier. In: IEEE International Conference on Software Engineering and Service Science, pp. 457–460 (2015)
11. Tantawi, M.M., Revett, K., Salem, A.B., Tolba, M.F.: A wavelet feature extraction method for electrocardiogram (ECG)-based biometric recognition. Sig. Image Video Process. **9**, 1271–1280 (2015)
12. Page, A., Kulkarni, A., Mohsenin, T.: Utilizing deep neural nets for an embedded ECG-based biometric authentication system. In: Biomedical Circuits and Systems Conference, pp. 1–4 (2015)
13. Jahiruzzaman, M., Hossain, A.B.M.A.: ECG based biometric human identification using chaotic encryption. In: International Conference on Electrical Engineering and Information Communication Technology (2015)
14. Zheng, G., Chen, Y., Dai, M.: HRV based stress recognizing by random forest. Fuzzy Syst. Data Min. II, 444–458 (2016)

Ear Alignment Based on Convolutional Neural Network

Li Yuan[1(⊠)], Haonan Zhao[1], Yi Zhang[1], and Zeyu Wu[2]

[1] School of Automation and Electrical Engineering,
University of Science and Technology Beijing, Beijing, China
lyuan@ustb.edu.cn
[2] School of Artificial Intelligence,
Hebei University of Technology, Tianjing, China

Abstract. The ability of biometric systems has recently been dramatically improved by the emergency of deep learning. In the process of ear verification, the accuracy is often lower than expected because of the influence of pose variation and occlusion. In this paper, we propose a novel ear alignment approach. According to the morphological characteristics and the geometric characteristics of the ear, we define six key points on the ear, three located in the inner ear region, and three located on the outer contour of the ear. In order to detect these key points on the ear image automatically, we train a cascaded convolutional neural network using our newly released USTB-Helloear database. Then the alignment of the test ear image is accomplished by radiological transformation which will minimize the mean square error of the six key points between the test image and the template image. Experimental results show that using ear alignment, the accuracy of the ear verification system can be improved.

Keywords: Ear verification · Cascaded convolutional neural network
Ear alignment · USTB-Helloear

1 Introduction

In recent years, as an emerging biometric identification technology, ear recognition has received more and more attention [1–4]. The ear recognition system is composed of structures such as ear detection, ear alignment, feature extraction, ear recognition/ear verification and so on; the research on ear alignment is relatively rare.

As we all know, deep convolutional neural networks have made great progress in face recognition [5–8]. Naturally, we would like to apply convolutional neural networks to ear recognition. In real applications, occlusion, lighting and pose variations are very common. Therefore, ear recognition under uncontrolled conditions is an urgent problem to be solved. The previous ear image database [9] has limited changes in lighting and posture, and it can only be used for ear recognition under controlled conditions. In the paper, we propose an ear alignment approach. Firstly, we apply R-FCN to detect ear regions on the image. Then we use cascading strategy to detect the key points through a two-level cascade convolutional neural network. Lastly, each test ear image is aligned according to the template ear image.

© Springer Nature Switzerland AG 2018
J. Zhou et al. (Eds.): CCBR 2018, LNCS 10996, pp. 562–571, 2018.
https://doi.org/10.1007/978-3-319-97909-0_60

The remainder of this paper is organized as follows: Sect. 2 introduce the related works to date. In Sect. 3, we introduce the process of ear alignment. Experimental results are presented in Sect. 4. We conclude our work in Sect. 5.

2   Related Works

In the field of ear alignment, Yuan et al. [10] proposed two methods for normalizing ear images in 2006, the line marking method based on the long axis of the outer ear and the point marking method based on the starting point of the contour of the outer ear. Gao et al. [11] proposed a normalization technique based on the improved active shape model in 2006. The algorithm established a point distribution model for the ear feature points in the training set and then searched out the outer ear contour in the test image. Finally, the ear image was normalized to the standard size and direction on the basis of the external ear long axis. In 2008, Tian et al. [12] proposed a human ear recognition method based on the fusion of SIFT features and geometric features, which could extract key points that were stable, free from light, scale, and rotation. In 2016, Tian et al. [13] proposed ear recognition based on deep convolutional neural network, which consisted three convolution layers, a fully connected layer, and a soft-max classifier. Experimental results at the USTB ear database showed that the proposed method was easier to achieve high accuracy and is superior to the traditional method in dealing with partial occlusion problems. In 2017, Zhang et al. [14] proposed a large-scale ear database, USTB-Helloear database, in which images were photographed under uncontrolled conditions with different poses and occlusion, they fine-tuned and modified some deep models on the proposed database through the ear verification experiments.

3   Methodology

3.1   System Flow Chart

In this paper, we propose a two-phase ear alignment approach. In the training phase, we firstly mark the key points on the training images, then use the annotated data to train a two-level cascade convolutional neural network. In the alignment phase, the key points

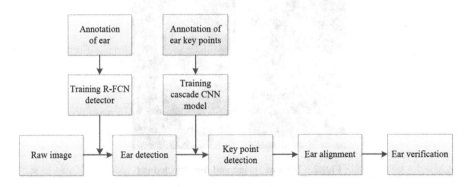

Fig. 1. System flow chart

are firstly detected using the trained network model, and then get aligned to the template image. The system flow chart is shown in Fig. 1.

3.2   USTB-Helloear Database

The USTB-Helloear database [15] was collected by us in cooperation with Xi'an Musheng Electronic Technology Co., Ltd. in October 2016. The database contains 612,661 profile images from 1570 Chinese people. The images in this database are extracted from video sequences and each ear extracted an average of 150 images in 10 s video, there are about 300 images of left and right ears in each person. The entire database is divided into two parts. The subset A consists of 336,572 human ears of 1,104 individuals, and the subset B consists of 275,909 human ears of 466 individuals. The ear image of the subset A only has change in posture, and the subset B contains posture and occlusion changes.

In the paper, during the training phase, we randomly selected 1000 left ear images in subset B. In order to avoid the risk of overfitting due to lack of training data, we augmented the data that was calibrated in the subset B by changing the brightness of each image, increasing Gaussian noise, rotating a small range, and finally constructed a training dataset of 8000 images. We firstly use CNN to train the key points detection models on the training dataset, then conduct the ear alignment experiments on subset A.

3.3   Ear Detection Based on R-FCN

For most people, the left and right ears of a same person are of the same shape [16]. Therefore, in the paper, all of the experiments were done on the left ear. We used 300 left ear images in the USTB-Helloear subset B to train, experimental results showed that 300 left ear images to train can reach a good result on the test set. Based on the R-FCN method [17], we used a trained model for ear detection and the detection time of each picture was about 50 ms. The result of the detection is shown in Fig. 2. For more details about ear detection, readers are referred to Ref. [14].

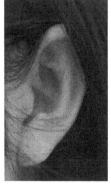

Fig. 2. The raw image and the detected ear

3.4 Ear Key Points Detection

Definition of Key Points. Different from the key points of face, since the color and texture of the ear are almost indistinguishable from each part, and the key points depend more on the semantic features, so the selection of the key points is particularly important. According to the morphological characteristics and the geometric characteristics of the ear, we define six key points on the ear, three located in the inner ear region, and three located on the outer contour of the ear, as shown in Fig. 3.

These key points are determined through extensive experiments. The distribution of these six key points is even. They can still be clearly found even when the angle of the ear changes greatly. The three points on the outer ear and the three points in the inner ear constitute two isosceles triangles respectively, The line between point 3 and point 6 is perpendicular to the line between point 1 and point 2. The line between point 1 and point 2 is the longest axis for the outer ear contour.

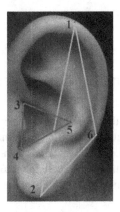

Fig. 3. Ear key points: Point 1: upper ear long axis endpoint, Point 2: lower ear long axis endpoint, Point 3: anterior auricular incisor, Point 4: intertragic notch, Point 5: the last point of the ear concha cavity, Point 6: the closest point between the outer ear and the concha cavity

Cascade Convolutional Neural Network

Level 1. In this paper, we use a cascade regression approach for ear key point detection with two levels of convolutional neural network. In Level 1, the convolutional neural network takes the cropped ear image as input, extracts the high-level features of the deep architecture globally, and the constraint relation of the key points will also be implied.

The task of predicting key points is a regression process. The last full connected layer output of CNN is the 12 coordinate value of the 6 point. The loss function we use is the Euclidean distance loss function, which is calculated as follows:

$$L = \frac{1}{2n} \sum_{i=1}^{n} \| \hat{y}_i - y_i \|_2^2 \tag{1}$$

The network structure of Level 1 is shown in Fig. 4:

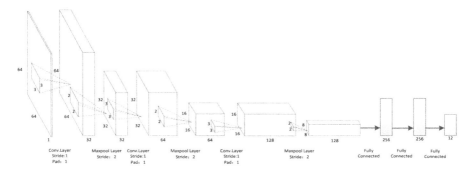

Fig. 4. The network structure of Level 1

Level 2. In level 2, we select those training patches that are centered at positions randomly shifted from the ground truth position. The maximum shift in both horizontal and vertical directions is 0.05 at Level 2. Centered on the key points detected in Level 1, we crop the images surrounding them and scale them to 15 * 15. The length and width of the cropped images are 0.06 times and 0.08 times the length and width of the original

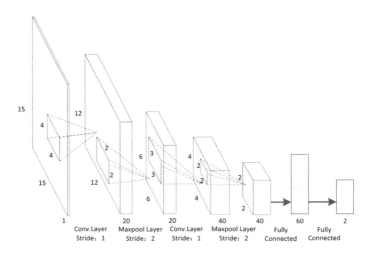

Fig. 5. The network structure of a CNN in Level 2

image. For each key point, we average the CNN prediction results of two different patch. Finally, the coordinate of the key point in the original image is obtained through coordinate transformation. Level 2 consists of 12 CNNs, two CNNs for detecting one key point. The network structure of one CNN in Level 2 is shown in Fig. 5:

Ear Alignment. The ear template is shown in Fig. 3. Using the key points coordinates of the unaligned images and the key point coordinates of the standard ear, we calculate the affine transformation matrix, using the least square method to minimize the distance between the detected points and the target points, therefore unaligned images can be aligned with standard ear through translation, scaling and rotation transformation.

Affine transformation is a linear transformation from two-dimensional coordinates (x, y) to two-dimensional coordinates (u, v). The affine transformation matrix form is as follows:

$$\begin{bmatrix} u \\ v \end{bmatrix} = \begin{bmatrix} a_1 & b_1 & c_1 \\ a_2 & b_2 & c_2 \end{bmatrix} \begin{bmatrix} x \\ y \\ 1 \end{bmatrix} = s \begin{bmatrix} cos\theta & -sin\theta \\ sin\theta & cos\theta \end{bmatrix} \begin{bmatrix} x \\ y \end{bmatrix} + \begin{bmatrix} t_1 \\ t_2 \end{bmatrix} = sR \begin{bmatrix} x \\ y \end{bmatrix} + T \quad (2)$$

In formula (2), s is the scaling ratio, θ is the rotation angle, T is the translation matrix and R is an orthogonal matrix.

$$R^T R = I \quad (3)$$

We use the least squares method to determine the effect of the alignment. Suppose P and Q represent the shape matrices of the test image and the template image. Each row of the matrix represents the horizontal and vertical coordinates of a key point. Since we have 6 key points, so $P \in R^{6 \times 2}$. The objective function of the alignment process is as follows:

$$\text{argmin}_{s,\theta,T} \sum_{i=1}^{6} ||sRp_i^T + T - q_i^T||^2 \quad (4)$$

In formula (4), p_i is the ith row of P and q_i is the ith row of Q.

4   Experimental Results and Analysis

In this section, we used a total of 172551 left ear images in subset A for key point detection and ear alignment. For the convenience of comparison, we randomly generated 3000 matched pairs and 3000 unmatched pairs from subject A for ear verification.

4.1   Analysis of Experimental Results

The results of the key point detection based on the cascade convolutional neural network are shown in Fig. 6.

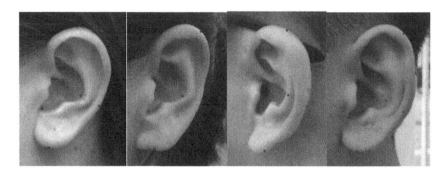

Fig. 6. The results of the key point detection

As shown in Fig. 7, we randomly selected 1104 left ear images in the subset A, and we evaluated the accuracy of key points for each test image. We can easily find that the accuracy of point 1 and point 6 is lower than other points, this is mainly due to the fact that these two points are often obscured in the ear and are not easy to be located when the angle of posture changes greatly.

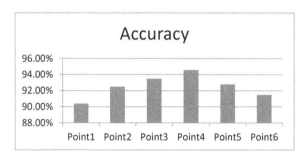

Fig. 7. The detection accuracy of key points

The result of ear alignment is shown in Fig. 8.

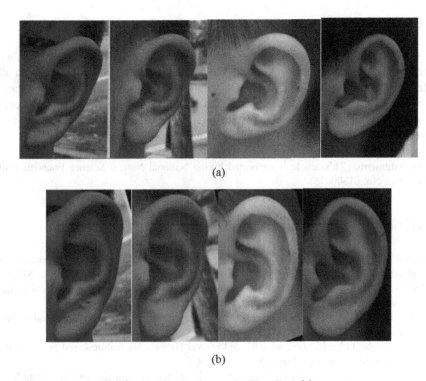

(a)

(b)

Fig. 8. (a) The raw image (b) The aligned image

4.2 Ear Verification

We conduct ear verification with reference to Zhang [15]. Before ear verification, CNN is used to convert the input ear image into a 128-dimensional feature vector, this process is called feature extraction. During the verification process, two images were sent to the trained model and feature vectors were extracted. Then the cosine distance was used to measure the similarity of the two ear feature vectors. Finally, the verification program determined whether the two ears belong to the same subject. The ear verification results are presented in Table 1.

Table 1. Accuracy of ear verification before and after alignment

Test set	Raw images (%)	Aligned images (%)
Subset A	83.23	92.17

It is shown that using the aligned ear image, we get higher accuracy of ear verification than with the raw image. This is mainly because the aligned ear image reduces the interference from the non-ear region and can represent the ear feature better.

5   Conclusion

The work in this paper is based on our previous work in Ref. [15]. In the paper, we propose a novel ear alignment approach. We define six key points on the ear, and all the test ears are aligned to the template ear with minimum mean distance among these key points. The automatic key points detection is realized by a cascaded convolutional neural network model. Experimental results on the USTB-Helloear database show that ear verification performance can be enhanced with ear alignment.

Acknowledgments. This article is supported by the National Natural Science Foundation of China (Grant No. 61300075).

References

1. Nixon, M.S., Bouchrika, I., Arbab-Zavar, B., et al.: On use of biometrics in forensics: gait and ear. In: 2010 European Signal Processing Conference, pp. 1655–1659. IEEE (2010)
2. Huang, H., Liu, J., Feng, H., et al.: Ear recognition based on uncorrelated local Fisher discriminant analysis. Neurocomputing **74**(17), 3103–3113 (2011)
3. Lakshmanan, L.: Efficient person authentication based on multi-level fusion of ear scores. IET Biometrics **2**(3), 97–106 (2013)
4. Mu, Z.: Robust classification for occluded ear via Gabor scale feature-based non-negative sparse representation. Opt. Eng. **53**(6), 061702 (2014)
5. Taigman, Y., Yang, M., Ranzato, M., et al.: DeepFace: closing the gap to human-level performance in face verification. In: IEEE Conference on Computer Vision and Pattern Recognition, pp. 1701–1708. IEEE Computer Society (2014)
6. Sun, Y., Wang, X., Tang, X.: Deep learning face representation from predicting 10,000 classes. In: IEEE Conference on Computer Vision and Pattern Recognition, pp. 1891–1898. IEEE Computer Society (2014)
7. Sun, Y., Wang, X., Tang, X.: Deep learning face representation by joint identification-verification, vol. 27, pp. 1988–1996 (2014)
8. Sun, Y., Wang, X., Tang, X.: Deeply learned face representations are sparse, selective, and robust. In: Computer Vision and Pattern Recognition, pp. 2892–2900. IEEE (2015)
9. Emeršič, Ž., Štruc, V., Peer, P.: Ear recognition: more than a survey. Neurocomputing **255**, 26–39 (2017)
10. Yuan, L., Mu, Z., Liu, L.: Ear recognition based on kernel principal component analysis and support vector machine. J. Eng. Sci. **28**(9), 890–895 (2006)
11. Gao, S., Mu, Z., Yuan, L., et al.: Normalization of ear image based on active shape model. In: National Conference on Image and Graphics, p. 4 (2006)
12. Tian, Y., Fan, W.: Ear recognition based on fusion of scale invariant feature transform and geometric feature. J. Opt. **28**(8), 1485–1491 (2008)
13. Tian, L., Mu, Z.: Ear recognition based on deep convolutional network. In: International Congress on Image and Signal Processing, Biomedical Engineering and Informatics, pp. 437–441. IEEE (2017)
14. Zhang, Y., Mu, Z., Yuan, L., et al.: Ear verification under uncontrolled conditions with convolutional neural networks. IET Biometrics **7**, 185–198 (2018)

15. Zhang, Y., Mu, Z., Yuan, L., Yu, C., Liu, Q.: USTB-Helloear: a large database of ear images photographed under uncontrolled conditions. In: Zhao, Y., Kong, X., Taubman, D. (eds.) ICIG 2017. LNCS, vol. 10667, pp. 405–416. Springer, Cham (2017). https://doi.org/10.1007/978-3-319-71589-6_35
16. Qi, N., Li, L., Zhao, W.: Chinese adult auricular morphology measurement and classification. Tech. Acoust. 29(5), 518–522 (2010)
17. Dai, J., Li, Y., He, K., et al.: R-FCN: object detection via region-based fully convolutional networks (2016)

Evaluation of Outdoor Visible Light Communications Links Using Actual LED Street Luminaries

Jupeng Ding[1(⊠)], Chih-Lin I[2], Chi Zhang[1], Baoshan Yu[1], and Huicheng Lai[1]

[1] College of Information Science and Engineering,
Xinjiang University, Urumqi 830046, China
jupeng7778@163.com
[2] Green Communication Research Center,
China Mobile Research Institute, Beijing 100053, China

Abstract. In existing indoor & outdoor visible light communications (VLC) works, the LED luminaries are almost all modeled following conventional Lambertian beam pattern. However, for providing energy efficient illumination and controlling lighting pollution, the beam patterns of the commercially available LED street luminaries are almost all application-oriented designed which can only be profiled by more sophisticated mathematical representation. In this paper, for the first time, to the best of our knowledge, the link coverages of the outdoor VLC with actual LED street luminaries are modeled and evaluated. Numerical results identify that, compared to the conventional Lambertian case the beam pattern of typical actual LED street luminary is superior to concentrate the emitted power in the served cell by sharp cell edge, naturally limit the inter cell interference to quite low level and provide highly link quality uniformity within each cell.

Keywords: Visible light communications · LED street luminaries
Angular intensity profile · Optical wireless · Link characteristics

1 Introduction

In 5G mobile communications age, more attenuation is focused on sufficiently utilizing existent infrastructure to reduce the operation expenditures (OPEX) and the Capital expenditures (CAPEX). In this technology trends, LED illumination infrastructure based visible light communications (VLC) technologies are continuously discussed and investigated by the academia and industry [1]. In outdoor environment, the VLC technologies can be incorporated in the building of smart city to provide green and ubiquitous wireless connection [2]. Specifically, in a large scale outdoor domain, the LED street luminaries can be modified and networked to provide various and low-cost services (video broadcasting, stream media, real time voice, high precision positioning and so on) to the pedestrians and the grounding vehicles in moving or static status [1, 3].

© Springer Nature Switzerland AG 2018
J. Zhou et al. (Eds.): CCBR 2018, LNCS 10996, pp. 572–579, 2018.
https://doi.org/10.1007/978-3-319-97909-0_61

To date, some preliminary works of outdoor VLC have been reported. For simplicity, the LED street luminaries are usually viewed as generalized Lambertian optical source. Such approximation processing is efficient and valid in short range indoor VLC based on indoor illumination infrastructure which is quite sensitive to the cost and expected to lighting the working zones as large as possible. Moreover, in most indoor scenarios, the emitted white light is restricted by the surrounding opaque walls, furniture or inner structures, and the influence of original beam illumination to the surrounding rooms and outdoor space is almost negligible [4–6]. Nevertheless, for the outdoor public illumination, the lighting area is tightly restricted for preventing the occurrence of lighting pollution to the domains outside the street. Therefore, the commercially available LED street luminaries from main manufacturer are usually carefully designed and optimized while the respective beam patterns cannot be simply matched by the Lambertian mode [7].

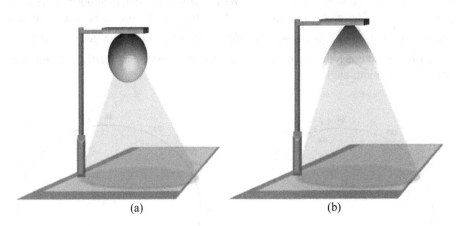

(a)   (b)

Fig. 1. Single LED street luminaries with: (a) ideal Lambertain optical beam, (b) actual optical beam

In this paper, to the best of our knowledge, for the first time, the beam pattern of actual LED street luminaries is introduced into the outdoor VLC modeling and analysis. Furthermore, the 2D & 3D intensity pattern of actual luminaries is represented in the mathematical architecture of outdoor VLC link. Compared to the familiar Lambertian pattern, the superiority of the actual LED beam pattern in the link coverage characteristics including the naturally served cell shape, the sharp cell edge and the coverage uniformity, is numerically illustrated in envisioned typical street scenario.

The remainder of this paper is organized as follows. In Sect. 2, besides the beam pattern of the conventional Lambertian luminary, the 2D & 3D beam patterns of typical actual street luminary are presented. And then the studied beam patterns are adopted to describe the outdoor visible light communication links. In Sect. 3, the numerical results obtained by simulation are presented and discussed. Conclusion is given in Sect. 4.

2 Description of Outdoor Visible Light Communication Links Using LED Street Lighting

2.1 Beam Pattern of Lambertian Luminary

In conventional VLC link models for both indoor and outdoor scenarios, the transmitter i.e. LED sources are usually profiled to emit Lambertian beams. This profile is approximately valid in some basic circumstances [1, 3]. Such beams can be described by the respective beam pattern (also known as angular intensity profile or radiation pattern) given by:

$$I(\theta) = \frac{(n+1)}{2\pi} \cos^m(\theta).$$ (1)

where $I(\theta)$ is radiant intensity in units of W/sr, and θ is the spherical polar angle for a given direction. The mode number m is related to $\theta_{1/2}$, the source semiangle at half intensity, by $n = \ln(2)\big/\ln(\cos\phi_{1/2})$ [4, 6]. Apparently, the above generalized Lambertian beam pattern follows uniaxial symmetry. This means its intensity is independent of the azimuth angle.

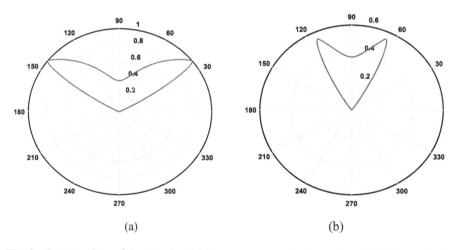

(a)   (b)

Fig. 2. Cross sections of the actual optical beam along (a) the long axis and (b) the short axis

2.2 Beam Patterns of Actual Street Luminary

As for street lighting application, for controlling light pollution, visibility, and light utilization efficiency, the beam patterns of commercially available street lamps are sophisticated, which cannot be profiled by concise Lambertian pattern any more. Without loss of generality, following the work of [7], the identified 2D beam pattern of typical LEDs streetlight i.e. LD48 luminary from major manufacturer BBE LEDs can be given by:

$$I(\theta) = UG(\theta) + (1 - U)G(\theta_p) \exp\left[-g_5(|\theta| - \theta_p)^2\right].$$ (2)

where θ is the polar angle in a coordinate system centered in the LED lamps, θ_p is the characteristic peak angle of 2D intensity curves.

And the function G is a Gaussian, given by:

$$G(\theta) = g_1 - g_2 \exp\left[-g_3(|\theta| - g_4)^2\right].$$ (3)

and function U is a simple step function, defined as:

$$U = \left\{ \begin{array}{ll} 1 & \text{if } |\theta| < \theta_p \\ 0 & \text{if } |\theta| \geq \theta_p \end{array} \right\}.$$ (4)

Coefficients g_1 to g_5 mainly decided by the specific shape of the LED luminary emission. As for LD48 luminary of BBE LEDs, the relevant coefficients of Eq. (2) are $g_1 = 1.515$, $g_2 = 1.14$, $g_3 = 0.0003$, $g_4 = 0$, and $g_5 = 0.015$, respectively. Specifically, cross sections of this actual optical beam along two perpendicular axes are shown in Fig. 2 explicitly. For the short axis cross section, $\theta_p = 23°$ and for the long axis cross section, $\theta_p = 51.5°$. These coefficient values normalize the intensity and make Eq. (2) a function of angle θ in degrees.

Apparently, the profiled intensity of actual street luminary has an asymmetric beam pattern unlike the discussed Lambertian pattern. To fully model the optical beam in 3D space, the advanced beam pattern can be given as:

$$I(\theta, \phi) = UG(\theta) + (1 - U)G[\theta_p(\phi)] \exp\left\{-g_5(\phi)[|\theta| - \theta_p(\phi)]^2\right\}.$$ (5)

where θ and ϕ are the direction angles in spherical coordinates. Function G is given by Eq. (3), and g_5 become the function of ϕ as:

$$g_5(\phi) = \frac{g_{x5}g_{y5}}{\sqrt[2]{(g_{x5} \sin \phi)^2 + (g_{y5} \cos \phi)^2}}.$$ (6)

Gx_5 and gy_5 are the parameters related to the mentioned perpendicular cross sections. The step function U is given by:

$$U = \left\{ \begin{array}{ll} 1 & \text{if } |\theta| < \theta_p(\phi) \\ 0 & \text{if } |\theta| \geq \theta_p(\phi) \end{array} \right\}.$$ (7)

where the peak angle function $\theta_p(\phi)$ determines the illumination distribution shape of the actual street luminary to a large extent, which is given by:

$$\theta_p(\phi) = \arctan\left[\frac{\tan\theta_{px}\tan\theta_{py}}{\sqrt[m]{(\tan\theta_{px}\sin\phi)^m + (\tan\theta_{py}\cos\phi)^m}}\right]. \tag{8}$$

Where θ_{px} and θ_{py} are the peak angles in the both perpendicular cross sections, and m is an even integer to give the rectangular contour shape. In Fig. 1(b) including LD48 luminary, the coefficients of Eq. (7) are $g_1 = 1.491$, $g_2 = 1.122$, $g_3 = 0.0003$, $g_4 = 0$, $g_{x5} = g_{y5} = 0.015$, which are the same for both the perpendicular cross sections. The parameter of rectangular shape is $m = 6$. The left parameters are $\theta_{px} = 23°$ and $\theta_{py} = 51.5°$, respectively [7].

2.3 Outdoor Visible Light Communication Links

In typical outdoor street scenario, the multipath propagation effect is limited due to the sufficient open space. Therefore, the optical signals emitted by the optical source directly reach the receiver via the line of sight (LOS) path. In the time domain, the impulse response of the channel is adopted to characterize the OWC channel. If a LOS path exists, the VLC link gain due to this path between optical source S and receiver R can be given by [4, 5]:

$$H(S, R) = \frac{A_R}{d_0^2}I(\theta, \phi)\cos\psi_0 rect(\frac{\psi_0}{FOV}) \tag{9}$$

where A_R is the effective receiver area, d_0 is the direct distance from source to receiver, and ψ_0 is the angle of incidence on the receiver location. FOV is the field of view of the receiver.

As a matter of fact, the typical street is usually illuminated by multiple adjacent street luminaries simultaneously, as illustrated in Fig. 3. In this situation, the sum VLC link gain for one receiver location can be further derived as:

$$H(R) = \sum_{i=1}^{N}\frac{A_R}{d_{0i}^2}I_i(\theta_i, \phi_i)\cos\psi_{0i} rect(\frac{\psi_{0i}}{FOV}) \tag{10}$$

where N is the amount of working street luminaries, $I_i(\theta_i, \phi_i)$ is the pattern intensity of the ith luminary in the LOS emission direction, d_{0i} is the LOS distance from the ith luminary to the receiver, and ψ_{0i} is the link incidence angle of the ith luminary on the receiver location. FOV is the field of view of the receiver.

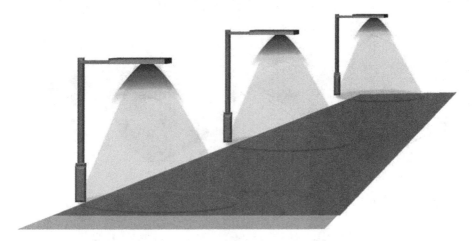

Fig. 3. Multiple adjacent street luminaries in typical outdoor scenario

3 Numerical Results and Discussion

In this section, the link coverage outdoor VLC is numerically evaluated in scenarios including single and multiple street LED luminaries with actual beam pattern, separately. Table 1 presents the main parameters setting for the following simulation evaluation.

3.1 Basic Link Coverage of Outdoor VLC

In basic case, only one LED street luminary are considered. Without loss of generality, this luminary pole is located in the side line center of the envisioned street, as shown in Fig. 2. Specifically, the luminary mounting height is 10 m, while the width and the length of this street are 14 m and 30 m respectively. Other main link configuration parameters are included in Table 1. By numerical simulation, the received power on the floor under the conventional Lambertian and the modeled actual optical beam cases are presented in Fig. 4. From Fig. 4 (a), it can be observed that in the original setting with the 0 m arm length, the cell shape of outdoor VLC link with conventional Lambertian is semicircle and the edge of this coverage is unclear since the Lambertian beam is symmetric and smoothly changed among various directions. As for the actual street luminary case, the VLC cell shape is basically similar to the right part of one rectangular and the cell edge is observable in both contrary directions along the envisioned street.

Table 1. Parameters for link characteristics simulation

Parameters	Value	Parameters	Value
Detection area of receiver	1 cm^2	Street width	14 m
FOV of receiver	85°	Street length	30 m
Elevation of receiver	90°	Height of LED source	10 m
Azimuth of receiver	0°	Elevation of LED source	−90°
Height of receiver	0 m	Azimuth of LED source	0°

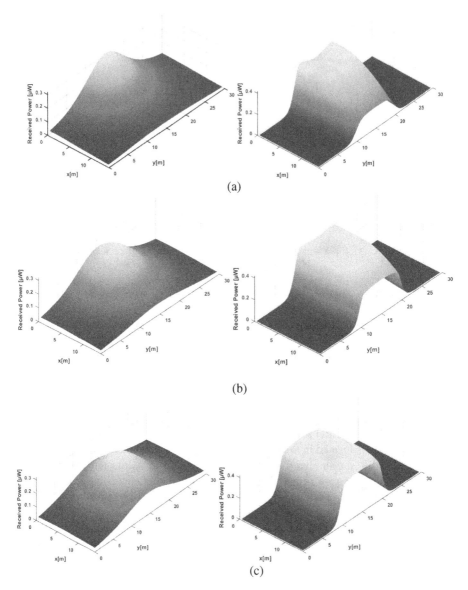

Fig. 4. Received power comparison between Lambertian and actual optical beam under different street lamp arm length setting: (a) 0 m, (b) 3.5 m, and (c) 7 m

As shown in Fig. 4 (b), with the street lamp arm length is increased from 0 m to 3.5 m, the VLC cell shape of the Lambertian beam pattern is more closed to one whole circle since the 3D coordinates of the luminary is closer to the street middle line, while there is still transitional zone at the cell edge which is liable to cause potential significant interference to the surrounding cell. On the other side, when arm length is up to

3.5 m, the cell shape of the actual luminary beam looks more like the most part of one rectangular and the cell edge is quite clear in mentioned two directions. By observation, the cell size is about 14 m × 10 m.

When the street lamp arm length is further increased to 7 m, as presented in Fig. 4 (c), the VLC cell shape of the Lambertian beam pattern is almost one circle and the cell radius is about 5 m without clear edge in all directional. As for the latter case, the VLC cell shape is almost perfect rectangular which tightly cover one section of the envisioned street. The cell edge can be easily identified in four main directions respect to the four sides of the rectangular, which means significant reduced inter cell interface to the other cells.

4   Conclusions

In this paper, one novel degree of freedom i.e. LED luminaries beam pattern, is systematically incorporated in the outdoor VLC link design and analysis. Due to the more strict regulation for outdoor illumination compared to indoor counterpart, the beam pattern is carefully designed to lighting the street domain which naturally form the sharp VLC cell edges, the regular cell shape and the satisfactory coverage uniformity within one cell. In advance, the street lamp arm length has the potential to be carefully designed to modify and optimize the outdoor VLC cell planning as well.

Acknowledgments. This work was supported in part by National Natural Science Foundation of China (Grants No. 61561048).

References

1. Do, T.H., Yoo, M.: Visible light communication based vehicle positioning using LED street light and rolling shutter CMOS sensors. Opt. Commun. **407**, 112–126 (2018)
2. Yaqoob, I., Hashem, I.A.T., Mehmood, Y., Gani, A., Mokhtar, S., Guizani, S.: Enabling communication technologies for smart cities. IEEE Commun. Mag. **55**(1), 112–120 (2017)
3. Zhu, N., Xu, Z., Wang, Y., Zhuge, H., Li, J.: Handover method in visible light communication between the moving vehicle and multiple LED streetlights. Optik **125**(14), 3540–3544 (2014)
4. Barry, J.R., Kahn, J.M., Krause, W.J., Lee, E., Messerschmitt, D.: Simulation of multipath impulse response for indoor wireless optical channels. IEEE J. Sel. Areas Commun. **11**(3), 367–379 (1993)
5. Ding, J., I, C.-L., Xu, Z.: Indoor optical wireless channel characteristics with distinct source radiation patterns. IEEE Photonics J. **8**(1), 1–15 (2016)
6. Ding, J., Wang, K., Xu, Z.: Accuracy analysis of different modeling schemes in indoor visible light communications with distributed array sources. In: Proceedings 2014 9th International Symposium on Communication Systems, Networks Digital Signal Processing, Manchester, July, pp. 1005–1010 (2014)
7. Moreno, I., Avendaño-Alejo, M., Saucedo-A, T., Bugarin, A.: Modeling LED street lighting. Appl. Opt. **53**(20), 4420–4430 (2014)

Readback Error Classification of Radiotelephony Communication Based on Convolutional Neural Network

Fangyuan Cheng, Guimin Jia$^{(\boxtimes)}$, Jinfeng Yang, and Dan Li

Tianjin Key Lab for Advanced Signal Processing, Civil Aviation University of China, Tianjin, China
gmjia_cauc@163.com

Abstract. The readback errors of radiotelephony communication result in serious potential risk to the air transportation safety. Therefore, it is essential to establish a proper model to identify and also to classify the readback errors automatically so as to improve the flight safety. In this paper, a new scheme, which has two channels to process the instructions and the readbacks (I-R pairs) respectively based on one-layer convolutional neural network (CNN), is proposed for the readback error classification. The semantics of the I-R pairs are learned by the one-layer CNN encoder. Then, the classification decision is made according to a matching vector of the I-R pairs. A new method of input is also tested. Extensive experiments have been conducted and the results show that the proposed scheme is effective for automatic readback error classification and the average classification accuracy on a Chinese civil radiotelephony communication dataset is up to 95.44%.

Keywords: Radiotelephony communication
One-layer convolutional neural network · Semantic vector
Readback error classification

1 Introduction

According to the reports of Aviation Safety Reporting System (ASRS) and Federal Aviation Administration (FAA), the radiotelephony communication errors are the main factor of resulting in aviation incidents. Meanwhile, the readback errors take a half percent of the total radiotelephony communication errors [1, 2]. Readback errors refer to the incorrect readbacks that the pilots make in conversation with air traffic controllers during flight. Here, the common readback errors can be usually divided into five types: heading information error, runway information error, call sign information error, altitude information error and partial information loss [3–6]. To reduce this kind of aviation incidents caused by readback errors, it has to analyze the error tendency of readbacks

---

F. Cheng and G. Jia—These authors contributed equally to this work and should be considered co-first authors.

© Springer Nature Switzerland AG 2018
J. Zhou et al. (Eds.): CCBR 2018, LNCS 10996, pp. 580–588, 2018.
https://doi.org/10.1007/978-3-319-97909-0_62

to improve the communications among the air traffic controllers and the pilots. The conventional way deals with this problem by analyzing the voice tapes of communication manually [4–6], which requires a lot of efforts in listening to the voice tapes. Thus, it is meaningful to establish a model for automatic readback error classification. Unfortunately, there are few proper models of this problem in the aviation field by now.

The task of readback error classification is similar to the sentence matching issue in natural language processing (NLP), which has been studied for a long time. Sentence matching aims to identify the relationship between the sentence pairs by matching the semantics of sentences. Recently, deep neural networks are widely used and the CNNs have achieved remarkable performance in computer vision and sentence matching [7–13]. Some CNNs first represent the sentence pairs as sentence-level semantic vectors, and then identify the relationship based on the semantic vectors, such as ARC-I [8] and CNTN [9]. Some CNNs take the multiple-granularity into account for identifying the relationship, such as Bi-CNN-MI [10] and MultiGranCNN [11]. Bi-CNN-MI and Multi-GranCNN are complicated in architecture and there are too many parameters to be tuned in training. In these works, the square kernel is widely used of CNN to model the sentences. Whereas the latest works have proved that one-layer CNN, whose kernel width is equal to the dimensionality of the word vectors, is more effective in semantic modeling [12, 13].

According to the analysis above, a novel scheme is proposed to classify the readback errors for I-R pairs based on one-layer CNN. It mainly consists of semantic modeling and semantic matching. For semantic modeling, the I-R pairs are processed respectively to generate their semantic vectors by a two channel model that has the same one-layer CNN encoder. In addition, for the input of the one-layer CNN, a doubling strategy is applied to improve the representations of the I-R pairs. For semantic matching, a matching vector, which contains semantic vectors of the I-R pairs and a similarity information, is generated and then the classification decision is made using the softmax function.

2   The One-Layer Convolutional Neural Network

The architecture of the one-layer CNN is described in this section. As illustrated in Fig. 1, it is composed of input layer, one convolutional layer and one pooling layer.

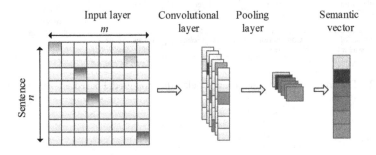

Fig. 1. The architecture of one-layer CNN

The input of the one-layer CNN is a sentence matrix. The sentence matrix $\mathbf{S} \in \mathbb{R}^{n \times m}$ is formed by concatenating word vectors of all words in the sentence, where n is the (zero-padded) sentence length and m is the dimension of the word vector. Then, the sentence matrix is fed into the convolutional layer.

In convolutional layer, a rectangle kernel which size is $h \times m$ is taken on the sentence matrix $\mathbf{S}$. The kernel regards the single word vector as a pixel. It slides several words under each convolution to generate a new feature. For example, a feature c_i can be generated from a window of words $\mathbf{S}_{i:i-h+1}$ by Eq. (1)

$$c_i = \sigma(\mathbf{W} \cdot \mathbf{S}_{i:i-h+1} + b) \quad i = 1, 2, \ldots, n - h + 1, \tag{1}$$

where h denotes the 'height' of the kernel, $\mathbf{W} \in \mathbb{R}^{h \times m}$ stands for the weight matrix in convolutional layer, σ represents an active function such as ReLU, and $b \in \mathbb{R}$ is the bias. The filter is applied to each possible window of words in sentence matrix $\mathbf{S}$ and then the feature map is produced by Eq. (2)

$$\mathbf{c} = [c_1, c_2, \ldots, c_{n-h+1}], \tag{2}$$

where $\mathbf{c} \in \mathbb{R}^{n-h+1}$. To make the extracted features abundant, we can use multiple kernels to learn complementary features with the same region or the varying region. The convolutional layer produces a set of feature maps of dimension $(n + h - 1) \times 1$.

The output of the model is a semantic vector, which is put into the pooling layer to reduce the dimension and over fitting. There are many strategies used for pooling operations, such as Max, k-Max and average etc. Finally, these features are further concatenated to a semantic vector.

3   The Proposed Method for Readback Error Classification

The architecture of readback error classification model based on one-layer CNN is shown as Fig. 2. It consists of two modules: semantic modeling module and semantic matching module.

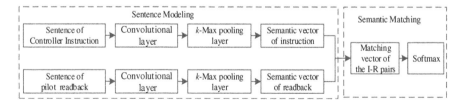

Fig. 2. The architecture of readback error classification model based on one-layer CNN

3.1 Semantic Modeling

In sentence modeling module, we propose an augmented one-hot encoding method to represent the words in the sentence. A doubling strategy is also applied to obtain the sentence matrix **S**.

In verification task of radiotelephony communication, it has been reported that the one-hot word vector outperforms word2vec [14, 15]. These works do not take the abbreviation of some keywords into account, which is listed in Table 1. To increase the correlation between the standard keywords and their abbreviated keywords, flags are added after the one-hot vector, as listed in Table 1. In this way, the correlation between the standard keywords and their abbreviated keywords can be improved significantly. Meanwhile, the misclassification is reduced.

Table 1. The examples of abbreviation words

	keywords	one-hot vector	augmented one-hot vector
Standard keywords	修正/海压	{0,1,0,0,0,...,0,0}/{0,0,1,0,0,...,0,0}	{0,1,0,0,0,...,1,0}/{0,0,1,0,0,...,0,1}
Abbreviated keywords	修/压	{0,0,0,1,0,...,0,0}/{0,0,0,0,1,...,0,0}	{0,0,0,1,0,...,1,0}/{0,0,0,0,1,...,0,1}

For building sentence matrices, three different input strategies are used here to find the best semantics representation of the sentences. They are Original Sentences, Doubling Instruction and Doubling Readback respectively. The doubling strategy is applied to strengthen the semantics of the words in [16, 17]. An example of Original Sentences is listed in Table 2. In doubling strategy, the input sentence is represented twice in **S** when the sentence length is shorter than the max-length of the pairs. This method can emphasize the information of the short sentences twice so that the model can extract better representations of semantics. For Doubling Readback, the readback is represented twice in the sentence matrix and the matrix of instruction is unchanged as listed in Table 2.

Table 2. The example of I-R pairs

Instruction	吉祥 1147 离场 跑道 32 地面 风 290 度 4 节 修正 海压 1022 温度 负 2 露点 负 3 跑道 视程 550 米 时间 27
Readback	跑道 32 修 压 1023 吉祥 1147
Doubling Readback	跑道 32 修 压 1023 吉祥 1147 跑道 32 修 压 1023 吉祥 1147

In convolutional layer, multiple kernels of an identical region are used to learn complementary features. The output of the convolutional layer is fed into a k-Max pooling layer to detect the top k important features. Then, these features are concatenated to a semantic vector. The semantic vectors of the instruction and readback can be represented as $\mathbf{x}_I$ and $\mathbf{x}_R$ respectively.

3.2 Semantic Matching

The matching vector, which can represent the relationship between the I-R pairs, is generated by aggregating $\mathbf{x}_I$, $\mathbf{x}_R$ and cosine similarity between the semantic vectors. The aggregating operation is defined as Eq. (3)

$$\mathbf{x}_{input} = \left[\mathbf{x}_I \oplus sim \oplus \mathbf{x}_R\right], \tag{3}$$

where $\oplus$ is the concatenation operator. sim stands for the cosine similarity between the semantic vectors. The cosine function is defined as Eq. (4)

$$sim(\mathbf{x}_I, \mathbf{x}_R) = \frac{\mathbf{x}_I^T \cdot \mathbf{x}_R}{\|\mathbf{x}_I\| \cdot \|\mathbf{x}_R\|}, \tag{4}$$

where $\|\cdot\|$ represents the l_2 norm. Then, the matching vector is fed into a fully connected layer and the softmax function is used to output a vector, which denotes the probability of input I-R pair belonging to each kind of matching category. The function can be expressed as Eq. (5)

$$p(y = j|\mathbf{x}) = \frac{e^{\mathbf{x}^T \theta_j}}{\sum_{m=1}^{M} e^{\mathbf{x}^T \theta_m}} \quad j = 1, 2, \ldots, 6, \tag{5}$$

where θ_m is a weight vector of m-th label and $p(y = j|\mathbf{x})$ stands for the probability that the input $\mathbf{x}$ belongs to label j. $\mathbf{x}$ can be thought of as a final representation of the readback pairs. Finally, the error type of the input I-R pair can be obtained according to the index of the max value in the vector.

4 Experiments

4.1 Dataset

Due to the vacancy of the Chinese civil radiotelephony communication (CCRC), we built the CCRC dataset according to the recordings of radiotelephony communication between air traffic controllers, and pilots and the training books for radiotelephony communications are also consulted to establish the dataset. In this dataset, there are six types of readback pairs: correct readback, heading information error, runway information error, call sign information error, altitude information error and partial information loss. There are 1300 correct I-R pairs, and there are 500 I-R pairs for each kind of readback errors, which means there are 2500 incorrect I-R pairs that are inconsistent in semantics.

4.2 Parameter Settings and Test Protocol

Here, the embedding size of augmented one-hot vector is 1005. The other parameters of the proposed model are as follows: in convolutional layer, the value h of the rectangle kernel is set to 14 and the number of the feature maps is 50. In k-Max pooling layer, the value of k is 7. To train the model, the minibatch Gradient Descent (GD) is used for optimization and the batch size is 100. Besides, the learning rate is 0.1 and the dropout rate is 0.5.

The training set contains 3100 I-R pairs, in which there are 1100 correct I-R pairs and 400 incorrect I-R pairs with one type of errors. The test set is made up by the rest 700 I-R pairs. To verify the accuracy and stability of the proposed model, we conduct the experiments using random 'sampling protocol' for thirty times. The evaluation metrics of the experimental results are Average test accuracy (Ave.) of thirty tests, Mean square error (MSE) and F.

$$\text{test accuracy} = \frac{\text{Correct classification numbers of test samples}}{\text{Total numbers of test samples}}, \tag{6}$$

$$F = \frac{2RP}{R + P}, \tag{7}$$

MSE denotes the stability of the model and F is the geometric mean of the precision and recall rate of a certain matching category.

4.3   Analysis of Parameters h and k

The original sentences are used as the input to analyze the influence of the parameters h and k. The value of h varies from 6 to 18, and the k in k-max pooling layer is set to 1. From Fig. 3(a), it can be noted that the performance is better when larger value of h is used in convolutional layer. We recommend the h is set to 14. Besides that, Fig. 3(a) shows the test accuracy of augmented one-hot is better than one-hot. The value of k is from 1 to 14. As illustrated in Fig. 3(b), the performance is better when larger k is used in k-Max pooling. It is observed that the improvement is quite limited for the value of k over 7. The more features are remained in k-Max pooling layer, the more neural nodes are needed in the final fully connected layer so that the model cost more training and testing time. In this paper, k is set to 7 by making a tradeoff between the costing time and the test accuracy.

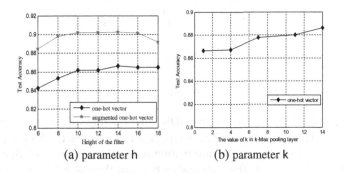

(a) parameter h   (b) parameter k

Fig. 3. Analysis of the parameters h and k

4.4   Classification Performance

First, to test the performance of the augmented one-hot vector for word representation in our task, as well as the performance of the proposed new model, the ARC-I [8] model is used for comparison. The experimental results are listed in Table 3. Here, the input strategy is fixed to original sentences.

Table 3. Experimental results on CCRC

Model	Ave. (%)	MSE (%)
ARC-I (one-hot)	74.71	0.72
ARC-I (augmented one-hot)	77.50	0.69
Ours (one-hot)	88.60	0.65
Ours (augmented one-hot)	90.21	0.61

From Table 3, it can be noted that the proposed method outperforms the baseline method, ARC-I. This is mainly due to the rectangle kernel and the k-max pooling. Furthermore, the model using the augmented one-hot encoding has a higher test accuracy and lower MSE. The reason is that the augmented one-hot word vector can represent the relations of the abbreviated words better. The augmented one-hot vector is used in the following experiments.

Then, three different input strategies are compared. The experimental results are illustrated in Fig. 4 and Table 4. The test accuracy of thirty random validations is shown in Fig. 4. The F-value and MSE of each kind of errors are listed in Table 4. The Correct stands for the type of correct readback, and Error type1 to type5 denote the five given error types: heading information error, runway information error, call sign information error, altitude information error and partial information loss.

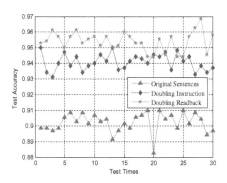

Fig. 4. Test accuracy of the proposed model with three input strategies

From Fig. 4 and Table 4, it can be noted that the doubling strategies can improve the test accuracy and the F-value of each error type. The reason is that the doubling strategies can emphasize and strengthen the information of the short sentences twice for better representations. As a result, the relationship between the I-R pairs can be expressed better. At the same time, it can be seen that Doubling Readback achieves higher performance than Doubling Instruction. This is because the model can emphasize the difference and the semantics of the sentences twice via Doubling Readback strategy when the readback error is not obvious. That is, it can provide more class-discriminative information.

Table 4. F-value and MSE of each kind of errors

Label	Original sentences		Doubling instruction		Doubling readback	
	F (%)	MSE (%)	F (%)	MSE (%)	F (%)	MSE (%)
Correct	87.12	1.69	90.89	1.31	93.08	0.79
Error type1	96.51	1.79	97.64	1.14	98.29	1.18
Error type2	93.91	0.56	96.05	0.96	96.46	0.68
Error type3	80.62	2.57	89.90	2.28	91.77	1.73
Error type4	96.39	0.60	96.74	0.62	96.43	1.12
Error type5	92.29	0.75	96.54	1.31	98.71	0.68
All samples	90.21	0.61	94.25	0.61	**95.44**	**0.52**

5   Conclusions and Future Work

In this paper, a new scheme has been proposed for classifying readback errors of radiotelephony communication. Based on the CCRC dataset, a series of experiments were conducted to evaluate the performance of the new scheme. The experimental results have shown that the proposed method is effective for automatic readback error classification and give a new solution for classifying readback errors. While, some improvements can be made in the future work. The kernel with different region can be used in the model to extract the semantics of the I-R pairs, and the method of the matching vector generation is also a key point to improve the performance of the model.

Acknowledgements. This work is supported by National Natural Science Foundation of China (No. U1433120, No. 61502498, No. 61379102) and the Fundamental Research Funds for the Central Universities (No. 3122017001).

References

1. National Transportation Safety Board: Review of U.S. Civil Aviation Accident, Calender Year 2010. Annual Review NTSB/ARA-12/01, Washington, DC (2012)
2. Billings, C.E., Cheaney, E.D.: Information transfer problems in the aviation system, Technical report 1875, National Aeronautics and Space Administration (1981)
3. Cardosi, K., Falzarano, P., Han, S.: Pilot-controller communication errors: an analysis of Aviation Safety Reporting System (ASRS) reports. Aviat. Saf. **119**, S518–S519 (1998)
4. US Federal Aviation Administration: Altitude deviation study: a Descriptive Analysis of Pilot and Controller incidents, Final report, October 1992
5. Morrow, D., Lee, A., Rodvold, M.: Analysis of problems in routine controller-pilot communication. Int. J. Aviat. Psychol. **3**(4), 285–302 (1993)

6. Pope, J.A.: Research identifies common errors behind altitude deviations. Flight Saf. Digest. **12**, 1–13 (1993)
7. Luan, S.Z., Chen, C., Zhang, B.C., Han, J.G., Liu, J.Z.: Gabor convolutional networks. IEEE Trans. Image Process. **27**, 4357–4366 (2018)
8. Hu, B.T., Lu, Z.D., Li, H., Chen, Q.C.: Convolutional neural network architectures for matching natural language sentences. In: International Conference on Neural Information Processing Systems, pp. 2042–2050 (2015)
9. Qiu, X., Huang, X.: Convolutional neural tensor network architecture for community-based question answering. In: AAAI Conference on Artificial Intelligence, pp. 1305–1311 (2015)
10. Yin, W., Schütze, H.: Convolutional neural network for paraphrase identification. In: Conference of the North American Chapter of the Association for Computational Linguistics, pp. 901–911 (2015)
11. Yin, W., Schütze, H.: MultiGranCNN: an architecture for general matching of text chunks on multiple levels of granularity. In: International Joint Conference on Natural Language Processing, pp. 63–73 (2015)
12. Kim, Y.: Convolutional neural networks for sentence classification. In: Conference on Empirical Methods in Natural Language Processing, Doha, Qatar, pp. 1746–1751 (2014)
13. Zhang, Y., Roller, S., Wallace, B.: MGNC-CNN: a simple approach to exploiting multiple word embeddings for sentence classification. arXiv preprint arXiv:1603.00968 (2016)
14. Lu, Y.J.: Semantic Representation and Verification of Aviation Radiotelephony Communication Based on RNN. Civil Aviation University of China (2017)
15. Jia, G.M., Lu, Y.J., Lu, W.B., et al.: Verification method for Chinese aviation radiotelephony readbacks based on LSTM-RNN. Electron. Lett. **53**(6), 401–403 (2017)
16. Zaremba, W., Sutskever, I.: Learning to execute. arXiv preprint arXiv:1410.4615 (2014)
17. Liu, Y., Sun, C.J., Lin, L., Wang, X.L.: Learning natural language inference using bidirectional LSTM model and inner-attention. arXiv preprint arXiv:1605.09090 (2016)

Determination of Sex Discriminant Function Analysis in Chinese Human Skulls

Wen Yang, Xiaoning Liu$^{(\boxtimes)}$, Fei Zhu, Guohua Geng, and Kang Li

College of Information Science and Technology, Northwest University,
Xi'an 710127, China
920759301@qq.com, xnliu@nwu.edu.cn

Abstract. Introduction: Human identity and sex determination are crucial for forensic investigations. The human skull is a useful tool for identities in natural disasters and criminal investigations. **Aim:** Using stepwise Fisher and logistic regression to build multivariate linear discriminant function to achieve sex determination for Uighur adult skull of Turpan, Xinjiang. **Methods:** Using CT equipment to acquire and reconstruct 267 (114 males and 153 females) three-dimensional skull models. Sixteen measurement indicators were measured and computed. Stepwise Fisher and logistic regression was performed to build the sex discriminant function and leave-one-out cross validation was used to evaluate accuracy. **Results:** Average of fifteen measurement indicators of male was bigger than that of female. Only one measurement indicator of male was smaller than female. Except two indicators (X7 and X13), the other existed significant difference ($p < 0.01$). According to sex discriminant function consisting of four indicators (X1, X4, X10, X11), using stepwise Fisher method, the accuracy of male was 86.8% and female was 86.2%. According to sex discriminant function consisting of five indicators (X4, X6, X12, X15, X16), using Logistic method, the accuracy of male was 89.4% and female was 90.2%. According to sex discriminant function consisting of incomplete skull with only frontal and mandibular, using stepwise Fisher method, the accuracy of male was 67.9% and female was 69.1%. Using Logistic method, the accuracy of male was 68.7% and female was 70.4%. **Conclusion:** By combining computer software with machine learning classification algorithm, the sex discrimination of complete skull and incomplete skull can be realized. In the gender identification of the Uygur population, the Logistic regression method is better than the stepwise Fisher method.

Keywords: Forensic anthropology · 3D skull model · Measurement indicators
Sex determination · Logistic regression · Stepwise Fisher

1 Introduction

The most important step in the identification of skeletonized remains. Previous studies [1, 2] indicate that pelvis is the most reliable indicator of sex assessment, and skull is the second one. However, not all forensic cases provide a complete skeleton due to breakage or postmortem destruction, while the skull can be well preserved in most cases since it is composed of hard tissue. So the skull is the most commonly used skeleton part in forensic anthropological analysis.

© Springer Nature Switzerland AG 2018
J. Zhou et al. (Eds.): CCBR 2018, LNCS 10996, pp. 589–598, 2018.
https://doi.org/10.1007/978-3-319-97909-0_63

Traditional skeletal sex assessments principally rely on visual assessments of sexually dimorphic traits. Krogman [3] used morphological methods to perform sex identification on 750 skulls of known gender. The correct rate was 82–87%. Ramsthaler et al. [4] use kappa statistics to quantify the disagreement in sex classification performed by two different observers after visual assessment, and the agreement reaches only 90.8%. However, gender determination may be problematic in some cases, because the classification standard of this method is somewhat subjective and some of the bone samples may show features between males and females. In addition, there are some scholars using the measurement method for sex identification of the skull [5, 6]. By measuring the characteristics of the skull with gender differences, a discriminant function was established to determine gender. Li et al. [5] measured sixty-seven indicators of maximal length, maximum width and cranial height in 67 skulls with clear gender. A gender discrimination equation was established and backtested. The accuracy of male discrimination was 89.2%, and the accuracy of female discrimination was 90.0%. Anabel [6] measured 6 characteristic indexes for 109 cases of skull. Discriminant analysis was performed and cross-validation was used to evaluate the discriminative power of selected variables. The discriminant accuracy rate was 75.7%, of which the male accuracy rate was 77.8% and the female accuracy was 73.7%. However, this measurement method is cumbersome and it'll cause secondary damage to the skull.

With the rapid development of computer technology, computer-aided measurement is increasingly used for sex identification of skulls. Compared with the morphological method, the main advantage of the anthropometric method is that it can obtain more objective results and be more efficient. Many studies on anthropometric methods are still being reported and their results are currently widely used in actual forensic cases [7–11].

Although anthropometric methods are helpful for sex estimation, they can have limitations when applied to actual cases. Many genetic and environmental factors are considered to influence skeletal shape, including the effects of migration and heterosis, nutritional condition, diet, and changes in these factors may degrade the reliability of the method. Consequently, we need to generate population-specific discriminant functions

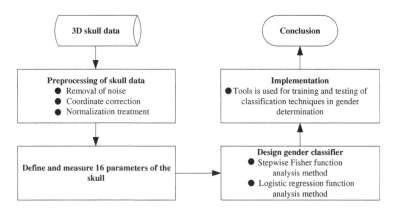

Fig. 1. Research framework

and sufficiently validate the classification accuracy. Because of the lack of reliable discriminant function in sex estimation of skulls in modern China. We have attempted to generate a new set of functions by using Chinese anthropometric measurements collected during recently adult skulls. In this paper, the framework flow chart as shown in Fig. 1.

2 Materials and Methods

2.1 Materials

It is carried out on a database of 267 whole skull CT scans (153 females and 114 males) on voluntary persons that mostly come from Uighur ethnic group in North of China, age 18–88 years for females and 20–84 years for males. The images of each subject are restored in DICOM format with a size of approximately $512 \times 512 \times 250$. Each 3D skull surface is extracted from the CT images and represented as a triangle mesh including about 220,000 vertices. All the skulls are substantially complete; that is, each skull contains all the bones from calvarias to jaw and has the full mouth of teeth. In this paper, all skull samples are unified and normalized using reference paper [12].

2.2 Methods

The sex of the adult preserved skull was initially determined by standard morphological traits. A total of 16 craniometric parameters were included in the study. All craniometric parameters are measured automatically by computer software. The parameters studied were orbital breadth (dacryon-ectoconchion), interorbital breadth (dacryon-dacryon), upper facial height (nasion-prosthion), Protruding of eyebrow, frontal chord (nasion-bregma), inter-mastoid width, nasal breadth (alare-alare), frontal arc (nasion-bregma), occipital protruding angle, mandibular angle width, mandibular height, maximum cranial length (glabella-opisthocranion), maximum cranial breadth (euryon-euryon), basion-bregma height (basion-bregma), cranial base length (basion-nasion), maximum cranial circumference.

All the measurements were taken to the nearest millimeter and were converted to centimeter and the range of angles is [0,180]. In order to reduce the measurement error, all skulls are measured three times, and then averaged as the final measurement data.

The data was tabulated in Microsoft excel worksheet and the statistical analysis was done using the statistical package for social sciences software IBM SPSS 22.0 for Windows. The general descriptive statistics was done for all the craniometric measurements providing mean and standard deviation (S.D) separately for both male and female skulls. Student's t test was performed to check if any significant differences exist ($p \leq 0.05$) among genders. Using stepwise Fisher and Logistic regression methods to establish gender discriminant function. The results were cross-validated using leave-one-out method to ensure their validity and usefulness outside the reference group on which they were calculated.

3 Results

3.1 Statistical Analysis

Using computer software to measure various craniometric parameters of 3D skull digital model, 16 craniometric parameters of male and female were obtained. The results are shown in Table 1.

Table 1. Means, Standard deviations and p values of craniometric parameters by sex in North of China population

Index	Parameters	Male		Female		p value
		Mean	SD	Mean	SD	
X_1	Orbital breadth	98.7	3.1	95.2	3.5	<0.01
X_2	Inter-orbital breadth	24.9	2.69	23.8	2.1	<0.01
X_3	Upper facial height	106.3	5.1	103.8	4.6	<0.01
X_4	Protruding of eyebrow	32.3	8.9	29.4	5.6	<0.01
X_5	Frontal chord	113.5	4.9	110.1	5.6	<0.01
X_6	Inter-mastoid width	110.9	5.9	107.9	4.9	<0.01
X_7	Nasal breadth	29.9	2.7	29.4	8.9	0.083
X_8	Frontal arc	26.5	2.1	25.7	1.7	<0.01
X_9	Occipital protruding angle	167.0	11.1	177.8	3.1	<0.01
X_{10}	Mandibular angle width	102.3	6.4	97.7	5.8	<0.01
X_{11}	Mandibular height	45.7	3.9	43.6	3.3	<0.01
X_{12}	Maximum cranial length	178.1	7.4	168.6	5.7	<0.01
X_{13}	Maximum cranial breadth	138.7	6.3	136.4	5.5	0.062
X_{14}	Basion-bregMa height	13.4	3.6	12.9	2.9	<0.01
X_{15}	Cranial base length	9.6	2.6	9.2	3.1	<0.01
X_{16}	Maximum cranial circumference	52.3	4.4	50.2	4.1	<0.01

Notes: The unit of measurement for distance is mm; the angle range is [0,180].

A direct comparison of the collected measured data depicted in Table 1 shows a significant difference in size between male and female crania. As can be seen from the table, there are 15 parameters in the 16 craniometric parameters more men than women, and only one craniometric parameter named occipital protruding angle is more women than men. This is consistent with the results of Li [13]. Analysis of the significance of the 16 craniometric parameters showed that there was no significant difference in the mean of the 2 parameters ($p > 0.05$), and the significance of the remaining 14 parameters was greater in men than in women ($p < 0.01$). Here we use the t-test method in statistics to obtain the p value result by looking up the corresponding cut-off table. The p value is a decline index of the result reliability. The smaller the value of p, the more significant the result. In many research areas, $p = 0.05$ is generally considered to be acceptable in the wrong boundary level, so we also choose 0.05 as the boundary value in this article. From the table, it can be seen that the p values of Nasal breadth and

Maximum cranial breadth are both greater than 0.05, so there is no significant difference between men and women in these two items; the gender differences were not statistically significant, which is consistent with the findings of Li et al. [5]. The other 14 craniometric parameters except Nasal breadth and Maximum cranial breadth were significant, and the difference was statistically significant. There are overlaps in the values of the craniometric parameters for men and women.

3.2 Discriminant Function Analysis

From the 267 skull models, 178 skulls (76 male, 102 female) were selected as training samples, and the remaining 89 skull models were used as test samples. The stepwise Fisher method and Logistic regression method were used to establish multivariate discriminant equations.

3.2.1 Stepwise Fisher Function Analysis

The Fisher discriminant method uses projection methods to project n m-dimensional data into a space, so that the projection results have the properties of maximum discrimination between classes and minimal intraclass distance. Because there are many defined craniometric parameters and the contribution of each indicator is not the same, this article adopts a gradual introduction. The stepped Fisher discriminating method, which measures the index and used as a discriminant factor, removes the insignificant craniometric parameters, thereby improving the accuracy of the gender discrimination. The specific steps of the Fisher discriminant analysis are shown in Fig. 2.

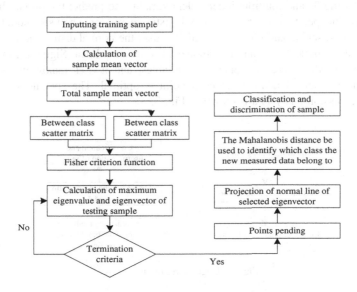

Fig. 2. Fisher discriminant procedure

For the 178 skull data sets, a stepwise Fisher discriminant method was used to establish a gender discrimination equation with Orbital breadth, Protruding of eyebrow, Mandibular angle width, and Basion-bregma height as factors:

$$Z1 = 3.976 \cdot X_1 + 4.722 \cdot X_4 + 4.005 \cdot X_{10} + 8.629 \cdot X_{14} - 532.436$$
$$Z2 = 3.883 \cdot X_1 + 4.462 \cdot X_4 + 3.714 \cdot X_{10} + 8.905 \cdot X_{14} - 443.598$$
$$(1)$$

When Z1 > Z2, the skull to be detected is male; when Z1 < Z2, the skull to be detected is female.

Stepwise Fisher analysis method classified 85.2% of the skulls (84.2% males and 86.2% females). Leave-one-out cross-validations proved that the model was highly reliable with 86.5% of skulls being correctly classified as shown in Table 2.

Table 2. Classification accuracy of craniofacial parameters in North of China population by Stepwise Fisher discriminant function analysis

Craniofacial parameters and functions	Male (n %)		Female (n %)		Total (%)
Stepwise Fisher function analysis	32/38	84.2	44/51	86.2	85.2
Cross-validated	33/38	86.8	44/51	86.2	86.5

3.2.2   Logistic Regression Function Analysis

Logistic regression analysis uses a multiple regression relationship formed between a dependent variable and multiple independent variables to predict the probability of an event. The independent variable of the logistic regression analysis model can be continuous or discrete, and it doesn't need to satisfy the normal distribution, so it has a wider range of application than other models. It uses a nonlinear Sigmoid function for the analysis of the two-class dependent variables, and it uses maximum likelihood estimation to ensure that the fit at each point is optimal. The specific steps of the Logistic regression analysis are shown in Fig. 3.

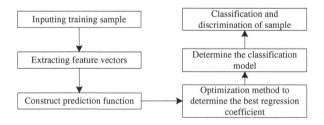

Fig. 3. Logistic regression steps

In this study, Logistic regression was applied to identify the sex of cranium, and the accuracy of the test was verified by experimental results. For the 178 skull models, the forward stepwise regression based on maximum likelihood estimation established Protruding of eyebrow, Inter-mastoid width, maximum cranial length, cranial base length, maximum cranial circumference as the independent variable regression equation is as follows:

$$P(y = 1|x) = \frac{e^{-0.081 \cdot X_4 + 0.638 \cdot X_6 + 0.194 \cdot X_{12} + 0.201 \cdot X_{15} + 0.343 \cdot X_{16} - 107.376}}{1 + e^{-0.081 \cdot X_4 + 0.638 \cdot X_6 + 0.194 \cdot X_{12} + 0.201 \cdot X_{15} + 0.343 \cdot X_{16} - 107.376}}$$

$$P(y = 0|x) = \frac{1}{1 + e^{-0.081 \cdot X_4 + 0.638 \cdot X_6 + 0.194 \cdot X_{12} + 0.201 \cdot X_{15} + 0.343 \cdot X_{16} - 107.376}}$$

$$(2)$$

Logistic regression analysis method classified 85.2% of the skulls (84.2% males and 86.2% females). Leave-one-out cross-validations proved that the model was highly reliable with 86.5% of skulls being correctly classified as shown in Table 3.

Table 3. Classification accuracy of craniofacial parameters in North of China population by Logistic regression function analysis

Craniofacial parameters and functions	Male (n %)		Female (n %)		Total (%)
Logistic regression function analysis	33/38	86.8	45/51	88.2	87.5
Cross-validated	34/38	89.4	46/51	90.2	89.8

3.3 Sex Determination of Incomplete Skulls

In actual criminal cases, incomplete skulls are often encountered, while sex identification methods used generally do not involve gender identification of non-integrated skulls. In order to verify the universality of the proposed algorithm, we use the two methods above to identify the skulls without mandibular and frontal bone respectively. Of course, this method can also be applied to incomplete skulls with missing parts. Due to the lack of examples of incomplete skulls, the incomplete skull model data used in this paper was processed using software for the complete skull. For skulls with frontal bone only, two craniofacial parameters of the frontal chord and the frontal arc can be measured to establish a discriminant equation. For the skull with mandible only, the craniofacial parameters of mandibular angle width and mandibular height can be measured to establish the discriminant equation. The results are shown in Table 4.

From the table above, it can be seen that stepwise Fisher method and Logistic regression method can both achieve sex identification of incomplete skulls with high accuracy and can provide reference for practical applications. For the incomplete skulls in northern China, the stepwise Fisher method is better and the accuracy is higher than the Logistic regression method. The accuracy of mandibles used for gender identification is higher than that of the frontal bones. However, the actual situation still needs to be verified.

Table 4. The discriminant function and accuracy of the two methods

Methods	The frontal bone		Mandible	
	Discriminant Function	Accuracy Rate	Discriminant Function	Accuracy Rate
Stepwise Fisher	$Z1 = 1.436 \cdot X_5 + 11.734 \cdot X_8 - 68.149$ $Z2 = 1.422 \cdot X_5 + 10.918 \cdot X_8 - 31.723$	67.9%	$Z1 = 5.252 \cdot X_{10} + 3.565 \cdot X_{11} - 121.854$ $Z2 = 5.187 \cdot X_{10} + 3.384 \cdot X_{11} - 79.324$	69.1%
Logistic Regressi on	$P(y = 1 \mid x) =$ $\dfrac{e^{0.433 \cdot X_5 + 1.316 \cdot X_8 - 78.885}}{1 + e^{0.433 \cdot X_5 + 1.316 \cdot X_8 - 78.885}}$ $P(y = 0 \mid x) =$ $\dfrac{1}{1 + e^{0.433 \cdot X_5 + 1.316 \cdot X_8 - 78.885}}$	68.7%	$P(y = 1 \mid x) =$ $\dfrac{e^{0.196 \cdot X_{10} + 0.168 \cdot X_{11} - 28.22}}{1 + e^{0.196 \cdot X_{10} + 0.168 \cdot X_{11} - 28.22}}$ $P(y = 0 \mid x) =$ $\dfrac{1}{1 + e^{0.196 \cdot X_{10} + 0.168 \cdot X_{11} - 28.22}}$	70.4%

4 Discussion

In this study, we generated a new set of sex discriminant functions for the skull by using recent anthropological measurements of Chinese skulls. Based on the results presented above, we can conclude that China population has a pronounced sexual dimorphism. When measuring skull indicators, two principles should be followed. First, it is convenient to define and measure. Many previous reports [14–16] have mentioned the importance of generating practical discriminant functions that utilize measurable characteristics from clearly identifiable landmarks. Second, measurements must be effective on partially broken skulls. In actual forensic cases, we often encounter parts of bones that are broken and so only a limited number of discriminant functions can be applied.

In addition to broken bones, we frequently see cases where only the frontal bone or mandible is found. In consideration of this, separate discriminant functions were established for the variables associated with these two parts of the skull. Several other reports have established discriminant functions for the skull [16–19]. The accuracy in these reports ranged from 83.07 to 89.71% for functions constructed with four or five variables [16], from 84.1 to 83.7% with five or seven variables [17], from 83.5 to 87.6% with three to eight variables [18], and from 81.1 to 85.7% with three or six variables [19]. Although the variables selected in these previously established functions are not the same as those selected in this study, the classification accuracies of the functions are similar.

In this paper, the accuracy rate of gender discrimination is between 85% and 90% for complete skull and about 70% for incomplete skull. It basically meets the application requirements and can provide reference for practical work. However, in practical applications, the higher the accuracy is, the better the accuracy of this article is. There is still some gap between the accuracy of this article and the ideal value. This is also the motivation and direction for future research. Twisha et al. [20] used Logistic regression and discriminant functions to perform skull sex discrimination on 901 healthy Gujarati. The accuracy of male discrimination was 92%, and the accuracy of female discrimination was 80.9%. Ren et al. [21] combined the non-measurable and non-measurable characteristics, combined the nonlinear dimensionality reduction and non-linear classification methods to perform gender discrimination on the skulls of 94 Han adults. The highest accuracy rate was 96.4%. Although the accuracy rate varies from different researcher, different races, different sample sizes and different methods, it is of reference value in the application.

Based on the study, we can conclude that the North China population has a pronounced sexual dimorphism. It is imperative to use the discriminant functions only to the similar population. In other words, the population groups with similar sexual dimorphism can use this formula.

5 Conclusion

Summarizing the results above, we can conclude that the Uygur skulls in Chinese present a well-defined sexual dimorphism. The discriminant function established in this paper still needs a large number of test samples to verify, and the application of the actual case can confirm its application value. Further research may consider expanding the skull training sample sets and test sample sets to increase credibility. For incomplete skulls, the skull can be divided into regions. Apart from the frontal bone and mandible, sex identification can be performed on other cranial regions. In addition, it is necessary to further improve the performance and accuracy of the discriminant method. We hope our study can contribute to further population data studies, or can even contribute to skull gender recognition in other populations.

Acknowledgement. This work was supported by the National Natural Science Foundation of China (61363065) and Shaanxi Provincial Natural Science Foundation of China (2014JM8358) and Shaanxi Province International Cooperation Project (2013KW04-04) and Shaanxi provincial science and Technology Department Project (2010JQ8011) and the Graduate Scientific Research Foundation of Northwest University (no. YZZ17181) and Shaanxi Provincial Natural Science Basic Research Project (2018JM6061).

References

1. Ubelaker, D.H., Volk, C.G.: A test of the Phenice method for the estimation of sex. J. Forensic Sci. **47**(1), 19–24 (2002)
2. Sangvichien, S., Boonkaew, K., Chuncharunee, A., et al.: Sex determination in Thai skulls by using Craniometry: multiple logistic regression analysis. Jpn. J. Appl. Phys. **51**(12), 2407–2423 (2007)
3. Krogman, W.M.: Book Reviews: The Human Skeleton in Forensic Medicine, vol. 4, 3rd edn. Charles C Thoms, US (1962). pp. 287–288
4. Ramsthaler, F., Kettner, M., Gehl, A., et al.: Digital forensic osteology: morphological sexing of skeletal remains using volume-rendered cranial CT scans. Forensic Sci. Int. **195**(1–3), 148–152 (2010)
5. Li, M., Fan, Y.N., Yu, Y.M., et al.: Sex assessment of adult from southwest area of China by bones of facial cranium. Chin. J. Forensic Med. **27**(2), 132–134 (2012)

6. Anabel, A.: Sexual dimorphism in base of skull. Anthropol. Anz. **74**(1), 9–14 (2017)
7. Kharosha, M.A., Almadani, O., Ghaleb, S.S., et al.: Sexual dimorphism of the mandible in a modern Egyptian population. J. Forensic Leg. Med. **17**(4), 213–215 (2010)
8. Spradley, M.K., Jantz, R.L.: Sex estimation in forensic anthropology: skull versus postcranial elements. J. Forensic Sci. **56**(2), 289–296 (2011)
9. Raghavendra Babu, Y.P., Kanchan, T., Attiku, Y., et al.: Sex estimation from foramen magnum dimensions in an Indian population. J. Forensic Leg. Med. **19**(3), 162–167 (2012)
10. Akhlaghi, M., Bakhtavar, K., Moarefdoost, J., et al.: Frontal sinus parameters in computed tomography and sex determination. Leg. Med. **19**, 22–27 (2016)
11. Tanya, K., Arpita, K., Uday, G., et al.: Cephalometric analysis for gender determination using maxillary sinus index: a novel dimension in personal identification. Int. J. Dent. **2017**(1), 1–4 (2017)
12. Liu, X.N., Zhu, L.P., Lu, Y.N., et al.: Hierarchical skull registration method with a bounded rotation angle. In: Intelligent Computing Methodologies, pp. 561–571 (2017)
13. Li, J.S., Zhang, F.S., Zhu, B.M., et al.: Observation and measurement of men's and women's skull. J. Shanxi Datong Univ. (Natural Science) **28**(4), 45–46 (2012)
14. Hanihara, K., Kimura, K., Minamidate, T.: The sexing of Japanese skeleton by means of discriminant function. Nihon Hoigaku Zasshi **18**(2), 107–114 (1964)
15. Tanaka, T., Hanihara, K., Koizumi, K.: Sex determination of the modern Japanese skull by means of discriminant function. Sapporo Med. J. **48**, 582–593 (1979)
16. Hanihara, K.: Sexual diagnosis of Japanese skulls and scapulae by means of discriminant function. Anthropolgical Sci. **67**(4), 191–197 (2008)
17. Iscan, M.Y., Yoshino, M., Kato, S.: Sexual dimorphism in modern Japanese crania. Am. J. Hum. Biol. **7**, 459–464 (1995)
18. Giles, E., Elliot, O.: Sex determination by discriminant function analysis of crania. Am. J. Phys. Anthropol. **21**, 53–68 (1963)
19. Steyn, M., Iscan, M.Y.: Sexual dimorphism in the crania and mandibles of South African whites. Forensic Sci. Int. **98**(1–2), 9–16 (1998)
20. Twisha, S., Patel, M.N., Nath, S., et al.: Determination of sex using cephalo-facial dimensions by discriminant function and logistic regression equations. Egypt. J. Forensic Sci. **6**(2), 114–119 (2016)
21. Ren, R.R., Zhou, M.Q., Geng, G.H., et al.: Nonlinear sex determination and three dimensional quantitative representation of the skull morphology. J. Beijing Normal Univ. (Natural Science) **53**(1), 19–23 (2017)

Fast and Robust Detection of Anatomical Landmarks Using Cascaded 3D Convolutional Networks Guided by Linear Square Regression

Zi-Rui Wang[1][✉], Bao-Cai Yin[2], Jun Du[1], Cong Liu[2],
Xiaodong Tao[2], and Guoping Hu[2]

[1] NELSLIP, University of Science and Technology of China, Hefei, China
cs211@mail.ustc.edu.cn, jundu@ustc.edu.cn
[2] iFLYTEK AI Research, Hefei, China
{bcyin,congliu2,xdtao,gphu}@iflytek.com

Abstract. Detecting anatomical landmarks on structural magnetic resonance imaging (MRI) is an important medical computer-aid technique. However, for some brain anatomical landmarks detection, linear/non-linear registration with skull stripping across subjects is usually unavoidable. In this paper, we propose a novel method. Starting from the original MRI data, a series of 3D convolutional neural networks (cascaded 3D-CNNs) are adopted to iteratively update the predicted landmarks. Specially, the predicted landmarks of each 3D-CNN model are used to estimate the corresponding linear transformation matrix by linear square regression, which is very different from traditional registration methods. Based on the estimated matrix, we can use it to transform the original image for getting the new image for the next 3D-CNN model. With these cascaded 3D-CNNs and linear square regression, we can finally achieve registration and landmark detection.

Keywords: Anatomical landmark detection · Cascaded 3D-CNNs
Linear square regression · Fast · Robust

1 Introduction

Recently, deep learning [1] is increasingly used for landmarks detection in medical analysis [2–6]. Interesting, a data-driven manner is utilized to generate discriminative landmarks [6] between Alzheimer's disease (AD) [8] and normal control, which can effectively improve the performance of AD diagnosis. This kind of landmark detection is also the topic of this paper.

In [6], Zhang et al. defined discriminative landmarks between AD and healthy control (HC) via a data-driven manner and then used a regression-forest algorithm to identify those landmarks. Furthermore, similar method can be effectively used with the help of longitudinal structural MR images [9]. But, in order

© Springer Nature Switzerland AG 2018
J. Zhou et al. (Eds.): CCBR 2018, LNCS 10996, pp. 599–608, 2018.
https://doi.org/10.1007/978-3-319-97909-0_64

to cover landmarks in different locations, many random forests have to be trained and used. Besides, massive image patches have to be extracted for training these models. Moreover, some additional fine processes have to be employed to make the algorithm have final good performance. As an improved scheme, a fully convolutional network (FCN) has also been adopted to jointly predict all landmarks at the same time in [7]. However, the FCN was completed by two stage training, due to limited medical imaging data. But, in the first training stage, massive image patches still need to be extracted for training.

In addition to the above mentioned problems, as a basic step for brain MRI preprocessing, linear/non-linear registration with skull stripping across subjects is usually unavoidable. To address this critical issue, we propose a novel method to directly work on original MRI data (with little preprocessing), for iteratively estimating landmarks with cascaded 3D-CNNs. In particular, landmarks predicted by each 3D-CNN model are used to estimate the corresponding linear transformation matrix by linear square regression. Based on the estimate transformation matrix, we can use it to transform the image and obtain the new image for the next 3D-CNN model. Finally, a linear transformation matrix can be estimated. This registration strategy is very different from traditional linear registration methods [10]. They usually try to hard search a best transformation which can yield the minimum cost for a given cost function while our registration can be regarded as a learning-based method. The whole procedure can be regarded as fast linear image registration and seamlessly achieve landmark detection at the same time.

2   Materials

All subjects used in this study are obtained from the publicly available dataset, ADNI-1[1]. Totally, there are 199 AD, 229 HCs and 404 MCI subjects, each with 1.5T T1-weighted MR image. All these images are conducted with some necessary preprocessing, i.e., reorientation and resampling to $256 \times 256 \times 256$ (with a voxel resolution $1 \times 1 \times 1 \, mm^3$). A preprocessed MR image and its corresponding landmarks are shown in Fig. 1. As we can see, many landmarks are concentrated around the hippocampus. These areas play important roles in memory and are related to AD [8]. We call these images as original images (ori-images) and the images after linear registration (the Colin27 template [14] for reference) as lin-images.

In experiments, we randomly select 420 subjects from 428 AD and HC subjects as our training set, and use the remaining 8 subjects as validation set to tune the parameters of our networks. Totally, 404 new MCI subjects are used as our testing set to evaluate our approach, demonstrating its robustness. For all the training subjects, their corresponding 100 anatomical landmarks in ori-images (ori-landmarks) and lin-images (lin-landmarks) respectively are defined by [6]. For all the testing subjects, we use their corresponding 100 ori-landmarks

---

[1] http://adni.loni.usc.edu.

defined by the same way as the ground truth to evaluate the performance of our approach. All these landmarks can be represented as follows:

$$L = [(x_1, y_1, z_1)^{\mathrm{T}}, .(x_i, y_i, z_i)^{\mathrm{T}}.., (x_{100}, y_{100}, z_{100})^{\mathrm{T}}] \tag{1}$$

where $(x_i, y_i, z_i)^{\mathrm{T}}$ denotes the coordinate of the i-th landmark. For simplicity, we use L_{ori} and L_{lin} to represent the ori-landmarks and the lin-landmarks, respectively.

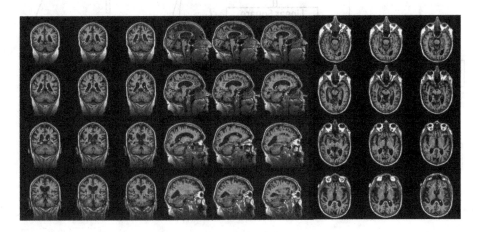

Fig. 1. Example anatomical landmarks on different slices with 3 mm striding.

3 Method

3.1 Overview

The pipeline of proposed method is shown in Fig. 2, which is composed of a number of similar blocks $(1,...,n)$. The input images of each block come from the output images of its previous block. Each block consists of two main parts, namely a 3D-CNN model and a landmark-based linear transformation estimation with linear square regression (LSR), except the last block that only contains a 3D-CNN model. The structure of 3D-CNN is the same for all the blocks. The details of the 3D-CNN and the LSR will be described in Sects. 3.2 and 3.3.

In the training stage, for the 3D-CNN in the first block, we use the ori-images and their corresponding L_{ori} (L_{lin}^1) to train the first 3D-CNN. Once completing this training step, the trained 3D-CNN is used to predict the landmarks L_{pre}^1 of the training ori-images. Then, we can conduct the LSR between the L_{pre}^1 and their corresponding lin-landmarks L_{lin} and get the corresponding transformation matrix W_1 and biases $\boldsymbol{b}_1$ for each subject in the first block. Based on the estimated matrix W_1, biases $\boldsymbol{b}_1$ and the ori-images, we can get a set of new training data (through linear transformation) for the next 3D-CNN. By applying the same corresponding matrix W_1 and biases $\boldsymbol{b}_1$ to the L_{lin}, the labels

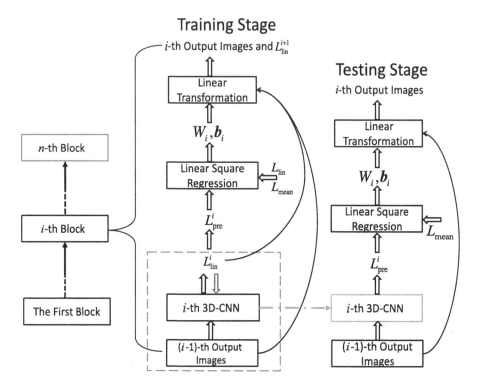

Fig. 2. The pipeline of proposed method.

L_{lin}^{2} of the second 3D-CNN in the second block can be obtained. Next, we keep training the second 3D-CNN. Especially, the weights of the first 3D-CNN are used to initialize the weights of the second 3D-CNN, which is very important as shown in Sect. 4.3. But, there is a problem in the testing stage, since we don't know their lin-landmarks L_{lin}, to address this problem, we use the average landmarks L_{mean} of all training lin-landmarks L_{lin} as our targets in the LSR for every testing subject. This could cause a potential issue since the targeted landmarks are changing across subjects. To further handle this problem and get better performance, we propose a novel data augmentation, i.e., we also use the L_{mean} as targets in the LSR to augment our training data for the second 3D-CNN, which helps our model to see more data based on different transformations and thus enhance the generalization ability of our model. In this way, the amount of training data of the second 3D-CNN are also doubled, compared with the training data of the first 3D-CNN, since no data augmentation is used for the first 3D-CNN. The same training/testing strategies are used for the blocks 3 to n.

3.2   3D-CNN

The conventional convolutional neural network (CNN) [11] consists of successively stacked convolutional layers, optionally followed by spatial pooling, one or more fully-connected layers and a softmax layer. For convolutional and pooling layers in the usual 2-dimensional CNN (2D-CNN), each layer is a three-dimensional tensor organized by a set of planes called feature maps, while convolutional and pooling layers in the 3D-CNN are the four-dimensional tensors organized by a set of cubes, which is naturally suitable to deal with 3D MR images. The fully-connected layer and the softmax layer are the same with the common deep neural network (DNN). Inspired by the locally-sensitive, orientation-selective neurons in the visual system of cats, each unit in a feature map is constrained to connect a local region in the previous layer, which is called the local receptive field. Two contiguous local receptive fields are usually shifted for s pixels (referred as stride) along a certain direction. All units in the same feature map of a convolutional layer share a set of weights, each computing a dot product between its weights and local receptive field in the previous layer and then followed by nonlinear activation functions (e.g., rectifier). Meanwhile, the units in a pooling layer perform a spatial average or max operation for their local receptive field to reduce spatial resolution and noise interferences. Accordingly, the key information for identifying the pattern can be retained. We formalize the convolution operation in 3D-CNN as:

$$Y_{i,j,h,k} = \sum_{m,n,q,l} X_{(i-1)\times s+m,(j-1)\times s+n,(h-1)\times s+q,l} K_{m,n,q,k,l}$$

where $X_{i,j,h,k}$ is the value of the input unit in feature map k at row i, column j and height h, while $Y_{i,j,h,k}$ is corresponding to the output unit. $K_{m,n,q,k,l}$ is the connection weight between a unit in feature map k of the output and a unit in channel l of the input, with an offset of m rows, n columns and q heights between the output unit and the input unit. Similarly, the pooling operation can be conducted by using a max operation in this study. The 3D-CNN model used in this paper is shown in Fig. 3.

3.3   Linear Square Regression

As shown in Fig. 4, given D source points (blue points) $S_d = (x_{s\_d}, y_{s\_d}, z_{s\_d})^T$ $(d = 1, ..., D)$ and their corresponding target points (red points) $T_d = (x_{t\_d}, y_{t\_d}, z_{t\_d})^T$ $(d = 1, ..., D)$, the LSR tries to find a 3×3 matrix W and a 3-dimensional vector b to minimize the Eq. (2) so that the new transformed points Tr_d (green points) can get close to the target points.

$$Loss = \frac{1}{2} \sum_{d=1}^{D} |WS_d + b - T_d|^2 \tag{2}$$

namely:

$$(W^*, b^*) = \underset{(W,b)}{\arg\min} \; Loss \tag{3}$$

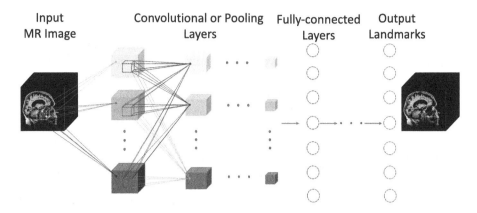

Fig. 3. Schematic diagram of 3DCNN for landmark detection.

The Eq. 3 has closed solution. So the transformed points:

$$\mathrm{Tr}_d = WS_d + \boldsymbol{b} \quad (d = 1, ..., D) \tag{4}$$

In the i-th block, for the input image j, the source points are the predicted landmarks $L^{i,j}_{\mathrm{pre}}$ of the i-th 3D-CNN while the target points are the lin-landmarks L^j_{lin} or the average landmarks L_{mean}. Based on the transformation matrix W^j_i and the bias vector $\boldsymbol{b}^j_i$, we can transform the input image j and the corresponding landmarks $L^{i,j}_{\mathrm{lin}}$ for training the $(i+1)$-th 3D-CNN in the training stage. Obviously, the transformed landmarks $L^{(i+1),j}_{\mathrm{lin}}$ can be directly obtained by using the Eq. (4), and the transformed image can also be obtained by using this equation. As shown in Fig. 5, we can assume a point $\mathrm{P_T}$ in the transformed image, corresponds to its corresponding location $\mathrm{P_S}$ in the image j, which can be obtained by tracing back based on the W^j_i and $\boldsymbol{b}^j_i$, thus, we can get the intensity value for the point $\mathrm{P_T}$ ($\mathrm{P_S}$) according to image interpolation.

4 Experiments

4.1 Evaluation Criteria

In the experiments, we focus on evaluating our approach in detecting anatomical landmarks for the ori-images. For example, for the testing subject j, based on the predicted landmarks $L^{n,j}_{\mathrm{pre}}$ of the last 3D-CNN model and a series of estimated transformation matrices W^j_i ($i = 1, ..., n-1$) and biases $\boldsymbol{b}^j_i$ ($i = 1, ..., n-1$), the final predicted landmarks in the ori-images can be traced back according to the following formula:

$$L^{i,j}_{\mathrm{pre}} = \left(W^j_i\right)^{-1} * \left(L^{(i+1),j}_{\mathrm{pre}} - \boldsymbol{b}^j_i\right) \quad (i = n-1, ..., 1)$$

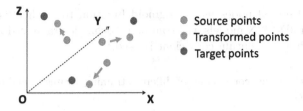

Fig. 4. The diagram of the linear square regression. (Color figure online)

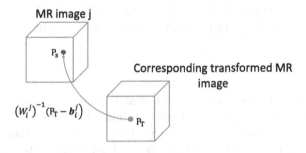

Fig. 5. The diagram about how to find corresponding points between MR image and transformed MR image by using the transformation matrix and bias.

To quantitatively evaluate detection performance, we use the mean Euclidean distance to measure the detection error (DE) between all final predicted landmarks and the ground truth landmarks in the ori-images:

$$DE = \sum_{p=1}^{P} \sqrt{(x_p - \tilde{x}_p)^2 + (y_p - \tilde{y}_p)^2 + (z_p - \tilde{z}_p)^2}$$

(x_p, y_p, z_p) is the ground truth landmark and $(\tilde{x}_p, \tilde{y}_p, \tilde{z}_p)$ is the predicted landmark. There are P (40400) landmarks in all for 404 MCI subjects, each with 100 landmarks.

4.2   Experimental Setup

All 3D-CNN models in our approach have the same structure, i.e., five convolutional layers in the front. Their local receptive fields, feature maps and strides are [(5,5,5),24,1], [(5,5,5),64,1], [(5,5,5),128,1], [(3,3,3),256,1], [(3,3,3),512,1], respectively. The first four convolutional layers are followed by a pooling layer while the last convolutional layer is followed by two fully-connected layers with 1024 neural nodes. All convolutional layers are equipped with batch normalization. All pooling layers have local receptive field (2,2,2) and stride is 2, except the first pooling layer which has local receptive field (3,3,3) and stride 3. The activation functions of the convolutional and fully-connected layers are ReLU, while the output layer with 300 neural nodes uses a sigmoid function to predict landmarks. In the training of 3D-CNN models, the common stochastic gradient descent (SGD) algorithm with a momentum coefficient is used.

Table 1. The DE (mm) comparison of different training strategies and different total numbers of blocks.

	Block1	Block2	Block3	Block4	Block5
Structure1	3.20	2.86	2.72	2.66	2.66
Structure2	3.20	2.82	2.68	2.57	2.57
Structure3	3.20	2.70	2.27	2.02	**1.95**

4.3   Results

Table 1 lists the DE comparison of different training strategies and different total numbers of blocks. For structure1, we don't use data augmentation and all CNN models are randomly initialized. That is, in the training stage, only lin-landmarks L_{lin} are used as targets in the LSR while both L_{lin} and L_{mean} are used in the structure2. Further more, in the structure3, not only the data augmentation strategy is used in the training stage, but also the weights of the $(i-1)$-th 3D-CNN are used to initialize the weights of the i-th 3D-CNN. For all structures (1–3), with the increase of the number of blocks, the performance of our approach can become better and better. In the structure3, the DE can be reduced to 1.95 mm (block5) from 3.20 mm (block1), which shows the usefulness of the cascaded 3D-CNNs in this task. When the number of blocks is increased to 5, the performance keeps unchanging (for structure1 and structure2) or just small increment (i.e., for structure3). Moreover, when the number of blocks is set to 5, compared with the structure1, the DE of the structure2 can be reduced to 2.57 mm from 2.66 mm due to the use of data augmentation strategy, which enhances the generalization ability of our model. Finally, the improvement of the structure3 is significant, compared with the structure2, due to two main reasons. First, the i-th 3D-CNN can get better initial weights than random initialization and thus can be trained easily. Second, more importantly, we think the training data of the i-th 3D-CNN is augmented based on the training data of the $(i-1)$-th 3D-CNN, which allows our model to cover more possible transformations. All these make our 3D-CNN models improve the performance gradually.

Table 2 lists the average detection time for the whole process in our proposed approach, using a computer with the processor of Intel(R) Xeon(R) E5-2650 2.20 GHz and NVIDIA GPU P40. It should be noted that each individual time includes the time cost of reading and writing data. As we can see, our proposed approach is free of traditional image registration and has very low detection error.

We tentatively only use the traditional linear registration (TLR) method including skull stripping to detect landmarks. First, all testing images are skull-stripped and then the FLIRT [13] is used to achieve linear registration based on the Colin27 template. Finally, we take the average landmarks of all training lin-landmarks as our detected landmarks in lin-images for every testing image and then their landmarks in corresponding ori-images can be found by utilizing linear registration matrix. In Table 3, we can see the detection result 2.93 mm is unsatisfactory if we only use TLR. Further more, if we train a 3D-CNN model based on these lin-images, the detection result can reduce to 2.05 mm while the 3D-CNN model based on ori-images only can achieve 3.20 mm as shown in Table 1, which means linear registration is very important. Comparing with our method, the traditional linear registration with skull-stripping needs more processes and gets higher detection error than our proposed method. So we think our method has more advantages and the whole procedure can be regarded as fast linear registration and seamlessly achieve landmark detection at the same time.

Table 2. The average detection time of the whole process of our proposed system.

Procedure	Implementation	Individual time	Total time
3D-CNNs (1–5) prediction	C++/MXNet [12]	13.3 s	15.9 s
LSR (block 1–4)	Python	2.3 s	
Final prediction	Python	0.3 s	

Table 3. The comparison of different methods.

Method	DE
TLR	2.93 mm
TLR+3D-CNN	2.05 mm
Our proposed method	**1.95** mm

5   Conclusion

In this study, we propose a novel and effective approach to fast detect anatomical landmarks and estimate linear transformation for image registration. It's interesting we find a clever and effective way to combine landmarks detection and linear registration. Our experimental results show a competitive advantage. For the future work, we will verify our algorithm on other anatomical landmarks and enhance our deep learning model.

Acknowledgments. This work was supported in part by the National Key R&D Program of China under contract No. 2017YFB1002202, in part by the National Natural Science Foundation of China under Grants 61671422 and U1613211, in part by the MOE-Microsoft Key Laboratory of USTC. The authors would like to thank Dr. Dinggang Shen for the contributions on implementation.

References

1. LeCun, Y., Bengio, Y., Hinton, G.: Deep learning. Nature **521**, 436–444 (2015)
2. Riegler, G., Urschler, M., Ruther, M., Bischof, H., Stern, D.: Anatomical landmark detection in medical applications driven by synthetic data. In: IEEE International Conference on Computer Vision Workshops, pp. 12–16 (2015)
3. Zheng, Y., Liu, D., Georgescu, B., Nguyen, H., Comaniciu, D.: 3D deep learning for efficient and robust landmark detection in volumetric data. In: Navab, N., Hornegger, J., Wells, W.M., Frangi, A.F. (eds.) MICCAI 2015. LNCS, vol. 9349, pp. 565–572. Springer, Cham (2015). https://doi.org/10.1007/978-3-319-24553-9_69
4. Payer, C., Štern, D., Bischof, H., Urschler, M.: Regressing heatmaps for multiple landmark localization using CNNs. In: Ourselin, S., Joskowicz, L., Sabuncu, M.R., Unal, G., Wells, W. (eds.) MICCAI 2016. LNCS, vol. 9901, pp. 230–238. Springer, Cham (2016). https://doi.org/10.1007/978-3-319-46723-8_27
5. Ghesu, F.C., Georgescu, B., Mansi, T., Neumann, D., Hornegger, J., Comaniciu, D.: An artificial agent for anatomical landmark detection in medical images. In: Ourselin, S., Joskowicz, L., Sabuncu, M.R., Unal, G., Wells, W. (eds.) MICCAI 2016. LNCS, vol. 9902, pp. 229–237. Springer, Cham (2016). https://doi.org/10.1007/978-3-319-46726-9_27
6. Zhang, J., Gao, Y., Gao, Y., Munsell, B.C., Shen, D.: Detecting anatomical landmarks for fast Alzheimers disease diagnosis. IEEE Trans. Med. Imaging **35**(12), 2524–2533 (2016)
7. Zhang, J., Liu, M., Shen, D.: Detecting anatomical landmarks from limited medical imaging data using two-stage task-oriented deep neural networks. IEEE Trans. Image Process. **26**(10), 4753–4764 (2017)
8. Hyman, B.T., Van Hoesen, G.W., Damasio, A.R., Barnes, C.L.: Alzheimer's disease: cell-specific pathology isolates the hippocampal formation. Science **225**, 1168–1171 (1984)
9. Zhang, J., Liu, M., An, L., Gao, Y., Shen, D.: Alzheimer's disease diagnosis using landmark-based features from longitudinal structural MR images. IEEE J. Biomed. Health Inform. **21**(6), 1607–1616 (2017)
10. Jenkinson, M., Bannister, P., Michael, B., Stephen, S.: Improved optimization for the robust and accurate linear registration and motion correction of brain images. Neuroimage **17**(2), 825–841 (2002)
11. LeCun, Y., Bottou, L., Bengio, Y., Haffner, P.: Gradient-based learning applied to document recognition. Proc. IEEE **86**(11), 2278–2324 (1998)
12. Chen, T., Mu, L., et al.: Mxnet: a flexible and efficient machine learning library for heterogeneous distributed systems. arXiv preprint arXiv:1512.01274 (2015)
13. Fischer, B., Modersitzki, J.: FLIRT: a flexible image registration toolbox. In: Gee, J.C., Maintz, J.B.A., Vannier, M.W. (eds.) WBIR 2003. LNCS, vol. 2717, pp. 261–270. Springer, Heidelberg (2003). https://doi.org/10.1007/978-3-540-39701-4_28
14. Holmes, C.J., Hoge, R., Collins, L., Woods, R., Toga, A.W., Evans, A.C.: Enhancement of MR images using registration for signal averaging. J. Comput. Assist. Tomogr. **22**(2), 324–333 (1998)

An Automated Brain Tumor Segmentation Framework Using Multimodal MRI

Haifeng Zhao[1,2], Shuhai Chen[1,3(✉)], Shaojie Zhang[1,2],
and Siqi Wang[1]

[1] Key Lab of Intelligent Computing and Signal Processing of MOE
and School of Computer and Technology, Anhui University,
Hefei 230039, People's Republic of China
senith@163.com, cshl8315913353@163.com,
86073224@qq.com, wangsiqi_1112@163.com
[2] Key Lab of Industrial Image Processing and Analysis of Anhui Province,
Hefei 230601, People's Republic of China
[3] Anhui University, Jiulong Road 111, Shushan District,
Hefei City, Anhui Province, China

Abstract. An automated region of interest (ROI) segmentation framework is proposed for edema detection and brain tumor segmentation from brain magnetic resonance images (MRI). In order to further improve the accuracy of the framework, multimodal MRI data are applied in this framework. The framework mainly contains three stages. First the cluster algorithm and morphological operation are used for detecting the abnormal tissue i.e. edema so as to automatically initialize the level set method. Then edge-based level set method combining regional information is used for edema segmentation from Fluid Attenuated Inversion Recovery (FLAIR) MRI. The final segmentation result of brain tumor is obtained by using the cluster method, filling algorithm and opening (morphology) operation at T1 contrast-enhanced (T1c) MRI. The experiments are carried out on two modalities MRI slices of 8 true patients, which have the matching ground truth of the edema and tumor. Experimental results demonstrate the effectiveness of our algorithm.

Keywords: Level set · Brain tumor · Image segmentation · MRI

1 Introduction

Image segmentation is one of the elementary techniques in computer vision and image analysis. The definition of image segmentation is partition an image into distinct non-overlapping regions where each region containing each pixel with similar attributes. In mathematical terms, image segmentation can be described using set theory models [1]. There is an image I and a set of similarity constraints C_i ($i = 1,2,...$), image segmentation is the process of dividing I into multiple parts. That is, $\bigcup_{j=1}^{N} R_j = I, R_j \cap R_k = \emptyset, \forall j \neq k, j, k \in [1, N]$. Here, R_j is a set of connected pixels that satisfy all

© Springer Nature Switzerland AG 2018
J. Zhou et al. (Eds.): CCBR 2018, LNCS 10996, pp. 609–619, 2018.
https://doi.org/10.1007/978-3-319-97909-0_65

the similarity constraint at the same time, which is what we call the image region. N is an integer not less than 2, indicating the number of divided regions.

The medical images segmentation is a common task in medicine for extracting a specific region to be analyzed. Generally, medical image segmentation methods can be roughly categorized into thresholding [2], region growing [3], clustering [4], edge detection [5], and model-based methods [6–14]. At present, most of the basic methods of medical image segmentation are for two-dimensional (2D) images. Brain MRI is usually blurred a nonuniform in intensity and brain tumor in MRI usually exhibit unclear and irregular boundaries, which can increases the difficulty in tumor segmentation. The traditional single method is difficult to achieve accurate segmentation. Due to the above limitations, this paper proposes an automated method for brain tumor segmentation based on 2D multimodal magnetic resonance images. In this study, a novel automated brain tumor segmentation framework is proposed. Initially, Fuzzy C-means (FCM) cluster [4] algorithm is introduced to segment the possible lesion region in FLAIR MRI then obtaining binary image which may contain lesion tissue and healthy tissue. Secondly, morphological operations [15] are applied to extract lesion region. Then, the extracted region is utilized to initialize the improved level set function. Li et al. [7] proposes the distance regularized level set evolution (DRLSE) model which removes the reinitialization. We use DRLSE algorithm combined with region information of MRI to propose an improved active contour model. Finally, the brain tumor is segmented using T1c MRI based on segmentation results on FLAIR MRI.

2 Proposed Method

2.1 Automatic Initialization of Level Set Function (LSF)

The initialization of the LSF plays a crucial role in the process of segmentation. Most of traditional initialization methods require manual intervention which is time-consuming and laborious. An automatic framework is introduced in this work with the aim to remove artificial participation and improve segmentation accuracy. The overall flowchart of the proposed initialization method is shown in Fig. 1. The process is composed by two main steps. The first step is to divide the image structures into several regions using FCM. In classification-based segmentation method, the FCM algorithm allows pixels to have relation with multiple clusters with varying degree of memberships and thus more reasonable in applications of medical images [4]. After that the image is converted to a binarized image which contains ROI. Then on the binarized image morphological operations [15] is applied and based on information on solidity and areas of the plausible locations, only ROI are kept. Then the LSF is initialized by the ROI.

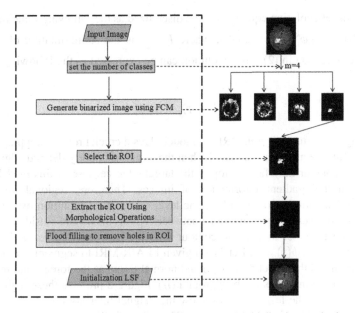

Fig. 1. The overall flowchart of the proposed initialization method

2.2 Edge-Based Level Set Method Combining Regional Information (EBLSM-CRI)

The level set method (LSM) embeds the evolution curve $C(s,t)$ into a function $\Phi(x,y,t)$ whose dimension is higher than $C(s,t)$. In level set function $\Phi(x,y,t)$, a closed curve C is represented implicitly by the zero level set function $\Phi(x,y,t)$: $C(s,t) = \{(x,y) \mid \Phi(x,y,t) = 0\}$. The variational level set methods [4] to transform the evolution of LSF into a problem of minimizing an energy function defined as

$$\frac{\partial \phi}{\partial t} = -\frac{\partial E}{\partial \phi} \tag{1}$$

Exiting image segmentation models using LSM can be categorized into edge-based level set methods [7–9, 12, 14] and region-based level set methods [6, 10, 11, 13].

In this work DRLSE model is used to drive the contour curve toward target edge during its evolution. The level set evolution equation of the DRLSE method is obtained as

$$\frac{\partial \phi}{\partial t} = \mu div(d_p(|\nabla\varphi|)\nabla\varphi) + \lambda\delta_\varepsilon div(g\frac{\nabla\varphi}{|\nabla\varphi|}) + \beta g\delta_\varepsilon(\varphi) \tag{2}$$

where $d_p(*)$ is the derivative of potential function defined by $d_p(s) = \frac{p'(s)}{s}$, μ, λ and β are the coefficients of distance regularization energy $div(d_p(|\nabla\varphi|)\nabla\varphi)$, length term $\delta_\varepsilon div(g\frac{\nabla\varphi}{|\nabla\varphi|})$, and the area term $g\delta_\varepsilon(\varphi)$, respectively.

The level set evolution equation can be discretized as the following finite difference equation $\left(\phi_{i,j}^{k+1} - \phi_{i,j}^{k}\right)\big/\tau = L(\phi_{i,j}^{k})$, where $L(\phi_{i,j}^{k})$ is the approximation of the right hand side of equation in (2). This evolution can be expressed as the following iterative equation:

$$\phi_{i,j}^{k+1} = \phi_{i,j}^{k} + \tau L(\phi_{i,j}^{k}) \tag{3}$$

The edge stop function g in DRLSE model plays a crucial role in stopping contour evolution. But, the model has a defect when the target has poorly defined edge in used images. The contour may fail to stop at the target edge because of this model merely relating with the gradient information of images. Therefore, regional information parameter Dif is introduced controlling the level set function evolution, which defines the difference of average intensity value between regions inside and outside the contour C. Within the level set model, the contour C is the zero level curve of ϕ which is expressed by $s \in \Omega, \phi(s) = 0$. Let I be a given FLAIR MRI to segment, we define the abnormal tissue as the target region (I_t) and normal tissue as the foreground region (I_f) and the rest of the image as the background (I_b). Figure 2 presents these regions using simulation image. The lesion regions show high signal intensity on FLAIR. Figure 2 depicts two possible initialization contours. The value of Dif is gradually increased with the curve evolution to the target edge. However, once the contour crosses the edge of the target, the value of Dif will decrease. So, The Dif value, which is calculated by using Eq. (4), is used to control evolutionary destination.

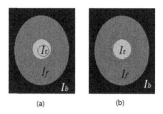

(a)   (b)

Fig. 2. Illustration of 2 kinds of configuration.

The value of Dif is calculated as follows

$$Dif = \left|\overline{O_s} - \overline{B_s}\right| \tag{4}$$

Where $\overline{O_s}$ and $\overline{B_s}$ are calculated from Eqs. (5) and (6), respectively.

$$\overline{O_s} = average(I_s) \quad in\{\phi \geq 0\} \tag{5}$$

$$\overline{B_s} = average(I_s) \quad in\{\phi < 0\} \tag{6}$$

The proposed method can be implemented by using the following steps.

Step 1: Initialization. Initialize an LSF ϕ to a function ϕ_0 using the proposed automatic initialization method.

Step 2: Calculate $\overline{O_s}$ and $\overline{B_s}$. Calculate $\overline{O_s}$, $\overline{B_s}$ by (5) and (6) respectively.

Step 3: Calculate values of difference *Dif*. Calculate *Dif* by (4).

Step 4: Update the LSF. Update level set function by (3).

Step 5: Determine the termination of iteration. If either the level set function is stable or k exceeds a prescribed maximum number of iterations or $Dif^k - Dif^{k-1} < 0$ then stop the iteration.

2.3 Brain Tumor Segmentation

The framework of this study is composed by three main steps. In the step (1), The FCM is employed to categorize the FLAIR MR image structures into four regions. Next, the binary image is obtained by keeping only pixels classified in the high intensity. But the obtained binary image may contain other structures different from the abnormal tissues, hence morphological operations are applied to select only abnormal structures in the obtained binary image. At last the LSF is initialized by the binary image only containing abnormal structures. Figure 1 shows the overall flowchart of the proposed method of LSF initialization. The final contour of the abnormal region on FLAIR MR image is given by the result of proposed LSM, which is illustrated in step (2). At last step (3) the outline of the abnormal tissue on FLAIR is used to extract the same region on T1c. It well locates the tumor region and removes the tissues which is not lesion on T1c. This greatly reduces the impact of normal tissue on segmentation results. Then the segmentation result of brain tumor on extracted region is obtained by using the FCM cluster method. The final tumor region is extracted and refined using opening (morphology) operation and filling algorithm. The flowchart of this step is shown in Fig. 3 for an MR image.

Fig. 3. The overall flowchart of the tumor segmentation

3 Experimental Results

Experimental data used in this study is obtained from the MICCAI 2012 Challenge [16]. It includes four MR image modalities which are T1, T2, T1c and FLAIR respectively. T1 with better visualization of anatomy structure and the tumor is better visualized in the T1c. T2 is sensitive to edema and fluid, however, the vast majority of diseased tissues contain more water and display high signal. Thus T2 is easy to visualize lesions. FLAIR is mainly used to inhibit the free water in human tissues and making it a low signal. However, the water in diseased tissue is bound water that is not inhibited and remains a high signal to fully expose the lesion. Therefore the edema is better visualized in the FLAIR than T2 [17]. In [6] T1c and T2 are used to enhance visualization of the tumor by combining the information of multimodal images. In our work, two different modal images, T1c and FLAIR, are used because our study focuses on lesions and tumor segmentation.

All experiments are performed on a total of 88 slices image data of 8 patients (considering 11 consecutive slices of each patient). The FLAIR is first filtered using Anisotropic Diffusion Filter to reduce contrast between consecutive pixels. The resolutions of the MR images used in this study are 176×216 or 230×230 pixel. Two objectively metrics are used for quantitatively evaluate the segmentation accuracy i.e. the Jaccard coefficient (Jac) and the Dice coefficient (Dice). Letting S and T be the segmented and ground truth images, respectively. They are defined by

$$Jac = \frac{|S \cap T|}{|S \cup T|} \tag{7}$$

$$Dice = \frac{2|S \cap T|}{|S| + |T|} \tag{8}$$

where $|\cdot|$ shows the number of pixels. The range of Jac and Dice is from 0 to 1, the greater the better.

First, we analyze the influence of the LSF initialization on the segmentation result of abnormal tissue. As the LSM is sensitive to initialization, different initializations are used in order to test the influence of our method. Eight possible initializations and their segmentation result are illustrated in Fig. 4. The selected original image data and its ground truth are shown in the first column on the right hand. In row 1 the red contour illustrates the initialization and in row 2 the red contour illustrates the evolution result achieved by the proposed LSM. We randomly select eight initial contours (in row 1: from left to right 1–7). The second column on the right hand illustrates the initial contour achieved by the proposed automatic initialization method and the result of evolution, respectively. Table 1 shows the comparisons of segmentation accuracy with respect to different initializations. We can see that initialization has great influence on

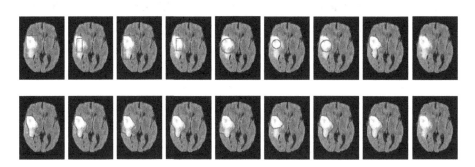

Fig. 4. Result of different LSF initializations on FLAIR MRI. (Color figure online)

Table 1. Accuracy and run time of different initialization methods.

Num	1	2	3	4	5	6	7	8
Dice	0.8246	0.9267	0.8169	0.9312	0.8628	0.7434	0.9266	**0.9533**
Jaccard	0.7015	0.8634	0.6905	0.8712	0.7586	0.5916	0.8632	**0.9108**
Run time(s)	19.2438	19.0432	21.9240	18.4819	21.7920	20.5017	21.9007	**11.3573**

segmentation result and our proposed initialization method perform better than other initializations.

Second, we analyze the behavior of our proposed EBLSM-CRI comparing with other level set algorithm such as Caselles method [9], Chan & Vese (C-V) method [10], Lankton method [11] and the DRLSE method mentioned in this paper. This phase of the experiment is carried out on FLAIR MR image of real patient data with brain lesion. To ensure the fairness of the comparison of the obtained result, the same automatic active contour initialization as proposed in this study is used in all experiments. The parameters values of the proposed method in this study is set to $\sigma = 3$, $\mu = 0.04$, $\alpha = 1.3$, $\varepsilon = 1.5$ and $\lambda = 3$. For Caselles, C-V, LanKton method the parameters for each modality are carefully chosen. For DRLSE method, the parameters are identical with our method. Figure 5 presents the segmentation results obtained by (from (a) to (e)) the Caselles method, the C-V method, the Lankton method, the DRLSE and the proposed method. The ground truth of brain lesion, as made by a physician, is shown in Fig. 5(f). It is observed that the circumscription (in red) of the proposed method is more robust than the comparative methods. Segmented results obtained by DRLSE and the proposed method are illustrated in Fig. 5(d) and (e), respectively. We can obviously notice that when the brain lesions with poorly defined boundaries, the segmented result by the DRLSE is always considerably larger than the actual region, as marked in Fig. 5(d). Table 2 provides the comparative accuracy (in terms of Jac and Dice) obtained for each comparative method in the segmentation of 8 patients data.

Last, we compare the proposed automated brain tumor segmentation framework with Subhashis Banerjee et al. [2] proposed semi-automatic MR brain tumor segmentation framework using multi-level thresholding technique and Elisee Ilunga-Mbuyamba et al. [6] proposed automatic MR brain tumor segmentation framework using region-based active contour model. The experiment is carried out on the MRI of real patients with tumor. We randomly select 8 patients brain MRI data. Elisee Ilunga-Mbuyamba et al. propose localized active contour model with background intensity compensation method (LACM-BIC) fuses the T1c and T2 using $I = T1c + \kappa T2$ equation, where $\kappa = 0.2$. Only T1c is used on Subhashis Banerjee et al. proposed single seed delineation with multi-thresholding method (SSDMT). The FLAIR and T1c are used on our proposed method. Figure 6 shows the performance comparison of existing and proposed method for brain tumor segmentation. It can be observed that our proposed approach is able to segment brain tumorous tissue more accurately than the comparative methods.

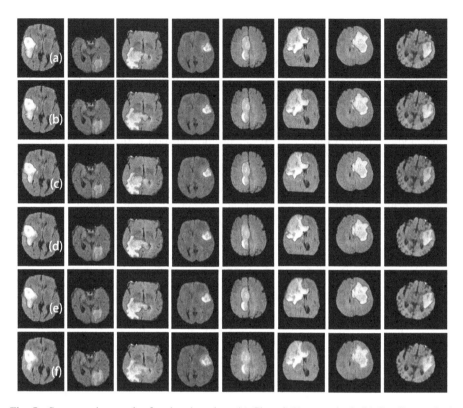

Fig. 5. Segmentation result of real patient data. (a) Chan & Vese method, (b) Caselles method, (c) Lankton method, (d) DRLSE method, (e) Proposed method, (f) Ground truth (Color figure online)

Table 2. Accuracy of different methods over T1c slice of 8 patients.

Patient #	Init+CV		Init+Caselles		Init+LanKton		Init+Li		Init+Proposed	
	Jaccard	Dice	Jaccard	Dice	Jaccard	Dice	Jaccard	Dice	Jaccard	Dice
1	0.7852	0.8797	0.7955	0.8861	0.8171	0.8994	0.8568	0.9229	**0.9108**	**0.9533**
2	0.6529	0.7900	0.7884	0.8817	**0.8649**	**0.9276**	0.5650	0.7221	0.8583	0.9237
3	0.7424	0.8521	0.7393	0.8501	0.6956	0.8204	0.8485	0.9180	**0.8725**	**0.9319**
4	**0.8248**	**0.9062**	0.7382	0.8494	0.7445	0.8535	0.6415	0.7816	0.7726	0.8717
7	0.8129	0.8968	0.8095	0.8947	0.8901	0.9418	0.7070	0.8284	**0.9047**	**0.9559**
9	0.8492	0.9185	0.8876	0.9405	0.9020	0.9485	0.9098	0.9528	**0.9163**	**0.9563**
11	0.8395	0.9127	0.9052	0.9502	**0.9261**	**0.9616**	0.8935	0.9437	0.9161	0.9562
23	0.7589	0.8629	0.8069	0.8931	0.8556	0.9222	0.7462	0.8547	**0.8893**	**0.9414**

Table 3 provides a quantitative comparison results obtained for each comparative method in the segmentation of 8 patients data, based on the two measures of Eqs. (7) and (8). It is found that the proposed method is better than the existing method for brain

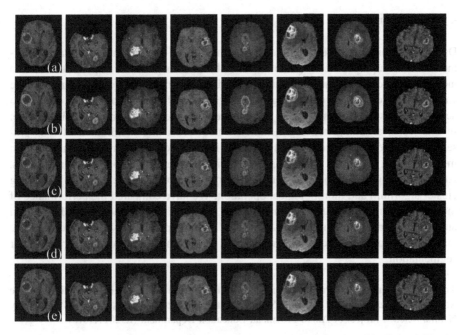

Fig. 6. Segmentation result of real patient data. (a) Original image, (b) Ground Truth, (c) Proposed Method, (d) SSDMT, (e) LACM-BIC.

Table 3. Accuracy of different methods over T1c slice of 8 patients.

Patient	SSDMT		LACM-BIC		Init+Proposed	
#	Jaccard	Dice	Jaccard	Dice	Jaccard	Dice
1	0.9091	0.9524	0.9465	0.9725	**0.9508**	**0.9748**
2	0.8692	0.9300	0.8089	0.8944	**0.9537**	**0.9763**
3	0.8780	0.9351	0.8378	0.9118	**0.8993**	**0.9470**
4	0.8253	0.9043	0.6324	0.7748	**0.8357**	**0.9105**
7	0.8391	0.9125	0.866	0.9282	**0.9017**	**0.9583**
9	0.8186	0.9003	0.8406	0.9134	**0.8831**	**0.9379**
11	0.8047	0.8918	0.7984	0.8879	**0.8336**	**0.9093**
23	0.8207	0.9015	0.8908	0.9423	**0.9013**	**0.9481**

tumor segmentation. Table 3 shows that for patient 4 the Jaccard coefficient value of 0.8357 achieved by the proposed method is the highest and the value of 0.6324 reached by LACM-BIC is the lowest, the difference in values between the highest and the lowest is 0.2033.

4 Conclusion

Due to the complex diversity of medical images and the difficulty of manual segmentation, computer-aided segmentation method has become an important means to increase the accuracy and efficiency of medical diagnosis. In recent years, a wide variety of approaches have been suggested for brain MRI segmentation. It is difficult to achieve the desired results by using a single method to segment a single medical image. In this work, an automated segmentation framework using multimodal MRI is presented. We propose an edge-based level set method combining regional information method, which is adapted for handling the region of interest with poorly defined edges. And the proposed method with automated initialization is implemented by utilizing cluster algorithm and morphological operation. We have compared the performance of the proposed method with a semi-automatic segmentation method SSDMT and an automatic segmentation method LACM-BIC. The experimental results demonstrate that the proposed method performs better for edema detection and brain tumor segmentation.

Acknowledgments. The Project Sponsored by the Scientific Research Foundation for the Returned Overseas Chinese Scholars, State Education Ministry (NO. 48, 2014-1685), the Key Natural Science Project of Anhui Provincial Education Department (KJ2017A016).

References

1. Pal, N.R., Pal, S.K.: A review on image segmentation techniques. J. Patt. Recogn. **26**(9), 1277–1294 (1993)
2. Banerjee, S., Mitra, S., Shankar, B.U.: Single seed delineation of brain tumor using multi-thresholding. J. Inf. Sci. **330**, 88–103 (2016)
3. Zhu, S.C., Yuille, A.: Region competition: unifying snakes, region growing, and Bayes/MDL for multiband image segmentation. J. IEEE Trans. Patt. Anal. Mach. Intell. **18**(9), 884–900 (1996)
4. Gong, M., Liang, Y., Shi, J., et al.: Fuzzy c-means clustering with local information and kernel metric for image segmentation. J. IEEE Trans. Image Process. **22**(2), 573–584 (2013)
5. Senthilkumaran, N., Rajesh, R.: Edge detection techniques for image segmentation–a survey of soft computing approaches. Int. J. Recent Trends Eng. **1**(2), 250–254 (2009)
6. Ilunga-Mbuyamba, E., Avina-Cervantes, J.G., Garcia-Perez, A., et al.: Localized active contour model with background intensity compensation applied on automatic MR brain tumor segmentation. J. Neurocomput. **220**, 84–97 (2017)
7. Li, C., Xu, C., Gui, C., et al.: Distance regularized level set evolution and its application to image segmentation. J. IEEE Trans. Image Process. **19**(12), 3243–3254 (2010)
8. Pratondo, A., Chui, C.K., Ong, S.H.: Robust edge-stop functions for edge-based active contour models in medical image segmentation. J. IEEE Sig. Process. Lett. **23**(2), 222–226 (2016)
9. Caselles, V., Kimmel, R., Sapiro, G.: Geodesic active contours. Int. J. Comput. Vis. **22**(1), 61–79 (1997)
10. Chan, T.F., Vese, L.A.: Active contours without edges. J. IEEE Trans. Image Process. **10**(2), 266–277 (2001)

11. Lankton, S., Tannenbaum, A.: Localizing region-based active contours. J. IEEE Trans. Image Process. **17**(11), 2029–2039 (2008)
12. Li, C., Xu, C., Konwar, K.M., et al.: Fast distance preserving level set evolution for medical image segmentation. In: 2006 9th International Conference on Control, Automation, Robotics and Vision, ICARCV 2006, pp. 1–7. IEEE Press, Singapore (2006)
13. Li, C., Kao, C.Y., Gore, J.C., et al.: Minimization of region-scalable fitting energy for image segmentation. J. IEEE Trans. Image Process. **17**(10), 1940–1949 (2008)
14. Yang, X., Gao, X., Tao, D., et al.: An efficient MRF embedded level set method for image segmentation. J. IEEE Trans. Image Process. **24**(1), 9–21 (2015)
15. Spencer, A.: Morphological Theory: An Introduction to Word Structure in Generative Grammar. Wiley-Blackwell (1991)
16. MICCAI 2012 Challenge. http://www.imm.dtu.dk/projects/BRATS2012
17. Li, Y., Jia, F., Qin, J.: Brain tumor segmentation from multimodal magnetic resonance images via sparse representation. J. Artif. Intell. Med. **73**, 1–13 (2016)

Video-Based Pig Recognition
with Feature-Integrated Transfer
Learning

Jianzong Wang$^{(\boxtimes)}$, Aozhi Liu, and Jing Xiao

Ping An Technology (Shenzhen) Co., Ltd, Shenzhen, China
{wangjianzong347,liuaozhi092,xiaojing661}@pingan.com.cn

Abstract. Automatic detection and recognition of animals has long been a popular topic. It can be used on different areas, such as ecosystem protection, farming industry, insurance industry, etc. Currently, there is still no robust and efficient method for this problem. Deep neural network, a recently rapid developing technology, has shown its great power on image processing, but suffers from low training speed problem. Recently, transfer learning has become popular because it avoids training the network from scratch, which significantly speeds up the training speed. In this paper, we focus on the pig recognition contest organized by a Chinese finance company. Applying all frames for training the neural networks with VGG-19 will result in an accuracy lower than 60% in the prediction steps. With experiments, we find out a key to enhance the accuracy of the video-based pig recognition task is that the frames have to be carefully selected with a certain algorithm. To take advantage of the strengths of different network architectures, we apply feature integration method with the deep neural networks of DPN131, InceptionV3 and Xception network together. We then implement the integrated feature to train the labelled dataset which are frames extracted from the videos of 30 pigs. The resulted model receive an prediction accuracy of 96.41%. Experiments show that the best performance of our proposed methods outperforms all classic deep neural networks training from scratch.

Keywords: Pig recognition · Automatic detection
Feature-integration · Video-analysis

1 Introduction

Getting accurate and real-time information about the behavior and location of animals is of great value in the fields of biology, ecology, zoology sciences and farming industry [6, 7]. Driven by the increasing demand of ecological surveillance and biodiversity monitoring, more and more images are collected with the aid of advanced imaging system. Currently, most of the related work is done by manual detection from recorded videos and images, it is of course prohibitive to rely on

© Springer Nature Switzerland AG 2018
J. Zhou et al. (Eds.): CCBR 2018, LNCS 10996, pp. 620–631, 2018.
https://doi.org/10.1007/978-3-319-97909-0_66

experts manual handling to annotate these data. With the recent development of machine learning technology, automatic and accurate animal detection becomes possible.

Deep learning, a revolutionary machine learning methodology, has been developed greatly thanks to the advancement of hardwares and the explosion of information. It shows its great power in natural language, image and video processing tasks [8–10]. Many researches has used different deep learning methodology to realize automatic animal detection. For example, Poon *et al.* [11] used deep neural network to estimate sheep pain levels using facial action unit detection. Recently, Kaggle organized dog breed recognition competition. Therefore, an automatic way to analyze the animal images is of great potential.

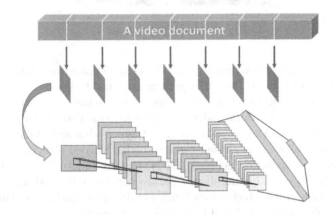

Fig. 1. Transfer learning.

In this paper we focus on the pig face recognition contest organized by a Chinese finance company. The data provided are videos with pigs. Two extracted frame images are shown in Fig. 1. Since the pigs in the videos are moving, it is necessary to find the optimal frames selection method from the extracted frames. After experimenting with I-frame, P-frame, B-frame and different extracting intervals, we find the optimal method to extract video frames is extracting the frames with an interval of 5. A comparison is shown in Table 1. Finally, $9w$ images are extracted from the videos as our training set. We try to investigate the deep learning methodology to automatically detect and recognize pigs from the images, the whole process is shown in Fig. 1. Many researchers have already done a lot of researches on human face recognition [12,13], These researches have generated great commercial value. However, there is a lack of study related to animal recognition. Our work contributes the literature in this area.

Recently, many researchers experiment on combining different networks together to take advantage of the strength of different networks at the same time. Some successful networks include DPN(Dual Path Network) [4] and Inception net [3]. Inspired by their success, we build a deep neural network that combines some well-known networks together, in order to fully utilize the information from the input image. Our experiment shows that the combination of a Dual path network, a InceptionV3 network and a Xception network performs the best. To relieve the over-fitting problem, we use data augmentation as shown in Fig. 6.

Fig. 2. Sample pig images.

Transfer learning, which means transferring the knowledge learned from one task to the target task, has been increasingly popular during recent years, especially in the context of deep learning. It means extracting the parameters from a well-trained source network and transfer them to a new target network (as illustrated in Fig. 3.). The intuition is that there is similarity among different learning tasks, thus we can transfer the knowledge learned from one task to the others. Training deep neural network (DNN) usually suffers from the burden of calculation due to the large number of parameters to be trained, even with the advancement of hardware technology (such as GPU and cloud computing). However, this problem can be relieved by transfer learning because it avoids training the network from scratch. Literatures show that the training process can be sped up significantly by proper using of transfer learning [14,16].

2 Related Work

2.1 Animal Detection and Recognition

Norouzzadeh et al. [19] investigated the methodology to automatically identify, count, and describe wild animals in camera-trap images. They were the first to show that deep neural networks can perform good on the SS dataset, as well they showed the great potential to deploy deep neural network on such subjects. Table 1 shows the target and method in two specific animal detection problems.

Lu et al. [11] extended techniques for recognizing human facial expressions to encompass facial action units in sheep, which can then facilitate automatic estimation of sheep pain levels. They first detect sheep faces, localize facial landmarks, and then extract facial features. The final pain levels are determined by Support Vector Machine. This study shows the capability of automatically analyzing animal facial expression, which is also used in our study.

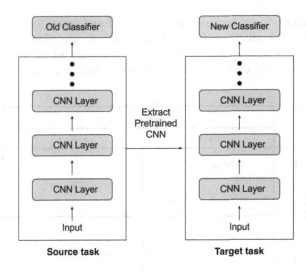

Fig. 3. Transfer learning.

Table 1. Specific animal detection literature

	Horse [2]	Sheep [11]
Target	Distinguish horses in camera videos	Estimate sheep pain level
Method	1. Gabor filter for face characterization;	1. Viola-Jones object detection framework for face detection;
	2. DNN for vector extraction;	2. Caascade Pose Regression for facial landmark detection;
	3. Linear SVM for classification	3. Histogram of Oriented Gradient(HOG) feature descriptor;
		4. SVM classification

2.2 Transfer Learning

Pan and Yang [5] gave a rigorous definition of transfer learning. Denote the domain of source task and the target task as $\mathcal{D}_S$ and $\mathcal{D}_T$ respectively. More specifically, $\mathcal{D}_S = \{(x_{S_1}, y_{S_1}), (x_{S_2}, y_{S_2}), ..., (x_{S_n}, y_{S_n})\}$ and $\mathcal{D}_T = \{(x_{T_1}, y_{T_1}), (x_{T_2}, y_{T_2}), ..., (x_{T_n}, y_{T_n})\}$, where x_{S_n} is the n_{th} data instance, y_{S_n} is the corresponding class label in the classification task, x_{T_n} is the input data and y_{T_n} is the corresponding output.

Given a source domain $\mathcal{D}_S$ and learning task $\mathcal{T}_S$, a domain $\mathcal{D}_T$ and learning task $\mathcal{T}_T$, transfer learning aims to help improve the learning of the target predictive function $f_T(\cdot)$ in $\mathcal{D}_T$ using the knowledge in $\mathcal{D}_S$ and $\mathcal{T}_S$, where $\mathcal{D}_S \neq \mathcal{D}_T$, or $\mathcal{T}_S \neq \mathcal{T}_T$.

Some commonly used techniques based on if the target or the source task dataset have labels is shown in Fig. 4. Yang, Hanneke and Carbonell [1] explore a transfer learning setting, in which a finite sequence of target concepts are sampled independently with an unknown distribution from known family.

		Source Data	
		labelled	unlabeled
Target Data	labelled	Fine-tune	Self-taught learning
		Multitask Learning	
	unlabeled	Domain-adversarial training	Self-taught Clustering
		Zero-shot learning	

Fig. 4. Common techniques for transfer learning.

Shin *et al.* [14] examined when and why transfer learning from pre-trained ImageNet (via fune tuning) can be useful. They studied two specific computer-aided detection (CADe) problem, namely thoraco-abdominal lymph node (LN) detection and interstitial lung disease (ILD) classification. Their empirical study shows that cross-dataset CNN transfer learning are indeed beneficial.

3   Approach

In this section, we introduce our methodology of video-based pig recognition step by step, including the network we use, transfer learning method, feature extraction method and feature integration method. Firstly we will discuss about the theory of why feature integration has outstanding performance, then we will provide the detail implementation of the feature concatenation approach.

3.1   Theoretical of Feature Integration in Transfer Learning

The problem of DNN training from scratch can be described as the following optimization problem:

3.2   Theoretical of Feature Integration in Transfer Learning

The problem of DNN training from scratch can be described as the following optimization problem:

$$\theta^{\star} = \arg\min_{\theta \in \Theta} E_{(x,y) \in D}[l(x, y, \theta)] \tag{1}$$

where $l(x, y, \theta)$ is a loss function that depends on the parameter θ, D are the training dataset. Transfer learning is still a 'blackbox' without too much mathematical exploration, but fine tuning can be deemed as a combination of two optimization stages, which is:

$$\theta_1 = \arg \min_{\theta_1 \in \Theta_1} E_{(x,y) \in P}[l(x, y, \theta_1)] \tag{2}$$

where $\theta_1 = (\theta^{pre}, \theta^{drop})$, and

$$\theta^\star = \arg \min_{\theta^{new} \in \Theta_2} E_{(x,y) \in D}[l(x, y, \theta_2)] \tag{3}$$

where $\theta_2 = (\theta^{pre}, \theta^{new})$.

The experimental success of transfer learning based on the assumption that D and P have similarity. If D and P are homogeneous, then

$$\sup_D |\theta_{new} - \theta_{drop})| < \epsilon \tag{4}$$

the two optimization degenerate to one. Here we fix θpre and expect the difference between θ^{drop} and θ^{new} can address the difference of D and P. The final layer of the network is actually a linear regression, where the estimation of parameters is:

$$\beta_{est} = (X'X)^{-1}X'Y \tag{5}$$

where X is the input of the last layer and Y is the label. To avoid singular $X'X$, it is better to have higher dimension of X'. Thus, we concatenate the output of second to last layer of well-known three networks together, then feed to the final fully connected layer. Experiment shows that our approach performs much better than single network.

3.3   Network Architecture and Fine-Tuning

The networks we use include Inception-V3 [21], Xception [4] and DPNs131 [4]. The weights and bias are transferred from networks pre-trained on ImageNet for all the layers before the final fully connected layer. Concretely, only the parameters from the final layer are adjusted during the training process.

Transfer learning is re-implementing the knowledge learned from one dataset into a new dataset. It avoids training the network from scratch, which significantly improves the training speed. A widely used skill to implement transfer learning is the fine-tuning. Conservative training, a technique of fine-tune which means minimizing the difference between the source data and the target data with a few modification of the Neural Networks, are used in our problem. Concretely, we firstly extract features from the training data set with the pre-trained weights of the champion networks trained on ImageNet.

However, this approach is with limitation that the combination of different networks is hard. It is not easy to quantitatively integrate the advantages of different deep neural networks. To address this issue, we implement feature extraction approach instead of directly fine-tuning the pre-trained neural network.

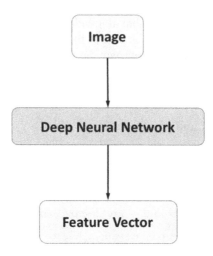

Fig. 5. Feature extraction with convolutions.

3.4   Feature Extraction

Many experiments show that convolution operation can extract the abstract features from the images. This is the well-known "black box" of deep learning. Still, there is no good explanation why deep neural network has such outstanding performance.

Classic feature extraction methods in computer vision include Histogram of Oriented Gradient(HoG), Local Binary Pattern(LBP), Haar-like and so on. Experiments show that features extracted by CNN contain the information of features extracted by traditional methods. Hence, we apply features extraction method using CNN as illustrated in Fig. 5.

3.5   Feature Integration

Feature integration is used by us to enhance the robustness of the training model. Concretely, a fine-tune operation at the training step will be applied on the final fully-connected layer, the dimension of input of which is $(1, N \times d)$, where N is the number of networks, $(1, d)$ is the dimension of output of each networks.

As shown in Fig. 5, every deep neural network(DNN) extracts a feature with a certain dimension. Later on, a merge operation is performed on the features. As a rule of thumb, N is selected as 3 for the best performance. The reason is that training with a larger number tends to overfit the model, even with more data augmentation.

The concrete operation of the integration is a concatenation of the vectors. Suppose the deep neural networks extract feature vectors of a, b and c, the integration is denoted as:

$$d = concat(a, b, c) = (a_1, ..., a_n, b_1, ..., b_n, c_1, ..., c_n) \tag{6}$$

$$a = (a_1, ..., a_n), b = (b_1, ..., b_n), c = (c_1, ..., c_n) \tag{7}$$

The beginning of b is concatenated to the end of a and the beginning of c is concatenated to the end of b. This concatenation will result in a integrated vector d. d is subsequently trained as the nodes of a fully-connected layer of the neural network with the labelled data set of the pigs (as shown in Fig. 6).

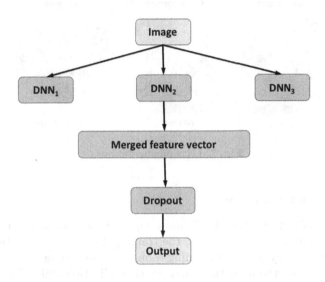

Fig. 6. Feature concatenation of neural networks.

4   Experiments

4.1   Dataset

The data set is provided from the challenge of a pig recognition competition. Finance. It contains 30 videos of pigs covering most parts of the whole body of pigs. Since the training data set are videos whereas the test set are images, frame extraction algorithms are necessary for converting videos to images. In our project, we have experimented 3 kinds of key frame selection methods including I-Frame, P-Frame and B-Frame extraction. Moreover, we try to select frames with an intervals of 2, 3, 4, 5, 6 frames. Finally, we find the optimal frame selection method is with an interval of 5. Experiment shows that frame selection plays an important role on the prediction accuracy. About $9w$ images are extracted by us as the training set, including 6000 images of pigs as our test set.

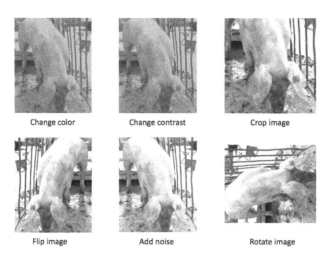

Fig. 7. Data augmentations.

4.2   Data Augmentations

Another step of data preparation is data augmentation. Data augmentation is widely used to prevent overfitting on the training data. Implementation of data augmentation is a key point for training robustness because of the variety of pig images. To improve the robustness and the generalization ability of the trained model, we apply the methods of rotation, reflection, flipping, zooming and shifting, as shown in Fig. 7.

4.3   Feature Extractions with Several Models

It is significant to get the best combination of network architectures to realize the best performance. We use *log(loss)* as the criterion to choose the best 3 architectures for feature combination. The *logloss* evaluation method is applied as a supplement. The equation of *logloss* is:

$$logloss = -\frac{1}{N}\sum_{i=1}^{N}\sum_{j=1}^{M} y_{i,j}log(p_{i,j}) \tag{8}$$

where N is the number of images, M is the number of classification. $p_{i,j}$ is the predicted probability that the ith image is identified as the jth pig.

Experiment shows that train the VGG-19 network from scratch with all the 90000 images results in an prediction accuracy lower than 60%. Therefore, using all extracted frames is considered a inaccurate solution. We tested three kinds of training methods: DPN-131(training from scratch), DPN-131(fine tune from parameters trained on ImageNet) and feature concatenation based on DPN-131, Xception and Inception-V3(as shown in Fig 8).

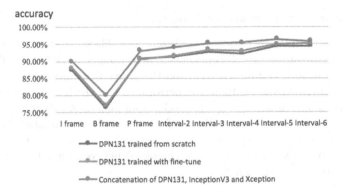

Fig. 8. Comparison of accuracy of frames selections.

Table 2. Comparison of the accuracy of different networks with fine-tune.

DNN	Accuracy	Loss
VGG19	87.21%	0.38
Resnet152	87.21%	0.25
InceptionV3	94.74%	0.19
Xception	94.80%	0.19
DPN131	95.17%	0.17
Densenet	83.42%	0.42

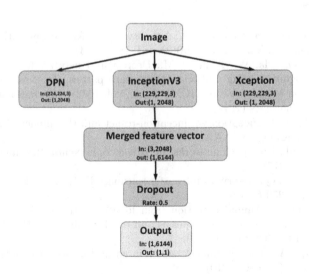

Fig. 9. Feature concatenation with three models.

4.4 Examination of Features Integration

A comparison of different networks is shown on Table 2. As shown in the table, the top 3 architectures are Inception V3, Xception and DPN131. Therefore, feature integration is conducted based on the above three networks.

We did experiment to evaluate the performance of the feature concatenation approach in comparison with single model approaches. As shown in Fig. 9., a fully-connected layer containing 6144 nodes is trained with 30 labeled classifications. The accuracy and *logloss* of the integrated model are 96.41% and 0.13, respectively. It is shown in Fig. 8, the combined network has obvious improvement compared with single network.

5 Conclusion

As the experiments show, the frame selection is the key for good performance in video-based image recognition task. In our experiment, key frames extraction method has contribution to improve the accuracy that training the neural networks with all frames. However, a method sampling frames with 5-frame interval has reachieved an maximal accuracy in our experiments. Moreover, the transfer learning approach with pre-trained parameters has more robustness than training the parameters from scratch. With features integration approach, the accuracy of video-based pig recognition results in an decent accuracy of 96.41% in the 6000 test set of pig images.

References

1. Yang, L., Hanneke, S., Carbonell, J.: A theory of transfer learning with applications to active learning. Mach. Learn. **90**(2), 161–189 (2013)
2. Jarraya, I., Ouarda, W., Alimi, A.M.: Deep neural network features for horses identity recognition using multiview horses face pattern. In: Ninth International Conference on Machine Vision (ICMV 2016), vol. 10341. International Society for Optics and Photonics (2017)
3. Szegedy, C., et al.: Inception-v4, inception-resnet and the impact of residual connections on learning. In: AAAI, vol. 4 (2017)
4. Chen, Y., et al.: Dual path networks. In: Advances in Neural Information Processing Systems (2017)
5. Pan, S.J., Yang, Q.: A survey on transfer learning. IEEE Trans. Knowl. Data Eng. **22**(10), 1345–1359 (2010)
6. Zhang, Z., et al.: Animal detection from highly cluttered natural scenes using spatiotemporal object region proposals and patch verification. IEEE Trans. Multimedia **18**(10), 2079–2092 (2016)
7. Wichmann, F.A., et al.: Animal detection in natural scenes: critical features revisited. J. Vis. **10**(4), 6–6 (2010)
8. Socher, R.: CS224d: Deep Learning for Natural Language Processing
9. Zhang, W., et al.: Distributed embedded deep learning based real-time video processing. In: 2016 IEEE International Conference on Systems, Man, and Cybernetics (SMC). IEEE (2016)

10. He, K., et al.: Deep residual learning for image recognition. In: Proceedings of the IEEE Conference on Computer Vision and Pattern Recognition (2016)

11. Lu, Y., Mahmoud, M., Robinson, P.: Estimating Sheep Pain Level Using Facial Action Unit Detection. In: 2017 12th IEEE International Conference on Automatic Face and Gesture Recognition (FG 2017). IEEE (2017)

12. Poon, B., Ashraful Amin, M., Yan, H.: Improved methods on PCA based human face recognition for distorted images. In: Proceedings of the International Multi Conference of Engineers and Computer Scientists, vol. 1. (2016)

13. Mandal, B.: Face recognition: perspectives from the real world. In: 2016 14th International Conference on Control, Automation, Robotics and Vision (ICARCV). IEEE (2016)

14. Shin, H.-C., et al.: Deep convolutional neural networks for computer-aided detection: CNN architectures, dataset characteristics and transfer learning. IEEE Trans. Med. Imaging **35**(5), 1285–1298 (2016)

15. Kumar, S., Gao, X., Welch, I.: Learning under data shift for domain adaptation: a model-based co-clustering transfer learning solution. In: Ohwada, H., Yoshida, K. (eds.) PKAW 2016. LNCS (LNAI), vol. 9806, pp. 43–54. Springer, Cham (2016). https://doi.org/10.1007/978-3-319-42706-5_4

16. Long, M., et al.: Deep transfer learning with joint adaptation networks. arXiv preprint arXiv:1605.06636 (2016)

17. Zhou, Y., Xie, L., Fishman, E.K., Yuille, A.L.: Deep supervision for pancreatic cyst segmentation in abdominal CT scans. In: Descoteaux, M., Maier-Hein, L., Franz, A., Jannin, P., Collins, D.L., Duchesne, S. (eds.) MICCAI 2017. LNCS, vol. 10435, pp. 222–230. Springer, Cham (2017). https://doi.org/10.1007/978-3-319-66179-7_26

18. Dahl, G.E., Sainath, T.N., Hinton, G.E.: Improving deep neural networks for LVCSR using rectified linear units and dropout. In: 2013 IEEE International Conference on Acoustics, Speech and Signal Processing (ICASSP). IEEE (2013)

19. Norouzzadeh, M.S., et al.: Automatically identifying wild animals in camera trap images with deep learning. arXiv preprint arXiv:1703.05830 (2017)

20. Simonyan, K., Zisserman, A.: Very deep convolutional networks for large-scale image recognition. arXiv preprint arXiv:1409.1556 (2014)

21. Szegedy, C., et al.: Rethinking the inception architecture for computer vision. In: Proceedings of the IEEE Conference on Computer Vision and Pattern Recognition (2016)

Integrating Multi-scale Gene Features
for Cancer Diagnosis

Peng Hang[1], Mengjun Shi[1], Quan Long[3], Hui Li[2], Haifeng Zhao[1(✉)],
and Meng Ma[1,2(✉)]

[1] Key Lab of Intelligent Computing and Signal Processing of MOE and School of Computer
and Technology, Anhui University, Hefei 230039, People's Republic of China
senith@163.com, mengma2@gmail.com
[2] Icahn School of Medicine at Mount Sinai, New York 10029, USA
[3] Departments of Biochemistry & Molecular Biology, Medical Genetics, and Mathematics
& Statistics, Alberta Children's Hospital Research Institute and O'Brien Institute for Public
Health, University of Calgary, Calgary T2N1N4, Canada

Abstract. Cancer is one of the major diseases that threaten human life. The
advancement of high-throughput sequencing technology provides a way to accurately diagnose cancer and reveal the pathogenesis of cancer at the molecular
level. In this study, we integrated the differentially expressed genes, and differential DNA methylation patterns, and applied multiple machine learning methods
to conduct cancer diagnosis. The experimental results show that the performance
of cancer diagnosis can be significantly improved with the integrated multi-scale
gene features of RNA and epigenetic level. The AUC of classifier can be increased
by 7.4% with multi-scale gene features compared to only differentially expressed
genes, which verifies the effectiveness of the integration of multi-scale gene
features for cancer diagnosis.

Keywords: Cancer diagnosis · Machine learning · Gene expression
DNA methylation · High-Throughput sequencing technology

1 Introduction

The development of the Human Genome Project and the maturity of various bioinformatics technologies have spawned a variety of new medical diagnostic techniques. High-
Throughput Sequencing Technology, also known as Next Generation Sequencing
(NGS), can be used to perform detailed analysis of the whole transcriptome and genome.
The emergence of high-throughput sequencing technology has not only improved the
accuracy and efficiency of disease diagnosis, but also promoted the in-depth study of
pathogenic mechanisms in human diseases [1, 2]. Extracting gene feature information
from massive sequencing data generated by high-throughput sequencing technology to
construct a predictive model for precise diagnosis of cancer is a focus of current cancer
research.

At present, a variety of machine learning methods have been applied to cancer diagnosis based on only microarray data or RNA-Seq data. Maglogiannis et al. used support

© Springer Nature Switzerland AG 2018
J. Zhou et al. (Eds.): CCBR 2018, LNCS 10996, pp. 632–641, 2018.
https://doi.org/10.1007/978-3-319-97909-0_67

vector machines (SVM) to design an intelligent system for diagnosing breast cancer and compared it with Bayesian networks and artificial neural networks [3]. Chen et al. developed a new multitasking learning technique to predict leukemia and prostate cancer [4]. Hijazi et al. discussed some semi-supervised machine learning methods for cancer prediction [5]. Nakkeeran et al. combined several classification algorithms of machine learning for feature selection and classification of cancer [6]. Kourou et al. systematically elaborated the effects of machine learning methods for the diagnosis and prognosis of cancer [7].

The three core steps in the gene expression process are transcription, splicing, and translation. Gene expression is a highly regulated process in which multiple regulatory signals are involved. As a change in epigenetic control, DNA methylation plays a key role in transcriptional regulation, chromosomal stability and genomic imprinting [8] and has been shown to be associated with many human diseases, including various types of cancer [9–11]. In this study, we integrated gene expression and DNA methylation features, using a variety of machine learning classification models for cancer prediction, to identify whether the fusion of multi-scale gene features contributes to cancer diagnosis. We downloaded RNA-Seq and DNA methylation sequencing data of tumor and normal control samples of cancer patients from TCGA, and identified differentially expressed genes from RNA-Seq data and detected two differential DNA methylation patterns including Differentially Methylated Loci (DML) and Differentially Methylated Region (DMR), then applied multiple machine learning models constructed based on the integrated features of the differential DNA methylation patterns and differentially expressed genes to predicting cancer. The experimental results show that compared to cancer diagnosis based on only gene expression data, there is a significantly improve of cancer diagnosis based on multi-scale features including gene expression and DNA methylation patterns which testifies the effectiveness of multi-scale gene features for cancer diagnosis.

2   Method

2.1   Experimental Steps

(1)   Download patient samples with available both RNA-Seq and DNA Methylation sequencing data from TCGA. We focused on four types of cancer including Breast invasive carcinoma (BRCA), Liver hepatocellular carcinoma (LIHC), Prostate adenocarcinoma (PRAD), and Thyroid carcinoma (THCA).

(2)   According to the barcodes of the TCGA samples, we further filtered patients and adopted only patients with available tumor and normal control samples which were sequenced at both RNA and DNA methylation levels.

(3)   Differential gene expression analysis and differential DNA methylation analysis were performed on sequencing data of the four types of cancer. For each type of cancer, we constructed three feature sets. The first set contains top 30 differentially expressed genes. The second set contains top 15 differentially expressed genes and 15 DML with the largest absolute values of the improved relative entropy. The third

set contains top 15 differentially expressed genes and 15 DMRs with the most CpG sites.

(4) Because the size of available sample set of each type of cancer is not big enough, we merged samples of the four types of cancer together for the construction of machine learning prediction models. However, the selected features of different types of cancer are not the same with each other, and cannot be simply combined. Accordingly, we merged the samples of four cancers for each type of feature set, separately. Taking the gene expression data as an example, we combined the 30 differentially expressed genes of BRCA, LIHC, PRAD and THCA into one gene list which contains 120 genes. For each type of cancer, the genes in the list are used as their first type of features. It means that only a quarter of the features in the list truly belong to some specific cancer type, while the remaining features may not to be informative for the classifier learning of such cancer type.

(5) Train multiple classifiers for learning based on the three types of features respectively, and then apply the mature machine learning classifiers to predict tumor and control normal samples.

(6) Compare the performance of the classifiers for cancer diagnosis.

Figure 1 shows the analysis flowchart of this study.

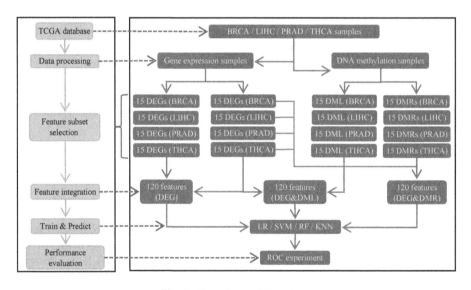

Fig. 1. Experimental flowchart.

2.2 Identify Differentially Expressed Genes

Differential gene expression means that there is a significant difference of gene expression between cases and controls. In the studies of cancer diagnosis based on machine learning, differentially expressed genes are often used as input features for classifiers. In this study, we first identified normal control and tumor samples from the same

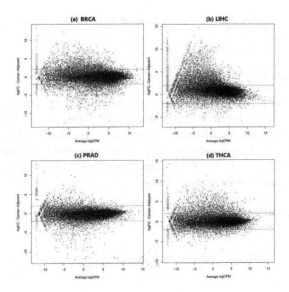

Fig. 2. Differential analysis of gene expression data using edgeR. Red dots with fold change greater than 2 and p-value less than 0.01 indicate up-regulated differentially expressed genes, red dots with fold change less than 0.5 and p-value less than 0.01 indicate down-regulated differentially expressed genes, and black dots are non-differentially expressed genes. The horizontal axis shows the average expression level of the genes, and the vertical axis represents the logarithm of the fold change in gene expression between cases and controls. (Color figure online)

individual based on the TCGA barcodes, and all the corresponding samples are combined into a data matrix. Then downloaded RNA-Seq data for all the samples and conducted differential expression gene analysis for each cancer type. In this study, we used the edgeR package in the Bioconductor platform to perform differential gene expression analysis for the four types of cancer [12]. As shown in Fig. 2, the red dot in each figure represents the differentially expressed genes that are suggested by edgeR. All the red dots basically fall outside the two blue lines, indicating that the ratio of the expression of these genes in different phenotypes exceeds two or less than 0.5. In combination with p-values we can finally determine whether the difference in the expression of a gene is statistically significant. In this experiment, not all of the differentially expressed genes were captured, but the top 30 differentially expressed genes with the smallest p-value were selected for each type of cancer. Their p-values are all less than 0.01. In addition, we found that the differentially expressed genes of LIHC were mostly up-regulated, but the number of differentially expressed genes up-regulated and down-regulated in BRCA or THCA was not much different. For example, there were 7674 up-regulated differentially expressed genes in LIHC, but only 559 genes were down-regulated. Unlike LIHC, the number of up-regulated differentially expressed genes was 2833 and 2158 in BRCA and THCA, and 2514 and 1523 genes were down-regulated, respectively. In THCA, the number of down-regulated differentially expressed genes was even 1055 more than the up-regulated genes. The results of this experiment reflect the tendency of different tumor differentially expressed genes to have different expression status.

2.3 Identification of DML

Currently, the identification of DML is mainly based on statistical theory [13–15]. In addition, some entropy-based methods were also proposed and showed excellent performance. Zhang et al. quantified the differences in the status of CpG sites between cases and controls based on the principle of relative entropy [16]. This method can retain the information of the original CpG sites and has a high accuracy. The main formulas for improved relative entropy are as follows:

$$MD_{DML}(M_i^1, M_i^0) = MD_{KL}(M_i^1 \parallel M_i^0) - MD_{KL}(M_i^0 \parallel M_i^1). \tag{1}$$

$$MD_{KL}(M_i^1 \parallel M_i^0) = \sum_{j=1}^{n} m_{ij}^1 \cdot \log_2(\frac{m_{ij}^1}{m_{ij}^0}). \tag{2}$$

$$MD_{KL}(M_i^0 \parallel M_i^1) = \sum_{j=1}^{n} m_{ij}^0 \cdot \log_2(\frac{m_{ij}^0}{m_{ij}^1}). \tag{3}$$

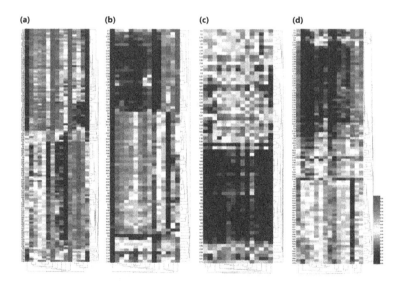

Fig. 3. Methylation levels measured at 15 CpG sites exhibit a significant difference between tumor and controls in breast (a), liver (b), prostate (c), and thyroid (d) cancers, respectively. Each row represents a sample. *Ci* and *Ni* are the labels of samples and represent the *i-th* matched pair of cancer and normal samples, respectively. Each column represents a site. Using the CpGs we performed hierarchical clustering on the samples. The heat map of the methylation values for these CpGs clearly distinguishes the sample types.

Among them, m_{ij}^0 and m_{ij}^1 represent the beta values of the j-th sample in the control and case group for the i-th CpG site, respectively. As a measure of the methylation level at each CpG site, the beta value ranges continuously from 0 to 1, with 0 denoting totally unmethylated and 1 denoting completely methylated. MD_{DML} is a quantitative representation of the differential methylation status of the CpG sites.

We generated heat maps for the methylation data of the DML which identified by the improved relative entropy, and hierarchical clustering was performed across the samples. As shown in Fig. 3, the tumor samples and the normal samples were clearly separated, indicating that the experiment identified CpG sites with significant differences in methylation status. These CpG sites can be considered as informative features for cancer diagnosis.

2.4   Detection of DMRs

Classical methods for identifying DMRs include bumphunting by Jaffe et al., A-clustering by Sofer et al., and Ong et al.'s algorithm [17–19]. In recent years, Wang et al. have designed a smooth function model to determine candidate DMRs by combining different signal features of CpG sites [20]. The function model shows superior performance in identifying DMRs. In this study, we used the method proposed by Wang [20] to detect DMRs. However, this algorithm requires the m values of the methylation level, and the methylation level in our experimental data is represented by the beta values. Therefore, the conversion of the methylation data from beta values to m values was conducted using the method proposed by Du [21].

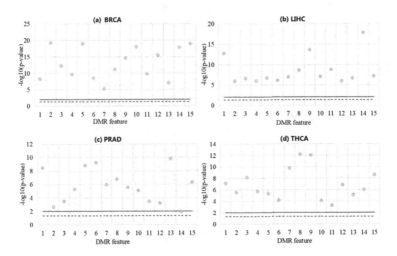

Fig. 4. Statistically significant analysis of selected DMRs. The red solid line indicates the threshold at which differences in methylation status become statistically significant in normal and matched cancer samples (T-test at 99% level). In all four cancer types, the vast majority of DMRs are above the solid line, indicating that the selected DMRs are statistically significant. (Color figure online)

We performed a T-test across samples of the selected DMRs for each cancer type, and then used the negative logarithm function to convert the p-values. As shown in Fig. 4, the red dotted line indicates a p-value of 0.05, and the solid red line indicates a p-value of 0.01. In addition to a DMR of No.14 for PRAD, the p-values of all other features are less than or equal to 0.01. The results of the T-test indicate that these methylated regions show statistically significant differences between normal and tumor samples, and can be informative for classifier learning.

2.5   Construct Machine Learning Classifiers

In this study, four machine learning packages developed with R language, Logistic Regression, SVM, Random Forest, and K-Nearest Neighbor (KNN), are used to construct classifier based on the three types of feature sets. In order to compare the predictive performance of the classifiers on the three features sets, we conducted Receiver Operating Characteristic (ROC) analysis. The larger the Area Under Curve (AUC) under the ROC curve, the better performance of the classifier. As shown in Fig. 5, the green, red, and purple curves are plotted by each classifier based on three types of feature sets. The green curves represent ROC featured by only differentially expressed genes, the red curves represent ROC featured by differentially expressed genes and DML, and the purple curves represent ROC featured by differentially

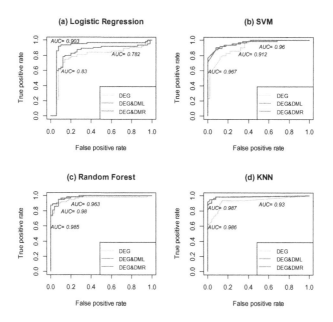

Fig. 5. Classifier performance based on different three types of input feature sets. Each panel shows the ROC experiment result for each classifier based on different feature sets. Green curves represent data of differentially expressed genes, red curves represent data of differentially expressed genes and DML, and the purple curves represent data of differentially expressed genes and DMRs. The corresponding AUC area of each curve is marked alongside. (Color figure online)

expressed genes and DMRs. The total AUCs of the green, red, and purple curves in the four classifiers are 3.587, 3.757, and 3.841 respectively, and DEG&DMR is with a gain of 7.4% compared to only DEG. The experiment of ROC analysis leads to such conclusion that the feature sets of differentially expressed genes and DML/DMRs outperform the feature sets of only differentially expressed genes for cancer diagnosis. Using the integrated feature sets, the predictive performance of the classifiers is greatly improved. Besides, the Logistic Regression, SVM, and Random Forest experimental results suggest that the integration of features of differentially expressed genes and DMRs was superior to the integration of differentially expressed genes and DML for cancer diagnosis.

3 Material

RNA-Seq and DNA methylation sequencing data in TCGA database can be downloaded from https://portal.gdc.cancer.gov/ [22] (Table 1).

Table 1. The statistics of experiment samples from TCGA.

	Normal samples with RNA-Seq	Tumor samples with RNA-Seq	Normal samples with DNA Methylation-Seq	Tumor samples with DNA Methylation-Seq
BRCA	64	64	64	64
LIHC	41	41	41	41
PRAD	36	36	36	36
THCA	49	49	49	49

4 Discussion

In recent years, the integration of multi-level biometric information has become a hot topic at bioinformatics research field [23–26]. In this study, we fused the two kinds of cancer risk marker information: differentially expressed genes and differential methylation patterns. We used multiple classification models in the field of machine learning to classify and predict tumor samples with different features. Based on the experimental results, we have gotten to the conclusion that the fusion of multi-scale gene features can significantly improve the diagnostic efficacy of cancer. In addition, similar prediction results from different classifiers also demonstrate the robustness of the integrated features. Our research provides new ideas for precision medicine. The disadvantage of this experiment is that the matched tumor/normal samples are not sufficiently enough, so we have merged samples of different cancer types as experimental data. Although we have proposed solutions, we should still collect more abundant samples and perform detailed studies on specific tumors. This paper is mainly based on cancer research, but our experimental methods can also be applied to the diagnosis of other complex diseases.

Acknowledgments. The project sponsored by the Scientific Research Foundation for the Returned Overseas Chinese Scholars, State Education Ministry (NO. 48, 2014-1685) and the Key Natural Science Project of Anhui Provincial Education Department (KJ2017A016).

References

1. Schuster, S.C.: Next-generation sequencing transforms today's biology. J. Nat. Methods **5**(1), 16–18 (2008)
2. Zhou, X.G., Ren, L.F., Li, Y.T., et al.: The next-generation sequencing technology: a technology review and future perspective. J. Sci China Life Sci. **53**(1), 44–57 (2010)
3. Maglogiannis, I., Zafiropoulos, E., Anagnostopoulos, I.: An intelligent system for automated breast cancer diagnosis and prognosis using SVM based classifiers. J. Appl. Intell. **30**(1), 24–36 (2009)
4. Chen, A.H., Huang, Z.-W.: A new multi-task learning technique to predict classification of leukemia and prostate cancer. In: Zhang, D., Sonka, M. (eds.) ICMB 2010. LNCS, vol. 6165, pp. 11–20. Springer, Heidelberg (2010). https://doi.org/10.1007/978-3-642-13923-9_2
5. Hijazi, H., Chan, C.: A classification framework applied to cancer gene expression profiles. J. Healthcare Eng. **4**(4), 255–284 (2013)
6. Nakkeeran, R., Victoire, T.A.A.: Hybrid approach of data mining techniques, PCA, EDM and SVM for cancer gene feature selection and classification. J. Eur. J. Sci. Res. **79**, 638–652 (2012)
7. Kourou, K., Exarchos, T.P., Exarchos, K.P., Karamouzis, M.V., Fotiadis, D.I.: Machine learning applications in cancer prognosis and prediction. Comput. Struct. Biotechnol. J. **13**, 8–17 (2015)
8. Kuan, P.F., Wang, S., Zhou, X., Chu, H.: A statistical framework for Illumina DNA methylation arrays. J. Bioinform. **26**, 2849–2855 (2010)
9. Baylin, S.B., Ohm, J.E.: Epigenetic gene silencing in cancer - a mechanism for early oncogenic pathway addiction. J. Nat. Rev. Cancer **6**, 107–116 (2006)
10. Kulis, M., Esteller, M.: DNA methylation and cancer. J. Adv. Gene. **70**, 27–56 (2010)
11. Wang, S.: Method to detect differentially methylated loci with case-control designs using Illumina arrays. J. Genet. Epidemiol. **35**, 686–694 (2011)
12. Robinson, M.D., McCarthy, D.J., Smyth, G.K.: EdgeR: a Bioconductor package for differential expression analysis of digital gene expression data. J. Bioinform. **26**, 139–140 (2010)
13. Wang, D., Yan, L., Hu, Q., et al.: IMA: an R package for high-throughput analysis of Illumina's 450K Infinium methylation data. J. Bioinform. **28**(5), 729–730 (2012)
14. Ahn, S., Wang, T.: A powerful statistical method for identifying differentially methylated markers in complex diseases. J. Pac. Symp. Biocomput. 69–79 (2013). NIH Public Access
15. Huang, H., Chen, Z., Huang, X.: Age-adjusted nonparametric detection of differential DNA methylation with case-control designs. J. BMC Bioinform. **14**, 86–94 (2013)
16. Zhang, Y., Zhang, J., Shang, J.: Quantitative identification of differentially methylated loci based on relative entropy for matched case-control data. J. Epigenomics **5**, 631–643 (2013)
17. Jaffe, A.E., Murakami, P., Lee, H., et al.: Bump hunting to identify differentially methylated regions in epigenetic epidemiology studies. J. Int. J. Epidemiol. **41**(1), 200–209 (2012)
18. Sofer, T., Schifano, E.D., Hoppin, J.A., et al.: A-clustering: a novel method for the detection of co-regulated methylation regions, and regions associated with exposure. J. Bioinform. **29**(22), 2884–2891 (2013)

19. Ong, M.L., Holbrook, J.D.: Novel region discovery method for Infinium 450K DNA methylation data reveals changes associated with aging in muscle and neuronal pathways. J. Aging Cell. **13**(1), 142–155 (2014)

20. Wang, Y., Teschendorff, A.E., Widschwendter, M., Wang, S.: Accounting for differential variability in detecting differentially methylated regions. J. Brief. Bioinform. (2017). bbx097

21. Du, P., Zhang, X., et al.: Comparison of Beta-value and M-value methods for quantifying methylation levels by microarray analysis. J. BMC Bioinform. **11**, 587–596 (2010)

22. The Cancer Genome Atlas Research Network., Weinstein, J.N., et al.: The cancer genome atlas Pan-Cancer analysis project. J. Nat. Genet. **45**(10), 1113–1120 (2013)

23. Ge, S., Xia, X., Ding, C., et al.: A proteomic landscape of diffuse-type gastric cancer. J. Nat. Commun. **9**(1), 1012–1028 (2018)

24. Mertins, P., Mani, D.R., Ruggles, K.V., et al.: Proteogenomics connects somatic mutations to signalling in breast cancer. J. Nature **534**, 55–62 (2016)

25. Zhang, H., Liu, T., Zhang, Z., et al.: Integrated proteogenomic characterization of human high-grade serous ovarian cancer. J. Cell. **166**(3), 755–765 (2016)

26. Zhang, B., Wang, J., Wang, X., et al.: Proteogenomic characterization of human colon and rectal cancer. J. Nature **513**, 382–403 (2014)

Behavioral Biometrics

A Novel Multiple Distances Based Dynamic Time Warping Method for Online Signature Verification

Xinyi Lu[1], Yuxun Fang[1], Qiuxia Wu[2], Junhong Zhao[1(✉)],
and Wenxiong Kang[1]

[1] School of Automation Science and Engineering,
South China University of Technology, Guangzhou 510641, China
jhzhao@scut.edu.cn
[2] School of Software Engineering, South China University of Technology,
Guangzhou 510641, China

Abstract. In this paper, a novel Multiple Distances Based Dynamic Time Warping (MDB-DTW) method is proposed for signature verification. In order to obtain more discriminative and complementary information, we take accounts of the multiple distance measurements on the Euclidian distance based DTW path. In addition, two classifiers (SVM-based classifier and PCA-based classifier) are adopted to fuse the useful information and remove the noise from the multiple dissimilarity vector space. The comprehensive experiments have conducted on three publicly accessible datasets MCYT-100, SUSIG and SVC-task2 with the obtained EER results are 1.87%, 1.28% and 6.32% respectively, which further demonstrates the robust and effectiveness of our proposed MDB-DTW method.

Keywords: Online signature verification · Multiple distance measurements
Dynamic time warping · Biometrics

1 Introduction

Automatic signature verification has been an active research area due to its social and legal acceptance, and the written signatures are also in widespread use as a personal authentication method. There are many types of research on signature verification [1–3] while it still remains a challenging task, owing to the large intra-class variations and, when considering skilled forgeries, small inter-class variations [4].

There are two different kinds of signatures depending on different data formats [5]. The off-line signature verification mainly deals with the signature images scanned from documents and papers. While the on-line signature verification utilizes specific devices like touch screens and digital tablets to capture dynamic time sequences (e.g. x, y coordinates and pressure, etc.). Therefore, it can utilize richer dynamic information with more accurate results comparing with the off-line mode. When considering the

---

X. Lu and Y. Fang—Contributed equally to this paper.

J. Zhou et al. (Eds.): CCBR 2018, LNCS 10996, pp. 645–652, 2018.
https://doi.org/10.1007/978-3-319-97909-0_68

forged signatures, it can be divided into two categories, namely random and skilled forgeries. It's obvious that the skilled forgeries are more challenging due to its small inter-class variations and thus, we will focus on the skilled forgeries for on-line signature verification.

For the on-line signature verification system, the users first should be registered with genuine samples, referred as a reference set. Then, when a user presents a signature referred as a test sample, claiming to be a particular individual, the test sample will be compared with the reference set of that claimed individual. If the dissimilarity score is above a predefined threshold, this test sample will be rejected as a forgery.

So far many methods have been proposed to extract discriminative features and design effective classifiers for on-line signature verification. Fierrez et al. [6] proposed a function-based feature set, including three basic and four extended time sequences and applied this 7-dimension feature vector into a HMM-based model. To alleviate the instability of the signature length, Fischer et al. [7] utilized distance normalization as well as the DTW algorithm to verify a user. A well-designed SVM classifier is used in [8] and won the first prize in the first international signature verification competition. There are also various DTW-based signature verification algorithms. For example, Sharma et al. [9] exploited the information from the DTW cost matrix, while in [10], a GMM-DTW method was proposed to extract discriminative features.

In this paper, we propose a simple but effective feature fusion strategy based on multiple distance measurements and dynamic time warping algorithm (MDB-DTW). This strategy utilizes seven different kinds of distance measurements to extract discriminative information and then two different classifiers are implemented for making full use of the obtained information for the final decision, respectively.

The rest of the paper is organized as follows: Sect. 2 introduces the proposed MDB-DTW method, including seven different distance measurements, fusion strategy and two different classifier structures. The experimental results and analysis are presented in Sect. 3 and followed by conclusion in Sect. 4.

2   The MDB-DTW Method

In this section, we will introduce the novel feature fusion strategy for the multiple distances based dynamic time warping algorithm. We first calculate the DTW dissimilarity and the aligned DTW path based on the Euclidian distance. With the Euclidian distance based aligned DTW path, we can calculate other six different distances based DTW dissimilarity and fuse them into a SVM-based classifier and a PCA-based classifier separately.

2.1   The Original DTW Dissimilarity

To align two sequences more precisely, we first extract a 7-dimension feature vector $[x_i, y_i, p_i, \theta_i, v_i, \rho_i, \alpha_i]$ in Table 1 for each ith sequence point [6] before implementing the DTW algorithm. The dot superscript in Table 1 can be calculated by formula (1).

Table 1. The description of the features

Features	Formulas
Path-tangent angle θ	$\theta_i = \arctan(\dot{y}_i/\dot{x}_i)$
Path velocity magnitude v	$v_i = \sqrt{\dot{x}_i^2 + \dot{y}_i^2}$
Log curvature radius ρ	$\rho_i = \log\left(v_i/\dot{\theta}_i\right)$
Total acceleration magnitude α	$\alpha_i = \sqrt{\dot{v}_i^2 + \left(v_i \cdot \dot{\theta}_i\right)^2}$

x, y, p denotes the (x, y) coordinates and the pressure.

$$\dot{f}_i = \frac{\sum_{\varepsilon=1}^{2} \varepsilon(f_{i+\varepsilon} - f_{i-\varepsilon})}{2 \cdot \sum_{\varepsilon=1}^{2} \varepsilon^2} \tag{1}$$

As we all know, the signature length is variable even written by the same user. Therefore, the dynamic time warping is a suitable and efficient method to align two sequences with different lengths. Specifically, for two sequences $S = \left(s_{1,z}, s_{2,z}, \ldots s_{n,z}\right)$ and $T = \left(t_{1,z}, t_{2,z}, \ldots t_{n,z}\right)$, the distance matrix d can be calculated by formula (2) based on Euclidian distance where z denotes the zth feature dimension. Then the DTW dissimilarity $D(m, n)$ and the aligned DTW path W (Fig. 1) can be calculated by (3).

$$d(i,j) = \sum_{z=1}^{k} \left\| s_{i,z}, t_{j,z} \right\|_2 \tag{2}$$

$$D(i,j) = d(i,j) + min \begin{cases} D(i, j-1) \\ D(i-1, j-1) \\ D(i-1, j) \end{cases} \tag{3}$$

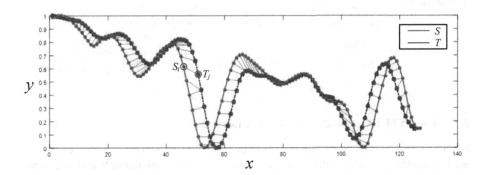

Fig. 1. The pair points of the aligned DTW path

2.2   The Multiple Distances Based DTW Dissimilarity

As we have observed that different distance measurements have different characteristics in measuring sequences and multiple distance measurements can comprise a complementation group, which can gain more powerful discriminative ability for signature verification, so we proposed to use multiple distance measurements in this paper. Besides, we have made an assumption that the Euclidian distance based DTW can well align two sequences for two reasons: (a) the Euclidian distance is the simple and straightforward way for understanding; (b) it could achieve better results in the single distance based signature verification system. Therefore, we choose it to align the signature sequences for verification.

To make full use of the Euclidian distance based aligned DTW path, we finally choose another six different distance measurements as listed in Table 2 to calculate $d(i,j)$ in (2). Considering the characteristic of different measurements, we divide these seven distance measurements into 2 groups, namely absolute numerical group and shape distribution group. The absolute numerical group mainly focuses on the numerical distance between two sequences, while the shape distribution group lays emphasis on the sequence shape and statistical distribution. Hence, the signature sample will be characterized more precisely by our proposed two different group descriptors.

Table 2. Introduction of seven distance measurements

Group	Distance No.	Formula
Absolute numerical measurement	1. Euclidian distance	$d(i,j) = \left\| S_i - T_j \right\|_2$
	2. Manhattan distance	$d(i,j) = \left\| S_i - T_j \right\|$
	3. Chebyshev distance	$d(i,j) = \max_z \left\| S_{iz} - T_{jz} \right\|$
	4. Standardized Euclidian distance	$d(i,j) = \sqrt{\sum_z \frac{(S_{iz}-T_{jz})^2}{std([S_{iz},T_{jz}])}}$
Shape distribution measurement	5. Cosine distance	$d(i,j) = 1 - \frac{S_i \cdot T_j}{\sqrt{\sum_i S_i^2}\sqrt{\sum_i T_i^2}} = 1 - \frac{\langle S,T \rangle}{\|S\| \cdot \|T\|}$
	6. Correlation coefficient	$d(i,j) = 1 - \frac{\sum_i (S_i-\bar{S}_i)(T_i-\bar{T}_i)}{\sqrt{\sum (S_i-\bar{S}_i)}\sqrt{\sum (T_i-\bar{T}_i)}} = 1 - \frac{\langle S-\bar{S},T-\bar{T} \rangle}{\|S-\bar{S}\| \cdot \|T-\bar{T}\|}$
	7. Bhattacharyya coefficient	$d(i,j) = \frac{1}{4}\frac{(\bar{S}_i-\bar{T}_j)^2}{\text{var}(S_i)+\text{var}(T_j)} + \frac{1}{2}\log\left(\frac{\text{var}(S_i)+\text{var}(T_j)}{2 \cdot \sqrt{\text{var}(S_i) \cdot \text{var}(T_j)}}\right)$

2.3   The SVM-Based and PCA-Based Classifiers

It cannot be ignored that indeed, these seven distance measurements are highly correlated with each other. In other words, the information calculated by multiple distance measurements is overlapped and noisy. To extract the tiny but useful information of a high dimension space, we first apply the support vector machine (SVM) to the 7-dimension dissimilarity space inspired by [8]. Besides, considering to remove the correlation, we also adopt the principle component analysis (PCA) inspired by [11]. Finally, a distance normalization *DN-1* and a decision formula *ID2* proposed in [12] are used to calculate the decision score as shown by formula (4) and formula (5), respectively. In formula (4), i denotes the ith and j^{th} sample in reference set and test set respectively, l denotes the length of the sample and n denotes the nth subject. In formula (5), the parameters (u_t, σ_t) and (u_r, σ_r) are corresponding to $D_{ref,ref} \sim N(u_r, \sigma_r^2), D_{ref,test} \sim N(u_r, \sigma_r^2)$ respectively. In summary, Algorithm 1 presents the whole procedure of our proposed MDB-DTW algorithm.

Algorithm 1: The MDB-DTW-SVM/PCA algorithm

Inputs: the x, y, p data of reference i^{th} sample R_n^i and test j^{th} sample T_n^j of subject n.

Outputs: the decision score $SCORE_n^j$ of R_n^i and T_n^j.

1. Extract the 7-D feature vectors F_n^i, F_n^j with $F = [x, y, p, \theta, \nu, \rho, \alpha]$ in Section 2.1.

2. Calculate the Euclidian distance based DTW dissimilarity $DTW\text{-}DIST_1^{i,j}$ and the corresponding aligned DTW path $W^{i,j}$.

3. **FOR** distance 2 to 7 in Table 1:

   Calculate the other distance based DTW dissimilarity using Euclidian distance based aligned DTW path $W^{i,j}$: $DTW\text{-}DIST_{n,k}^{i,j} = \sum_{w \in W_n^{i,j}} d_k\left(F_n^{i,w_1}, F_n^{j,w_2}\right)$

4. **IF** MDB-DTW-SVM:

   Use $\left[DTW\text{-}DIST^{R,R}, DTW\text{-}DIST^{R,F}\right]_m^*$ as training data to train the SVM model.

   Transform the $DTW\text{-}DIST^{i,j}$ with the SVM model: $Dtrans_n^{i,j} = SVM\left(DTW\text{-}DIST^{i,j}\right)$

   Elif MDB-DTW-PCA:

   Apply PCA algorithm to $\left[DTW\text{-}DIST^{R,R}\right]_r^{**}$ and calculate the PCA coefficient: *coeff.*

   Transform the $DTW\text{-}DIST^{i,j}$ with the *coeff*: $Dpca_n^{i,j} = coeff \times DTW\text{-}DIST_n^{i,j}$.

   Use the first dimension of $Dpca_n^{i,j}$ as $Dtrans_n^{i,j} = \left[Dpca_n^{i,j}\right]_1$.

5. Apply distance normalization to $Dtrans_n^{i,j}$ with formula (4): $Dsn_n^{i,j} = DN\text{-}1\left(Dtrans_n^{i,j}\right)$.

6. Calculate the SCORE by formula (5): $SCORE_n^j = ID2\left(Dsn_n^{R,R}, Dsn_n^{R,j}\right)^{***}$.

---

* m denotes the randomly-selected 10 subjects, R,R denotes one randomly-selected pair sequence in reference set, R,F in both reference and test set.

** r denotes 100 randomly-selected subjects (allow repeat), R,R denotes one randomly-selected pair sequence in reference set

*** $Dsn_n^{R,R} \sim N(u_r, \sigma_r^2)$ is calculated via reference set, and $Dsn_n^{R,j} \sim N(u_t, \sigma_t^2)$ is calculated between test sample and reference set.

$$DN-1: \quad dist_n^{i,j}/l_n^j \tag{4}$$

$$ID2: \quad D = (u_t - u_r) \times \left(\frac{\sigma_t}{\sigma_r}\right)^{0.4}, \quad if \quad \frac{\sigma_t^2}{\sigma_r^2} > T1$$

$$D = (u_t - u_r) \times \left(\frac{\sigma_r}{\sigma_t}\right)^{0.4}, \quad if \quad \frac{\sigma_t^2}{\sigma_r^2} < T1 \tag{5}$$

$$T1 = \left(\frac{(u_r - u_t)^2}{\sigma_r^2} + 1\right) \times 0.7$$

3   The Experimental Results

Three different online signature databases are used to evaluate our proposed MDB-DTW-SVM and MDB-DTW-PCA algorithm. Also, to make the experimental results more convincing, we set two strict protocols with fixed reference set and test set.

3.1   Database and Protocol Description

The MCYT-100 database [13] is comprised of 100 subjects and each subject contains 25 genuine samples and 25 skilled forged samples. The SUSIG database [14] consists of 94 subjects, 20 genuine samples and 10 skilled forged samples per subject, and the SVC-task2 [15] database contains 40 subjects, 20 genuine samples and 20 skilled forged samples per subject.

We have defined two protocols P5 and P10 for our experiments. For the protocols, we use the first 5 and 10 genuine samples as a reference set, and the rest of the genuine samples and all of the skilled forged samples of the corresponding subject as the test set, namely P5 and P10 respectively. To compare with other signature verification systems, we have reported the EER under the above-mentioned P5 and P10 protocols.

3.2   The Experimental Results

The EER results under the P5 and P10 protocols are listed in Table 3. It seems that the original DTW outperforms our proposed MDB-DTW method a little under the P5 protocol for MCYT-100 and SUSIG databases. This is expected because our MDB-DTW aims to dig the minor but discriminative information from the multiple distance measurements and it's reasonable that the more samples we used, the more information our MDB-DTW will capture to enhance the accuracy. The results further confirm our expectations.

We also compare our proposed MDB-DTW with other signature verification approaches as listed in Table 4. To be noted that most evaluation protocols choose reference set randomly and thus it's unfair to directly compare the EER results. The randomly-chosen reference set is unreliable while our fixed protocols P5 and P10 are more convincing. In Table 4, our proposed MDB-DTW achieves the state of the art results except for the P5 protocol of MCYT-100 and P10 protocol of SVC-task2, even comparing with the randomly-chosen reference set. What's more, our proposed MDB-DTW performs well in all three common signature databases, which further demonstrates the robust and effectiveness of our proposed MDB-DTW method.

Table 3. The EER (%) of the proposed MDB-DTW

Database	MCYT-100		SUSIG		SVC-task2	
Protocol	P5	P10	P5	P10	P5	P10
Original-DTW*	**2.98**	1.95	**1.91**	1.33	6.36	6.71
MDB-DTW-SVM	3	**1.84**	2.04	1.38	**6.26**	6.64
MDB-DTW-PCA	3	1.87	1.99	**1.28**	6.33	**6.32**

*The original-DTW refers to only use Euclidian distance based DTW and *ID2* decision formula in [12].

Table 4. EER (%) summary of different signature verification approaches

Method	EER (%)		
	MCYT-100	SUSIG	SVC-task2
Path-DTW [9]	**2.76^5***	–	7.8^5*
SC-DTW [7]	$3.94^5/2.74^{10}$	$3.09^5/2.13^{10}$	–
KL-DTW [12]	$3.16^5/2.25^{10}$	$2.13^5/1.6^{10}$	–
DCT + Sparse representation [16]	–	2.98^{10}*	**5.61^{10}***
SVC2004 [15]	–	–	6.9^5
MDB-DTW- SVM [this work]	**3.00^5/1.84^{10}**	$2.04^5/1.38^{10}$	**6.26^5/6.64^{10}**
MDB-DTW-PCA [this work]	**3.00^5/1.87^{10}**	**1.99^5/1.28^{10}**	$6.33^5/6.32^{10}$

*Select the reference set randomly
The superscript 5 and 10 denote the P5 and P10 protocol respectively

4 Conclusions

In this paper, we have proposed a novel MDB-DTW method, to extract discriminative information for signature verification. We found that multiple distance measurements can be complementary to each other and thus via the SVM or PCA method, more discriminative information can be utilized to enhance the accuracy. The experimental results show that our proposed MDB-DTW-SVM/PCA is robust and effective.

Acknowledgements. This work was supported by the National Natural Science Foundation of China (Nos. 61573151 and 61503141), the Guangdong Natural Science Foundation (No. 2016A030313468), Science and Technology Planning Project of Guangdong Province (No. 2017A010101026).

References

1. Tolosana, R., et al.: Exploring recurrent neural networks for on-line handwritten signature biometrics. IEEE Access **6**, 5128–5138 (2018)
2. Fang, Y., et al.: A novel video-based system for in-air signature verification. Comput. Electr. Eng. **57**, 1–14 (2017)
3. Ahrabian, K., Babaali, B.: On usage of autoencoders and siamese networks for online handwritten signature verification. arXiv preprint arXiv:1712.02781 (2017)
4. Lu, X., Fang, Y., Kang, W., Wang, Z., Feng, D.D.: SCUT-MMSIG: a multimodal online signature database. In: Zhou, J., et al. (eds.) CCBR 2017. LNCS, vol. 10568, pp. 729–738. Springer, Cham (2017). https://doi.org/10.1007/978-3-319-69923-3_78
5. Zhang, Z., Wang, K., Wang, Y.: A survey of on-line signature verification. In: Sun, Z., Lai, J., Chen, X., Tan, T. (eds.) CCBR 2011. LNCS, vol. 7098, pp. 141–149. Springer, Heidelberg (2011). https://doi.org/10.1007/978-3-642-25449-9_18
6. Fierrez, J., et al.: HMM-based on-line signature verification: Feature extraction and signature modeling. Pattern Recogn. Lett. **28**(16), 2325–2334 (2007)
7. Fischer, A., et al.: Robust score normalization for DTW-based on-line signature verification. In: International Conference on Document Analysis and Recognition (2015)
8. Kholmatov, A., Yanikoglu, B.: Identity authentication using improved online signature verification method. Pattern Recogn. Lett. **26**(15), 2400–2408 (2005)
9. Sharma, A., Sundaram, S.: On the exploration of information from the DTW cost matrix for online signature verification. IEEE Trans. Cybern. **48**, 611–624 (2017)
10. Sharma, A., Sundaram, S.: A novel online signature verification system based on GMM features in a DTW framework. IEEE Trans. Inf. Forensics Secur. **12**, 705–718 (2017)
11. Chan, T.H., et al.: PCANet: a simple deep learning baseline for image classification? IEEE Trans. Image Process. **24**(12), 5017 (2015)
12. Tang, L., Kang, W., Fang, Y.: Information divergence-based matching strategy for online signature verification. IEEE Trans. Inf. Forensics Secur. **13**(4), 861–873 (2018)
13. Ortega-Garcia, J., et al.: MCYT baseline corpus: a bimodal biometric database. IEE Proc. Vis. Image Sig. Process. **150**(6), 395–401 (2003)
14. Kholmatov, A., Yanikoglu, B.: SUSIG: an on-line signature database, associated protocols and benchmark results. Pattern Anal. Appl. **12**(3), 227–236 (2009)
15. Yeung, D.-Y., et al.: SVC2004: first international signature verification competition. In: Zhang, D., Jain, A.K. (eds.) ICBA 2004. LNCS, vol. 3072, pp. 16–22. Springer, Heidelberg (2004). https://doi.org/10.1007/978-3-540-25948-0_3
16. Liu, Y., Yang, Z., Yang, L.: Online signature verification based on DCT and sparse representation. IEEE Trans. Cybern. **45**(11), 2498–2511 (2015)

The Detection of Beard Behavior of Taxi Drivers Based on Traffic Surveillance Video

Zuyun Wang[1], Xunping Huang[2,3,4,5], Kebin Jia[2,3,4,5(✉)], Pengyu Liu[2,3,4,5], and Zhonghua Sun[2,3,4,5]

[1] Traffic Execution BR Gade of Beijing, Beijing, China
[2] Faculty of Information Technology, Beijing University of Technology, Beijing 100124, China
kebinj@bjut.edu.cn
[3] Beijing Laboratory of Advanced Information Networks, Beijing 100124, China
[4] Beijing Advanced Innovation Center for Future Internet Technology,
Beijing University of Technology, Beijing 100124, China
[5] Beijing Key Laboratory of Computational Intelligence and Intelligent System,
Beijing University of Technology, Beijing 100124, China

Abstract. This paper presents a method for automatic detection of taxi drivers beard behavior. First, Haar-Adaboost algorithm is used to locate the special window area of taxi. Secondly, the image is preprocessed by multi-scale retina enhancement algorithm on image value channel, then face feature points and chin area are extracted from the window area, and the beard pixel is segmented by skin tone and gray threshold method. Finally, The method was tested by real traffic surveillance video and the validity was proved

Keywords: Beard behavior · Window area · Face feature points · Chin area

1 Introduction

The taxi industry is an important part of the transportation industry. In the first-tier cities such as Beijing, due to the large population, public transport can't stand the huge crowd pressure, it has led to an increasing demand for taxis, and the law enforcement personnel's law enforcement difficulty and work intensity have greatly increased [1, 2]. At the same time, the taxi industry belongs to the category of service industry. Therefore, the appearance and dress of taxi drivers are also included in the enforcement of the traffic law enforcement department. The beard behavior is one of them. Therefore, if the automatic detection of the taxi driver's beard behavior can be realized, it will relieve the law enforcement pressure of the traffic department.

At present, The detection of beard behavior is not a hot research point, especially for special groups. Most of the domestic and foreign research focuses on the beard detection of simple environments. In document [3], a beard detection algorithm based on facial feature points and skin color segmentation is proposed. The algorithm is more

---

Z. Wang—Professor-level senior engineer, Computer science and technology.

© Springer Nature Switzerland AG 2018
J. Zhou et al. (Eds.): CCBR 2018, LNCS 10996, pp. 653–661, 2018.
https://doi.org/10.1007/978-3-319-97909-0_69

dependent on the color information, so the detection accuracy is easily affected by the light. Document [4] proposes a beard detection method combined with convolutional neural network, but this method detects face data sets and is difficult to apply in practice. In view of the above problems, this paper proposes a method of automatic detection of beard behavior of taxi drivers. This method proposes to use the window area detection instead of the complete taxi detection to accurately locate the taxi driver. Secondly, use the MSR (Multi-Scale Retina) enhancement algorithm based image value channel (MSRBVC) for image enhancement to reduce the effect of light on the image. Then use the libfacedetection face detection library to accurately locate the chin region, and finally use the combination of skin color information and gray threshold segmentation to determine whether the driver has beard behavior.

This paper describes the structure as follows. Section 2 describes the detection of taxi window area based on Haar-Adaboost algorithm. Section 3 describes the MSRBVC algorithm. Section 4 describes the extraction of the chin area and the beard segmentation based on skin color information and gray threshold method. Section 5 shows the experimental results. The last section summarizes the full text.

2   Window Area Detection

In the traffic surveillance video, the scene has a certain degree of complexity. So it is necessary to accurately locate the taxi cab, that is, to accurately position the taxi driver. In this paper, we use the unique dome light design and window area of the taxi (The latter is referred to as window area), proposed a window area detection method based on the Haar-Adaboost algorithm. At the same time, in order to reduce the false detection rate, a sliding color histogram matching method based on the dome light is proposed.

2.1   Haar-Adaboost Algorithm

The Haar feature [5, 6] refers to a rectangular feature whose value is expressed as the difference between the gray value of the black rectangular region and the gray value of the white rectangular region, thereby generating an image feature matrix. The commonly used Haar features are shown in Fig. 1.

Fig. 1. Common Haar features: (picture 1) Linear feature, (picture 2) Edge feature, (picture 3) Diagonal feature, (picture 4) Central feature.

Adaboost algorithm [7] is an improved Boosting algorithm. The algorithm does not need any prior knowledge of weak classifiers. Its core is training different weak classifiers for the same training set, and then classifies these weak classifiers into a stronger final classifier. Figure 2 is a process of cascade and detection of taxi by classifier.

Fig. 2. Process of cascade and detection of taxi by classsifier.

Multiscale scanning is carried out by using different sizes of rectangular windows on the image to be detected, and the cascade classifier is used to judge each of the rectangular windows of the scan. If a rectangular window feature passes all cascade classifiers, it indicates that the area is the taxi window area, and the location of the taxi in the current image is obtained.

2.2 Training and Preliminary Test

Taking account of the fact that the taxi is partial cover by each other in the real environment, we choose the taxi window area which is not easy to be sheltered and use the specific area as the positive sample feature extraction area. In this paper, the training set contains 2767 window area positive samples and 7219 environmental negative samples, In order to make the classifier more adaptable to the environment, these samples were taken from the actual traffic surveillance video. Some samples are shown in Fig. 3.

Fig. 3. (row 1) Partial positive samples and (row 2) partial negative samples.

The trained classifier is used to detect traffic surveillance video. The experimental results are shown in Fig. 4.

Fig. 4. Preliminary detection results of window area.

From the experimental results, it can be seen that the classifier has a good recognition degree for taxi, but there still exists the problem of identifying the environment and conventional vehicle into taxi.

2.3 Sliding Color Histogram Matching

The similarity of the color histogram can reflect the similarity of the two images [8]. This paper uses the window area of the previous section segmented, and segmenting out the part containing the dome light, and setting this part as the ROI. Through the proposed sliding color histogram matching for ROI, in order to delete the false detection area. The ROI partition and matching process is shown in the left of Fig. 5.

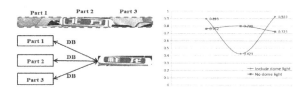

Fig. 5. (left) ROI partition and matching process, (right) histogram matching result.

The matching curve can be obtained by dividing the ROI into three equal parts and matching each part with the dome light for color histogram matching (using the Bhattacharyya distance calculation matching similarity). Use 100 ROI images with dome light and 100 ROI images without dome light to perform the above matching. Finally, take the matching results for each part to average. The experimental results are shown in the right of Fig. 5.

The experimental results show that the difference between the sliding color histogram matching results of the ROI including the dome light and no dome light is mainly reflected in Part 2. The Bhattacharyya distance calculated by the part include the dome light is significantly smaller than the other parts, use this difference to set the criteria for distinguishing whether or not include a dome light:

$$P(x) = \begin{cases} 1 \ if \ (DB_2 \leq 0.2) \\ or \ (DB_3 - DB_2 \geq 0.3 \ and \ DB_1 - DB_2 \geq 0.3) \\ 0 \ else \end{cases} \tag{1}$$

DB_i is the Bhattacharyya distance calculated by $Part_i$. Among them, $i = 1, 2, 3$. $P(x) = 1$ means that the ROI includes dome light, otherwise $P(x) = 0$.

The algorithm proposed in this paper is used for taxi detection in traffic surveillance video again. The experimental results are shown in Fig. 6. It can be seen from the experimental results that the previous false detection has been eliminated.

Fig. 6. Secondary detection results of window area.

3   MSR Algorithm Based on Image Value Channel

In the actual environment, the taxi driver is in a semi-enclosed space, which causes the phenomenon of light imbalance in the space. It will greatly interfere with subsequent pixel point determination. Therefore, images need to be preprocessed. The MSR algorithm [9, 10] based on the image value channel is used in this paper. The image of the window area is transferred to the HSV color space, and MSRBVC image enhancement algorithm is performed to reduce the effect of light on the image.

According to Retinex theory, the brightness of a human-perceived object depends on the illumination of the environment and the reflection of the irradiated light on the surface of the object. Its mathematical expression is:

$$I(x, y) = L(x, y) * R(x, y) \tag{2}$$

In the formula (2): $I(x, y)$ represents the image signal observed or received by the camera; $L(x, y)$ represents the illumination component of the ambient light; $R(x, y)$ represents the reflection component of the target object carrying the image detail information. To take the logarithm of both sides of formula (2) can throw away the nature of the incident light to get the original appearance of the object, that is formula (3):

$$Log[R(x, y)] = Log[I(x, y)] - Log[L(x, y)] \tag{3}$$

Applying this technique to image processing is to calculate the corresponding $R(x, y)$ for the image data $I(x, y)$ we have obtained so that $R(x, y)$ is considered to be enhanced image, the author of Retinex theory points out that this $L(x, y)$ can be obtained by Gaussian blurring the image data $I(x, y)$. Multiscale refers to a variety of Gaussian blur radii. Therefore, MSR image enhancement by separating the V channel can not only restore the details of the light affected by the image, but also preserve the original color of the image. Figure 7 is an image enhancement of the taxi affected by light. It can be seen that the details of the taxi driver's face and taxi are restored to a large extent.

Fig. 7. MSRBVC algorithm test results: (left) original frame, (right) enhanced frame.

4   Chin Area Extraction and Beard Segmentation

The development of face detection has been relatively mature. This paper uses libfacedetection face detection library to extract facial feature points. This library is 2–3 times faster than Haar-Adaboost algorithm(based on Opencv library) in detection speed [11, 12]. Face detection results from libfacedetection library will mark 68 feature points. In this paper, the 3–13 and 31–35 feature points are connected to form the outer contour of the chin region. The 48–59 feature points are connected to form the inner contour (lip region) of the chin region. The outer contour includes the region minus the inner contour. The area constitutes the chin area. As shown in Fig. 8.

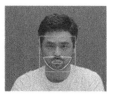

Fig. 8. (left) outer contour, (right) inner contour and outer contour.

The chin area extracted in this paper can only include skin color information and beard. Therefore, this paper uses a combination of direct and indirect verification methods to split the beard, directly verifying use the information that the pixel value of beard are deeper than the skin, therefore using the gray threshold method to split beard pixel. Indirectly verify use the non-skin color pixels in the chin region are treated as beard pixel.

The gray threshold method converts the original color image into a single-channel gray image, uses gray information of beard and skin color to be distributed in different gray levels, sets a suitable threshold value, and separates the beard pixel. The line 1 of Fig. 9 shows the splitting effect of beard under different thresholds. Based on the experimental results, this paper will set the threshold to 100.

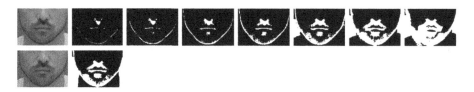

Fig. 9. (row 1) Beard segmentation under different thresholds: From the column 2 to the column 8, the thresholds are 50–110, (row 2) skin color detection results.

This paper is based on the Ycrcb color space to detect skin color, because the space is less affected by the brightness, skin color will produce a good clustering. According to experience, the CrCb value of the pixel satisfies: $133 \leq Cr \leq 173$, $77 \leq Cb \leq 127$, then this point is considered as a skin color pixel, Otherwise beard pixel. The test results are shown in the line 2 of Fig. 9.

The skin color detection result and the gray threshold segmentation result are combined Bitwise AND calculated to obtain the final beard segmentation image. Finally, the proportion of pixels in the chin area occupied by the beard pixels is counted to achieve the illegal condition, and it is determined that the driver has beard behavior.

5 Analysis of Experimental Results

By integrating the above algorithm, a complete automatic detection algorithm of taxi driver's beard behavior is constructed. In order to verify the validity of the detection method of taxi driver beard behavior proposed in this paper, four traffic surveillance video of different scenes was selected as the test set. The video information as shown in the Table 1.

Table 1. The surveillance video information.

Video number	Bearded driver number	Beardless driver number	Weak light
1	1	53	Y
2	1	47	N
3	0	68	Y
4	0	51	N

And the same time, we compare the methods proposed in this paper with a method proposed by CAI. Some of the experimental results are shown in Fig. 10 and Table 2.

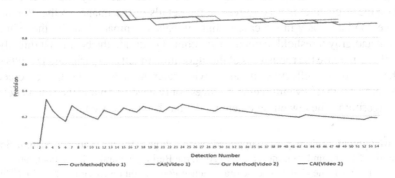

Fig. 10. The accuracy trend of our method and CAI's method.

Table 2. Experimental results of the four surveillance videos.

Video number	Detected number of bearded driver		Detected number of beardless driver	
	Our method	CAI's method	Our method	CAI's method
1	5	45	49	9
2	4	5	44	43
3	5	51	63	17
4	3	4	48	47

In this paper, we use Precision to describe the performance of algorithm. The definition of Precision in formula 4.

$$\mathrm{Pr}\,ecision \;=\; True\;Detection\;Number/Detection\;Number \tag{4}$$

It can be seen from the accuracy curve that our method is obviously superior to CAI's method in the weak light environment. In a normal environment, our method is also slightly better than CAI's. Table 2 is a summary of all experimental data.

The above data show that the proposed method of this paper has stronger environmental adaptability. Moreover, since other algorithms do not have the function to identify taxi drivers, Therefore, when comparing the experimental results, the default detection object of this paper is taxi driver.

Combined with the above mentioned taxi detection, this paper realizes the accurate detection of the taxi driver's beard behavior.

6   Conclusion

This paper proposes an automatic detection method for taxi driver's beard behavior. This method proposes a taxi window area detection instead of the traditional vehicle detection, which can solve the partial occlusion problem of the vehicle and quickly locate the driver's position, At the same time, a method of sliding color histogram matching is proposed to reduce the error detection of window area. Secondly, the MSR algorithm based on the V channel is used to restore the details of the image, so that the method can have good accuracy in the case of light imbalance impact. Finally, the skin color detection and gray threshold method are combined to divide the beard that directly and indirectly to increase the robustness of the algorithm. Finally, experimental results show that the algorithm is effective. It can provide references for traffic law enforcement departments, So that law enforcement officers only need to review the results detected by the algorithm, The law enforcement model has been improved.

Acknowledgment. This paper is supported by the Project for the National Natural Science Foundation of China under Grants No. 61672064, the Beijing Natural Science Foundation under Grant No. 4172001, the China Postdoctoral Science Foundation under Grants No. 2016T90022, 2015M580029, the Beijing Postdoctoral Science Foundation under Grants No. 2015ZZ-23, the Science and Technology Project of Beijing Municipal Education Commission under Grants No. KZ201610005007, and Beijing Laboratory of Advanced Information Networks under Grants No. 040000546617002, and Beijing Municipal Communications Commission Science and Technology Project under Grants No. 2017058.

References

1. This newspaper's commentator: Correctly understanding the relationship between the transportation power and the socialist modernization power (Chinese). China Water Transport, (001), 13 November 2017
2. Huang, Q.: Current situation and improvement of non-site enforcement (Chinese). J. Shanghai Public Secur. College **17**(3), 79–81 (2007)
3. Cai, X., Gan, K., Yang, C.: The beard detection algorithm based on feature point location and skin color segmentation (Chinese). Video Eng. **40**(3), 116–121 (2016)

4. Gu, Y., Qiu, W.: Beard and hat detection based on CNN (Chinese). Inf. Technol. **9**, 121–124 (2017)
5. Lienhart, R., Maydt, J.: An extended set of Haar-like features for rapid object detection. In: International Conference on Image Processing, Proceedings, vol. 1, pp. I-900–I-903. IEEE (2002)
6. Viola, P., Jones, M.: Robust real-time face detection. Int. J. Comput. Vis. **57**(2), 137–154 (2004)
7. Freund, Y., Schapire, R.E.: A desicion-theoretic generalization of on-line learning and an application to boosting. In: Vitányi, P. (ed.) EuroCOLT 1995. LNCS, vol. 904, pp. 23–37. Springer, Heidelberg (1995). https://doi.org/10.1007/3-540-59119-2_166
8. Li, Z., Qiu, H.: Research on fast image matching based on correlation coefficient (Chinese). J. Beijing Inst. Technol. **27**(11), 998–1000 (2007)
9. Jobson, D.J., Rahman, Z.-u., Woodell, G.A.: A multiscale retinex for bridging the gap between color images and the human observation of scenes. IEEE Trans. Image Process. **6**(7), 965–976 (1997)
10. Qin, X., Wang, H., Du, Y.: Retinex structured light image enhancement algorithm in HSV color space (Chinese). J. Comput. Aided Des. Comput. Graph. **25**(4), 488–493 (2013)
11. Li, Y., Lai, J., Ruan, B.: Multi template ASM algorithm and its application in face feature points detection (Chinese). J. Comput. Res. Dev. **44**(1), 133–140 (2007)
12. Liu, C., Zhang, L.: An improved feature point location method for face. J. Fudan Univ. (Nat. Sci.) **45**(4), 457–463 (2006)

Robust Recognition Algorithm
for Fall Down Behavior

Wei Yan$^{(\boxtimes)}$, Jianbin Xie, Peiqin Li, and Tong Liu

College of Electronic Science and Engineering,
National University of Defense Technology, Changsha 410073, China
wei.yan@nudt.edu.cn

Abstract. Detecting fall down behavior is a meaningful work in the area of
public video surveillance and smart home care, as this behavior is often caused
by accident but usually trigger serious result. However, the uncertain individual
behavior, the difference between different cameras, and the complexity of real
application scene make the work absolutely hard. In this paper, a robust fall
down behavior recognition algorithm is proposed based on the spatial and
temporal analysis of the Key Area of Human Body (KAHB). Firstly, a modified
ViBe method is applied to extract motion area. Then a pre-trained human body
classifier combined with histogram tracking is used to locate the KAHB and
extract its normalized spatial and temporal features. Finally, a SVM classifier is
employed to find the fall down behavior.

Keywords: Fall down behavior recognition · Visual computation
Smart surveillance

1 Introduction

The fall down behavior should be paid more attention, as it often caused by accident.
The fall down person such as a lonely old man usually cannot help himself and need
immediate help. The human behavior recognition method based on visual computation
is helpful to this problem. However, in authentic application, the fall down posture
varies greatly from person to person. Since the different cameras have different optics
parameters and installation parameters, thus the scenes are usually complex. All these
negative effect makes the recognition of fall down behavior absolutely hard.

Without loss of generality, we assume that the recognizable fall down behavior has
two restrictions: (1) At the beginning of the video, the target human must be standing.
(2) The fall down behavior must not be covered. In this paper, a robust fall down
behavior recognition algorithm is proposed based on the spatial and temporal analysis
of the Key Area of Human Body (KAHB). The proposed method include two key
steps: KAHB detection and behavior recognition, as Fig. 1 shows. In the first step, a
modified ViBe method is used, which can effectively resist the effect caused by ghost
and shadow, and can extract motion area. Then pre-trained human body classifier is
applied to locate the KAHB. In the second step, histogram tracker is employed to track
KAHB and extract the normalized spatial and temporal features. Meanwhile, a SVM
classifier is employed to classify these features and find the fall down behavior.

© Springer Nature Switzerland AG 2018
J. Zhou et al. (Eds.): CCBR 2018, LNCS 10996, pp. 662–668, 2018.
https://doi.org/10.1007/978-3-319-97909-0_70

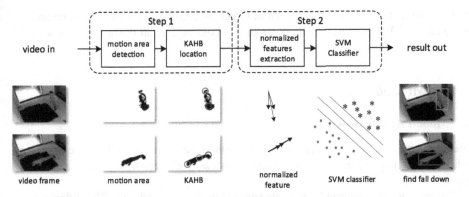

Fig. 1. Flow diagram of proposed algorithm. Step 1, extracts motion areas from input video frame, and locate the KAHB. Step 2, extract normalized features of KAHB and use SVM classifier to find fall down behavior. The green square frame in result image represent the human target, while the red one represent the detected fall down behavior. (Color figure online)

The contributions of our method are as follows: (i) The method has no special restrictions for application and the camera installation. (ii) The method can recognize different fall down postures.

2 Relate Work

Computer recognition of human activities is an important research area in computer vision. J. K. et al. categorized human activities into four different levels: gestures, actions, interactions, and group activities by complexity, and review the early representative researches [1]. They pointed out that most methods are valid only for single person in controlled environments. Bo Yao et al. use interval type-2 fuzzy logic classification systems to recognize behaviors robustly [2]. In recent years, many researchers attempt to recognize human behaviors by real 3d information. Chen Xiao et al. adopted Kinect to acquire and analyze the similarities of human body posture [3], C. H. Kuo et al. applied multiple depth cameras to acquire time-variant skeleton vector projection [4]. Changji Wen et al. use smart phones with built-in sensor to recognize the behaviors of the phone user [5]. However, when they get benefits from the special hardware, the area of application is limited at the same time.

For the fall down behavior recognition based on visual computation, there exist a few published achievements. According to our searching scope, Wei Quan et al. used custom made sensor to detect fall down indoor [6]. Hongxia Chu et al. propose da behavior recognition algorithm based on block matrix, which can deal with fall down behavior [7].

In the previous research work, a fast suspicious behavior recognition method for high definition videos is proposed. It analyses the motion vectors extracted from compressed video data and can be used for fall down behaviors recognition [8]. However, due to the fact that the motion vector feature is a kind of statistics feature, which cannot distinguish the special area of target, and easily be effected by scene and camera change. The proposed method can only recognize the fall down behavior with some special postures.

3 Our Method

3.1 Motion Area Extraction

ViBe is a powerful motion area extraction method based on spatial and temporal random sample [9], but the extraction accuracy is easily effected by the ghost and the shadow.

The ghost is often caused by the foreground target in initial frame. The difference between ghost and real target is that the ghost area has the similar texture with the background surround it. Therefore, for each extracted area, the follow formulas are adopted to calculate the static property S and the grad property G, where p_{ij}^t represents the point at (i, j) in frame t, a_n is all point number in the area, th_s and th_g is the preset threshold. The bigger S means the area is more like a dead target, and the bigger G means the area has little difference between surround area. Thus when S and G big enough, the area can be regard as ghost area (as Fig. 2a show), and the ViBe model should re-initial it.

$$s_{ij} = \begin{cases} 0 & \left| p_{ij}^t - p_{ij}^{t-1} \right| \leq th\_s \\ 1 & else \end{cases} \quad , \quad S = \sum_{area} s_{ij} \Big/ a\_n \qquad (1)$$

$$g_{ij} = \begin{cases} 1 & grad\left(p_{ij}^t\right) \leq th\_g \\ 0 & else \end{cases} \quad , \quad G = \sum_{area} g_{ij} \Big/ a\_n \qquad (2)$$

The common shadow removal method generally compares the color property of current frame with reference frame in HSV space. However, the problem is how to obtain valid reference frame. For each point, 3 value (1 for each color channel) from the ViBe background array are randomly sampled, and combined as current reference frame, and the frame is used to remove the shadow (as Fig. 2b shows).

(a)   (b)

Fig. 2. Motion area extraction sample of modified ViBe method. (a) ghost remove, (b) shadow remove.

3.2   KAHB Location

The head area, waist area and the foot area are defined, as the Key Area of Human Body (KAHB), because these areas can effectively represent the fall down posture of human body.

In the motion area, a pre-trained detector is adopted based on Haar descriptor to extract human body area. Since the detector may extract more than 1 different human body in signal area, several results are recorded in adjacent frames. Then the similarity of those results are analyze to pick out the final human body area.

In the human body area, the top 1/5 is selected as head area, and the bottom 1/5 as foot area. The question is how to define the waist area. Obviously, when people are walking, the arms and the legs are swinging, which makes the width of the human body vary in each frame, while the width of the waist area changes little. Therefore the area width of same human body is analyzed in frame sequence, and the position has small width and small change will be selected as waist area. If the human body keeps standing for a long time, the middle area of the human body is selected as waist area.

When the human body does not keep standing posture, the detector can hardly extract the human body area. In the view of the restriction 1, here a histogram tracker is employed to find the KAHB in current frame.

3.3   Extract Normalized Features

The human body area has three KAHB, and for each KAHB, the centroid point is calculated, which can be defined as P_H, P_W and P_F. Then we can gain three vectors, $\overrightarrow{P_H P_F}$, $\overrightarrow{P_W P_F}$ and $\overrightarrow{P_H P_W}$. The follow formula is used to normalize those vectors, here the X represents the original vectors.

$$\tilde{X} = normalize(X) = X \Big/ \left| \overrightarrow{P_W P_F} \right| \tag{3}$$

The fall down behavior includes three states, standing, falling down and lying on the ground. The three vectors of each state should be very different. Thus for the same target, the normalized vectors in current frame is combined with the vectors belonging to the previous frame at preset space, and $f_{t,m}$ is used to represent the human body state change (Eq. 4), where t is for current frame number, m for frame space.

$$f_{t,m} = \left\{ \left(\widetilde{\overrightarrow{P_H P_F}} \right)_{t-m}, \left(\widetilde{\overrightarrow{P_W P_F}} \right)_{t-m}, \left(\widetilde{\overrightarrow{P_H P_W}} \right)_{t-m}, \left(\widetilde{\overrightarrow{P_H P_F}} \right)_{t}, \left(\widetilde{\overrightarrow{P_W P_F}} \right)_{t}, \left(\widetilde{\overrightarrow{P_H P_W}} \right)_{t} \right\} \tag{4}$$

In Eq. 4, small m means short time behavior feature, while big m means long time behavior feature. Therefore in order to represent the entire features of fall down behavior, all the human body state changes in certain period of time have been searched, as Eq. 5 shows, where N is the preset period.

$$F_{t,N} = \{f_{t,i}\}, \ i = 1, 2, \ldots, N \tag{5}$$

3.4   Behavior Classify

As to fall down behavior, high-dimension features can hardly be classified by methods based on minimum distance or template matching. To solve this problem, SVM is used as the classifier. For non-liner SVM classifiers, the decision function is as follows:

$$f(x) = \text{sgn}\left\{ \sum_{i=1}^{n} y_i \alpha_i^* K(x_i \cdot x) + b^* \right\} \tag{6}$$

Where $x \in R^N$ is a feature vector, n is the number of support vectors, x_i is the support vectors, $y_i \in \{-1, 1\}$ is class label (-1 means negative sample and 1 means positive sample). α_i^* and b^* are found by using a SVC learning algorithm. $K(\cdot)$ is kernel function, which can be used to change the computation from high dimension to low dimension. In this paper, Gauss radial basis function is used, which is the most popular kernel function and is perfectly suitable for non-linear classification application problems.

$$K(x_i \cdot x) = \exp\left\{ -\frac{|x_i - x|^2}{2\sigma^2} \right\} \tag{7}$$

Through the classifier training, upon methods are applied to extract each human body's features frame by frame, and set a label to them. The label scope is standing, falling, fall down, and other actions, and only the feature with fall down label will be regard as positive sample.

4   Experiment

There exist many databases, such as KTH actions database, UCF sport actions database, Hollywood2 actions database, suspicious behavior databases ESCAPES and CACIAR et al. But fall down behavior is not included in any of these databases in previous work, we build a suspicious behavior database including 50 fall down video clips. The database is extended by collecting 300 new fall down samples in 3 different scene in this article. Each sample's resolution is 1920*1080, with 300 frames.

In the experiment, all fall down video clips are divide into train dataset and test dataset at first. Each dataset has same sample amount, and use the train dataset to obtain the optimal parameter of the proposed method. Then the trained method to classify the test dataset is employed. Figure 3 illustrates samples of experiments. For comparison, the dataset is also used to test other three method. Table 1 shows the results, which indicate that the new method has better performance. In Table 1, the speed of new method is slower than method 3 in that the method 3 is carried out in compressed region. However, the speed of new method is still fast enough for real time system.

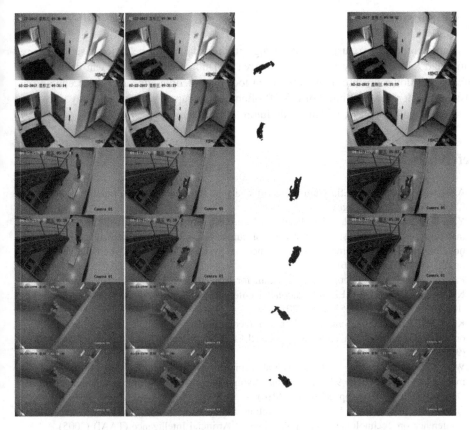

Fig. 3. Samples of experiments. Column 1 is the standing frame, column 2 is falling down frame, column 3 is the extracted target mask, column 4 is the detected result.

Table 1. Experiment results. Bold is better

Method	LAR (leak alarm rate)	FAR (false alarm rate)	Speed (frame per second)
Bo Yao [2]	7.9%	8.8%	18.1
Hongxia Chu [7]	5.1%	9.4%	15.7
Chundi Mu [8]	19.6%	13.3%	**45.6**
This paper	**4.8%**	**7.2%**	30.2

5 Conclusion

This paper proposes a robust recognition algorithm for fall down behavior based on the spatial and temporal analysis of the Key Area of Human Body, which can deal with different fall down posture. However, when too many people appear in the scene and mask each other, the continuity of KAHB often be interrupted and the accuracy rate of this method will decrease, which needs future effort to improve.

References

1. Aggarwal, J.K., Ryoo, M.S.: Human activity analysis: a review. ACM Comput. Surv. **43**(3) (2011). Article 16, 43 pages
2. Yao, B., Hagras, H., Lepley, J.J., Peall, R., Butler, M.: An evolutionary optimization based interval type-2 fuzzy classification system for human behaviour recognition and summarization. In: 2016 IEEE International Conference on Systems, Man, and Cybernetics (SMC), pp. 004706–004711 (2016)
3. Fan, C., Zhou, Y.: A recognition algorithm for behaviors with high similarities based on Kinect. In: 2016 2nd IEEE International Conference on Computer and Communications (ICCC), Chengdu, pp. 1255–1259 (2016)
4. Kuo, C.H., Chang, P.C., Sun, S.W.: Behavior recognition using multiple depth cameras based on a time-variant skeleton vector projection. IEEE Trans. Emerg. Topics Comput. Intell. **PP** (99), 1 (2017)
5. Wen, C., Yuan, H., Gao, Y., Li, J.: The abnormal behavior recognition based on the smart mobile sensors. In: 2016 9th International Symposium on Computational Intelligence and Design (ISCID), vol. 1, pp. 390–393 (2016)
6. Quan, W., Kubota, N.: Fall down detection for surveillance of health care. In: 2015 Conference on Technologies and Applications of Artificial Intelligence (TAAI) (2005)
7. Chu, H., Yang, Y., Xie, Z., Zhang, R., Liu, F.: Research of behavior recognition algorithm based on block matrix. In: 2016 IEEE International Conference on Mechatronics and Automation, pp. 1716–1720 (2016)
8. Mu, C., Xie, J., Yan, W., Liu, T., Li, P.: A fast recognition algorithm for suspicious activity in high definition videos. J. Multimedia Syst. (2015)
9. Barnich, O., Van Droogenbroeck, M.: ViBe: a universal background subtraction algorithm for video sequences. IEEE Trans. Image Process. **20**(6), 1709–1724 (2011)

Multi-source Interactive Behavior Analysis for Continuous User Authentication on Smartphones

Xiaozi Liu, Chao Shen[✉], and Yufei Chen

Xi'an Jiaotong University, Xi'an 710049, China
{xzliu,cshen,yfchen}@sei.xjtu.edu.cn

Abstract. Analyzing smartphone users' behavioral characteristics for recognizing the identities has received growing interest from security and biometric researchers. Extant smartphone authentication methods usually provide one-time identity verification in some specific applications, but the authenticated user is still subject to masquerader attacks or session hijacking. This paper presents a novel smartphone authentication approach by analyzing multi-source user-machine usage behavior (i.e., power consumption, physical sensors, and touchscreen interactions), which can continuously verify the presence of a smartphone user. Extensive experiments are conducted to show that our authentication approach can be up to a relatively high accuracy with an equal-error rate of 5.5%. This approach can also be seamlessly integrated with existing authentication methods, which does not need additional hardware and is transparent to users.

Keywords: Continuous authentication · Motion sensor · Smartphone security

1 Introduction

As more and more sensitive private data are stored in users' smartphones, the risk of information leakage has sparked significant concerns from the public. To alleviate this problem, many authentication methods have been developed and implemented. However, most existing smartphone authentication mechanisms just examine a single certification at the entry-point and fail to assure the safety of the users' privacy during a long time, while the cybercrimes become increasingly frequent and complex.

Recent studies have shown that most entry-point authentication methods become restricted when applied to mobile devices in the practical application. Muslukhov et al. [1] showed that smartphone users are also concerned about sharing mobile phones with guest users. Karlson et al. [2] thought that the entry-point authentication is too rough and inflexible to meet the security and privacy demands for smartphone users.

Recently, researchers propose new approaches to overcome these disadvantages. One increasingly popular approach is called *continuous authentication* [3–8], which continuously verifies the user while the smartphone is in use. It can analyze the user's smartphone usage habit and conduct the user surveillance in the background during the whole time.

© Springer Nature Switzerland AG 2018
J. Zhou et al. (Eds.): CCBR 2018, LNCS 10996, pp. 669–677, 2018.
https://doi.org/10.1007/978-3-319-97909-0_71

In this paper, we propose a novel technique to authenticate users via user behavior analysis of touchscreen interactions, inertial sensors and power consumption. We explore the applicability of multimodal behavior for active smartphone authentication under various application conditions. The basic idea behind this work is to reveal biometric behavior discrimination between different users from multiple perspectives: Physical sensors could detect the users' gestures of holding and operating smartphone, kinematic patterns and even life styles [8–11]. Touch dynamics and power consumption behavior can reflect interesting contents on the screen and which applications are running. It should be noted that the whole data collection procedure is being conducted implicitly in the background without interruption during the user's normal use of smartphone, which we can call user-friendly.

To distinguish between legitimate users and attackers, we propose a multimodal authentication mechanism on Support Vector Machine (SVM) one-class classifier. Besides, we use the decision fusion method in order to make serial authentication decisions. Moreover, a degradation model is introduced to solve the problem of non-synchronized decisions between heterogeneous features [9].

The major contributions of this paper are three folds. First, we examine the applicability of the analysis of user-machine usage behavior for continuously authenticating smartphone users. It can run as an enhancement for extant smartphone authentication systems. Second, we characterized and combined user-machine usage behavior from three aspects (i.e., power consumption, physical sensors, and touchscreen interactions), to depict users' identities in a robust and accurate manner. Third, we developed an objective assessment method to evaluate the accuracy and usability of the proposed method.

2   Background and Related Work

Besides of traditional password-based authentication mechanisms and widely used physiological biometrics (e.g., fingerprint), recently *behavioral biometric* authentication methods have arisen (e.g., touchscreen), which can authenticate continuously and implicitly. Our method belongs to behavioral biometrics.

Murmuria et al. [12] introduced a system that performed authentication on smartphones by analyzing user behavior characteristics, such as touch interaction and power consumption. They used data collected from 73 volunteers and finally achieved good results via an outlier detection algorithm. However, their evaluation of authentication methods is limited to two specific applications (Google Browser and Facebook). In the practical situation, there are numerous applications and hence the feasibility of their approach remains unclear. Feher et al. [13] used individual mouse actions as a feature for continuous authentication. 25 volunteers collected data in their experiment and they used Random Forest Classifier for data analysis. They achieved an Equal-Error-Rate (EER) of 8.53% (for 30 actions). What's more, Alzubaidi et al. [14] discussed the development of several behaviors biometric approaches which can be used to implement authentication.

These efforts confirm that man-machine usage behavior has a rich potential for continuous authentication on smartphones. This study, differing from existing work: (1) characterizes and combines multi-source usage behavior by proposing a set of descriptive features, to characterize a user's identity in a robust and accurate manner; (2) models usage behavior from different perspectives, and develops a multiple decision procedure on the decision level to obtain the authentication result; (3) provides extensive experiments on more subjects and samples to verify the validity of our approach in practice.

3   Biometric Behavior Architecture Analysis

From mobile phones' embedded sensors, we can record the users' kinematic information. We can also obtain the voltage and current information from built-in battery driver to investigate the power consumption patterns.

3.1   Touch Screen Information Extraction

From our preliminary study, we found that touch-interaction behaviors mainly consist of clicking and sliding. For android devices, all these data could be collected via the built-in touch event interface of the system. And then, the system sampled the touch screen data ten times per second.

In addition, if the touch down point is very close to the lifting point, we consider this movement as *tapping*. When the distance between someone's touch down point and lifting point is relatively large, this movement can be recognized as a sliding touch. Plenty of features can be extracted from these two touch behaviors, which will be discussed in part 4.

3.2   Kinematic Information Extraction

For the kinematic modality, we can obtain sensor data from the *SensorEvent* API. The API can report values from the built-in hardware sensors including accelerometer and so on. We collected data from accelerometer, magnetic field sensor, orientation sensor and gyroscope. The accelerometer sensor measures the acceleration and the gyroscope sensor measures the rate of rotation. The magnetometer measures the presence of the magnetic field of a determinate area in SI units (A/m), while the orientation sensor measures the azimuthal, pitch and the roll in degrees.

3.3   Power Consumption Information Extraction

For the power consumption modality, theoretically, it is sufficient to get voltage and current to model the power consumption. The current and voltage sensors interface exists as a character device under*/sys/class/power_supply/Battery* and can be read by any system user. The voltage reading is gradually declining while the current data depend on what the user is doing on the phone. We get the current data as well as voltage data per second so that power consumption value can be calculated by them.

4   Active Authentication Architecture

After we got the data and extracted the valid features, one-class SVM classifier algorithm would be deployed to implement the authentication.

4.1   Design of One-Class SVM Classifier

The term of one-class classification was coined by Moya & Hush [16]. The objective of this algorithm is to identify objects belonging to a specific class by learning from a training set containing only the objects of that class. The one-class classifier can calculate a decision boundary that encloses all legitimate user's data samples [14–22]. In order to distinguish between authorized users and impostors, we collected the authorized user's data and used the one-class SVM model to train the data.

4.2   Data Normalization and Feature Construction

The range of all features should be standardized so that each and every feature can assist nearly proportion to the final distance [15]. Here we used the maximum and minimum regularization method. For the touch behavior modality, the whole touch data can be divided into two parts: tapping and sliding touch. The model for tapping can only extract two features: the duration time and the pressure of the click. For slide model, we extracted 7 features from each touch gesture as listed in Table 1.

Table 1. Touch features

Features	Description
X	Displacement in X-axis
Y	Displacement in Y-axis
st	Angle of rotation for a gesture
vm	Mean value of velocity
vd	Variance of velocity
pm	Mean value of pressure
pd	Variance of pressure

For the physical sensor model, the collected temporal data are three dimensional and we processed data of each axis as follows: the collected data will be separated at regular intervals which is w. We take every w data items as a group and swipe $w/2$ data entries at a time. Within each sliding window, we extracted 5 features (as listed in Table 2) from the movement series. These features include maximum value along each axes, for all the physical sensors.

4.3   Model Integration and Degradation

We adopted the Decision-level integration classification architecture in our system. For each feature, we can get an authentication result and adjust the threshold to plot a

Table 2. Kinematic and power consumption features

Category	Statistic features	Description
Kinematic features	Mean	Extract statistics feature in a window
	Variance	
	Median	
	Mode	
	Number of local Peaks	Count the number of local peaks and crests
Power features	Mean	Extract the mean value and variance value in a window
	Variance	

Receiving Operating Characteristic (ROC) curve. All these results can be sent to a central processor, where we use weighted summation method for final decision making.

At the same time, the amounts of data collected from different modalities were significantly different because the frequencies of collecting data on different sensors and device drivers are not identical. Another reason is that users may generate data of very large or small size for different kinds of modalities. We handled this problem by using a degradation model, where we used the last decision made by a detector if it failed to provide a current authentication result and we reduced its weight accordingly. At the beginning, the weights for all features are set to be 1/3. When some detectors obtain the results, we increase the weights of these detectors while reduce the weights of the others. The whole authentication process is carried out every five seconds.

5   Experiments

In this section we describe our experiment steps, which are mainly about data collection and feature selection.

5.1   Data Collection

An accurate data collection process is needed so as to objectively evaluate our authentication model, which in our experiments were performed on the Android 6.0 platform. During the whole experiment, the smartphone used by each volunteer was the same.

We collected data from ten volunteers for this experiment and all participants were allowed to collect data for three hours. To make the experiments realistic, all these participants were not restricted to use specific applications and they all used the smartphone in our laboratory so as to shield environment interference. Our developed application was able to collect data unobtrusively in the background and all the data would be stored and processed in the following steps.

All our volunteers were aged between 20 s and 30 s, covering different professions. Each user was assigned an identity number between 1 and 10 without real name recorded.

5.2 Data Preprocessing

In our experiments, we collected and stored data on the smartphone. After standardizing the dataset and extracting features, a similar amount of data would be analyzed in our experiments. If a user's data were pretty small or abnormally large, a new set of data would be collected. Finally, we used 60% of each user's dataset to train the model. The remaining 40% from each user was used to test the model.

6 User Diagnosis

We employed one-class SVM algorithm to generate the boundary between legitimate and illegal users, and LIBSVM [22] library was utilized here. We calculated the False Reject Rate (FRR) and False Accept Rate (FAR) and changed the threshold to plot the ROC curve. We calculated the EER point where the rate FAR and FRR are equal.

After we respectively implemented the authentication task using collected data, we made the overall decision and utilized the degradation model based on the technology of data fusion which was mentioned before. The final result we obtained was a probability value.

7 Results and Analysis

We used metrics such as EER introduced above to evaluate the overall performance of our authentication system.

First, we utilized data of a single characteristic to implement the authentication task and then we performed data fusion and made the final decision. Table 3 shows the average EERs of authentication for each detector and integrated classifier for all users. The highest accuracy was marked in boldface in the table. Additionally, Fig. 1 shows the ROC curve for each detector and the entire model.

Table 3. Recognition result of each modality

User ID	Equal-error rate (%)			
	Power	Kinematic	Touch	Ensemble
3	8.23	7.10	**5.9**	**5.50**
4	7.65	**6.20**	6.11	5.82
5	**6.81**	6.31	6.24	6.21
7	6.94	6.47	6.57	6.35
1	7.06	6.84	6.65	6.60
8	7.15	7.12	7.01	6.99
2	7.26	7.56	7.15	7.12
6	7.39	7.91	7.52	7.36
10	8.14	8.12	7.99	7.56
9	8.19	9.51	8.14	8.01

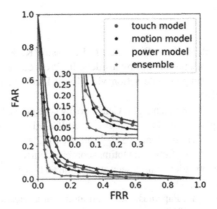

Fig. 1. The ROC curve of the ensemble

The first observation is that the best performance on the dataset has an EER of 5.50%. The system based on all these three features provides the most accurate authentication of a user. Experimental results also show that the authentication result based on the kinematic characteristic was better than others over all subjects.

8 Conclusion

A novel system has been introduced which implements authentication on smartphone by capturing user's behavior patterns through three distinct modalities: power consumption, touch dynamics, and physical movements via motion sensors. The data were collected unobtrusively and authentication was carried out without confining users to specific applications, which improved the reliability and applicability of the system. We also developed an efficient features extraction method and integrating the distinct characteristics to accomplish a powerful authentication system. The performance evaluation shows it can achieve good performance with an equal error rate between 5.50% and 8.01%, suggesting its feasibility and applicability.

Acknowledgments. This research was supported in part by National Natural Science Foundation of China (U1736205, 61773310, 61403301), China Postdoctoral Science Foundation (2014M560783), Special Foundation of China Postdoctoral Science (2015T81032), Natural Science Foundation of Shaanxi Province (2015JQ6216), Application Foundation Research Program of SuZhou (SYG201444), Open Projects Program of National Laboratory of Pattern Recognition, and Fundamental Research Funds for the Central Universities (xjj2015115). Chao Shen is the corresponding author.

References

1. Muslukhov, I., Boshmaf, Y., Kuo, C., Lester, J., Beznosov, K.: Know your enemy: the risk of unauthorized access in smartphones by insiders. In: Proceedings of the 15th International Conference on Human-computer Interaction with Mobile Devices and Services, pp. 271–280. ACM, New York (2013)
2. Karlson, A.K., Brush, A.B., Schechter, S.: Can I borrow your phone?: understanding concerns when sharing mobile phones. In: Proceedings of the SIGCHI Conference on Human Factors in Computing Systems, CHI 2009, pp. 1647–1650. ACM (2009)
3. Liu, J., Yu, F.R., Lung, C.-H., Tang, H.: Optimal combined intrusion detection and biometric-based continuous authentication in high security mobile ad hoc networks. IEEE Trans. Wirel. Commun. 8(2), 806–815 (2009)
4. Papadopoulos, S., Yang, Y., Papadias, D.: Continuous authentication on relational streams. J. VLDB. 19(2), 161–180 (2010)
5. Frank, M., Biedert, R., Ma, E., Martinovic, I., Song, D.: Touchalytics: on the applicability of touchscreen input as a behavioral biometric for continuous authentication. IEEE Trans. Inf. Fore. Secur. 8(1), 136–148 (2013)
6. Shen, C., Cai, Z., Guan, X.: Continuous authentication for mouse dynamics: a pattern-growth approach. In: Proceedings of IEEE/IFIP DSN (2012)
7. Clarke, N., Furnell, S.: Advanced user authentication for mobiledevices. Comput. Secur. 26(2), 109–119 (2007)
8. Tsapeli, F., Musolesi, M.: Investigating causality in human behavior from smartphone sensor data: a quasi-experimental approach. EPJ Data Sci. 4(1) (2015)
9. Yu, C.C.: Degradation model for device reliability. In: Proceedings of 18th International Reliability Physics Symposium, pp. 52–54 (1980)
10. Damera-Venkata, N., Kite, T.D., Geisler, W.S., Evans, B.L., Bovik, A.C.: Image quality assessment based on a degradation model. IEEE Trans. Image Process. 9(4), 636–650 (2000)
11. Hu, C., Tam, S.C., Hsu, F.C., Ko, P.K., Chan, T.Y., Terrill, K.W.: Hot-electron-induced MOSFET degradation-model, monitor, and improvement. IEEE Trans. Electron Devices ED-32, 375–385 (1985)
12. Murmuria, R., Stavrou, A., Barbará, D., Fleck, D.: Continuous authentication on mobile devices using power consumption, touch gestures and physical movement of users. In: Bos, H., Monrose, F., Blanc, G. (eds.) RAID 2015. LNCS, vol. 9404, pp. 405–424. Springer, Cham (2015). https://doi.org/10.1007/978-3-319-26362-5_19
13. Feher, C., Elovici, Y., Moskovitch, R., Rokach, L., Schclar, A.: User identity verification via mouse dynamics. J. Inform. Sci. 201(19), 19–36 (2012)
14. Alzubaidi, A., Kalita, J.: Authentication of smartphone users using behavioral biometrics. J. IEEE Commun. Surv. Tutorials 1998–2026 (2016)
15. [Online]. https://en.wikipedia.org/wiki/Feature_scaling
16. Moya, M., Hush, D.: Network constraints and multi-objective optimization for one-class classification. J. Neural Netw. 9(3), 463–474 (1996)
17. Poggio, T., Torre, V., Koch, C.: Computational vision and regularization theory. Nature 317(6035), 314–319 (1985)
18. Provencher, S.: A constrained regularization method for inverting data represented by linear algebraic or integral equations. Comput. Phys. Commun. 27(3), 213–227 (1982)
19. Poggio, T., Girosi, F.: Regularization algorithms for learning that are equivalent to multilayer networks. Science 247(4945), 978 (1990)

20. Jones, M., Poggio, T.: Regularization theory and neural networks architectures. Neural Comput. **7**(2), 219–269 (1995)
21. Castanedo, F.: A review of data fusion techniques. Sci. World J. **2013**, 1–19 (2013)
22. Chang, C.C., Lin, C.J.: LIBSVM: a library for support vector machines. ACM Trans. Intell. Syst. Technol. **2**(3) (2011)

Character-Based N-gram Model
for Uyghur Text Retrieval

Turdi Tohti[1,2(✉)], Lirui Xu[1], Jimmy Huang[2], Winira Musajan[1],
and Askar Hamdulla[1]

[1] School of Information Science and Engineering,
Xinjiang University, Ürümqi, China
turdy@xju.edu.cn
[2] Information Retrieval and Knowledge Management Research Lab,
York University, Toronto, Canada

Abstract. Uyghur is a low resourced language, but Uyghur Information Retrieval (IR) is getting more and more important recently. Although there are related research results and stem-based Uyghur IR systems, it is always difficult to obtain high-performance retrieval results due to the limitations of the existing stemming method. In this paper, we propose a character-based N-gram model and the corresponding smoothing algorithm for Uyghur IR. A full-text IR system based on character N-gram model is developed using the open-source tool Lucene. A series of experiments and comparative analysis are conducted. Experimental results show that our proposed method has the better performance compared with conventional Uyghur IR systems.

Keywords: Uyghur · Information retrieval · Stemming · N-gram
Lucene

1 Introduction

With the rapid development and popularization of information technology, a significant amount of text information in Uyghur language has gradually emerged in digital form. The accumulated vast amounts of text information recorded on paper are also beginning to be digitized, and the emergence of websites in Uyghur language increased the popularity of the Internet and provided Uyghur people with the convenience of sharing information in their mother tongue. Therefore, accurate and fast search user-wanted information from the enlarging volume of electronic texts in Uyghur language has become a scientific issue that needs to be solved urgently.

At present, there are no web search services in Uyghur language provided by internal search engines like Baidu or Sougou. Although Google provides a simple Uyghur text search service, the performance is still insufficient. Nowadays, information retrieval theory and technology are more advanced, but for a specific language, it needs to study the specific language characteristics.

Uyghur is an agglutinating (adhesive) language with abundant morphological and grammatical rules. In Uyghur, the word is the smallest language unit, and the stem expresses the lexical meaning of a word, so stemming is one of the most significant

© Springer Nature Switzerland AG 2018
J. Zhou et al. (Eds.): CCBR 2018, LNCS 10996, pp. 678–688, 2018.
https://doi.org/10.1007/978-3-319-97909-0_72

tasks in Uyghur natural language processing. Uyghur has flexible ways of word formation itself, and there are more adopted foreign words from English, Russian and other languages, this will make stemming more difficult in Uyghur language, and this is one of the reasons for present stemming technique weak to produce a satisfactory stemming effect [1].

Conventional method in Uyghur text retrieval system is to make a simple word segmentation first (take the inter-word space as a natural separator), then carry out the batch operation of stemming, and then texts are indexed by stems. Therefore, words in text and user query statement are needed stemming before indexing and searching, and the shortcomings and difficulties of stemming are mainly manifested in the following aspects:

(1) Stemming has a high dependence on the stem library, and poor stem segmentation will lead the removal of words from the text.
(2) The similarity of Uyghur character shapes and the accent differences very efficiently produce spelling errors. Single using stemming is not the solution to the problem, and there is no convincing tool for automatic spelling error correction yet.
(3) Although words in the Uyghur text are separated by space regularly, the incorrect concatenation of two or more words affects the accuracy of segmentation.

Naturally, stemming in large-scale text data will produce certain computational complexity, and the limitations of stemming tool itself also can produce some mistakes, so it is difficult to improve the efficiency of Uyghur text retrieval system.

The main work of this paper is to implement two Uighur text retrieval systems respectively use the open-source tool Lucene; one is a traditional system with stemming and the other is a new system using the character-based N-gram model and the corresponding smoothing algorithm without stemming. Experimental results on the same dataset show that the new system has higher retrieval efficiency than the traditional system.

The main contribution of this paper is three-fold. First, we demonstrate that the stemming process can be eliminated in Uyghur text retrieval system. Second, a character-based N-gram IR model is proposed for Uyghur IR. Third, the suitable size of N, the most suitable smoothing method, and the parameter settings are also investigated. To the best of our knowledge, it is the first attempt to explicitly model the Uyghur text retrieval system under the framework of N-gram model.

2 Related Work

In the study of the minority language full-text retrieval system, Laboratory of Multilingual information processing of Xinjiang University has started and realized multilingual text search engine which serves Uyghur, Kazak, and Kyrgyz text search service also is a traditional system with stemming [2]. In their work, many technical problems related to multilingual search indexing and query processing has been addressed and improved the performance of this full-text information retrieval system by using VSM-based improved document similarity measuring approach [3]. However, compared with Chinese and English related work [4, 5], the research of Uyghur text retrieval technology is still in early age both in theory and specific technology, and need further research and exploration.

Recently, the statistical language model has been applied to handle relevant information retrieval tasks and contributed to making reasonable recall and precision. In the statistical language model-based information retrieval, each text is regarded as a small language model, and the last searching results are listed by comparing the probability of generating specific query message of each model. For the application of statistical language model, Ponte and Croft proposed a query probabilistic search model in 1998 [6]. Miller used a two-state implicit Markov model and proposed a simple language model in 1999 [7]. Berger and Lafferty used to associate query documents and translation, put forward a statistical translation model [8]. Jin et al. proposed a document title language model based on statistical translation model in 2002 [9]. A correlation model proposed by Lavrenko and Croft [10]. Ren [11], Li [12] and other scholars applied statistical language models for Chinese information retrieval system and achieved excellent results.

In this paper, we introduce the character N-gram model into the Uyghur text retrieval system, by smoothing and selecting the best parameters, we get a better retrieval efficiency than the traditional system.

3   N-gram Model for Uyghur Language

3.1   Traditional N-gram Model

Statistical Language model is a probabilistic model supported by the probability distribution of text corpus. The advantage of the statistical language model is that it is not influenced by language, but the shortcoming lies in the lacking of expression at the semantic level. N-gram model uses Markov chain to construct language model. In N-gram model, a sentence is divided into corresponding units by particular word length, and the generation probability of the sentence is calculated by the maximum likelihood estimation. The simplicity and effectiveness of N-gram model are based on the assumption that the probability of a word in this model is affected by the previous word, except for the 1-gram model. The formula of N-gram model is usually written as:

$$P(x_1 \ldots x_n) = P(w_1) \times P(w_2 \mid w_1) \times \ldots \times P(w_n \mid w_{n-1}) \tag{1}$$

In the study of N-gram model on Uyghur language, Ablimit et al. [13] proposed the morpheme-based language model in Large-vocabulary Uyghur speech recognition system and validated that it is resulting in a significant reduction of word error rate without a drastic increase of the vocabulary size. For Uyghur N-gram model smoothing, Zhang [14] compared the efficiency of several smoothing approaches on Uyghur N-gram model, and the result was that the perplexity of statistic model is decreased significantly by using the Kneser-Ney smoothing approach.

It is simple in technique to build a word-based N-gram language model, and there is no need to do prior stemming from samples. However, it is weak to build a language model with low confusion for Uyghur which has vibrant morphological features, random distribution of words in a sentence as well as the massive vocabulary of itself. Therefore, it is always challenging to build an Uyghur 2-gram or 3-gram language model with lower confusion.

3.2   Character-Based N-gram Model

Since the stem-based N-gram model has limited efficiency on Uyghur text search, this paper used character-based N-gram model and experienced its efficiency. Considering a regular Uyghur word consists three or more characters, the minimum value for N is set as 3.

For English, Feisong applied word-based binary N-gram model and implemented linear interpolation technique [15]. For the searching query of length 2, the following formula was applied.

$$P(t_{i-1}, t_i \,|\, d) = \lambda \times P_1(t_i \,|\, d) + (1 - \lambda) \times P_2(t_{i-1}, t_i \,|\, d) \tag{2}$$

Where $P\,(t_{i-1},\, t_i \,|\, d)$ represents the generation probability of 2-lengthed word by the document d, $P_1(t_i \,|\, d)$ represents the probability that document d generates the second character of the word, while $P_2(t_{i-1},\, t_i \,|\, d)$ represents the probability that document d generates that word. He believes that in the information retrieval, the length of 2 corresponds to the majority of the word retrieval information, while the length of 1 corresponds to a smaller number of retrieval information. So, he set his score factor $P_2(t_{i-1},\, t_i \,|\, d)$ with higher coefficient when testing. He noticed the information retrieval system performed best when the $\lambda = 0.9$. His research proved the fact that word N-gram model ($N > 1$) is not ideal for retrieval system and demands more time to be established. Also, the often case of concatenating two words into one word in Uyghur influences the accuracy of word N-gram model. So, this paper only applies the character N-gram model for the word 1-gram.

A character group of 3 or 4 (grouping 3 or 4 characters together) reflects the word-stem or suffix of Uyghur words. In our approach, Segmenting character groups with the length of 3 or 4, and in some degree, this equals to the segmentation of stem and suffix with n-gram model. There is one problem has to be taken into account: if only one 1-gram model with a length of 3 characters is created for retrieval, the search results will appear in disorder. Because the document which includes this query character groups much more has the high-ranking score and retrieval accuracy is wrongly influenced. To avoid this situation, the ranking scores are averaged by creating 1-gram models with longer character length. Of course, setting the length too long for character segmentation will lead to a character group contains too much information, resulting in the decline of retrieval efficiency and also occupy a lot of indexing space.

3.3   Smoothing Approach

Smoothing corpus is the very first task to build N-gram language model. The absence of specific words in corpus will cause the data sparseness, and the smoothing is a necessary process to solve this case. Usually, word frequency is implemented as main characteristics in building a language model.

Information retrieval system aims to find the corresponding document according to the keywords and query phrases, however too much focusing on word frequency and smoothing on it is not an ideal solution to get good retrieval results. For information retrieval system, smoothing through corpus model is advisable for compensating the data sparseness. According to the study of Zhai [16], the degree of smoothness between document model and corpus model will affect search results. A higher degree of smoothing is appropriate for longer sentences with more adjectives or adverbs and reduces the effect of a single word on search results; while a lower degree of smoothing is good for more accurate query statements, such as title, and strengthens the effect of a single word to the ranking of search results.

With limited corpus resources, the selection of smoothing algorithm will directly affect the retrieval results. The establishment of many language models also focuses on the design of smoothing algorithm. In the study of Zhai, it is found that the smoothing algorithm plays two essential roles in building a language model. One is that it makes the language model more conformed to the characteristics of the corpus; The second is that in adjusting query words, the sensitivity of different smoothing algorithms to the proportional parameters of common words and stop words is different.

Suppose that a query phrase q is generated by document d through language model so that the problem of information retrieval can be simplified into a simple probability calculation using Bayesian formula, as shown in formula (3):

$$P(d \mid q) \propto P(q \mid d)P(d) \tag{3}$$

In this formula, $P(d \mid q)$ represents the probability of d can be an "ideal" document for the query q; $P(q \mid d)$ represents the probability of d would generate query q. $P(d)$ is the prior probability of a document and noted that all documents have same prior probability. So, $P(d \mid q)$ and $P(q \mid d)$ are approximately equal.

After the query is split into character groups, the probability of generating query q by document d can be converted as:

$$P(q \mid d) = \sum_i (w_i \mid d) \tag{4}$$

Then the maximum likelihood method is used to establish the 1-gram language model, and the document model and corpus model are smoothed by two different smoothing approach:

(1) Dirichlet smoothing

$$P_s(w \mid d) = (1 - \lambda)P_{ml}(w \mid d) + \lambda P(w \mid c) \tag{5}$$

Where $P_s(w \mid d)$ represents a smoothed document model, w represents a word, $P_{ml}(w \mid d)$ represents the document model using maximum likelihood estimation, d represents documents, c represents corpus, λ is the main parameters of the algorithm.

(2) Jelinek-Mercer smoothing

$$P_s(w \mid d) = \frac{c(w; d) + uP(w \mid c)}{\sum_w c(w; d) + u} \tag{6}$$

Where $P_s(w \mid d)$ represents smoothed document model, w represents a word, $c(w; d)$ represents all the w in a document, and u is the primary parameter of the algorithm.

Since models are built using a different length of character groups, the evaluation score is averaged according to the number of the models with different lengths, as shown in Eq. (7):

$$S_{score} = \frac{1}{n} \sum_{i=1}^{n} (M_1 + M_2 \ldots + M_i) \tag{7}$$

Where S_{score} is the total score and M_i is the character model.

4 Experiments and Analysis

Text retrieval systems (stem-based traditional system and new system uses character-based N-gram model) are realized using the open-source tool Lucene with version4.7. System development and experiments are carried out on the environment of the Windows10 operating system, supported by CPU of I5-4590 and frequency of 3.3 GH, and with 4G RAM.

For the data set, there are currently no published Uyghur standard data sets for comparison and analysis, so 15,000 news documents (61 MB) collected from Xinjiang People's Daily (http://uyghur.people.com.cn).

In our task, 20 different Uyghur words are selected for text retrieval test, and the text retrieval systems are evaluated by the average precision of top 10 search results. 1-gram language models with different length of character segments are tested to check their effect on search results. First, a model with a length of 3 is established and checked, and then models with longer lengths are successively built on it and checked for retrieval performance.

684   T. Tohti et al.

The Dirichlet smoothing algorithm with $\lambda = 2000$ is implemented for all tests. The test results are shown in Tables 1 and 2:

Table 1. Search precision of new models with different character lengths

Character length	3	4	5	6	7	8
Average precision	70.5%	73%	71%	69%	68%	68%

Table 2. Building time cost and index size of new models with different character lengths

Character length	Building time	Index size
3	15.8 s	107 MB
4	25.2 s	179 MB
5	34.8 s	242 MB
6	44.1 s	260 MB
7	51.9 s	326 MB
8	58.3 s	351 MB

The experimental results show that the model with the shortest length of 3 and the most extended length of 4 produced the highest precision for searching. Models with the shortest length of 3 and most extended length of 5 are also useful in the score.

A particular case has occurred in the model with a length of 3 characters. A document in search result has been scored very high for it includes too much character groups from query statement. The above situation indicates that only using one model will have a certain degree of defects on searching and combination of multiple models is recommended.

By comparing the modeling time and index size of different models with different segmentation length, it can be found that the modeling time and index size increase as model scale grows.

Then, based on the combination of 1-gram with segmentation length of 3 and 4, the effects of smoothing parameters using Dirichlet and Jelinek-Mercer smoothing are compared, as shown in Tables 3 and 4:

Table 3. Average precision using different Dirichlet smoothing parameters

λ	2000	3000	4000
Average Precision	73.5%	73.2%	73.2%

Table 4. Average precision using different Jelinek-Mercer smoothing parameters

μ	2000	3000	4000
Average precision	71.7%	70.5%	70.3%

The experimental results show that the smoothing effect of the Dirichlet algorithm is better than that of the Jelinek-Mercer algorithm. It is also found that the retrieval system is not sensitive to the parameter setting, which may be caused by the modest volume of the corpus. It is worth to note that the precision rate of nouns is higher than that of verbs, which may be because news corpus is more standardized for nouns.

To compare the effects of the new system with the traditional full-text retrieval system, a tradition full-text retrieval system based on TFIDF model has been realized using Lucene open-source toolkit. The new system was configured with parameters of the shortest segmentation length of 3 and longest of 4 and the Dirichlet smoothing value of 2000. Comparing test results are given in Tables 5 and 6.

Table 5. Average precision using new and traditional retrieval systems

Evaluation criteria	Traditional retrieval systems	New (character-based N-gram) retrieval systems
Average precision of Top10	70%	73.5%
Average precision of Top20	67.7%	73.4%
Average precision of Top40	65.8%	73.3%
Recall	52%	78%

Through comparison, the new retrieval system stands higher in average precision than the traditional system by 3 points, proving that the method is feasible, and avoided the problem of influenced retrieval result caused by the limited stemming effect in traditional retrieval system to a certain extent. The proposed system proved that it costs shorter time to build the search index than the traditional system, this can be attributed as new system eliminated stemming and stem-matching procedures which always generate massive time consumption for traditional systems.

Table 6. Other results using new and traditional retrieval systems

Evaluation criteria	Traditional retrieval systems	New (character-based N-gram) retrieval systems
Average number of documents	3343	12386
Number of searched items	27091	389942
The time cost of index building	260.4 s	25.2 s
Size of index	34.7 MB	107 MB

When comparing the average precision of TopN retrieval results of these two retrieval systems, it is found that the matching degree of the search results and query words of the new system decreases with the increase of N, and the decrease is smoother. The matching result of the traditional system and the matching degree of the query word also decrease with the increase of N, but the reduction rate is relatively large. This phenomenon is related to the retrieval method of the statistical language model. In the proposed model, the search results are sorted by comparing the generation probability of query words by different documents, and this shows a gentler change in ranking than TFIDF model. So, the two models have a different degree of variations, shown in Fig. 1.

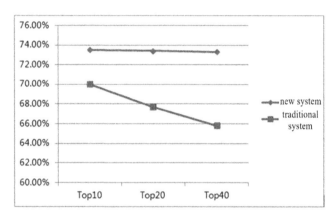

Fig. 1. Comparison of the average rate of change between the new system and the traditional system.

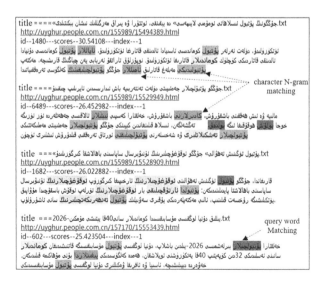

Fig. 2. Retrieval examples in the new system.

When testing new system with query word پۇتبولچىلار (football players), a document which includes too much character groups from query word is got top ranking, but the document which has same query word was ranked lower and listed in following positions, as shown in Fig. 2. Although this phenomenon indicates the fact that new system has certain limitations, considering this is the only case among all tested query words, it is reasonable to say that the proposed system is still reliable in most cases.

According to above search example, the new system has the following advantages and disadvantages, compared with the traditional system.

(1) Some documents appear with many character groups (character N-gram) from query word, as shown in the first item of a search result in Fig. 2, which result in higher rankings for these documents than the more relevant ones.

(2) New search system segmented the query word by a certain length, so search results return not only the documents containing same words but also more documents include character groups from query word, result in that new system has even higher recall rate than traditional one.

(3) In contrast, the retrieval system using the traditional stemming method can match searching results according to the index items after stemming and cannot match the documents with the same character groups.

5   Conclusions and Future Work

Compared to the stem-based traditional Uyghur text retrieval system, the new system eliminated the needs for stemming and realized to create index directly through character N-gram, it is improved not only the time efficiency of pretreatment and indexing but also solved the low search efficiency caused by the stemming problem to a certain extent. Above good results are obtained because this method indirectly extracts the affix and stem of a word by dividing the text with an appropriate length of characters, and constructs N-gram language model which is similar to morphemes, thus obtained better search results than the conventional method. However, the above work was done on a relatively small-scale text corpus. It is hoped that a large-scale search test will be carried out in the future study and the enhanced language model will be proposed to achieve better retrieval results in Uyghur.

Acknowledgments. This work has been supported by the National Natural Science Foundation of China (61562083, 61262062), Western Region Talent Cultivation Special Projects of China Scholarship Council (201608655002).

References

1. Tohti, T., Musajan, W., Hamdull, A.: Design and implementation of Uyghur, Kazak, Kyrgyz web-based full-text search engine. Comput. Appl. Softw. **26**(6), 96–98 (2009)
2. Tohti, T., Musajan, W., Hamdull, A.: Key techniques of Uyghur, Kazak, Kyrgyz full-text search engine retrieval server. Comput. Eng. **34**(21), 45–47 (2008)
3. Tohti, T., Hamdull, A., Musajan, W.: Research on web text representation and the similarity based on improved VSM in Uyghur web information retrieval. In: Chinese Conference on Pattern Recognition (CCPR 2010), pp. 984–988 (2010)
4. Huang, X., Peng, F., Schuurmans, D., Cercone, N., Robertson, S.: Applying machine learning to text segmentation for information retrieval. Inf. Retr. **6**(3), 333–362 (2003)
5. Beaulieu, M., Gatford, M., Huang, X., Robertson, S., Walker, S., Williams, P.: Okapi at TREC-5. In: Proceedings of the 5th Text Retrieval Conference, National Institute of Standards and Technology (NIST), pp. 238–500, 143–166. NIST Special Publication (1997)
6. Ponte, J.M., Croft, W.B.: A language modeling approach to information retrieval. In: Proceedings of the 21st Annual International ACM SIGIR Conference on Research and Development in Information Retrieval, pp. 275–281 (1998)
7. Miller, D.R.H., Leek, T., Schwartz, R.M.: A hidden Markov model information retrieval system. In: Proceedings of the 22nd Annual International ACM SIGIR Conference on Research and Development in Information Retrieval, pp. 214–221 (1999)
8. Berger, A., Lafferty, J.: Information retrieval as statistical translation. In: Proceedings of the 22nd Annual International ACM SIGIR Conference on Research and Development in Information Retrieval, pp. 222–229 (1999)
9. Jin, R., Hauptmann, A.G., Zhai, C.X.: Language model for information retrieval. In: Proceedings of the 25th Annual International ACM SIGIR Conference on Research and Development in Information Retrieval, pp. 42–48 (2002)
10. Lavrenko, V., Croft, W.B.: Relevance based language models. In: Proceedings of the 24th Annual International ACM SIGIR Conference on Research and Development in Information Retrieval, pp. 120–127 (2001)
11. Ren, Z.F., Cang, Y.Q., Fan, A.W.: N-Gram statistical information retrieval model based on bayesian theory. J. Zhengzhou Univ. **42**(1), 21–23 (2010)
12. Li, X.G., Wang, D.L., Yu, G.: Information retrieval based on statistical language model. Comput. Sci. **32**(8), 124–127 (2005)
13. Ablimit, M., Hamdull, A., Kawahara, T.: Morpheme concatenation approach in language modeling for large-vocabulary Uyghur speech recognition. In: International Conference on Speech Database and Assessments (Oriental COCOSDA), pp. 112–115 (2011)
14. Zhang, Y.J.: Study on N-gram language model of Uygur language. Comput. Knowl. Technol. **7**(17), 4177–4179 (2011)
15. Song, F., Croft, W.B.: A general language model for information retrieval. In: Proceedings of the Eighth International Conference on Information and Knowledge Management, pp. 316–321 (1999)
16. Zhai, C., Lafferty, J.: A study of smoothing methods for language models applied to ad hoc information retrieval. In: Proceedings of the 24th Annual International ACM SIGIR Conference on Research and Development in Information Retrieval, pp. 334–342 (2001)

Multi-task Network Learning Representation Features of Attributes and Identity for Person Re-identification

Junqian Wang[✉] and Mengsi Lyu

Shenzhen Graduate School, Bio-Computer Research Center,
Harbin Institute of Technology, Shenzhen, China
wangjunqian@stu.hit.edu.cn

Abstract. Person re-identification (re-ID) has become increasingly popular due to its significance in practical application. In most of the available methods for person re-ID, the solutions focus on verification and recognition of the person identity and pay main attention to the appearance details of person. In this paper, we propose multi-task network architecture to learn powerful representation features of attributes and identity for person re-ID. Firstly, we utilize the semantic descriptor on attributes such as gender, clothing details to effectively learn representation features. Secondly, we employ joint supervision of softmax loss and center loss for person identification to obtain deep features with inter-class dispersion and intra-class compactness. Finally, we use the convolutional neural network (CNN) and multi-task learning strategy to integrate the person attributes and identity to complete classifications tasks for person re-ID. Experiments are conducted on Market1501 and DukeMTMC-reID to verify the efficiency of our method.

Keywords: Person re-identification · Convolutional neural network
Multi-task learning · Person attributes

1 Introduction

Person re-ID [1] is a technique for searching the same person under different cameras with a provided query image. It has received much attention because its significance in fields of video analysis. Despite years of research, person re-ID is still a challenging task due to the large variation in human body pose, illumination, occlusion and background clutter. Moreover, person images captured by the surveillance video cameras usually have low resolution and some facial detail components are indistinguishable [2]. Fortunately, the application of the person re-ID task can use the constraint with respect to time and spatial. Thus, the appearance and visual features of a person will not change significantly in a certain period. This constraint condition inspired many researchers to utilize visual appearance to extract distinctive features for person re-ID.

Most existing methods for person re-ID focus on extracting powerful representation features to handle the variation of human body pose, illumination and background clutter [3–5]. And some effective metric algorithms have been proposed to combine with extracted features for improving performance of person re-ID [6–9]. Recently,

© Springer Nature Switzerland AG 2018
J. Zhou et al. (Eds.): CCBR 2018, LNCS 10996, pp. 689–699, 2018.
https://doi.org/10.1007/978-3-319-97909-0_73

deep learning methods have been popular in computer vision [10–12]. CNN-based deep learning methods also have obtained outstanding performance in person re-ID [13–15]. In the early days, since re-ID datasets only provide two images for each person, some deep learning methods for person re-ID tend to learn an embedded structure with representation and distance metric as the Siamese model [16–18]. Given image pairs or triplets as input, the Siamese model methods directly learn image representation through contrastive loss or triplet loss and use distance metric such as Euclidean metric for comparison [17, 19, 20]. With the increasing sample size of re-ID datasets, some research show that learning of features from multi-class person identification task are easier and superior than the Siamese models [13, 21]. Zheng et al. [22] proposed the descriptor which is extracted features from person identification CNN model as ID-discriminative Embedding (IDE). Zheng et al. [14] learned the IDE feature for the video-based person re-ID. Xiao et al. [13] and Zheng et al. [15] learned the IDE feature from an entire framework for pedestrian detection and person re-ID. Moreover, person attributes are also used as auxiliary information for person re-ID [16, 23, 24]. Matsukawa et al. [24] improved the CNN features by embedding person attributes for person re-ID. Lin et al. [25] also proposed effective method i.e. attribute-person recognition (APR) network which combines person identification and attribute recognition on the loss level can improve the performance of person re-ID.

In this paper, we propose multi-task network to learn powerful representation features of attributes and identity for person re-ID. Firstly, we exploit some appearance attributes such as age, gender, color and style of the clothes which are stable and discriminate ability for learning representation features [26]. Secondly, we employ to joint supervision of softmax loss and center loss for person identification to obtain the deep features with inter-class dispersion and intra-class compactness which can achieve improving performance [27]. Finally, we use CNN and multi-task learning strategy [28] to integrate the person attributes and identity to complete classifications tasks for person re-ID. Multi-task learning can improve the generalization capability of CNN by sharing parameters among different learning tasks. Our work is similar to Liu et al. [25]. Furthermore, we use joint super vision method to enhance the accuracy of person identification task. The experiments results on Market1501 and DukeMTMC-reID show that the methods we proposed for person identification can achieve better result than APR for person re-ID.

2   Proposed Method

2.1   Baselines Model

In this paper, we focus on learning powerful representation features via person attribute recognition and identification, and we employ Resnet50 [12] as the base network in our paper. In this subsection, we present two baselines to describe two main features learning tasks proposed in this work. And we will provide the comparative results between baselines and our method for person re-ID in the subsequent experiment.

Baseline1. The person identification feature extraction network for person re-ID task. During training, we use a CNN embedding to learn the discriminate features, i.e. learning IDE features. During testing, the IDE features are extracted from the last hidden layer, pool5 layer of Resnet50, we employ Euclidean distance as similarity calculation for person re-ID. We also propose two sub-baselines based on IDE, where Baseline1-A is denoted that the single softmax loss function in CNN to learn the IDE features and Baseline1-B is defined as the joint supervision loss function of softmax loss and center loss in CNN to learn the IDE features.

Baseline2. The person attributes recognition feature extraction network for person re-ID task. During training, we use a multi-task CNN architecture to learn M attributes recognition. For multi-task attribute recognition CNN, we use softmax loss as loss function and loss weight is set to $1/M$ for each attribute. During testing, features are extracted from the last hidden layer, pool5 layer of Resnet50. Then we employ Euclidean distance as similarity calculation for person re-ID.

2.2   Network Architecture

The outline of our method architecture is shown in Fig. 1. We use the Resnet50 as the base network and the input images are resized as 224×224. From the figure of outline CNN architecture, we can see the green dashed box is the full convolutional layers connected to pool5, which is used to learn and extract common features. The red dashed line indicates the loss function calculating for attribute recognition and person identification of the entire network. We employ softmax loss for multiple attribute recognition and joint supervision of softmax loss and center loss for person identification. By setting hyper parameters, we can balance the contribution of multiple tasks and optimize learning parameters of our method. Thus, the method we proposed can achieve better results for person re-ID.

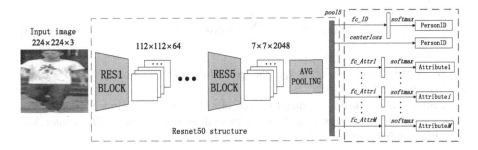

Fig. 1. Multi-task representation feature learning network architecture

2.3   Loss Computation

In this part, we will propose the detail description of the loss function for our present network. Assume there are n images of G person identities. Each person identity has M attributes. We let $T_i = \{x_i, g_i, l_i^{g_i}\}$ represents the training set, where x_i denotes the

i-th image, g_i denotes the person identity of image x_i, and $l_i^{g_i} = \{l_1, l_2, \cdots, l_M\}$ is a group of M attribute-labels of image x_i. For person attribute recognition task, we suppose one certain attribute M_c has m classes and use p $(j|x)$ to denote the probability that image x belongs to class $j \in 1, \cdots, m$ of attribute M_c, and c_j means the output from the corresponding attribute fc_AttrM_c layer. So we can calculate $p(j|x)$ as follow:

$$p(j|x) = \frac{\exp(c_j)}{\sum_{j'=1}^{m} \exp(c_{j'})} \tag{1}$$

The cross entropy loss function of each attribute can be formulated as follow:

$$L_A(f, x, y_{M_c}) = -\sum_{j=1}^{m} (\log(p(j|x))) q(j|x) \tag{2}$$

When the given label of M_c is y_{M_c}, the ground-truth distribution $q(y_{M_c}|x) = 1$ and $q(j|x) = 0$ for all $y_{M_c} \neq j$.

For person identification task, we employ joint supervision of softmax loss and center loss to improve the accuracy of person identification. Softmax loss of person identification is similar to the attribute recognition. We use p $(g|x)$ to denote the probability that image x belongs to class $g \in 1, \cdots, G$ of person identity, and z_g is the output from fc_ID layer. So we can calculate $p(g|x)$ as follow:

$$p(g|x) = \frac{\exp(z_g)}{\sum_{g'=1}^{G} \exp(z_{g'})} \tag{3}$$

And the softmax loss function of person identity can be formulated as follow:

$$L_{ID}(f, x, y_{ID}) = -\sum_{g=1}^{G} (\log(p(g|x))) q(g|x) \tag{4}$$

When the given label g is y_{ID}, the ground-truth distribution $q(y_{ID}|x) = 1$ and $q(g|x) = 0$ for all $y_{ID} \neq g$.

Center loss can learn a center for each class and it can minimize the distances between the deep features and their corresponding class centers. The center loss formula is as follows:

$$L_C(f, x, y_{ID}) = -\frac{1}{2} \sum_{i=1}^{b} \|f - z_{g_i}\|_2^2 \tag{5}$$

Where z_{g_i} denotes the feature center of g_i person classes, and b is the batch size. It calculates the center of the samples come from the same class for each batch, so that the distance of image features for the same person identity is reduced, and the distance of image features for different person identities is increased.

By using multiple attribute loss function and joint supervision of softmax loss function and center loss function for person identification, our network is trained to predict attribute and identity labels. So the final loss function is defined as:

$$L = \frac{1}{M} \sum_{i=1}^{M} L_A + \lambda_1 L_{ID} + \lambda_2 L_C \tag{6}$$

Where hyper-parameter λ_1 and hyper-parameter λ_2 represent the contribution balance factors for the center loss and softmax loss for person identification in the entire multi-tasks person re-ID network, respectively. Wen et al. [5] also mentioned to avoid the perturbations caused by a few mislabeled samples, there is another hyper-parameter α to control the learning rate of the centers, and in this paper we set hyper-parameter α to 0.5. In addition, when we set hyper-parameter $\lambda_2 = 0$ it can be seen as the APR method in paper [25].

3 Experiments

3.1 Datasets and Protocols

In this paper, we evaluate our proposed method on current largest person re-ID datasets including Market1501 [7] and DukeMTMC-reID [18]. Market1501 contains 1,501 identities which captured by 6 cameras in Tsinghua Campus. There are 32,668 person images in total. Each person has 3.6 images on average at each camera. Market1501 dataset provided 751 identities for training and 750 identities for testing. DukeMTMC-reID contains 1,404 identities which captured by 8 cameras in Duke Campus. There are 36,361 person images in total. It also provided 702 identities for training and 702 identities for testing by manual annotation of person bounding boxes. Liu et al. [25] provided the 27 manual annotation person attributes for Market1501, and provides 23 manual annotation person attributes for DukeMTMC-reID.

In our experiments, we extract a 2048-dims feature vector from pool5 layer. And we calculate the Euclidean distance between the given query and gallery images' features, before a ranking up. For each dataset, we adopt two evaluation protocols for comparison. The first one is Cumulative matching characteristic (CMC) curve. The second one is mean average precision (mAP). The detailed calculation process of mAP is shown below. We first define average precision (AP) for evaluation single person query ranking results as follow:

$$AP = \left(\frac{t_1}{loc_1} + \frac{t_2}{loc_2} + \cdots + \frac{t_n}{loc_n} \right) / n \tag{7}$$

where t_i represents the i-th image which is matching with the query image, loc_i represents the location of corresponding matching image ranking order and n denotes as the number of matching images to the query image. Then when testing set has m query images, we can calculate the mAP as follow:

$$mAP = \frac{1}{m} \sum_{i=1}^{m} AP_i \tag{8}$$

3.2   Training Parameters

We adopt the Resnet50 network architecture which is pre-trained on ImageNet dataset. The number of epoch is set to 55 and batch size is set to 20. We employ the multi-step strategy for learning rate update. The initialized learning rate is 0.001 and we changed it to 0.0001 after 45 epochs learning. During training, we randomly select 1 to 3 images of each identity as the validation set for network parameter evaluation and update.

3.3   Parameter Adjustment

The hyper-parameter λ_1 dominates contribution weight of the person identity recognition task in our proposed network architecture and hyper-parameter λ_2 controls the intra-class variations of person identification. Both of them are essential to our model. So we conduct the following experiments to adjust the appropriate values for our network. For facilitating adjustment of parameter $\lambda_1$and parameter λ_2, we use the training set of Market1501 dataset for model training and testing.

Table 1. Person re-ID accuracy of rank-1, rank-5, rank-10, rank-20 and mAP on Market1501 when parameter $\lambda_2 = 0$ and parameter λ_1 varies.

λ_1	Rank-1 (%)	Rank-5 (%)	Rank-10 (%)	Rank-20 (%)	mAP (%)
1	77.94	89.96	93.61	96.11	56.12
2	81.53	92.13	94.95	96.85	59.80
3	81.35	92.01	94.63	96.67	60.35
4	82.13	92.13	94.92	97.00	60.99
5	81.47	92.43	95.19	96.85	60.63
6	81.95	91.51	94.63	96.82	60.73
7	**82.57**	92.64	95.31	**97.18**	**61.76**
8	82.21	**93.32**	**95.46**	**97.18**	61.18
9	80.93	91.39	94.21	96.50	59.71
10	81.50	91.51	94.69	96.94	59.77

Table 2. The re-ID accuracy of rank-1 and mAP on Market1501 when parameter $\lambda_1 = 7$ and various parameter λ_2.

λ_2	Rank-1(%)	mAP(%)
0	82.57	61.76
0.001	83.91	63.39
0.003	83.31	63.90
0.005	82.48	62.89
0.008	81.95	60.73
0.0001	82.21	62.28
0.0003	82.19	62.31
0.0005	**84.14**	**64.07**

To simplify the parameter adjustment process, we first set parameter $\lambda_2 = 0$. We take the different values of parameter λ_1 for training models, and we evaluate the corresponding results of rank-1, rank-5, rank-10, rank-20 and mAP. The results of parameter λ_1 for person re-ID are shown in Table 1. It obviously that we set parameter $\lambda_1 = 7$ the model on rank-1, rank-20 and mAP can get best results, and when parameter $\lambda_1 = 8$, the model on rank-5 and rank-10 can get better results. Later, we fixed parameter $\lambda_1 = 7$ and $\lambda_1 = 8$ respectively and choose the different values of parameter λ_2 to evaluate the person re-ID task. The person re-ID result of parameter $\lambda_1 = 7$ and various parameter λ_2 is shown in Table 2 and the person re-ID result of parameter $\lambda_1 = 8$ and various parameter λ_2 is shown in Table 3. From the results of the tables, we can find when parameter $\lambda_1 = 7$ and parameter $\lambda_2 = 0.0005$, our proposed network can get the best result on rank-1 and mAP than others in Market1501 dataset.

Table 3. The re-ID accuracy of rank-1 and mAP on Market1501 when parameter $\lambda_1 = 8$ and various parameter λ_2.

λ_2	Rank-1 (%)	mAP (%)
0	82.21	61.18
0.001	83.11	**64.04**
0.003	**83.61**	63.82
0.005	83.28	63.86
0.008	79.60	58.57
0.0001	79.13	57.17
0.0003	83.40	62.79
0.0005	83.02	62.68

3.4   Experiment Results of Person Re-ID

Based on our previous work results, we fixed parameter $\lambda_1 = 7$ and parameter $\lambda_2 = 0.0005$ in our proposed network on Market1501, and fixed parameter $\lambda_1 = 7$ and parameter $\lambda_2 = 0.0001$ in our proposed network on DukeMTMC-reID. Then we provide re-ID results with the IDE features from Baseline1-A and Baseline1-B where the balance parameter between joint supervisor loss function of softmax loss and center loss is also set to 0.003. Moreover, we compare re-ID results with the attributes features from Baseline2 where parameter $\lambda_1 = 0$ and parameter $\lambda_2 = 0$ and APR [25] where parameter $\lambda_1 = 7$ and parameter $\lambda_2 = 0$. We also proposed the comparison results with the state-of-the-art methods on two datasets which are shown in Tables 4 and 5, respectively.

Table 4. The comparison results with state-of-the-art methods on Marter1501.

	Rank-1 (%)	mAP (%)
S-CNN [17]	65.88	39.55
GAN [30]	84.29	64.67
PAN [31]	82.81	66.07
Triplet [14]	**90.53**	76.42
Baseline1-A	75.77	50.84
Baseline1-B	76.01	54.84
Baseline2	50.65	27.69
APR [25]	82.57	61.76
Ours	84.14	64.07
Ours+re-rank	86.02	**77.90**

Table 5. The comparison results with state-of-the-art methods on DukeMTMC-reID.

	Rank-1 (%)	mAP (%)
Bow+kissme [7]	25.16	12.17
LOMO+XQDA [6]	30.75	17.04
GAN [30]	67.68	47.13
PAN [31]	71.59	51.51
Baseline1-A	63.28	43.40
Baseline1-B	66.16	44.54
Baseline2	55.97	34.89
APR [25]	70.33	49.91
Ours	73.56	52.87
Ours + re-rank	**77.69**	**68.93**

From the results, we can find the performance of joint supervision loss function of softmax loss and center loss in CNN is much better than the single softmax as loss function. The comparison between Baseline1-A and Baseline1-B further proves that our proposed method in this paper will achieve better performance than APR. Furthermore, by comparing with the experiments of APR, our method improves the performance on rank-1 accuracy is 1.57% and 2.31% on Market1501 respectively, and our method also improves the performance on rank-1 accuracy is 3.23% and 2.96% on DukeMTMC-reID respectively. Our method obtains quite remarkable results. It is verified that the joint supervision of softmax loss and center-loss can learn the more discriminative identity features than the single softmax loss for person re-ID, and the powerful representation features can be learned from multi-task learning network via person attribute recognition and identification.

We also used the person re-rank algorithm [29] to improve accuracy results for person re-ID of our proposed network. For Market1501, we obtain the improvement results after re-rank on rank1 = 86.02% and mAP = 77.90%. For DukeMTMC-reID, we get impressive results after re-rank on rank1 = 77.69% and mAP = 68.93%. In this sense, our method achieves the state-of-the-art performance. Despite our method is simple, the experiment results further prove that the auxiliary attributes and identity joint supervisor loss function are significant for learning the powerful representation features.

4 Conclusion

In this paper, we propose the multi-task network architecture to learn powerful representation features of attributes and identity for person re-ID. We employ person attributes as auxiliary features and joint supervision of softmax loss and center loss for person identification. Our method integrates the multi-task learning strategy to enhance the generalization and performance with the single CNN for person re-ID. We achieve very remarkable experiment results. We have further proved that the auxiliary attributes and identity joint supervisor loss function are significant for learning the powerful representation features.

Acknowledgments. This work is supported in part by Natural Science Foundation of Guangdong Province (Grand no. 2017A030313384) and Guangdong Province high-level personnel of special support program (NO. 2016TX03X164).

References

1. Gheissari, N., Sebastian, T.B., Hartley R.: Person re-identification using spatiotemporal appearance. In: Proceedings of the IEEE Computer Society Conference on Computer Vision and Pattern Recognition, pp. 1528–1535. IEEE Press, New York (2006)
2. Li, D., Chen, X., Zhang, Z., Huang, K.: Learning deep context-aware features over body and latent parts for person re-identification In: Proceedings of 30th IEEE Conference on Computer Vision and Pattern Recognition, pp. 7398–7407. Institute of Electrical and Electronics Engineers Inc., Honolulu (2017)
3. Zhao, C., Wang, X., Miao, D., Wang, H., Zheng, W., Xu, Y., Zhang, D.: Maximal granularity structure and generalized multi-view discriminant analysis person re-identification. Pattern Recogn. **79**, 79–96 (2018)
4. Zhao, R., Ouyang, W., Wang, X.: Learning mid-level filters for person re-identification. In: Proceedings of 27th IEEE Conference on Computer Vision and Pattern Recognition, pp. 144–151. IEEE Computer Society, Columbus (2014)
5. Liu, C., Gong, S., Loy, C.C., Lin, X.: Person re-identification: what features are important? In: Fusiello, A., Murino, V., Cucchiara, R. (eds.) ECCV 2012. LNCS, vol. 7583, pp. 391–401. Springer, Heidelberg (2012). https://doi.org/10.1007/978-3-642-33863-2_39

6. Liao, S., Hu, Y., Zhu, X., Li S.Z.: Person re-identification by local maximal occurrence representation and metric learning. In: Proceedings of IEEE Conference on Computer Vision and Pattern Recognition, pp. 2197–2206. IEEE Computer Society, Boston (2015)

7. Zheng, L., Shen, L., Tian, L., Wang, S., Wang, J., Tian, Q.: Scalable person re-identifitcation: a benchmark. In: Proceedings of IEEE International Conference on Computer Vision, Santiago (2015)

8. Liao, S., Hu, Y., Zhu, X., Li, S.Z.: Person re-identification by local maximal occurrence representation and metric learning. In: Proceedings of the IEEE Computer Society Conference on Computer Vision and Pattern Recognition, pp. 2197–2206. IEEE Computer Society, Boston (2015)

9. Chen, D., Yuan, Z., Chen, B., Zheng, N.: Similarity learning with spatial constraints for person re-identification. In: Proceedings the IEEE Computer Society Conference on Computer Vision and Pattern Recognition, pp. 1268–1277. IEEE Computer Society, Las Vegas, (2016)

10. Chu, M., Wu, S., Gu, Y., Xu, Y.: Rich features and precise localization with region proposal network for object detection. In: Zhou, J., et al. (eds.) CCBR 2017. LNCS, vol. 10568, pp. 605–614. Springer, Cham (2017). https://doi.org/10.1007/978-3-319-69923-3_65

11. Zhong, Z., Zhang, B., Lu, G., Zhao, Y., Xu, Y.: An adaptive background modeling method for foreground segmentation. IEEE Trans. Intell. Transp. Syst. **18**(5), 1109–1121 (2017)

12. He, K., Zhang, X., Ren, S., Sun, J.: Deep residual learning for image recognition. In: Proceedings of 29th IEEE Conference on Computer Vision and Pattern Recognition, pp. 770–778. IEEE, Las Vegas (2016)

13. Xiao, T., Li, H., Ouyang, W., Wang, X.: Learning deep feature representations with domain guided dropout for person re-identification. In: Proceedings of 29th IEEE Conference on Computer Vision and Pattern Recognition, pp. 1249–1258. IEEE Computer Society, Las Vegas (2016)

14. Zheng, L., et al.: MARS: a video benchmark for large-scale person re-identification. In: Leibe, B., Matas, J., Sebe, N., Welling, M. (eds.) ECCV 2016. LNCS, vol. 9910, pp. 868–884. Springer, Cham (2016). https://doi.org/10.1007/978-3-319-46466-4_52

15. Zheng, L., Yang, Y., Hauptmann, A.G.: Person re-identification: past, present and future. arXiv preprint arXiv:1610.02984 (2016)

16. Su, C., Yang, F., Zhang, S., Tian, Q., Davis, L.S., Gao, W.: Multi-task learning with low rank attribute embedding for person re-identification. In: Proceedings of 2015 IEEE International Conference on Computer Vision, pp. 3739–3747. IEEE Computer Society, Santiago (2015)

17. Varior, R.R., Haloi, M., Wang, G.: Gated siamese convolutional neural network architecture for human re-identification. In: Leibe, B., Matas, J., Sebe, N., Welling, M. (eds.) ECCV 2016. LNCS, vol. 9912, pp. 791–808. Springer, Cham (2016). https://doi.org/10.1007/978-3-319-46484-8_48

18. Hermans, A., Beyer, L., Leibe, B.: In defense of the triplet loss for person re-identification. arXiv preprint arXiv:1703.07737v4 (2017)

19. Cheng, D., Gong, Y., Zhou, S., Wang, J., Zheng, N.: Person re-identification by multi-channel parts-based CNN with improved triplet loss function. In: Proceedings of 29th IEEE Conference on Computer Vision and Pattern Recognition, pp. 1335–1344. IEEE Computer Society, Las Vegas (2016)

20. Varior, R.R., Shuai, B., Lu, J., Xu, D., Wang, G.: A siamese long short-term memory architecture for human re-identification. In: Leibe, B., Matas, J., Sebe, N., Welling, M. (eds.) ECCV 2016. LNCS, vol. 9911, pp. 135–153. Springer, Cham (2016). https://doi.org/10.1007/978-3-319-46478-7_9

21. Xiao, T., Li, S., Wang, B., Lin, L., Wang, X.: End-to-end deep learning for person search. arXiv preprint arXiv:1604.01850 (2016)
22. Zheng, L., Zhang, H., Sun, S., Chandraker, M., Tian, Q.: Person re-identification in the wild. arXiv preprint arXiv:1604.02531 (2016)
23. Layne, R., Hospedales T.M., Gong, S.: Re-id: hunting attributes in the wild. In: Proceedings of 25th British Machine Vision Conference, BMVA, Nottingham (2014)
24. Matsukawa, T., Suzuki, E.: Person re-identification using CNN features learned from combination of attributes. In: Proceedings of 23rd International Conference on Pattern Recognition, pp. 2428–2433. IEEE, Cancun (2017)
25. Lin, Y., Zheng, L., Zheng, Z., Wu, Y., Yang, Y.: Improving person re-identification by attribute and identity learning. arXiv preprint arXiv:1703.07220 (2017)
26. Reid, D.A., Nixon, M.S., Stevenage, S.V.: Soft biometrics; human identification using comparative descriptions. IEEE Trans. Pattern Anal. Mach. Intell. **36**(6), 1216–1228 (2014)
27. Wen, Y., Zhang, K., Li, Z., Qiao, Y.: A discriminative feature learning approach for deep face recognition. In: Leibe, B., Matas, J., Sebe, N., Welling, M. (eds.) ECCV 2016. LNCS, vol. 9911, pp. 499–515. Springer, Cham (2016). https://doi.org/10.1007/978-3-319-46478-7_31
28. Caruana, R.: Multitask learning. Mach. Learn. **28**(1), 41–75 (1997)
29. Zhong, Z., Zheng, L., Cao, D., Li, S.: Re-ranking person re-identification with k-reciprocal encoding. In: Proceedings of the 30th IEEE Conference on Computer Vision and Pattern Recognition, pp. 3652–3661. Institute of Electrical and Electronics Engineers Inc., Honolulu (2017)
30. Zheng, Z., Zheng, L., Yang, Y.: Unlabeled samples generated by GAN improve the person Re-identification baseline in vitro. In: Proceedings of the IEEE International Conference on Computer Vision, pp. 3774–3782. Institute of Electrical and Electronics Engineers Inc., Venice (2017)
31. Zheng, Z., Zheng, L., Yang, Y.: Pedestrian alignment network for large-scale person re-identification. arXiv preprint arXiv:1707.00408v1 (2017)

BoVW Based Feature Selection for Uyghur Offline Signature Verification

Shu-Jing Zhang[1], Mahpirat[2], Yunus Aysa[1], and Kurban Ubul[1($\boxtimes$)]

[1] School of Information Science and Engineering,
Xinjiang University, Urumqi 830046, China
kurbanu@xju.edu.cn
[2] Academic Affairs Division, Xinjiang University, Urumqi 830046, China

Abstract. As an important research direction in the field of biometrics, offline signature verification plays an important role. This paper proposes BoVW based on feature selection algorithm MRMR for offline signature verification. In this paper, eigenvectors were formed by extracting visual word features and the features were obtained by building a visual word bag of signature samples. In order to improve the relevance between eigenvectors and categories, and reduce the redundancy between features, the Maximum Relevance and Minimum Redundancy algorithm was used to select features of visual word eigenvectors. The algorithm can find the optimal feature subset. The experiments were conducted using 1200 samples from in our Uyghur signature database, and comparison experiments were carried on selecting 2640 samples from CEDAR database. It was obtained 93.81% of ORR from Uyghur signature and 95.38% of ORR using Latin signature from CEADER database respectively. The experimental results indicated the efficiency of proposed method in this paper.

Keywords: Offline signature verification · BoVW · MRMR · Feature selection

1 Instruction

As an important part of biometric research, signature verification has important research value. The signature identification method studied in this paper is a biometric identification method, which is mainly aimed at the verification of Uyghur signatures commonly used by ethnic minorities in Xinjiang. And Uyghur signature verification has a wide range of regional applications. Handwritten signature verification is mainly divided into two types: online handwritten signature verification and off-line handwritten signature verification. Offline signature samples lose the dynamic features of signatures, and can only extract their static features. Through recent researches, offline signature studies with common languages have come to perfection. But the research on Uyghur signatures is still at a stage of development.

Maergner et al. [1] used the graph method to process the signature and extracted endpoints, intersections, and points on the circular structure as key points for signature samples. The method was matched by a bipartite graph to obtain good experimental results. Ma et al. [2] used local binary patterns (LBP) to extract local texture features of signatures in 2017 and classify them using a deep belief network (DBN) training

© Springer Nature Switzerland AG 2018
J. Zhou et al. (Eds.): CCBR 2018, LNCS 10996, pp. 700–708, 2018.
https://doi.org/10.1007/978-3-319-97909-0_74

model. The recognition rate error on the MCYT database was 9.3%. Zois et al. [3] used the grid template to encode and divide the fine geometric structure of the signature to form a 5*5 binary mask. The EER of the method was 9.42% on the GPDS300 database. Okawa [4] published the latest research results in 2018. He extracted the signature foreground image and background image, and used the Fisher vector model based on KAZE feature to identify the signature. The EER was 5.47%. Kumar et al. [5] and Hafemann et al. [6] systematically reviewed offline signature verification techniques in recent years.

At the same time, the research, which is about the verification and recognition of offline Uyghur handwritten signatures, has also made some progress. From 2012 to 2017, Ubul et al. [7–11] used local statistical features, such as local central line feature and corner curve feature, to identify and recognize Uyghur handwritten signatures. These experimental results were good and the total accuracy were above 90%. Gheni et al. [10] proposed an improved 16-dimensional directional feature based on Uyghur. And the ORR was the 92.58%. Yimin et al. [11] used 112-dimensional ETDT features to extract features of Uyghur signature. And he used the cosine similarity measure to recognize offline Uighur signatures. The recognition rate was 94.1%.

As a pattern recognition problem, a complete offline signature verification system is mainly composed of four parts: signature sample collection, signature sample preprocessing, signature sample feature extraction, and signature sample classification. The main flow of the signature authentication system is shown in the Fig. 1.

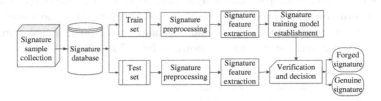

Fig. 1. Offline signature verification process

2 Feature Extraction

2.1 Preprocessing

Preprocessing image can remove the interference factors in the image and preserve the key information of the signature image more effectively. The preprocessing methods used in this paper are the steps of normalized, graying, binarization, smoothing and denoising. When the image is normalized, the size of the signature image is normalized to 384*96 pixels. The weighted average method is used to grayscale the signature sample, and the Otsu algorithm is used to convert the signature image into a binary image. The bilateral filtering method is used to denoise the binary image.

2.2   The Bag of Visual Words

The bag of words was first used in the natural language processing and was a method of describing text documents. In order to solve the semantic understanding of the image, Fei-Fei et al. [13] used the bag of words to form the bag of visual words in the field of image. And the method was used to extract the semantic features of the image. It is widely used in image retrieval and image classification.

The model is mainly composed of three steps in the extraction of signature samples, which will be described below.

Underlying Features Extraction. In order to build a more effective bag of visual words with signature samples, visual words are formed by extracting the underlying features of the image. This has a great influence on the quality of the extracted visual word features. After analyzing underlying features extraction algorithms and characteristics of feature descriptors, the SIFT operator is used to extract underlying features [14].

The Bag of Visual Words Generation. After extracting the underlying features of all training images, all the extracted features are encoded and quantified to form visual word bags. The underlying local features are clustered to group the extracted underlying features into different categories. As shown in Fig. 2(a), the same shape in the Uyghur handwritten signature can be used as a category of graphs. This process is similar to the graph composed of different shapes in Fig. 2(b). By clustering, as shown in Fig. 3(a), the same shape parts can be aggregated together. All visual words make up the image form a bag of visual words, as shown in Fig. 3(b). This paper uses the k-means clustering method to cluster Uyghur signature images. The visual words and visual word bag generation process are shown in Figs. 2 and 3.

(a)   (b)

Fig. 2. The underlying features of the image turn into visual word features

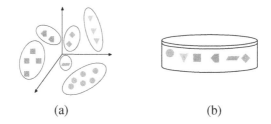

(a)   (b)

Fig. 3. The Bag of Visual Word generated by clustering

Visual Word Frequency Statistics. According to the extraction of visual word, the semantic content of the training image and testing image can be described. Then the visual word features of the image are constructed. After the Bag of Visual Words is generated in the previous section, all feature points in each image will have unique corresponding words in the Bag of Visual Words. Every feature points is used as a visual word, and the number of all visual words in the bag of words is counted. Then a K-dimensional word frequency statistic result can be obtained. These are the signature visual words features.

2.3 Maximum Relevance and Minimum Redundancy

As a filter feature selection algorithm, the Maximum Relevance and Minimum Redundancy algorithm was proposed by Peng [15] in 2005. The algorithm can get an optimal feature subset for classification.

The maximum relevance refers to the maximum relevance between the feature subset and the class which it belongs to. W is feature subset and c is the class, so $\max D(W, c)$ is the maximum relevance.

Minimal redundancy refers to minimizing the relevance between all features in a feature vector. Therefore, in order to ensure mutual exclusivity between features, the feature of the minimum relevance between features is denoted by $\min Q(W)$.

In the Maximum Relevance and Minimum Redundancy algorithm, D and Q are optimized at the same time, so as to obtain the optimal feature subset. If n-1 features are selected from the feature vector W, the optimization criterion function for the n-th feature is as follows. Then the best values of the formula is calculated, and the best subset of features can be chose.

$$\max_{f_j \notin W_{n-1}} \left[\Psi(f_j, c) - \frac{1}{n-1} \sum_{f_i \in W_{n-1}} \Psi(f_i, f_j) \right] \tag{1}$$

3   SVM

The classifiers used for signature verification are mainly divided into two categories, writer-dependent and writer-independent. The first method, writer-dependent, is adopted in this paper. The classification method uses the writer's genuine signature and forged signature to train the writer's verification model. This model is used to identify the authenticity and forgery of the signature writer. In this paper, Support Vector Machines are used for writer-dependent signature verification.

Support Vector Machine (SVM) is a highly efficient learning method [16] that is used as the classifier to verify in this paper. This is a two-class problem classifier that applies the principle of structural risk minimization in statistics. It has fast training speed and strong generalization ability. SVM solves the optimal classifying hyper-plane in the high-dimensional feature space, and makes its classification accuracy optimal. The optimal hyper-plane of SVM can be calculated and defined as follows:

$$\min \frac{1}{2} \|w\|^2 + C \sum_{i=1}^{l} \xi_i$$
$$s.t. \begin{cases} y_i \cdot ((w \cdot \varphi(x)) + b) \geq 1 - \xi_i \\ \xi_i \geq 0, \end{cases}, i = 1, 2, \ldots, l \tag{2}$$

Among them, $\xi_i = (\xi_1, \ldots, \xi_d)$ is a slack variable and C is a penalty factor. $\varphi(x)$ is a mapping function that maps the input feature vector to a high-dimensional feature space.

The SVM model is commonly used for linearly separable classification problems. If the classification problem to be solved is a linearly inseparable problem, it is necessary to select a proper kernel function to process the feature vector. The kernel function chosen in this paper is Gaussian Radial Basis Function (RBF). The formula is shown below.

$$K(x, z) = \exp\left(\frac{-\|x - z\|}{2\sigma^2}\right) \tag{3}$$

4   Experiment

4.1   Database and Evaluation Standards

In this paper, 20 individuals' signature sample images were selected from the Uyghur handwriting signature database. Each of them has 20 genuine signature sample images, 20 simple forged signature sample images, and 20 skilled forged signature sample images. The total number of samples used for the experiment was 1200. The comparative experiment used the database CEDAR for Latin signature verification. The database contains a total of 55 writers, each of whom had 24 genuine signatures and 24 forged signatures. In this experiment, 12 genuine samples and 12 forged samples of each person were collected to form training set, and other signatures were test sets.

The False Rejection Rate (FRR) and False Acceptance Rate (FAR) were used to evaluate the results of signature verification. The FRR represented the error rate of which the genuine signatures were mistaken as forged signatures, and the FRR represented the error rate of which the forged signatures were mistaken as genuine signatures. And the Overall Right Rate (ORR) were used to evaluation system performance here. The formulas for calculating the three evaluation criteria are as follows.

$$\text{FRR} = \frac{\text{The number of genuine signature sample errors}}{\text{The number of genuine signatures sample}} \times 100\% \tag{4}$$

$$FAR = \frac{\text{The number of forgery signature sample errors}}{\text{The number of forgery signatures sample}} \times 100\% \qquad (5)$$

$$ORR = \left(1 - \frac{FRR + FAR}{2}\right) \times 100\% \qquad (6)$$

4.2 Experimental Results and Analysis

In this paper, the training set contained a total of 480 signature samples, and the rest of the signature samples made up the test set. The training sets were used to extract eigenvectors and train the classification model. The trained classification model can be used to predict the type of test samples. In this experiment, when feature points were extracted from handwritten signatures in different languages, the number of feature points were different. In the experiment, different K values were used for feature extraction of Uyghur and Latin signatures. Afterwards, MRMR was used to select features. There were a total of 25 different size feature subsets. The results of the feature vector selection method extracted by the BoVW algorithm were analyzed.

Table 1. BoVW based offline signature verification in Uyghur database

The number of visual words	200	300	400	500	600	700	800
FRR (%)	8.75	10.63	10.63	8.75	4.38	6.88	10.63
FAR (%)	11.96	12.86	13.75	15.36	11.46	11.79	11.43
ORR (%)	89.64	88.26	87.81	87.95	**92.08**	90.67	88.97

Table 2. BoVW based offline signature verification in CEDAR

The number of visual words	100	200	300	400	500
FRR (%)	7.73	8.18	10.76	11.21	11.21
FAR (%)	9.70	10.91	12.88	10.91	14.39
ORR (%)	**91.29**	90.45	88.18	88.94	87.20

Table 1 can be seen, for offline Uyghur signature verification, when BoVW algorithm extracted 600-dimensional visual word features, the best ORR was 92.08%. At this time, the FRR was 4.38% and the FAR was 11.46%. The results of the CEDAR signature verification in Table 2 achieved the best result when the K value was 100, and the ORR was 91.29%. This was because the uncertainty of the number of extracted feature points in different training sample sets.

The signatures obtained by the optimal feature subset were shown in Tables 3 and 4. Compared with the data in Tables 1 and 2, the ORR with the different K values can increase 1.63% on average in the Uyghur signature verification. When performing feature selection experiments in the CEDAR database, the ORR increased by an average of 5.63%. It was proved that this feature selection method MRMR was effective for

Table 3. Using MRMR to Select Optimal Feature Subset in Uyghur database

The number of visual words	200	300	400	500	600	700	800
The best feature subset	56%	60%	84%	68%	80%	88%	72%
FRR (%)	5.63	8.75	8.13	3.13	3.58	6.13	7.74
FAR (%)	13.57	12.86	12.68	15.00	8.81	9.61	11.21
ORR (%)	90.40	89.20	89.60	90.94	**93.81**	92.13	90.52

Table 4. Using MRMR to Select Optimal Feature Subset in CEDAR

The number of visual words	100	200	300	400	500
The best feature subset	56%	72%	28%	32%	56%
FRR (%)	4.75	3.13	4.38	2.63	4.38
FAR (%)	6.97	6.88	5.93	6.62	5.93
ORR (%)	94.14	95.00	94.85	**95.38**	94.85

off-line signature verification. The result of the Latin signature using this method was higher than Uyghur signature verification results. Finally, the FRR of 2.63% and FAR of 6.62% were obtained in Uyghur signature verification experiments. And the best Overall Right Rate on the CEDAR database was 95.38%.

Table 5. Comparison of other research results

Method	Database	Train and test	FRR (%)	FAR (%)	ORR (%)	AER (%)	EER (%)
Fisher vector + KAZE [4]	MCYT	Train:20 Test:10	–	–	–	–	5.47
Gradient Features [16]	CEDAR	Train:16 Test:32	–	–	–	6.99	–
Directional Features [10]	Uyghur	Train:30 Test:30	5.75	9.09	92.58	–	–
The proposed method	Uyghur	Train:24 Test:36	3.58	8.81	93.81	6.19	–
The proposed method	CEDAR	Train:24 Test:24	2.63	6.62	95.38	4.62	–

Table 5 shows the comparison between the proposed method and other research methods. It can be seen that [10] used 16-dimensional Directional Features to authenticate 10 Uyghur signatures, and the ORR obtained is 92.58%. Using the method proposed in this paper, the ORR of 20 Uyghur handwritten signatures was 93.81%, which was higher than that in [10]. Compared with [16], AER was also 2.37% higher than 6.99% of [16]. It can be seen that this method can effectively improve the verification results of Uyghur and Latin.

5 Conclusion

This paper studied the application of the Bag-of-Visual-Word based on the Maximum Relevance and Minimum Redundancy algorithm in Uyghur signature verification. Using this method, experiments were performed in a Uyghur signature database containing 20 people and a CEDAR database containing 55 persons. The ORR obtained from the selected optimal feature subsets were 93.81% and 95.38%, respectively. Then the results were better. In the future research work, the idea of feature fusion can be added when generating the underlying features of the word bag model. And the feature vectors can also be merged when extracting features. At the same time, different classifiers are used to compare the classification performance of feature vectors.

Acknowledgments. This work was supported by the National Natural Science Foundation of China (No. 61363064, 61563052, 61163028).

References

1. Maergner, P., Riesen, K., Ingold, R., et al.: Offline signature verification based on bipartite approximation of graph edit distance. In: International Graphonomics Society Conference (2017)
2. Ma, X., Sang, Q.: Handwritten signature verification algorithm based on LBP and deep learning. Chin. J. Quant. Electron. **34**(1), 23–31 (2017)
3. Zois, E.N., Alewijnse, L., Economou, G.: Offline signature verification and quality characterization using poset-oriented grid features. Pattern Recogn. **54**(C), 162–177 (2016)
4. Okawa, M.: Synergy of foreground-background images for feature extraction: offline signature verification using fisher vector with fused KAZE features. Pattern Recogn. **79**, 480–489 (2018)
5. Kumar, R.: Signature verification using support vector machine (SVM). Int. J. Sci. Res. Manage. Stud. **4**(6), 1771–1773 (2017)
6. Hafemann, L.G., Sabourin, R., Oliveira, L.S., et al.: Offline handwritten signature verification-literature review. In: International Conference on Image Processing Theory (2017)
7. Ubul, K., Yibulayin, T., Mahpirat: Uyghur off-line signature verification based on modified corner line features. In: 2016 International Conference on Artificial Intelligence and Computer Science (AICS 2016), pp. 465–469 (2016)
8. Ubul, K., Abudurexiti, R., Mamat, H., Yadikar, N., Yibulayin, T.: Uyghur off-line signature recognition based on modified corner curve features. In: You, Z., et al. (eds.) CCBR 2016. LNCS, vol. 9967, pp. 417–423. Springer, Cham (2016). https://doi.org/10.1007/978-3-319-46654-5_46
9. Ubul, K., Zhu, Y.-l., Mamut, M., Yadikar, N., Yibulayin, T.: Uyghur off-line signature recognition based on local central line features. In: Zhou, J., et al. (eds.) CCBR 2017. LNCS, vol. 10568, pp. 750–758. Springer, Cham (2017). https://doi.org/10.1007/978-3-319-69923-3_80
10. Gheni, Z., Mahpirat, N.Y., Ubul, K.: Uyghur off-line signature verification based on the directional features. J. Image Signal Process. **6**(2), 121–129 (2017)
11. Yimin, A., Mamut, M., Aysa, A., et al.: High-dimensional statistical features based uyghur handwritten signature recognition. J. Front. Comput. Sci. Technol., 308–317 (2017)

12. Fei-Fei, L., Fergus, R., Perona, P.: Learning generative visual models from few training examples: an incremental Bayesian approach tested on 101 object categories. In: Computer Vision and Pattern Recognition Workshop on Generative-Model Based Vision (2004)
13. Lowe, D.G.: Distinctive image feature from scale-invariant keypoints. Int. J. Comput. Vis. **60**, 91–100 (2004)
14. Peng, H., Long, F., Ding, C.: Feature selection based on mutual information: criteria of max-dependency, max-relevance, and min-redundancy. IEEE Trans. Pattern Anal. Mach. Intell. **27**(8), 1226–1238 (2005)
15. Chauhan, V.K., Dahiya, K., Sharma, A.: Problem formulations and solvers in linear SVM: a review. Artif. Intell. Rev. **6**, 1–53 (2018)
16. Serdouk, Y., Nemmour, H., Chibani, Y.: New gradient features for off-line handwritten signature verification. In: International Symposium on Innovations in Intelligent Systems and Applications, pp. 1–4. IEEE (2015)

Research on the Methods for Extracting the Sensitive Uyghur Text-Images for Digital Forensics

Yasen Aizezi[1], Anniwaer Jiamali[1], Ruxianguli Abdurixiti[1], and Kurban Ubul[2(✉)]

[1] Department of Information Security Engineering,
Xinjiang Police College, Ürümqi 830011, China
[2] School of Information Science and Engineering,
Xinjiang University, Ürümqi 830046, China
kurbanu@xju.edu.cn

Abstract. With the continuous development of filtration technology for text information, many criminal offenders made much harmful text information in Uyghur involving extreme religion and terrorism information by image editing software. In order to recognize the Uyghur text-images effectively, a scheme for recognizing printed Uyghur based on the features extracted by histogram of oriented gradient (HOG) and the multilayer perceptron (MLP) neural network is put forward. Firstly, preprocess the Uyghur text-images to obtain the binary images after eliminating noise. After that, segment the text-line by horizontal projection integral method and segment the words and characters by vertical projection integral method to obtain independent characters. Next, extract the features of characters by HOG. Finally, recognize the characters through the trained MLP neural network classifier and according to features extract by HOG. The experimental results showed that we could recognize Uyghur characters accurately by the method put forward.

Keywords: Printed Uyghur · Recognition · Character segmentation
Histogram of oriented gradient (HOG) · Multilayer perceptron (MLP)

1 Introduction

The Optical Character Recognition (OCR) is a research field crossed by image processing, pattern recognition and machine learning, which is used to convert the document characters on images to the editable electronic document format [1]. Due to the continuous improvement of computer technology, OCR for printed text-image develops rapidly, which improves the efficiency to type characters greatly.

With the deepening of anti-terrorism, in order to avoid information filtering, many criminals disseminate much harmful and sensitive Uyghur information containing reactionism by image file [2]. For this purpose, an intelligent system to recognize and extract Uyghur automatically is needed. At present, the recognition technology for English, Chinese and some other majority languages has been researched much and

© Springer Nature Switzerland AG 2018
J. Zhou et al. (Eds.): CCBR 2018, LNCS 10996, pp. 709–718, 2018.
https://doi.org/10.1007/978-3-319-97909-0_75

maturing [3]. However, because Uyghur is an agglutinative language, which is different from the languages composed of traditional characters obviously, the recognition technology for Uyghur is not mature [4].

At present, some scholars have put forward some methods for recognizing printed Uyghur. For example, a method for recognizing Uyghur based on template matching was put forward in the literature [5]. With this method, people can extract the shapes and structure features of the characters and match them with the characters in text-image library to recognize them. However, the features extracted cannot express the characters well. In the literature [6], people took the distribution density of characters and their features of local direction to build a Uyghur character sorter by Hidden Markov Model. However, people didn't explain that how to get the single characters from the text image.

For this purpose, a scheme for recognizing printed Uyghur based on the features extracted by histogram of oriented gradient (HOG) and the multilayer perceptron (MLP) neural network is put forward. In the scheme, people can segment the characters in the images by projection integral method, extract the features of character by HOG, and recognize the character by the classifier MLP trained by the character library. The experimental results showed that this method was effective and feasible.

2   The Frame of the Scheme to Recognize Uyghur

Uyghur is an agglutinative language, which is different from English and other languages composed of mutually independent characters, and which is composed of mutually connective characters [7]. Uyghur is composed of 32 characters and 20 additional strokes. In a Uyghur word, the additional stroke is above, under or in the character body and is not connected with the body [8], as shown in Fig. 1. Moreover, every character can be written by 4 different forms at most according to the location of the Uyghur character in the word, and there are 126 forms in all.

Fig. 1. Uyghur words composed of characters and additional strokes

Because of the uniqueness of Uyghur, it cannot be recognized by traditional English recognition technology. For this purpose, a recognition method for printed Uyghur based on character segmentation, HOG and MLP classifier has been put forward. Its basic process as shown in Fig. 2, which is divided into 4 parts: preprocessing, character segmentation based on the integral projection method, the features extracted by HOG and character recognition based on MLP classifier.

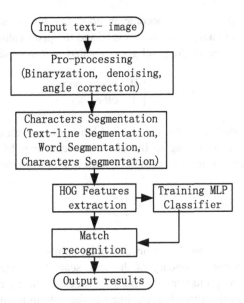

Fig. 2. The process flowchart of the method

The printed Uyghur text was converted into images by image scanner and other equipment and uploaded into the recognition software in the computer as data input. Because the image capture equipment is inconsistent with the environment, the text image needs to be preprocessed.

The preprocessing process includes image binaryzation, noise reduction, angle correction, normalization, etc. In the process of binaryzation, translate the pixel in the text image into 0–255 grey level at first, and then convert the image into the black-white binary image with 192 as the threshold value for judgment [9]. In the process of noise reduction, take median filter to remove the noise points in the image. In the process of angle correction, adjust the angle of the image according to the written base line of Uyghur to avoid incline [10]. In the process of normalization, zoom image by high-order interpolation algorithm to normalize the words.

3   Character Segmentation Based Projection Integral Method

Because in Uyghur, characters are agglutinative mutually, there are many similar characters, and the width and height of the characters are not same, there is no obvious boundary between characters. For this purpose, before recognizing the text, it is needed to segment the characters in the words. In this article, we segment characters by pixel integral projection method [11], including segmenting text lines, segmenting words, and segmenting characters.

After preprocessing, the image become an noise-free binary image, on which, the pixel value of the white background points is 0, and the pixel value of black character points is 1. The expression of the pixel $g(i,j)$ located at row i and column j is:

$$g(i,j) = \begin{cases} 0 & background \\ 1 & other \end{cases} \tag{1}$$

Step 1: line segmentation. Confirm the top and bottom boundaries by horizontal projection integral method according to the blank between lines to complete line segmentation. The integral projection method of each line is expressed as follows:

$$F(i) = \sum_{j=1}^{l} g(i,j) \tag{2}$$

In the expression, l means the number of pixel points.

To confirm the bottom boundary of the text, scan the image pixel from top to bottom line by line through judging the threshold value. If there are continuous n lines according with following expression, the line i is the bottom boundary of the text.

$$(F(i) > p) \cap (F(i+1) > p) \cap \ldots \cap (F(i+n-1) > p) \tag{3}$$

To confirm the top boundary of the text, scan the image pixel from bottom to top line by line. If there are continuous n lines according with following expression, the line i is the top boundary of the text.

$$(F(i) < r) \cap (F(i+1) < r) \cap \ldots \cap (F(i+n-1) < r) \tag{4}$$

In this expression, the threshold values, p and r are confirmed by the experiment effect. In this article, they are set as 2.

Figure 3 shows the results of horizontal projection and line segmentation of a text-image.

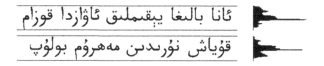

Fig. 3. The line segmentation of a text image based on horizontal projection integral method

Step 2: word segmentation. After line segmentation, implement word segmentation. Namely, segment every word. Because there are obvious spaces between the words of printed Uyghur, and the spaces between characters are bigger than that between words,

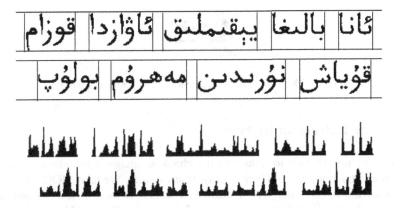

Fig. 4. The word segmentation of a text-image by vertical projection integral method

we implement word segmentation by vertical projection integral method. The segmentation process by vertical projection is similar with that by horizontal projection. Figure 4 shows the results of vertical projection and word segmentation of a text image.

Step 3: character segmentation. Segment the characters of the words obtained after line segmentation and word segmentation to get independent characters. Some characters in the words are interconnected, but all these connected parts are on the base line. Therefore, we can get the segmentation points according to the locations of vertical projection and base line.

Firstly, segment the characters with spaces in the words by vertical projection integral method. After that, set the base line of characters connected mutually in while, namely base line whitening, and segment them by vertical projection. Figure 5 shows the process to segment a connected character, in which, (a) is the word, (b) is the word without base line, and (c) is the result of vertical projection and vertical segmentation.

After segmenting every character vertically, build the top and bottom boundary frames by horizontal projection, and get the independent characters as shown in Fig. 6.

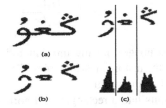

Fig. 5. The sketch map to segment the connected characters in a word

Fig. 6. The final result to segment the characters in a word

4 Feature Extraction by HOG

Feature extraction is used to transform the character image input into a feature set, which is an important part of Uyghur recognition system. We take (HOG) [12] to test and extract the features of Uyghur characters, which is used to test the profile by calculating the local gradient information of the image. Divide the characters segmented into small connected units, generate a gradient histogram for every pixel in the units, and then connect these histograms in series to form a rectangle, so as to get the features characters by HOG.

Firstly, calculate the pixel gradient of the character image. Calculate the direction and magnitude of the maximum strength change of the gradient by Sobel filter to get the horizontal component (H) and vertical component (H^T) of the gradient. After that, convoluted every pixel with H and H^T to get the horizontal and vertical gradient values, G_x and G_y. The expression is shown as follows:

$$G_x(x, y) = H * I(x, y)$$
$$G_y(x, y) = H^T * I(x, y)$$

(5)

In the expression, $I(x, y)$ is the single character segmented, so the magnitude value of the character gradient, $G(x, y)$ can be expressed as follows:

$$G(x, y) = \sqrt{\left(G_x^2(x, y) + G_y^2(x, y) \right)}$$

(6)

The gradient direction is expressed as follows:

$$\theta(x, y) = \tan^{-1} = \frac{G_x(x, y)}{G_y(x, y)}$$

(7)

Secondly, divide the text-image into the units in 8 * 8, and calculate the pixel gradient in each unit through the histogram with 9 bins. The histogram is voted with the gradient value of every pixel as the weight.

Finally, combine these units into a rectangle, and normalize the pixel gradients in all overlapped rectangles. Next, aggregate the vector quantity of the histograms of all rectangles, and form a big HOG feature vector finally.

5   Character Recognition Based on MLP Classifier

In the scheme put forward, we build a classifier based on a type of the multilayer feedforward artificial neural network (MFANN) [13]. After converting every character extracted into rectangular HOG, there will be 576 values in the vector quantity of HOG as the input features of the classifier. MLP is a common feedforward network. Its typical frame is composed of input layer, hidden layer and output layer as shown in Fig. 7, in which, x is the input vector, y is the output vector, and $\Delta\omega$ is the weight connecting the layers.

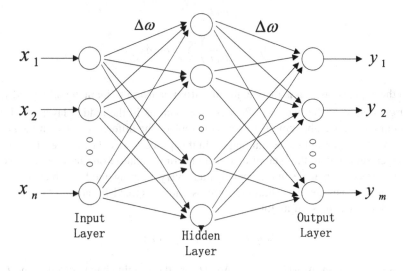

Fig. 7. The structure of MLP neural network

The neurons in the input layer are used to buffer the signals $x_i = (1, 2, 3 \ldots, n)$, and input these signals in classification into the neurons of the hidden layer. For each neuron in the hidden layer, the input signal x_i shall be weighted $\Delta\omega_{ji}$ according to the connection strength, and aggregated to form the output y_i. The expression of output y_i is shown as follows:

$$y_i = f\left(\sum_{i=1}^{n} \omega_{ji} xi\right) \tag{8}$$

In the expression, f can be a simple threshold function S-shape function or hyperbolic tangent function.

Back-propagation algorithm is a gradient descent method, which is used to adjust the connection weight, $\Delta\omega_{ji}$ between the neurons, i and j in MLP training process, which is expressed as follows:

$$\Delta\omega_{ji} = \eta\delta_j x_i \tag{9}$$

In the expression, η is a parameter of learning rule, and the feature δ depends on the type of the neuron j. For example, the corresponding δ_j of a hidden neuron or an input neuron is:

$$\delta_j = \left(\frac{\partial f}{\partial net_j}\right)\left(y_j^{(t)} - y_j\right) \tag{10}$$

$$\delta_j = \left(\frac{\partial f}{\partial net_j}\right)\sum_q \omega_{jq}\delta_q \tag{11}$$

In the expression, net_j is the weight sum from neuron j to input signal x_i, and $y_j^{(t)}$ is the target output of the neuron j. Because the neurons in the hidden layer don't have target output, the weight sum of δ_q is used to replace the difference between the neuron j in the hidden layer and the actual output. In this process, calculate δ of each neuron in each layer, and update the weight of the connecting iteration one by one. The weight updating process shall be implemented after every training model, which is model-based training. The network training process can be spread by adding "momentum" terms, which is expressed as follows:

$$\Delta\omega_{ji}(I+1) = \eta\delta_j x_i u\Delta\omega_{ji}(I) \tag{12}$$

In the expression, $\Delta\omega_{ji}(I+1)$ and $\Delta\omega_{ji}(I)$ are the weight change of $I+1$ and I, and u is the "momentum" coefficient.

6   Simulation and Analysis

In order to assess the performance of the recognition scheme for printed Uyghur, we took tool Matlab8.0 to build the experimental environment. In the experiment, we took 4 pictures from Uyghur magazines as the examples, including 528 words and about 1762 characters in ALKATIP typeface. In addition, we took the standard Uyghur block character library with additional strokes as the training set, and trained the MLP neural network classifier by the features extracted by HOG.

Compare the scheme in this article with the scheme with structure features and template matching put forward in literature [5]. Moreover, to verify the performance of the MLP classifier, we compared it with the SVM classifier. Make statistics on FAR (False Acceptance Rate), TAR (True Acceptance Rate) and FRR (False Rejection Rate) recognized by characters to be the performance indexes.

Table 1. The recognition results of printed Uyghur

Recognition methods	FAR	FRR	TAR
Proposed method (HOG+MLP)	10.95%	8.14%	96.15%
HOG+SVM	15.95%	9.14%	95.64%
Structure features+Template matching	17.23%	10.64%	93.95%

Table 1 shows the comparative results of the three methods. It is observed that the scheme put forward has high performance, and the performance of the MLP classifier is better than that of the SVM classifier. Because we segment Uyghur characters accurately and expressed the features of the characters by HOG to provide efficient features for MLP neural network classifier, it has a high correct recognition rate.

7 Conclusion

In this article, a recognition system for printed Uyghur is put forward. Firstly, segment every character in the text-image by projection integral method to extract the HOG features of every character, and then recognize the characters by MLP classifier. After the experiment on some images taken from Uyghur magazines, the results showed that the correct recognition rate in this scheme was 96.15%, so the scheme has high practical value.

Acknowledgments. This paper is supported by the National Natural Science Foundation of China (NSFC) (No. 61762086), the National Social Science Fund of China (No. 13CFX055) and the Science Research Program of the Higher Education Institute of Xinjiang (No. XJEDU 2016I052, XJEDU2016S090, XJEDU2017M046).

References

1. Song, Y., Liu, Y., Wang, Y., Chen, Y.: A high performance text detection system based on SWT for RGB-D image. Microcomput. Appl. **31**(9), 33–36 (2015)
2. Liu, W., Li, H.: Uighur character recognition based on multi-template normalization. J. Chin. Inf. Process. **30**(1), 56–61 (2016)
3. Yu, B.: Research on Form and Chinese Characters Recognition in Printed Chinese Document Recognition System. Harbin Engineering University, 12 March 2011
4. Ubul, K., Adler, A., Abliz, G., et al.: Off-line Uyghur signature recognition based on modified grid information features. In: International Conference on Information Science, Signal Processing and Their Applications, pp. 1056–1061. IEEE (2012)
5. Chen, Q., Yuan, B., Li, X., Ren, H., Zhang, J.: Printed Uyghur characters recognition based on template matching. Comput. Technol. Dev. **22**(4), 119–122 (2012)
6. Kadier, N., Peng, L., Halimulati: Uyghur and Arabic recognition methods based on HMM and statistical language model. Comput. Appl. Softw. **32**(1), 171–174 (2015)
7. Jiang, Z., Ding, X., Peng, L.: Character model optimization for segmentation-free uyghur text line recognition. J. Tsinghua Univ. (Sci. Technol.) **55**(8), 873–877 (2015)

8. Su, P., Mamat, H., Saypidin, A., Wang, J.: A Uyghur words feature extraction method based on the conjoined section. J. Xinjiang Univ. (Nat. Sci. Edn.) **32**(4), 462–468 (2015)

9. Simayi, W., Ibrayim, M., Tursun, D., et al.: Research on on-line Uyghur character recognition technology based on center distance feature. In: IEEE International Symposium on Signal Processing and Information Technology, pp. 293–298. IEEE (2013)

10. Wan, J.: The Research and Implementation of the Key Technology in the printed Uyghur character recognition System. Xinjiang University, pp. 20–21 (2013)

11. Li, X., Yuan, B., Chen, Q., Ren, H., Zhang, J.: A segmentation method of printed Uyghur character based on projection histogram of pixels. Comput. Technol. Dev. **22**(4), 41–49 (2012)

12. Liu, J., Bai, X.: Fuzzy Chinese character recognition of license based on Histogram of oriented gradients and Gaussian pyramid. J. Comput. Appl. **36**(2), 586–590 (2016)

13. Kong, L., Tang, Y.: A Method for 3D Occlusion Face recognition based on wavelet transform and wavelet Neural network. Nat. Sci. Xiangtan Univ. **37**(4), 82–86 (2015)

14. Mao, Y., Gui, X., Li, Q., He, X.: Study on application technology of deep learning. Appl. Res. Comput. **33**(11), 3201–3205 (2016)

A Study on the Printed Uyghur Script Recognition Technique Using Word Visual Features

Halimulati Meimaiti[1,2(✉)]

[1] College of Information Science and Engineering, Xinjiang University, Urumqi 830046, China
halmuratm@xju.edu.cn
[2] Key Laboratory of Multilanguage Information Technology, Urumqi, Xinjiang, China

Abstract. This paper proposes a recognition technique which applies a combination of image processing and pattern recognition to visual features of individual words. Uyghur script is naturally cursive, and its characters have uneven width. Therefore, in image format, precisely cutting Uyghur words into characters is difficult. To avoid such problem, we use word models instead of character models. Besides, this technique does not need a large amount of training samples: prepared text samples are converted to image samples which are used to construct individual word models .

Keywords: Uyghur · Visual features · Recognition

1 Introduction

Uyghur, Kazak and Kirgiz scripts are based on Arabic and Persian characters, and widely used in Xinjiang Uygur Autonomous Region of China. Arabic based scripts are used by 1/7 of the world population. Therefore, recognition technique of the Uyghur script has significance in both theory and practice.

Uyghur characters have various shapes; characters have uneven width and height. Besides, Uyghur script is naturally cursive because it is written by connecting characters. Using structural and statistical features of characters will result in a low recognition rate and slow speed. We studied the printed Uyghur script, and realized that using word visual features has the following benefits. First, we can avoid the problem of traditional techniques: using a large amounts of training samples. Our technique only needs a small amount of training samples. Second, by focusing on words, it is easy to obtain visual structural features such as the number of sub-words, the number of characters in sub-words and others. Third, post-processing is simpler: n-gram is used to verify recognition results. Figure 1 illustrates a method for Uyghur word recognition.

J. Zhou et al. (Eds.): CCBR 2018, LNCS 10996, pp. 719–726, 2018.
https://doi.org/10.1007/978-3-319-97909-0_76

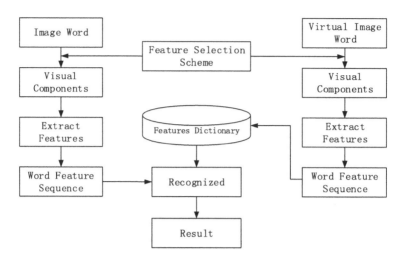

Fig. 1. A Method for Uyghur Word Recognition

Chinese character recognition techniques are mature and already used in practice. However, research on the recognition of Uyghur script is insufficient. Ding [1–4] and other scholars studied the recognition of the printed Uyghur script with multiple fonts, and achieved certain results. These works are applied the idea of the printed Chinese and English recognition techniques: vertical projection extracts sub-words, then sub-words are cut into characters, and word recognition is obtained using character models. Kadier [5] created a statistical model of Uyghur and Arabic scripts using HTK, which was used to improve the recognition results: the increment from 78.28% to 97.45% was reported.

Most Uyghur script recognition techniques are based on the idea of "segment first and then recognition". However, it is not easy to have a clear segmentation of characters in the case of Uyghur/Arabic scripts. There are two shortcomings. First, over-segmentation, which means that characters are cut into smaller blocks, so creating character models is difficult. Second, spaces between sub-words are tend to falsely identified as usual spaces: a single word is often recognized as several words which severely affects post-processing.

Naz et al. [6] pointed out that the OCR of Latin and Chinese is mature unlike the OCR of cursive scripts such as Arabic. However, segmentation techniques of Arabic scripts generate inaccurate outputs. There are two kinds of work. The first kind is segmentation-based approaches. Shatnawi et al. [7] compared the five skeleton extraction algorithms in the pre-processing of Arabic recognition to find an efficient algorithm which keeps the body shape of the Arabic script without generating redundant parts. The second kind is segmentation-free approaches. These methods use a sliding window to extract features in a local area, and HMM forms the basis of recognition. Maqqor et al. [8] proposed to scans the lines of the input image text, then extracts the local density statistical features through a sliding window. The recognition results are obtained through Hidden Markov Model toolkit (HTK). In this case, it is difficult to use HMM based technique because the shape of Arabic characters depend on their positions in a word which leads to a tremendous challenges in the parameter estimation of HMM. Ahmad et al. [9] extracted sub-character features, re-grouped sub-characters by their similarity in pattern thus greatly reduced the number of basic elements in the HMM. Jiang et al. [10] use an improved bootstrap method to solve the difficulty of model parameters training in HMM. The results show a significant improvement in Arabic script recognition. Ait-Mohand et al. [11] use semi-supervised learning technique using a small amount of tagged samples to improve and optimize model parameters and structure of the existed HMM. Moysset et al. [12] segmented the text line images into non-overlapping pieces in their multilingual OCR system A2iA, and then used the RNN classifier for learning.

To sum up, more work are needed in the OCR techniques of Uighur/Arabic. One point is that all these techniques tried to avoid the problem of segmentation. This paper proposes a technique based on word recognition as shown in Fig. 1: (1) there are no scanning a large number of samples for training. (2) Recognition focuses on words rather than on characters, so avoids the segmentation problem. (3) Our post-processing technique further improves the recognition accuracy.

2   The Research

2.1   Text Line Segmentation and Word Segmentation

Preprocessing removes noise from an input Uyghur text image, and identifies text area, image area and others. The direct method of identifying gaps between lines is applying horizontal projection. However, there are a large number of additional parts of characters in the Uyghur text. Therefore, it is possible that white spaces between main body of characters and additional parts of characters will be identified as blank between the lines. That means a single line could split into two lines during the preprocessing. A threshold is used to solve such problem: the width of an identified blank is larger than the threshold, then such blank is a true blank between lines. Otherwise, ignored as a false blank.

Uyghur script, which has 8 vowels and 24 consonant characters, is written from right to left, and characters are connected to each other on the baseline. According to its position in a word, e.g. the first position of a word, in the middle of a word, or at the final position of a word, each letter has a different shape. Some letters have only an independent shape and a final shape. Many Uyghur characters have similar shapes, many of these letters have the same main body but with different additional parts. For example, common additional parts include a single dot, two dots or three dots over or below the main body of characters. There are spaces between words.

Some characters have only an independent shape and middle shape. These characters will split a word into sub-words because they don't connect to other characters appearing before and after them. The features of Uyghur scripts including uneven width of characters, cursive style, gaps between sub-words and gaps between punctuation marks bring difficulty for the separation of the words and punctuation.

We use a method of dynamic threshold of word segmentation. First, calculate the frequency of the uneven width of gaps between sub-words. Second, calculate the value of a threshold using the OTSU algorithm to identify space between words and space between sub-words. Finally, use the threshold to figure out words and sub-words.

Figure 2 illustrates word and sub-word identification. In the figure, the horizontal coordinates are the gap width between sub-words, and the vertical coordinates are the gap frequency. When the width value is less than the obtained threshold, there are two peaks. From left to right, the first peak area has higher frequencies, which is the most wide value region between sub-words. The second peak area is the area of width between the symbols and the word, and varies with the proportion of the punctuation. The minimum values of the first peak area and the second peak area are set as the word boundary value.

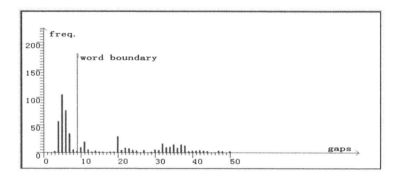

Fig. 2. Histogram of gap width (pixel) and frequency

To distinguish between words and punctuation marks, take out the left and right boundary values of sub-words, analyze the word width frequency, and then use the OTSU algorithm to calculate the width threshold as the boundary value of words and punctuation marks, which is because the punctuation mark usually has only one sub-word.

Figure 3 shows the results of the segmentation of words and punctuation marks. For the first 2 lines in a scan image page, the red rectangle represents the external rectangle of the word, the green rectangle inside is a sub-word, and the blue rectangle is the external rectangle of the punctuation mark.

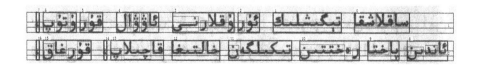

Fig. 3. Words and punctuation mark segmentation (Color figure online)

2.2   Word Parts and Word Feature Extraction

How to extract features from Uyghur script is one of the key problems, and the feature extraction method needs to adapt to the cursive characteristics of Uyghur script. We propose a solution for extracting the global and local features based on the visual parts of the word.

A Uyghur word is composed of one or several sub-words. Because of the uneven width and its cursive connected feature, it is hard to draw a character border in a sub-word. After applying further segmentation to a sub-word, most characters become a single visual part, and several characters are divided into two or three visual parts. In Fig. 4, (a) each character is a visual part, (b) segments each character into two parts, (c) segments each character into three parts, and the visual component is extracted as the basic unit of the word. Therefore, a word tag has a pair of multiple visual parts as shown in Fig. 5.

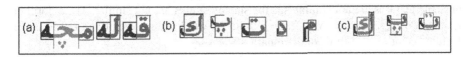

Fig. 4. Character and the visual parts

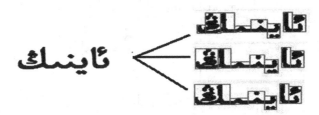

Fig. 5. One-to-many multi-visual component words

Whether it's printed or handwritten, characters are written and connected alongside a horizontal line called baseline. Therefore, it is natural to find baselines first, and make a vertical projection on pixels excluding the baseline, producing one or more detached projection peaks [13], and a peak area is a part. A sub-word is segmented into parts, there are two or four parts: independent part, starting part (from right to left), middle part and end part. From these, we construct vertical position feature. By the text line, the image is divided into upper, middle and lower regions, these describe the vertical position of word parts. The number of sub-word segments, transverse position charac-teristics and longitudinal position characteristics of a word are considered as global features. Each part includes contour, hole, corner point, and additional parts over or below the baseline, these are called local features. Using the obtained the global and local features of the visual parts, we formed a visual part based on word feature vector.

2.3 Word Recognition

How to transform Uyghur word feature vector into word text is a core issue. In this study, we abandoned the traditional recognition method based on the segmentation of the characters. For large amount Uyghur script recognition problem, the solution is to use statistical pattern classification method to establish the image words feature dictionary.

We use features which are easy to extract and have a high recognition rate as the stable feature. According to the number of the most stable sub-words in words, divide the feature dictionary into multiple subclasses with corresponding index tables. In the test set, we sorted the word feature vectors in the subclass. Similar classification is also applied word images, then find the corresponding subclasses in the feature dictionary using their index. Using the similarity relationship between stable and unstable features to some degree reduces the ill-effect instable features caused by noise thus could improve the recognition rate. The similarity comparison of word features has 3 cases. (1) Both stable and unstable features are similar; (2) the stable features are similar, and the unstable features are not similar; (3) the stable features are not similar. The algorithm is shown in Fig. 6, where WFi is the i-th image word feature vector and DWFj is the feature vector in the j-th word dictionary.

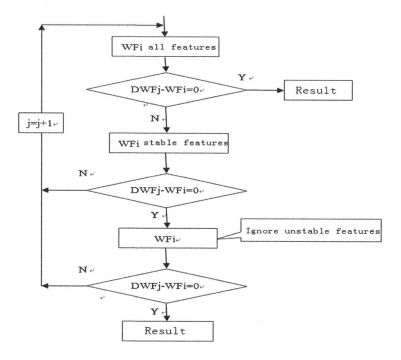

Fig. 6. Word feature comparison algorithm

In this work, the feature dictionary has more than 28,000 sorted and compared words, and the uniqueness of vector is verified.

3   Virtual Sample Generation

The cost of obtaining training samples usually consumes a large amount of human resources. Therefore, training samples tend to be small, lack of variety, and it is difficult to reflect the changes of the printed script in practice. To solve such problem, we can use virtual sample technology. The idea of the virtual sample technology is to combine the prior knowledge on the research subject and specific techniques to generate virtual samples of simulate real world situations.

The document image degradation model is as follows.

$$g(x, y) = h(x, y) * f(x, y) + n(x, y) \tag{1}$$

Where, $f(x, y)$ is the original clear image, $h(x, y)$ is the convolution template that embodies the characteristics of the imaging process which is simulated by the two-dimensional Gaussian function, $*$ is a convolution operation, and $n(x, y)$ is additive noise.

The virtual sample generation is as follows.

1. Input the image IMG which is obtained from text and a specific system font mapping.
2. Apply binary processing to IMG;
3. Apply the two-Gaussian function to IMG to simulate the blur effect.
4. Apply N (x, y) to IMG to add noise.

As Fig. 7 shows, the algorithm simulates the effect of noise on the sample. For example, two points of characters became one after treatment, and irregular gaps occurred in some linear parts, which are common in the poorly printed scripts.

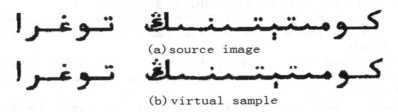

(a) source image

(b) virtual sample

Fig. 7. Virtual sample generation instance

4   Conclusion

In this study, we introduce a technique to improve printed Uyghur script recognition. We work on two main points. First, we use word models instead of character models. Second, we opt for virtual samples to simulate real world situations, where text samples are converted into image samples which are then used to train individual word models. In the test with the small amount of samples, the recognition rate is about 90%, that is due to the fact that authenticity of the virtual word samples needs to be improved and perfected to closely resemble real word situation.

References

1. Ding, X., et al.: Character Recognition: Principles Methods and Practice. Tsinhua University Press (2017)
2. Wang, H., Ding, X.: Multi-font multi-typeface printing Uyghur character recognition. J. Tsinghua Univ. **44**(7), 946–949 (2004)
3. Jin, J., Wang, H., Ding, X., Peng, L.: Printed Arabic document recognition system. In: DDR2005, pp. 48–55 (2005)
4. Arzigul, H.: Research and development of multi-font printing Uyghur character recognition system. Chin. J. Comput. **11**,1480–1484 (2003)
5. Kadier, N., Peng, L.: A method of Uyghur and Arabic recognition based on HMM and statistical language model. Comput. Appl. Softw. **32**(1), 171–174 (2015)
6. Naz, S., et al.: The optical character recognition of Urdu-like cursive scripts. Pattern Recognit. **47**(3), 1229–1248 (2014)
7. Al-Shatnawi, A.M., et al.: Skeleton extraction: comparison of five methods on the Arabic IFN/ENIT database. In: 2014 6th International Conference on Computer Science and Information Technology (CSIT), pp. 50–59 (2014)
8. Maqqor, A., et al.: Using HMM toolkit (HTK) for recognition of Arabic manuscripts characters. In: 2014 International Conference on Multimedia Computing and Systems (ICMCS) (2014)
9. Ahmad, I., Fink, G.A., Mahmoud, S.A.: Improvements in sub-character HMM model based Arabic text recognition. In: 2014 14th International Conference on Frontiers in Handwriting Recognition (ICFHR) (2014)
10. Jiang, Z., Ding, X., Peng, L., Liu, C.: Modified bootstrap approach with state number optimization for hidden markov model estimation in small-size printed arabic text line recognition. In: Perner, P. (ed.) MLDM 2014. LNCS (LNAI), vol. 8556, pp. 437–441. Springer, Cham (2014). https://doi.org/10.1007/978-3-319-08979-9_33
11. Ait-Mohand, K., Paquet, T., Ragot, N.: Combining structure and parameter adaptation of HMMs for printed text recognition. IEEE Trans. Pattern Anal. Mach. Intell. **36**(9), 1716–1732 (2014)
12. Moysset, B., et al.: The A2iA multi-lingual text recognition system at the second maurdor evaluation. In: 2014 14th International Conference on Frontiers in Handwriting Recognition (ICFHR) (2014)
13. Mamat, H., Xiaojiao, C.: A method for printed Uyghur character segmentation. In: Liu, C.-L., Zhang, C., Wang, L. (eds.) CCPR 2012. CCIS, vol. 321, pp. 539–547. Springer, Heidelberg (2012). https://doi.org/10.1007/978-3-642-33506-8_66

Multilingual Offline Handwritten Signature Recognition Based on Statistical Features

Kurban Ubul, Xiao-li Wang, Ahat Yimin, Shu-jing Zhang, and Tuergen Yibulayin[✉]

School of Information Science and Engineering, Xinjiang University, Urumqi, China
turgun@xju.edu.cn

Abstract. Signature recognition is an identity authentication method widely used in various fields such as finance, judiciary, banking, insurance so on, and it plays an important role in society as a behavioral trait. In order to improve the accuracy of multilingual off-line handwritten signature recognition, this paper was proposed the high-dimensional statistical feature extraction methods to multi signature samples. The signature image is preprocessed firstly. Then, 128 dimensional local center point features and 112 dimensional ETDT features were extracted from the mixture (English, Chinese and Uyghur) signatures, and a high dimensional feature vector is formed after combining this two features. At last, the different distance based metric learning methods were used to train and recognize the multilingual signature. It was obtained 91.50%, 95.75% and 97.50% of recognition rates respectively using mixed Chinese-English signature dataset, Chinese-Uyghur mixed signature dataset and the English-Uyghur mixed signature dataset separately. The experimental results indicated that the algorithm proposed in this paper can identify mixed signature effectively, and it is suitable for identifying multilingual handwritten signature.

Keywords: Handwritten signature · Multilingual signature
Distance metric learning · Statistical features

1 Instruction

The design of a fast and effective signature recognition system has important application value in various fields such as finance, judiciary, banking, insurance so on, and it plays an important role in society as a behavioral trait. In the actual handwriting signature recognition, the writer will be based on different countries, different regions and different ethnic groups to write different kinds of signatures. Therefore, how to recognize the mixed signatures of different languages is a difficult point in handwriting signature recognition. According to the regional characteristics of Xinjiang in China, this paper selects the Chinese, Uyghur and English languages to do the experiments of multi-language handwritten signature recognition. The samples used for off-line handwritten signature recognition are still images, which only have the static features such as the shape and texture of the signature sample, which increases the difficulty of handwritten signature recognition [1].

© Springer Nature Switzerland AG 2018
J. Zhou et al. (Eds.): CCBR 2018, LNCS 10996, pp. 727–735, 2018.
https://doi.org/10.1007/978-3-319-97909-0_77

Since handwritten signature recognition technology has undergone more than thirty years of research and development, and identification of single languages signature such as English, Chinese and Arabic has gradually matured. Marušić et al. combined feature extraction of global feature, mesh feature and SIFT feature, using SVM for classification and recognition with the highest accuracy of 88.97% [2]. Miah et al. used rotational and size-independent feature extraction methods to identify numbers and signatures in check information, and the correct recognition rate of signatures was 96% [3]. Mohammad and Bharti have got better accuracy in recognizing off-line signatures using two different feature extraction methods, DTW and MSER [4]. Daqrouq et al. proposed a signature recognition method based on probabilistic neural network (PNN) and averaged frame-forming entropy of wavelet transform (AFE), with the best recognition rate of 92% [5]. Ubul and others have achieved initial results [6–9] for Uyghur handwritten signature recognition and verification. In 2016, the corner curve feature (CCF) and modified corner curve feature (MCCF) of different 3D vectors were extracted from handwritten signature [7]. Ubul et al. extracted the local centerline characteristics of two horizontal centers (2LCLF-16H, 2LCLF-24H and 2LCLF-32H) and two vertical centerlines in 2017, and used Euclidean distance for similarity measurement, with an accuracy rate of 96.8% [8].

In practical applications, a signature is usually written using a language that oneself is good at, rather than one single type of text. Therefore, it is necessary to study the recognition of multilingual signatures. In 2015, Ohyama et al. [10] extracted three gray gradient features from the entire signature image and two segmented signature images, left and right, to identify the signatures of both Chinese and Dutch languages, and the recognition rate was high. Pan and Chen extracted global features and grid features from the signatures of Chinese, Japanese and Dutch, and used SVM to verify them [11]. Experiments show that this method can better describe the effective information of the above three languages and achieve better verification results. Xin et al. proposed a text-independent grid-based microstructure identification method for handwriting Chinese, English, Tibetan and Uyghur texts for handwriting recognition with an accuracy rate of 94.20% [12]. In 2013, Bhattacharya proposed a signature recognition method based on improved mesh information features, which has good experimental results in multilingual hybrid signature recognition [13].

2   Feature Extraction

In order to reduce the influence of external factors, the local central point feature and the ETDT feature are extracted in this paper [6, 14].

2.1   Preprocessing

It is necessary to remove the invalid information and noise in the image in, which is the preprocessing step. In this paper, the weighted average method is used to grayscale the signature samples, and then the median filter of the neighborhood 3*3 is used to smooth the image. The global thresholding method is used to binarize the signature image. Finally, the Hilditch refinement algorithm will refine the signature to extract the skeleton.

2.2   Local Central Point Features

The process of extracting local central point features is mainly divided into the following steps. The center point of the rectangular window is found out from the projection result in the window, and the horizontal coordinate and the vertical coordinate of the 64 central points are taken as the features respectively to form a 128-dimensional eigenvector, which can be expressed as:

$$X_n^m = [x_{m1}, x_{m2}, \dots, x_{mc}], m = 1, 2, \cdots, 10, \cdots, 32 \tag{1}$$

where, m is refer to the writer corresponding to all training signature samples; c is the dimension of the eigenvector. N represents the number of personnel involved in the training. For the training signature sample, the feature vector is:

$$X = [X_1^m, X_2^m, \dots, X_k^m] \tag{2}$$

where, k is the total number of training samples. Assuming that the size of signature is $h \times w$ after segmentation, the horizontal and vertical projections of the signature curve segment $T(x, y)$ in the small window can be represented by $T_s[y]$ and $T_c[x]$:

$$T_S[y] = \sum_{x=1}^{h} blackpixel[T(x, y)]$$
$$T_C[x] = \sum_{y=1}^{w} blackpixel[T(x, y)] \tag{3}$$

Where, *blackpixel* represents the black pixel in the signature sample. It can be calculated in each widget contains the center of the signature segment.

$$\begin{cases} Z_h = \sum_{y=1}^{h} (y.T_S[y]) \Big/ \sum_{y=1}^{h} T_S[y] \\ Z_v = \sum_{x=1}^{w} (x.T_C[x]) \Big/ \sum_{x=1}^{w} T_C[x] \end{cases} \tag{4}$$

In formula (4), Z_h and Z_v represent the abscissa and ordinate of the center point, respectively. $T_s[y]$ and $T_c[x]$ is the number of black pixels calculated by horizontal

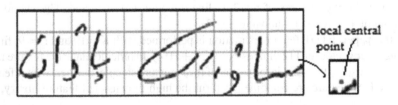

Fig. 1.   Feature extraction of 128 dimensional local center point

projection and vertical projection of each small window respectively. The feature extraction of 128 dimensional local center point indicated as the following Fig. 1.

2.3   ETDT Feature Extraction

The ET feature is a feature that describes the external shape information of the signature image. In contrast, the DT feature describes the internal shape feature of the image. Therefore, the ETDT feature can fully describe the features contained in the external and internal shape information of the signature sample.

ET Feature. The ET feature extraction method divides the image into columns of the same width K. For each part, the number of white pixels N in each column from the upper edge to the first black dot is accumulated from top to bottom and N is divided by the total number of pixels in each pixel to normalize them. By analogy, the same process is done from the bottom to the top. Finally, 2*K features can be obtained, and 2*K is the feature vector. Then the same signature image is divided into H sections with the same height by rows, and the same operation as the column direction is performed from left to right and from right to left. A total of 2*H features are obtained, forming a feature vector. ET feature extraction is indicated as the following Fig. 2.

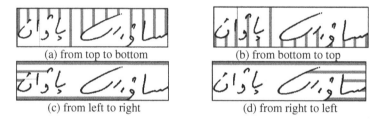

(a) from top to bottom   (b) from bottom to top

(c) from left to right   (d) from right to left

Fig. 2. ET feature extraction from 4 direction

DT Feature. Firstly, the signature images are divided into K parts of the same width. For each part, in accordance with the order from top to bottom, the number of white pixels between accumulated in each column from the first black and white pixels to second white black pixels, and then divided by the total number of pixels of each part are normalized to. By analogy, the same processing can be done from the bottom to the top, and a total of K*2 features are obtained and the feature vectors are formed. Then the same signature image is divided into H sections with the same height by rows, and the same operation as the column direction is performed from left to right and from right to left. Finally, the features of the 2*H line direction are extracted. The DT feature extraction of 4 direction is shown in Fig. 3.

In this paper, ETDT feature extraction is performed with K = 19 and H = 9, finally forming eigenvectors of 112 dimensions (L*4 + H*4). In order to make the feature more effective to display the valid information of the signature sample, the local center feature and the ETDT feature are combined to form the high-dimensional feature library, and

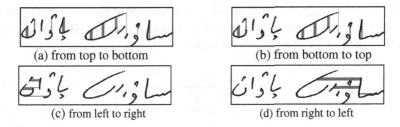

<table>
<tr><td>(a) from top to bottom</td><td>(b) from bottom to top</td></tr>
<tr><td>(c) from left to right</td><td>(d) from right to left</td></tr>
</table>

Fig. 3. DT feature extraction from 4 direction

the classification and identification experiments are performed using different distance and similarity measures.

3 Classification and Recognition

In this paper, training samples are trained using the KNN algorithm [15]. In order to achieve the purpose of classification and recognition, this paper uses the commonly used distance measurement methods (Manhattan distance, Euclidean distance) and similarity measure (Cosine measure) to calculate the distance and similarity between training samples and test samples.

Suppose that the eigenvector of a test signature sample is:

$$X = [x_1, x_2, \ldots, x_W] \quad (W = 1, 2, \ldots, N) \tag{5}$$

The feature vectors of the training signature sample are:

$$Y = [y_1, y_2, \ldots, y_W] \quad (W = 1, 2, \ldots, N) \tag{6}$$

In the above equation, N is the feature dimension contained in the independent eigenvectors. The distance measures used to calculate the distance between them are as follows:

- Manhattan distance:

$$d(X_i, Y_i) = \sum_{i=1}^{W} |x_i - y_i| \tag{7}$$

- Euclidean distance:

$$d(X_i, Y_i) = \sqrt{\sum_{i=1}^{W} (x_i - y_i)^2} \tag{8}$$

In the above formula, x_i is the data of each dimension of the test sample X, and y_i represents the various dimensions of the training sample Y, and the W is the dimension of the eigenvector. Cosine similarity measure is:

$$cos\theta = d\left(X_i, Y_i\right) = \sum_{i=1}^{W} \frac{x_i.y_i}{\sqrt{\sum_{i=1}^{W} x_i^2} \sqrt{\sum_{i=1}^{W} y_i^2}} \tag{9}$$

In the Cosine similarity measure formula, x_i is the data of each dimension of the test sample X, and y_i represents the various dimensions of the training sample Y, and the W is the dimension of the eigenvector.

4   Experiment Results

The database used in this experiment includes Uyghur handwritten signature database of 50 people, Chinese signature database of 50 people and GPDS English database of 50 people. Each of them has 20 signatures, and each of language has 1000 signatures. During the experiment, the handwritten signatures of the three languages were combined into three experimental groups to form a mixed-signature experimental group in Chinese and English, a mixed-signature experimental group in Chinese and Uyghur and a mixed-signature experimental group in Uyghur and English. Each experimental group contains 100 people's handwritten signature samples, a total of 2000 signature sample images, and in which 16 signatures are selected for each person, a total of 1600 signature samples are trained, and the remaining signature samples are used for testing. The 128 dimensional local center feature and 112 dimensional ETDT feature of each signature image are extracted, and KNN classifier is used to identify it based on distance measurement and similarity measure when the value of K is different. The experimental results of signature recognition experiments on three experimental groups was indicated as the following Tables 1, 2 and 3 separately.

Table 1. Recognition rates of Chinese and English handwriting signature

Chinese and English				
Classifier		The value of K		
		1	3	5
Training set 1600	Manhattan distance	**91.50%**	78.25%	75.00%
	Euclidean distance	89.25%	74.25%	69.50%
	Cosine angle metric	88.00%	72.75%	67.00%

As can be seen in Table 1, when randomly selected 1,600 signed samples in the mixed experimental group of Chinese and English signatures for training, the 128-dimensional local center points and 112-dimensional ETDT features of the signed samples in the experimental group are extracted to construct a high-dimensional feature vector library. In the case of different values of K, three distance measures and one measure of similarity are used to calculate the distance and the similarity between the test sample and the training sample respectively. In the experiment, the values of K were compared with the values of 1, 3, and 5. The average recognition rate under different K values is obtained by a large number of statistical operations. It can be seen that when K = 1, the recognition rate of Chinese-English handwritten signature images using Manhattan distance is the highest, which is 91.50%.

Table 2. Recognition rates of Chinese and Uyghur handwriting signature

Chinese and Uyghur		The value of K		
Classifier		1	3	5
Training set 1600	Manhattan distance	**95.75%**	85.00%	80.50%
	Euclidean distance	86.50%	76.25%	72.50%
	Cosine angle metric	94.75%	79.75%	75.25%

Table 3. Recognition rates of English and Uyghur handwriting signature

English and Uyghur		The value of K		
Classifier		1	3	5
Training set 1600	Manhattan distance	**97.50%**	84.25%	80.25%
	Euclidean distance	88.50%	73.50%	72.75%
	Cosine angle metric	**97.50%**	78.50%	73.00%

The above Table 2 shows that the experimental group of Chinese and Uyghur mixed signature randomly selects 1,600 signed images for training, and the different K values was selected to recognition the mixed language handwritten signatures by distance measure and similarity measure. The Manhattan distance, Euclidean distance and cosine angle metric are used to classify and identify the signature samples. When K = 1, 2, 3 different values, the average recognition rate is also very different. It can be seen from the data in the table that when K = 1, the Manhattan distance measure is used to recognize Chinese and Uyghur handwritten signature recognition rate is higher than other metrics algorithm, the average recognition rate of 98.75%.

It can be seen from the data in Table 3, the signature recognition results of the mixed handwritten signature images of English and Uyghur are higher than the recognition rates of the other two experimental groups. When the training signature samples are extracted from the high-dimensional feature vector that combines the local center point feature and the ETDT feature, the KNN classifier is used to classify the test signature samples. Especially when K = 1, the highest recognition rate is reached, and the accuracy of Manhattan distance measurement and cosine measurement method are the same, which are all 97.50%. It can be seen that the algorithm of Manhattan distance measurement has more remarkable advantages than other distance measurement algorithms in the multilingual offline handwritten signature recognition.

5 Conclusion

The recognition of mixed offline handwritten signatures in three different languages of Chinese, English and Uyghur was proposed in this paper. A feature vector is composed of 128 - dimensional local central point feature and 112 - dimensional ETDT feature extracted from the signature sample separately. The KNN classifier is used to classify the feature vectors of the multilingual mixed handwritten signature training set, and the identification experiments were performed respectively using distance metric learning methods such as, the Manhattan distance, the Euclidean distance and the cosine angle metric. Finally, It was obtained 91.50%, 95.75% and 97.50% of recognition rates respectively using mixed Chinese-English signature dataset, Chinese-Uyghur mixed signature dataset and the English-Uyghur mixed signature dataset separately. It can be seen from the experimental results that the proposed algorithm is an effective method for mixed signature handwriting recognition in Chinese, English and Uyghur signature. In the future work, in order to get a better accuracy of signature recognition, it can be combined with other feature extraction methods and adopt different classifier recognition. The signature will also expand the sample database, for more different languages mixed handwritten signature recognition.

Acknowledgments. This work was supported by the National Natural Science Foundation of China (No. 61563052, 61163028, 61363064), the Funds for Creative Research Groups of Higher Education of Xinjiang Uyghur Autonomous Region (XJEDU2017T002).

References

1. Kumar, A., Bhatia, K.: A survey on offline handwritten signature verification system using writer dependent and independent approaches. In: International Conference on Advances in Computing, Communication, & Automation, pp. 1–6. IEEE (2016)
2. Marušić, T., Marušić, Ž., Šeremet, Ž.: Identification of authors of documents based on offline signature recognition. In: International Convention on Information and Communication Technology, Electronics and Microelectronics, pp. 1144–1149. IEEE (2015)
3. Badrulalammiah, M., Yousuf, M.A, Mia, M.S: Handwritten courtesy amount and signature recognition on bank cheque using neural network. Int. J. Comput. Appl. **118**, 21–26 (2015)
4. Basil, M., Gawali, B.: Comparative analysis of MSER and DTW for offline signature recognition. Int. J. Comput. Appl. **110**(5), 13–17 (2015)
5. Daqrouq, K., Sweidan, H., Balamesh, A., Ajour, M.: Off-line handwritten signature recognition by wavelet entropy and neural network. Entropy **19**(6), 252 (2017)
6. Ubul, K., Adler, A., Yadikar, N.: Effects on accuracy of Uyghur handwritten signature recognition. Commun. Comput. Inf. Sci. **321**(321), 548–555 (2012)
7. Ubul, K., Abudurexiti, R., Mamat, H., Yadikar, N., Yibulayin, T.: Uyghur off-line signature recognition based on modified corner curve features. In: You, Z., et al. (eds.) CCBR 2016. LNCS, vol. 9967, pp. 417–423. Springer, Cham (2016). https://doi.org/10.1007/978-3-319-46654-5_46

8. Ubul, K., Zhu, Y.-L., Mamut, M., Yadikar, N., Yibulayin, T.: Uyghur off-line signature recognition based on local central line features. In: Zhou, J., et al. (eds.) CCBR 2017. LNCS, vol. 10568, pp. 750–758. Springer, Cham (2017). https://doi.org/10.1007/978-3-319-69923-3_80

9. Ohyama, W., Ogi, Y., Wakabayashi, T., Kimura, F.: Multilingual signature-verification by generalized combined segmentation verification. In: International Conference on Document Analysis and Recognition, pp. 811–815. IEEE (2015)

10. Pan, W., Chen, G.: A method of off-line signature verification for digital forensics. In: International Conference on Natural Computation, Fuzzy Systems and Knowledge Discovery, pp. 488–493. IEEE (2016)

11. Xin, L.I., Ding, X.Q., Peng, L.R., et al.: A microstructure feature based text-independent method of writer identification for multilingual handwritings. Acta Automatica Sinica 35(9), 1199–1208 (2009)

12. Bhattacharya, P.P.: An Approach Towards Offline Multilingual Signature Recognition Based on Modified Grid Information Features (2013)

13. Esmailzadeh, A., Rahnamayan, S.: Center-point-based simulated annealing. In: Electrical & Computer Engineering, pp. 1–4. IEEE (2012)

14. Fang, B., Leung, C.H., Tang, Y.Y., Kwok, P.C.K.: Offline signature verification with generated training samples. In: IEE Proceedings - Vision, Image and Signal Processing, vol. 149, no. 2, pp. 85–90, April 2002

15. Zhang, S., Li, X., Zong, M., Zhu, X., Cheng, D.: Learning k for kNN classification. ACM Trans. Intell. Syst. Technol. 8(3), 43 (2017)

HMM-Based Off-Line Uyghur Signature Recognition

Long-Fei Mo[1], Hornisa Mamat[1], Mutallip Mamut[2], Alimjan Aysa[3], and Kurban Ubul[1(✉)]

[1] School of Information Science and Engineering,
Xinjiang University, Urumqi 830046, China
kurbanu@xju.edu.cn
[2] The Library of Xinjiang University, Urumqi 830046, China
[3] The Network and Information Center of Xinjiang University,
Urumqi 830046, China

Abstract. Signature as a new biometric-based feature, due to its convenience, reliability, and non-invasion, signature recognition has been accepted by people. It is widely used in many fields such as commercial, financial, judicial, insurance and other aspects, so offline signature recognition has important theoretical significance and practical value. In this paper, an offline signature recognition system based on Hidden Markov Models is established to extract the DCT features of off-line signatures. This method takes all the fonts in the offline signature image as a whole, uses image processing techniques to segment the entire font area, and then calculates the number of pixels in each font part. The whole is modeled by a Hidden Markov Model, the best state chain is obtained using viterbi segmentation, and the EM algorithm is used to train the model. There are 2000 Uyghur signatures from 100 different people, 1000 English signatures from 50 different people, the highest recognition rates were 99.5% and 97.5%, respectively. The experimental results show that Hidden Markov Model can accurately describe the characteristics of Uygur signatures.

Keywords: Offline signature · Hidden Markov Model
Discrete cosine transform

1 Introduction

Biometrics is a hot topic of research in recent years. It involves fingerprints, palm veins, iris, face, and voice. Signature recognition can be divided into online and offline categories. On-line signature requires a specially crafted tablet for signatures, it extracts the dynamic characteristics of the signature, such as speed, acceleration, pressure and direction of movement, etc., use dynamic programming [1] for training. Offline signatures use a scanner to obtain electronic images, first graying, binarization, refinement and other preprocessing operations [2], extract the location, shape, stroke and other characteristics of the signature, then classify training through neural network and SVM. For off-line signatures, it is difficult to obtain the dynamic characteristics of the signature, for example, the pressure of the signer's writing, the sequence of strokes, the

© Springer Nature Switzerland AG 2018
J. Zhou et al. (Eds.): CCBR 2018, LNCS 10996, pp. 736–744, 2018.
https://doi.org/10.1007/978-3-319-97909-0_78

angle of holding the pen, and the personality of the author's signature. Therefore, offline signature recognition technology is difficult and the recognition rate is not high.

Ismail et al. proposed a new offline signature recognition method based on multi-scale Fourier descriptors and wavelet transform, which has a better recognition rate [3]. Bernardete Ribeiro et al. proposed a deep learning model that can extract off-line handwritten signature recognition from advanced representations and improved the error classification rate in the famous GPDS database [4]. Zhang et al. proposed an offline signature recognition method based on multiple features [5]. Przemysław Kudłacik et al. proposed a new fuzzy method for off-line handwritten signature recognition, which is based on feature extraction [6].

2 Introduction of Hidden Markov

The Hidden Markov Model [7] is a parametric model used to describe the statistical characteristics of stochastic processes. Hidden Markov process is a dual random process: one potential process is called "state" process, and the other observable process is called "observation sequence". Observed sequence is determined by implicit state process.

The HMM can be expressed in the form of a parameter of $\lambda = (A, B, \pi)$. The observation sequence is described by the most common mixed Gaussian probability density function [8]:

$$b_j(o) = \sum_{m=1}^{M} C_{jm} b_{jm}(o) \tag{1}$$

Where M represents the number of mixtures of mixed Gaussian probability density functions, the mixing coefficient satisfies:

$$\sum_{m=1}^{M} C_{jm} = 1 \tag{2}$$

Bj(o) is a single Gaussian probability density function for the mth component of the jth state.

2.1 Determination of the Best State Chain

Payment one piece Observation hierarchy $O = O_1 O_2 \ldots O_T$ Waki one piece HMM number of participants λ, how to choose a piece maximum condition $Q = q1q2 \ldots qt$ coming visit observation ranking O, ordinary adaptive calculation method viterbi algorithm. Definition:

$$\delta_t(i) = \max_{q_1 q_2 \cdots q_{t-1}} p(q_1 q_2 \ldots q_t = i, o_1 o_2 \ldots o_t \mid \lambda) \tag{3}$$

Step 1: Initialization

$$\delta_1(i) = \pi_i \cdot b_i(o_1) \quad 1 \leq i \leq N \tag{4}$$

$$\Psi(i) = 0 \tag{5}$$

Step 2: guessing

$$\delta_t(j) = \max_i \left[\delta_{t-1}(i)a_{ij}\right]b_j(o_t) \quad 2 \leq t \leq T, 1 \leq i \leq N \tag{6}$$

$$\Psi_t(j) = \arg\max_{1 \leq i \leq N} \left[\delta_{t-1}(i)a_{ij}\right] \quad 2 \leq t \leq T, 1 \leq i \leq N \tag{7}$$

Step 3: bundle

$$p^* = \max_{1 \leq i \leq N}\left[\delta_T(i)\right] \tag{8}$$

$$q_t^* = \arg\max_{1 \leq i \leq N}\left[\delta(i)_t\right] \tag{9}$$

Step 4: Road diameter retrograde (Best condition definite)

$$q_t^* = \Psi_{t+1}\left(q_{t+1}^*\right) \tag{10}$$

The viterbi algorithm can not only determine an optimal state chain for the observation sequence O, but also obtain the probability P(O|λ) of the O of the observation sequence at the same time.

2.2   HMM Parameter Estimation

The optimization problem of HMM parameters, that is, how to adjust the model parameter λ = (A, B, π), maximizes P(O|λ). In fact, given any finite-length observation sequence as a training number, it is impossible to obtain an optimal parameter estimate. In general, use the EM algorithm to obtain a local optimal solution.

EM algorithm flow

Step 1: Initialize the distribution parameters

Step 2: Step E: Calculate the posterior probability of the implicit variable based on the initial value of the parameter or the model parameters of the previous iteration, which is actually the expectation of the hidden variable. Current estimate as a hidden variable:

$$\theta_i\left(z^i\right) = p\left(z^{(i)}x^i; \theta\right) \tag{11}$$

M-step: Maximize the likelihood function to obtain a new parameter value:

$$\theta = \arg\max_{i} \sum_{i} \sum_{i} Q_i(z^i) \log \frac{p(x^i, z^i;\ \theta)}{Q_i(z^i)} \tag{12}$$

Through continuous iteration, the parameter θ that maximizes the likelihood function L(θ) can be obtained.

3   Data Acquisition and Preprocessing

The Uyghur handwritten signature [9] database used in this paper includes 100 individuals (20 individuals per year) with a difference in age and a total of 2000 signature samples. These sample signatures are scanned using a scanner (with a scanning accuracy of 300 dpi), then stored on a computer in the BMP (256-bit bitmap) format and the specified serial number, and collected into a signature image library. The main purpose of preprocessing is to provide the feature extraction stage with valid information contained in the sample image, removing invalid information and noise interference. Therefore, preprocessing the signature image is necessary. The preprocess of the signature image is shown in the Fig. 1.

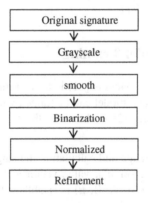

Fig. 1. Pretreatment process

4   Feature Extraction Based on Discrete Cosine Transform

The DCT for Discrete Cosine Transform [10] is a transform associated with the Fourier transform that is similar to the DFT for Discrete Fourier Transform but uses only real numbers. The discrete cosine transform is equivalent to a discrete Fourier transform that is approximately twice its length. This discrete Fourier transform is performed on a real-even function (because the Fourier transform of a real-even function is still a real-even function. In some variants, it is necessary to shift the input or output position by half a unit (DCT has 8 standard types, of which 4 are common). Discrete cosine transforms are often used by signals and image processing to perform lossy data compression on signals and images (including still and moving images). This is due to the fact that the discrete cosine transform has a strong "energy concentration" characteristic. Most of the natural signal (including sound and image) energy is concentrated in the third-order part of the discrete cosine transform, and when the signal has a close Markov process In the statistical feature of (Markov processes), the decorrelation of the discrete cosine transform is close to the KL transform.

For a M × N digital image f(x, y), the two-dimensional discrete cosine transform formula is as follows:

$$F(\text{u}, v) = c(u)c(v) \sum_{x=0}^{M-1} \sum_{y=0}^{N-1} F(\text{x}, f) \cos \frac{(2x+1)u\pi}{2M} \cos \frac{(2y+1)v\pi}{2N} \tag{13}$$

Among them, u = 0, 1, 2, ..., M−1; v = 0, 1, 2 ..., N−1. The corresponding two-dimensional discrete cosine inverse transform (IDCT) formula is as follows:

$$f(x, y) = \sum_{u=0}^{M-1} \sum_{v=0}^{N-1} c(u)c(v)F(c, v) \cos \frac{(2x+1)u\pi}{2M} \cos \frac{(2y+1)v\pi}{2N} \tag{14}$$

Among them, x = 0, 1, 2, ..., M−1; y = 0, 1, 2, ..., N−1. F(u, v) in the above two formulas is called DCT coefficient.

5   Hidden Markov Model Training

The training of Hidden Markov Models [11] is to determine a set of optimized HMM parameters for each person. Each model can be trained with single or multiple blessing images. The training flowchart [12] is shown in the figure below. The calculation is performed as follows:

(1) Sampling the signature image and calculating the singular value of each sampling window matrix, using the singular value vector as the observation sequence.
(2) A general HMM model λ = (A, B, π) is established to determine the number of states of the model, allowable state transitions, and the size of the observation sequence vector.
(3) The training data is evenly divided, corresponding to N states, and the initial parameters of the model are calculated. An initial distribution can be given, for example:

$$\Pi_0 = \begin{bmatrix} 1 & 0 & 0 & 0 & 0 \end{bmatrix} \tag{15}$$

Since the time length of the observation sequence in our experiment is T = 108. The initial value of the observation probability matrix B can be calculated according to the following formula:

$$b_j(o_j) = \frac{1}{\sqrt{(2\pi)^n \left|\sum_j^l\right|}} EXP\left\{-\frac{1}{2}(o_i - u_j)^T {\sum}_J^{-1} (o_i - u_i)\right\} \qquad (16)$$

Where T_j is the length of the sequence corresponding to each state after even division.

(4) Replace the uniform segmentation with viterbi segmentation and re-initialize the parameters.
(5) Baum-Welch algorithm is used to re-evaluate parameters. Iteratively adjust model parameters to maximize

The HMM parameter [13] of this process is used to represent the signature in the database. See the following figure for the flowchart of HMM training. The flowchart of HMM training is indicated as the following Fig. 2.

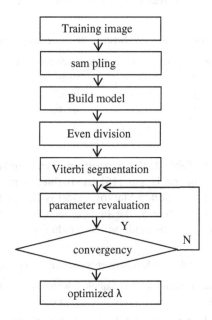

Fig. 2. The flowchart of HMM training

6 Experimental Results and Analysis

There are three contents in this experiment. The first experiment is to use 1000 Uyghur signature images to identify. The second experiment is to use 1000 English signature images to identify. The third is to increase Uyghur database is a total of 2000 signatures. The signature images are identified and the experimental results are as follows:

Table 1. 1000 Uygur handwritten signature image recognition

State number	Training time	Recognition rate
N = 2	11.5 s	98%
N = 3	12 s	98%
N = 4	27.1 s	99%
N = 5	34 s	99.5%

As can be seen from Table 1, the experiment uses a hidden Markov model to extract the DCT features of the Uygur [14] handwritten signature image. When the number of states of the model hidden Markov model is changed, different recognition rates can be obtained. When N = 5, the highest recognition rate is 99.5%. As the number of states decreases, the recognition rate gradually decreases.

Table 2. 1000 English handwritten signature image recognition

State number	Training time	Recognition rate
N = 2	6.81 s	95%
N = 3	6.94 s	96.67%
N = 4	7.8 s	97.5%
N = 5	8.27 s	97.5%

As can be seen from Table 2, the experiment uses a hidden Markov model to extract the DCT features of the Uygur [15] handwritten signature image. When the number of states of the model hidden Markov model is changed, different recognition rates can be obtained. When N = 5, the highest recognition rate is 99.5%. As the number of states decreases, the recognition rate gradually decreases (Table 3).

Table 3. 2000 Uygur handwritten signature image recognition

Training samples	Test samples	Recognition rate
700	1300	73.92%
800	1200	78.75%
900	1100	84.09%
1000	1000	87.7%
1100	900	85.89%
1200	800	83.88%
1300	700	79.57%

It can be seen from the above that when the number of Uyghur test and training samples is changed, the recognition rate is different [16]. When the training set and the test set respectively select 1000 signature samples, the highest recognition rate is 87.7%.

7 Conclusion and Future Work

Through the above three experiments, it can be found that for Uighur and English, when the number of states gradually increases, the recognition rate gradually becomes higher. When N = 5, the highest recognition rate is 99.5% and 97.5%. This method has an effect on Uyghur. Better recognition effect. By increasing the Uighur database, the recognition rate decreases. When the training set and the test set respectively select 1000 samples, the highest recognition rate is 87.7%.

In future work, on the basis of this article, we will increase the number of signature types and the number of signature databases, find more features suitable for Hidden Markov extraction, and change the parameters to perform more experiments.

Acknowledgments. This work was supported by the National Natural Science Foundation of China (No. 61563052, 61163028, 61363064), the Funds for Creative Research Groups of Higher Education of Xinjiang Uyghur Autonomous Region (XJEDU2017T002).

References

1. Basil, M., Gawali, B.: Comparative analysis of MSER and DTW for offline signature recognition. Int. J. Comput. Appl. (0975–8887) 110(5) (2015)
2. Marušić, T., Marušić, Ž., Šeremet, Ž.: Identification of authors of documents based on offline signature recognition. In: MIPRO 2015, 25–29 May 2015, Opatija, Croatia (2015)
3. Zeinstra, C.G., Meuwly, D., Ruifrok, A.C., Veldhuis, R.N., Spreeuwers, L.J.: Forensic face recognition as a means to determine strength of evidence: a survey. Forensic Sci. Rev. 30(1), 21–32 (2018)
4. Ribeiro, B., Gonçalves, I., Santos, S., Kovacec, A.: Deep learning networks for off-line handwritten signature recognition. In: San Martin, C., Kim, S.-W. (eds.) CIARP 2011. LNCS, vol. 7042, pp. 523–532. Springer, Heidelberg (2011). https://doi.org/10.1007/978-3-642-25085-9_62
5. Zhang, Y., Xu, Y., Bao, H.: Offline handwritten signature recognition method based on multi-features. J. Converg. Inf. Technol. 8(5) (2013)
6. Kudłacik, P., Porwik, P.: A new approach to signature recognition using the fuzzy method. Pattern Anal. Appl. 17, 451–463 (2014)
7. Hafemann, L.G., Luiz, R.S., Oliveira, S.: Offline Handwritten Signature Verification-Literature Review. arXiv:1507.07909v2 [cs.CV], August 2015
8. Bertolini, D., Oliveira, L.S., Justino, E., Sabourin, R.: Reducing forgeries in writer-independent off-line signature verification through ensemble of classifiers. Pattern Recogn. 43(1), 387–396 (2010)
9. Abril, G.: Uyghur Offline Signature Recognition Technology. Xinjiang University (2012)

10. Serdouk, Y., Nemmour, H., Chibani, Y.: New off-line handwritten signature verification method based on artificial immune recognition system. Expert Syst. Appl. **51**, 186–194 (2016)
11. Yi, A.Y.: Uyghur Offline Handwritten Signature Recognition. Xinjiang University (2014)
12. Justino, E.J.R., Bortolozzi, F., Sabourin, R.: A comparison of SVM and HMM classifiers in the off-line signature verification. Pattern Recogn. Lett. **26**(9), 1377–1385 (2005)
13. Kessentini, Y., Burger, T., Paquet, T.: A Dempster-Shafer theory based combination of handwriting recognition systems with multiple rejection strategies. Pattern Recogn. **48**(2), 534–544 (2015)
14. Kumar, R., Sharma, J.D., Chanda, B.: Writer-independent off-line signature verification using surroundedness feature. Pattern Recogn. Lett. **33**(3), 301–308 (2012)
15. Aini, Z.: Research on Uyghur Off-Line Handwritten Signature Authentication Based on Statistical Features. Xinjiang University (2017)
16. Yimin, A.: Research on Uyghur Handwritten Signature Recognition Based on Multiple Features. Xinjiang University (2017)

Author Index

Abdurixiti, Ruxianguli 709
Aizezi, Yasen 709
An, Weizhi 137
Aysa, Alimjan 736
Aysa, Yunus 700

Bai, Shanglin 497

Cao, He 11
Cao, Lu 11
Chen, Caikou 257
Chen, Chao 545
Chen, Fuxuan 349
Chen, Jianyun 223
Chen, Sheng 428
Chen, Shuhai 609
Chen, Song 399
Chen, Xilin 358
Chen, Xing-rong 536
Chen, Yudong 231
Chen, Yufei 669
Chen, Zhicheng 387
Chen, Zhihong 294
Cheng, Fangyuan 580
Cheng, Miaomiao 214
Chu, Yuna 486
Cui, Jiyun 358
Cui, Qing 175

Dai, Min 553
Deng, Qiyao 311
Deng, Wenbo 11
Ding, Jupeng 517, 572
Ding, Tong 441
Du, Haishun 189
Du, Jun 599
Du, Xuefeng 48
Duan, Xiaodong 367

Fang, Peiyu 247
Fang, Xiaozhao 206
Fang, Yuchun 387
Fang, Yuxun 645

Fei, Chun 157
Fei, Lunke 206
Feng, Zhanxiang 409
Feng, Ziqing 418
Fu, Jingru 239

Gan, Junyin 11
Gao, Farong 545
Gao, Junxiong 476
Gao, Xiang 428
Geng, Guohua 589
Guo, Jianzhu 275
Guo, Wei 528

Hamdulla, Askar 678
Han, Aili 450
Han, Feilin 450
Han, Hu 358
Han, Shujie 265
Han, Zhen 428
Hang, Peng 632
Hao, Haifan 497
He, Yan 66
He, Yuqing 128
He, Zhixiang 340
Hou, Tao 22
Hou, Xielian 257
Hu, Guoping 599
Hu, Haifeng 79, 294
Hu, Min 109
Huang, Di 399
Huang, Jimmy 678
Huang, Ming 198
Huang, Rui 409
Huang, Xunping 653
Huang, Yongzhen 137
Huo, Guang 441

I, Chih-Lin 517, 572

Ji, Shengzhen 553
Jia, Guimin 29, 580
Jia, Kebin 653

Jia, Wei   239
Jia, Xi   321
Jiamali, Anniwaer   709
Jian, Meng   331
Jiang, Peilin   497
Jiang, Shoukun   22
Jiang, Xiaochen   3
Jin, Changlong   56
Jing, Liping   214

Kang, Bing   22
Kang, Peipei   206
Kang, Wenxiong   645
Kim, Hakil   56
Kong, Heng   231
Kong, Xiangwen   56

Lai, Huicheng   517, 572
Lai, Jianhuang   409
Lai, Zhihui   231
Lei, Zhen   275, 285
Li, Dan   580
Li, Guodong   189
Li, Haoxuan   3
Li, Hui   632
Li, Huibin   377
Li, Jingshan   257
Li, Kang   589
Li, Li   459
Li, Meng   265
Li, Peiqin   662
Li, Pengfei   349
Li, Qi   148, 311
Li, Shengguang   459, 468
Li, Shuyi   29
Li, Stan Z.   275, 285
Li, Ting   536
Li, Weixin   399
Li, Xiaopeng   128
Li, Xin   148
Li, Xingguang   468
Lian, Ying   486
Liang, Xu   66
Liao, Rijun   137
Liao, Wenzhe   476
Liu, Aozhi   620
Liu, Bing   497
Liu, Cong   599
Liu, Fei   148

Liu, Feng   38
Liu, Fu   22
Liu, Guoqun   175
Liu, Jing   468
Liu, Jing-Wei   198
Liu, Mingkang   311
Liu, Pengyu   653
Liu, Shuai   441
Liu, Tong   662
Liu, Wanquan   367
Liu, Xiaoning   589
Liu, Xiaozi   669
Liu, Yang   428
Liu, Yanqiong   175
Liu, Yuanning   441
Liu, Zhen   441
Long, Quan   632
Lu, Guangben   387
Lu, Xinyi   645
Luo, Nan   66
Luo, Qi   223
Luo, Xu   349
Lv, Xiaoyu   476
Lyu, Mengsi   689

Ma, Hui   11
Ma, Meng   632
Ma, Yukun   331
Mahpirat   700
Mamat, Hornisa   736
Mamut, Mutallip   736
Meimaiti, Halimulati   719
Meng, Xiangyu   528
Miao, Yu-Qing   87
Min, Chen   214
Mo, Long-Fei   736
Mu, Zhichun   507
Musajan, Winira   678

Piuri, Vincenzo   11

Qiu, Kang   87
Qiu, Yaru   96

Scotti, Fabio   11
Shan, Shiguang   358
Shao, Wei   387
Shen, Chao   669
Shen, Linlin   38, 321

Sheng, Yuhong   175
Shi, Gang   175
Shi, Mengjun   632
Song, Yonghong   96
Su, Wen   302
Sun, Chunling   545
Sun, Ting   486
Sun, Xiaoxia   553
Sun, Ying   553
Sun, Zhenan   148, 311
Sun, Zhonghua   653

Tan, Jiaqi   166
Tan, Lin   459
Tang, Hong   536
Tang, Yan   321
Tang, Yunqi   528
Tao, Xiaodong   599
Teng, Shaohua   206
Tian, Ming   157
Tohti, Turdi   678
Tu, Xiaokang   387

Ubul, Kurban   700, 709, 727, 736

Wan, Xinxin   148
Wang, An   87
Wang, Fei   497
Wang, Haowen   109
Wang, Hongxia   223
Wang, Jianzong   620
Wang, Jiawei   166
Wang, Jie   265
Wang, JingJing   157
Wang, Jinxin   11
Wang, Junqian   689
Wang, Qi   486
Wang, Rongsheng   56
Wang, Sheng   189
Wang, Siqi   609
Wang, Xianliang   340
Wang, Xiaohua   109
Wang, Xiaojing   265
Wang, Xiao-li   727
Wang, Xing   321
Wang, Yan   399
Wang, Yiding   3
Wang, Yuehai   367
Wang, Yuhong   399
Wang, Yumeng   56

Wang, Zengfu   302
Wang, Zi-Rui   599
Wang, Zuyun   653
Wu, Gang   66
Wu, Lifang   331
Wu, Qiuxia   645
Wu, Qiuxuan   545
Wu, Zeyu   562

Xia, Qing   157
Xiao, Jing   620
Xiao, Meihong   189
Xie, Jianbin   662
Xie, Lingjiang   377
Xie, Ruiyue   517
Xie, Xiaohua   409
Xu, Lirui   678
Xu, Xiangxi   231
Xu, Xiao-ke   536
Xu, Yong   206
Xue, Mingliang   367

Yan, Wei   662
Yang, Anran   450
Yang, Jinfeng   29, 580
Yang, Jucheng   265
Yang, Tingting   247
Yang, Wen   589
Yang, Yuan   48
Yi, Kaijun   476
Yibulayin, Tuergen   727
Yimin, Ahat   727
Yin, Bao-Cai   599
Yin, Dong   87
Yip, Chitung   294
Yu, Baoshan   572
Yu, Cuican   377
Yu, Jian   214
Yu, Shiqi   137, 166
Yuan, Li   562
Yuen, Pong C.   137

Zeng, Junying   11
Zeng, Zhiguo   468
Zhai, Yikui   11
Zhang, Bob   239
Zhang, Chi   517, 572
Zhang, Dexin   120
Zhang, Haifeng   302

Zhang, Haigang   29
Zhang, Haoxiang   120
Zhang, He   468
Zhang, Hongwen   148
Zhang, Hu   340
Zhang, Hui   468
Zhang, Junxuan   79
Zhang, Kuo   441
Zhang, Lei   239
Zhang, Lingchao   265
Zhang, Ping   157
Zhang, Shaojie   609
Zhang, Shifeng   285
Zhang, Shu-Jing   700
Zhang, Shu-jing   727
Zhang, Wei   148, 206
Zhang, Xiangde   486
Zhang, Xiaodian   128
Zhang, Xuetao   497
Zhang, Yi   562
Zhao, Haifeng   609, 632

Zhao, Haonan   562
Zhao, Junhong   645
Zhao, Qian   128
Zhao, Qijun   349, 418
Zhao, Shiwei   459
Zhao, Yuanhao   38
Zheng, Gang   553
Zheng, Yubao   206
Zhi, Yihang   11
Zhong, Dexing   48
Zhou, Guoxiang   109
Zhou, Qianli   468
Zhou, Shengwei   257
Zhu, Fei   589
Zhu, Jihua   377
Zhu, Qinping   507
Zhu, Wei-Jian   198
Zhu, Xiangyu   275, 285
Zhu, Xiaodong   441
Zhuang, Chuan-Zhi   198
Zhuang, Chubin   285

Printed in the United States
By Bookmasters